# The Use of Force in UN Peace Operations

# The Use of Force in UN Peace Operations

Trevor Findlay

OXFORD UNIVERSITY PRESS

2002

# OXFORD
UNIVERSITY PRESS

Great Clarendon Street, Oxford OX2 6DP
Oxford University Press is a department of the University of Oxford.
It furthers the University's objective of excellence in research, scholarship,
and education by publishing worldwide in

Oxford New York
Auckland Bangkok Buenos Aires Cape Town Chennai
Dar es Salaam Delhi Hong Kong Istanbul Karachi Kolkata
Kuala Lumpur Madrid Melbourne Mexico City Mumbai Nairobi
São Paulo Shanghai Taipei Tokyo Toronto

Oxford is a registered trade mark of Oxford University Press
in the UK and certain other countries

Published in the United States
by Oxford University Press Inc., New York

British Library Cataloguing in Publication Data
Data available

Library of Congress Cataloguing-in-Publication Data
Data available

ISBN 0-19-829282-1

Typeset and originated by Stockholm International Peace Research Institute
Printed in Great Britain on acid-free paper by
Biddles Ltd., Guildford and King's Lynn

# Contents

# Preface

This book is a product of SIPRI's Project on Peacekeeping and Regional Security, which was led from its inception in 1993 to 1997 by Dr Trevor Findlay, the author. The aim of the study is to examine the use of force in all its forms—in self-defence, in defence of the mission and as a tool of peace enforcement.

One of the most troubling issues that faced the international community in the closing decade of the 20th century was the use of force by the United Nations peace operations in situations where the ultimate goal was the alleviation or ending of armed conflict. Such missions were dubbed 'peace enforcement'. The difficulty is that they were carried out by peacekeepers—UN forces designed for the relatively benign function of monitoring borders between states after conflict has ended. Complex civil wars in Somalia, Bosnia and Rwanda, in which UN peacekeeping missions were deployed with disastrous results, raised several stark questions. When and how should UN peacekeepers use force to protect themselves or protect their mission, or, most troublingly, to ensure the compliance of recalcitrant parties with peace accords? Is a 'peace enforcement' role for peacekeepers impossible? Is there a middle ground between peace-keeping and enforcement or is there a stark 'Mogadishu Line' across which peacekeeping should never stray? More recent UN operations in East Timor and Sierra Leone have kept such issues at the forefront of international concern.

This project was made possible by the funding received from various sources. We are indebted to all the external funders involved for supporting this study. The Australian Government funded a conference organized by SIPRI on the subject in Stockholm in April 1995 which was attended by senior academics, former UN force commanders, and UN and government officials. The then Australian Foreign Minister, Senator Gareth Evans, opened and participated in that meeting. Funding for subsequent research was provided by the US Institute of Peace in Washington, DC, and by an Evans-Grawemeyer Travel Award to Dr Findlay by the Australian Department of Foreign Affairs and Trade.

We would like to thank Dr Findlay for the invaluable work he has done to bring this project to completion. In publishing this book he makes a significant contribution to both the theory and the practice of the use of force in peace operations.

Adam Daniel Rotfeld
Director of SIPRI
to June 2002

Alyson J. K. Bayles
Director of SIPRI
August 2002

# Acknowledgements

I am indebted to a many individuals for their support and inspiration and material contribution to this project over seven years. They include: Datuk Jelani Asmawi, Abdul Razak Abdulla Baginda, Mike Bailey, Meli Bainimarama, Maurice Baril, Mats Berdal, Runo Bergstrom, Anneli Berntson, Billie Bielckus, Wolfgang Biermann, Christine-Charlotte Bodell, Gerard van Bohemen, Hugh Borrowman, Göran Bäckstrand, Soon Lian Cheng, Jarat Chopra, Christopher Coleman, R. R. Crabbe, Sarah Croco, Robert Dalsjö, Don Daniel, Murray Denyer, Charles Dobbie, Rick Dobbie, William Durch, Renata Dwan, Douglas Dyer, Gareth Evans, Marie Fagerström, Steve Feller, Genevieve Forde, Trond Furuhuvde, Joshua Gabriel, Thierry Germond, Marrack Goulding, Percurt Green, Andrew Greene, Kelly Groll, Tui Gucake, Marilla Guptil, Olga Hardardottír, Chesley Harris, Mohamed Jawhar Hassan, Brad Hayes, Damien Healy, John Hillen, Kristina Hinds, Jonathan Howe, Trevor Hughes, Robert Hunter, Joachim Hütter, Peni Jikoiono, Eve Johansson, Leonard Kapunga, Jaana Karhilo, Mike Kelly, Bill Kirk, Kathryn Klebacha, Guy Lavender, Mark Lavender, Peter Leentjes, Milton Leitenberg, Sasha Lezhnev, Elisabeth Lindenmeyer, Joan Link, Mohamed Yunus Bin Long, Andrea Lupo, David McBrien, Andrew Mack, John Mackinlay, John McKinnon, Laila Manji, Isaac Mattiakabara, Vicky Melton, Robert Merrillees, Rosanne Milano, Tony Miles, Christopher Moore, Alex Morrison, Bernard Myet, Fred Naceba, Andrew Natsios, Matthew Neuhaus, Peter Noble, Mak Joon Num, Michael O'Brien, Bo Pellnäs, Dave Phillips, Mirak Raheem, Christopher Reberger, Andrew Renton-Green, Indar Jit Rikhye, Michael Rose, Adam Daniel Rotfeld, John Russell, John Sanderson, Erwin Schmidl, Taylor Seybolt, Apahr Sidhu, Bjørn Skogmo, Hugh Smith, Rupert Smith, Takao Takahra, Filipo Tarakinikini, Shashi Tharoor, Shinichi Tsurada, Brian Urquhart, Matt Vaccaro, James Vaile, Jonas Waern, Connie Wall, Philip Wilkinson, Luke Williams, Michael Williams, David Wimhurst and Susan Woodward.

Trevor Findlay
June 2002

# Acronyms and abbreviations

| | |
|---|---|
| ACDA | Arms Control and Disarmament Agency (USA) |
| ADL | Armistice Demarcation Line (Egypt–Israel) |
| ANC | Armée Nationale Congolaise |
| APC | Armoured personnel carrier |
| ASEAN | Association of South-East Asian Nations |
| BHC | Bosnia and Herzegovina Command |
| CENTCOM | US Central Command |
| CINCSOUTH | Commander-in-Chief South (NATO) |
| CIS | Commonwealth of Independent States |
| CivPol | Civilian police |
| DFF | De Facto Forces (Lebanon) |
| DPKO | Department of Peace-keeping Operations (UN) |
| DRC | Democratic Republic of the Congo |
| ECOMOG | ECOWAS Military Observer Group |
| ECOWAS | Economic Community of West African States |
| EISAS | Executive Committee on Peace and Security (ECPS) Information and Strategic Analysis Secretariat (UN) |
| FALINTIL | Forças Armadas de Libertação Nacional de Timor Leste (Armed Forces of Liberation of East Timor) |
| ICJ | International Court of Justice |
| ICRC | International Committee of the Red Cross |
| IDF | Israeli Defence Forces |
| IFOR | Implementation Force (Bosnia) |
| INTERFET | International Force for East Timor |
| IPA | International Peace Academy |
| JNA | Yugoslav National Army |
| JTF | Joint Task Force (Somalia) |
| KFOR | Kosovo Force |
| KR | Khmer Rouge |
| MMWG | Mixed Military Working Group |
| MNF | Multi-National Force (in Beirut) |
| MNF | Multi-national Force (in Haiti) |
| MONUC | UN Observer Force in the Democratic Republic of Congo |
| NAC | North Atlantic Council |
| NATO | North Atlantic Treaty Organization |

| NGO | Non-governmental organization |
| Nordbat | Nordic Battalion |
| ONUC | UN Operation in the Congo |
| OOTW | Operations other than war |
| OP | Observation post |
| PDD | Presidential Decision Directive |
| PE | Peace enforcement |
| PK | Peacekeeping |
| PLO | Palestine Liberation Organization |
| PsyOps | Psychological operations |
| QRF | Quick Reaction Force (Somalia) |
| ROE | Rules of engagement |
| RPF | Rwanda Patriotic Front |
| RRF | Rapid Reaction Force (UNPROFOR) |
| RUF | Revolutionary United Front |
| SAM | Surface-to-air missile |
| SDS | Strategic Deployment Stock |
| SFOR | Stabilization Force |
| SHIRBRIG | Stand-by High Readiness Brigade |
| SNA | Somali National Alliance |
| SOC | State of Cambodia |
| SOFA | Status of forces agreement |
| SOP | Standing (or standard) operating procedures |
| SRSG | Special representative of the secretary-general |
| SWAPO | South West African Peoples' Organization |
| UAR | United Arab Republic |
| UNAMET | UN Mission in East Timor |
| UNAMIR | UN Assistance Mission for Rwanda |
| UNAMSIL | UN Mission in Sierra Leone |
| UNCRO | UN Confidence Restoration Operation (Croatia) |
| UNDOF | UN Disengagement Force |
| UNDP | United Nations Development Programme |
| UNEF | UN Emergency Force |
| UNF | UN Force (Congo) |
| UNFICYP | UN Force in Cyprus |
| UNHCR | UN High Commissioner for Refugees |
| UNIDIR | United Nations Institute for Disarmament Research |
| UNIFIL | UN Force in Lebanon |
| UNITAF | United Task Force (Somalia) |

| | |
|---|---|
| UNMEE | UN Mission in Eritrea and Ethiopia |
| UNMIH | UN Mission in Haiti |
| UNOSOM | UN Operation in Somalia |
| UNPA | UN protected area |
| UNPF | UN Peace Forces |
| UNPREDEP | UN Preventive Deployment Force (Former Yugoslav Republic of Macedonia) |
| UNPROFOR | UN Protection Force (former Yugoslavia) |
| UNRWA | UN Relief and Works Agency |
| UNSAS | UN Standby Forces Arrangements System |
| UNSCOM | UN Special Commission on Iraq |
| UNTAC | UN Transitional Authority in Cambodia |
| UNTAES | UN Transitional Administration for Eastern Slavonia, Baranja and Western Sirmium |
| UNTAET | UN Transitional Administration in East Timor |
| UNTAG | UN Transitional Assistance Group (Namibia) |
| UNTSO | UN Truce Supervision Organization |
| USC | United Somali Congress |
| WFP | World Food Programme |

# 1. Introduction

Traditionally, the United Nations has shied away from allowing the military forces under its command to use force. The whole bias of the UN Charter is, quite rightly, towards the peaceful resolution of disputes. The effect of this was magnified by the cold war, which dramatically reduced the options (beyond negotiation and mediation) that might otherwise have been open to the UN for maintaining international peace and security. The result was the invention of peacekeeping. Dag Hammarskjöld, the UN Secretary-General who oversaw its advent and was by personal inclination conflict-averse, saw in peacekeeping a role for the UN which was quasi-military but avoided the use of force.

While UN peacekeepers have always had the right to use force in self-defence,[1] it has been used sparingly, even in extreme life-and-death circumstances where it would be universally perceived as legitimate and warranted. The chief concern of commanders at all levels has been to avoid exacerbating a situation and damaging the consent of the parties to the UN's presence, both at the tactical and, more dangerously, at the strategic level. Overall, the use of force has been marked more by its absence than by its presence. However, it has been a central issue and a source of abiding controversy in UN peace operations. While principles and practices have evolved, they have been subject to the vicissitudes of time and place as various missions across almost half a century have struggled to fulfil the mandate of a Security Council that often seemed oblivious to the facts of the situation in the field.

The three peace operations in which the UN's disinclination to use force was overcome on a significant scale—in the Congo in 1960–64, in Bosnia and Herzegovina in 1992–95 and in Somalia in 1993–95—were traumatic experiences for the UN. During the cold war era, even though the UN operated in a number of intra-state environments, only the Congo mission triggered significant debate about the use of force by peacekeepers. With the end of the cold war, the sheer number, level of ambition and complexity of UN missions occasioned public and often passionate debate. Argument centred not just on how and when the UN should use force, but on whether and how various types of mission might be categorized in terms of the degree of force they used. Controversy about the non-use of force by particular missions, as in Rwanda and Bosnia,[2] was often as heated as the controversy surrounding missions, such as that in Somalia, which were generally felt to have used too much force.

This book examines the use of force by UN peacekeepers, from the first armed mission under UN command to the present. It investigates every mission in which substantial force has been used and the major incidents which affected

---

[1] See section V below.

[2] Although the official name of the country is the Republic of Bosnia and Herzegovina, the term 'Bosnia' is used hereafter in this volume for the sake of brevity.

the way in which the mission was conducted. In parallel, it traces the development of UN norms concerning the use of force and considers how these have been applied in practice, both in missions where they have been transgressed and in missions where they have not been used to full advantage. The book also follows the wider debate about the use of force by UN troops at various stages of the UN's existence, but especially since the end of the cold war. In doing so it traces the UN's struggle towards a peace operations 'doctrine' which might provide a basis for use-of-force norms in broader UN political and military strategy. It concludes with some proposals as to how, in the early 21st century, the use of force by UN missions might be made more credible in terms of both doctrine and capability.

The focus is on peace operations mandated by the Security Council and operating under UN command, but two non-UN missions, in Somalia and East Timor, are considered in detail because they were germane to the way in which UN follow-on operations used force and because they seem to suggest models for future UN missions.

This introductory chapter explains the terminology of UN peace operations used in this volume, describes how the use of force is mandated and regulated by the UN, explores the legal and military origins of the self-defence norm of UN peacekeeping, and looks at some of the myths, puzzles and paradoxes of the use-of-force question. Chapter 2 examines the emergence and application of the self-defence norm in the first armed UN peacekeeping operation, the UN Emergency Force (UNEF I) in Sinai from 1956 to 1967.[3] The chapters which follow relate how the norm operated and evolved in subsequent operations and illustrate some of the legal, political and military complexities encountered. Chapter 3 describes the first major peace enforcement operation by forces under UN command—in the Congo in the early 1960s—described elsewhere as the 'Blue Helmets' first war'.[4] Chapter 4 traces the evolution of the UN's use-of-force doctrine after the Congo in missions such as those in Cyprus and Lebanon. Chapter 5 deals with the impact of the end of the cold war on the use of force in peace operations, most notably in Namibia, in Cambodia, and in the early years of the missions in Somalia and the former Yugoslavia. Chapter 6 deals with the first major excursion into peace enforcement after the Congo in the second UN Operation in Somalia (UNOSOM II) as well as the US-led multilateral force which preceded it. Chapter 7 examines the almost contemporaneous imbroglio in Bosnia, dealing with the use of force on the ground and from the air. Chapter 8 looks at the complex missions that followed in Rwanda, East Timor, Sierra Leone and elsewhere. Chapter 9 analyses the debate about the UN's use of force after Somalia, Bosnia and Rwanda, and the UN's institutional response. Finally, chapter 10 assesses the use of force by the UN over the

---

[3] The UN Truce Supervisory Organization (UNTSO), established in 1948, and UN Military Observer Group in India and Pakistan (UNMOGIP), established in 1949, used only unarmed military observers.

[4] Findlay, T. C., *The Blue Helmets' First War? Use of Force by the UN in the Congo 1960–64* (Canadian Peacekeeping Press: Clementsport, 1999).

past half-century, considers how improvements might be made in the future and speculates on the type of use-of-force doctrine that might be most appropriate.

Each of the main case studies in this book details the mandate(s) of the operation, the type of military force fielded and the use-of-force rules provided. Where appropriate, command and control arrangements are also described. Each case study analyses the use of force by the mission and any accompanying evolution of the use-of-force rules that occurred.

This book does not deal with all the peace operations deployed since the UN was founded. Operations are only considered (*a*) if force was used to any significant degree, (*b*) if the use-of-force issue was compelling (whether or not force was actually used), or (*c*) if the mission affected the use-of-force rules in subsequent UN missions (again, whether or not force was used). Hence attention is devoted both to Somalia, where substantial military operations were mounted, and to Rwanda, even though that mission failed to use force.

Although it is often difficult to disaggregate the various elements, the case studies do not cover the entirety of each mission's activities, particularly those relating to the non-military sphere, nor do they try to identify the requirements for the success of peace operations overall. Even in relation to military matters, each case study deals with military operations and capabilities only as they relate to the use-of-force issue.

Finally, the focus on the use of force does not suggest that it is the most important issue facing the shaping of peace operations into a more effective tool to promote international peace and security. Nor should it be taken as advocating the use of force to resolve the dilemmas faced by peace operations in all or most circumstances. Indeed, a convincing argument can be made that the more willing and able UN operations are to use force the less likely they are to have to use it.

## I. Peace operations: a typology

'Peace operations' is the umbrella term this book applies to all UN missions involving military personnel, whether they be otherwise described as peacekeeping, traditional peacekeeping, expanded peacekeeping, humanitarian missions or peace enforcement missions. The term usefully avoids prejudging whether a particular mission is traditional or non-traditional or has become, either inadvertently or by design, peace enforcement. It also coincides with nomenclature widely used for non-UN missions, such as those conducted by the North Atlantic Treaty Organization (NATO) or by ad hoc coalitions of states, whether with a Security Council mandate or not.

### Peacekeeping

The UN has traditionally defined peacekeeping as missions 'involving military personnel, but without enforcement powers, undertaken by the United Nations to help maintain or restore international peace and security in areas of conflict'.[5] Attempts at a more cogent definition have always been bedevilled by its peculiar nature. Peacekeeping is not mentioned in the UN Charter; it has never been guided by established theory or doctrine; the term was invented long after praxis had begun; and improvisation has characterized its evolution ever since. The UN membership has been reluctant to further explicate peacekeeping since 'to define it would be to impose a straitjacket on a concept whose flexibility made it the most pragmatic instrument at the disposal of the world organisation'.[6] This partly explains the widespread confusion and debate about the use of force by UN peacekeepers.

The three key characteristics of peacekeeping are considered to be: (a) the more or less voluntary consent of all parties to the presence and activities of the mission; (b) the peacekeepers' impartiality in their relationships with the parties; and (c) the minimum use of force, only as a last resort and only in self-defence. Peacekeeping is a tool of conflict prevention, management and resolution. Peacekeepers are intended to be enablers rather than enforcers. They have no enemies and are not there to win. Their effectiveness depends on voluntary cooperation. This in turn enables them to act impartially, since they threaten no one. 'Impartiality', Charles Moskos notes, 'means that the peacekeeping soldiers have no apparent interest in seeing the moral vindication or material triumph of either of the disputants'.[7] Shashi Tharoor, an official in the UN Department of Peace-keeping Operations (DPKO), has called impartiality the 'oxygen' of peacekeeping: 'The only way peacekeepers can work is by being trusted by both sides, being clear and transparent in their dealings, and keeping lines of communication open'.[8] The abandonment of impartiality, whether deliberate or inadvertent, runs the risk of turning the peace force into an enemy of one or more of the parties.

The consent of the parties enables peacekeepers to be deployed and carry out their mandate without the need for substantial military capability. Peacekeepers, according to the original understanding of the term, were to be equipped only for personal self-defence, on the assumption that being 'lightly armed and impartially disposed' would allow them to 'move freely and negotiate dispassionately'.[9] For Sir Brian Urquhart, former UN Under Secretary-General for Special Political Tasks: 'The real strength of a peacekeeping force lies not in its capacity to use force, but precisely in its *not* using force and thereby remaining above the conflict and preserving its unique position and prestige'.[10]

---

[5] United Nations, *The Blue Helmets: A Review of United Nations Peace-keeping*, 2nd edn (United Nations: New York, 1990), p. 4.

[6] Tharoor, S., 'Should UN peacekeeping go "back to basics"?', *Survival*, vol. 37, no. 4 (winter 1995/96), p. 56. The intergovernmental Special Committee on Peace-Keeping Operations has every year rejected the idea of a declaration on the principles of peacekeeping.

[7] Moskos, C. C., Jr, *Peace Soldiers: The Sociology of a United Nations Military Force* (University of Chicago Press: Chicago, Ill. and London, 1976), p. 3.

[8] Tharoor (note 6), p. 58.

[9] Mackinlay, J. and Chopra, J., 'Second generation multinational operations', *Washington Quarterly*, summer 1992, p. 115.

[10] Urquhart, B., *A Life in Peace and War* (Weidenfeld & Nicolson: London, 1987), pp. 178–79.

This description of peacekeeping has been complicated, however, by the emergence of two widely recognized subdivisions—'traditional' and 'expanded'.

## Traditional peacekeeping

The term 'traditional' peacekeeping is used in this book to refer to UN peace operations involving the deployment of military contingents to monitor, supervise and verify compliance with ceasefires, ceasefire lines, withdrawals, buffer zones and related military agreements. Having completed their relatively limited role in implementing a truce or peace settlement, such missions often have a limited life and are withdrawn promptly. Sometimes, however, they end up 'freezing' in place erstwhile combatants and their lines of control, often for decades, pending agreement on a peaceful solution. In either case, peacekeepers are not permitted under any circumstances to alter the political or military situation in which they find themselves, whether by military or by non-military means. Long-standing examples of traditional operations include the UN Military Observer Group in India and Pakistan (UNMOGIP), deployed in Kashmir since 1949, and the UN Truce Supervision Organization (UNTSO) and UN Disengagement Force (UNDOF), both deployed in the Middle East, since 1948 and 1974, respectively. Traditional-style missions continue to be mandated today. Examples are the UN Aouzou Strip Observer Group (UNASOG), which monitored Libyas handover of a border area to Chad in 1994, and the UN Mission of Observers in Prevlaka (UNMOP), mandated in 1996 to observe a ceasefire between Croatia and the Federal Republic of Yugoslavia on the Prevlaka Peninsula.

## Expanded peacekeeping

After the cold war there emerged what has been widely recognized as a new form of peacekeeping, although it had some cold war precursors, most notably the Congo mission in the 1960s.[11] The UN holding operation was suddenly superseded by the multifunctional operation linked to and integrated with an entire peace process. Where peacekeepers once studiously avoided tackling the root causes of armed conflict in favour of containment and de-escalation, they were now mandated to seek just and lasting resolutions. Such an operation would aim to establish or re-establish democratic, accountable governance, promote the growth of civil society and provide impetus to restart economic reconstruction and development. In some cases this amounted to the resuscitation of failed states or nation-building. Troubling to some UN member states, including China and other key developing countries, such missions were characterized in some cases by an apparent increased willingness on the part of the UN to breach rigid interpretations of the right of states to non-interference in their internal affairs or see its peacekeepers use force beyond self-defence.

[11] For arguments that dispute the novelty of the 'new peacekeeping' see James, A., 'Is there a second generation of peacekeeping?', *International Peacekeeping*, vol. 1, no. 4 (Sep./Nov. 1994), pp. 110–13.

In addition to a UN military force, there were often deployments of UN civilian police (CivPols) and an array of components to manage everything from the holding of elections and the safeguarding of human rights to the implementation of economic and social reconstruction programmes. Examples of such missions include the UN Transitional Authority in Cambodia (UNTAC), the UN Mission in Mozambique (ONUMOZ), the UN Protection Force (UNPROFOR) in the former Yugoslavia, UNOSOM II in Somalia, the UN Mission in Haiti (UNMIH) and the UN Transitional Administration in East Timor (UNTAET).

Heated debate occurred between those who saw expanded peacekeeping as simply a linear expansion of a long-standing technique and those who believed that it might require an adjustment of the traditional peacekeeping concept, involving less concern for the obtaining of consent from all parties, a rethinking of the notion of impartiality and greater flexibility in the use of force (meaning, inevitably, greater use of force). Those who wished simply to describe the broader range of activities involved called such missions 'second-generation', 'extended', 'wider', 'advanced' or 'broader'. Those who wished to emphasize a new attitude or inclination towards the use of force by some of these missions called them 'protected', 'aggravated', 'enforced' or 'muscular'.

Humanitarian operations, in which the principle goal is the relief of human suffering, are considered part of expanded peacekeeping.

## Peace enforcement

Although the term 'peace enforcement' is used in widely differing ways and overlaps with the 'robust' characteristics of 'expanded' peacekeeping just mentioned, it is used in this book to refer to peace operations, mandated by the Security Council, which aim to induce one or more parties to adhere to a peace arrangement or agreement previously consented to by using means which include the use or threat of military force.[12] It is in this sense that such missions aim to 'enforce the peace'. They do not attempt to militarily defeat the party concerned, but rather to coerce it to comply with the will of the international community and with its previously agreed commitments. They usually attempt to act impartially in dealing with all the parties, in the manner of an umpire, but in doing so may be forced to penalize one or more of them, including through the use of force. They are not normally only involved in peace enforcement, but will undertake the range of activities involved in expanded peacekeeping, including humanitarian assistance and 'nation-building'. Like peacekeeping operations, they employ both positive and negative inducements (the proverbial 'carrot' and 'stick'), but they also have the use and threat of the use of force as the ultimate negative inducement.

---

[12] Don Daniel identifies several variants of peace enforcement: 'peace inducement', 'coercive inducement', 'peace restoration', 'peace implementation', 'muscular peacekeeping', 'aggravated peacekeeping', 'gray area operations', 'middle ground operations', 'hybrid operations' and 'multifunctional peacekeeping'. Daniel, D. C. F., 'Wandering out of the void? Conceptualizing practicable peace enforcement', eds A. Morrison, D. A. Fraser and J. D. Kiras, *Peacekeeping with Muscle: The Use of Force in International Conflict Resolution* (Canadian Peacekeeping Press: Clementsport, 1997), p. 2.

There are few, if any, pure examples of such operations to date, but a number of UN missions have exhibited some of their characteristics at some point, including UNOSOM II, UNPROFOR, UNTAET and the UN Mission in Sierra Leone (UNAMSIL). One of the aims of this book is to help identify more clearly exactly what those missions were and which elements of their undertakings might be characterized as peace enforcement.

**Enforcement**

For the purposes of this study, the terms 'enforcement' and 'enforcement operations' are used (in contrast to '*peace* enforcement' and '*peace* enforcement operations') to designate military operations mandated by the Security Council, either implicitly or explicitly, under Chapter VII of the UN Charter, to use force or the threat of force to impose the will of the international community on a single errant state or sub-state party.[13] In such missions there is no pretence at neutrality or impartiality. If necessary, force is authorized to bring about military defeat of the designated 'enemy'—a key difference between such operations and peace enforcement operations. They will usually be organized from the outset to conduct war against such parties, although clearly 'war' can vary in intensity and purpose. The Security Council has never itself commanded such an enforcement operation, but has authorized member states to do so. The two examples are the UN operation in the 1950–54 Korean War, which sought to repel North Korea's invasion of South Korea, and the coalition operation in the Persian Gulf War which drove Iraq from Kuwait in early 1991.

Except by way of contrast, this book does not deal with such missions.

## II. Mandating the use of force by UN peace operations

The use of force by a UN peace operation is governed in the broadest sense by the mandate given to the operation by the Security Council. The drafting of such mandates is an intensely political process, driven by various considerations that are not relevant to the use-of-force issue. In addition to the 'normal' politicking and horse-trading that occur whenever states are required to agree on any matter, peace operations' mandates tend to be shaped by a reluctance on the part of many or all members of the Security Council to become too deeply involved in a particular conflict, a preoccupation with certain elements of a mandate, such as humanitarian assistance or the holding of an election, and in every case the likely financial costs.

Although Security Council mandates rarely mention a specific chapter of the UN Charter under which they are authorized, a convention has arisen whereby peacekeeping forces are assumed to be authorized under Chapter VI on the 'pacific settlement of disputes'. Decisions by the Security Council under this chapter are considered to be recommendatory and not enforceable, as the

---

[13] Chapters VI and VII of the UN Charter are reproduced in appendix 4 in this volume.

chapter deals only with cooperative measures to resolve conflict. Hence a peacekeeping operation authorized by the Security Council under Chapter VI is normally only deployed with the consent of the parties involved in the conflict. In terms of its authorization to use force, a Chapter VI operation is assumed to be limited to self-defence, as it may use force beyond this only with the consent of the parties. Since for the parties this would be tantamount to authorizing the use of force against themselves, such consent is unlikely to be granted.

In contrast to peacekeeping, the use of military force by the UN for enforcement purposes is seen as deriving its legality from Chapter VII of the UN Charter, 'action with respect to threats to the peace, breaches of the peace, and acts of aggression'. This is the chapter under which the Security Council makes decisions which are enforceable, including the imposition of economic sanctions and the taking of military action.[14] A Chapter VII operation, in contrast to a Chapter VI operation, may therefore be authorized to use force beyond self-defence for enforcement purposes. This understanding was confirmed by the International Court of Justice (ICJ) in July 1962 when it ruled that, while the UN has an inherent capacity to establish, assume command over and employ military forces, these may only exercise 'belligerent rights' when authorized to do so by the Security Council acting under Chapter VII.[15] This ruling suggests that the use of force by a Chapter VI peacekeeping operation beyond self-defence is illegal under the UN Charter. Along with impartiality and the consent of the parties, the self-defence rule may thus be seen as a key criterion that distinguishes peacekeeping from peace enforcement.

Despite these conventions, Security Council resolutions which envisage the use of force never specifically mention it. Usually they mandate a mission simply to use 'all necessary means' to accomplish its mandate. Hence they refrain from specifying in advance the appropriate level of force to be used.[16] While the mandate for UNPROFOR in Bosnia authorized 'all measures necessary' and that for UNOSOM II in Somalia authorized 'all necessary means', the ways in which force was used in the two theatres were quite different.

The situation has been complicated since the end of the cold war by the tendency of the Security Council to afford Chapter VII mandates to what have been perceived essentially as peacekeeping operations. This strategy has been resorted to for three purposes. The first is to supposedly reinforce, from the outset of a mission, its right to use force in self-defence. An example is the UN

---

[14] The General Assembly, whose decisions are never enforceable, may also establish peacekeeping operations (and has done so), but as practice has evolved it has become the exclusive preserve of the Security Council. 'The Charter has given to the Security Council means of enforcement and the right to take decisions with mandatory effect. No such authority is given to the General Assembly, which can only recommend action to Member Governments, which, in turn, may follow the recommendations or disregard them'. United Nations, Report of the Secretary-General in pursuance of General Assembly resolutions 1124 (XI) and 1125 (XI), UN document A/3527, 11 Feb. 1957, para. 19.

[15] International Court of Justice, 'Certain expenses of the United Nations (Article 17, para. 1), Advisory Opinion of 20 July 1962', *Reports of Judgements, Advisory Opinions and Orders* (International Court of Justice: The Hague, 1962), p. 177.

[16] Warbrick, C., 'Current developments: public international law', *International and Comparative Law Quarterly*, vol. 43 (Oct. 1994), p. 947.

Transitional Administration for Eastern Slavonia, Baranja and Western Sirmium (UNTAES). Arguably this is a misuse of the UN Charter, since peacekeepers already have the right of self-defence under their (implicit) Chapter VI authorization. Second, some peacekeeping missions originally deployed under Chapter VI have later acquired revised mandates authorized under Chapter VII, usually after they have begun experiencing difficulties—again, allegedly to strengthen their right of self-defence. A prime example was the mandate given to UNPROFOR in Bosnia once it began to experience difficulties with the local parties. Third, peacekeeping operations have acquired Chapter VII mandates to permit them to conduct what is in effect peace enforcement. This was true of UNOSOM II, UNTAET and UNAMSIL.

The essential problem with the UN Charter in relation to the use of force by UN peacekeepers is that neither peacekeeping itself nor the problems which have attended its evolution were foreseen when it was drafted. Like many national constitutions, it is both inflexible and almost impossible to amend and, as a consequence, has been and is being successively reinterpreted to sanction undertakings which, on the face of it, were never intended.

## III. Command and control of the use of force

The chain of command for UN peace operations runs from the UN Security Council through the UN Secretary-General and his representatives in the field to the military contingents supplied by UN member states.

### The UN Security Council

In theory, the Security Council is responsible for the command and control of military forces put at the disposal of the UN by member states. Article 47 of the UN Charter provides for the establishment of a Military Staff Committee, comprising the chiefs of staff of the five permanent members of the Security Council—China, France, Russia, the United Kingdom and the United States— to assist the Security Council in deploying and managing such military forces. Such a system has, however, never operated.[17]

For enforcement operations which have demanded the sustained and massive use of force to implement its writ, the Security Council has 'contracted out' command and control of the operation, either to a single member state or to a 'coalition of the willing'. The operation in Korea in the early 1950s was conducted under the UN flag by what purported to be a UN command but was, to all intents and purposes, a US-led and -run operation. In Operation Desert Storm against Iraq in 1991, the US-led coalition force was authorized to act by the Security Council but was not under the UN flag. Even some peacekeeping and/or peace enforcement operations have been contracted out to individual member states or coalitions, as in the cases of the United Task Force (UNITAF)

[17] For an analysis see Boulden, J., *Prometheus Unborn: The History of the Military Staff Committee*, Aurora Papers no. 19 (Canadian Centre for Global Security: Ottawa, 1993).

in Somalia, led by the USA, and the International Force for East Timor (INTERFET), led by Australia. The executive wing of the UN, the Secretary-General and Secretariat, have been kept at arm's length during such operations.

The UN as an organization has traditionally been entrusted only with peace-keeping (and latterly peace enforcement operations which were seen to be relatively easy), since that is all it has been judged capable of undertaking.

## The Secretary-General

Ever since Dag Hammarskjöld took responsibility for UNEF I, command and control of UN peace operations has come to be vested in the UN Secretary-General. This occurred more by serendipity than by design—in the absence of a functioning Military Staff Committee there simply was no one else. Hence the Secretary-General is in effect the commander-in-chief of UN peace operations.

While most operations have in reality required only token command from New York, sometimes the Secretary-General has become actively involved in command decisions, especially when force has been used. 'The organization's operations in both Somalia and Bosnia found the Secretary-General conducting himself as commanding general and making the final decision having to do with the application of air power, the disposition of ground forces and the dismissal of commanding officers.'[18] This also happened in the Congo under Hammarskjöld. The degree of the Secretary-General's involvement will depend to a great extent on his personality and attitude. He can be interventionist, as Hammarskjöld and Boutros Boutros-Ghali were, or at the other extreme, as in the cases of Kurt Waldheim and Perez de Cuellar, can largely remove himself from day-to-day command and management of operations. The attitude of the current Secretary-General, Kofi Annan, appears to fall somewhere between these two extremes.

## Special representatives of the Secretary-General and force commanders

For each operation the Secretary-General appoints a head of mission, normally called the Special Representative of the Secretary-General (SRSG), and a force commander to lead the military component. The former may come from within the UN system or from a UN member state; the latter is always chosen from the military hierarchy of a member state, often one of those contributing troops to the operation. Both posts may be occupied by a single individual for the duration of a mission, although the military tend to be rotated more frequently. The Secretary-General in theory devolves command authority down to the SRSG and/or force commander. An SRSG has command authority over the force commander, although sometimes the latter doubles as head of mission. As well as receiving orders from the Secretary-General, the SRSG and force

---

[18] Rosenau, J. N., 'Governance in the twenty-first century', *Global Governance*, vol. 1, no. 1 (winter 1995), p. 35.

commander provide military and other advice on their mission up the chain of command to the Secretary-General as well as the UN Secretariat.

The SRSG and/or force commander are usually given a high degree of autonomy in establishing, managing and commanding an operation. The UN has never had an appropriate Headquarters staff or communications system for providing tight command and control from UN Headquarters in New York. Such autonomy has been both advantageous and disadvantageous, permitting operations a degree of flexibility when required (useful both to the mission itself and to UN Headquarters for purposes of deniability), but has also resulted in many missions being 'orphaned', either continuously or at critical junctures. Both phenomena will be examined in this book.

The Secretary-General's representatives in the field may either faithfully reflect the views of their superior or have their own approach to the use of force. The relationship between the SRSG and force commander and their respective attitudes towards the use of force can be critical. There tends to be a constant tension between the perspectives of the political leadership and those of the military leadership towards the threat and use of force, although not necessarily in a way the stereotypes might suggest.

At the operational level, the force commander has considerable latitude in interpreting the UN guidelines on the use of force. Some force commanders are willing to countenance more robust use of force than others. The nationality, personality and previous experience of the commander are thus important variables in determining the mode of operation of each mission.

## The UN Secretariat

The UN Secretariat inherited the idealism of the League of Nations Secretariat, and was also greatly constrained by the cold war. These factors and the multinational nature of its composition tended to produce safe, lowest-common-denominator approaches. Its ethos as regards the settlement of international disputes and the deployment of peacekeepers alike became the following: always seek negotiation and mediation as first, middle and last resort; take everything declared by states (and even sub-state actors) at face value, at least in public; base all planning on best-case scenarios; shield the Security Council from unsettling information lest it be required to act on it; and uphold the sanctity at all cost of the three precepts of peacekeeping. The Secretariat has been widely perceived as being averse to the use of force—an attitude approved of and fostered by member states, most of which considered the Secretariat simply a functional, bureaucratic arm of the UN rather than an initiator of policy.

The Secretariat's capability for analysing and dealing with military issues during the cold war, including with regard to the use of force, was limited. Its staff was almost entirely civilian, lacking even a rudimentary capacity to handle military issues, much less mount, command, control or communicate satisfactorily with a UN military operation in the field. The Secretariat's role was dependent to a great extent on the personalities and capabilities of key individuals. The Secretary-General was at times advised by a military adviser, a senior military commander based at UN Headquarters, as well as by his regular staff, including self-made peacekeeping experts such as Urquhart. With the end of the cold war and the increased use of force in peace operations, the Secretariat found itself (as it did in the 1960s Congo operation) forced to deal with issues requiring greater military expertise, including complex command and control challenges.

In March 1992 UN peacekeeping expertise was gathered for the first time into a separate DPKO, headed by an under secretary-general, in an attempt to professionalize what had clearly become a permanent, time-consuming and costly UN endeavour.[19] Specialist units were set up in the department in an attempt to improve the management, including command and control, of UN peacekeeping operations.[20] In 1993 a Situation Centre was established to provide 24-hour communication, seven days a week, between UN Headquarters and missions in the field. An attempt was also made to acquire military expertise by recruiting military personnel to the DPKO and by seconding military personnel from member states at their expense (although this proved controversial among developing countries and after 1999 was scaled back). Since the release of the Brahimi Report in 2000[21] there has been a significant increase in professional military staffing levels in the department.

As in the case of national systems, decision making about the use of force has not always been in accordance with the formal command structure. Often an SRSG or force commander has dealt directly with officials in the UN Secretariat on use-of-force matters not seen as requiring the personal involvement of the Secretary-General. In some cases Secretariat officials have been critically involved in making and communicating decisions to missions in the field about use-of-force issues, particularly during periods of crisis. The operation of this somewhat loose chain of command has given rise to 'an almost continuous discussion' on the division of responsibilities, exemplified in the peacekeeper's adage that 'when New York is in doubt, the issue is left to the force headquarters, which is always wrong'.[22]

## National contingents

At the bottom end of the chain of command in UN peace operations are the individual national contingents headed by contingent commanders. While in

---

[19] Initially, it was called the Office of the Under Secretary-General for Peacekeeping Operations. On peacekeeping policy and administration before the DPKO was established see Durch, W. J., 'Running the show: planning and implementation', ed. W. J. Durch, *The Evolution of UN Peacekeeping: Case Studies and Comparative Analysis* (St Martin's Press for the Henry L. Stimson Center: Washington, DC, 1993).

[20] On the administrative structure of and arrangements for peacekeeping after 1992 see Annan, K. A., 'Challenges for the new peacekeeping', eds O. A. Otunnu and M. W. Doyle, *Peacemaking and Peacekeeping for the New Century* (Rowman & Littlefield: Lanham, Md., 1998).

[21] United Nations, Report of the Panel on United Nations Peace Operations, UN document A/55/305, S/2000/809, 21 Aug. 2000. On the Brahimi Report see also chapter 9 in this volume.

[22] Skogmo, B., *International Peacekeeping in Lebanon, 1978–1988* (Lynne Rienner: Boulder, Colo. and London, 1989), p. 84.

theory all contingents are subject to command and control by the UN, in practice the extent to which this occurs depends on the attitude of the government
contributing the troops and/or the contingent commander. Although all contingents will be expected to keep in regular contact with their national military
authorities, there are varying degrees to which UN orders will be checked with
national capitals. The greater the actual or potential use of force in the mission,
the greater the tendency to seek instructions from home. This has resulted in
some notorious cases of 'second guessing' by national authorities, in which UN
orders were countermanded or undermined. While some force commanders turn
a blind eye to such behaviour, others treat it as tantamount to rebellion and seek
the help of the Secretary-General in restoring proper command and control.

## IV. Regulating the use of force

Security Council resolutions authorizing the establishment of peacekeeping
operations not only rarely mention the chapter of the UN Charter under which
this is done but also usually fail to mention the specific type of operation
envisaged or the broad guidelines for the use of force under which it should
operate. Such broad guidelines are usually contained, instead, in a report by the
Secretary-General on his proposals for the force. These are normally requested
by the Security Council before it definitively authorizes the deployment of a
mission. The guidelines are drafted for the Secretary-General by the UN Secretariat, drawing on relevant precedents. Security Council resolutions normally
simply cite and/or endorse the Secretary-General's reports (although sometimes
they may be sent back to the Secretary-General for revision). Similarly, when
guidelines for the use of force are changed during the life of a mission they are
usually contained in a report of the Secretary-General endorsed by the Security
Council, but these are rarely set out or quoted in a Council resolution.

Guidelines for the use of force based on the broad concepts contained in the
Secretary-General's proposal may be reiterated in a Status of Forces Agreement
(SOFA) or Status of Mission Agreement (SOMA) between the UN and the state
hosting the peacekeeping operation.[23] Often, however, any reference they might
make to the use-of-force issue is extremely general. For the Congo mission in
the 1960s, during which a great deal of force was used, the SOFA simply provided that: 'The UN shall not have recourse to the use of force except as a last
resort and subject to the restrictions imposed by its mandate and by the
resolutions of the Security Council and the General Assembly'.[24] Mostly the
SOFAs make no mention of the use of force at all, undoubtedly to avoid raising
the fears of the host country.

More detailed guidelines for the use of force are usually contained in standing
(or standard)[25] operating procedures (SOP) issued to the UN force by the force

[23] US Department of the Army, *Peace Operations*, FM 100-23 (Department of the Army: Washington, DC, Dec. 1994), p. 66.

[24] Seyersted, F., *United Nations Forces in the Law of Peace and War* (Sijthoff: Leyden, 1966), p. 72.

[25] Military usage tends to oscillate between the 2 terms, seemingly unintentionally.

commander. The SOP define what is meant by force and the principles governing its use. They are meant to explain in detail the circumstances in which force may be used and establish the level of responsibility for taking the decision to use it. The SOP should also include instructions on the manner in which weapons are to be used, for example, in regard to the use of warning shots, the controlling of fire, prohibitions on the use of automatic weapons and/or high explosives, and the action to be taken after firing. Orders and directives in peace operations will almost always include admonitions to contingent and/or local commanders to exhaust all peaceful means first, including negotiation and mediation. Peaceful interpositioning is also a common recommendation.

The rules for the use of force, as formulated by the force commander, may be called rules of engagement (ROE) and be issued in written form to troops in the field. ROE are defined as 'directives specifying the circumstances and limitations under which military forces will initiate and/[or] maintain combat with the enemy'.[26] Simplified versions of ROE may be issued to individual soldiers for everyday reference, usually in the form of a readily accessible laminated card. These may be known as orders for opening fire (OFOF). Instructions relating to the use of force in specific operational activities or for specific occasions may also be issued by the force commander down through the chain of command as the need arises. Contrasted with those for normal military operations, the ROE for peace operations aim to embody two important principles of peackeeping—restraint and legitimacy.[27]

## V. The origins of the self-defence norm

A hallmark of UN peacekeeping and a key characteristic that distinguishes it from enforcement is the norm constraining peacekeepers from using force except in self-defence. Even in self-defence, force may only be used as a last resort. It is also to be used proportionately: only sufficient force may be employed to achieve the objective of ending the immediate threat and prevent, as far as possible, loss of life or serious injury. Force should not be initiated, except possibly after continuous harassment, when it may become necessary to restore a situation so that the UN can fulfil its responsibilities. Force should not be used to punish or retaliate for previous incidents. The principal tools of the peacekeeper are negotiation and persuasion, not the use of force.

Initially self-defence meant simply defence of the peacekeeper's own person and those of his colleagues, using his own personal weapon. Experience quickly

---

[26] Zurick, T., *Army Dictionary and Desk Reference* (Stackpole Books: Harrisburg, Pa., 1992), p. 176. The term 'rules of engagement' derives from the US military. Its first informal use in the Department of Defense may have been in connection with the issuing of 'Intercept Engagement Instructions' for the US Navy on 23 Nov. 1954. Its first formal use was in 1958 in the Joint Chiefs of Staff (JCS) precursor to what is now JCS Pub 1, the 'Dictionary of military and associated terms'. The US Air Force in South Korea developed ROE in 1960–63. The US Navy issued ROE for the Bay of Pigs landing in Cuba in 1961, and in 1962 the JCS promulgated 'Peacetime ROE for Seaborne Forces'. The US Army only started to use the term in the past few years. Information provided by Don Daniel, Director, Strategic Research Department, Center for Naval Warfare Studies, US Naval War College, Newport, R.I.

[27] Allard, K., *Somalia Operations: Lessons Learned* (National Defense University, Institute for National Strategic Studies: Washington, DC, 1995), p. 36.

demonstrated the need to broaden this to permit peacekeepers to use force to frustrate attempts to disarm them; to defend their posts, vehicles and equipment against seizure or armed attack; and to support UN troops from other contingents.[28] This was further expanded to permit them to defend UN civilian agencies and personnel from attack, although the decision on where to draw the line was left to individual force commanders.

The norm restricting the use of force by peacekeepers to self-defence is integral to the concept of peacekeeping as originally conceived. It is a logical concomitant of the principle that peacekeepers should be deployed and operate only with the consent of the parties to a conflict and should observe strict impartiality in their dealings with the parties. At a practical level, traditional peacekeeping is simply not sustainable if it leads to an uncontrolled escalation of violence, especially if, as a result, ill-equipped and ill-protected peacekeepers are perceived to have become parties to the conflict. For UN peacekeeping veteran Brian Urquhart: 'The moment a peacekeeping force starts killing people it becomes a part of the conflict it is supposed to be controlling and thus a part of the problem'.[29] In such circumstances, it is feared, consent is lost and impartiality forfeited.

The application of the self-defence norm to UN peacekeeping is also the inevitable result of the use of armed personnel for such operations. Military forces under UN command derive the right of self-defence from several sources. Military personnel, like anyone else, are considered to have a natural, inherent right of individual and collective self-defence. The origins of this concept may be traced to the writings of Dutch philosopher Hugo Grotius (1583–1645). He regarded preservation of the self as a natural right of individuals that could not be abrogated or limited by law.[30] He also posited the right of states to self-defence, a concept now embodied in international law, including in Article 51 of the UN Charter. Since armed forces are the main defenders of the state, they are assumed to derive their collective right of self-defence from the right of states to self-defence. Armed personnel are assumed to enjoy this right even when acting on behalf of the UN. Although some observers insist that this is 'more akin to a personal right of self-defence' than the much wider right of a state to self-defence,[31] others argue that the UN itself, like states, enjoys an inherent right of self-defence and its personnel, by implication, thus enjoy the right of individual and collective self-defence.[32]

By precedent, argument and international law, the right of self-defence was therefore from the outset the minimum that the UN was obliged to accord its

---

[28] International Peace Academy, *Peacekeeper's Handbook* (Pergamon Press: New York, 1984), p. 57.

[29] Quoted in Meister, S., 'Crisis in Katanga', *Soldiers for Peace*, Supplement to *Military History Quarterly*, vol. 5, no. 1 (autumn 1992), p. 54.

[30] Alexandrov, S. A., *Self-Defense Against the Use of Force in International Law* (Kluwer Law International: The Hague, 1996), pp. 5–6. Grotius defined such a right as 'the right of self-defense [which] has its origin directly, and chiefly, in the fact that nature commits to each his own protection, not in the injustice or crime of the aggressor'.

[31] McCoubrey, H. and White, N. D., *The Blue Helmets: Legal Regulation of United Nations Military Operations* (Dartmouth: Aldershot, 1996), p. 84.

[32] Seyersted (note 24), p. 406.

peacekeepers. However, the exercise of this right, as in the case of other uses of military force, is subject to certain conditions which have been codified by international law and practice. The most significant of these are necessity and proportionality. Force must only be used in self-defence when absolutely necessary, as a last resort and in proportion to the threat. What is notable is the provisional character of self-defence: 'It is triggered only upon certain require-ments being fulfilled (armed attack or imminent threat), and the fact that the final judgment of the legality of the use of force in self-defense is made by the international community'.[33]

Quite apart from these legal considerations, from the perspective of practical politics it has been clear since the advent of peacekeeping that states are unwilling to provide forces to the UN if they are not accorded the right of self-defence. 'It would be very doubtful if any nation would contribute its soldiers to a peace-keeping force without this minimal guarantee of recourse to arms'.[34] On the other hand, states are also concerned that the UN should not use their national contingents for purposes involving use of force beyond self-defence.[35]

When it comes to providing troops for UN peace operations, states are risk-averse, not wishing to incur casualties as a result of activity that moves beyond traditional peacekeeping and concerned that the world organization might begin to usurp the state's monopoly on the use of force if it is provided with a robust military capability. Self-defence is relatively easy, safe and cheap.

One of the aims of this book is to explore how this basic self-defence norm has been applied to UN peacekeeping, how it has evolved, how it has been stretched or transgressed, and the resulting implications for UN peace opera-tions.

## VI. Myths, puzzles and paradoxes about the UN's use of force

Ever since its inception there have been myths, puzzles and paradoxes about the use of force in UN peacekeeping, and they have rarely been scrutinized. There seems to have been a taboo about questioning the principles of peacekeeping too rigorously for fear that to do so might destroy a delicate instrument that was proving, despite its flaws, to be useful.

### Peacekeeping as a Chapter VI activity?

From the point of view of the UN Charter, the original conception of peace-keeping as a Chapter VI activity seems questionable. Hammarskjöld's original notion was that Chapter VI was appropriate because peacekeeping would be voluntary and non-enforceable. The deployment of a peacekeeping mission would follow a ceasefire or peace agreement and a voluntary request by the

---

[33] Alexandrov (note 30), p. 296.
[34] Moskos (note 7), p. 131.
[35] Some countries, e.g., Japan, are sensitive about their troops using force beyond personal self-defence.

parties. The troop-contributing countries were not compelled to volunteer their personnel. All this suggested non-enforcement and consent.

Hammarskjöld recognized, however, that such operations could equally be mandated under Article 40 of Chapter VII regarding 'provisional measures' that could be taken prior to the Security Council taking more drastic enforcement measures under Article 39. Hence the widespread idea that somehow peace-keeping might be viewed as a 'Chapter VI and-a-half' activity, somewhere between voluntarism and compulsion. Unfortunately Hammarskjöld did not live to flesh out his emerging theory of peacekeeping and it was left as it was. His conclusions about the moral duty of peacekeepers to ensure, if necessary through the use of force, the protection of civilians at risk in the Congo in the 1960s indicate the direction he might have taken.

The mantra of peacekeeping's 'essential' three attributes was adopted by an international community that was relieved to find some mechanism to assist in the implementation of ceasefires, withdrawals and peace agreements. Once this happened, however, peacekeeping tended to be applied simplistically to situations which did not necessarily suit it, such as the Congo and Lebanon, but for which no alternatives were deemed possible. Robust peacekeeping, or peace enforcement, was too far-reaching an option to be contemplated during the cold war, as it is for many states even now. In this situation, with peacekeeping operations dispatched to undertake missions for which they were not designed, the original use-of-force parameters became surreal.

The description of peacekeeping as a Chapter VI activity has never been entirely convincing. While both Egypt and Israel accepted the need for the deployment of UNEF I and II, it was hardly entirely voluntary: both had to be persuaded to accept it. The Congo mission was deployed without the consent of the Katangans and only reluctantly agreed to by Belgium, while the Congolese Government gave its consent only under the impression that it was to be a peace enforcement operation. The deployment of the UN Force in Lebanon (UNIFIL) was sought by Lebanon but shunned by Israel. Egypt had the right to ask UNEF I to leave—a right that it invoked in 1967. The Khmer Rouge only grudgingly accepted the deployment of UNTAC; Somali warlords acquiesced to the deployment of UNOSOM I and II in similar vein. Indonesia's acceptance of INTERFET and UNTAET is a more recent case of such 'coerced consent'.

**The right of freedom of movement**

One particularly puzzling dilemma, especially for force commanders, has been the so-called right of freedom of movement for peacekeepers. Supposedly an inherent right for all peacekeepers since it was established for UNEF I (by agreement with the Egyptian Government), it has since been enshrined in various forms in SOFAs with various host governments. It has rarely been mentioned, however, in Security Council resolutions or mission mandates, except when it has begun to be infringed. In the field it has been inconsistently asserted and often poorly understood. It is still not clear, after all these years, whether freedom of movement (*a*) means that the mission's military can move freely between the ports of entry and its bases along main thoroughfares, (*b*) extends only to ensuring that the mission can resupply itself unhindered, (*c*) extends to providing convoy protection (in effect transferring the UN troops' right of freedom of movement to others, such as those supplying humanitarian relief), or (*d*) connotes the right of UN troops to have access 'anywhere, any time, any place' within its theatre of operations.

Furthermore, if freedom of movement, however defined, is forcefully blocked, does the use of force in self-defence then apply? The UN has been loath to clarify the right, presumably for fear of then being obliged to enforce it.

### Self-defence as deterrence

The theory of deterrence holds that, for party A to successfully deter party B, it must convince B that it faces unacceptable consequences if it fails to comply with A's wishes.[36] The deterred party must be convinced that it will lose more of what it values than it will gain if it flaunts the wishes of the deterring party. The ability to deter successfully relies on clearly communicating the objective and the threat and demonstrating both capability and will. In particular, the deterring party must demonstrate that it will not be self-deterred through fear of the unanticipated consequences of taking action. In a military context, basic deterrence seeks to prevent attacks against oneself, while extended deterrence aims at preventing attacks against others.

From a military perspective, the deterrent effect of peacekeeping remains a puzzle. Why deploy armed peacekeepers if those arms are not to be used? If consent is obtained and impartiality maintained as it should be, there should be no need for weapons at all, even in self-defence. If opposition to the presence of peacekeepers develops, according to the theory of peacekeeping, negotiation and withdrawal are the only options. The use of force in self-defence can only be a short-term palliative to a loss of consent and indeed may cause consent to deteriorate even faster. Lightly armed UN peacekeepers have thus traditionally stood no chance of deterring in a military sense (although moral and political deterrence, which is not dependent on military capability or a willingness to use force, has also been presumed to be a factor).

The reason why armed troops are used for peacekeeping (apart from a soldier's personal security, which in relatively rare cases is threatened) can only be that there is always some implicit threat of the use of force. There is, it appears, an implicit uncertainty in the deployment of armed troops as to whether or not, and under what circumstances, they will use their weapons. An implicit deterrent effect may be at work which is probably enhanced rather than harmed by the element of uncertainty.

---

[36] Schelling, T., *Arms and Influence* (Yale University Press: New Haven, Conn., 1966).

Peacekeepers have a decidedly mixed record in handling the deterrence issue. They have often been both openly unwilling to defend themselves and patently militarily incapable of doing so, and thus unable to deter attacks against themselves by using force in self-defence. Even where they have been militarily capable of defending themselves, they have often signalled, by their behaviour and even pronouncements, that they were unwilling to defend even their fellow UN peacekeepers, much less anyone else, thereby destroying any extended deterrent effect they might have had. On occasions, however, the uncertain deterrent effect of the presence of peacekeepers has been used effectively by force commanders. This occurred notably in the Congo, Cyprus and Cambodia, where the right of a UN force to use force in self-defence was employed to signal resolve and effectively compel a party to act or refrain from acting in a particular way. This could be seen as a form of peace enforcement. Notably, however, it involves a dangerous element of bluff, since it is not clear that the threat of the use of force will actually be followed through, whether the force contemplated or used will be sufficient to bring about the desired compliance, whether the use of force will trigger retaliation and escalation or, perhaps most importantly, whether the Security Council will support the mission politically and (if necessary) militarily if deterrence fails.

## Defence of the mission

After 1973, as the chapters that follow show, the self-defence rule was expanded to encompass 'defence of the mission'. For the first time, self-defence would include resistance to attempts by forceful means to prevent a peace-keeping mission from discharging its duties under its Security Council mandate. While this was presumably designed to explicitly expand the self-defence rule rather than allow peacekeeping missions to suffer from 'mission creep', the effect was to create greater uncertainty for force commanders. In the absence of guidance from the Security Council, the Secretary-General or the Secretariat, they were left to interpret 'defence of the mission' according to their own predilections.

The difficulty is that the concept could in effect be used to justify the use of force for any purpose. If the mandate is to assist in the delivery of humanitarian relief, then force can in theory be used to ensure that relief gets through. If the mission is to ensure the disarmament and demobilization of erstwhile belligerents, then force can apparently be used if they attempt to thwart the mission by refusing to hand over their weapons and return to civilian life. If the mandate authorizes a peace operation to deploy throughout the whole of the mission area and that deployment is resisted by force, the new rule can be used to justify a forceful intervention.

# 2. The emergence of the self-defence norm: UNEF I

UNEF I, which was deployed in the Middle East from 1956 to 1967, laid the foundations for the development of norms for UN peacekeeping, including those relating to the use of force. Although it was not the first UN peacekeeping operation, nor the first to involve military personnel, it was the first in which military personnel were armed.[1] UNEF's deployment was therefore the first occasion on which the question of the use of force by UN troops arose.[2]

## I. Genesis and mandate

UNEF I was established by the UN General Assembly in November 1956 in response to an invasion of Egypt by British, French and Israeli forces, and subsequent agreement by the four states to a ceasefire and restoration of the *status quo ante*.[3] The idea for UNEF came from Lester B. Pearson, Canadian Secretary of State for External Affairs, soon after the crisis broke out. Recognizing the need in this case for something more than an unarmed observer force, he described UNEF as a 'a truly international peace and police force . . . large enough to keep these borders at peace while a political settlement is being worked out'.[4] Details of the concept were refined at UN Headquarters between Pearson, Secretary-General Dag Hammarskjöld, Executive Assistant to the Secretary-General Andrew Cordier and Under Secretary-General Ralph Bunche.[5] Initially, Hammarskjöld was 'not too enthusiastic' about the proposal and pessimistic about its chances of success. However, once convinced, he took on the project with his usual élan. On 4 November the General Assembly asked him to produce a plan for UNEF within 48 hours. He drafted it himself immediately, in consultation with Bunche, Cordier, Pearson and UN Legal Counsel Constantin Stavropoulos, and submitted it the same day.[6] The Assembly

---

[1] The UN Truce Supervisory Organization (UNTSO), established in 1948, and UN Military Observer Group in India and Pakistan (UNMOGIP), established in 1949, used only unarmed military observers.

[2] Unarmed personnel, as in the very earliest UN observer missions, presumably also have a right of self-defence but no means of exercising it.

[3] UN General Assembly Resolution 1000 (ES-1), 5 Nov. 1956, known as the 'Uniting for Peace resolution'. Proposed by the USA, it bypassed the Security Council, in which 2 of the protagonists in the conflict, Britain and France, had a veto. The precedent was not followed in the establishment of subsequent UN peacekeeping operations, presumably because it was regarded as a usurpation of the Security Council's ultimate responsibility for international peace and security.

[4] Munro, J. A. and Inglis, A. I. (eds), *Mike: The Memoirs of the Right Honourable Lester B. Pearson, Vol. 2, 1948–1957* (University of Toronto Press: Toronto, 1973), p. 247; and Urquhart, B., *Ralph Bunche: An American Life* (W. W. Norton: New York, 1993), p. 265.

[5] Burns, E. L. M. (Lt-Gen.), *Between Arab and Israeli* (George G. Harrap: London, 1962), p. 187.

[6] United Nations, Report of the Secretary-General on basic points for the presence and functioning in Egypt of the United Nations Emergency Force, UN document A/3289, 4 Nov. 1956. See also Urquhart (note 4), p. 267.

adopted the proposals on 5 November,[7] establishing a UN Command for UNEF and appointing as commander on an emergency basis the Chief of Staff of UNTSO, Canadian Major-General (later Lieutenant-General) E. L. Burns. It authorized him immediately to recruit a force, beginning with seconded UNTSO observers and adding larger troop contingents from UN member states as they became available.

The General Assembly requested a further report from the Secretary-General setting out the concept and guiding principles for UNEF, which he presented on 6 November.[8] Hammarskjöld proposed that the force be under an independent UN chief of command, that its troops be recruited from UN member states other than the permanent members of the Security Council and that its terms of reference be to 'secure and supervise the cessation of hostilities'. UNEF would have two main tasks. First, it would enter the areas occupied by the British and French forces as they withdrew, to maintain law and order prior to turning them over to Egypt. Second, it would supervise and follow the withdrawal of Israeli troops back across Sinai and from the Gaza Strip to the Israeli border, also permitting eventual handover to Egyptian control.

Hammarskjöld's report did not mention the use of force specifically but did include a caution that 'there was no intent in the establishment of the Force to influence the military balance in the current conflict, and thereby the political balance affecting efforts to settle the conflict'. Moreover:

The Force obviously should have no rights other than those necessary for the execution of its functions, in co-operation with local authorities. It would be more than an observer corps, but in no way a military force temporarily controlling the territory in which it was stationed; nor, moreover, should the Force have military functions exceeding those necessary to secure peaceful conditions on the assumption that the Parties to the conflict take all necessary steps for compliance with the recommendations of the General Assembly.[9]

Hammarskjöld's report was accepted at once by the General Assembly on 7 November 1956.[10] In the view of Brian Urquhart, Under Secretary-General for Special Political Tasks, it was 'a masterpiece in a completely new field, the blueprint for a nonviolent, international military operation'. 'Soldiers from national armies were being asked', he points out, 'to plunge into a critical situation without using force and under UN command. Such a venture touched on the most sensitive issues of military psychology and tradition, national sovereignty and international law'.[11] Pearson recalls that the original draft had called on the force to 'to enforce and supervise', but he spotted the slip just as the draft was about to be reproduced: 'Thank goodness I noticed it, because we

---

[7] United Nations, Report of the Secretary-General on basic points for the presence and functioning in Egypt of the United Nations Emergency Force, UN document A/3302, 6 Nov. 1956.
[8] Report of the Secretary-General (note 7).
[9] Report of the Secretary-General (note 7).
[10] UN General Assembly Resolution 1000 (ES-1) (note 3).
[11] Urquhart (note 4), pp. 267, 269.

would have been in the soup if this force had been charged with the job of "enforcing" anything!'[12]

As UNEF was established by the General Assembly, not the Security Council, it could not in any event have been an enforcement operation, since only the Security Council can take such action, under Chapter VII of the UN Charter. Rather, UNEF was mandated under Chapter IV, Article 14, which deals with the role and powers of the General Assembly.[13] UNEF has nonetheless come to be regarded as a quintessential Chapter VI operation. As early as 1957, states contributing troops to UNEF, such as Brazil and Colombia, were referring to it as such.[14]

The chain of command for the new force was to be as follows. Burns, as chief of command, would be answerable to the Secretary-General, who would in turn be responsible to the General Assembly. This chain of command has become the norm for peacekeeping operations, except that the Security Council rather than the General Assembly is at the apex and the Secretary-General is usually represented in the field by an SRSG with line authority over the force commander.

When asked by Hammarskjöld what type of force he would suggest, Burns thought it should be 'so strong that it would be in no danger of being thrust aside, pushed out, or ignored', as UNTSO had been.[15] In view of the military strength of Egypt and Israel he foresaw a need for a division, a brigade of tanks, and reconnaissance and fighter aircraft. It would be organized as 'an operational force capable of fighting'. Contingents, he felt, should be no smaller than battalion size since a force comprising many smaller units of different nationalities would be difficult to control administratively and tactically.[16] They should, moreover, be organized and trained to operate as a unit.

However, such a force was not possible, politically or in practice. The Secretary-General and the General Assembly clearly envisaged a symbolic, non-fighting force which would assist in implementing the withdrawal agreements rather than enforce them. In any case, no state would volunteer forces to engage the battle-hardened belligerents if they failed to comply with their undertakings. The militarily most capable states were all disqualified from involvement: of the five permanent members of the Security Council, France and the UK were parties to the conflict, China was uninterested, and the USA and the Soviet Union were locked in their cold war antagonisms. Nor was it

[12] Munro and Inglis (note 4), p. 259.
[13] This was confirmed by the ICJ in its Certain Expenses case. International Court of Justice, 'Certain expenses of the United Nations (Article 17, para. 1), Advisory Opinion of 20 July 1962', *Reports of Judgements, Advisory Opinions and Orders* (International Court of Justice: The Hague, 1962). See also Schneider, S. J., 'Congo Force and standing UN force: legal experience with ONUC', *Indian Journal of International Law*, vol. 4, no. 2 (Apr. 1964), p. 274.
[14] United Nations, Verbatim record, Meeting of the Advisory Committee for UNEF, UN Secretariat, New York, 16 Mar. 1957, p. 5.
[15] Burns (note 5), p. 188.
[16] Decades later, the Brahimi Report (United Nations, Report of the Panel on United Nations Peace Operations, UN document A/55/305, S/2000/809, 21 Aug. 2000) would make the same point. See chapter 9, section IV in this volume.

felt, initially, that Soviet and US allies could be involved (although NATO members Canada, Denmark and Norway eventually were). The candidates for providing forces were therefore smaller nations with less military power, as would become the norm for UN peacekeeping.

The force—it varied during its 10-year deployment from 3500 to 6000 troops—was small. The original 10 contributing countries were Brazil, Canada, Colombia, Denmark, Finland, India, Indonesia, Norway, Sweden and Yugo-slavia. Their contributions were of varying sizes, usually smaller than the battalions that Burns had requested, and nearly all infantry. The force was equipped with the normal regimental weapons and means of transport and recon-naissance, including vehicles and aircraft, but not heavy weapons. Yugoslavia provided a complete reconnaissance battalion, while Canada later supplied a fully-equipped, light-armoured squadron.[17] Naturally, they had no time to train together as an organized force prior to deployment.

This patched-together force was far from meeting Burns' requirement for a deterrent capability. He worried that 'by failing to provide a big enough force, and failing to express a firm enough attitude towards *both* parties, [the General Assembly] had created the danger that the UNEF might be thwarted, and in the end prove no more effective than the observer organization'.[18] That UNEF would not be expected to drive out any of the parties which disobeyed the General Assembly's demands for withdrawal was, he claims, 'fairly obvious', but it was not so clear what powers UNEF had to resist an attempt by one of the parties to reoccupy territory it had vacated.

UNEF was described as 'acting as a plate-glass window', not capable of withstanding assault but 'nevertheless a lightly armed barrier that all see and tend to respect'.[19] According to Arthur Lee Burns and Nina Heathcote, while the decision establishing UNEF made it clear that the operation was 'para-military', the 'absence of an explicit authorization to use offensive action and the legal basis on which the General Assembly took its decision restricted the Secretary-General to equipping the force for self-defense only'.[20]

## II. Use-of-force rules

As well as command, staff and logistical arrangements, the deployment by the UN of armed troops instead of unarmed observers required new principles and rules. Like other aspects of this first true peacekeeping operation, UNEF's use-of-force rules did not appear spontaneously, whether from the General Assembly, the Security Council or the UN Secretariat. Practice evolved grad-

---

[17] United Nations, *The Blue Helmets: A Review of United Nations Peace-keeping*, 3rd edn (UN Department of Public Information. New York, 1996), p. 43.

[18] Burns (note 5), p. 208. Emphasis in original.

[19] Seyersted, F., *United Nations Forces in the Law of Peace and War* (Sijthoff: Leyden, 1966), p. 48.

[20] Burns, A. L. and Heathcote, N., *Peacekeeping by UN Forces: From Suez to the Congo*, Princeton Studies in World Politics no. 4 (Praeger for the Center for International Studies, Princeton: New York, 1963), p. 21.

ually and was only later codified. 'Nothing could be more mistaken than the opinion that the self-defence doctrine was asserted from the very beginning.'[21]

Certain preconditions for UNEF's success were discussed in detail in the General Assembly and Security Council, such as the consent of the parties to UNEF's presence and activities, its right to freedom of movement and the fact that it was not an enforcement operation, but no particular attention was paid to whether and how force might be used. As in the later Congo mission, there was a tendency on the part of both bodies to 'leave it to Dag',[22] but in the urgent circumstances of UNEF's creation it was impossible for the Secretariat to draft guiding principles for the operation, including the use of force. As General Burns notes: 'So many matters relating to UNEF were improvised, and so much was dependent on political conditions, which were fluid and in the course of development'.[23]

## Policy making on the use of force

Hammarskjöld relied for advice on the establishment and management of UNEF on an informal military committee attached to his executive office, composed of military representatives of participating countries. It was headed by his military adviser, Major-General I. A. E. Martola of Finland, assisted by three other military officers.[24] Hammarskjöld also relied heavily on Bunche, who had set up and directed UNTSO and had devised its basic principles, procedures and rules of conduct. Although he was a civilian, he was in Urquhart's view 'the obvious choice to supervise this new type of international military venture'.[25]

The General Assembly also established an Advisory Committee composed of representatives of the main initial troop-contributing countries.[26] Chaired by the Secretary-General, it was supposed to advise on general policy for the operation.[27] It was intended that the Secretary-General would issue regulations and instructions to UNEF only after consultation with the committee, but in practice he convened it only when he needed its assistance. Hammarskjöld 'probably found it a useful device to ratify his policies but not control them'.[28] The tempo of his consultations with the committee changed according to the situation on the ground, increasing, for instance, when the first incidents occurred in Gaza.

Although Rosalyn Higgins claims that the Advisory Committee was consulted 'when the policy was formulated that UNEF should use force only in

---

[21] Goldmann, K., *Peace-keeping and Self-Defence*, Monograph no. 7 (International Information Center on Peace-keeping Operations: Paris, Mar. 1968), p. 10.

[22] Higgins, R., *United Nations Peacekeeping 1946–1967: Documents and Commentary. Vol. 1, The Middle East* (Oxford University Press: Oxford, 1969), p. 273.

[23] Burns (note 5), p. 218.

[24] *The Blue Helmets*, 3rd edn (note 17), p. 43.

[25] Urquhart (note 4), p. 266.

[26] These were Brazil, Canada, Ceylon, Colombia, India, Norway and Pakistan.

[27] Burns (note 5), p. 194.

[28] Cohen, M., 'The United Nations Emergency Force: a preliminary view', *International Journal*, no. 12 (spring 1957), p. 120.

self-defence',[29] the records reveal no such discussion. The use-of-force policy was formulated by Burns in consultation with Bunche, other members of the Secretariat and the Secretary-General, but without the benefit of the committee's advice. Certainly, when Burns and Bunche wanted to expand the policy to include meeting border incursions with armed force, the committee was consulted, resulting in firm instructions being sent to Burns to retain the original policy (see section III below). What is remarkable with hindsight is how little debate there was in the committee, or indeed in the General Assembly or Security Council, on the question of the use of force before UNEF was deployed or during its first months of operation. This is probably because UNEF was regarded as a 'one-off' initiative designed to meet the unique circumstances of the Israeli–Egyptian situation rather than a precedent that would permanently change the way the UN functioned in the peace and security field.

**The framework for UNEF's use-of-force policy**

Hammarskjöld and Bunche, in contrast, took immense pains to develop the legal basis for UNEF's presence and actions once it was deployed. They, at least, were 'conscious that the new institution they were building would also be a model for the future'.[30] UNEF's operational principles were, however, determined not according to some theoretical construct but by the practicalities of the situation, especially Egypt's sensitivity about encroachments on its sovereignty and the fact that two of the parties involved in the conflict were major military powers with permanent seats on the Security Council. These principles helped provide a framework for UNEF's eventual use-of-force policy.

Besides Hammarskjöld's two reports[31] and the General Assembly resolutions which established the force,[32] several agreements were concluded which, although they did not mention the issue specifically, contributed to such a framework.

The first was an oddly vacuous 'good faith agreement' negotiated by the UN with Egypt which essentially established that Egypt consented to the presence of UNEF on its territory.[33] The text is finely nuanced to preserve Egypt's prerogatives and pride. Hammarskjöld recognized that: 'There was an element of gambling involved which I felt I simply had to take in view of the danger that further delays might cause Egypt to change its mind . . . and throw our approach overboard'.[34] This is an indication that, contrary to conventional wisdom, peacekeeping has from the outset often been based on tenuous consent.

[29] Higgins (note 22), p. 275.
[30] Urquhart (note 4), p. 266.
[31] See notes 6 and 7.
[32] UN General Assembly resolutions 998 (ES-1), 4 Nov. 1956, and 1000 (ES-1) (note 3).
[33] United Nations, Aide-memoire on the basis for the presence and functioning of UNEF in Egypt, UN document A/3375, 20 Nov. 1956.
[34] 'View of Secretary General Dag Hammarskjöld on terms of UNEF withdrawal released by Ernest Gross and reprinted in June 1967 in the publication of the American Society of International Law', reprinted in Mezerik, A. G. (ed.), *The United Nations Emergency Force (UNEF): 1956—Creation, Evolu-*

Subsequent discussions were held to work out more detailed arrangements on UNEF's status in Egypt, resulting in an exchange of letters between Egypt and the UN on 8 February 1957.[35] These arrangements, which entered into force on 1 March 1957, constituted (although not in name) the first ever SOFA for a UN peacekeeping operation. They provided a pattern that was followed by subsequent missions in the Congo, Cyprus and elsewhere.[36] The SOFA covered a wide range of issues, including the premises of the force, the use of the UN flag, privileges and immunities, civil and criminal jurisdiction, and the settlement of disputes or claims. The provision that was to have the greatest impact on the UN's evolving use-of-force policy was the right of UNEF to full freedom of movement—essential in any peacekeeping operation, but especially so in the civil war contexts in which many subsequent operations were to be deployed.

A final piece of the documentation setting up the operation fell into place on 20 February 1957 when the Secretary-General issued regulations for the conduct of the force, devised in consultation with the Advisory Committee.[37] Again, no mention was made of the use of force. 'The self-defence doctrine thus came into existence in relative silence during the course of the operation.'[38] Hence, despite the wealth of documentation, there remained unresolved issues concerning the use of force which would require later negotiation with Egypt and to a lesser extent Israel, as well as makeshift approaches in the field by UNEF's command and troops.

## III. Application and evolution of the use-of-force rules

The UNEF mission had several discrete and chronologically distinct functions, each with its own imperatives (and dangers) in terms of the use of force. Different approaches and tactics were adopted for each and different precedents set for future UN use-of-force policy. In every case UNEF was 'inventing the wheel' for future peacekeepers. The three major tasks UNEF was to undertake were: (a) ensuring troop withdrawals; (b) providing assistance to the civil power; and (c) preventing border violations by infiltration or armed incursion.

### Ensuring troop withdrawals

UNEF's first challenge was to monitor and ensure the smooth withdrawal of the British, French and Israeli forces from the Egyptian territory they had occupied.

---

tion, End of Mission—1967, International Review Service, vol. 13, no. 97 (1969), p. 59. There is some doubt about the authenticity of this posthumously attributed comment on UNEF's withdrawal.

[35] United Nations, Letter dated 8 February 1957 from the Secretary-General to the Minister for Foreign Affairs of Egypt and Letter dated 8 February 1957 from the Minister for Foreign Affairs of Egypt to the Secretary-General, UN document A/3526, 8 Feb. 1957.

[36] United Nations, The Blue Helmets: A Review of United Nations Peace-keeping, 2nd edn (United Nations: New York, 1990), p. 56.

[37] United Nations, Regulations for the United Nations Emergency Force, UN document ST/SGB/UNEF/1, 20 Feb. 1957.

[38] Goldmann (note 21), p. 11.

*Ceasefire and withdrawal of the British–French force, December 1956*

UNEF's first task was to supervise the withdrawal of the British–French force from Port Said and the Suez Canal area. France and the UK had made their withdrawal conditional on their troops being replaced by an effective UN force. UNEF's first units arrived on 16 December and were sent immediately to the Suez Canal area, occupying a buffer zone between the British–French forces and the Egyptian forces. UNEF's role was limited to investigating, reporting and protesting about any incidents to the relevant authorities.[39] Some UNEF units entered Port Said and Port Fuad, and took responsibility for maintaining law and order in certain areas, in cooperation with the local authorities. The force also undertook guard duty at vulnerable installations and other points, provided security for public and private property, and exercised limited powers of detention.

During this period there were no instructions in place about the use of force for UNEF as a whole. Essentially, UNEF troops acted on national instructions issued by their contingent commanders. The standing orders of the Swedish contingent, for instance, permitted opening fire '(*a*) when UNEF personnel are fired upon; (*b*) when armed persons attack UNEF personnel; and (*c*) when armed persons approach UNEF personnel with the obvious intention of attacking them'.[40] It is not clear whether these instructions were common to all participating contingents.

There was one unusual use of armed UNEF personnel during this period. When Egypt refused to allow British and French naval forces to clear the Suez Canal of sunken vessels, UNEF provided small detachments of 'civilian guards' recruited from the Finnish and Swedish contingents to provide security. They wore civilian clothes but UN blue berets and armbands. No incident occurred in which they had to use force. There had been a suggestion that they should be authorized to open fire not only in self-defence but 'generally with wide powers', but this was clearly unacceptable to all sides.[41]

The first occasion on which a UN peacekeeping force ever used its weapons occurred in Port Said on 14 December 1956. Three hand-grenades were thrown and fire was opened on a Norwegian jeep patrol. Fire was returned, presumably in self-defence.[42] The following morning a Swedish patrol was fired on. There were no casualties in either incident. Burns protested 'energetically' to the Egyptian Government and requested that it broadcast instructions to the populace to refrain from acts of violence during the withdrawal. Hammarskjöld was kept informed of all such developments as they occurred, indicating an early awareness of the sensitivity of peacekeeping operations to even minor incidents involving the use of force. There appears, however, to have been no attempt to clarify the use-of-force rules immediately. This is surprising, since

---

[39] *The Blue Helmets*, 3rd edn (note 17), p. 50.
[40] Goldmann (note 21), p. 11.
[41] United Nations, Verbatim record, Meeting of the Advisory Committee for UNEF, UN Secretariat, New York, 18 Dec. 1956, p. 8.
[42] Verbatim record, Meeting of the Advisory Committee for UNEF, 18 Dec. 1956 (note 41), p. 1.

reports in the *New York Times* had created controversy by suggesting that force had been used for purposes other than self-defence.[43]

On 16 December there were several serious incidents in which British units were attacked in the Arab quarter of Port Said, resulting in both British and Egyptian casualties. UNEF troops were not involved, since it was not an area for which they had taken responsibility.[44] However, they subsequently took up positions between the Arab quarter and an area surrounded by barbed wire to which the British and French had retreated and began patrolling the two main arteries between these areas. UNEF troops were fired on, but Burns believed this to be from a sniper who was unaware of UNEF's presence and movements.

The British and French forces withdrew peacefully and in full cooperation with UNEF. There were no incidents involving the use of force between them. By 22 December all British and French troops had withdrawn. Administrative and police functions were turned over to the Egyptian authorities the next day.

### Withdrawal of Israeli forces from the Sinai Peninsula, November 1956–March 1957

Despite the General Assembly's repeated requests that the Israeli troops withdraw behind the armistice lines—from all of Sinai and the Gaza Strip—it took them much longer to withdraw than the British and French forces. On 3 December they moved back approximately 50 km east of the Suez Canal. UNEF immediately entered the evacuated area, although progress was slowed by minefields and destroyed roads. The force essentially carried out the same tasks that it had in the areas occupied by France and the UK. On 11 December Israel announced that it was ready to withdraw further into Sinai. Negotiations began between Burns and the Israeli commander, General Moshe Dayan, on 16 December to plan this phase and ensure that as Israel withdrew there would be no unforeseen contact with UNEF troops which might lead to misunderstanding and the opening of fire. UNEF forces were to move to within 5 km of the new Israeli positions. No incidents occurred, no doubt because of the precautions in the agreed plan.[45]

Israel then announced that it would withdraw from the remainder of Sinai over the next four weeks at the rate of approximately 25 km a week. Burns considered this inadequate. He recalls, however, that in attempting to persuade Israel to withdraw more quickly he had little bargaining power because of the military weakness of his force: 'There was no question of UNEF's being able to take offensive action, consequently it posed no military threat. Therefore I could do little but argue that the other side *ought* to withdraw more quickly'.[46] Israel eventually agreed, undoubtedly under US pressure, to a two-phase withdrawal. Accordingly, a further Israeli withdrawal took place on 7 and 8 January

[43] Goldmann (note 21), p. 10.
[44] Burns (note 5), p. 231.
[45] Burns (note 5), p. 241.
[46] Burns (note 5), pp. 229–30. Emphasis in original.

1957, leaving no Israeli forces west of El Arish. On 16 January the final withdrawal occurred except from the area of Sharm el Sheikh on the Gulf of Aqaba and the Gaza Strip.

On 24 January 1957, in a report on the situation, the Secretary-General expanded on UNEF's role. 'The use of military force by the United Nations other than that under Chapter VII of the Charter requires the consent of the States in which the force is to operate . . . It must, furthermore, be impartial, in the sense that it does not serve as a means to force settlement, in the interests of one party, of political conflicts or legal issues recognized as controversial.'[47] Hammarskjöld thus explicitly introduced for the first time the notions of consent and impartiality to the peacekeeping ethos, both key concomitants of the self-defence norm.

The first incident involving the use of force between UNEF and the Israeli forces occurred on 1 February, when a Swedish patrol intercepted five Israeli soldiers pursuing a group of refugees northwards.[48] The Swedes fired a warning shot, whereupon the Israeli troops opened fire with rifle and light machine-gun fire. A Swedish officer returned fire with a pistol. There were no casualties. Burns protested to Dayan against the opening of fire and the movement of Israeli troops west of agreed positions.

On 1 March 1957 Israel announced a complete withdrawal from Gaza and Sharm el Sheikh. Opposed to the resumption of Egyptian control, it only agreed to relinquish control to UNEF on the understanding that this would be maintained until an agreement on the future of the territory was reached. UNEF troops entered the Gaza Strip during curfew on the night of 6–7 March and took control of Sharm el Sheikh on 8 March. These operations were carried out according to plan and without incident.[49] As of 8 March, UNEF was deployed along the western sides of the Armistice Demarcation Line (ADL) and the international frontier between Israel and Egyptian Sinai. Its main role was to act as a buffer between the Egyptian and Israeli forces in order to avoid incidents, prevent illegal crossings by civilians from either side, and observe and report violations on land, sea or in the air.[50]

### Providing support to the civil power

UNEF's occupation of the Gaza Strip was to prove the most troublesome of its initial tasks and the source of incidents which eventually (but not at the time) stimulated the development of its use-of-force rules. UNEF's role was to replace the departing Israeli troops and briefly administer Gaza until arrangements could be made to transfer it to Egyptian control. In fact UNEF did not

---

[47] United Nations, Report of the Secretary-General in pursuance of General Assembly Resolution 1123 (XI), UN document A/3512, 24 Jan. 1957, para. 5(b).
[48] Incoming code cable no. UNEF 294, from Burns, Ballah to SecGen, 1 Feb. 1957, 1655 EST, UN Archives DAG1/2.2.5.5.0, #2.
[49] The Blue Helmets, 3rd edn (note 17), p. 49.
[50] The Blue Helmets, 3rd edn (note 17), pp. 53–54. UNEF assumed some of the duties previously performed by UNTSO, which had been monitoring the armistice agreement since 1949.

exercise complete authority, or even complete police authority, confining its activities to guard and check-post duty and patrolling to prevent mob disorders, incitement to violence and looting.[51] It confiscated some arms from civilians but did not attempt comprehensive disarmament. Normal law-and-order functions were carried out by the Palestinian police.

The duration of UNEF's 'control' over Gaza had not been agreed, being dependent on Egyptian–Israeli agreement on the territory's future. Israel declared that, if Gaza reverted to being a base for Palestinian fedayeen raids into Israel, it would resume 'full liberty of action to defend its rights'.[52] Egypt, on the other hand, was annoyed at Lester Pearson's suggestion that Gaza be internationalized and controlled by the UN. Fearing that the UN would never leave, Egypt surreptitiously stirred up agitation against its presence.[53]

On 10 March, barely four days after UNEF entered Gaza, a demonstration outside the building of the UN Relief and Works Agency for Palestine Refugees in the Near East (UNRWA) became threatening. Burns personally ordered the Danish–Norwegian (Danor) battalion to use tear gas bombs to break up the crowd.[54] The rioters scattered and a reserve Danor unit arrived and quickly advanced on them, firing rifles and sub-machine guns over their heads. This broke up the crowd completely. Although Burns concedes that firing over the heads of a crowd is not a recommended way of dealing with riots, in this case it worked. Later it was learned that a young Arab had been struck by a bullet, apparently a ricochet. He died two days later.

Involvement in maintaining law and order, or in British parlance 'assistance to the civil power', was not a role foreseen for the UN force, nor one that many of the contingents had experience of or were prepared to carry out. Several contingents were reportedly so disaffected with instructions from the chief of staff to fire in the air if crowds broke the curfew that a cable was sent to Cordier in New York urging with 'utmost seriousness' that the instructions be reviewed lest the future of UNEF be jeopardized.[55] It is not clear whether this cable was seen by Burns before it was dispatched. Nonetheless, it is the first instance of peacekeeping contingents being dissatisfied with the UN's use-of-force rules. As Hammarskjöld's successor, U Thant, later noted of the constraints on the use of force imposed on UNEF troops: 'It particularly causes some shock at first to well-trained military men and requires a considerable adjustment on their part to very unfamiliar ways'.

The UNEF military man was faced with a concept of soldiering which is entirely foreign to anything taught him in his national service. The soldier is basically trained to fight. In UNEF, however, he was ordered to avoid fighting in all circumstances, and

---

[51] United Nations, Verbatim record, Meeting of the Advisory Committee for UNEF, UN Secretariat, New York, 18 Mar. 1957, p. 1.
[52] Burns (note 5), p. 253.
[53] Burns (note 5), p. 253.
[54] Burns (note 5), pp. 262–63.
[55] Incoming code cable (unnumbered), from Reddy, Cairo to Cordier, 16 Mar. 1957, 1446 EST, UN Archives DAG1/2.2.5.5.0, #2.

indeed, to seek to prevent it. Though armed, he could use force only in the last resort in self-defense. He had no enemy. Under provocation he had to show discipline and restraint; his tasks had to be carried through with persuasion, tact, example, calm and soldierly bearing, but, if humanly possible, never by force.[56]

At around this time, during a visit to Gaza by Bunche, a trigger-happy Danish sentry accidentally killed an Arab man. Burns reported to the Secretary-General that the soldier's explanation for what had happened was 'somewhat improbable', but no other explanation had come to light.[57] Bunche reported to Hammarskjöld that, after discussions with Burns and others, he was convinced that because of the build-up of anti-UN, anti-UNEF sentiment there was a 'real danger' that UNEF in self-defence 'may have to use effective force with resultant certain emotional reaction and outcry against UNEF in Gaza and beyond once [a] local Arab is harmed'.[58] Burns felt that UNEF could not control such opposition except by using unacceptable force: 'It was plainly impossible to think of UNEF's checking disorders as the Israelis had done, by shooting enough rioters to cow the rest. It would be contrary to the whole idea of UNEF and the United Nations approach to the problem, and no doubt several contingents would have been withdrawn if such a policy had been tried'.[59] In addition, the local police would be unlikely to cooperate with UNEF in such activity. Burns and Bunche recommended the immediate creation of a local government under at least nominal Egyptian authority.[60]

The Egyptian Government, on the grounds that the UN had used force in suppressing disorder, pre-empted the UN by announcing the appointment of a new Egyptian governor. The day after his arrival on 14 March most of UNEF was redeployed to patrol the ADL.[61] Thus ended the UN's first brief foray into civil administration during a peacekeeping operation and its first armed encounter with civil conflict. Unprepared for such responsibilities, it sensibly withdrew before too much damage was done and before it was obliged to try to become an army of occupation. This was not to be the UN response in some subsequent operations.

*The Gyani instructions on crowd control*

In September 1962 Force Commander Lieutenant-General P. S. Gyani of India (who had replaced Burns in December 1959) issued what still must rate as the most detailed instructions on the use of force to control unruly crowds ever devised for a UN peacekeeping operation. Just why they were issued when UNEF's crowd control duties had largely ended is unclear, but they indicated

---

[56] United Nations, Final report by Secretary-General U Thant on UNEF, UN document A/6672, 12 July 1967, paras 10, 16.
[57] Urquhart (note 4), p. 280; and Incoming code cable no. UNEF 609, to Secretary-General from Burns, Gaza, 16 Mar. 1957, 1300 EST, UN Archives DAG1/2.2.5.5.0, #2.
[58] Incoming code cable no. UNEF 554, from Bunche, Gaza to Secretary-General, 11 Mar. 1957, 1133 EST, UN Archives DAG1/2.2.5.5.0, #2.
[59] Incoming code cable no. UNEF 554 (note 58).
[60] Goldmann (note 21), p. 19.
[61] Goldmann (note 21), p. 19.

the kind of detailed thinking about the role of peacekeepers that would be necessary if the founding principles of peacekeeping were to be upheld.

The sole objective of UNEF in controlling unruly crowds was, Gyani proclaimed, to restore order, 'first by the use of the maximum of persuasion and patience and then by the use of the *minimum* of military force'. Any such action taken by UNEF, the commander noted, 'would certainly have international repercussions, both favourable and unfavourable'. Gyani then set out the following principles:

(*a*) *Principle of necessity*
(i) There must be justification for each separate act;
(ii) Action must not be taken in one place with the object of creating an effect in another place;
(iii) No reprisals or unnecessary physical coercion;
(iv) Action is preventive and not punitive.
(*b*) *Principle of minimum force*
No more force may be used than is necessary in the circumstances. This refers to the degree of actual force used and not to the number of troops employed.
(*c*) *Principle of impartiality*
(i) The soldiers must be impartial;
(ii) Gifts or favours will never be accepted.
(*d*) *Principle of good faith*
(i) Nothing can be said to have been done or believed to have been done in good faith, which is done WITHOUT due care and attention.[62]

Gyani also stressed 'mutual understanding and cooperation' with the local authorities and populace: 'Since restoration of mutual confidence is of paramount importance the soldier must set an example by showing courage, honesty, efficiency and impartiality'.

The procedures for dispersing a crowd were systematically set out, involving several steps—warning, 'police action', use of tear gas and firing. If the warning and tear gas had no effect the commander was authorized to resort to firing, but it was to be strictly controlled. Fire orders were to give definite targets and state the number of rounds to be fired. Perhaps surprisingly, in the light of riot control techniques employed today, Gyani suggested that: 'The most effective targets are usually people at the front of the crowd, actually rioting or inciting to riot, or conspicuous ring leaders. Troops should shoot for effect; they should normally be directed to fire low, i.e. to wound and incapacitate rather than to kill; except in cases where firing is ordered at selected ring leaders who may be in the rear of the mob'.

Even more controversially, Gyani ruled that action could also be taken by UNEF in self-defence to prevent:

(*a*) other portions of a body of troops being surprised; (*b*) buildings etc. in military occupation, vessels, vehicles, aircraft or stores being captured or damaged; (*c*) vulner-

---

[62] UNEF Headquarters, Gaza, 'Instructions for the guidance of troops for protective duty tasks', ref. 2131/7(OPS), 1 Sep. 1962. Emphasis in original.

able points, centres of communications, power lines, etc. from being damaged, interfered with or entered (if these are located within the area placed under UNEF protection); and (*d*) persons from passing through a gate or barrier or any other passage which has lawfully been closed to them.

In addition, any commander, individual officer or soldier had the right to 'meet with force any attempt to interfere violently with any movement or action which he has been ordered to carry out or considers necessary in the execution of his duty'. Force might also be used to prevent persons in custody from escaping or being rescued.

Specific orders for the briefing of troops included an injunction that automatic weapons should be set at 'single shot' to 'ensure that troops are starting out imbued with the doctrine of minimum force'. However, if a threatening situation developed during reconnaissance and escort duties and they became surrounded or blocked the commander must decide whether to fire his machine-guns, use revolver fire or clear a passage otherwise.

Although intended solely as guidance for troops engaged in 'protective duty tasks', these instructions could be applied to many aspects of peacekeeping. The puzzle is that they were not used as a model for future peacekeeping operations, for instance, in the Congo. This was to prove typical of the UN. Its missions in the field would expend a great deal of energy, often through trial and error, in establishing detailed rules for the use of force in the various scenarios that they commonly faced, only to see such work disappear into the UN archives once the mission was wound up.

### Preventing border violations by infiltration or armed incursion/invasion

After relinquishing its administrative role in Gaza, UNEF's main task was to patrol the ADL and the international frontier to prevent border violations. The two key issues with regard to the use of force that it confronted were the day-to-day one of what to do about infiltrators (armed and unarmed) and the more theoretical one of how and whether to use force if a sizeable military incursion or invasion, either by Egyptian or Israeli forces, were attempted. Although these challenges were quite different and required different responses, they are considered together here since that is how they were dealt with at the time, often confusedly, by the key interlocutors.

The ADL was the more difficult challenge. It had seen the greatest number of infiltrations and raids in previous years, was near a large number of Palestinian refugees being assisted by UNRWA and was also the border across which an Israeli military incursion was most likely. By day the entire length of the 59-km ADL was kept under observation by some 72 inter-visible UNEF observation posts. Each post was manned during daylight; by night, the sentries were withdrawn and replaced by foot patrols of 5–7 men each. These covered the length of the ADL on an average of three rounds each night. Along the international frontier, in contrast, rough terrain and scattered minefields restricted access for potential infiltrators, who tended to use certain areas. These were covered by patrols day and night. Eight outposts were also established along the frontier. Motor patrols from these outposts covered the areas between them and certain tracks. In addition the frontier was patrolled by air reconnaissance daily (later reduced to three times a week).

In preparing for UNEF's role as a guardian of borders, Burns on 2 March issued Operations Instruction no. 10 dealing with infiltrators, the first detailed written instructions on the use of force issued by the UN command to UNEF and the first ever issued by a UN command to a peacekeeping operation. They also represented the first elucidation, albeit in particular circumstances, of what would become the self-defence norm of UN peacekeeping. On the 'use of arms', the instruction provided that:

1. In general, UNEF Troops shall NOT fire unless fired upon, and then ONLY for their own protection.
2. Warning shots shall NOT be used during daylight.
3. During darkness warning shots may be fired when unknown persons approach a UNEF position or are observed by a UNEF patrol or observation post, and the persons do not halt when called upon to do so.[63]

The instruction thus ruled out the action the Swedish patrol had taken in early February when it fired warning shots at an Israeli patrol in daylight hours. It also ruled out firing at night against infiltrators who refused to halt, except when such persons threatened UNEF troops and they could thus act in self-defence.

Instruction no. 10 was presumably a compromise drafted in consultation with Bunche and Hammarskjöld, as Burns and his troops thought it unsatisfactory. The restrictions on UNEF's ability to use force were, Burns says, 'naturally very frustrating to me, as commander'.[64] He expended much effort in subsequent months seeking to alter them. Burns wanted to be able to use force other than in self-defence in preventing infiltration, arguing that it was impossible for UNEF to control infiltrators effectively without the right to stop them, in the last resort by firing.[65] Infiltration was not a problem during the day, when individuals or groups could be easily spotted and warned or rounded up; it took place mostly at night. Burns thus constantly urged that UNEF be given the right to fire at persons who refused to halt when challenged in the prohibited zone at night.[66]

In the event of a more sizeable armed breach of a frontier, Burns—the first UN force commander ever to be placed in such a situation—was unsure what

---

[63] UNEF Headquarters, Operations Instruction no. 10 [untitled], HQ UNEF 1-0 (OPS), El Ballah, 2 Mar. 1957, UN Archives DAG13/3.11.1.1, #4. Burns (note 5, p. 275) records that the action of patrols was regulated separately on 9 July 1957 and that the regulation was reiterated on 12 Jan. 1960, but these documents have not been located.

[64] Burns (note 5), p. 273.

[65] Letter from Commander UNEF to Secretary-General, 27 Mar. 1957, UN Archives DAG1/2.2.5.5.2, #13.

[66] Burns (note 5), p. 275.

action UNEF should take. The problem applied especially to the Israeli forces, since Egypt was in no position to invade Israel. Burns says that he:

knew, of course, that UNEF, with no heavy weapons of any sort, and scattered over a wide area on public security tasks, could not resist a serious attack by the powerful and effective Israeli Army. On the other hand, the Israelis would never attempt to force the UNEF lines if to do so they had to fire on UNEF and cause casualties, which would bring the anger of the whole of the United Nations and the most powerful sanctions down on them at once. But if they thought that UNEF would make no armed resistance . . . they might, in the mood they were in, attempt to do so and re-establish their position on the Gaza Strip, at least. They had been accustomed to pushing UN Military Observers around, and an Emergency Force which couldn't use its weapons would be little more than a corp[s] of observers.[67]

Burns argued that UNEF, even with its existing composition and capabilities, could stop smaller-scale offensive actions, such as a raid or an attempt to create a fait accompli by occupying strategic positions with light forces.[68] Such acts, he noted, might conceivably be carried out by elements of armed forces acting without the sanction of central governments. He pointed out that UNEF was frequently compared to a police or paramilitary force and that such forces use weapons to resist lawbreakers or invaders.[69] Burns favoured giving UNEF the mandate to 'resist any attempt of armed forces to cross the demarcation line to the extent of its powers'.[70] He advocated that, at the very least, UNEF's right to fire in self-defence should be invoked if there was an attempt to remove its troops by force from positions they occupied (this would later become a key part of standard UN peacekeeping use-of-force instructions).

*The Advisory Committee considers the Burns proposals*

Backed by Bunche, Burns had put the following proposals, which were intended to deal with both infiltrators and invading forces, to the Secretary-General, who discussed them with the Advisory Committee on 15 March 1957:

(*a*) That the UNEF should have the right to fire at individuals or bodies crossing [the ADL] . . . ;

(*b*) That it be announced that UNEF has the right to fire in its own defence, and that it be decided that this would include right to fire at armed forces approaching positions with apparent intention to dislodge UNEF elements by force;

(*c*) That an attack on UNEF, or attempt to break through UNEF positions, should be considered an act involving automatic application of sanctions.[71]

---

[67] Burns (note 5), p. 273.

[68] Letter from Commander UNEF to Secretary-General, 27 Mar. 1957 (note 65).

[69] Burns in fact objected to the term 'paramilitary' to describe UNEF or its functions. The *Oxford English Dictionary*, he noted, defines 'paramilitary' as 'having a status or function ancillary to that of military forces'. UNEF, however, was 'unquestionably formed of military units, from the regular forces of the nations contributing'. Burns (note 5), p. 313, fn. 2.

[70] Burns (note 5), p. 273.

[71] United Nations, Verbatim record, Meeting of the Advisory Committee for UNEF, UN Secretariat, New York, 15 Mar. 1957.

Pearson, obviously influential in setting the tone of the committee's reaction, responded that: 'It would be quite impossible for UNEF to resist a military move by either side. To think otherwise is certainly not our understanding of the functions of their role as a *police force*'.[72] Hammarskjöld agreed, pointing out, as Burns had, that there were two distinct kinds of operation to be considered—'resisting a military move and exerting police functions with force'.[73] In the latter case he believed UNEF might assume such functions if Egypt and Israel agreed, perhaps in a 10-mile neutral zone astride the demarcation line. He told the committee: 'If we were to permit . . . UNEF people to use force, military force, to shoot, to fire, in other cases than those of self-defence, it is quite obvious that they cannot have a certain right in relation to Egyptian infiltrators without having a similar right in relation to Israeli infiltrators'.[74] He added: 'How the parties would agree to it when they both reserve their right to retaliation strikes me as somewhat dark'.

The representatives of Brazil and Colombia expressed concern about according UNEF 'military functions' and were relieved that Hammarskjöld spoke of avoiding the use of force altogether in all its functions. However, the Indian representative, Arthur Lall, noted that it would be wrong to say that UNEF could not take on direct military functions, since 'its mere presence there, does act as a deterrent. Of course it would have police functions because it has been agreed that it is more than a mere observer corps'.[75] Lall did not explain how UNEF could be anything more than a symbolic deterrent if it were not prepared to demonstrate credibility in the last resort by using force.

In the event no member of the Advisory Committee wanted any armed action against infiltrators, doubtless, according to Burns, 'because they thought it would result in an outcry against UNEF similar to that which had followed the firing over the heads of the crowd in Gaza on 10 March.[76] As a result of this debate, Hammarskjöld responded in a Top Secret cable to Bunche and Burns:

Primo. UNEF is not a combat force and is, under its terms of reference, not entitled militarily to resist troop movements from Egypt into Gaza or, indeed, from Israel into Gaza.

Secundo. Short of firing in cases mentioned in Tertio, UNEF has to exert its controlling and checking influence without resorting to firing at intruders or raiders. Shots in the air and the use of other disciplinary and deterrent measures of similar nature is another matter.

Tertio. If under Primo or Secundo, UNEF in emergencies must act in clear self-defence, they are to be considered as entitled to protect themselves by force.[77]

---

[72] Verbatim record, Meeting of the Advisory Committee for UNEF, 15 Mar. 1957 (note 71), p. 28. Emphasis added.
[73] Verbatim record, Meeting of the Advisory Committee for UNEF (note 71), pp. 29–30.
[74] United Nations, Verbatim record, Meeting of the Advisory Committee for UNEF, UN Secretariat, New York, 28 Mar. 1957, p. 4.
[75] Verbatim record, Meeting of the Advisory Committee for UNEF, 15 Mar. 1971 (note 71), pp. 34–35.
[76] Burns (note 5), p. 272.
[77] Outgoing code cable no. 503, from SecGen to Bunche, Burns, Gaza, 16 Mar. 1957, UN Archives DAG1/2.2.5.5.0, #2.

Hammarskjöld described the matter as 'extremely delicate' and noted that his views were shared by the whole Advisory Committee. The line advocated by Burns and Bunche, he said, 'might involve UNEF in impossible situations without preventing a military operation by Israel or Egypt'. 'The very presence of UNEF under "passive resistance"', he continued, 'is considered as the maximum deterrent we at present can introduce into the situation'.[78]

## Negotiations with Egypt on use-of-force issues

In talks between Hammarskjöld and Egyptian President Gamal Abdel Nasser in Cairo beginning on 22 March 1957, and during subsequent weeks of negotiations by Bunche and Burns with Egyptian officials, verbal agreements were reached on further details of UNEF's deployment in Sinai and Gaza.[79] Hammarskjöld decided to test Egypt on the issue of UNEF's handling of infiltrators, including the use of force against them. He asked Burns to 'set down on paper, without any political compromises being smuggled into his own thinking, what he considered as necessary at the demarcation line in order to be effective, and what he considered necessary, back of the demarcation line, in order to make this a sensible operation with full effect . . . '.[80]

Burns proposed that UNEF should have the right to take infiltrators into custody in a zone 750 metres deep on the Egyptian side of the ADL and hand them over to the Palestinian police for appropriate judicial action.[81] The 'right of UNEF to take action necessary for its own defence' should be made known to the population. He further proposed that UNEF should have the right to move freely by road and air throughout the Gaza Strip and Sinai.[82] In addition, UNEF should have the right to defend UN property and persons (including UNRWA's) in the event of civil disturbances which the Egyptian authorities could not control.[83] All these proposals were agreed to by Egypt.

With regard to Burns' proposals for UNEF to be given the right to open fire beyond self-defence to stop infiltrators, Egypt, as predicted, was lukewarm, but said it would agree if Israel agreed to the same policy on its side of the ADL. Instead it proposed mixed patrols of UNEF and Palestinian police on the Gaza side who might be given the right to fire. Hammarskjöld in any event seemed to doom Burns' proposals by telling Egypt (somewhat disingenuously, given his ability to sway opinion when he wanted to) that even if it had accepted them he would have had to submit them to the Advisory Committee and all troop-contributing countries for approval.[84]

---

[78] Outgoing code cable no. 503 (note 77).

[79] Burns (note 5), pp. 273–76; and Urquhart (note 4), pp. 281–84.

[80] Verbatim record, Meeting of the Advisory Committee for UNEF, 28 Mar. 1957 (note 74), p. 4.

[81] Memorandum concerning the functions, rights and responsibilities of the UNEF following the withdrawal of Israeli forces behind the Armistice Demarcation Line, 27 Mar. 1957, UN Archives DAG1/2.2.5.5.2, #13.

[82] Burns (note 5), p. 275.

[83] Incoming code cable no. UNEFCA 153, from Bunche, Cairo to Cordier, 26 Mar. 1957, 2310 (25th)-1129 (26th) EST, UN Archives DAG1/2.2.5.5.0, #2.

[84] Verbatim record, Meeting of the Advisory Committee for UNEF, 28 Mar. 1957 (note 74), p. 5.

Pending the acceptance by both sides of broader powers for UNEF, Burns agreed that cooperation between UNEF and the Palestinian police must be 'encouraged and systematized' and the feasibility of joint night patrols with the authority to fire 'seriously explored'. However, he ultimately changed his mind on the grounds that if the Israeli forces, who were patrolling right up to the ADL on their side, had learned that Palestinians were patrolling the other side there 'would certainly have been exchanges of fire across the ADL, causing casualties among UNEF personnel and a deteriorating situation'.[85]

On 6 May 1957 Israel finally replied to the UN's queries about its attitude to UNEF's right to fire against infiltrators with a letter which stated that:

The Government of Israel recognizes the competence of the United Nations Emergency Force to open fire on persons who enter from Israel territory into the UNEF security zone established along the Gaza side of the UNEF lines when such persons did not halt on being challenged by UNEF patrols. The above declaration is made on the basis of the information given by the Secretary-General that such authority will also be exercised by UNEF with respect to persons entering into the UNEF security zone from the direction of Gaza.[86]

However, as Burns pointed out, this did not give UNEF the right to fire across the line into Israel against persons threatening imminent transgression. The Israeli letter also erroneously assumed that a UNEF 'security zone' lay on the Egyptian side of the line. Most importantly, the Israeli position did not go far enough to secure Egypt's agreement. Thus, Burns concluded, there was dead-lock on the issue.

### Continuing difficulties with infiltrators

While the question of a sizeable violation of the ADL or the international fron-tier receded as the overall political situation improved, the problem of infil-tration remained. From March to July 1957 the number of incidents—thefts, firing, mining and captures of infiltrators—remained high.[87] Israel criticized the lack of UNEF action when infiltration allegedly occurred from the Gaza side.[88] The following incidents are examples of infiltration.

On 18 April 1957 a Swedish patrol encountered four or five men with two donkeys approaching the ADL.[89] The patrol leader challenged the group, which opened fire with sub-machine guns from approximately 100 metres away on the Israeli side of the line. The Swedish troops returned fire in self-defence and the group disappeared eastwards. On 17 June an Arab was seen approaching the Gaza Strip from Israeli territory, again east of Gaza township. A Danor patrol

[85] Burns (note 5), p. 275.
[86] United Nations, Verbatim record, Meeting of the Advisory Committee for UNEF, UN Secretariat, New York, 15 May 1957, p. 29.
[87] Burns (note 5), p. 276.
[88] Burns (note 5), p. 272.
[89] United Nations, Verbatim record, Meeting of the Advisory Committee for UNEF, UN Secretariat, New York, 23 Apr. 1957, p. 9.

fired a warning shot and saw the man throwing an object that appeared to be a hand grenade. The patrol opened fire, and the man was killed.[90] On 18 June two Arabs were shot by a UNEF patrol from the Danor battalion east of Gaza township, less than 500 metres from the ADL. The patrol saw six men moving in the direction of the ADL. When challenged to stop they converged in the direction of the patrol and threw a knife at it. The patrol opened fire immediately, and two Arabs were killed and one taken into custody.[91]

Contrary to the informal agreement with Egypt, nothing was ever officially made public about UNEF's powers, undoubtedly because of Egypt's extreme sensitivity about its sovereignty.[92] Burns notes, however, that the population seemed aware. After the incidents mentioned above, word spread and 'things became much quieter'.[93] There was no agitation about the incidents among the population.

However, UNEF's right to fire for reasons other than self-defence remained an unresolved issue for members of the force, all of whom were new to peacekeeping and its constraints. In May 1957 the new commander of the Danor battalion, Norwegian Lieutenant-Colonel J. Berg, questioned the adequacy of UNEF's instructions and the 'confusion' caused by the verbal orders that no firing was permitted, day or night, except in self-defence. He complained that such instructions seriously limited his troops' ability to stop infiltration and that the term 'self-defence' left 'wide scope for judgement':

In an actual situation this judgement today will be left to the private soldier. In my opinion this is a too big responsibility to place on a soldier who probably will have to act under confused conditions. Furthermore it does not safeguard our troops. It leaves all the chances to aggressive or irresponsible elements as the post or outpost virtually could be surrounded without having the legal right to fire. [There] is, in my opinion, a great need to get more clearly defined under which conditions a soldier can fire in self defence.[94]

Berg suggested that it would be best if UNEF forces were given 'freedom of action' (presumably to use force as they saw fit) within 500 yards of the ADL. If this were not possible it might help, he suggested, if around each post, outpost and company camp there were a marked area, with barbed wire and signs, inside which a soldier could use his weapons if someone tried to force an entry. By night, he suggested, patrols should, within a certain distance of the ADL, be allowed to fire on unauthorized persons who did not stop when challenged. These circumstances are uncannily like those encountered in Somalia by UNOSOM II decades later.

Burns replied sympathetically, noting that Berg's memorandum raised difficult questions for which no satisfactory solution had yet been found. He agreed

[90] UNEF Situation Report, 17 June 1957, UN Archives UNEF 1292.
[91] UNEF Situation Report, 18 June 1957, UN Archives UNEF 1312.
[92] Burns (note 5), p. 273.
[93] Burns (note 5), p. 275.
[94] Danor Battalion, Beit Hanun, 'In self defence', Memorandum no. 1199 to Commander, HQ, UNEF, Gaza, 25 May 1957, UN Archives DAG1/2.2.5.5.1, #19.

that it would be desirable to implement Berg's suggestion about giving UNEF freedom of action within 500 metres of the ADL, but noted that: 'Such drastic measures against the inhabitants cannot be undertaken without the agreement of those responsible for the government of the country, and such agreement has not been forthcoming'. He continued, pointing out a difficulty which has plagued peacekeeping operations ever since:

It is impossible to give a comprehensive statement of all the circumstances in which a soldier or group of soldiers of UNEF might be entitled to fire in self-defence. One very obvious situation, already quoted, is when they have been fired at. Another situation might be where a small group of soldiers were faced by a hostile group who were advancing in such a manner as to obviously threaten to disarm and do bodily harm to the UNEF soldiers, unless the latter used their arms.[95]

On 31 July 1957, in response to a letter from the Secretary-General which reviewed the main issues and arrangements affecting UNEF, Burns noted that the principal outstanding issue relating to the authority of UNEF was that of 'firing'. He then cannily attempted to use UNEF's 'unquestioned' right to self-defence to argue for wider powers to use force.[96] Since it was obvious that UNEF could not take orders from anyone other than its commander or the UN Secretary-General, he argued, it followed that: 'In the practical sense this right means that UNEF can fire if fired upon and also in resistance to any attempt to put the Force or any of its components out of function'. In what sounded like a plea for a new, wider, interpretation of the self-defence rule incorporating the need to 'defend the mission', Burns claimed that UNEF's authority would thus be 'adequate for dealing with a situation where one party raided the other with organized forces'. This was not the last time this argument was made as peacekeeping evolved.

Concerning night action within the right of self-defence, Burns reported that in April he had issued detailed and precise instructions to patrols on how to conduct themselves when infiltrators were encountered during darkness.[97] The memorandum claimed that these instructions were 'sufficiently flexible and broad in their interpretation of self-defence to afford the UNEF night patrols a reasonable basis for effectiveness' (although obviously not sufficient for Berg). It noted that all UNEF units were under instructions not to fire 'warning shots', since these were likely to 'bring about an unnecessary exchange of fire'.

Urquhart was wary of the leeway that Burns seemed to be giving UNEF troops, saying that: 'The UNEF people, now that they were well established, began to feel that they could do more or less as they liked, and often seemed unaware that a mistake or a false move could very easily jeopardize once again the whole enterprise'. Bunche, he records, continued to 'monitor and direct

---

[95] Commander UNEF, Gaza, 'Right of UNEF troops to fire in self-defence', Memorandum to Lt-Col J. Berg, Commander Danor Battalion, 11 June 1957, UN Archives DAG1/2.2.5.5.1, #19.

[96] Review of main issues and arrangements affecting UNEF, confidential UN document (unnumbered), 12 Aug. 1957, summarizing the views of Gen. Burns in his letter of 31 July 1957 to UN Secretary-General, UN Archives DAG1/2.2.5.5.2, #13.

[97] Review of main issues and arrangements affecting UNEF (note 96).

UNEF day and night', waging 'an indefatigable but kindly campaign to keep UNEF on the right track, scrutinizing each development and each incident and giving directions accordingly'.[98] It is not clear what particular incidents this refers to, but presumably it had something to do with a propensity on the part of some units in UNEF to exceed the use-of-force regulations. The official line of the Secretary-General was that UNEF 'often has had to move and act swiftly, but has done so always with the restraint required by the very nature of its status and role'. He noted that UNEF's 'unquestioned right to fire in self-defence' had, on occasions, been exercised.[99]

In any event the number of reported incidents dropped during and after July 1957, probably (in addition to the growing experience of UNEF) as a result of a stronger official Egyptian presence in the area and a change of Israeli policy whereby regular Israeli soldiers rather than irregular kibbutzim patrolled the line on their side. It appeared also that cooperation with the Egyptian authorities in Gaza and the Palestinian police, as proposed by Burns, was bearing fruit. Egypt had, as agreed, forbidden Gaza's inhabitants to be within 750 metres of the ADL during hours of darkness, and infiltrators apprehended by UNEF within 500 metres of the line were being handed over to the police. Burns' view was that relations between UNEF and the local population were now generally good and that the presence of UNEF under its existing terms of reference, 'despite occasional minor clashes, is accepted as a good thing by the majority of the inhabitants of the Gaza Strip'.[100] Burns again raised the question of wider authority for UNEF, including the need to deploy on the Israeli side, the erection of a fence with mines along the line and, yet again, authority for UNEF to fire during darkness at infiltrators from either direction, but he recognized that it would be futile to press Israel on these matters.

After the crucial year of 1957 UNEF settled into a regular pattern in which incidents, although they continued to occur, remained at a low and politically acceptable level.[101] Nonetheless, UNEF's use-of-force instructions were further clarified on 6 February 1958 as a result of continuing doubts among the troops as to the circumstances in which force could be used:

1. . . . In general, UNEF troops shall not fire except in self-defence, i.e. when they are fired upon first, or when they are threatened by the advance of an armed person or group of persons with the apparent intention to attack a UNEF sentry post, a patrol or an individual.

2. When a person is seen in the act of stealing/pilfering or loitering about in a suspicious manner in the proximity of UNEF installations or property being guarded by UNEF personnel, efforts should be made to apprehend him and to hand him over to the nearest police station. Fire, in this case, will not be resorted to except when the persons

---

[98] Urquhart (note 4), p. 288.

[99] United Nations, Report of the Secretary-General, UN document A/3694 and Add. 1, 9 Oct. 1957.

[100] Burns (note 5), p. 276.

[101] There was no appreciable reduction in the number of air violations or violations of territorial waters. In neither case could UNEF exercise any control other than by observing and informing the parties concerned, since it lacked air and naval forces.

are armed and danger to the safety of UNEF personnel is apparent, i.e. principle in para 1 above applies.

   3. In all cases, only that amount of force shall be used which the situation warrants. The principle of minimum force will always be borne in mind.[102]

   These were subsequently approved by Hammarskjöld and Bunche[103] and remained operative throughout the rest of the mission.[104]

   UNEF never did receive permission to use force beyond self-defence to apprehend infiltrators at night. A summary of UNEF standing orders as of April 1966 maintained that, while force could be used to apprehend infiltrators, fire could not be opened except in self-defence, specifically 'in response to fire upon UNEF personnel'. It continued: 'In all cases only that amount of force, including firing, will be used which the situation requires. The principle of use of minimum force is basic to the peacekeeping purposes of UNEF and will be impressed periodically on all members of the Force'. Finally, the regulations stressed that persons suspected of 'running away with UNEF property' must not be fired upon (which suggests that perhaps they had been in the past) and that 'warning shots will never be discharged'.[105]

   In some respects these instructions were narrower than ever. Warning shots were now ruled out altogether, even at night, and self-defence was narrowly defined as the use of fire only when fired on. This fell far short of the rights envisaged by Burns.

   The regulations were still being argued about at UNEF headquarters 10 years after the force was established. A memorandum from the military legal adviser to the Operations Section in March 1966 pointed out that a sentence in the rules indicating that UNEF troops should not 'resort to opening fire if the person is at a distance and cannot be stopped by using physical force' might imply that force could be used when they were at close range.[106]

## UNEF's forced withdrawal, June 1967

On 16 May 1967 General Indar Jit Rikhye, the new UNEF commander,[107] received a request from an Egyptian brigadier that all UNEF troops be withdrawn from their Observation Posts (OPs) immediately. Rikhye replied that he would have to seek the advice of the Secretary-General since he had no authority to order such a withdrawal. The new Secretary-General, U Thant, ordered

---

[102] UNEF Headquarters, Gaza, 'Use of force by UNEF personnel', HQ UNEF,1911/12-4 (OPS), 6 Feb. 1958, UN Archives DAG13/3.11.1.1, #4.

[103] Letter from Under-Secretary-General Ralph Bunche to Lt-General E. L. M. Burns, UNEF Commander, 28 Feb. 1958, UN Archives DAG1/2.2.5.5.1, #19.

[104] They were repeated verbatim, e.g., in UNEF Headquarters, Gaza, Operations Instruction no. 36 [untitled], no. 65/5-3 (OPS), 12 Jan. 1960, UN Archives DAG13/3.11.0.0, #9.

[105] UNEF Headquarters, Operations Section, 'Standing orders' (revised to Apr. 1966), UN Archives DAG13/3.11.0.0, #9.

[106] Memorandum from MLA to COO, 'Operational standing orders', 25 Mar. 1966, UN Archives DAG13/3.11.0.0, #9.

[107] Rikhye was appointed in Jan. 1966.

Rikhye to 'be firm in maintaining UNEF position while being as understanding and as diplomatic as possible in your relations with local [United Arab Republic] UAR officials'.[108]

The following day UAR troops occupied some UNEF OPs manned by Yugoslav troops, but later withdrew. More disturbingly, they positioned themselves around UNEF deployments and even moved up to the ADL itself. UNEF offered no resistance. On 18 May some UNEF soldiers were prevented by UAR troops from occupying their OP and from remaining in the area. The UN report on this incident says, almost resignedly, that: 'They did not resist by use of force since they had no mandate to do so'.[109] Burns' repeated attempts to seek authorization to use force in such instances had been to no avail. Other UNEF positions were visited by UAR officers who requested that the UN troops abandon them. Two artillery shells were fired between two Yugoslav positions. The same day two Israeli military aircraft tried to force an aircraft carrying Rikhye to land on the Israeli side of the ADL, including by firing warning shots.[110] The pilot of the UN aircraft, on instructions from Rikhye, ignored these efforts and landed safely at Gaza.

On 18 May, the UAR Foreign Minister, Mahmoud Riad, cabled U Thant explicitly 'terminating' the presence of UNEF in the territory of the UAR and the Gaza Strip.[111] After consultations with the Advisory Committee and troop-contributing countries, U Thant concluded that since Egypt's consent was withdrawn it was incumbent on him to order UNEF to withdraw. 'The consent of the host country', he said, 'is a basic principle which has applied to all United Nations peacekeeping operations'.[112] UNEF was 'after all, a peacekeeping and not an enforcement operation'. In withdrawing he cautioned the force commander and his subordinate officers to 'do their utmost to avoid a resort to the use of arms and any clash with the forces of the United Arab Republic or with the local civilian population'.[113]

U Thant was heavily criticized for this decision in some quarters, partly because he had not consulted the General Assembly and partly because it was believed that he had caved in precipitously to Egyptian demands. In response he assembled a lengthy refutation in which he argued that: 'There is a widespread misunderstanding about the nature of United Nations peacekeeping operations in general and UNEF in particular'. UNEF was based, he said:

---

[108] United Nations, United Nations Emergency Force: special report of the Secretary-General, addendum, UN document A/6669/Add. 3, 26 June 1967. Egypt and Syria had combined to form the UAR.

[109] United Nations Emergency Force: special report of the Secretary-General, UN document A/6669/Add. 3 (note 108).

[110] United Nations, United Nations Emergency Force: special report of the Secretary-General, UN document A/6669, 18 May 1967.

[111] Message reproduced in Higgins (note 22), p. 347.

[112] United Nations Emergency Force: special report of the Secretary-General (note 110).

[113] United Nations Emergency Force: special report of the Secretary-General, UN document A/6669/Add. 3 (note 108), annex, Cable containing instructions for the withdrawal of UNEF sent by the Secretary-General to the commander of UNEF on 18 May 1967, at 2230 hours New York time, para. 9.

entirely on its acceptance by the governing authority of the territory on which it oper-
ates and that is not in any sense related to Chapter VII of the Charter. It is a fact
beyond dispute that neither UNEF nor any other United Nations peacekeeping operation thus far undertaken would have been permitted to enter the territory involved if
there had been any suspicion that it had the right to remain there against the will of the
governing authority.[114]

Most UNEF troops were still awaiting repatriation when fierce fighting in
Gaza between Egyptian and Israeli forces erupted on 5 June 1967, marking the
outbreak of fully fledged war. Fifteen peacekeepers were killed and 17 wounded
during this period.[115] The casualties resulted from the strafing of a UNEF convoy by Israeli aircraft on 5 June, a mine explosion, and artillery and mortar fire
on UNEF camps and on UNEF headquarters in Gaza township. Israel insisted
that these were accidents caused by the 'fog of war'. UNEF troops were not
themselves engaged in fighting. When Canadian troops withdrew from Camp
Rafah, looting occurred which took Brazilian troops two days to control, but it
is not clear if force was used.[116] By 17 June UNEF had withdrawn completely.

## IV. UNEF's experience of the use of force

Despite its abrupt withdrawal, UNEF was an undoubted political and military
success, setting peacekeeping precedents that would be followed for decades.
Consent, impartiality and the use of force only in self-defence were registered
as key peacekeeping principles. By and large these unfamiliar requirements
were well met. U Thant noted that: 'It is an immensely encouraging fact that the
soldiers of UNEF, almost without exception, were able for over ten years to live
up to these unaccustomed and exacting standards and to carry out their duties
with extraordinary success and with a minimum of friction'.[117]

UNEF I discharged its mandate largely without using force for any purpose. It
successfully helped supervise, mostly without incident, the British, French and
Israeli withdrawals, provided 'assistance to the civil power' without becoming
embroiled in local conflict, and undoubtedly prevented infiltration and an
escalation of provocative incidents along the Egyptian–Israeli frontiers. In all
these respects it helped 'keep the peace'.

There were some incidents in which force was used, usually against infiltrators who had used or appeared to be ready to use force against UNEF troops.
On the whole, however, force was used extremely sparingly. UNEF suffered
89 fatalities and many wounded and injured, but only in the last desperate days
of the mission did these apparently result from the deliberate use of force
against it (although this was usually denied by the perpetrators). Freedom of
movement on the ground was largely unimpeded, except in the final days of the

---

[114] United Nations, Report of the Secretary-General, UN document S/7896, 19 May 1967, para. 12.
[115] United Nations, United Nations Emergency Force: special report of the Secretary-General,
addendum, UN document A/6669/Add. 2, 19 June 1967.
[116] Final report by Secretary-General U Thant on UNEF (note 56), para. 77.
[117] Final report by Secretary-General U Thant on UNEF (note 56), paras 10, 16.

mission. UNEF air movements were, however, watched closely by both Egypt and Israel and on occasions harassed or otherwise constrained.[118]

Until the outbreak of war in 1967 neither Egypt nor Israel attempted to breach the ADL or the international frontier in force, and no sizeable incidents involving fighting between UNEF and Egypt or Israel occurred. There were a few cases when Israeli patrols crossed the ADL and even fired at Arabs after crossing, but they always withdrew when requested by UNEF. The Israeli Defence Force authorities usually expressed regret, saying it was an error by some very junior officer.[119] Burns notes that gradually the force developed a system which made its troops on the ADL into a 'reasonably effective deterrent'.[120] He concluded at the end of his tenure that UNEF 'by and large' had accomplished its purpose in spite of its peculiar composition. 'I gradually realized', he wrote, 'that the force could achieve useful results, not by the exercise of military force, but so to speak as a political counter—that its moves and acts were dictated by a delicate balance of political pressures, whose resultant force it registered'.[121]

Yet, although UNEF inaugurated peacekeeping and laid the groundwork for further development of its ethos and norms, it did not successfully tackle all the dilemmas posed by the use-of-force issue. Among these were the use of force beyond self-defence to deter or prevent infiltration, the use of force in support of the civil power, and the question whether peacekeepers have the right to use force to prevent armed border incursions where their positions are overrun and/or their weapons and equipment are seized. At a strategic level the larger question of whether UN peacekeepers could use force to prevent the large-scale violation of agreed international frontiers and/or a ceasefire agreement, as Egypt had done while at the same time expelling UNEF I, lay completely unresolved and would occasion much controversy.

On the infiltration question, UNEF, through a series of cumulative decisions, eventually defined both its role in the mission area and its use-of-force policy, and gradually gained experience in handling infiltrators without using force. Yet the question of using force beyond self-defence in deterring or preventing such incidents was never decided to the satisfaction of any of the parties. Indeed, although attempts were made, notably by Gyani, to refine the self-defence norm, it still remained largely undeveloped by the end of UNEF. Certainly there was no agreement on the issue between UN Headquarters and UNEF military commanders. Not for the last time, there was a gulf between military and civilian views on the use of force in peacekeeping.

On the issue of assistance to the civil power, UNEF I provided some indication of the dilemmas that would face future peacekeepers, most immediately in the next UN mission, in the Congo, in discretely applying force to preserve law and order without becoming just another party in an ongoing civil war. It was

[118] Ghali, M., 'United Nations Emergency Force I: 1956–1967', ed. W. J. Durch, *The Evolution of UN Peacekeeping: Case Studies and Comparative Analysis* (St Martin's Press for the Henry L. Stimson Center: Washington, DC, 1993), p. 126.

[119] Burns (note 5), p. 273.

[120] Burns (note 5), p. 273.

[121] Burns (note 5), p. 208.

recognized, even on the basis of this limited experience, that any use of force could be provocative to the local populace and that without the support of the local authorities lightly-equipped UN peacekeepers were especially vulnerable to being made scapegoats, vilified and attacked. UNEF had the good fortune to be relieved of prolonged 'occupation' of areas experiencing civil unrest and was not required to seek solutions to this problem. This was left to subsequent missions.

As to whether peacekeepers had the right to resist armed incursions by regular forces (as contrasted with infiltration by irregulars) across frontiers that they were mandated to secure, this was resolved in the negative by UNEF. UN peacekeepers had not (yet) acquired the right to resist being overrun or dis-armed or to counter armed incursions that violated a frontier even when they themselves were not threatened or attacked. While UNEF may have had some deterrent effect against individual infiltrators, its deterrent effect in military terms against a determined invader was zero, as was demonstrated. Not only did UNEF troops not have the right to resist by force, unless directly attacked, but they were not equipped to do so (indeed, they were often not even in a position to defend themselves if directly attacked). While they could have mounted token resistance, as UN peacekeepers later did in Lebanon, or called the bluff of the belligerents, as they later did in Cyprus, this would ultimately only have delayed the inevitable. As Mona Ghali notes: 'To judge the withdrawal of UNEF as responsible for the outbreak of hostilities in June 1967 is both facile and naive'.[122]

The question whether UNEF I should have been mandated and equipped to forcefully resist an Egyptian or Israeli invasion is another matter. Burns felt to the end that: 'A stronger and more coherently organized force might have been a better instrument for the execution of UN policies'.[123] In a post-mortem on UNEF, he continued to urge that future UN peacekeeping forces should be organized 'with armaments and mobility superior or at least equal to those of the local forces which are engaged in or threatening to begin hostilities. The total manpower, or the number of units in the UN Force would not need to be equivalent to that of either combatant side, but it should be great enough to be a decisive factor in preventing renewed fighting or provocations, being prepared to use force if necessary. The mere presence of blue helmets or blue berets is not enough'.[124]

## V. Codification of the UNEF I experience

The codification of UNEF practice, including with regard to the use of force, came first in a 'summary study' of the UNEF experience written by Hammar-

---

[122] Ghali (note 118), p. 127.

[123] Burns (note 5), p. 190.

[124] 'Observations of General E. L. M. Burns, first Commander of UNEF and presently adviser to the Canadian Government on disarmament', *International Journal* (Canadian Institute of International Affairs), vol. 23, no. 1 (winter 1967/68), reproduced in Mezerik (note 34), p. 111.

skjöld and tabled in the General Assembly on 9 October 1958.[125] The study also drew on the Secretary-General's experience of the crises in Lebanon and Jordan in 1958, neither of which resulted in the establishment of armed peacekeeping forces, but which nonetheless Hammarskjöld deemed to have provided important lessons. The study set out the ethos of UN peacekeeping and the three rules which have governed it ever since. Hammarskjöld did not, however, use the term 'peacekeeping', which had not yet been invented, although clearly he was groping for a definition to distinguish the UNEF type of operation from an enforcement operation like that which the Security Council had authorized in Korea in 1950. However, while the terminology may not yet have evolved, the concept was crystallizing.

The summary study did not dwell in detail on the use-of-force issue to the extent of discussing concepts of operation and rules of engagement. Although Burns and Heathcote describe Hammarskjöld as having 'profoundly concerned himself with the UN's use of force',[126] he devoted in fact only one paragraph to the issue. Asserting that a right of self-defence exists for UN peacekeepers, he stated that:

In certain cases this right should be exercised only under strictly defined conditions. A problem arises in this context because of the fact that a wide interpretation of the right of self-defence might well blur the distinction between operations of the character discussed in this report and combat operations, which would require a decision under Chapter VII of the Charter, and an explicit, more far-reaching delegation of authority to the Secretary-General than would be required for any of the operations discussed here. A reasonable definition seems to have been established in the case of UNEF, where the rule is applied that men engaged in the operation may never take the initiative in the use of armed force, but are entitled to respond with force to an attack with arms, including attempts to use force to make them withdraw from positions which they occupy under orders from the Commander, acting under the authority of the Assembly and within the scope of its resolutions. The basic element involved is clearly the prohibition against any *initiative* in the use of armed force.[127]

He recommended that this definition be approved for future UN operations. Thus Hammarskjöld laid out for the first time the distinction between peacekeeping operations, which would be authorized to use force only in self-defence, and enforcement operations, which may use force beyond self-defence. Hammarskjöld recognized, though, even at this early stage, that the concept of self-defence was open to a variety of interpretations: 'There will always remain, of course, a certain margin of freedom for judgement, as, for example, on the extent and nature of the arming of the units and of their right to self-defence'.[128]

---

[125] United Nations, Summary study of the experience derived from the establishment and operation of the force, report of the Secretary-General, UN document A/3943, 9 Oct. 1958, reproduced in Mezerik (note 34), pp. 131–43.

[126] Burns and Heathcote (note 20), p. 22.

[127] Summary study (note 125), p. 139. Emphasis in original.

[128] Summary study (note 125), p. 139.

Some of the other principles enunciated in the study were also relevant to the use-of-force issue. Clearly, Hammarskjöld envisaged that UN peacekeepers would be deployed only with the consent of the host nation. Any UN force should be deployed under a clear-cut mandate 'which has entirely detached it from involvement in any internal or local problems, and which therefore enables it to maintain its neutrality in relation to international political issues'. A force of the UNEF type, he wrote, 'should not be used to enforce any specific political solution of pending problems or to influence the political balance decisive to such a solution'.[129] Even joint operations with government forces were to be abjured lest the force's neutrality be damaged. The neutrality principle had especially been necessary in the Gaza Strip and had informed the UN decision to withdraw from the administration of the area. Here Hammarskjöld was anticipating precisely the difficulties that were to beset future operations, including those in the Congo, Somalia, Bosnia and Lebanon. Hammarskjöld also drew from the UNEF experience the lesson that any UN force should have 'freedom of movement within its area of operations and all such facilities regarding access to that area and communications as are necessary for successful completion of the task'.[130] Such a principle would be critically important in the Congo.

While Hammarskjöld's study was a useful first attempt at describing the new phenomenon of peacekeeping, it was rambling, repetitive and at times incoherent. It was essentially a work in progress and not the definitive word that some observers today assume it to be. The self-defence doctrine did not in fact emerge very clearly from the document. 'The self-defence doctrine was left rather vague, and the report of 1958 had little to add.'[131] Hammarskjöld also skated over the difficulties in establishing UNEF, claiming somewhat disingenuously that differences of interpretation over its role had been resolved in consultation with contributing governments and the host government. Finally, since it was prepared well before the end of UNEF's tenure, the report did not encompass the whole UNEF experience, including the traumatic withdrawal in 1967. It therefore contained no recommendations on what to do when consent was withdrawn and a peacekeeping force was faced with a choice between using force or withdrawing.

At the end of the UNEF mission U Thant attempted to continue the codification process by publishing his own list of what he called 'fundamental principles of peacekeeping efforts' (by this stage the word 'peacekeeping' was in use). It is notable that, although he mentioned consent of the parties, voluntary provision of force contingents, the willingness of the parties to achieve peace and accept international assistance, exclusive UN command and control of its force, and a formal agreement on rights and privileges, including freedom of movement on land and in the air, he did not mention the use of force or indeed

---

[129] Summary study (note 125), p. 136.
[130] Summary study (note 125), p. 136.
[131] Goldmann (note 21), p. 21.

the problem of impartiality.[132] He did, however, anticipate some of the difficulties that would face future peacekeeping operations in regard to the use of force when he concluded that, on the basis of UNEF's experience, peacekeeping and Chapter VII enforcement 'cannot be mixed'.

## VI. Conclusions

As shown above, the theory of peacekeeping, including its self-defence norm, did not emerge fully formed with the deployment of UNEF I but evolved gradually from the initial assumptions of Pearson, Hammarskjöld, Bunche and others in the UN Secretariat about what might be possible in the context of the Suez conflict, especially given the hypersensitivity of both Egypt and Israel to any hint of infringement of their sovereignty and the severe constraints imposed by the cold war. Hence the extreme importance attached by Hammarskjöld to the only principles that would permit UNEF I to be deployed and operate—the consent of the parties, impartiality and the use of force only in self-defence. Although the limited principle of self-defence gained uneasy acceptance by the UN commanders and troops involved, and did work in practice in most circumstances that confronted UNEF I, its limits remained unclear and untested at the conclusion of the mission. While the self-defence norm had now arrived as a firm principle, it remained for future missions to explore both its limitations and its possibilities.

The surprising aspect, in fact, is that UN troops for UNEF I were armed in the first place. Presumably the decision to use formed military units for the world's first peacekeeping operation was taken because they were the only self-sustaining mechanism readily available to states for quick and organized deployment in the harsh environment of the Middle East. The idea that troops should monitor the withdrawal of other troops also had a certain logic to it. It is, however, difficult to see why such troops needed to be armed if, in fact, all they were doing was monitoring and facilitating a withdrawal. If they were only intended to symbolize the UN's moral authority and the Security Council's interest in the situation, it would seem that unarmed 'Blue Helmets' could have done the job just as well. In fact they might have done it better since they would pose no threat to heavily armed troops who had just fought a war. Especially as all the state parties involved had conventional military forces with good command and control systems, there would appear to have been no possibility of UNEF's deployment being opposed militarily or attacked by renegade units. While there was a need for UNEF I forces to be able to protect themselves against armed infiltrators across the agreed frontiers once the withdrawals had been carried out, this was not originally foreseen. Moreover, even the 'support to the civil power' functions that UNEF I assumed in Gaza, such as crowd control, were not only unforeseen in the original mandate, but could have been carried out by unarmed UN civilian police had such a concept been envisaged.

---

[132] Final report by Secretary-General U Thant on UNEF (note 56), para. 22.

There was, of course, an alternative to the Hammarskjöldian concept of UN peacekeeping, and it was broached from the outset. Force Commander Burns naturally assumed that there was a good reason for using armed forces to carry out his mission. That reason can only have been, from his military perspective, the need to be able to deter violations of the ceasefire and withdrawal agreement, to use force if necessary to warn off the violators, to express the Security Council's resolve and, depending on the situation, to enforce the will of the Security Council. Burns was genuinely surprised when his request for a force robust enough to pose a deterrent threat to the parties was refused. This problem was to be faced in dramatic fashion by the next UN mission after UNEF I, in the Congo.

# 3. Breaking the rules: peace enforcement in the Congo

While UNEF was still in the field and peacekeeping norms were still emerging, the UN deployed a mission that would break all the rules established so far, although not avowedly so, and take peacekeepers beyond peacekeeping into peace enforcement. Deployed in the newly independent former Belgian colony[1] from 1960 to 1964, the UN Operation in the Congo (ONUC)[2] used increasing amounts of military force to the point where it became, in strategy and tactics, indistinguishable from a standard military campaign.[3] Strangely, though, while the Security Council mandated the use of force for purposes beyond what is today considered peacekeeping, the UN maintained until the end that it was operating strictly in self-defence—by implication, in peacekeeping mode.

The mission was vastly different from UNEF. It was deployed in the middle of an incipient civil war overlaid with elements of foreign intervention. Since all the factions and breakaway provincial authorities had their own foreign backers, the use of force by troops under UN command inevitably became highly politicized and controversial, entangled in the ideological and decolonization struggles of the era. Legitimate questions were raised about ONUC's mandate and whether it had exceeded it, and exactly what the use of force was intended to achieve, but also about how far the UN could legitimately interfere in the internal affairs of a sovereign state without its consent, especially in the absence of a functioning national government. These controversies were to split the Security Council and the wider UN membership, almost bankrupt the organization and ensure that it refrained from the use of force on a comparable scale for decades. They also set back the search for a sensible and practicable use-of-force doctrine for the UN.

## I. Genesis, mandate and deployment

Within four days of the Congo gaining independence on 30 June 1960, the 25 000-strong Force Publique, which combined the functions of army and police force but was soon renamed the Armée Nationale Congolaise (ANC), mutinied against its Belgian officers. It began disintegrating into roving armed bands, attacking, raping and killing Europeans. The capital, Leopoldville, began to descend into chaos. Belgium promptly deployed its troops, still stationed at

---

[1] From 1971 to 1997 the country was called Zaire. After May 1997 it reverted to the Democratic Republic of the Congo.

[2] Originally Organisation des Nations Unies au Congo, later changed to Opération des Nations Unies au Congo.

[3] For a more detailed account of the Congo case see Findlay, T., *The Blue Helmets' First War? Use of Force by the UN in the Congo 1960–1964* (Canadian Peacekeeping Press: Clementsport, 1999).

bases at Kamina and Kitona, to 23 different locations throughout the country to protect its own and other foreign nationals.[4] These troop movements and later airlifts of reinforcements from Belgium were not authorized by the Congolese Government as required under the (unratified) Treaty of Friendship.[5] The Congolese were outraged, even though their own government was unable to control the situation. The deployment of Belgian troops to the mineral-rich province of Katanga in particular raised suspicions that Belgium was encouraging and supporting Katanga's independence.

On 13 July Secretary-General Dag Hammarskjöld invoked, for the first time in the UN's history, Chapter XV, Article 99 of the UN Charter, which provides that: 'The Secretary-General may bring to the attention of the Security Council any matter that in his opinion may threaten the maintenance of international peace and security'. His judgement that such a threat existed was based not on Belgium's actions or those of the Congolese but on the risk that the two cold war antagonists, the Soviet Union and the United States, and/or their allies and proxies, would be drawn into the conflict. Urging the Security Council to act with the utmost speed in view of the escalating crisis, he sought authorization to 'take the necessary steps, in consultation with the Government of the Congo, to provide the Government with military assistance'.[6] These would be 'stop-gap' measures until the national security forces were 'able to fully meet their tasks'. He proposed deploying a token group of troops immediately (those offered by Ghana, which were already on their way), while preparing a more substantial force, to be known as ONUC. Once UN troops were present he hoped Belgium would withdraw its forces. The Security Council adopted Hammarskjöld's proposals on 14 July in Resolution 143.[7]

Hammarskjöld subsequently proposed, in a plan requested by the Security Council, that ONUC should operate under the peacekeeping principles enunciated in his UNEF 'summary study' of October 1958.[8] The first four of these principles helped set the parameters for the policy on the use of force. According to these, ONUC would be present with the consent of the Congolese Government; take no action that would make it a party to internal conflict; be at all times under the exclusive command of the UN and not of the Congolese Government; and enjoy the freedom of movement and communications necessary for its operations (to be defined by agreement with the government).[9]

[4] Hoskyns, C., *The Congo Since Independence: January 1960 to December 1961* (Oxford University Press: London, 1965), pp. 124–25.

[5] Hoskyns (note 4), p. 124. The Treaty of Friendship, Assistance and Cooperation between the Kingdom of Belgium and the Republic of the Congo was signed on 29 June 1960.

[6] United Nations, Security Council, *Official Records* (SCOR), 873rd meeting, 13–14 July 1960.

[7] United Nations, Resolution adopted by the Security Council at its 873rd meeting on 14 July 1960, UN document S/4387, 14 July 1960 (SCOR, Supplement for July–Sep. 1960, p. 16).

[8] Published as United Nations, Summary study of the experience derived from the establishment and operation of the force, report of the Secretary-General, UN document A/3943, 9 Oct. 1958, reproduced in Mezerik, A. G. (ed.), *The United Nations Emergency Force (UNEF): 1956—Creation, Evolution, End of Mission—1967*, International Review Service, vol. 13, no. 97 (1969), pp. 131–43.

[9] United Nations, First report of the Secretary-General on the implementation of Security Council Resolution S/4387 of 14 July 1960, UN document S/4389, 18 July 1960 (SCOR, Supplement for July–Sep. 1960, pp. 16–24).

ONUC would use force only in self-defence and as a last resort, and not take 'military initiatives'. 'It follows', Hammarskjöld said, 'from the rule that the United Nations units must not become parties in internal conflicts, that they cannot be used to enforce any specific political solution of pending problems or to influence the political balance decisive to such a solution'.[10] A practical political reason for this, he pointed out, was that UN member states would not provide troops for an enforcement operation. Hammarskjöld seemed to believe, at least initially, that, as in the case of UNEF, the mere presence of UN troops, symbolizing the prestige and authority of the Security Council and the international community, would somehow solve the problem.[11]

On 22 July 1960, after considering Hammarskjöld's report, the Security Council passed Resolution 145, its second on the Congo crisis.[12] Far from explicitly establishing ONUC and giving it a definitive mandate, it simply commended the Secretary-General's report, thereby implicitly endorsing his plans, including, it must be presumed, his proposed constraints on the use of force. Like the initial resolution, this one provided no clues as to what the Congolese Government was to be helped to do or how ONUC was supposed to do it. The organization and management of the force was devolved to the Secretary-General, assisted by the UN Secretariat, under the principle 'leave it to Dag'.

Remarkably, by 26 July ONUC's military component had reached a strength of over 8000, comprising troops from Ethiopia, Ghana, Guinea, Ireland, Liberia, Mali, Morocco, Sweden and Tunisia, deployed in all provinces but rebellious Katanga.[13] It was one of the speediest peacekeeping deployments in UN history.[14] Unlike UNEF, which was headed by a force commander, ONUC would have as its head a civilian SRSG, later called the officer-in-charge. Ralph Bunche, appointed interim force commander until the arrival of Swedish General Carl von Horn, explained the role of UN troops in a radio broadcast in Leopoldville on 26 July: 'They will bear arms, but will only use them in self-defence . . . The UN forces in the Congo are forces for peace. They will do everything they can to help restore calm, harmony, and safety for all, whites as well as blacks in this troubled land'.[15] The weaponry and firepower ONUC eventually acquired would be unmatched by any peacekeeping operation for decades. They included artillery, armoured personnel carriers (APCs), tanks and a small international air force comprising 14 aircraft, both jet fighters and

[10] First report of the Secretary-General (note 9), para. 13.

[11] Schneider, S. J., 'Congo force and standing UN force: legal experience with ONUC', *Indian Journal of International Law*, vol. 4, no. 2 (Apr. 1964), p. 276.

[12] United Nations, Resolution adopted by the Security Council at its 879th meeting on 22 July 1960, UN document S/4405, 22 July 1960.

[13] Officially called the UN Force (UNF), it was mostly referred to simply as ONUC (despite the fact that it also had civilian and civilian police components)—a convention that is followed in this book.

[14] Burns, A. and Heathcote, N., *Peacekeeping by UN Forces: From Suez to the Congo*, Princeton Studies in World Politics no. 4 (Praeger for the Center for International Studies, Princeton: New York, 1963), p. 33.

[15] Ralph Bunche's broadcast message on the arrival of UN troops in the Congo, reproduced in Kanza, T., *Conflict in the Congo* (Penguin: Harmondsworth, 1972), appendix 3, p. 335.

bombers.[16] ONUC involved at its peak almost 20 000 troops, officers and specialized personnel from 28 countries. Because of the rotation of units, more than 93 000 military personnel served with the force.[17]

ONUC's mandate was progressively expanded in three further resolutions in 1960–61 (resolutions 146, 161 and 169),[18] which were increasingly controversial, forged through political compromise between widely varying viewpoints and thus not easily reconciled or interpreted by those charged with running the operation. They all failed to establish under which article of the UN Charter the force had been mandated and none even mentioned the Charter or its provisions. Even though they expanded ONUC's authorization to use force well beyond the new peacekeeping concept of self-defence, they still fell short of explicitly authorizing the use of force for enforcement purposes.

The question which chapter and article of the Charter the Security Council was acting under, if only implicitly, was answered piecemeal and apparently reluctantly by the Secretary-General himself. In a statement to the Council on 8 August 1960 he noted that its resolutions of 14 and 22 July were not explicitly passed under Chapter VII but 'on the basis of an initiative under Article 99'.[19] However, he then proceeded, inscrutably, to explain that he felt entitled nonetheless to cite three articles of Chapter VII because 'the problem facing the Congo is one of peace and war—and not only in the Congo'. The most important was Article 40, which permits the Security Council to decide on 'provisional measures'. Hammarskjöld's intention in citing this article was presumably to situate ONUC somewhere in Chapter VII but avoid articles 41 (on non-military sanctions such as embargoes) and 42 (military action). It also fitted well with his repeated references to ONUC as a temporary security force.[20] Surprisingly, despite Hammarskjöld's strong preference for peacekeeping, no consideration appears to have been given to mandating the Congo operation explicitly under Chapter VI.

The only authoritative interpretation of ONUC's mandate during the entire period of its existence came not from the Security Council but from the ICJ. In its advisory opinion of 20 July 1962 on certain expenses of the United Nations, it stated categorically that ONUC was not an '*enforcement* action' 'within the compass of Chapter VII' since its operations 'did not include a use of armed force against a State which the Security Council, under Article 39, determined

[16] Durch, W. J., 'The UN Operation in the Congo', ed. W. J. Durch, *The Evolution of UN Peacekeeping: Case Studies and Comparative Analysis* (St Martin's Press for the Henry L. Stimson Center: Washington, DC, 1993), p. 336.

[17] Lefever, E. W. and Joshua, W., *United Nations Peacekeeping in the Congo, 1960–1964: An Analysis of Political, Executive and Military Control. Vol. 2, Full Text* (Brookings Institution for the US Arms Control and Disarmament Agency (ACDA): Washington, DC, 30 June 1966), p. 1.

[18] UN Security Council resolutions 146, 9 Aug. 1960; 161, 21 Feb. 1961; and 169, 24 Nov. 1961.

[19] United Nations, Security Council, Verbatim records (provisional), 884th meeting, UN document S/PV.884, 8 Aug. 1960, pp. 9–10.

[20] He may also have seen the presumed establishment of UNTSO under Article 40 of the UN Charter as a precedent. Simmonds argues that the Korea operation was authorized under Article 39, the UN Observation Group in Lebanon (UNOGIL) under Chapter VI, UNEF under Article 14 and UNTSO probably under Article 40. Simmonds, R., *Legal Problems Arising from the United Nations Military Operations in the Congo* (Nijhoff: The Hague, 1968), p. 22.

to have committed an act of aggression or to have breached the peace'.[21] This ignored the fact that nowhere does Chapter VII refer to states as being the only threat to international peace and security—a fact taken advantage of by the Security Council in mandating peace enforcement operations in the 1990s.

## II. Policy and directives on the use of force

Although the Secretary-General's original reiteration of the self-defence norm and successive Security Council resolutions provided general guidance to ONUC on the use of force, the Congo mission was so politically sensitive and so much depended on ONUC's behaviour being seen as impartial, credible and beyond reproach that policy on the use of force could not be left to the military. It was therefore broadly determined by Hammarskjöld and his successor, U Thant. In close consultation with ONUC's civilian and military leadership, they each contrived, interpreted and supplemented the principles followed by ONUC in using force, approved directives for such use and attempted to manage—at times micromanage—their application in the field, with varying degrees of success. Policy was enunciated in operations directives issued to ONUC by the SRSG or the force commander and through ad hoc communications from the Secretary-General or UN Secretariat in response to developing situations. While precedents for the precise situation faced by ONUC were lacking, it is notable and surprising that the documents developed so painstakingly by UNEF, such as those relating to 'protective duty', were ignored.

Hammarskjöld was particularly influential in establishing use-of-force policy for the mission. Guided by his pacifist inclinations, he steadfastly retained his view of ONUC's essentially peaceable nature until his death. According to Sir Brian Urquhart: 'Hammarskjöld devoted much thought to the principles upon which the Congo operation should be carried out and throughout the hectic weeks that followed its establishment he did not cease to elaborate, largely for his own guidance, a firm basis in principles for all of the variety of actions that had to be taken'.[22] This applied especially to the use and non-use of force.

Hammarskjöld regularly consulted and reported to the Security Council. In August 1960 he also established a Congo Advisory Committee, similar to that established for UNEF, comprising representatives of troop-contributing countries. He attempted to consult it periodically, but it was often divided or unresponsive to his pleas for guidance.[23] Hammarskjöld's closest advisers were a handful of key Secretariat officials known as the Congo Club.[24] It evaluated

---

[21] International Court of Justice, 'Certain expenses of the United Nations (Article 17, para. 1), Advisory Opinion of 20 July 1962', *Reports of Judgements, Advisory Opinions and Orders* (International Court of Justice: The Hague, 1962), p. 177. Emphasis in original.

[22] Urquhart, B., *Hammarskjöld* (Alfred A. Knopf: New York, 1972), p. 403.

[23] It comprised representatives of Canada, Ethiopia, Ghana, Guinea, India, Indonesia, Ireland, Liberia, Mali, Morocco, Pakistan, Sudan, Sweden, Tunisia and the United Arab Republic.

[24] Lefever and Joshua, vol. 2 (note 17), p. 120; and O'Brien, C. C., *To Katanga and Back: A UN Case History* (Hutchinson: London, 1962), p. 50. The group included Andrew Cordier; Ralph Bunche; Heinz Wieschhoff (USA), senior director of the Trusteeship Department; C. V. Narsimhan (India), staff aide to

day-to-day events and formulated basic policy, which was discussed with the Advisory Committee where necessary.[25] Particularly influential in helping determine use-of-force policy were UNEF veterans Bunche and Indar Jit Rikhye as Military Advisor to the Secretary-General for the Congo operation.

The use-of-force instructions tended to be changed in response to developing conditions in the field rather than as a result of Security Council resolutions. The unique and rapidly changing character of ONUC's mission meant that, as in the UNEF case, they were essentially made up as the mission went along. Mostly they were issued in response to particular, unanticipated threats to the security and freedom of movement of ONUC and other unforeseen circumstances, such as attacks on civilians and inter-tribal conflict.

## Basic documents on the use of force

The key document establishing ONUC's use-of-force policy was Hammarskjöld's first report on the Congo situation of 18 July 1960. Its sole paragraph on the subject quoted directly from his 1958 summary study of the UNEF experience:

Men engaged in the operations may never take the initiative in the use of armed force, but are entitled to respond with force to an attack with arms, including attempts to use force to make them withdraw from positions which they occupy under orders from the Commander, acting under the authority of the Security Council and within the scope of its resolution. The basic element involved is clearly the prohibition against any *initiative* in the use of force.[26]

The use-of-force rules for ONUC, at least at the beginning, therefore exhibit a direct line of descent from UNEF. However, it very soon became apparent that they were grossly inadequate in the Congo. Unlike the UNEF case, there was no ceasefire line to monitor and no peace agreement, and the situation was extremely fluid rather than relatively stable, with armed rebels, ill-disciplined government troops and lawless civilians all posing a threat to lightly armed peacekeepers. Perhaps most troubling was the lack of consent.

While it requested and consented to ONUC's deployment, Belgium had not agreed to withdraw its troops unconditionally and had procrastinated for several weeks. The Congolese Government had unequivocally requested ONUC's presence and welcomed its arrival, but it was inexperienced, lacked understanding of international relations, was baffled by the circumlocutory style of Security Council resolutions and Hammarskjöld's lawyer's way with language, and

the Secretary-General; Brigadier Indar Jit Rikhye (India), Military Advisor to the Secretary-General for the Congo operation; Sir Alexander MacFarquhar (UK), special adviser on civilian operations in the Congo; and Robert Gardiner (Ghana), an economic and social affairs officer in the UN Secretariat. Francis Nwokedi of Nigeria and Taieb Sahbani of Tunisia joined later. Urquhart, B., *Ralph Bunche: An American Life* (W. W. Norton: New York, 1993), p. 341.

[25] Hoskyns (note 4), p. 183.

[26] United Nations, First report of the Secretary-General (note 9), para. 15. The text refers to the Security Council, which from now on would establish peacekeeping operations rather than the General Assembly (which had established UNEF). Emphasis in original.

above all was impatient to see results. It seriously misunderstood the role and powers of ONUC, expecting it to use force immediately to expel the Belgian regular forces, round up and deport foreign mercenaries, and end the Katangan and other secessions. It soon became disillusioned. This implied withdrawal of consent was later demonstrated by government-orchestrated political and military attacks on ONUC. As for the mutinous forces in the country, none of them, certainly not those in the rebellious province of Katanga, had agreed to the presence or mission of UN peacekeepers.

## Initial instructions on the use of force

The first instructions to ONUC were issued orally by Bunche in Leopoldville. Since the speed and improvised character of ONUC's initial deployment necessitated contingents transiting the capital only briefly on their way to the provinces, there was no time for extended briefing on local conditions—even if the UN had been aware of them—much less on peacekeeping techniques. The troops were told to attempt by 'diplomatic means' to restore law and order in the urban centres and then gradually fan out into surrounding areas; try to induce the Congolese troops to return to camp and keep warring elements apart; and give every assistance to the local authorities. They were given strict instructions not to use force except in cases of great emergency and self-defence, and were warned that firing by UN troops might prejudice the success of the whole operation.[27] In the first few days Bunche also issued specific operational orders, orally, to the force.[28] For instance, when the commander of the Ethiopian brigade in Orientale Province requested instructions from Bunche, he was simply told to maintain order. The biggest problem, the commander later reported, was the 'unclearness of our mission'.[29]

The interpretation of the UN mandate in the early days, when instructions from ONUC's Leopoldville headquarters were broad and vague, was therefore left to the national commands in each province, each of which tended to see its task according to its own military tradition and experience.[30] The Ethiopian and Tunisian troops in lower Leopoldville Province, for example, interpreted their mandate as being to act like a military government. As Rajeshwar Dayal, who became SRSG in September, reported, 'an immense responsibility . . . devolved upon local commanders and their men, and it is the best evidence of their devotion, discipline and judgement that no serious situations arose in any of the varied and delicate situations in which they found themselves at such short notice'.[31]

---

[27] Hoskyns (note 4), p. 134.
[28] Lefever and Joshua, vol. 2 (note 17), p. 302.
[29] Lefever and Joshua, vol. 2 (note 17), p. 314.
[30] Lefever and Joshua, vol. 2 (note 17), pp. 313, 372.
[31] United Nations, First progress report to the Secretary-General from his Special Representative in the Congo, Mr Rajeshwar Dayal, UN document S/4531, 21 Sep. 1960, para. 33.

**Operations directives**

Once the mission had settled in, the main instrument for transmitting policy on the use of force to ONUC was a series of written operations directives by successive force commanders, deputy commanders or chiefs of staff. Instructions relating to particular military operations were also issued in the form of operational orders.[32] Through these documents Hammarskjöld's UNEF-based guidelines and subsequent revisions were interpreted, embellished and expanded by ONUC into what would today be called rules of engagement. Subsidiary or territorial headquarters in the field sometimes issued additional directives to the forces under their command.

Although operations directives and operational orders were usually issued in the name of the force commander, they could be initiated either by him or by the SRSG or officer-in-charge. In any case they were always cleared in advance with the latter. At least one civilian head of mission, Bunche, issued an operations directive over the objection of Supreme Commander von Horn. Sometimes Rikhye was consulted. Both Hammarskjöld and U Thant appear to have been consulted in regard to operations directives, either before or after they had been issued, especially those that were particularly sensitive. Some specific directives were discussed in the Advisory Committee and the Congo Club.

The first operations directive, untitled and undated, was issued by von Horn, probably several days after he arrived. It simply stated, in relation to the 'use of arms', that: 'At all levels, Commanders are to be instructed that, on NO account, [are] weapons to be used unless in cases of great and sudden emergency and for the purpose of self-defence. In such cases, the commander on the spot will ensure that the greatest care and control are used'.[33]

*Bunche's directive on the protection of internal security, 2 August 1960*

Bunche's first major written edict on the use of force focused on what seemed to be the initial challenge faced by ONUC—the maintenance of security in case of 'unruly crowds, threatening demonstrations or riots'. It set out four principles for UN troops in assisting the Congolese Government in maintaining law and order. First, ONUC should 'exhaust all possible peaceful means of keeping order before any resort to force. Every effort should be exerted to avoid harm to anyone, since public reaction to the employment of force by United Nations personnel might well prove disastrous to the success of the entire United Nations operation'.[34] Second, it was normally the responsibility of the civilian police, either Congolese or UN, to maintain civil order. UN troops would only

[32] E.g., Operational Order no. 2 of 1963, 21 Aug. 1963, from the force commander, regarding the situation in Leopoldville and action to be taken in case of disturbances, UN Archives (file number unknown).
[33] ONUC, Operations Directive no. 1, untitled and undated, UN Archives DAG13/1.6.5.0.0, Ops Directives Aug. 1960–Jan. 1964, Box 3.
[34] ONUC, Directive on the protection of internal security, 2 Aug. 1960, UN Archives DAG/13.1.6.5.0.0, Ops Directives Aug. 1960–Jan. 1964, Box 3.

intervene at the request of the police when they felt they could no longer control the situation, at which point command of the situation would pass to the military. The third principle, which was to be interpreted 'in the light of the overriding force of the first principle', related directly to self-defence: 'Firing, even in self-defence, should be resorted to only in extreme circumstances. Any effort to disarm members of the United Nations Force is to be regarded as a legitimate cause for self-defence'. Fourth (in capital letters), 'firmness, tact and humour are essential qualities for controlling crowds peacefully'.

Bunche's guidelines ended by setting out in detail the methods of crowd control to be employed, including intelligence-gathering, mobile patrols, mobile loudspeakers, early identification of ring-leaders and promulgation of ONUC's purpose. Finally, more bold type: 'All officers and troops should be briefed in accordance with the above-stated principles and should be made constantly aware of the necessity for calm, discipline and the avoidance of bloodshed'.

Von Horn spent hours arguing with Bunche about this document, explaining that it was 'totally unsuitable for troops operating under active service conditions'.[35] Some of the soldiers, von Horn pointed out, came from 'remote villages in the Moroccan hills or from the bush districts of African states where the schoolhouse had as yet made little impact'. Faced with a hostile crowd, it was hardly likely that 'they would remember Ralph's document—let alone thumb their way through pages of legalistic argument'. Von Horn complained that:

Our rules were specific; force was *only* to be used in self-defence, nor were we allowed any latitude, however threatening the situation. As any soldier could have pointed out . . . orders like these present a commander with a distinct moral problem; whether to risk his men's lives by involving them in a situation where some of them are bound to get shot before having a chance to defend themselves—or whether to risk the failure of a mission (on whose success the lives of many civilians may depend) through a reluctance to expose his soldiers to what he considers an intolerable degree of risk.[36]

*Operations Directive no. 6*

The longest and most comprehensive document on the use of force issued during ONUC's tenure was Operations Directive no. 6 of 28 October 1960.[37] Issued under von Horn's name and with his approval, it was devised by Dayal in response to attacks on ONUC in Leopoldville earlier that month.[38] It also dealt with prevention of civil war and attacks on innocent civilians. The directive became the reference point for all subsequent ONUC operations directives. It began by setting out for UN personnel, for the first time, a considered official explanation for the deployment of an armed multinational force to the Congo:

[35] von Horn, C. (Maj.-Gen.), *Soldiering for Peace* (Cassell: London, 1966), p. 159.
[36] von Horn (note 35), pp. 150, 180. Emphasis in original.
[37] ONUC, Operations Directive no. 6, 'Security and maintenance of law and order', 28 Oct. 1960, UN Archives DAG13/1.6.5.0.0, Ops Directives Aug. 1960–Jan. 1964, Box 3. The directive is reproduced in appendix 2 in this volume.
[38] Dayal, R., *Mission for Hammarskjöld: The Congo Crisis* (Oxford University Press: London, 1976), p. 159.

The UN Force in the Congo is a peace force. It carries arms in order to lend weight to its authority and as a deterrent, but these arms may be used only in self-defence ... The UN Force is in no sense an occupying force. It seeks only to help achieve security in which government and administration can function effectively. Thus, its main purpose is to assist the government in creating conditions of peace in which Congolese people may themselves be able to develop their political freedom and economic prosperity. The UN force therefore must respect the sovereignty, independence and national integrity of the Republic of the Congo.

After declaring that the primary responsibility for law and order lay with the Congolese authorities, the directive explained that this did not prevent the UN from taking humanitarian measures to prevent bloodshed, such as acting as a buffer in inter-tribal conflict, lending its good offices to local disputants and arranging ceasefires. In the event of actual or potential disturbances, UN commanders were to rely in the first instance on the local Congolese authorities and encourage them to act. Only when they failed to do so would the UN become involved.

Specifically on the use of force, the directive repeated that ONUC 'may not take the initiative'. It was, however, 'entitled to use force in self-defence, but only as a last resort after other means viz., negotiation and persuasion, have failed'. The directive then proceeded, for the first time, to give specific cases in which UN troops were entitled to respond with force to an armed attack:

(a) attempts by force to compel them to withdraw from a position which they occupy under orders from their commanders, or to infiltrate and envelop such positions as are deemed necessary by their commanders for them to hold, thus jeopardising their safety;

(b) attempts by force to disarm them;

(c) attempts by force to prevent them from carrying out their responsibilities, as ordered by their commanders; and

(d) violation by force of United Nations' premises and attempts at arrest or abduction of UN personnel, civil or military.

This was the sort of expansion of the narrow self-defence rule that General Burns had unsuccessfully sought for UNEF. That such an expansion was approved indicates the very different threat facing the UN in the Congo.

The minimum force necessary was still required to be used in all such cases 'in order to prevent as far as possible the loss of human life or serious injury to person'. In the event of force being used, commanders were required to follow several principles:

(a) the object throughout is to deter and not to cause loss of life;

(b) it follows that firing should be low and not to cause loss of life;

(c) in the case of mob attack, the leaders should be picked out for deterrent action;

(d) firing must at all times be controlled and not indiscriminate;

(e) the officer in charge will keep a record of the number of rounds fired;

(f) firing into the air should be avoided as it may be provocative without strengthening respect for the force.

A separate section on 'Protection against marauders or armed bands' ordered that, if all attempts at peaceful settlement failed, UN commanders could recommend to the supreme commander that the threatened areas be placed under UN protection by deploying UN troops and then defended by 'resisting and driving off the attackers with such minimum use of force including firing, as may be necessary'. This is an early appearance of the interpositional strategy that would prove so successful as a peacekeeping technique.

If UN troops came across marauding bands attacking civilians or each other, and peaceful methods failing, commanders were ordered to 'immediately take appropriate steps to separate the combatants and to prevent further lawlessness, bloodshed, pillaging and looting'. If UN troops were then attacked: 'They may use such degree of force as may be necessary for the exercise of their right of self-defence, including firing'. Here, too, was a clear order for UN forces to interpose themselves in ways that would trigger the use of force in self-defence. Special instructions were also issued regarding looting. Persons observed looting, but not fighting, at the scene of armed clashes should be called upon by UN troops to desist and surrender. If they desisted and fled, firing should not be resorted to in order to apprehend them. If they refused to desist, force 'may be employed to stop them, and, if they attack, the principle of self-defence applies and resort may be had to the minimum firing necessary'. This was actually not self-defence at all. The instruction would have worked equally well without the reference to self-defence.

The directive recognized the difficulty that the lawless elements in the Congo were often ANC troops, declaring that ONUC's obligations to assist in the maintenance of law and order were 'in no way diminished' when the ANC was itself involved. If such elements were operating under any form of leadership, UN commanders were to use their good offices to stop all such activities, either directly or through higher Congolese authorities. If these endeavours failed, every effort should be made to disarm or neutralize them and confine them to barracks. Any further action should only be taken after specific instructions from the supreme commander. Finally, physical force could be used, if necessary, to protect UN property and installations and essential public utilities, extending to the 'minimum degree of firing necessary, as a last resort'.

The directive ended with a general enjoinder to UN troops to 'act with tact and moderation at all times'. It explained that: 'The very presence of armed and disciplined troops, skilfully deployed, can act as a powerful deterrent to the forces of disorder and violence. When force has to be used it should be kept to the minimum required for the attainment of the objective. It is expected that the action of the UN troops will always be inspired by the aims and purposes of the United Nations in the Congo'.

In this way ONUC, like UNEF, gradually acquired increasingly detailed regulations as to how it was to use force. However, ONUC's powers quickly outstripped those of UNEF, taking peacekeeping into new dimensions.

## III. The use of force in practice and the evolution of policy

In analysing ONUC's actual use of force it is necessary to treat its various functions separately, since each required a different approach. Some functions could be carried out entirely by peaceful means. Others required peaceful means backed by the threat, implicit or explicit, of force. Still others required the use of force in self-defence. Finally, some required force beyond self-defence.

Dividing ONUC's functions up in this way is necessarily arbitrary and artificial. Especially in the early months the force faced 'complete chaos' and often simply did what it felt it could do, particularly to save innocent lives.[39] Even after the mission settled into a recognizable pattern, its various functions overlapped and intertwined. For instance, preventing tribal conflict also helped prevent civil war as well as ensuring ONUC's security and freedom of movement. In ensuring freedom of movement ONUC could also, at times, be seen as upholding the territorial integrity of the Congo.

### Establishing and maintaining ONUC's presence and freedom of movement

ONUC's initial task was to establish its presence and freedom of movement throughout the Congo as quickly and peaceably as possible in an effort to calm and stabilize the situation. While the assumption was that ONUC was being deployed with the consent of the Congolese Government, the existence of rebellious ANC elements and provincial governments just beginning to assert their authority meant that consent was not assured. In view of the small size and military weakness of the ONUC units dispatched to most parts of the country, serious resistance would have been catastrophic. As it turned out, as UN troops fanned out across the vast Congolese territory they met no significant resistance either from the ANC or from other elements of the Congolese population. In general they were given a warm welcome, the atmosphere initially being more one of bewilderment and curiosity than of hostility.

Occasionally the ANC cooperated in ONUC's deployment and some units even voluntarily disarmed themselves. While there were incidents in which some force was used, within 10 days ONUC had established itself in Leopoldville and the provinces of Equateur, Kasai and Leopoldville. Later in Goma, in Kivu Province, a hostile crowd was metaphorically disarmed by the pipe band of the Irish 32nd Battalion in saffron kilts and with bagpipes—the ultimate alternative to the use of force.[40] Within weeks the initial and minimal objectives of the deployment were achieved except in South Kasai and South Katanga, where no attempt was made at this stage to deploy.

The replacement of the regular Belgian troops, who were providing security in key areas, proved to be ONUC's least difficult task and involved no use of force. To the consternation of Prime Minister Patrice Lumumba, the UN made

[39] Hoskyns (note 4), p. 130.
[40] von Horn (note 35), p. 177.

no attempt to use force to expel the Belgian irregulars from Katanga or from their bases at Kamina and Kitona.

It was in maintaining its presence once deployed that ONUC encountered difficulties. The security of UN troops and other UN personnel was a continuing concern, 'not entirely unlike that of an occupation army in an unfriendly country'.[41] Once in place ONUC's troops, civilian personnel and installations were attacked on numerous occasions. Random and essentially apolitical acts of violence by undisciplined individuals or units of the ANC were the main initial problem. Tribal attacks on UN personnel were also frequent, especially in Kasai and North Katanga. More serious in nature and more difficult to resolve were ANC attacks inspired by the central government, ONUC's putative host. These became a major problem from February to April 1961. Such a situation illustrated 'politically the extreme difficulty of conducting a peacekeeping operation in the face of host country opposition, and militarily the inability of a UN Force to protect itself and perform its mission because of inadequate strength and political limitations'.[42]

UN troops were obliged to use significant force in maintaining ONUC's presence and freedom of movement throughout the country. ONUC's response to specific incidents varied widely, from a failure to use force when it would have been justified to what some would consider excessive use of force and violation or at least a 'liberal interpretation' of the self-defence rule. In most cases ONUC used force legitimately in self-defence. Some incidents resulted in significant ONUC casualties. A report by the US Arms Control and Disarmament Agency (ACDA) claimed that, while ONUC's weakness in protecting itself and its installations was in some cases due to lack of adequate combat power, more often it was due to contingent commanders' confusion over the rules of engagement.[43] Lack of intelligence information was also a factor. In other cases it was due to lack of combat experience or proper military training, or incompetence. Three incidents are illustrative.

The first, in August 1960, was the first serious clash between ONUC and the ANC. It brought into public view the debate over ONUC's use-of-force rules. On 18 August ANC soldiers forced their way onto a UN aircraft at Leopoldville's Ndjili Airport, marched the Indian crew away at gunpoint, manhandled Moroccan civilians, and searched and beat several Canadian soldiers. Ghanaian troops nearby were slow to come to their defence but eventually rescued them. ONUC's chief of staff, Ethiopian Brigadier-General Iyassu Mengasha, and Rikhye negotiated the ANC's withdrawal and Sudanese troops were brought in to reinforce the UN position. The incident produced strong reactions among UN troops. Concerned about the divided loyalty and military capacity of the Ghanaian and Sudanese troops, Bunche cabled Hammarskjöld: 'Situation developing in such manner that we will quickly be faced with alternative of abandoning

[41] Lefever and Joshua, vol. 2 (note 17), p. 342.
[42] Lefever and Joshua, vol. 2 (note 17), p. 353.
[43] Lefever and Joshua, vol. 2 (note 17), p. 371.

Ndjili Airport altogether, thus closing it for all practical purposes, or employing force with *liberal interpretation of self-defence principle* to hold it'.[44]

General Harry T. Alexander, the British head of Ghana's defence force, in response to this incident criticized ONUC's use-of-force policy, describing it, disingenuously, as one of 'passive resistance' and 'non-interference' with the ANC. He alleged that the UN's instructions failed to give UN troops any liberty of action 'even for the use of minimum force'[45] and urged the use of force against the ANC rather than persuasion. British peacekeeper Brigadier Michael Harbottle noted that Alexander's attitude demonstrated 'a basic tendency among many professional soldiers to find difficulty in adapting to the concept of peaceable intervention and self-defence as practised in UN peacekeeping operations'.[46] Bunche strongly rejected Alexander's charges, saying that the UN command had issued orders to its troops that were 'very clear on the subject of the employment of force'. He accepted that he had tried to avoid 'getting elements of ONUC into the extreme position of having to shoot Congolese' and expressed regret that he had not always succeeded.[47]

Urquhart confirms that, while UN troops had so far acted with great restrain and Bunche was urging them to remain calm, tensions were rising dangerously and there was a notable tendency among the officers, from von Horn down, to 'rattle sabres'.[48] On 5 November 1960 von Horn, presumably in response to the Ndjili Airport incident, issued Operations Directive no. 7 concerning security measures at airports.[49] It reasserted that ONUC, including its civilian and military personnel, vehicles and aircraft, enjoyed freedom of movement throughout the Congo which was not subject to interference, inspection or control by any Congolese authority. The exercise of ONUC's right of self-defence, it said, included all necessary measures, consistent with Operations Directive no. 6 of 28 October 1960, to assure this freedom of movement. The directive also made clear that UN troops stationed at an airport could not 'stand aside as passive onlookers when arbitrary acts in violation of human dignity, freedom and security are committed in their presence'—a further expansion of ONUC's prerogatives and responsibilities.

The second notable incident, on 8 November, 1960, was devastating for ONUC.[50] Despite warnings from an experienced Swedish officer that they should be extremely careful in dealing with Baluba tribesmen, a 12-man Irish

[44] Quoted in Urquhart (note 24), p. 329. Emphasis added.
[45] United Nations, Report by Major General H. T. Alexander, UN document S/4445, 19 Aug. 1960, annex II (SCOR, Supplement for July, Aug. and Sep. 1960, pp. 101–102).
[46] Harbottle, M., *The Blue Berets* (Stackpole Books: Harrisburg, Pa., 1971), p. 42.
[47] United Nations, Observations by the Special Representative of the Secretary-General in the Congo on the report by Major General Alexander (S/4445, annex II), UN document S/4451, 21 Aug. 1960 (SCOR, Supplement for July, Aug. and Sep. 1960, pp. 113, 114).
[48] Urquhart (note 24), p. 329.
[49] ONUC, Operations Directive no. 7, 'Security measures at airports', 5 Nov. 1960, UN Archives no. 1001/11/OPS.
[50] For a basic account of the incident see Lefever, E. W. and Joshua, W., *United Nations Peacekeeping in the Congo, 1960–1964: An Analysis of Political, Executive and Military Control*, vol. 3 (Brookings Institution for the US Arms Control and Disarmament Agency (ACDA): Washington, DC, 30 June 1966), appendix P-7.

patrol in North Katanga allowed itself to be surrounded by them. The Baluba unexpectedly attacked, splitting the patrol into two groups and massacring all but two of the soldiers, who managed to escape. The ACDA report contends that this incident was due to the Irish officer's confusion over the rules of engagement.[51] Von Horn claims that it was due to the Irish troops' lack of battle experience. More capable vehicles, he claimed, would have afforded greater protection and allowed them to escape.[52] Other military commanders believed the massacre could have been avoided if the patrol had opened fire immediately instead of waiting until the last moment. They felt that the standing order to open fire only when fired on was unacceptable in the conditions prevailing in the Congo.[53]

A third, startling incident occurred in November 1960 when ANC troops under the orders of Congolese Army Chief of Staff Joseph Mobutu threatened to seize by force the Ghanaian Ambassador, Nathanial Welbeck, who had been declared *persona non grata*. Rikhye and von Horn believed that an adequate concentration of troops at the UN-guarded Ghanaian Embassy and a 'discreet show of force' could keep the situation within bounds.[54] Despite Hammarskjöld's cabled instructions to handle the situation cautiously, the outcome was the first sustained pitched battle between UN and central government soldiers. The commander of the Leopoldville ANC garrison, Colonel Justin Kokolo, was killed, along with a Tunisian UN soldier. Dayal claims that the episode fractured whatever remained of the professional bonds between UN and Congolese officers, causing the ANC to step up its harassment of ONUC and seriously degrading consent.[55]

Rikhye, in a report to the Secretary-General, noted that: 'Opening fire in such circumstances would be in accordance with standard military principles of self-defence to prevent an ONUC unit or position from being overwhelmed or effectively infiltrated'.[56] Hammarskjöld told the Congo Advisory Committee that: 'At a certain stage and a certain state of emotion a show of force is provocative, and even if there was no will to [take the] initiative on our side, obviously in the state of mind in which the Congolese troops found themselves, they regarded the accumulation of strength on the United Nations side as something which, so to speak, could release their military initiative. How the balance should be struck I dare not say'.[57]

Hammarskjöld was grappling with a fundamental dilemma of peacekeeping forces—how to use their military presence and strength as a deterrent without having to prove their willingness to use force by actually using it. That displays

---

[51] Lefever and Joshua, vol. 2 (note 17), p. 371.

[52] von Horn (note 35), p. 212.

[53] Hymoff, E., *Stig von Bayer* (James A. Heineman: New York, 1965), p. 109.

[54] Dayal (note 38), p. 128.

[55] Dayal (note 38), p. 131.

[56] United Nations, Situation in the Republic of the Congo, report to the Secretary-General from his Acting Special Representative in the Republic of the Congo, General Rikhye, 22 Nov. 1960, UN Archives DAG13/1.6.5.0.0, #4, p. 4.

[57] United Nations Advisory Committee on the Congo, Verbatim record, Meeting no. 15, 24 Nov. 1960, p. 81.

of military might or token shows of force are of little use when there is no willingness to actually use force in any significant way was demonstrated repeatedly in the Congo and replicated in Somalia and Bosnia.

## Restoring public order and preventing inter-tribal warfare and civil war

These functions had the potential to involve ONUC in significant use of force, but in the event it used force minimally, reluctantly and mostly in self-defence. Only in Katanga was there a different approach (see section IV).

### Restoration of public order

ONUC's initial public order functions included: patrolling areas threatened by disorder; disarming civilians and renegade military groups; rescuing civilians and evacuating them and the wounded and dead out of affected areas; and establishing and guarding UN protected areas and refugee camps where people in danger of arbitrary arrest or other persecution could take refuge.[58] Since the ANC was unable to discharge its internal security responsibilities, ONUC was in many cases obliged to assume all the normal law-and-order functions of a civilian police force, including apprehending and detaining violators of civilian law, establishing and enforcing curfews, and conducting short- and long-range patrols.[59] Sometimes the return of law and order followed naturally from the arrival of UN troops, the establishment of their presence and their persistence in asserting their freedom of movement. Their success in restoring public order varied from province to province.

ONUC was, however, severely limited in the measures it could take to preserve law and order. First, its powers were considerably more circumscribed than those of a normal police force: it had no powers of arrest, no jails to detain offenders and no legal authority to try suspects in a court of law. Second, it was bound by its instructions to use force only in self-defence, which were more restrictive than the use-of-force rules of many police forces. As Dayal told Hammarskjöld: 'The right to self-defence was too restricted as it did not even allow the arrest of criminals and hooligans or intervention to prevent arbitrary arrest'.[60] Third, it was not clear what law ONUC was supposed to uphold, since the new Congolese state had not had time to codify a Congolese version of the old Belgian law. The enforcement of old colonial laws by the UN would appear anomalous and provocative. Fourth, ONUC's thinness on the ground did not allow it cover all problem areas simultaneously or deal with major breakdowns in law and order. Fifth, the UN troops had not been trained in police duties. Finally, in all its law and order work the force needed to be constantly aware, in

---

[58] Seyersted, F., *United Nations Forces in the Law of Peace and War* (Sijthoff: Leyden, 1966), pp. 67–68.

[59] United Nations, Second progress report to the Secretary-General from his Special Representative in the Congo, Mr Rajeshwar Dayal, UN document S/4557, 2 Nov. 1960 (SCOR, Supplement for Oct., Nov. and Dec. 1960, pp. 22–23); and Lefever and Joshua, vol. 2 (note 17), p. 344.

[60] Dayal (note 38), p. 115.

a way that civilian police in a normal society would not have to be, that some of its legitimate policing activities could be construed as interference in internal politics.

Some civilian police functions were carried out by UN Civilian Police (Civ-Pols) provided by Ghana and Nigeria, who were part of ONUC for most of its mission. Arthur Lee Burns and Nina Heathcote claim that for most of the policing work the CivPols were 'worth twenty times their number of the best fighting infantry'.[61] Catherine Hoskyns concurs: 'It was . . . becoming increasingly apparent that in the situation of the Congo crack military regiments were not necessarily the most suitable and that in many cases highly trained riot police were what was really needed'.[62]

While some force was used in self-defence in curbing elements of the ANC, there were no cases of force being used to control or disarm ANC units. The implicit threat of force inherent in the presence of armed UN troops was apparently sufficient. A later public account of the Congo operation by the UN notes that ONUC 'refused to use force to subdue Congolese authorities, or the ANC under their orders. Even when its own personnel were attacked, ONUC intervened only to prevent further excesses and to urge the Congolese Government to take disciplinary action against the culprits'.[63]

Some observers considered that only disarmament of the entire ANC would satisfactorily address the Congo's law and order problem. Alexander campaigned vehemently and tirelessly for disarmament, using force if necessary.[64] Bunche equally strongly opposed him, arguing that, while it would be highly desirable, it could only be done with the consent of the Congolese Government, which was unlikely to be given.[65]

The debate about disarmament, as in the case of Somalia 30 years later, continued throughout and after the mission. In the view of Ernest Lefever: 'Had the ANC been disarmed and kept disarmed, there would have been no domestic military support for contending political factions which continued to tear the country apart. The restoration of order and the creation of a unified national government would have been less difficult'.[66] He argues that disarmament without coercion might have been possible if the Secretary-General had given it the highest priority, if it had been vigorously pursued at the diplomatic level in New York and at the political level in Leopoldville, and if all UN commanders had been instructed to engage in active persuasion toward this end.

An issue which provoked calls for the use of force beyond self-defence was the protection of civilians, both expatriates and Congolese, from ANC attacks. As in Rwanda three decades later, ONUC had to decide whether and how to use

[61] Burns and Heathcote (note 14), p. 185.

[62] Hoskyns (note 4), p. 295.

[63] United Nations, *The Blue Helmets: A Review of United Nations Peace-keeping*, 2nd edn (UN Department of Public Information: New York, 1990), p. 227.

[64] O'Brien (note 24), p. 312.

[65] Urquhart (note 24), p. 314.

[66] Lefever, E. W., *Crisis in the Congo: A United Nations Force in Action* (Brookings Institution: Washington, DC, 1965), p. 37.

force, including beyond self-defence, to protect civilians in grave danger, whether individuals, groups or entire populations. Hammarskjöld's view seemed to be that ONUC should act on humanitarian grounds to protect populations at risk, even to the extent of stretching the self-defence rule.[67] One way was to take them under UN protection in safe areas or camps and to use the self-defence rule if they were attacked. ONUC established such areas for both expatriate and Congolese civilians in late 1960 and early 1961. Approximately 1200 people in Bukavu, Bunia, Goma, Kindu, Leopoldville, Luena, Luluabourg and Stanleyville were protected in this way.[68] One of the largest was the Baluba camp on the outskirts of Elisabethville, which held up to 35 000 refugees. It posed a major challenge to ONUC's use-of-force rules because of the presence within and outside the camp of gangs of radical Baluba youth.

In February 1961 (the exact date is unclear) the force commander's Operations Directive no. 8 directed that, where feasible, every protection was to be afforded to unarmed groups subjected by any armed party to acts of violence likely to lead to loss of life.[69] In such cases, UN troops were to interpose themselves, using armed force if necessary, to prevent such loss of life.

*Prevention of inter-tribal conflict*

By late 1960 and early 1961 the law-and-order mission of ONUC had become closely entwined with, and often indistinguishable from, the more politically sensitive tasks of preventing tribal conflict and civil war, which were themselves closely linked.[70] On 17 August 1960 Operations Directive no. 3 set out ONUC policy on inter-tribal conflict. It declared that, while the subject was 'an internal matter with heavy political connotations', it was also one that ONUC could not ignore. When confronted with such conflict UN forces were to try to induce local authorities, including the police and the ANC, to assert control (even though at least some of the violence was inspired by ANC elements). ONUC should use its 'good offices' to prevent further violence. Finally, however, at the discretion of the local commander, it could '*intervene* more directly through the undertaking of patrols, guards and other preventive or protective actions using force in self-defence'.[71]

On reviewing the directives, Hammarskjöld objected to the word 'intervene' as going beyond the self-defence formula, since it implied taking the initiative in the use of force. Hammarskjöld drew a distinction between using force to intervene between factions involved in fighting and using force to support an agreed ceasefire: 'Were clashes between armed units to develop, the United Nations could not permit itself to become a third party to such a conflict. But

---

[67] Dayal (note 38), p. 180.

[68] Lefever and Joshua, vol. 2 (note 17), p. 346.

[69] ONUC, Operations Directive no. 8 [untitled, Feb. 1961], UN Archives DAG13/1.6.5.0.0, Ops Directives Aug. 1960–Jan. 1964, Box 3. Excerpts are reproduced in appendix 2 in this volume.

[70] Lefever and Joshua, vol. 2 (note 17), p. 345.

[71] ONUC, Operations Directive no. 3, 'ONUC policy with regard to inter-tribal conflict', 17 Aug. 1960, UN Archives DAG13/1.6.5.0.0, Ops Directives Aug. 1960–Jan. 1964, Box 3. The directive is reproduced in appendix 2 in this volume. Emphasis added.

the use of force in support of cease-fire arrangements should not therefore be excluded'.[72] Presumably the latter would be a clear use of force in self-defence, along traditional UNEF lines, whereas the former would not.

After a discussion in the Advisory Committee about preventing tribal conflict, Hammarskjöld authorized ONUC troops in Katanga to 'prevent the burning of villages and the killing of civilians by force if necessary' on the grounds that the attacks there had strong elements of genocide: 'We have no excuse to stand passive'.[73] This seemed to be a further development in Hammarskjöld's views and UN policy, based on moral considerations: 'Prohibition against intervention in internal conflicts cannot be considered to apply to senseless slaughter of civilians or fighting arising from tribal hostilities'.[74] In a plea similar to one heard from another Secretary-General in the 1990s in relation to Rwanda and Burundi, he told the Security Council that the massacres could not be viewed as merely internal political conflict but were a flagrant violation of elementary human rights and had elements of genocide. 'Should it be supposed', he asked, 'that the duty of the United Nations to observe strict neutrality in the domestic conflicts and to assist the Central Government means that the United Nations cannot take action in these cases?'[75] ONUC Operations Directive no. 6 of 28 October 1960 set out this new policy.[76]

Although ONUC was now explicitly authorized to prevent attacks on innocent civilians, this was still to be based on an interpositional strategy using force in self-defence. Urquhart confirms that force could still not be used directly by ONUC to prevent the killing of civilians when UN troops were not interposed between them and their attackers, since this would be an offensive use of force.[77] ONUC was, in the event, able to prevent widespread tribal conflict and in some cases defuse particular incidents. There are no reports of it using significant force in doing so, either in self-defence or beyond. This may have been because, as Conor Cruise O'Brien, the (civilian) Irish head of ONUC in Katanga, notes, ONUC's new interpositional policy was not implemented consistently by all units.[78] Lefever concludes that: 'It is probably correct to say that ONUC blunted the savagery, prevented some slaughter of the innocent, frustrated the designs of several politically motivated ANC units, and helped to deter what might have become a bloody civil war'.[79]

*Prevention of civil war*

From the beginning of ONUC's mandate the integrity of the Congo was threatened by the establishment of alternative power centres to Leopoldville and the

[72] SCOR, 16th year, 935th meeting, 15 Feb. 1961, para. 28.
[73] Dayal (note 38), p. 201. On the use of force in Katanga see section IV in this chapter.
[74] Urquhart (note 22), p. 438.
[75] United Nations, Security Council, Verbatim records (provisional), 896th meeting, UN document S/PV.896, 9–10 Sep. 1960, p. 58.
[76] Operations Directive no. 6 (note 37).
[77] Urquhart (note 22), p. 438.
[78] O'Brien (note 24), p. 147, fn. 1.
[79] Lefever (note 66), p. 65.

risk of civil war. The greatest danger came in September 1960, when the Congo was plunged into an 11-month constitutional crisis, leaving ONUC to conduct its mission in a political vacuum.[80] It began on 5 September when President Joseph Kasavubu peremptorily dismissed Prime Minister Lumumba and his government. Lumumba promptly obtained endorsement from the Congolese Parliament, leading to constitutional deadlock. On 14 September Mobutu announced that he was 'neutralizing' both Kasavubu and Lumumba, suspending all political institutions and appointing a College of High Commissioners to take over the government. The Congolese administration and the ANC thereafter split into a Leopoldville faction (led by Kasavubu), a Stanleyville faction (led by Lumumba's Deputy Prime Minister, Antoine Gizenga) and a military faction (led by Mobutu). Kasavubu and Mobutu later combined forces to rule jointly, while the College of High Commissioners quietly faded away. In November Lumumba left UN protection in Leopoldville to try to join his supporters in Stanleyville. He was detained en route, jailed by the Kasavubu government and secretly handed over to his enemies in Elisabethville, who murdered him in January 1961.

ONUC was now faced not only with trying to prevent tribal conflict without being seen as interfering in Congolese internal affairs, but also with trying to prevent civil war without favouring one side or the other. 'Deprived of a clearly defined host government, ONUC was effectively limited even further in the degree of armed force it could employ. In its residual mission of maintaining and restoring order, its chief office was to be "present". Never before so strong militarily, its military tasks were less patent than ever.'[81]

Although there was no question of ONUC using force to restore the Lumumba government, since it had neither the mandate nor the capacity to do so, it was roundly criticized for failing to use force to prevent Lumumba's arrest, imprisonment and death. ONUC also refrained from using force to prevent armed clashes between the different factions, opting instead for negotiations, at local, provincial and national levels, to restore constitutional government. Operations Directive no. 8 of February 1961 ordered UN forces to continue to try to prevent armed conflict by every means at their disposal other than the use of armed force.[82]

With civil war looming, and after visiting Leopoldville from 4 to 6 January 1961, Hammarskjöld asked for ONUC's hand to be strengthened to prevent arms being imported and 'eliminate' the new threat to order from the splintering of the government, but he again cautioned that the mandate should not be so broadened as to permit ONUC to take the 'military initiative'.[83] The Security Council, in paragraph A1 of Resolution 161 of 21 February 1961, authorized ONUC to 'take immediately all appropriate measures to prevent the occurrence of civil war in the Congo, including arrangements for cease-fires, the halting of

[80] Lefever and Joshua, vol. 2 (note 17), p. 46.
[81] Burns and Heathcote (note 14), p. 47.
[82] Operations Directive no. 8 (note 69).
[83] SCOR, 16th year, 928th meeting, 1 Feb. 1961.

all military operations, the prevention of clashes, and the use of force, if necessary, in the last resort'.[84]

This was the first time the Security Council had authorized a military operation under UN command to use force to carry out a Council decision. Despite this, the resolution authorized the use of force only to prevent civil war and even then only as a last resort. It did not authorize force in relation to any other part of the resolution and certainly not the imposition of a political solution on the Congo.

Dayal, too, felt that he could partly compensate for ONUC's weakness in numbers by giving the force 'additional powers and initiatives, particularly of a preventive nature'.[85] On 30 March 1961 he issued, without Security Council endorsement, Operations Directive no. 10, 'Action of the United Nations Force in the Congo to prevent armed clashes'. This envisaged the possibility of UN troops intervening in three circumstances—when civil war threatened to break out; when it had already broken out; and when an armed clash threatened to envelop ONUC forces.[86] Essentially Dayal established an interpositional policy for dealing with civil war clashes similar to that already in place for tribal fighting. Force would be used, in self-defence, when interposed UN positions came under attack. This seems to be both less than the Security Council had in mind in Resolution 161 and less revolutionary than Dayal's claim that ONUC was moving into 'high gear'.[87]

In the event, except in Katanga, the UN did not, after the 21 February resolution, use force beyond self-defence in its efforts to prevent civil war. ONUC in fact did not have to contend with an all-out conflict, but rather skirmishes and shows of force by the various sides.[88] Even so, its losses in such clashes were significant: more UN troops were killed by Leopoldville ANC soldiers, Stanleyville ANC soldiers and tribal elements than in the three major clashes that were to come between the UN and the gendarmerie in Katanga.[89]

## IV. The use of force in Katanga: a lapse into peace enforcement

The greatest use of force by UN troops in the Congo occurred in the secessionist province of Katanga. It was these military engagements that also generated the most heated controversies of the operation. ONUC was never mandated explicitly to end the Katangan secession, and certainly not by force. Nor was it explicitly mandated to help the Congolese Government militarily to end the

---

[84] United Nations, Resolution adopted by the Security Council at its 942nd meeting on 20–21 Feb. 1961, UN document S/4741, 21 Feb. 1961.

[85] Dayal (note 38), p. 200.

[86] ONUC, Operational [sic] Directive no. 10, 'Action of the United Nations Force in the Congo to prevent armed clashes', 30 Mar. 1961, UN Archives DAG13/1.6.5.0.0, Ops Directives Aug. 1960–Jan. 1964, Box 3. The directive is reproduced in appendix 2 in this volume.

[87] Dayal (note 38), p. 200.

[88] Burns and Heathcote (note 14), p. 75.

[89] Lefever and Joshua, vol. 2 (note 17), p. 342.

Katangan secession, since that would have been seen as interfering in the internal affairs of the country. With Katanga refusing to allow the entry of UN troops several months after their arrival, Hammarskjöld, convinced that he was not authorized to use force, returned to the Security Council in August 1960 for further instructions. The result was Security Council Resolution 146, of 9 August, which insisted that the entry of UN forces into Katanga was necessary. It cited Article 49 of Chapter VII, which provides that: 'The Members of the United Nations shall join in affording mutual assistance in carrying out the measures decided upon by the Security Council'. This was hardly helpful since no UN members stepped forward to help.

In fact the only Katanga-specific power to use force that ONUC acquired was in relation to the removal of foreign mercenaries. Paragraph A2 of Resolution 161 gave ONUC explicit authorization for the first time to take (unspecified) measures for the 'immediate withdrawal and evacuation from the Congo of all Belgian and other foreign military and paramilitary personnel and political advisers not under the United Nations Command, and mercenaries'. However, it did not specifically authorize ONUC to use force to remove them. Presumably, therefore, if force were used it could only be justified to assert ONUC's freedom of movement and maintain its positions, and beyond self-defence if necessary to prevent civil war. In theory it could be argued that attempting to remove the Katangan Government might prevent the central government attacking it and thereby prevent civil war, but an attempt by the UN to do so might very well ignite such a civil war if the Katangans resisted.

Despite these apparent legal constraints, ONUC did ultimately bring about the collapse of the Katangan secession through the use of force.

## ONUC's 'negotiated' entry

Eager to break the impasse over Katanga, Hammarskjöld made a dramatic personal intervention, flying to Elisabethville on 12 August 1960 to meet Moise Tshombe, the president of the province, accompanied by two companies of Swedish troops. He advised Tshombe that these would be in uniform but under his exclusive personal authority. They would have orders to use force 'only in the right of legitimate self-defence in the event—which I rule out as inconceivable—that they are attacked'.[90] His aircraft circled the airport while he negotiated landing rights for the second aircraft carrying the troops. Eventually the Katangans capitulated and no violence occurred. The main UN force entered Katanga peacefully three days later after Tshombe had at last agreed to their arrival on condition that there would be no interference in Katanga's 'internal affairs'.[91]

---

[90] United Nations, Telegram dated 10 August 1960 from the Secretary-General to the president of the provincial government of Katanga, UN document S/4417/Add.4, 10 Aug. 1960 (SCOR, 15th year, Supplement for July, Aug. and Sep. 1960, p. 45).
[91] O'Brien (note 24), p. 90.

In a sense the Secretary-General had employed purely diplomatic methods, based on bluff, courage and guile to achieve this breakthrough. However, the presence of armed Swedish troops was an implied threat of the use of force. While any military action by the Swedish troops at the airport could presumably have been justified as 'self-defence', it could have been regarded by the Katangans and the world at large as 'offensive' action or at the very least aggressive and risky pre-emption by the Secretary-General. The case illustrates cogently the difficulty of distinguishing between the use of force in self-defence and peace enforcement.

When it eventually became clear some months later that negotiations would not suffice to remove the Belgian and other mercenaries from Katanga, ONUC began moving quietly but determinedly, without the use of armed force (but undoubtedly with the implied threat of its use), to arrest and expel them from the province. The process was painstaking and frustratingly slow.

### 'Round One': Operation Rumpunch, August 1961

After a final attempt to convince Tshombe to cooperate in expelling the mercenaries, the UN launched a surprise military operation, but without the use of force. Operation Rumpunch began on 28 August 1961 with 'preventive measures' justifiable, according to ONUC, under the force's right of self-defence and its mandate to prevent civil war. As a first step Radio Katanga, the gendarmerie headquarters, the airport, the post office, the telephone system and other key points and installations in Elisabethville, as well as the villa of Information Minister Godefroide Munongo, were surrounded and placed under surveillance. This was a prelude to the rounding up of European officers serving with the Katangan forces. By the end of the day more than 60 officers had been arrested in Elisabethville and similar action had been carried out by UN troops in other parts of the province. By evening 70–100 persons had been taken to the Kamina base for expulsion.[92] The entire operation was accomplished without resort to military force, although the threat of its use was certainly implicit in the arrests (as would be the case in a normal civilian policing situation). Some physical force was used in effecting some of the arrests.

The move took the Katangans completely by surprise. ONUC supporters were pleased with the efficient and peaceful rounding up of a large proportion of the mercenaries. However, the operation evoked a 'wave of hostility' against the UN among the European expatriates and their supporters both in Katanga and abroad.

After Operation Rumpunch, ONUC's Swedish office in charge, Sture Linnér, proposed to Hammarskjöld an ultimatum to 'all foreigners who were still on the run' to come forward within 24 hours.[93] If these 'preliminary measures' did not

---

[92] Hoskyns (note 4), pp. 406–407.
[93] Alan James cites incoming and outgoing cables of 31 Aug. 1997 for details of this proposal. James, A., *Britain and the Congo Crisis, 1960–63* (St Martin's Press: London, 1996), pp. 101–102.

1. The mandate of the UN for the protection of law and order authorized it to deploy troops to protect civilians when they were threatened by tribal war or violence.

2. Paragraph 1A of the Security Council's resolution of February 21 also authorized preventive action by the UN to deal with incitement to or preparation of civil war.

3. The right of UN troops to use force in self-defence covered attempts to overrun or displace UN positions. It also covered attempts to injure or abduct UN personnel.

4. The act of self-defence against attack could include the disarming and, if necessary, the detention of those preparing to attack UN troops.

5. Incitement to or preparation for violence, including troop movements and confirmed reports of an impending attack, would warrant protective action by UN troops, but criticism of the UN, however pungently expressed, or peaceful demonstrations against the UN, could not be held to justify protective action.

6. The maintenance of law and order or the prevention of civil war might justify, in certain circumstances, the closing of radio stations and airports if it was clear they were being used to foment civil war or for other unlawful purposes. The legal basis for taking such measures would be strengthened when the competent authorities of the Central or the provincial government had requested or approved such measures.

7. Arrest or detention of civil leaders was only justifiable if they were engaged in overt military action or were caught *in flagrante delicto* inciting violence. Without such justifying circumstances, the detention of political leaders would run a serious risk of violating the ban on intervention in domestic conflicts.

8. Political leaders could be arrested by the UN if the UN was requested to do so by *both* the Central Government *and* the provincial authorities. However, it was doubtful if a warrant of arrest issued against a provincial leader by the Central Government alone was sufficient basis for the UN to carry out such an arrest, even if the arrest was requested by the Commissaire d'État appointed by the Central Government.

9. The appointment of a Commissaire d'État could not change the legal situation of the UN in conflicts between the Central Government and a provincial government, nor did it remove the obligation of the UN to abstain from interference in constitutional conflicts.

**Figure 3.1.** Summary of Secretary-General Dag Hammarskjöld's instructions to ONUC, 7 or 8 September 1961

*Source*: Sir Brian Urquhart, quoted in Abi-Saab, G., *The United Nations Operation in the Congo 1960–1964* (Oxford University Press: Oxford, 1978), p. 135.

work, ONUC would arrest all the leading figures in the Katangan regime except Tshombe. In preparation it would 'neutralize' the gendarmerie and police and seek Tshombe's 'confirmation' of arrest warrants issued by the central government. If he refused, a state commissioner appointed by the central government would act on behalf of the Katangan authorities: 'for a few hours this would amount to a take-over of the whole of the administrative apparatus'. Hammarskjöld reluctantly agreed that stronger measures might be necessary, but as usual added numerous qualifications (see figure 3.1). Many of these were ignored by ONUC's leadership.

**'Round One' continued: Operation Morthor, September 1961**

Operation Morthor, begun on 12 September without the express authorization of Hammarskjöld and contrary to his understanding of his instructions, marked a temporary lapse of ONUC from peacekeeping into peace enforcement. It involved significant use of force, caused hundreds of casualties and exponentially increased the dissent that had plagued the UN operation in the Congo from its inception. Harbottle called it 'possibly the most ill-judged action of the whole Congo operation'.[94]

Unlike Rumpunch, whose unfinished tasks it was supposed to complete, Operation Morthor met early and sustained resistance, so that the UN forces rather than the Katangans were taken by surprise. The UN officially blamed the outbreak of fighting on firing from a building housing the Belgian Consulate.[95] Both the radio station and the post office were taken only after heavy hand-to-hand fighting. Counter-attacks soon occurred.[96] There were allegations that Indian troops, possibly in panic, shot a number of gendarmes and police in cold blood and fired on an ambulance.[97]

Although the plan was to arrest all Katangan ministers, only Vice-President Jean-Baptiste Kibwe was captured, but he was released the following day. Tshombe first requested a ceasefire and agreed to proclaim the end of Katangan independence, then escaped to Northern Rhodesia. Undeterred by the failure of the operation, O'Brien, the officer in charge of the operation, nervously told journalists that it had been undertaken in accordance with ONUC's mandate, conferred by paragraph A1 of Security Council Resolution 161, to prevent civil war. He added, disingenuously, that 'the secession of Katanga was ended'.[98]

Serious military engagements continued for eight days between ONUC and Katangan forces led by white officers and Belgian mercenaries. The UN base at Kamina was attacked, as were the UN garrison and installations at Albertville. A lone Katangan Fouga Magister jet fighter, piloted by a Belgian, had aerial supremacy, bombing and machine-gunning UN forces in Elisabethville, Jadotville and Kamina.[99] By 14 September the UN's Katanga Command was issuing orders to Sector A Headquarters in Albertville to use 'full force if necessary', advising that no reinforcements were possible.[100] Sector B in Elisabethville was being ordered to block all roads to the post office by overturning civilian cars

---

[94] Harbottle (note 46), p. 51.

[95] United Nations, Report of the officer-in-charge of the United Nations Operation in the Congo, UN document S/4940, 14 Sep. 1961 (SCOR, Supplement for July, Aug. and Sep. 1961, p. 103). See also Lefever, E. W. and Joshua, W., *United Nations Peacekeeping in the Congo, 1960–1964: An Analysis of Political, Executive and Military Control*, vol. 4 (Brookings Institution for the US Arms Control and Disarmament Agency (ACDA): Washington, DC, 30 June 1966), p. 36.

[96] Message from HQ Katanga Command Elisabethville to ONUC Leopoldville, 13 Sep. 1961, UN Archives DAG13/1.6.5.7.1.0, #4.

[97] Lefever and Joshua, vol. 2 (note 17), p. 112; and Hoskyns (note 4), p. 419.

[98] Martelli, G., *Experiment in World Government: An Account of the United Nations Operation in the Congo 1960–1964* (Johnson Publications: London, 1966), p. 131.

[99] Lefever (note 66), p. 81.

[100] Flash message from HQ Katanga Command to HQ Sector A, 14 Sep. 1961, UN Archives DAG13/1.6.5.7.1.0, #4.

and vehicles to stop further counter-attacks.[101] Meanwhile a company of 150 Irish troops sent to protect Europeans at Jadotville, at the request of the European consuls, was surrounded and threatened by a superior force of gendarmerie commanded by white officers. It refused to surrender and, in a fierce 'Battle of Jadotville', lasting from 13 to 17 September, was attacked from the ground and the air. Miraculously, there were no fatalities.

Hammarskjöld only learned of Operation Morthor after landing in Accra, Ghana, for a refuelling stop on his way to the Congo. On arriving in Leopoldville he ordered UN troops to abstain from any new initiative and use force only in self-defence.[102] The operation was precisely what he had warned against— 'premature', 'provocative', and encumbered with the wrong legal justification. It was indeed beyond any reasonable interpretation of 'prevention of civil war' for the UN, as Linnér and O'Brien apparently planned, to pre-empt an attack by the central government on Katanga, taking over the province and handing it over to the government. Operation Morthor provoked strong protests from some UN member states, including France, Senegal and Congo (Brazzaville), which spoke of 'war operations conducted by the United Nations in Katanga'.[103] The international press was highly critical, in some cases hysterically so.

Meanwhile the Katangans continued to attack and harass ONUC's forces, forcing them to fight defensively. Dayal notes that the troops were 'chafing at the restraints which the Secretary-General had imposed and were eager to force a decision to end their defensive role'.[104] Hammarskjöld refused to countenance a military offensive so as not to exacerbate the situation, deciding instead to stake his full authority and prestige on negotiating a ceasefire by meeting Tshombe.[105] En route to Ndola in Northern Rhodesia on 17 September for such a meeting, he was killed when his aircraft crashed. A provisional ceasefire was announced on 20 September to take effect the following day. It virtually restored the *status quo ante*—an outcome unfavourable to the UN—requiring the UN to surrender all the positions ONUC had captured.

Nine UN troops were killed and 23 wounded in Operation Morthor.[106] On the Katangan side there were over 20 fatalities, including civilians, 500 wounded and 100 taken prisoner. Operation Morthor clearly took the UN beyond the use of force in self-defence into enforcement. The 1966 ACDA study concluded that: 'The sending of [UN Force] UNF troops to take over the post office and to apprehend cabinet ministers at four o'clock in the morning was hardly a use of force in self-defense'.[107] Burns and Heathcote describe Operation Morthor as a 'mistake or misappropriation of authority'.[108] It is probably more accurately

[101] Message from HQ Katanga Command to HQ Sector B, 14 Sep. 1961, UN Archives DAG13/1.6.5.7.1.0, #4. For O'Brien's version see note 24.

[102] Abi-Saab, G., *The United Nations Operation in the Congo 1960–1964* (Oxford University Press: Oxford, 1978), p. 143.

[103] Seyersted (note 58), p. 73.

[104] Dayal (note 38), p. 271.

[105] Dayal (note 38), p. 271.

[106] Lefever and Joshua, vol. 3 (note 50), appendix P, p. 21; and Martelli (note 98), p. 132.

[107] Lefever (note 66), p. 84.

[108] Burns and Heathcote (note 14), p. 165.

described as a case of mutually reinforcing misperceptions combined with hubris and bravado, which produced, seen in the best light, over-enthusiasm and poor judgement, and at worst a conspiracy to force the UN's hand in over-turning the Katangan regime. The lesson drawn at the time was that ONUC should not use force in such a way without proper command and control, military capability, legal authority and political support. All these elements would be attended to before ONUC next used significant force in Katanga.

With the failure of Operation Morthor and the death of Hammarskjöld, the UN operation in Katanga entered a new phase. ONUC gradually acquired new military capabilities and plans. On 24 November 1961 the Security Council passed Resolution 169 which further extended ONUC's mandate to use force, this time to remove foreign mercenaries from Katanga. It authorized Acting Secretary-General U Thant 'to take vigorous action, including the use of the requisite measure of force, if necessary, for the immediate apprehension, detention pending legal action and/or deportation of all foreign military and paramilitary personnel and political advisors not under the United Nations Command, and mercenaries . . . '. It also authorized him to 'take *all necessary measures* to prevent the entry or return of such elements under whatever guise and also of arms, equipment or other material in support of such activities'.[109]

The resolution gave ONUC the powers it had lacked when it used force in Operation Morthor, providing *ex post facto* justification for at least some aspects of that operation.[110] Yet it did not mandate ONUC to suppress the Katangan secession directly (which would unequivocally have been enforce-ment), but merely to eliminate its foreign support. It was perhaps the view of some that if this ended Katangan secession so much the better, but that was not its declared intention.

The new Secretary-General, U Thant, was less averse than Hammarskjöld to the use of force when the situation demanded it. He also had a different attitude towards the central government, telling the Security Council that ONUC's man-date to prevent civil war 'necessarily implies a sympathetic attitude on the part of ONUC toward the efforts of the Government to suppress all armed activities against the Central government, and all secessionist activities'.[111]

## 'Round Two': December 1961

Resolution 169 of 24 November had a galvanizing effect on the Katangans and their foreign supporters. Despite the ceasefire, the gendarmerie began to harass UN troops and restrict their movement in and around Elisabethville. Road-blocks were established across key routes in the city. Attacks were launched on the Baluba refugee camp. Anti-UN propaganda was repeatedly broadcast. On

---

[109] United Nations, Resolution adopted by the Security Council at its 982nd meeting on 24 Nov. 1961, UN document S/5002, 24 Nov. 1961. Emphasis added.

[110] Interoffice Memorandum from Oscar Schachter, Director, General Legal Division to Dr Ralph Bunche, Under Secretary-General, 14 Nov. 1961, UN Archives, Box 2, file 8.

[111] United Nations, Security Council, Verbatim records (provisional), 982nd meeting, UN document S/PV.982, 24 Nov. 1961, paras 71–80.

the evening of 28 November the two top UN civilian officials in the province, Urquhart and George Ivan Smith, were kidnapped and assaulted. U Thant instructed Linnér that indiscriminate arrest or molestation of UN civilians must be 'avoided and resisted by all possible means including use of force offensive and defensive as necessary'.[112] Linnér wrote to Tshombe telling him that if such attacks continued the UN would be forced 'to exercise its right of self-defence'.[113] After lengthy but fruitless negotiations with the Katangan authorities over removal of the roadblocks, Linnér concluded, in consultation with the UN military, that further talks would be 'both useless and dangerous' and that the roadblocks should be removed and further military measures taken to secure freedom of movement.[114] This time the Secretary-General's approval was sought in advance.

On 5 December U Thant authorized 'all counter-action—ground and aerial—deemed necessary' to restore complete freedom of movement in the area'.[115] Commending ONUC on its 'remarkable restraint in handling this very difficult situation amid protracted negotiations marked by such bad faith on the other side', the Secretary-General directed that ONUC insist on 'complete freedom of movement': 'You are free to take such action as you and our people in Elisabethville consider necessary and [are] able to take, including occupation of key points like the [railway] tunnel'.[116] Leaflets were to be dropped by air telling Katangans that ONUC was a 'force of peace' which 'did not come here to fight. But, because it has been attacked, it has no choice but to defend itself and fight back. The United Nations will remove the non-Congolese intruders who have brought misery to your country . . . [and] eliminate malevolent foreign influences'.[117] Force Commander Lieutenant-General Sean McEeoin ordered Indian Brigadier K. S. A. Raja in Elisabethville to 'use all the troops at your disposal to restore law and order. To achieve this you are authorized to use all force necessary'.[118] UN forces were no longer under orders, as in September, to shoot only in self-defence. The whole operation was understood to be a *pre-emptive* attack, justified as an act of self-defence, using whatever means were necessary.

For several days after 5 December ONUC restricted itself to holding its positions on the edge of town, keeping communications between them open and launching probing attacks while waiting for reinforcements to permit an attack

---

[112] Code Cable L-179, 30 Nov. 1961 from acting Secretary-General to Linner and MacFarquhar, Leopoldville, UN Archives DAG1/2.2.1, #10.

[113] Hoskyns (note 4), p. 448.

[114] Telex conversation Leopoldville–New York, 5 Dec. 1961, UN Archives DAG1/2.2.1, #34.

[115] Lefever (note 66), p. 94. For the official UN account of the operation see United Nations, *The United Nations and the Congo: Some Salient Facts* (United Nations: New York, 1963), p. 8.

[116] Telex Conversation Leopoldville–New York, 5 Dec. 1961, UN Archives DAG1/2.2.1, #34.

[117] Quoted in Franck, T. M. and Carey, J., 'Working paper: the role of the United Nations in the Congo. A retrospective perspective', ed. L. M. Tondel, Jr, *The Legal Aspects of the United Nations Action in the Congo, Background Papers and Proceedings of the Second Hammarskjöld Forum* (Oceana Publications for the Association of the Bar of the City of New York: New York, 1963), p. 39.

[118] Secret code message from the force commander to ONUC in Elisabethville, 5 Dec. 1961, UN Archives DAG13/1.6.5.2.0, #41.

on the city centre.[119] On 6 December ONUC's first air strike took place when Indian Canberra bombers destroyed the Katanga Fouga and three transport aircraft on the ground at Kolwezi airstrip.[120] By 8 December ONUC had gained command of the air over Katanga. Then, between 14 and 19 December, with reinforcements completed, ONUC carried out extensive military operations around Elisabethville to restore freedom of movement, capture the city centre and block Katangan escape routes. In a coordinated offensive Irish troops attacked the railway tunnel; Swedish troops seized Camp Massart, the heavily defended main base for the Katangan gendarmerie; the Indian contingent created diversionary attacks and blocked fleeing Katangan forces; and the Ethiopian forces secured the western part of the city.[121] When fighting halted on 18 December, only the radio station, the headquarters of the Belgian Union Minière mining company and Tshombe's residence remained to be captured.

The scale of the operation had been considerable and the fighting fiercer and more widespread than in September. Twenty-one UN troops were killed and 84 wounded. Among the Katangans, 206 gendarmes were killed and an unknown number wounded.[122] Raja had been given greater latitude in exercising military initiative than any previous commander in the Congo, or indeed any previous UN commander, allowing him to employ offensive tactics and to move his troops into previously unoccupied positions.[123]

On 18 December U Thant declared a unilateral 'temporary ceasefire', conditional on the Katangan authorities agreeing to negotiate with the central government. With the critical support of the USA and India behind him, U Thant wisely defended the operation on the ground of self-defence—the one undisputed right of UN troops. He denied vigorously that the action had had political aims.[124]

The campaign was criticized by Belgium, Congo (Brazzaville), France, Greece, Portugal, the Federation of Rhodesia and Nyasaland, and South Africa, which saw the operation as an attempt to overthrow the Katanga regime through the 'back door' of self-defence, notably combined with the assertion of ONUC's right of freedom of movement. The 1966 ACDA report concludes that there was some justification for West European fears that the action had overstepped the bounds of the permissible use of force and had become an effort to impose a political solution by military means.[125]

When it became clear after further months of fruitless negotiations that Tshombe did not intend to end the secession and that his forces were intent on continuing to harass ONUC, the UN began a significant military build-up for a final showdown. While hoping that the build-up itself would convince Tshombe

---

[119] Hoskyns (note 4), p. 452.
[120] [ONUC], Chief of Military Operations, Elisabethville, Summary of major events, 6–7 Dec. 1961, UN Archives DAG13/1.6.5.2.0.
[121] Lefever and Joshua, vol. 3 (note 50), appendix P-22; and Hymoff (note 53), p. 201.
[122] Lefever and Joshua, vol. 3 (note 50), appendix P-22.
[123] Lefever (note 66), p. 97.
[124] Burns and Heathcote (note 14), p. 134.
[125] Lefever and Joshua, vol. 2 (note 17), p. 122.

that resistance was useless, Bunche declared that the UN's behaviour would be 'more aggressively defensive'.[126] By October 1962 ONUC was again sustaining unacceptable levels of harassment and attack. On 28 December UN officials warned Tshombe that unless firing against ONUC ceased it would 'take all necessary action in self-defence and to restore order'.[127] The final straw came when radio intercepts revealed that the Katangan commander had ordered his air force to attack Elisabethville Airport on the night of 29 December.[128] Responding to an urgent request from Robert Gardiner, the new Ghanaian officer-in-charge, and Major-General Dewan Prem Chand, who had replaced Raja in May 1962, and with the full concurrence of Rikhye and Bunche, U Thant reluctantly ordered renewed military action by the UN.[129] That this was to be a standard military operation is revealed by the operational orders for ONUC's land and air forces.[130]

### 'Round Three': Operation Grandslam, December 1962–January 1963

The UN began Operation Grandslam on 28 December in accordance with its operational plan. This time it encountered little serious resistance. The mercenaries, now largely French and South African, were much less organized than in the two previous rounds.[131] Tshombe's much-feared appeals for a 'scorched earth' campaign were largely ignored. By the end of 29 December UN troops effectively controlled an area extending 20 km around Elisabethville. They also occupied the nearby towns of Kamina and Kipushi. Tshombe fled to Southern Rhodesia. At the same time ONUC conducted an air campaign. On 29 and 30 December Swedish jets destroyed the Katangan air force and all vital air installations at Katangan airbases.

On 30 December Gardiner made it clear that he was 'not going to make the mistake of stopping short this time'.[132] Yet on 31 December, pressed by Belgium and the UK, which feared that the gendarmes would blow up the valuable mining installations of the Union Minière, U Thant announced that UN military action had been successfully concluded. He issued an ultimatum, giving Tshombe two weeks for the Katangan armed force to surrender and for the expulsion of all mercenaries.[133]

---

[126] Quoted in James (note 93), p. 188, citing *Foreign Relations of the United States, 1961–63, Vol. 20: Congo Crisis* (US Government Printing Office: Washington, DC, 1994), p. 766 (19 Dec. 1962).

[127] Lefever (note 66), p. 108.

[128] Dorn, A. W. and Bell, D. J. H., 'Intelligence and peacekeeping: the UN Operation in the Congo, 1960–64', *International Peacekeeping*, vol. 2, no. 1 (spring 1995), p. 20.

[129] Nassif, R., *U Thant in New York: A Portrait of the Third UN Secretary-General* (C. Hurst: London, 1988), p. 99; and U Thant, *View from the UN* (David & Charles: London, 1978), p. 142.

[130] Undated instruction to UN forces in Katanga Area, no. 3330/Katanga/ops, UN Archives DAG13/1.6.5.2.0, #41; and ONUC headquarters, Leopoldville, Fighter Operations Order no. 16, 27 Dec. 1962, AHQ/6600/1/F-OPS, UN Archives DAG13/1.6.5.0.0, #9.

[131] Lefever (note 66), p. 111.

[132] Lefever (note 66), p. 108.

[133] Harbottle (note 46), p. 57.

In spite of this announcement and an explicit order from New York for UN troops to halt on the near side of the Lufira River, Prem Chand on the same day indicated his intention to 'capture Jadotville as early as possible', apparently because two gendarmerie battalions had retreated there.[134] Indian troops crossed the Lufira and continued towards Jadotville, occupying it unopposed on 3 January 1963. Soon afterwards the Katangan secession collapsed completely.

This final military action was a result of the 'miraculous breakdown of communication'[135] between UN Headquarters and ONUC which U Thant immediately sent Bunche to investigate. Bunche concluded that the commander's decision had been militarily sound since to halt would have exposed UN troops to unnecessary risk. The problem had purportedly arisen because UN troops had suddenly enjoyed more success than they were prepared for or were used to.[136]

In a White Book defending its actions in the Congo, the UN declared that force used in 'Round Three' was in self-defence and undertaken to establish complete freedom of movement.[137] On this reading, if the Katangans had never restricted ONUC's freedom of movement the UN would not have acted at all and Katangan independence would never have been challenged militarily. Lefever contends that Round Three, in contrast to the two previous clashes, was conducted with 'discipline and restraint' and by customary standards of military appraisal the casualties amongst both civilian and military were 'remarkably light'.[138] Ten UN troops had been killed and 77 wounded. Katangan casualties also appeared to be relatively low.[139] Nonetheless, U Thant commented that: 'For a peace force, even a little fighting is too much, and only a few casualties are too many'.[140]

With the Katangan secession ended, the Security Council was eager to wind up the contentious Congo mission. Its withdrawal began in March 1963 and was complete by June 1964. By September widespread internal conflict and chaos returned to the Congo, but the UN was safely out of it.

# V. Conclusions: lessons of the Congo

Until the Somalia and Bosnia missions in the 1990s ONUC was the most violent peacekeeping operation ever conducted by the UN. One hundred and

---

[134] [ONUC], HQ Indian Independent Brigade Group Operation Instruction no. 3, Op Grand Slam', document no. 1013/4/G S (0), 31 Dec. 1962, UN Archives DAG13/1.6.5.7.1.0, #9.

[135] Urquhart, B., *A Life in Peace and War* (Weidenfeld & Nicolson: London, 1987), p. 194.

[136] Urquhart (note 24), p. 359.

[137] *The United Nations and the Congo: Some Salient Facts* (note 115), p. 9.

[138] Lefever (note 66), p. 112.

[139] United Nations, *The Blue Helmets: A Review of United Nations Peace-keeping*, 3rd edn (UN Department of Public Information: New York, 1996), p. 195.

[140] United Nations, Report by the Secretary-General on the implementation of the Security Council resolutions of 14 July 1960, 21 Feb. and 24 Nov. 1961, UN document S/5240, 4 Feb. 1963 (SCOR, Supplement for Jan., Feb., Mar. 1963, p. 95).

twenty-seven UN military personnel died in action and 133 were wounded,[141] along with scores of European expatriates and hundreds of Congolese.[142]

ONUC began putatively as a conventional peacekeeping mission modelled on UNEF. Like UNEF, it was initially mandated to use force only in self-defence and as a last resort. The Congo, however, proved to be a very different theatre of operations, well beyond the relative simplicities of the UNEF case. The self-defence concept was considerably extended as new requirements arose, such as the need to prevent peacekeepers being disarmed and attacked, their posts and installations being besieged and their mandated activities being disrupted. It was later extended to permit peacekeepers to afford protection to civilians at risk of death, injury or gross violations of human rights. ONUC was sub-sequently authorized to use force beyond self-defence, if necessary, to prevent civil war and, later, to detain and expel foreign mercenaries. Ultimately, ONUC became, through accident and design, involved in military operations that differed little from standard warfare.

The lessons of the Congo with regard to the use of force are uncomfortably familiar to those who witnessed the UN operations in Somalia, the former Yugoslavia, Rwanda and Sierra Leone 30 years on. Indeed, had the lessons of the Congo been learned and retained the mistakes of the latter missions might never have occurred.

1. The first and most widely drawn lesson was that operations designed to do peacekeeping should not be permitted, either deliberately or inadvertently, to move into enforcement or peace enforcement—the 'mission creep' of more recent parlance. As Hammarskjöld feared, such a transformation risks damaging or destroying two of the requirements of peacekeeping—the consent of the parties and impartiality. The Congo mission first moved beyond peacekeeping in Operation Morthor as a result of the misreading or deliberate misuse of instructions by local ONUC officials, rather than as a result of a deliberate decision by ONUC headquarters in Leopoldville or UN Headquarters in New York. Supporters of Katanga saw it as taking sides against the province and violating the principle of consent. Subsequent enforcement campaigns, rounds two and three, were sanctioned by UN Headquarters and were within the new powers accorded to ONUC by the Security Council, but brought down even greater controversy on the UN, partly because the action was so deliberate but also because it was portrayed in some quarters as exceeding the UN's assigned role, or at the very least its hitherto peaceable ethos.

2. A second lesson, also related to consent and impartiality, is that the use of force is a blunt instrument for pursuing discrete political aims in a peace opera-tion. In the Congo ONUC's opponents were expected to understand and accept the subtle and highly implausible notion that ONUC's use of force did not involve interference in the internal affairs of the country, but was rather an

---

[141] *The United Nations and the Congo: Some Salient Facts* (note 115), p. 12.

[142] UNIFIL had by June 1990 incurred 130 fatalities through hostile action but these were spread over 12 years, rather than 4 in the case of the Congo. *The Blue Helmets*, 2nd edn (note 63), p. 427.

attempt to ensure ONUC's freedom of movement, prevent civil war and end external interference.

Such situations are particularly problematic when Security Council mandates give the clear impression that the UN is already biased towards one side. In the Congo the UN clearly favoured Congolese territorial integrity and sovereignty, yet ONUC was expected to act impartially towards all the Congolese factions. Invariably, when the UN uses force it will be seen to be acting partially in favour of one party against another, even when pursuing supposedly neutral goals, such as preventing civil war.

3. A third lesson which is resonant of later, similarly troubled operations is that the military capability of peace operations should match the expectations of their mandates (and the parties in the theatre of operations) with regard to the threat or use of force. In ONUC's case its military weakness—it was a relatively lightly armed peacekeeping force deployed across a territory the size of Western Europe—prevented it on several occasions from using force even in self-defence, and even more from carrying out the more ambitious goals mandated by the Security Council. Even the technique of interposing itself between warring parties required more military capability than ONUC was able to muster. This presaged the dilemmas of UNPROFOR 30 years later in trying to protect humanitarian convoys, exclusion zones and 'safe areas' in Bosnia, all of which had been mandated by a Security Council that was unwilling to provide the requisite military means. ONUC needed better logistics, command and control, intelligence-gathering, protective equipment and weaponry along with a better-trained and integrated force if it was to carry out more than an observation role.

As discussed in chapter 2, besides ensuring that military tasks are carried out with maximum effectiveness and efficiency, a major reason for having a militarily capable force is deterrence. Deterrence works in peace operations much as it does in normal military circumstances: the more powerful the force the greater the deterrent and the less likely it is that force will need to be used. In a peacekeeping operation, however, there needs to be greater awareness that shows of force may be unnecessarily provocative, as in the Ghanaian Embassy incident in the Congo. The Swedish Military History Commission concludes from the ONUC experience that: 'UN units must be of such strength, quality and conduct that they earn the respect of all parties affected. In the Congo some of the fighting could probably have been avoided if the weakness of the UN units had not encouraged the parties to [commit] acts of violence'.[143]

4. A fourth lesson relates to the timing of the deployment and use of military force, especially in achieving a conflict prevention effect. ONUC's very deployment, achieved so rapidly and effectively, clearly had such an effect without force being used. Lessons to be drawn from its later use of force are less clear. Hoskyns argues that, if a fraction of the pressure used against

[143] Sköld, N., *Med FN i Kongo: Sveriges medverkan i den fredsbevarande operationen 1960–1964* [With the UN in the Congo: Sweden's participation in the peacekeeping operation 1960–64] (Probus: Stockholm, 1994), p. 80.

Katanga in 1961 had been used in 1960, the whole story would have been very different: 'Ironically enough, Hammarskjöld's sensitivity about intervention in internal affairs in 1960 meant that the situation could only be restored in 1961 by action which came very close to the intervention he had tried to avoid'.[144] Superficially, the lesson is that early and decisive military intervention should be undertaken. However, ONUC was severely constrained by political and military considerations from taking robust action earlier and to have done so would have courted disaster. In Lefever's view: 'The effectiveness of the use of force against Tshombe was determined partly by the UNF's military capability and the legal restraints of its mandate, and partly by the interplay of political pressures among interested governments'.[145]

5. The UN needed a doctrine for the use of force which would set out in advance the rationale for it, notably the circumstances under which it was appropriate or inappropriate to use force under varying mandates. This doctrine should in turn be reflected in a concept of operations, standard operating procedures and rules of engagement. In the Congo the instructions on the use of force, as in later operations, were improvised as the operation proceeded, since there were no UN precedents to draw on, for example, in preventing inter-tribal conflicts. While UN member states, especially the UK, had a great deal of experience as a result of the decolonization process which could, in theory, have been harnessed for ONUC's purposes, cold war politics and the non-aligned countries' fears about re-colonization prevented this being exploited.

6. Efforts in the political arena can make the use of force more effective, lessen the need for substantial use of force or even render it unnecessary. The UN did attempt this, in some respects extremely effectively. The involvement of the Secretary-General at critical junctures, including on-site, prevented even greater disasters unfolding in the Congo. Efforts were also made after September 1960 by experienced political operators such as Bunche and Urquhart to re-establish a functioning national government through negotiation and mediation. Other possibilities were neglected. An effective UN public information campaign, including by media such as the radio, is particularly vital. If this had been in place from the outset much violence in Katanga might have been avoided, as might those incidents in the early days of the mission in which UN troops were mistaken for Belgians. Only today is the UN finally learning such lessons after further bitter experiences.

7. A seventh lesson concerns command and control. Peacekeeping operations are more politically sensitive than normal military campaigns and therefore warrant tight political control. Better command and control, along with better civilian leadership, would have ensured better cooperation with the military and avoided incidents such as Operation Morthor. The Swedish Military History Commission argues that there should be competent political leadership on the spot for day-to-day monitoring of a peacekeeping force's conduct of military

---

[144] Hoskyns (note 4), p. 476.
[145] Lefever (note 66), p. 113.

operations.[146] Yet micromanagement of military operations by civilians once they are under way can seriously undermine military effectiveness, morale and safety. A balance clearly needs to be struck between preserving overall civilian control and adherence to the mandated goals of the mission, on the one hand, and, on the other hand, the military's need, in accordance with its own expertise and experience, to conduct the most efficient and effective military operation.

8. The self-defence principle, the bedrock of peacekeeping, is apparently infinitely malleable. It therefore needs careful definition and management. In the Congo it was constantly expanded, eventually to the point where it was used to mask peace enforcement. As Oscar Schachter, a former director of the UN Legal Division, notes, because of the UN's great reluctance to go beyond self-defence as the touchstone of peacekeeping, the concept of self-defence was stretched 'to incredulity and beyond its usual legal meaning'.[147]

9. A ninth lesson relates to air power and its uses in peacekeeping. It was discovered early on in the Congo that air power has its own complexities as an instrument for the achievement of UN goals. While enabling the UN to project force at a relatively safe distance, thereby avoiding casualties, it is more politically sensitive than use of force by ground troops. The Congo revealed, too, that air power can be worryingly inaccurate and thus its widespread use is constrained by the dangers of striking civilians, friendly forces or UN forces. Traditional self-defence rules are also difficult to apply to the use of air power. Since the greatest danger to aircraft is other airborne aircraft, self-defence may involve pre-emptively destroying both aircraft on the ground and ground-based weapons—an action which those opposed to the UN may readily portray as offensive. Clearly more thought needed to be given to the use of air power by and in support of peacekeeping missions.

10. A tenth lesson is the value of civilian police in internal conflict situations, especially where anarchy rather than armed conflict is the main problem. This is a lesson the UN appears to have learned, as CivPols were deployed in the UN Force in Cyprus (UNFICYP) the year the Congo operation ended and have since been used effectively in many missions. Even when CivPols do not have executive functions,[148] they can, through monitoring, assistance and training, enable the local police to perform better, thereby relieving peacekeeping troops of arduous and dangerous duties for which they are not trained or equipped.

What is most extraordinary about the Congo experience is that, having obtained elements of what might today be considered a peace enforcement mandate, ONUC went on to actually conduct an enforcement operation—in the sense of defeating a breakaway regime and reasserting the authority of the

---

[146] Sköld (note 143), p. 80.

[147] Schachter, O., 'Authorized uses of force by the UN and regional organizations', eds L. F. Damrosch and D. Scheffer, *Law and Force in the New International Order* (Westview Press: Boulder, Colo., 1991), p. 84.

[148] On executive police functions see Dwan, R., 'Introduction', ed. R. Dwan, *Executive Policing: Enforcing the Law in Peace Operations*, SIPRI Research Report no. 16 (Oxford University Press: Oxford, forthcoming, 2002), pp. 1–11.

central government—while all along denying that it was doing more than acting in self-defence and preserving its freedom of movement.[149] Even its 'prevention of civil war' mandate was played down. This deliberate playing down of the significance of ONUC's military operations by two successive secretaries-general and their staffs was clearly designed to avoid further controversy. U Thant especially was wily enough to realize that the downfall of the Katangan regime, which was becoming a noose around the UN's neck, might be accomplished as a happy by-product of a robust effort, perhaps more robust than was strictly necessary, to putatively re-establish ONUC's prerogatives. His strategy ultimately worked because the military operations were a success and because he had the backing of the USA (which mollified the other Western powers) and India (which took care of the non-aligned countries). None of this, however, was particularly helpful to the orderly development of UN peace operations doctrine. Indeed, it discredited that endeavour by demonstrating that political machinations could ultimately render Security Council resolutions and peacekeeping mandates and norms irrelevant.

[149] Lefever and Joshua, vol. 2 (note 17), p. 139.

# 4. The Congo to Lebanon: from self-defence to 'defence of the mission'

The 20 years between the end of the Congo mission and 1984, when the same major dilemmas over the use of force began to arise in Somalia, may appear at first glance to have been relatively unproductive in terms of the use-of-force issue. However, this is far from the case. Two missions were deployed during the period, in Cyprus and Lebanon, which raised similar dilemmas to those encountered in the Congo, although they were resolved in different ways. More significantly, the self-defence rule was overtly transformed from its narrow origins to encompass a much wider variety of possibilities, known collectively as 'defence of the mission'.

## I. The impact of the Congo on the UN's use-of-force norms and rules

The impact of the Congo mission on the theory and practice of the use of force by the UN was powerful. It operated in two, apparently contradictory but in fact complementary, ways.

The first impact was negative, encapsulated in the slogan 'no more Congos'. So traumatic and enervating was the Congo mission that it produced a ground-swell of opinion that the UN should never again become involved in messy internal conflicts involving peace enforcement, whether mandated explicitly by the Security Council or not. George Martelli, a partisan supporter of Katangan independence, expressed the conclusion of many: 'The results of this, the first experiment in world government, should discourage any repetition; the United Nations should in future confine itself to genuine peace-keeping operations, in which the use of force to impose policies is excluded'.[1] The Congo experience, combined with continuing and in some cases worsening cold war suspicions, had a sobering effect on UN peacekeeping for decades.

The UN operations fielded between the Congo mission and the end of the cold war in 1989 were mainly small observation or goodwill missions, most of them involved in post-conflict monitoring.[2] None of them had the remotest

---

[1] Martelli, G., *Experiment in World Government: An Account of the United Nations Operation in the Congo 1960–1964* (Johnson Publications: London, 1966), p. 239.

[2] Between the establishment of ONUC in July 1960 and Jan. 1989, the following UN peacekeeping missions were established: the UN Security Force in West New Guinea (West Irian), Oct. 1962–Apr. 1963; the UN Yemen Observation Mission (UNYOM), July 1963–Sep. 1964; the Mission of the Representative of the Secretary-General in the Dominican Republic (DOMREP), May 1965–Oct. 1966; the UN India–Pakistan Observer Mission (UNIPOM), Sep. 1965–Mar. 1966; the UN Disengagement Observer Force (UNDOF), June 1974 to the present; the UN Good Offices Mission in Afghanistan and Pakistan (UNGOMAP), May 1988–Mar. 1990; and the UN Iran–Iraq Military Observer Group (UNIIMOG), Aug. 1988–Feb. 1991.

chance of becoming involved in peace enforcement. Moreover, between the Congo and Somalia operations the Security Council mandated only two operations in civil war situations—in Cyprus and Lebanon. In both cases the Congo experience was very much a consideration in the crafting of the mandate and mode of operation, to the extent that any hint of force being used for peace enforcement purposes was anathema.

Not only were no new Congo-like missions established, but there was no recognition that the Congo mission had been of a new type which might be described as 'peace enforcement'. It was regarded as an aberration rather than a flawed first attempt at creating a useful new tool—beyond traditional peacekeeping—which might be conceptualized and developed.[3] The UN Secretariat and the UN member states were, on the whole, 'more interested in forgetting than learning, more interested in avoiding future ONUCs than in doing them better'.[4] Even the unofficial bible of peacekeeping, the *Peacekeeper's Handbook*, produced by the non-governmental International Peace Academy (IPA) in New York, treated the Congo as if it had been only a token, inadvertent violation of traditional peacekeeping precepts:

There were occasions in the Congo when ONUC did initiate enforcement operations against the Katangese, and though in some cases the operations exceeded the principle of use of force, in others they were the result of prolonged and unprovoked harassment action against ONUC which had resulted in ONUC suffering a number of casualties. Force was also used in the Congo against the mercenaries and mercenary led bands, who represented an external interference in the affairs of a sovereign state, and as such constituted a direct threat to the UN operation.[5]

No sustained attempt was thus made to produce a UN military doctrine, refine concepts of operation or even improve the managerial and organizational aspects of peacekeeping to permit larger, more complex operations to be mounted, whether they included peace enforcement or not. Numerous studies of the Congo operation outside the UN did identify ways in which future peacekeeping operations could be improved, but, as the Swedish Military History Commission bemoaned, in the UN Secretariat itself the Congo experience was never evaluated.[6]

In January 1964 Ralphe Bunche reportedly attempted to combine the UNEF and ONUC standard operating procedures (SOP) into a model for future operations. It was recognized, however, that: 'As no two UN peace operations are alike, it is obvious SOP would have to be expressed in general terms which would assist in training and preparation of standby forces; and which would be

---

[3] Sköld, N., *Med FN i Kongo: Sveriges medverkan i den fredsbevarande operationen 1960–1964* [With the UN in the Congo: Sweden's participation in the peacekeeping operation 1960–1964] (Probus: Stockholm, 1994), p. 79.
[4] Durch, W. J. (ed.), *The Evolution of UN Peacekeeping: Case Studies and Comparative Analysis* (St Martin's Press for the Henry L. Stimson Center: Washington, DC, 1993), p. 349.
[5] International Peace Academy, *Peacekeeper's Handbook* (Pergamon Press: New York, 1984), p. 38.
[6] Sköld (note 3), p. 79.

useful to Commanders and staffs of any future UN peace forces'.[7] It is not clear whether such documents were ever finalized and distributed.

In any event the UN lacked the military staff to develop a credible peace operations doctrine. In 1960 Hammarskjöld had re-established the post of Military Advisor with the appointment of Major-General Indar Jit Rikhye. However, his office never consisted of more than four persons. Although they did, according to Charles Moskos, help design standby peacekeeping programmes for contributing nations and guidelines on peacekeeping requirements in the field, they did not work on doctrinal issues.[8] In 1969 the office of Military Advisor was abolished. Outside the Military Advisor's office, the UN's small peacekeeping staff were always too preoccupied with emergencies and current missions to consider such arcane issues as doctrine. The Secretariat, when called on to establish a new mission, continued to improvise.

Even if it had systematically absorbed the doctrinal lessons of the Congo, a combination of institutional lethargy, the enveloping atmosphere of the cold war, and the negative attitudes of France and the Soviet Union towards peacekeeping would have ensured that they were never implemented.

The one area where the UN did learn and apply lessons from ONUC was with regard to the self-defence norm, which, depending on one's perspective, had been clarified, expanded or distorted by the Congo experience. The Secretary-General's instructions and various force commanders' directives during the Congo mission were used as precedents for subsequent UN operations, although not always consistently or all at the same time. It is in this sense, perhaps, that Marrack Goulding, former Under Secretary-General for Political Affairs, claims that: 'The necessary lessons were learnt from the Congo experience'.[9]

The first test case was Cyprus.

## II. The UN Force in Cyprus (1964 to the present)[10]

Surprisingly, during the final year of the Congo operation and despite the misgivings of France and the Soviet Union, the UN Security Council established the UN Force in Cyprus (UNFICYP) in a civil war situation.

In December 1963 inter-communal conflict erupted between the Greek and Turkish communities on Cyprus, supported by the Greek and Turkish governments, respectively. On 24 December the Turkish national troop contingent, stationed in Cyprus under the 1960 Treaty of Alliance, left its camp and took up

[7] United Nations, New York, Interoffice memorandum, Standard operating procedures from Dr Ralph J. Bunche, Under-Secretary [General] for Special Political Affairs to Major General J. T. U. Aguiyi-Ironsi, Force Commander, ONUC and Major General C. F. Paiva Chaves, Force Commander, UNEF, 16 Jan. 1964, UN Archives DAG13/3.11.0.0, #9.

[8] Moskos, C. C., Jr, *Peace Soldiers: The Sociology of a United Nations Military Force* (University of Chicago Press: Chicago, Ill. and London, 1976), p. 5.

[9] Goulding, M., 'The use of force by the United Nations', *International Peacekeeping*, vol. 3, no. 1 (spring 1996), p. 8.

[10] UNFICYP remains deployed at the time of writing but consideration is given here only to its history to 1969.

positions in the northern outskirts of the capital, Nicosia. A report on the situation by Lieutenant-General P. S. Gyani of India for Secretary-General U Thant described the situation in January 1964 as deteriorating rapidly, 'involving scattered inter-communal fighting with heavy casualties, kidnappings and the taking of hostages (many of whom were killed), unbridled activities by irregular forces, separation of the members of the two communities, and disintegration of the machinery of government, as well as fears of military intervention by Turkey or Greece'.[11] With international mediation failing and a British peace-keeping force unable to keep the peace, the Security Council, at the request of the Republic of Cyprus, unanimously established UNFICYP on 4 March 1964.

## The mandate

UNFICYP's mandate was: 'In the interest of preserving international peace and security, to use its best efforts to prevent a recurrence of fighting and, as necessary, to contribute to the maintenance and restoration of law and order and a return to normal conditions'.[12] The wording strongly suggested a Chapter VI rather than Chapter VII operation, but as usual this was not made explicit.

U Thant expressed dissatisfaction with it:

UNFICYP was given a very heavy responsibility without any precise definition of its general mandate to guide it so that it might know clearly just what it is entitled to do and how far it may go, particularly in the use of force. This inadequacy and lack of clarity in the mandate of the Force has been, obviously, a handicap to its operation. The Force, of course, has been subjected to much pressure from those, on the one hand, who would wish it to go much further than it has gone, particularly in the employment of armed force, and those on the other, who would feel that at times the Force tries to go too far on the territory of a sovereign State.[13]

This all sounded rather familiar to those who had experienced the Congo. In this case it was Turkey which expected UNFICYP to use force—to restore the constitutional prerogatives of the Turkish community which they believed the Cypriot Government had removed. Momentarily forgetting his own Congo experience, U Thant told the Security Council that: 'The United Nations Force in Cyprus is in the most delicate position that any United Nations mission has ever experienced, for it is not only in the midst of a bitter civil war but it is dangerously interposed between the two sides of that war. In that situation, the United Nations has had to exert every effort to maintain objectivity, to serve fairness and justice, and to avoid taking sides while doing all possible to alleviate suffering'.[14]

---

[11] United Nations, *The Blue Helmets: A Review of United Nations Peace-keeping*, 3rd edn (UN Department of Public Information: New York, 1996), p. 151.

[12] UN Security Council Resolution 186, 4 Mar. 1964.

[13] United Nations, Report by the Secretary-General on the United Nations Operation in Cyprus, UN document S/5950, 10 Sep. 1964, p. 61.

[14] Report by the Secretary-General on the United Nations Operation in Cyprus (note 13), p. 63.

While perhaps not on the scale of the Congo crisis, the situation facing a UN peacekeeping mission in Cyprus combined a mix of elements that had not been encountered before, including what would now be known as ethnic cleansing as the two communities tried to expel each other from their homes and villages. The use-of-force rules for UNFICYP would therefore need careful elaboration.

## The force

The force did not become operational until late March 1964, almost a month after the mandating resolution was passed.[15] Between 1964 and 1974 UNFICYP's total strength, including civilian police, never exceeded 6275.[16] It clearly lacked sufficient military power to compel the warring parties to submit to an agreement imposed on them, even if the Security Council had wanted it to make such a foolhardy attempt.

The original troop contingents came from Austria, Canada, Denmark, Finland, Ireland, Sweden and the UK, with CivPols from Australia, Austria, Denmark, New Zealand and Sweden. The force was deployed throughout the island, its areas of responsibility, to the extent possible, matching the island's administrative districts.[17] In Nicosia its troops were positioned as observers along a 'green line' separating the two sides. In two other districts, Kyrenia and Lefka, UN posts were also established between the Greek and Turkish lines, from which observation and patrolling took place. On the rest of the island UNFICYP was deployed in such a way as to enable it to interpose itself between the warring sides in areas of tension and where incidents might cause a recurrence of fighting. Observation squads, backed by mobile patrols, were regularly dispatched to such areas.

CivPols, who became operational in April 1964, were available from the outset to help the military component in its attempts to extinguish inter-communal strife. They established liaison with the local police, observed them when they conducted searches of vehicles, manned police posts in certain sensitive areas and conducted investigations into incidents involving members of the opposing communities.[18] Compared with UN missions where military contingents are solely responsible for policing and where their inexperience in such matters may increase the likelihood of the use of force, in Cyprus the availability of unarmed CivPols attenuated the use-of-force issue somewhat.

## Use of force instructions: U Thant sets out an expanded self-defence norm

As was so often the case, the resolution establishing UNFICYP did not contain any reference to the carrying of arms by the force or the appropriate modus operandi for their use. Unlike the case with other missions, even the Secretary-General's report on establishing the mission did not contain such information. It

---

[15] *The Blue Helmets*, 3rd edn (note 11), p. 152.
[16] *The Blue Helmets*, 3rd edn (note 11), p. 160.
[17] *The Blue Helmets*, 3rd edn (note 11), p. 154.
[18] Birgisson, K. Th., 'United Nations Peacekeeping Force in Cyprus', ed. Durch (note 4), p. 228.

was not until 11 April 1964, almost a month after the first troop deployments, that U Thant, in an aide-memoire, set out the mission's use-of-force rules.

It proved to be a revelation. Despite the ill-favour with which the mission in the Congo was viewed, U Thant's instructions clarified and widened the pre-Congo understanding of the self-defence norm. According to Goulding, U Thant had expounded a 'new use of force doctrine' which 'clearly reflected the Congo experience'.[19] Drawing almost verbatim on ONUC's Operations Directive no. 6 of 28 October 1960, U Thant authorized UNFICYP to use force in the case of:

(a) attempts by force to compel them to withdraw from a position which they occupy under orders from their commanders, or to infiltrate or envelop such positions as are deemed necessary by their commanders for them to hold, thus jeopardizing their safety;

(b) attempts by force to disarm them;

(c) attempts by force to prevent them from carrying out their responsibilities as ordered by their commanders; and

(d) violation by force of UN posts, premises and vehicles and attempts to arrest or abduct UN personnel, civil or military.[20]

In certain cases, U Thant said, it might be 'possible to enforce a cease-fire by interposing UNFICYP military posts between those involved', but 'normally' this should not be done if interposition was unacceptable to the parties: this seemed little more than traditional peacekeeping. The Secretary-General also authorized the use of force in self-defence to maintain 'such unrestricted freedom of movement as may be considered essential by the Force Commander to the implementation of the mandates of the Force' and to enable it 'to remove positions and fortified installations where these endanger the peace'. This elaborated the concept of freedom of movement in a way that was never possible in the UNEF case because of Egyptian and Israeli sensitivities. Yet UN freedom of movement on Cyprus, as in the UNEF case, still needed to be negotiated with the Cypriot authorities, which it was in March and November 1964.[21]

In September 1964, U Thant elaborated on these powers: to prevent a recurrence of fighting the commander could create buffer zones in which the presence of armed forces of either side would be prohibited.[22] He stressed, though, that: 'When acting in self-defence, the principle of minimum force shall

---

[19] Goulding (note 9), p. 8.

[20] United Nations, Note by Secretary-General concerning certain aspects of the function and operation of the United Nations Peacekeeping Force in Cyprus, UN document S/5653, 11 Apr. 1964.

[21] The issue was the topic of an exchange of letters on 31 Mar. between the Secretary-General and the Cypriot foreign minister. Subject to a minor qualification regarding large troop movements, it entitled UNFICYP to use all roads, bridges and airfields on the island. Further clarifying UNFICYP's rights, on 10 Nov. Force Commander Gen. K. S. Thimayya of India reached an agreement with the commander of the Cyprus National Guard which declared the whole island open to UNFICYP except for certain militarily sensitive areas (covering about 1.65% of the country) which would be accessible only to the force commander or senior UNFICYP officers. *The Blue Helmets*, 3rd edn (note 11), p. 157.

[22] United Nations, Report by the Secretary-General on the United Nations Force in Cyprus, UN document S/5950, 10 Sep. 1964, p. 68.

always be applied and armed force will be used only when all peaceful means of persuasion have failed. The decision as to when force may be used in these circumstances rests with the Commander on the spot'.

This was the first time a Secretary-General had publicly clarified the range of situations in which UN peacekeepers were permitted to use force in self-defence. He did so presumably to give them added weight and serve notice on the belligerents. He made it very clear that force could be used if belligerents attempted to forcibly disarm peacekeepers—something that had occurred at the end of UNEF I's tenure without UN resistance. Peacekeepers could also now create buffer zones, which presumably they could defend by using force in self-defence. Moreover, UN civilian personnel were now definitely to be protected by UN peacekeepers using force if necessary. Finally, force could be used if attempts were made to prevent peacekeepers from carrying out their 'responsibilities' as ordered by their commanders, rather than simply defending 'positions' as ordered by the commanders. Strangely, there was now no mention of commanders' acting under the authority of the Security Council and its resolutions, as in Hammarskjöld's formulations. Overall, the new rules suggested a more independent, less passive, less defensive posture by peacekeepers than in the past.

Antonia and Abram Chayes note that: 'The judicious use of such expanded interpretations of consent and self-defense would permit a peacekeeping force to adopt a much more aggressive posture, when necessary, without moving to large-scale combat'.[23] Moskos has argued that U Thant's guidelines increased the prospect of force being used since they permitted the defence of dynamic peacekeeping activities rather than just static positions. This meant that, although 'the criteria on the minimum use of force remained anchored on the fundamental principle of nonaggression', 'self-defense could be situation-specific and not limited to defense against unprovoked assault'.[24]

Gerald Draper comments that the new right of freedom of movement itself amounted to 'a considerable extension of the circumstances in which self-defensive force might be used legitimately' and was a 'telling example of the expanding nature of the right of self-defence'.[25] Whether that right would permit UN troops to intentionally put themselves in harm's way or to fight their way through a massed opposing force is not clear. This raises the question whether an effective defence of the UN's freedom of movement can involve anticipatory, offensive action. As Draper notes: 'It is readily admitted by military experts that effective defensive action may have to be anticipatory and, as such, is frequently resorted to in combatant activities'.[26]

[23] Chayes, A. H. and Chayes, A., 'Alternatives to escalation', in *The United States and the Use of Force in the Post-Cold War Era*, Report by the Aspen Strategy Group (Aspen Institute: Queenstown, Md., 1995), p. 213.

[24] Moskos (note 8), pp. 87–88.

[25] Draper, G. I. A. D., 'The legal limitations upon the employment of weapons by the United Nations in the Congo', *International and Comparative Law Quarterly*, vol. 12 (1963), p. 401.

[26] Draper (note 25), p. 402.

Yet, whatever the expansiveness of the new doctrine, it was hardly a licence for peace enforcement. U Thant himself emphasized that: 'It would be incongruous, even a little insane, for that Force to set about killing Cypriots, whether Greek or Turkish, to prevent them from killing each other'.[27] However, as the UN's own publication, *The Blue Helmets*, notes, this really *was* the dilemma facing UNFICYP, which 'could not stand idly by and see an undeclared war deliberately pursued or innocent civilians struck down'.[28] This was closer to the Congo scenario, from which the UN was at that moment attempting to extricate itself, than anyone was prepared publicly to admit.

### UNFICYP's standard operating procedures

UNFICYP's SOP define force—somewhat surprisingly, given that it was supposed to be restricted to self-defence—as 'the use of physical means to impose the will of the UN'.[29] In order of severity, force could be categorized as unarmed, 'weaponed', or involving the opening of fire.

Unarmed force was the 'employment of all means other than weapons to impose the UN's will'. Examples included the construction of barricades, manhandling, the use of engineer equipment to remove obstacles and the use of tear-gas grenades. 'Weaponed force' was defined as 'the use of any physical instrument, military or non-military, to impose the UN's will, such as clubs, batons, rifle butts and bayonets'. These lower levels of force might be used, but not necessarily, when all peaceful means of persuasion had failed. In no situation was the UN to initiate the opening of fire. The guiding principle was that peacekeeping relies on preventing or stopping incidents by negotiation and persuasion rather than force.[30]

The SOP did authorize the opening of fire as an extreme measure when troops were under direct attack. All means of warning, such as emplacement of barbed wire, loudspeakers and tear gas were to be used whenever possible before opening fire. Should it be necessary to open fire, warning shots were to be used before resorting to 'aimed' fire, which would any case be directed low, at the legs of the attackers. Firing should at all times be controlled and discriminate. In all cases it was to continue only so long as necessary to achieve its immediate objective. The commander on the spot was required to keep a record of the number of rounds fired and an attempt was to be made to collect and count empty cartridges after each incident.

When time did not permit reference to higher authority, the commander on the spot was authorized to decide the amount of force necessary for immediate defence. Commanders at all levels were enjoined, however, to anticipate dangerous situations and obtain advance clearance from UNFICYP headquarters to use force should it be necessary. Automatic weapons or explosive

---

[27] United Nations, Report by the Secretary-General on the United Nations Force in Cyprus, UN document S/5671, 29 Apr. 1964.

[28] *The Blue Helmets,* 3rd edn (note 11), p. 156.

[29] Described in Moskos (note 8), p. 88.

[30] Moskos (note 8), pp. 88–89.

projectiles were to be used only if a UN position was unmistakably, deliberately and directly attacked. Their use required the personal authorization of the force commander. In all circumstances the overriding principle of minimum force was to be applied.

However, the question UNFICYP contingent commanders really wanted answered, and which the mandate did not touch on, was whether their troops should attempt to stop government forces from expelling Turks from particular villages and areas. This was a dilemma that the UN would later face in Bosnia. Colonel Jonas Waern, chief of Sector B of ONUC's Katanga Command, claims that U Thant refused to resolve the issue, but left it to the force commander to decide.[31] Presumably this was to establish 'plausible deniability' should the use of force exceed strict self-defence guidelines and create international controversy.

## UNFICYP's use of force

Despite numerous appeals from the Security Council and the Secretary-General, fighting continued in Cyprus as UNFICYP was being deployed, although it was not required to fight its way in. From 1964 to 1974 the force valiantly tried to keep communal peace between Greek and Turkish Cypriots, although violence was never far from the surface. The mission was successful in damping down local conflict, protecting Turkish enclaves and helping restore law and order and a sense of normality to the island. Negotiations and mediation were, as required, UNFICYP's preferred techniques. UNFICYP commanders also often deliberately interposed their troops between the warring sides in an effort to stop the fighting, even when they were likely to be shot at. As a result UN troops often found themselves caught up in outbreaks of armed conflict in which they would be fired at by both sides. They were often forced to return fire in self-defence. Several were killed in major incidents in May 1964 alone.[32]

UNFICYP was also subjected to deliberate harassment and obstruction of its freedom of movement. In some cases troops were intentionally fired at or man-handled.[33] This occurred in 1967, when serious fighting broke out after the Cypriot National Guard moved into the Kophinou area to attempt to 'normalize' conditions.[34] Violence quickly spread in what amounted to a major breakdown of the ceasefire.

By and large UNFICYP troops stuck scrupulously to their (newly enhanced) self-defence rules. Moskos, in a sociological study of UNFICYP peacekeepers published in 1976, based in part on interviews, concluded that: 'No deviation from UNFICYP regulations on the use of force was permitted, and all unit commanders were required to transmit the relevant UNFICYP guidelines to all troops under their command. Virtually every UN soldier I talked to had

---

[31] Waern, J. (Col), personal communication with the author, Stockholm, 24 Nov. 1995.
[32] *The Blue Helmets*, 3rd edn (note 11), p. 156.
[33] *The Blue Helmets*, 3rd edn (note 11), p. 157.
[34] Birgisson (note 18), p. 234.

received such instruction and understood its terms and import'.[35] Although he seems to have underestimated both the use and the threat of use of force by UNFICYP, he records that: 'By far and away the typical UNFICYP field duty revolved around managing incidents through third-party negotiations, recourse to Cypriot authorities to control their armed elements, and moral one-upmanship. Or as one long-term UNFICYP officer indelicately phrased it: "Bullshitting, bullshitting, all the time"'.[36]

Moskos' study revealed several counter-intuitive developments among UNFICYP peacekeepers with regard to the use of force.[37] First, he discerned the emergence of a 'constabulary ethic' over the course of their tours of duty. 'Behavioural adherence to the minimum-of-force concept', he notes, 'was virtually universal and, over time, increasingly normative as well'. This applied whether they were civilian reservists from the Nordic countries or regular soldiers of the 'Atlantic' contingents.[38] He comments that the emergence of adherence to the norm across national lines was all the more remarkable in view of the wide divergences among UNFICYP soldiers in their military backgrounds and motivations for being in Cyprus.

Moskos' second illuminating observation was that there were definite stages in the evolution of the soldiers' attitudes towards the use-of-force norm. When first exposed to it, their reactions ranged from dutiful compliance to outright disbelief. Later, ironically, as cynicism about their role grew, the restraints on the use of force became 'routinely acceptable'. Towards the end of the tour of duty the 'modal reaction' was one of 'quizzical tolerance of the perceived antics of the Cyprus disputants coupled with a reluctance to use force even if hypothetically so ordered'. 'On numerous occasions I heard UN soldiers on duty wonder aloud if they would fire upon a Cypriot—barring self-defense—no matter what the provocation. By the time they left the island, most UNFICYP soldiers appeared to have consciously absorbed the constabulary ethic while possessing mixed views towards the efficacy of the peacekeeping enterprise'.[39]

Moskos' third major finding was that informal learning arising out of the field situation was a greater determinant in forging the constabulary ethic than peacekeeping training prior to arrival in Cyprus. This held true despite the major differences between the various national contingents in their military organization and prior peacekeeping training.

Finally, Moskos concluded that, despite widespread assumptions that there is a disjuncture between military professionalism and peacekeeping, the UNFICYP officer corps demonstrated how military professionalism contributed

[35] Moskos (note 8), p. 87. Moskos' claim (p. 88) that in a decade of peacekeeping in Cyprus there appeared, as of 1976, to have been no case in which an UNFICYP soldier even returned fire is clearly wrong. His claim (p. 89) that there had been fewer than half a dozen instances in which UN troops were deployed in a fashion that threatened the use of force is also suspect.

[36] Moskos (note 8), p. 89.

[37] Moskos (note 8), p. 93.

[38] This tends to contradict the widespread perception that the Nordic troops are best suited to peacekeeping because of their cultural disinclination to use force.

[39] Moskos (note 8), pp. 94, 95.

to, rather than handicapped, adaptation to peacekeeping. While he notes that there was some private expression of resentment over the limitations on the use of force, 'the overriding reality was how capably the United Nations soldiers performed their peacekeeping assignments in an impartial and noncoercive manner'. Moskos pleads that, rather than giving weight to preconceptions of an inflexible 'military mind', what is needed is a more grounded understanding of the norms of military professionalism. He notes that peacekeeping, despite its pacific connotations, can call for demonstrations of sheer physical courage. His conclusions, he says, confirm what has become the peacekeeper's adage: 'Peacekeeping is not a soldier's job, but only a soldier can do it'.[40]

## UNFICYP's changed role after the 1974 Turkish invasion

In 1974 UNFICYP faced its most serious dilemmas with regard to the use of force when inter-communal strife was supplemented by large-scale hostilities between two conventional military forces. On 20 July, in response to a Greek-sponsored *coup d'état* by the Cypriot National Guard against the Cypriot Government of Archbishop Makarios, Turkey invaded the island. Turkish troops occupied the main Turkish Cypriot enclave north of Nicosia and areas to the north, east and west of the enclave, including Kyrenia. In response, the National Guard began attacking Turkish villages and areas.

Never before had an invading army encountered a UN force already in place, or vice versa (although this was not to be the last time). Pending consideration of the new situation by the Security Council, the new UN Secretary-General, Kurt Waldheim, was unable to issue new directions to UNFICYP. Brian Urquhart, Under Secretary-General for Special Political Affairs, records that: 'All we could do was to tell [Force Commander Lieutenant-General Dewan] Prem Chand to "play it by ear" and do his best to limit violence and protect civilians'.[41] UNFICYP was placed on full alert, took extra security precautions and did what it could to arrange local ceasefires, help evacuate foreign missions and protect civilians.

UNFICYP was in any case in no position, politically or militarily, to oppose the Turkish invasion. Unlike the UN Force in Lebanon (UNIFIL) in 1982, UNFICYP did not, with one significant exception described below, attempt to delay the Turkish advance with passive resistance. It confined itself to helping delineate the positions of the parties and maintaining extensive patrolling throughout the island to monitor the situation and act as some sort of deterrent to excessive actions by either party.

On 22 July the Security Council called for a ceasefire and the withdrawal of foreign forces, as well as urging all parties to cooperate with UNFICYP, indicating that the force was to carry on despite the changed circumstances. In his instructions to UNFICYP that evening the Secretary-General stressed that the

---

[40] Moskos (note 8), pp. 136–39.
[41] Quoted in Henn, F., 'Eyewitness: the Nicosia Airport incident of 1974: a peacekeeping gamble', *International Peacekeeping*, vol. 1, no. 1 (spring 1994), p. 83.

first priority was to consolidate the ceasefire by interposing UN troops wherever possible on the belligerents' opposing lines. This resulted in UNFICYP suffering 'severe casualties' when it was caught up in resumed heavy fighting in August.[42]

One area that the Turkish troops had been unable to capture in their initial advance was Nicosia International Airport. Not only was this of strategic importance to the parties as the only international airport on Cyprus, but the area contained British military bases and three UNFICYP facilities. With the British personnel withdrawn from the area, a dangerous vacuum appeared which Turkey would be tempted to fill. The Greek National Guard based at the airport would be likely to try to stop Turkish troops seizing it and UNFICYP would be caught in the middle. Prem Chand, recalling a precedent set in the Congo, took the bold decision to declare the airport a 'UN-protected area', thus pre-empting a battle for it.[43] UN Headquarters gave its immediate approval after receiving support from troop-contributing countries.[44] A multinational but necessarily token group of 150 UN soldiers (mostly British, Canadian, Finnish and Swedish), the majority of them from logistics units, was deployed to the airport and a large UN flag hoisted over the terminal. UN roadblocks were set up to block entry and the runways were obstructed with vehicles.

An announcement of the UN's unilateral move was made on the local media and the two parties were informed. It was made clear that Secretary-General Waldheim had instructed UNFICYP to resist, by force if necessary, any attempt by either side to seize the airport (they were instructed to open fire if fired on or if the Turkish troops refused to halt their advance). Remarkably, Waldheim had done so without consulting the Security Council, presumably afraid that a Council debate could drag on for too long and fail to avert disaster.

Initially the two sides accepted the announcement and the Greek National Guard units withdrew. Nonetheless a dangerous stand-off between UNFICYP forces and Turkish troops began, including tank advances and incidents in which the Turkish forces barely held their fire.[45] The situation only eased with a series of diplomatic and military moves: the UK promised air support to the UN troops if attacked (and dispatched 12 Phantom aircraft to Cyprus for the purpose); additional UN troops, mostly British, were deployed to the airport; delicate negotiations were conducted at the local level; and high-level démarches were made by British Prime Minister Harold Wilson and Waldheim to Turkish Prime Minister Bulent Ecevit.[46] The crisis ended and the airport, now disused, remains in UN hands to this day.

The Nicosia Airport incident revealed the importance of ensuring that the credibility of UN forces is maintained, if necessary through the threat of the use

---

[42] *The Blue Helmets*, 3rd edn (note 11), pp. 161, 163.

[43] Henn (note 41), p. 88.

[44] Rikhye, I. J. (Gen., former Military Advisor to the UN Secretary-General), personal communication with the author at the Lester B. Pearson Canadian International Peacekeeping Training Centre, Nova Scotia, 15 May 1996.

[45] Henn (note 41), p. 88.

[46] Henn (note 41), pp. 88–90.

of force and displays of credible determination to carry through such threats. Although even the reinforced UN force at the airport would ultimately have been overwhelmed militarily by the Turkish troops, they would have put up stiff resistance and, more importantly, brought the wrath of the international community down on Turkish heads. Wilson later indicated that war between Turkey and the UK would also have been likely.

The incident also illustrated the possibilities for creative use of interpositional strategies, combined with the threat of the use of force in self-defence, to achieve peacekeeping goals. This, of course, could best be done when the mission had the active support of the Secretary-General, the Security Council and major powers.

UNFICYP was eventually given a new mandate which included the establishment and control of a security zone between the forces of the two sides.[47] This in effect changed the mission into a classic peacekeeping operation, involving monitoring a ceasefire line between two conventional armies—in this case the famous 180-km Green Line which bisected Cyprus, ranging in width from a few metres in parts of Nicosia to several kilometres. UNFICYP also remained deployed throughout the island to continue to reduce inter-communal violence. The use-of-force rules have remained unchanged from those established by U Thant in 1964.

### Conclusion

UNFICYP conducted peacekeeping using minimal force and by and large strict adherence to the self-defence rule. It saw its mission area and mandate dramatically transformed by a major military invasion from ameliorating and preventing intra-national conflict across a wide area to more traditional peacekeeping duties along a ceasefire line. Its relatively vague mandate enabled it to be flexible and avoid becoming involved in armed conflict with the warring parties, but at the same time inhibited its ability to change the situation. While it is most renowned for its creative use of patrolling and negotiation techniques to reduce inter-communal violence and for its patient oversight of the Green Line, the fact that UNFICYP witnessed the first codification, after the Congo operation, of an expanded self-defence concept gives it a special place in UN peacekeeping history.

## III. The UN Emergency Force II (1973–79)

Ironically, it was a relatively trouble-free peacekeeping mission, in traditional mode, established 13 years after UNFICYP, which produced a further expansion in the use-of-force concept for UN peacekeepers, by incorporating the notion of defence of the mission. Unlike UNFICYP, the UN Emergency Force II (UNEF II) had little need of it.

---

[47] UN Security Council Resolution 355, 1 Aug. 1974.

UNEF II was established in Sinai after the October 1973 war between Israel and Egypt. Its mandate was to supervise the implementation of Security Council Resolution 340 (1973), which demanded that an immediate and complete ceasefire be observed and that the parties return to the positions they had occupied on 22 October 1973.[48] UNEF was to help separate the Egyptian and Israeli forces, act as a buffer between them and monitor the staged 'disengagement' of Israeli forces from Sinai in January 1974 and September 1975.

### Use-of-force guidelines: Waldheim inaugurates 'defence of the mission'

Although UNEF II would appear only to have required the application of existing precedents, Waldheim issued a new concept, approved by the Security Council, which was copied by all subsequent UN peacekeeping operations. While in all other respects the mission would be a traditional peacekeeping operation, Waldheim proposed for UNEF II that: 'Self-defence would include resistance to attempts by forceful means to prevent it from discharging its duties under the mandate of the Security Council'.[49] Whereas previously force could be used to defend the 'responsibilities' or the 'positions' of the mission as ordered by the force commander, now the authority of the Security Council itself was invoked to raise matters to a higher plane.

Given that UNEF II was a standard, traditional peacekeeping operation, it is not immediately apparent why the decision was taken at this point to expand the self-defence norm. Certainly the UN was not expecting any particular difficulties with Egypt or Israel, which had experienced peacekeeping operations in the region and, after an initial settling-down period, had been largely compliant. Moreover, the peacekeeping force would clearly be too small and lightly armed to do anything but defend itself from relatively minor attacks. Urquhart explains that the Secretariat—more specifically, he and his staff—had long felt that the 'only in self-defence' formulation was 'ridiculously weak'.[50] They therefore put the new formulation into the Secretary-General's proposals for establishing the force. Urquhart recalls that at the time Security Council members were extremely worried about the Middle East situation and the 'antics' of the super-powers, and were therefore unusually well disposed to peacekeeping and receptive to the Secretary-General's report.[51] The new wording sailed through unchallenged.

The UN itself and many observers have since regarded the new formulation as a sea change in the UN's use-of-force 'doctrine'. The UN's General Guide-

---

[48] United Nations, Report of the Secretary-General on the implementation of Security Council resolution 340 (1973), UN document S/11052/Rev. 1, 27 Oct. 1973.

[49] Like its predecessor, UNEF II would proceed on the assumption that the conflicting parties, Egypt and Israel, consented to its presence. It would also attempt to act with complete impartiality and avoid actions which could prejudice the rights, claims and positions of the parties. The Secretary-General also proposed to the Security Council that, like UNEF I, UNEF II be 'provided with weapons of a defensive character only' and 'shall not use force except in self-defence'. Report of the Secretary-General (note 48).

[50] Urquhart, B., personal communication with the author, 15 July 2002.

[51] Urquhart, B., personal communication with the author, 15 July 2002.

lines for Peace-keeping Operations of 1995 note that: 'This is a broad conception of "self-defence" which might be interpreted as entitling United Nations
personnel to open fire in a wide variety of situations' (although they also note
that in practice commanders have been reluctant to do so).[52] Former UN
Assistant Secretary-General for Special Political Affairs F. T. Liu notes that in
expanding the self-defence definition the Security Council 'intended to increase
the clout of UN peacekeepers', but (without further elucidation) claims that this
'also made the application of self-defence more hazardous and more difficult'.[53]
He also credits Waldheim with 'obviously' wanting to make peacekeeping
'more effective'.[54] Goulding notes that the 1973 change was in the direction of
a 'wide definition of "self-defence"'.[55] Urquhart comments that: 'This change,
theoretically at any rate, gave peacekeepers a much stronger basis to react to
interference if they wanted to'.[56]

The UNEF II formulations also signalled a closer connection between the use
of force by peacekeepers and the Security Council, which had previously
devolved the use-of-force issue largely to the force commander. Urquhart
points out that the UNEF II formula for establishing the respective authority of
the Secretary-General and the Security Council in directing peacekeeping
operations was novel.[57] The Secretary-General slipped this, too, into his report,
ignoring the fact that the General Assembly's Special Committee on Peacekeeping Operations had been trying unsuccessfully for nearly 10 years to agree
such a change.

To some observers the new use-of-force formulation appeared to lower the
barriers to peace enforcement: if force could be used to help a UN mission fulfil
its mandate, was this any different from peace enforcement? Peace enforcement
was, after all, the imposition of the will of the Security Council on a belligerent
party or parties. In Moskos' view, the new formulation was more problematic
than the previous one in that it seemed to imply that:

While fire cannot be initiated under any circumstances by UN troops, such troops can
be ordered to perform missions which may draw fire. In that event, return fire may be
allowable . . . If the mission is to be pursued, however, the peacekeeping commander
must seek to maneuver his men initially into a tactically defensive posture from which
armed self-defense then becomes permissible. . . Calculations become very fine indeed
when trying to determine what are the outer boundaries to which a peacekeeping
mission can be pushed without [provoking] attack.[58]

---

[52] United Nations, Department of Peace-keeping Operations, *General Guidelines for Peace-keeping
Operations*, UN document 95-38147, Oct. 1995, p. 20.

[53] Liu, F. T., 'The use of force in UN peacekeeping operations: a historical perspective', Paper prepared
for the Tokyo Symposium on New Dimensions of United Nations Peacekeeping, Tokyo, 19–20 Jan. 1995.

[54] Liu, F. T., *United Nations Peacekeeping and the Non-Use of Force*, Occasional Paper, International
Peace Academy (Lynne Rienner: Boulder, Colo., 1992), pp. 25–26.

[55] Goulding, M., 'The evolution of United Nations peacekeeping', *International Affairs*, vol. 69, no. 3
(1993), p. 455.

[56] Urquhart, B., personal communication with the author, 15 July 2002.

[57] Urquhart, B., personal communication with the author, 15 July 2002.

[58] Moskos (note 8), pp. 131–32.

White is blunter: 'Allowing a force to take positive action in defence of its purpose is no different from allowing them to enforce it'.[59]

Since 1973 and the establishment of UNEF II, the guidelines approved by the Security Council for all peacekeeping forces have stipulated that self-defence is deemed to include what has become known as 'defence of the mission'. The implications of the new concept did not, however, become apparent until the missions in Somalia and Bosnia decades later slid into peace enforcement.

## Concept of operations

As was becoming usual in UN peacekeeping missions, initially there appeared to be no concept of operations for UNEF II, although it is unclear why those for UNEF I could not have been dusted off and reused. Force Commander Lieutenant-General Ensio Siilasvuo of Finland reportedly simply ordered his Finnish and Swedish battalions to 'go there and make peace': 'Siilasvuo: "We do not know where the front is. Fighting is going on. Your task: Get there. Get in between. Separate them. See that they stop shooting. Solve the problem as you see best and use your imagination. Any questions?"'[60]

UNEF II's undated use-of-force instructions, issued in the earliest days of the operation when its headquarters were temporarily located in Cairo, clearly derived from those of UNFICYP.[61] They incorporated, almost word for word, the broad use-of-force guidelines promulgated by U Thant in his aide-memoire of 11 April 1964. They also duplicated many of the detailed provisions of UNFICYP's use-of-force instructions as described by Moskos.[62] Indeed, they did not reflect the new 'defence of the mission' concept. Nowhere is the term 'defence of the mission' even mentioned. UNEF troops were still only authorized to use force 'when attempts are made to prevent them from carrying out their responsibilities as ordered by their commanders'.

Interestingly, the UNEF II instructions did permit force to be used 'when specific arrangements accepted by both communities have been, or in the opinion of the commander on the spot, are about to be violated'. This hints at peace enforcement. The reference to 'both communities' also indicates that the instructions were simply taken wholesale from the UNFICYP model without adaptation to the specific circumstances of UNEF II—which was not expected to deal with 'communities' but only with the regular military forces of Egypt and Israel. It appears, then, that the new 'defence of the mission' ethos for UNEF II failed to filter down to the military on the ground.

Although this indicated a worrying disconnection between strategy and tactics, in practice it appeared to matter little.[63] Certainly in the first days of

---

[59] White, N. D., *The United Nations and the Maintenance of International Peace and Security* (Manchester University Press: New York, 1990), p. 201.

[60] Stjernfelt, B., *The Sinai Peace Front: UN Peacekeeping Operations in the Middle East, 1973–1980* (Hurst: London, 1992), pp. 31–32.

[61] The instructions are reproduced in appendix 2 in this volume.

[62] Moskos (note 8), pp. 87–88.

[63] Ghali, M., 'United Nations Emergency Force II: 1973–1979', ed. Durch (note 4), p. 143.

UNEF II it appeared as if the mission might need the new self-defence concept. Constant violations of the ceasefire by both Egypt and Israel, and particularly Israel's continuing operations against the entrapped Egyptian Third Army, 'seriously hampered the Force's effectiveness'.[64] For a day or two the fighting threatened to erupt again into full-scale hostilities. Finnish troops were involved in a hand-to-hand skirmish with Israeli troops in the very first hours of their deployment.[65]

Thereafter, under pressure from the Soviet Union and the USA, the two warring parties settled into a lasting ceasefire. Bertil Stjernfelt reports that: 'As far as is known, UNEF II never had to use armed force to carry out its task. Warning shots were fired, usually to prevent infiltration or theft or destruction of UN property'.[66] Mona Ghali records that there were occasional shootings near UNEF II outposts and patrols that provoked official protests.[67] However, overall UNEF II enjoyed particularly favourable conditions for peacekeeping, including high-level political and technical support, and for the most part the cooperation of the parties. The mission was withdrawn in July 1979 after less than six years, having successfully fulfilled its mandate. Its legacy with regard to the use of force in self-defence was, paradoxically, more lasting than those of other more complex and violence-prone missions, since it introduced the concept of defence of the mission into what passed as UN peacekeeping doctrine.

## IV. The UN Interim Force in Lebanon (1978 to the present)

After UNFICYP, UNIFIL was the next UN peacekeeping mission to be deployed in a civil war or internal conflict situation.[68] Its establishment was rushed and its mandate obscure and unachievable. The tasks it faced were rife with the types of danger and complexity that had confronted ONUC in relation to the use of force. That UNIFIL was able to avoid being drawn into fighting a war in Lebanon is miraculous.

Although the force was established to deal with the consequences of the Israeli invasion of southern Lebanon in March 1978, its area of deployment was contested not just by these two states but also by several Lebanese and non-Lebanese forces. These included the Palestine Liberation Organization (PLO) and an Israeli-supported Christian Lebanese militia led by Major Saad Haddad

---

[64] Ghali (note 63), p. 143.

[65] This incident is recounted in Greenberg, K. E., 'The essential art of empathy', *Soldiers for Peace*, Supplement to *Military History Quarterly*, vol. 5, no. 1 (autumn 1992), p. 45, and is confirmed by Sir Brian Urquhart, personal communication with the author, 15 July 2002. See also Stjernfelt (note 60), p. 18.

[66] Stjernfelt (note 60), p. 151.

[67] Ghali (note 63).

[68] UNIFIL remains in Lebanon at the time of writing (spring 2002), 23 years after its deployment. In 2000 Israel, without warning to the UN or anyone else, suddenly withdrew from Lebanon. The pro-Israeli Haddad forces quickly collapsed, leaving UNIFIL to fill the vacuum. While the problem of harassment by Israeli and right-wing militias has thus considerably eased (although peacekeepers are still caught up in Israeli shelling from across the border), UNIFIL continues to face familiar problems with the various pro-Palestinian militias, which now anarchically 'control' southern Lebanon, and a pusillanimous Lebanese Government, heavily influenced by Syria, which refuses to assert control over its own territory.

(in UN parlance the De Facto Forces, DFF). UNIFIL was thus obliged to deploy 'in a most unorthodox manner, facing four directions as well as looking inward'.[69] Urquhart warned that Lebanon was likely to be a 'peacekeeper's nightmare':

Governmental authority, an important condition for successful peacekeeping, did not exist in southern Lebanon, where a tribal, inter-confessional guerrilla war was raging. The terrain of southern Lebanon—hilly, with many ravines and gullies with citrus groves along the coast—was ideal for guerrilla activity and very difficult for conventional forces. The PLO, a dominating factor in the area, was under no formal authority. Another important element, the Israeli-sponsored Christian militia of the volatile Major Saad Haddad, though illegal, would certainly be strongly supported by Israel. A force of the size and with the mandate necessary for the job was unlikely to be agreed upon by the Security Council.[70]

With pressure from the Lebanese and US governments and helped by fortuitous British chairmanship of the Security Council, the decision to deploy UNIFIL was unusually rapid. Little more than 24 hours passed between the USA proposing it and the Council adopting its mandate and guidelines.[71]

**The mandate**

On 19 March 1978 the Security Council decided 'in the light of the request of the Government of Lebanon, to establish immediately under its authority a United Nations interim force for southern Lebanon for the purpose of confirming the withdrawal of Israeli forces, restoring international peace and security and assisting the Government of Lebanon in ensuring the return of its effective authority in the area'.[72]

Although the resolution used the expression 'international peace and security', which is found in Chapter VII of the UN Charter, it did not invoke the specific language of Chapter VII or other parts of that chapter. UNIFIL was therefore from the beginning not regarded as a Chapter VII operation.

The problems with this resolution, and the subsequent one which actually set up the operation,[73] were legion, effectively hampering UNIFIL from the outset. First, the speedy adoption of the resolutions was at the expense of agreement among the parties—Israel, the PLO and the Lebanese factions—as to the purpose of the force. Second, the resolution avoided mentioning the real problems on the ground: the PLO was effectively given the right to maintain its presence in southern Lebanon, which in turn gave Israel an excuse to maintain the Christian militias as a counterbalance. Third, the Security Council failed to define UNIFIL's area of operation.

---

[69] Skogmo, B., *International Peacekeeping in Lebanon, 1978–1988* (Lynne Rienner: Boulder, Colo. and London, 1989), p. 55.

[70] Urquhart, B., *A Life In Peace and War* (Weidenfeld & Nicolson: London, 1987), p. 288.

[71] Skogmo (note 69), p. 13.

[72] UN Security Council Resolution 425, 19 Mar. 1978.

[73] UN Security Council Resolution 426, 19 Mar. 1978.

In setting out guidelines for the force, Waldheim, eager to avoid the UN becoming dragged into the labyrinthine Lebanese politics, emphasized the principles of the non-use of force and non-interference in the internal affairs of the host country.[74] The UN Secretariat, hurriedly drafting the guidelines, was guided by the precedents of previous missions, especially those in the Middle East and Cyprus, simply setting out three of the conditions now felt to be necessary for a successful peacekeeping operation—that it should have at all times the full confidence and backing of the Security Council, operate with the full cooperation of all the parties, and be able to function as an integrated and efficient military unit.[75] Oddly, nothing was said about consent or impartiality.

Like other peacekeeping missions, UNIFIL would not be authorized to use force, except in self-defence. However, following the UNEF II precedent, it could use force to resist attempts by forcible means to prevent it from discharging its duties under the Security Council's mandate. The Secretary-General's report to the Council of 19 March 1978 contained the following wording, identical to that for UNEF II: 'The Force will be provided with weapons of a defensive character. It will not use force except in self-defence. Self-defence would include resistance to attempts by forceful means to prevent it from discharging its duties under the mandate of the Security Council. The Force will proceed on the assumption that the parties to the conflict will take all necessary steps for compliance with the decisions of the Council'.[76]

Any formulation that deviated from the UNEF II model would probably have required lengthy consultations with the Security Council, for which there was no time. The use of the customary formulations also reduced the concerns of troop-contributing countries, which would have been much less willing to put their soldiers at the UN's disposal if they were to be given more offensive tasks. Moreover, after the experience of the Congo, the Soviet Union would have been disinclined to approve a stronger mandate for UNIFIL. In a statement to the Security Council as early as May 1976, Soviet Ambassador Oleg Troyanovsky stressed that: 'Attempts to embroil the United Nations troops in the internal affairs of Lebanon could lead to the most undesirable and dangerous complications'.[77] The Soviet attitude was summed up by Foreign Minister Andrey Gromyko, who always harked back to the Congo: 'What kind of so-called peacekeeping operations are we talking about? No mention is made of such things in the UN Charter. Remember in the Congo we saw how UN troops could be used against the progressive forces'.[78]

Urquhart, in helping to draft UNIFIL's mandate, tried to include a provision authorizing UNIFIL to prevent the incursion of any armed personnel into its zone of operations, which presumably would have involved the use of force if

[74] United Nations, *The Blue Helmets: A Review of United Nations Peace-keeping*, 2nd edn (UN Department of Public Information: New York, 1990), p. 113.

[75] United Nations, Report of the Secretary-General on the implementation of Security Council Resolution 425 (1978), UN document S/12611, 19 Mar. 1978.

[76] Report of the Secretary-General (note 75), para. 4.

[77] Skogmo (note 69), p. 59.

[78] Quoted in Shevchenko, A., *Breaking with Moscow* (Alfred A. Knopf: New York, 1985), p. 257.

necessary. This was opposed by Lebanon on the grounds that the PLO would certainly object.[79] Kuwait, which was important in obtaining Arab support for the text, also objected.[80] In the event, there was no discussion in the Security Council on the use-of-force issue in connection with the adoption of Resolution 426.[81] According to Bjørn Skogmo, its implementation was left, again, almost entirely to the Secretary-General and his staff.[82] Marianne Heiberg notes that:

Perhaps inevitably the sense of urgency and haste surrounding the establishment of UNIFIL seems to have precluded adequate, advance planning and a careful examination of the military and political factors necessary for successful execution of the Force's mandate and for precision in operational guidelines. Indeed, almost every assumption upon which UNIFIL was based and most of the guidelines the Force received proved to be insufficient, inappropriate or unworkable.[83]

**The force**

UNIFIL was given an initial strength of just 4000 and mandated initially for six months. The first force commander was Lieutenant-General Emmanuel Erskine of Ghana, an experienced peacekeeper who had been deputy commander of UNEF II and chief of staff of UNTSO in the Middle East, established in 1948. Although conceived as a traditional interpositional peacekeeping force, UNIFIL was ultimately more heavily armed than would normally be expected. Its heaviest weapons were 120-mm mortars (although Erskine notes that these were often unusable because they are an 'area weapon' that might endanger civilians).[84] In addition, the Secretary-General eventually convinced the Security Council that UNIFIL should have APCs for defensive actions and to protect troops from small-arms fire and landmines. Finally, the Dutch contingent, on replacing French troops in March 1979, brought TOW anti-tank guns, which were to prove their worth at the At-Tiri confrontation in April 1980.[85]

UNIFIL was established by redeploying personnel from the two existing peacekeeping forces in the Middle East, UNTSO and UNEF. On 19 March UNIFIL immediately set up temporary headquarters at Naqoura in southern Lebanon, on the site of an UNTSO out-station, with 45 military observers.[86] They were initially reinforced by additional UNTSO observers, a reinforced company from the Iranian UN Disengagement Force (UNDOF) contingent and another from the Swedish UNEF contingent. Eventually France, Nepal, Nigeria, Norway and Senegal provided contingents. The authorized strength of the force has varied over the years between 4000 and 7000.

[79] Urquhart (note 70), p. 290.

[80] Skogmo (note 69), p. 13.

[81] Skogmo (note 69), p. 83.

[82] Skogmo (note 69), p. 243.

[83] Heiberg, M., *Peacekeeping in Southern Lebanon: Past Present and Future?*, NUPI Paper no. 453 (Norwegian Institute for International Affairs (NUPI): Oslo, Nov. 1991), p. 3.

[84] Erskine, E. A. (Lt-Gen.), *Mission with UNIFIL: an African Soldier's Reflections* (St Martin's Press: New York, 1989), p. 121.

[85] Erskine (note 84), p. 114.

[86] *The Blue Helmets*, 3rd edn (note 11), p. 85.

## UNIFIL's understandings with the parties

UNIFIL's major task was to keep its area of deployment demilitarized in order to avoid it being used by any of the conflicting parties as a base for military operations. It was also obliged to ensure freedom and safety of movement for the local population as well as its own personnel. In the absence of a clear mandate, an agreed ceasefire or peace settlement and the consent of all the parties to its presence, a vital tool for UNIFIL in 'restoring international peace and security' was the negotiation of understandings with the parties about its role. Such agreements included attempts to establish its freedom of movement and define its area of operation, in addition to setting limits to the often anarchic behaviour of the parties.

First, this involved negotiations with the PLO. The task of 'restoring international peace and security', the most vaguely defined aspect of the mandate, was in fact an oblique reference to the need to stop guerrilla or terrorist attacks from PLO bases in southern Lebanon against Israel. UNIFIL's task therefore was to stop attempts to infiltrate arms or armed personnel into its area and to limit supplies to Palestinians to strictly non-military goods. Although the PLO was not happy about this, according to Skogmo it realized it had little choice and could derive greater political benefits from cooperating with UNIFIL than by openly obstructing it.[87] Hence, in an agreement with UNIFIL the PLO agreed not to initiate hostile acts against Israel from southern Lebanon and not to infiltrate armed elements into UNIFIL's area of operations, implying that it recognized UNIFIL's mandate.[88]

Between 1978 and 1982 the PLO and other armed elements regularly broke the agreement. Part of the problem was that the Palestinians operated in small groups, not all of them under full control of the PLO leadership in Beirut. A long series of confrontations with UNIFIL personnel occurred, many of them serious and leading to the use of force and to casualties and loss of UNIFIL lives. The Secretary-General's reports to the Security Council repeatedly contained long lists of infiltration attempts and separate chapters on 'exchanges of fire across the UNIFIL area'. Negotiations with the PLO to establish calm were more or less continuous.[89]

UNIFIL's relationship with local Lebanese armed militias was also fraught, despite negotiated agreements. It reached an agreement with the Shi'ite Muslim Amal, for instance, by which the group instructed its members not to carry weapons in UNIFIL's area. UNIFIL continued to confiscate the weapons of such members crossing its checkpoints, although, as in the PLO case, personal weapons were returned after a certain period. Other groups, more fundamentalist than Amal, were a bigger problem. Hezbollah for instance, supported by Iran, was unwilling to establish a formal agreement with UNIFIL.

---

[87] Skogmo (note 69), p. 41.
[88] United Nations, Progress report of the Secretary-General on the United Nations Interim Force in Lebanon, UN document S/12620/Add. 5, 13 June 1978.
[89] Skogmo (note 69), p. 45.

Finally, UNIFIL tried to reach various kinds of agreement, arrangement or understanding—tacit or explicit—with the Israeli and Lebanese governments, often with only temporary results. In the case of Israel this was much more difficult because of its perception of the UN as anti-Israel, even though the UN was helping to secure Israel's northern borders with both Lebanon and Syria.

## The use of force by UNIFIL

### Early incidents

Urquhart reports that initially UNIFIL troops were outraged by the violent activities of both the PLO and Haddad, and had to be restrained from reacting with force against them. He comments that at this early stage the UN soldiers 'had not yet appreciated that the moment they drew blood their special status of being above the conflict would collapse, and with it their only source of authority'.[90] He reports meeting Colonel Jean Servan of the French Parachute Regiment. Having not yet grasped the nature of, and the necessary attitude for, UN peacekeeping, Servan spoke of the 'enemy' in relation to both Haddad and the PLO. Urquhart took him aside and pointed out that peacekeepers had no 'enemies', just a series of 'difficult and sometimes homicidal clients'.[91]

The rules for the use of force were debated several times during UNIFIL's early tenure in response to several incidents between its peacekeepers and Israel or various militias. One peacekeeping challenge peculiar to the Middle East is the tradition of seeking revenge for deaths caused, accidentally or otherwise. The local parties applied this philosophy to incidents involving UN troops even when they were clearly using force in self-defence in reaction to militia provocation. This had the potential to spiral out of control and drag the UN forces into tit-for-tat incidents and ultimately into the civil conflict itself. An instance occurred in April 1979, when Ghanaian UN troops returned fire in response to widespread Israeli shelling of UNIFIL's area of operations. UNIFIL's counter-fire led to the death of a member of Haddad's forces.[92] In response, the vulnerable UN headquarters at Naqoura was fiercely attacked by the Israeli-supported militia. The headquarters defence battalion fought back fiercely, supported by the French logistics battalion. After another of his soldiers was killed, Haddad demanded monetary compensation from UNIFIL to avoid 'blood revenge'. Three Dutch UN soldiers were later abducted to press the point. On his way to a meeting with Haddad to resolve the issue, Erskine was physically assaulted by Haddad supporters. UNIFIL resolved the issue by paying the requested blood money. Critics contend that these events reinforced the notion that any party could obstruct UNIFIL's operations with impunity. Ghali says that: 'The Force's vulnerability to external obstruction and its capitulation to Haddad's demands compromised its authority and credibility'.[93]

---

[90] Urquhart (note 70), p. 291.
[91] Urquhart (note 70), p. 293.
[92] Erskine (note 84), pp. 65–70.
[93] Ghali (note 63), p. 194.

*Support for greater use of force by UNIFIL*

Some countries were prepared to consider tougher rules of engagement for UNIFIL, especially during periods of crisis. In several of the Security Council debates in 1978–82 frustration over the parties' lack of cooperation ran so high that several countries indicated a willingness to consider stronger measures. Among the permanent five members of the Security Council, France expressed a readiness to 'strengthen UNIFIL's capacity', although it also stressed that this must be seen in the context of the 'security of its personnel'.[94]

Among the other troop contributors, a statement in April 1980 by the ambassador of Fiji, which had the highest casualty rates of all contributors, was probably the strongest endorsement of revising the rules to permit greater use of force:

In calling for such a review, we are mindful that UNIFIL's central character as a peace-keeping force should neither be compromised nor brought into question. At the same time, my Government is concerned at the seeming ease with which the *de facto* forces appear to have moved into UNIFIL's area of operation and taken up positions without any apparent reaction from UNIFIL, until too late. We believe that we have long passed the point beyond which UNIFIL should not be expected to tolerate the harassment both verbal and physical to which it has been subjected, especially in recent weeks.[95]

The Fijian troops, with a strong and continuing warrior tradition, were, however, a special case. Deployed in Lebanon almost from the start of UNIFIL, they were new to peacekeeping and 'tested' by the local parties in ways that more experienced peacekeepers were not; yet they soon gained a reputation for toughness, sometimes using force beyond what other peacekeepers considered appropriate. For their part, they considered themselves 'naively apolitical' in their peacekeeping role, more willing than others to take advantage of the use-of-force rules to the letter, more inclined to consider the option of using force when negotiations failed, and less reluctant to risk their lives for the mission than other contingents, whom they considered less devoted to peacekeeping.[96]

In response to repeated demonstrations of apparent UN helplessness, the Lebanese Government also demanded a more 'dynamic' interpretation of UNIFIL's ROE. In a letter of 7 May 1979 to the Security Council it said:

It is . . . clear to us that a certain measure of 'peaceenforcing' was not precluded at the very inception of UNIFIL . . . The military option should not be foreclosed by the exclusive use of the (so far) limited diplomatic option. In the light of the tragic experiences accumulated since, we think that UNIFIL should have a greater military credibility. A serious deterrent capability can alone enable the Force to discourage any

---

[94] United Nations, Security Council, Verbatim records (provisional), 2232nd meeting, UN document S/PV.2232, 17 June 1980.

[95] United Nations, Security Council, Verbatim records (provisional), 2218th meeting, UN document S/PV.2218, 18 Apr. 1980.

[96] Conversations between the author and Fijian peacekeepers at the headquarters of the Royal Fiji Military Force, Queen Elizabeth Barracks, Nabua, Fiji, Dec. 1995, 18 Jan. 1996.

challenge to its authority and prevent attacks on its men and installations, let alone prevent it from pursuing its mission . . . If, however, obstruction should come from irresponsible elements, armed illegitimately, then it becomes vital that UNIFIL should not be allowed to find itself in a position of inferiority or inadequacy . . . The time has now come for the Security Council to give UNIFIL the means of carrying out its mission to the end, forcefully, with confidence and assured success.[97]

Ironically, the Lebanese Government stressed that it did not seek a fundamental change in UNIFIL's mandate.

Such Lebanese plaints were generally met with great scepticism in the UN Secretariat, which naturally felt responsible for the safety of UN peacekeepers. Urquhart was 'very conscious that our soldiers were taking risks the Lebanese themselves were not prepared to take'.[98] He expressed exasperation that: 'The Lebanese in their impotence continued to make impossible demands and criticism of UNIFIL which was, unlike the Lebanese army, actually being shot at'.[99] It is also clear that the Lebanese Government intended that UNIFIL be strengthened in order to deal with Israel and its client militia and not the PLO or other armed elements in the south.[100]

Cynically, Israel also at times advocated a more forceful profile for UNIFIL because of the force's alleged weakness vis-à-vis the PLO.[101] Israeli diplomats on other occasions indicated that they thought peacekeeping in the Middle East was not viable without a certain amount of peace enforcement.[102] This was clearly self-serving, given that Israel had never permitted a UN peacekeeping mission to operate on its territory and had given only marginal cooperation to UNIFIL. Moreover, as Skogmo notes, for obvious reasons Israel never pressed officially for a stronger peace enforcement role for UNIFIL.[103]

### Confrontation with Israeli forces and creation of the Force Mobile Reserve

A serious confrontation between UNIFIL and Israeli forces on 9 May 1979 illustrated the dangers of escalation.[104] When an Israeli battalion was detected moving into the UN zone, Erskine immediately ordered his mobile reserve of Dutch, Nigerian and Senegalese soldiers to mount their APCs and reinforce an Irish contingent already on the spot. When the Israeli battalion arrived at the Irish roadblock, instead of encountering the expected lightly-manned checkpoint that could have been pushed aside or bypassed, it faced a well-deployed, substantial force with anti-tank guided missiles, heavy machine guns and

[97] United Nations, Letter dated 7 May 1979 from the Permanent Representative of Lebanon to the United Nations addressed to the President of the Security Council, UN document S/13301, 7 May 1979.
[98] Urquhart (note 70), p. 292.
[99] Urquhart (note 70), p. 301.
[100] Skogmo (note 69), p. 88.
[101] Skogmo (note 69), p. 89.
[102] Skogmo (note 69), p. 89.
[103] Skogmo (note 69), p. 89.
[104] The incident is recounted in Paschall, R., 'UN peacekeeping tactics', *Soldiers for Peace*, Supplement to *Military History Quarterly*, vol. 5, no. 1 (autumn 1992), p. 29.

120-mm mortars. The battalion halted and an uneasy stand-off developed. Meanwhile, Erskine alerted UN Headquarters in New York.

The deadlock ended when the UN offered to search for the guerrillas whom the Israeli troops had been intending to look for in nearby houses. When the UN search revealed that Israeli intelligence had been mistaken, the Israeli troops withdrew. Erskine later commented that: 'A show of force, depending on how one plays it, can be an effective means of self-defence'.[105] On other occasions, however, Israeli forces crashed through UN roadblocks unperturbed. Fijian Colonel Isikia Savua noted that: 'We had to put up a semblance of resistance by placing barricades in the roads, and the Israelis would plow over them with trucks. Then the only thing we could do was stand back and watch. This was an observer mission, not an enforcement action'.[106]

The May 1979 incident led to establishment of a permanent Force Mobile Reserve (FMR) for UNIFIL,[107] a composite mechanized company drawn from all six infantry battalions and equipped with APCs. It was deployed quickly to areas of tension and given other special tasks when required. The Lebanese ambassador to the United Nations, Ghassan Tueni, claims that UNIFIL's problems were caused by the fact that it was given a 'dynamic mission' but essentially 'static means' to do the job.[108] The FMR was designed to address this problem. Some of the incidents in which it was subsequently involved are described below.

*The At-Tiri Incident, April 1980*

One of the most infamous violent incidents between the UN and the DFF occurred in the strategically situated village of At-Tiri in the Irish sector on 6 April 1980. Tension began to build when a DFF tank and two jeeps arrived at the main intersection controlling movements into and out of At-Tiri, which was guarded by an Irish post. The tank pushed an Irish personnel carrier out of the way to allow the jeeps to enter the village. Irish troops immediately surrounded the DFF men and began negotiations to evict them. After an investigation by UNIFIL's troubleshooting 'Team Zulu', the FMR was deployed in and around the village. Melodramatically, and quite inaccurately given UNIFIL's mandate and ROE, Erskine declares that: 'UNIFIL was at war'.[109] On 7 April a heavy exchange of small arms fire took place, initiated by the DFF, to which UNIFIL responded.

During the fighting nine Irish soldiers were taken prisoner by Haddad's forces. In negotiations Haddad attempted to trade their freedom for establishment of a command post in At-Tiri. UNIFIL's negotiator, Norwegian Brigadier Ole Nielsen, refused and demanded the men's unconditional release. He warned

---

[105] Erskine (note 84), p. 121.
[106] Greenberg (note 65), p. 43.
[107] Erskine (note 84), p. 120.
[108] Tueni, G., *Une guerre pour les autres* [A war for others] (Jean-Claude Lattes: Paris, 1985), p. 203, cited in Skogmo (note 69), p. 90.
[109] Erskine (note 84), p. 71.

Haddad that if the DFF did not withdraw by the following morning, 8 April, at 1100 hours, UNIFIL would seal off the area, thereby preventing supplies getting through to his men. If armed confrontation ensued, UNIFIL would respond with 'full force'. Erskine notes that: 'Security Council Resolution 425 had to be defended whatever happened, and in any case the loss of At-Tiri would have meant a serious encroachment which, on top of the encroachments we had already suffered, would harm the credibility of UNIFIL operations. Our stand on At-Tiri was non-negotiable'.[110]

Waldheim was informed and Urquhart commended Erskine for his handling of the crisis. The Secretary-General urgently requested Israel to call off its allies and the USA was informed. Although three of the Irish captives were released early on 8 April, the Irish battalion in the area was attacked. The Irish commander ordered his force to open controlled fire on the DFF attackers. A local ceasefire was arranged but subsequently broke down. Further incidents occurred on 10 and 11 April, resulting in the death of a Fijian soldier. This provoked the Dutch troops into using their TOW anti-tank missiles in a battle against DFF tanks.

This was followed by a major DFF attack on UNIFIL headquarters at Naqoura the following day, 12 April, including the use of mortars, artillery, tanks, heavy machine guns and small arms. For more than four-and-a-half hours the headquarters and most of the adjacent supporting elements were subjected to continuous and indiscriminate firing. UNIFIL fought back fiercely. The Ghanaian battalion and French logistics battalion used every weapon at their disposal except the 120-mm mortars, which it was feared would cause civilian casualties. Extensive damage was done to the headquarters and equipment. Luckily, the UN incurred no deaths and only one peacekeeper was wounded. The attack on Naqoura led the UN to establish a permanent headquarters defence unit, initially comprising a French detachment.

Security Council Resolution 467 was adopted in April 1980 after further serious incidents which culminated in the abduction and murder of two Irish UNIFIL soldiers. It included a paragraph that called 'attention to the provisions in the mandate that would allow the force to use its rights of self-defence'.[111] Although this was nothing more than a restatement of the obvious, it was, according to Skogmo, 'meant as a reminder that the mandate and guidelines of UNIFIL did not exclude more forceful action'.[112] In response to the attacks on its troops the Irish Government convened an unprecedented summit of UNIFIL troop contributors in Dublin in May 1980.[113] While this gave UNIFIL additional political support and served notice on Israel and Haddad, it did not lead to any change in the use-of-force rules or military reinforcements.

Erskine later claimed that the At-Tiri incident illustrated some important peacekeeping principles. First, UNIFIL's determination to hold At-Tiri demon-

[110] Erskine (note 84), p. 73.
[111] UN Security Council Resolution 467, 24 Apr. 1980.
[112] Skogmo (note 69), p. 86.
[113] Erskine (note 84), p. 87.

strated the principle of firmness, undoubtedly facilitated by the importance of the village 'both strategically and for ensuring that UNIFIL's credibility did not suffer', which was 'well understood' by both sides. Second, he commended the unswerving support of the UN Secretary-General, the Under Secretary-General and troop contributors. Third, he pointed to the importance of an integrated command. Fourth, he praised the parallel negotiating 'track' in New York to resolve the issue while UNIFIL's defensive operations were continuing. Fifth, he claimed, the incident demonstrated that a UN peacekeeping force 'is able to fight in defence of its mandate and of its troops and equipment whenever that becomes absolutely necessary. When the case is right, the full support of the Secretary-General and the contributing countries can be assured'. He concluded that: 'The fighting at At-Tiri presented a practical demonstration, as well as definition, of the use of force in self-defence in UN peacekeeping operation operations'.[114] This, of course, begs the question when the conditions can be judged to be right. Much presumably depends on the fine judgements of the force commander as to the appropriateness of using force at any particular juncture.

## Attempts to 'refine' the use-of-force rules

In his June 1980 report to the Security Council on UNIFIL, the Secretary-General commented on the use of force, giving as clear a view as any of the attitude of UN officials to its increased use:

Measures are . . . being considered to enable the contingents of UNIFIL to react firmly and consistently to threats or actions designed to interfere with the discharge of the duties of the Force. . . [H]owever . . . the use of force in self-defence will not by itself achieve significant progress in the implementation of the UNIFIL mandate. A peace-keeping operation must achieve its major objectives through means other than the use of force, and this consideration certainly applies to UNIFIL. While consolidating UNIFIL and taking the necessary steps to render its position as strong as possible, I believe that the main road to full implementation of the UNIFIL mandate lies in pol-itical and diplomatic efforts. These efforts must secure genuine co-operation with the Force and implant the conviction that such co-operation represents, in the long run, the best guarantee of security and normality for all concerned.[115]

The new measures were informally discussed with Security Council members and troop contributors in mid-1980. They included changing the standing orders to allow UNIFIL to open fire in specified situations—for instance, when other forces shot at them to kill or tried to infiltrate the UNIFIL area to set up new positions, or when UNIFIL posts were denied necessary provisions. Reactions among troop-contributing countries were negative. The USA, which did not have troops in UNIFIL but feared that such steps would lead to increased con-frontations between UNIFIL and the Israeli forces, was also less than enthusi-

---

[114] Erskine (note 84), pp. 78–79.
[115] United Nations, Report of the Secretary-General on the United Nations Interim Force in Lebanon, for the period from 11 December 1979 to 12 June 1980, UN document S/13994, 12 June 1980.

astic. The Security Council and troop contributors reiterated their strong support for the existing use-of-force policy outlined in the Secretary-General's original report.[116] Ironically, all the new measures proposed were perfectly possible within the existing mandate and the March 1978 guidelines.

In 1982, again under Lebanese pressure, the Security Council, as well as increasing UNIFIL's strength to 7000 troops, in its Resolution 501 quoted verbatim the relevant paragraphs of the Secretary-General's original report on the use of force.[117] According to Skogmo, even if no new elements were introduced, this elevated the use-of-force guidelines to a slightly higher status, since they were quoted in a resolution and not simply in a report.[118] However, they were useless in preventing Israeli incursions.

### The second Israeli invasion of Lebanon, 1982

In June 1982 UNIFIL Force Commander Lieutenant-General William Callaghan of Ireland was informed by the Israeli Defence Forces (IDF) Chief of Staff, General Rafael Eitan, that Israel intended to launch its second invasion of Lebanon within half an hour. Eitan intimated that Israeli forces would pass through or near UNIFIL positions and he expected UNIFIL to 'raise no physical difficulty' for his advancing troops. Callaghan protested strongly and ordered all UNIFIL troops to block the advancing IDF, adopt defensive measures and remain in position unless their safety was 'seriously imperilled'.[119]

In accordance with these instructions UNIFIL troops took various measures to stop or at least delay the Israeli advance. On the coastal road to Tyre, Dutch soldiers planted obstacles before an advancing Israeli tank column and damaged one tank. During the encounter Israeli tank barrels were trained on the Dutch soldiers while Israeli troops pushed the obstacles aside. Other UNIFIL battalions also put up various obstacles which were forcibly removed or bulldozed. A small Nepalese position guarding the Khardala bridge stood its ground despite continued harassment and threats. Only after two days were the Israeli tanks able to cross the bridge after partially destroying the Nepalese post.

Despite these efforts, the UN officially records: 'UNIFIL soldiers with their light defensive weapons could not withstand the massive Israeli invading forces, and the UNIFIL positions in the line of the invasion were bypassed or overrun within 24 hours'.[120] One Norwegian soldier was killed by shrapnel on 6 June. In commenting on the invasion in his report of 14 June 1982 to the Security Council, the Secretary-General stated that UNIFIL, like all UN peacekeeping operations, was based on certain fundamental principles, foremost of which was the non-use of force, except in self-defence: 'The Force was not meant to engage in combat to attain its goals; it had a strictly limited strength,

---

[116] Skogmo (note 69), p. 88.
[117] UN Security Council Resolution 501, 25 Feb. 1982.
[118] Skogmo (note 69), p. 87.
[119] *The Blue Helmets*, 3rd edn (note 11), p. 101.
[120] *The Blue Helmets*, 3rd edn (note 11), p. 101.

armed only with light defensive weapons . . . Once the Israeli action commenced, it was evident that UNIFIL troops could, at best, maintain their positions and take defensive measures, seeking to impede and protest the advance'.[121] Erskine pleads that: 'Perhaps UNIFIL could have offered more resistance, taken some casualties and made a few more "martyrs", thus consoling some critics who have accused it of doing nothing to stop the IDF. Whether such casualties, in a show of force designed for political convenience, are justifiable is a highly debatable issue'.[122]

Once the IDF had occupied the area, UNIFIL troops could do little to affect the situation. They were instructed not to block IDF movements but only observe and report. They generally followed Israeli troops wherever they went. When the latter went beyond what UNIFIL considered allowable in their dealings with Lebanese civilians, UNIFIL often tried to intervene, at times by placing themselves between the IDF troops and the civilians to prevent violence and to permit mediation to commence.[123] In some cases UNIFIL personnel interposed themselves physically to prevent the IDF demolishing the houses of suspected anti-Israeli guerrillas, leading to heated arguments and sometimes direct confrontation.[124] In mid-February 1985, in the village of Burj Rahhal, French UNIFIL soldiers engaged in fisticuffs with IDF soldiers in an attempt to stop such demolitions.[125]

## Intensified civil war, 1986

As the conflict between Lebanese resistance groups, on the one hand, and the IDF and South Lebanon Army (SLA) forces, on the other, intensified in 1986, UNIFIL personnel were subjected to increasing attacks from both sides. In August two men, one of them a local Amal leader, were shot by a French sentry in a confrontation at a UNIFIL checkpoint.[126] In the following days UNIFIL positions came under fire, particularly in the French sector, but also in the Fijian, Finnish, Irish and Nepalese contingent areas. In September four French soldiers were killed by remote-controlled bombs, several more were wounded and the French contingent continued to be harassed. Hezbollah militia were suspected of involvement.

In his report to the Security Council, the Secretary-General spoke of the 'major crisis' facing UNIFIL and presented a list of immediate measures proposed by the force commander, including regroupment of UNIFIL positions and contingents, a crash programme for additional reinforced shelters and increased reliance on APCs.[127] The Council authorized the Secretary-General to proceed. There was also discussion about reassessing aspects of the SOP, one

---

[121] *The Blue Helmets*, 3rd edn (note 11), pp. 101–102.
[122] Erskine (note 84), p. 112.
[123] United Nations, Report of the Secretary-General, UN document S/17093, 11 Apr. 1985.
[124] Skogmo (note 69), p. 35.
[125] Skogmo (note 69), p. 35.
[126] Skogmo (note 69), p. 53.
[127] United Nations, Report of the Secretary-General, UN document S/18348, 18 Sep. 1986.

suggestion being to acquire heavy weapons. In the opinion of Force Commander Major-General Gustav Hägglund of Finland, UNIFIL should not acquire such weapons, given its need for the cooperation and consent of the local population. He believed instead that UNIFIL's strategy should be to avoid violence by being able to deploy superior force quickly when needed.[128]

The measures introduced in late 1986 and early 1987 to enhance UNIFIL's effectiveness and improve its security included: (*a*) a major redeployment in late 1986 as a result of the withdrawal of the French contingent from its sector;[129] (*b*) a revision of the SOP to ensure that the tasks assigned to individual units were realistic and practicable in the prevailing circumstances of southern Lebanon; and (*c*) steps to ensure that these procedures were carried out consistently by all units of the force.[130] When the cold war ended in 1989 UNIFIL was still in place, effectively overshadowed by the emergence of new missions with even more difficult use-of-force issues to confront.

### Conclusions on UNIFIL's use of force

UNIFIL used force, where necessary, to defend itself and its mission. Most of its fatalities were incurred at its own roadblocks, designed to check the entry of weapons, ammunition and armed personnel into its area of operation.[131] In some cases force was not used where it might have been, even according to a conservative interpretation of the self-defence rule. Skogmo reports that there were cases where UNIFIL units were 'not sufficiently firm to establish respect'.[132] There were also several reports of incidents in which UNIFIL contingents, in response to repeated provocation, used more force than UN and UNIFIL headquarters realized. By June 1990 UNIFIL had incurred 130 fatalities through hostile action, the highest toll of any UN mission at that time.[133]

Sound political judgement and military professionalism on the part of UNIFIL officers were two equally important requirements in handling incidents involving the use of force. Also crucial in performing its preventive duties without the use of force was early warning of the build-up of Israeli or militia forces prior to an incursion. When successful, this resulted in UNIFIL being able to boost its presence in the area under threat, including through the use of

---

[128] Report of the Secretary-General (note 127).

[129] Skogmo (note 69), pp. 89–90.

[130] None of this helped UNIFIL in Feb. 1992 when Israel launched another large-scale incursion. Lewis, P., 'A short history of United Nations peacekeeping', *Soldiers for Peace*, Supplement to *Military History Quarterly*, vol. 5, no. 1 (autumn 1992), p. 20. UNIFIL was humiliated when an Israeli armoured column broke through its roadblocks on its way to punish Hezbollah guerrilla groups. Israeli attacks on UNIFIL troops occurred periodically thereafter, some apparently deliberate. In Apr. 1996 an Israeli artillery barrage against the Fijian battalion's headquarters at Qana killed 100 refugees and injured several peacekeepers. A report by the Secretary-General's Military Advisor, Major-Gen. Franklin van Kappen, expressed doubt that the attack had been as accidental as Israel claimed. United Nations, Annex to Letter dated 7 May 1996 from the Secretary-General addressed to the President of the Security Council, UN document S/1996/337, 7 May 1996.

[131] Erskine (note 84), p. 107.

[132] Skogmo (note 69), p. 88.

[133] *The Blue Helmets*, 2nd edn (note 74), p. 427.

its FMR—a precedent that has been followed in subsequent peacekeeping operations in Bosnia, Somalia, Cambodia, Eastern Slavonia and East Timor, with varying results.

Skogmo concludes that the Secretary-General's guidelines and SOP were sufficiently flexible to allow each battalion commander a relatively high degree of latitude. In a situation as volatile as that in southern Lebanon, this was an operational necessity, particularly as local challenges to the authority of the individual battalions tended to develop quickly.[134] Erskine immodestly expresses satisfaction that the 'near perfect' concept of operations and SOP devised at the inception of UNIFIL remained largely intact.[135] This he notes, provided continuity of policy, an essential factor in the 'complex, tense and ever changing situation in South Lebanon'. John Mackinlay, on the other hand, criticizes the lack of mission-wide SOP for dealing with armed confrontations.[136]

Operational practice in fact varied strikingly from one national contingent to its successor contingent.[137] Ghali argues that this undermined UNIFIL's military coherence and credibility. She notes that most battalions were rotated every six months, meaning that: 'Once troops have reached a stage where they can be effective, the continuity and consistency of field operations are disrupted'.[138] This often coincided with increased violence as the militia and others tested the newcomers for their resilience and resolve. Ghali claims, too, that the Norwegian battalion became 'rather independent in its actions', especially since it was physically separated from the rest of UNIFIL, while others developed characteristic ways of dealing with the various armed elements in the early days of the operation before UNIFIL was in effective communication with its own contingents.[139] This continued until the mid-1980s.

Heiberg differentiates between passive and aggressive battalions. The latter include the Fijian and Norwegian troops, who pursued 'a policy contrary to official norms in preventing by all means available the establishment of non-UNIFIL forces in their areas of operation'.[140] Erskine unwittingly reveals the variability of his force when he notes that the Fijian troops 'had a no-nonsense professional attitude to their duties which I always admired and respected'.[141] By contrast, the Irish are characterized by Heiberg as a passive battalion.[142]

Paul Lewis accuses governments of undercutting the force commander by giving their forces special instructions to stay out of danger and minimize casualties. He also contends that UNIFIL has been 'plagued by poor morale'; its soldiers, well aware that they are virtually powerless to stop the hostilities,

---

[134] Skogmo (note 69), p. 88.
[135] Erskine (note 84), p. 100.
[136] Mackinlay, J., *The Peacekeepers: Peacekeeping Operations at the Arab–Israeli Interface* (Unwin Hyman: London, 1989), pp. 59, 65.
[137] Heiberg (note 83), p. 6.
[138] Ghali (note 63), p. 191.
[139] Ghali (note 63), p. 191.
[140] Heiberg (note 83), p. 34.
[141] Erskine (note 84), p. 99.
[142] Heiberg (note 83), p. 34.

put survival first'.[143] Erskine pleads that: 'Self-defence within the context of UN peacekeeping operations has always been a difficult, sensitive and sometimes rather confusing issue', particularly in southern Lebanon. He concedes that a major constraining factor was sensitivity to casualties:

As commander of a peacekeeping force operating in an arms-infested territory full of nervous, untrained, trigger-happy little boys, I was reasonably sensitive to casualties. Heavy casualties were acceptable to the armed elements since blood did not mean much to some of them. It was my strong and unshakeable feeling that contributing countries would be prepared to accommodate a few casualties in the cause of UNIFIL troops defending [their] mandate, themselves and UN/contingent property, but that casualties suffered outside this spectrum of operational activities could provoke national political difficulties and serve as a catalyst for the collapse of the mission. There was no way contributing countries would be prepared to receive sealed coffins from Naqoura at their respective international airports on a daily basis.[144]

While UNIFIL cannot be credited with contributing to the long-term solution to the complex situation in southern Lebanon, it helped dampen conflict, protect and sustain local populations, and maintain an international deterrent and observational presence without being drawn into armed conflict itself through the inappropriate use of force. While from the outset there were periodic calls for greater use of force, the Security Council resisted. As Skogmo notes, had UNIFIL adopted such a course, it would have run the risk of perpetuating the same stalemate and balance of forces as existed but at a higher level of violence.[145] In general both the members of the Security Council and troop contributors supported the existing use-of-force guidelines. In truth, the force was always too small, too lightly armed and too dispersed and disintegrated to do much more.

UNIFIL's problems, Skogmo says, were caused more by lack of agreement among the parties on the basic objectives of UNIFIL's mission than by the force's means and capabilities.[146] Indeed, the requirements of the Secretary-General for a successful mission were only ever partly met. The permanent members of the Security Council never gave their full support to the mission, the parties to the conflict never cooperated fully with UNIFIL and some created major problems, and the restrictions placed on UNIFIL's movements prevented integration between the force headquarters and its individual contingents.[147]

## Implications of the UNIFIL experience for UN thinking on the use of force

The difficult conditions of UNIFIL did not generate attempts to reconsider use-of-force issues within the UN. Despite decades of experience in the Lebanese

[143] Lewis (note 130), p. 20.
[144] Erskine (note 84), pp. 114–15.
[145] Skogmo (note 69), p. 90.
[146] Skogmo (note 69), p. 90.
[147] Skogmo (note 69), p. 254.

peacekeeping 'laboratory', no attempt was made to draw up a doctrine for the use of force by UN peacekeepers in civil war situations based on that experience. No novel rules of engagement were developed and no substantive debate arose about the use of force for enforcement purposes. UNIFIL was simply left to maintain its presence and fulfil its mandate as best it could. As a relatively minor player in the wider Middle East arena, the mission was forgotten and neglected until periodically an incident or crisis arose. Once these abated UNIFIL fell back into obscurity.

The reasons why the Lebanon mission was unlikely, from the outset, to generate new thinking about the use of force are obvious. First, the UN Secretariat was from the outset unenthusiastic about and perplexed by the mission. It was seen as a case of the UN being involved in an impossible mission as a favour to the great powers. Second, the case was regarded as *sui generis* and unlikely to be a model that anyone would wish to emulate. Third, the involvement of a US ally, Israel, in the conflict, made the case sensitive and special. Fourth, the mission was able to get by without becoming involved in the civil war, thereby avoiding the crisis in peacekeeping that the Congo had produced, but also thereby avoiding the need for hard-headed reconsideration of the appropriateness of 'traditional peacekeeping'—the question which the Somalia, Bosnia and Rwanda cases would raise later. Finally, the mission was simply involved in holding the line in a conflict that was but a subset of a much larger regional imbroglio involving considerably higher stakes than those pertaining to southern Lebanon.

Although it was not a UN force, the Multi-National Force (MNF), deployed in Beirut in 1982–84, demonstrated the result that would have been likely if UNIFIL had been allowed to drift into peace enforcement. The force comprised 1800 US Marines and some 4000 British, French and Italian troops. The MNF was militarily far more powerful than UNIFIL or any UN peacekeeping operation in the Middle East. It was dispatched, without UN endorsement, to support the Lebanese Government in the wake of the assassination of President-Elect Bechir Gemayal and the massacres of Palestinian civilians in refugee camps by Lebanese Phalangists. Once deployed, the force could do little more than hunker down in fixed, vulnerable positions near Beirut Airport.[148] The MNF's considerable firepower was soon used, initially as a means of reprisal, both to protect itself and to assist the Lebanese Government against its opposing forces, but later for overtly political aims. By August 1983, less than a year after their arrival, MNF troops were exchanging fire with various factions in Lebanon's civil war.[149] By September, US warships and carrier-based aircraft were bombing these factions and Syrian air defence units to help the Lebanese Armed Forces maintain control of the heights overlooking Beirut Airport.

The narrow Western political base of the MNF led most people in the Middle East to perceive it as a Western, NATO operation. Their activities on arrival led

---

[148] Haass, R. N., *Intervention: The Use of American Military Force in the Post-Cold War World* (Carnegie Endowment for International Peace: Washington, DC, 1994), p. 24.
[149] Haass (note 148), p. 24.

it to appear to be allied to the Christian-dominated Lebanese Government. The MNF therefore became another party to the long-running Lebanese civil war. The US forces and part of the French contingent in particular came to be perceived as partisan; the British and Italian troops were more successful in maintaining impartiality. On 2 October 1983, 241 US Marines were killed when a huge truck bomb demolished their barracks in Beirut. Total MNF deaths in 1983 were over 300 (French and US).[150] Four months later the MNF withdrew in disgrace. Urquhart notes that the MNF should never have been called a peacekeeping force:

It was called a peacekeeping force but was based on the US Marines (and three aircraft carriers), who were not used to taking insults without doing something about it. Quite right, too. I used to go to see the marines stewing in the airport in Beirut, and just longing to get the bastards who were mortaring them all the time. They finally did, and they became part of the problem. The point of peacekeeping is to remain above the problem.[151]

Erskine is also highly critical of the MNF:

The glaring absence of a force commander in the MNF and the corresponding absence of a force standing operating procedure resulted in each contingent responding to enemy fire according to the political wishes emanating from Rome, London, Paris or Washington. Thus the troops on the ground were in grave danger. Peacekeeping missions should be commanded on the ground by the military and not by politicians and ambassadors, as was done with the MNF.[152]

He also notes that the way the MNF used fire in self-defence contrasted sharply with the UN's application of the use of force. The use of heavy weapons, he says, had the unfortunate effect of provoking the armed groups in Lebanon and consequently drawing the MNF into a 'reprisal game'. Peacekeeping forces, he declares, 'should retain the right to defend the mandate, themselves and their equipment, but the commander must always bear in mind at the same time that excessive use of fire is a double-edged weapon'.[153] Lorenz notes that in fact the US ROE for Beirut were 'highly restrictive and politically driven' and limited the collective and individual right of self-defence in a way that should never be repeated.[154] The USA's experience in Beirut in 1982–84, along with its deeper fears of becoming trapped in a Viet Nam-like quagmire, was to have a profound impact on the use of force in UN operations in the 1990s, shaping the US approach both to its own involvement and that of the UN in Somalia, Rwanda and the former Yugoslavia.

---

[150] Erskine (note 84), p. 123.

[151] Quoted in Morrow, L., 'An interview: the man in the middle', *Soldiers for Peace*, Supplement to *Military History Quarterly*, vol. 5, no. 1 (autumn 1992), p. 27.

[152] Erskine (note 84), p. 124.

[153] Erskine (note 84), p. 125.

[154] Lorenz, F. M. (Col), 'Law and anarchy in Somalia', *Parameters: US Army War College Quarterly*, vol. 23, no. 4 (winter 1993/94), p. 41, fn 27.

## V. UN doctrine on the use of force by the 1980s

Despite having engaged in peacekeeping for more than 30 years, the UN still had no use-of-force doctrine for such operations by the time the cold war ended in 1989. While there was a widely understood distinction between Chapter VI peacekeeping and Chapter VII enforcement, beyond this vague delineation Security Council resolutions consistently failed to offer guidance on the use of force. Hammarskjöld's summary study with its pioneering conceptualization of the key requirements of traditional peacekeeping—consent, impartiality and use of force only in self-defence—remained the conventional wisdom.[155]

After UNIFIL no new UN peacekeeping operations were established for a decade. This led naturally to a decline in interest in peacekeeping principles and practices. Certainly the UN itself was under no pressure to establish a clear doctrine or more detailed procedures for armed peacekeepers, who seemed to be a disappearing breed. The UNEF II guidelines became the standard, to the extent that they were needed at all.

Beyond this, successive force commanders were left to contrive their own SOP and ROE. There were no model SOP or ROE on which missions could draw. As ever, each new mission tended to reinvent the wheel, adopting its own rules and regulations regarding the use of force without regard to precedent. Although after 1973 the self-defence concept had been expanded to include 'defence of the mission', this was itself subject to interpretation and was implemented inconsistently within and between missions. Finally, no official UN training manuals existed to help potential troop contributors prepare for the use of force in UN missions, whether in self-defence or beyond.

There were, however, two repositories of received wisdom on peacekeeping outside the official UN system which illustrate the prevailing view about the use of force in UN operations in the final decade of the cold war.

### The *Peacekeeper's Handbook*

One of the few institutions that kept a close eye on peacekeeping during this fallow period was the International Peace Academy, established in New York in 1971. Its *Peacekeeper's Handbook*, first published in 1984, sets out the received wisdom on peacekeeping, based on decades of UN experience.[156] Although this was done on an unofficial basis, the IPA has always had close links to the UN Secretariat and a good appreciation for official views on peacekeeping. This was particularly due to the fact that Major-General Rikhye was for many years its director-general.

With regard to the use-of-force issue, the *Handbook* simply duplicates the standard UN line, with no attempt to be innovative or analytical. The only novel element seems to be the suggestion that force might be used when 'specific

---

[155] See chapter 2, section V, in this volume.
[156] International Peace Academy, *Peacekeeper's Handbook* (Pergamon Press: New York, 1984).

**Table 4.1.** The *Nordic UN Tactical Manual* situation schedule for the use of force

| Activity | Use of armed force | Negotiation | Use of non-armed force |
| --- | --- | --- | --- |
| 1 | Warning | Contact | Block, close, stop |
| 2 | 1st warning shot | Contact | Enclose |
| 3 | 2nd warning shot | Contact | Superiority of [*sic*] |
| 4 | Fire for effect | Contact | Press, push on |

*Source:* Joint Nordic Committee for Military UN Matters (NORDSAMFN), *Nordic UN Tactical Manual* (Gummerus Kirjapaino Oy: Jyväskylä, 1992).

arrangements' accepted by both parties involved in a dispute 'have been, or in the opinion of the commander on the spot, are about to be violated'.[157] The *Handbook* fails to mention the post-1973 conception of 'defence of the mission', thereby reflecting the conservative spectrum of peacekeeping opinion. It also neglects to deal with the tortured question of what peacekeepers should do if they witness gross violations of human rights, or even 'ordinary' attacks on civilians, much less flagrant violations of a peace agreement or an internationally agreed frontier.

## Nordic peacekeeping doctrine

The other repositories of peacekeeping experience, including in relation to the use of force, were the Nordic countries, Denmark, Finland, Norway and Sweden, all of them active in peacekeeping from its inception. Many other countries looked on them as peacekeepers par excellence and sought their advice when first offering contingents for UN peacekeeping. Nordic UN tactical manuals were thus used to train peacekeepers not just from the Nordic countries but from a wide variety of others.[158] The principles they established for the conduct of peacekeeping were all eminently sensible—firmness, impartiality, clarity of intention, anticipation, recognition of the host government's authority and integration of the force.[159] The manuals reflect the Nordic countries' conservative, almost proprietorial view of peacekeeping dogma.

What is remarkable is how unsophisticated, incomplete and often incoherent with regard to the use of force issue the manuals are, even as late as the 1992

---

[157] *Peacekeeper's Handbook* (note 156), p. 58. The full list is as follows: '(*a*) when compelled to act in self-defence: (*b*) when the safety of the Force or its members is in jeopardy; (*c*) when attempts by force are made to compel a withdrawal from a position which has been occupied under orders from their commanders, or to infiltrate and envelop such positions as are deemed necessary by their commanders for them to hold, thus jeopardizing their safety; (*d*) when attempts by force are made to disarm them; (*e*) when attempts by force are made to prevent them from carrying out their responsibilities as ordered by their commanders; (*f*) when a violation by force against United Nations premises takes place; (*g*) when attempts are made to arrest or abduct UN personnel, civil or military; and (*h*) when specific arrangements accepted by both parties involved in the dispute have been, or in the opinion of the commander on the spot, are about to be violated'.

[158] Joint Nordic Committee for Military UN Matters (NORDSAMFN), *Nordic UN Tactical Manual* (Gummerus Kirjapaino Oy: Jyväskylä, Finland, 1992), vols 1 and 2.

[159] *Nordic UN Tactical Manual* (note 158), vol. 1, p. 27.

editions, despite years of Nordic experience in the field. Table 4.1, a 'situation schedule' for the use of force, is illustrative. Even conceding language difficulties, some of the terms used, such as 'non-armed force' and the apparently oxymoronic 'non-violent use of force', border on the incomprehensible. Since English is the common language used by Nordic peacekeepers in their training and in most UN peacekeeping operations, this is perplexing.

While repeating the mantra that force is to be used as a last resort and as little as possible, the manuals contain two different sets of rules for when force might be used in self-defence which are confusing and overlapping. They also fail to deal with any of the real-life dilemmas that are likely to be faced by peacekeepers, such as whether to protect non-uniformed UN personnel, whether to prevent civilians from being massacred or what to do when repeated violations of an agreement occur. They contain no warnings about the risks of using force to compel local parties to do the UN's bidding, the difficulties of 'pre-emptive self-defence' or the subtleties of interpositional techniques. There is no mention of how far 'defence of the mission' or the principle of freedom of movement could and should be taken by peacekeepers. In any event, these traditional rules, even if they had been well expressed, would have been no match for the new demands on peacekeeping which arose at the end of the cold war.

By this time other countries had also clearly gained much experience in peacekeeping. However, there is little evidence that they established peacekeeping doctrines or training programmes. Short of sending their troops to the Nordic training schools, most simply briefed their troops immediately prior to departure, but without formal training. This was the situation when the cold war suddenly ended and a new era of UN peacekeeping began.

# 5. After the cold war: use-of-force dilemmas resurface

With the end of the cold war and the ushering in of a purported 'new world order', peacekeeping burgeoned. Freed of the shackles of Security Council vetoes and hypersensitivity to the sovereign affairs of states, it suddenly became the conflict resolution tool of choice. However, the old dilemmas about when and how to use force soon resurfaced, as the UN increasingly became involved in attempting to end brutal civil wars and engage in nation-building.

## I. The immediate post-cold war missions and the use of force

Between April 1989 and the end of 1992 the Security Council authorized several operations involving armed peacekeepers—the UN Transitional Authority in Cambodia (UNTAC), UNPROFOR in Croatia and Bosnia, and the UN Operation in Somalia (UNOSOM I)—which, although they did not, by and large, use force beyond self-defence, provided the first inklings that the issue of the use of force would again become significant.[1]

### The UN Transitional Authority in Cambodia (1991–94)

The UN Transitional Authority in Cambodia (UNTAC) was the first case after the end of the cold war in which the possibility of the use of force was seriously raised. Comprising at its peak 22 874 international personnel, including

[1] Several new missions were established in 1988–89, but all were small and involved mostly unarmed military observers. The use-of-force issue did not therefore arise. The first new mission after UNIFIL was the UN Good Offices Mission in Afghanistan and Pakistan (UNGOMAP), established in May 1988 and more a diplomatic than military affair. It was followed by a traditional border-monitoring operation, the UN Iran–Iraq Military Observer Group (UNIIMOG), established in Aug. 1988, which was mandated to observe the ceasefire between Iran and Iraq at the end of their protracted war but mostly comprised unarmed military observers. In Jan. 1989 came the first UN Angola Verification Mission (UNAVEM I), designed to verify the withdrawal of Cuban troops from Angola, also involving only unarmed military observers. In Nov. 1989 another unarmed observer mission, the United Nations Observer Group in Central America (ONUCA), was deployed.

The UN Transitional Assistance Group (UNTAG) in Namibia (1989–90) was the first comprehensive UN peace operation since the Congo. The use-of-force issue arose in this case not because UN peacekeepers, who had barely begun deploying, became involved, but because the UN had to authorize South Africa to use force against the South West African Peoples Organization (SWAPO), which had broken the ceasefire and had begun infiltrating its forces in large numbers back into Namibia from Angola. Another large peacekeeping operation with a significant armed military component, the UN Operation in Mozambique (UNOMOZ), was deployed in Dec. 1992, but essentially did not contribute to the use-of-force debate. It accomplished its mission peaceably and successfully, and departed in Dec. 1994. It is not considered further in this volume. In Feb. 1993 the Security Council expanded the mandate of the UN Iraq–Kuwait Observation Mission (UNIKOM), deployed on the Iraq–Kuwait border, from border monitoring to a mandate designed to deter and if necessary deal with small-scale Iraqi incursions, presumably using force if necessary. Since it had its basis in a Chapter VII enforcement action, it was an unusual blend of traditional peacekeeping and enforcement. To date it has not had to use force to fulfil its mandate.

approximately 16 000 troops, UNTAC would be the largest peacekeeping force since ONUC.[2] It was deployed to assist in implementing the 1991 Paris Peace Accords.[3] The mission, like ONUC, was complex. There were many parties involved; there had been a long-running civil war between indigenous forces backed by external powers; and the compliance of one of the parties, the genocidal Khmer Rouge (KR), was in great doubt as the peace operation began.

UNTAC's mandate, like that of the UN Transitional Assistance Group (UNTAG) in Namibia, was to monitor a ceasefire, assist in the cantonment, disarmament and demobilization of armed personnel, and organize an election to create a new, democratic government. Unlike the Namibia operation, however, UNTAC was to have administrative oversight of the country, protect and foster human rights, and attend to the return of refugees and economic reconstruction and rehabilitation.[4] A Supreme National Council, comprising representatives of all the parties, was required to delegate to the UN 'all powers necessary to ensure the implementation' of the Paris Peace Accords.[5] Taken to its logical extreme this could have meant that UNTAC could have enforced its will on the Cambodians, including, presumably, by military means. However, as James Schear notes, although 'somewhat at odds with the tenor of the Paris Accords', the Security Council at no time conferred on UNTAC the 'compulsory authority' provided for in Chapter VII of the UN Charter.[6]

The rules governing UNTAC's use of force were the standard UN rules. UNTAC was authorized to use force in self-defence and in resisting forceful attempts to prevent it from accomplishing its mission. Significantly, and no doubt reflecting Cambodia's tortured history, UNTAC's ROE for the first time in a UN operation specifically identified the prevention of 'crimes against humanity' as warranting the use of 'all available means', including armed force.[7] Such crimes would include executions and attacks on refugee columns, cantonment areas or combatants who had laid down their weapons, including prisoners of war under UNTAC's care. The force commander, Lieutenant-General John Sanderson of Australia, also assumed that the ROE permitted defence of 'anyone going about their legitimate business under the Paris Agreement', including

[2] For a comprehensive account of UNTAC see Findlay, T., *Cambodia: The Legacy and Lessons of UNTAC*, SIPRI Research Report no. 9 (Oxford University Press: Oxford, 1995).

[3] The Paris Peace Accords consisted of 4 documents: (*a*) the Final Act of the Paris Conference on Cambodia, 23 Oct. 1991; (*b*) the Agreement on a Comprehensive Political Settlement of the Cambodia Conflict, Paris, 23 Oct. 1991; (*c*) the Agreement Concerning the Sovereignty, Independence, Territorial Integrity and Inviolability, Neutrality and National Unity of Cambodia, Paris, 31 Oct. 1991; and (*d*) the Declaration on the Rehabilitation and Reconstruction of Cambodia, Paris, 23 Oct. 1991. All were published as annexes to United Nations, Letter dated 91/10/30 from the permanent representatives of France and Indonesia to the United Nations addressed to the Secretary-General, UN document A/46/608, S/23177, 30 Oct. 1991. The texts are reproduced in Findlay (note 2), pp. 173–89.

[4] UN Security Council Resolution 745, 28 Feb. 1992.

[5] Agreement on a Comprehensive Political Settlement of the Cambodia Conflict (note 3), part 1, section III, article 6.

[6] Schear, J., 'Riding the tiger: the UN and Cambodia', ed. W. J. Durch, *UN Peacekeeping, American Policy, and the Uncivil Wars of the 1990s* (St Martin's Press: New York, 1996), p. 143.

[7] Schear (note 6), p. 145.

non-uniformed UN personnel and Cambodians.[8] He was quick to stress publicly, however, that none of this changed UNTAC's mission: 'The mission is not defending Cambodia. Therefore the UNTAC Military Component will not be drawn into internal security operations. Nor is the mission to defend the political process but we are in Cambodia to defend an electoral process'.[9]

## UNTAC and the use of force

Unlike UNTAG, UNTAC did use some force, but only in self-defence when fired on. Low-level ceasefire violations by both the KR and the State of Cambodia (SOC) forces occurred almost throughout the entire period of UNTAC's deployment, sometimes involving UNTAC in the crossfire. UNTAC invariably used direct negotiations and contacts with the parties' military representatives on the Mixed Military Working Group (MMWG) to end these transgressions. On at least one occasion it used the tried and proven peacekeeping method of interposing a company-sized unit between the two sides, which considerably calmed the situation.

In May 1992 a much-discussed confrontation took place between the KR and the SRSG, Yasushi Akashi of Japan, accompanied by the force commander, at a KR roadblock on the road to Pailin in north-west Cambodia. The two heads of mission had hoped that their presence would persuade the KR to reverse its earlier obstinately-held position and let a Dutch battalion deploy into the area, as provided for under the Paris Peace Accords, but, in what was widely seen as a humiliation for UNTAC, they were turned away at a bamboo pole across the road. UNTAC was criticized for not using force to drive its way through. However, Sanderson, who had fought in Viet Nam, recognized the futility of UNTAC joining a guerrilla war against the KR in its jungle redoubt.

Soon afterwards, French Brigadier-General Jean-Michel Loridon, UNTAC's deputy force commander, was relieved of his position after advocating the use of force against the KR.[10] Loridon was quoted as saying that he would accept the deaths of up to 200 soldiers, including his own, to end the KR threat once and for all. Akashi said he was startled by the general's remarks, since a military plan that cost 200 lives would be 'a failure, a bankruptcy, of a peacekeeping operation'. Notably, however, Akashi did not completely rule out the use of force but said rather: 'It's premature to consider military enforcement. That would change the rules of the game so completely. Some of the countries that have contributed might try to remove their troops. It is not a decision that should be made lightly'.[11]

---

[8] Sanderson, J. M. (Lt-Gen.), 'A review of recent peacekeeping operations', Paper presented to the Pacific Armies Management Seminar (PAMS) 18th Conference, Dacca, Jan. 1994, p. 8.

[9] Sanderson, J. M. (Lt-Gen.), 'Preparations for, deployment and conduct of peacekeeping operations: a Cambodia snapshot', Paper presented at the conference on UN Peacekeeping at the Crossroads, Canberra, 21–24 May 1993, p. 10.

[10] Findlay (note 2), p. 37; and United Nations, Second progress report of the Secretary-General on the United Nations Transitional Authority in Cambodia, UN document S/24578, 21 Sep. 1992, p. 5.

[11] Quoted in 'A Japanese envoy's impossible job: keeping the peace in Cambodia', New York Times, 4 Oct. 1992, p. IV-8.

Akashi has been reported as admitting that UNTAC initially interpreted self-defence in a very strict manner and that its troops failed to resist severe harassment from Khmer Rouge elements.[12] Uneven application by UNTAC military units of the mission's ROE created uncertainty among UNTAC civilian personnel, some of whom complained that the military seemed overly passive, even to the point of failing to defend UNTAC storage areas. In April 1993 a Japanese volunteer electoral officer, just before he was murdered, had appealed to Indonesian troops for protection; they told him that that was not their role.[13] When armed attacks became a serious impediment to the accomplishment of its duties, UNTAC started to actively defend itself, resulting in KR casualties. The inconsistency of application of the ROE by different contingents was a problem that plagued UNTAC until the end of its mission, despite Sanderson's best efforts. From UNTAC onwards, the importance of appropriate, credible and consistently applied ROE became a much-discussed element of the debate on the use of force by UN peacekeepers.

When the KR decided to boycott the UN-run elections scheduled for late May 1993, Sanderson, fearing a military attack to disrupt them, decided to redeploy UNTAC's Military Component to 'protect' the 'electoral process'. This was described as keeping a 'line of distance', both physically and psychologically, between KR areas and those where electoral preparations were taking place.[14] The new deployment was meant to: (a) act as a deterrent; (b) make more effective the protection of UNTAC activities through escorts and patrols; (c) ensure rapid reaction at potential trouble spots; and (d) permit direct contact and negotiation with those threatening the electoral process. In addition to establishing 12 local mobile reserves, Sanderson also created a Force Commander's Mobile Reserve on '60 minutes' notice to move.[15]

Initially, the new measures increased the number of peacekeepers in contested areas, leading the KR to initiate a 'cat-and-mouse game of taking peacekeepers hostage and then releasing them'.[16] These incidents were resolved not through the use of force but through discussions in the MMWG and between UNTAC's liaison officers and the parties, proving, says Sanderson, 'the power . . . of negotiation'.[17]

Perhaps most radically of all, and echoing the Namibia precedent somewhat, UNTAC also decided to allow the SOC forces and those of the other two parties (the Front Uni National pour un Cambodge Indépendent, Neutre, Pacifique et Coöpératif, FUNCINPEC, and the Khmer People's National Liberation Front, KPNLF) to repulse KR forces to secure the safety of polling stations. In April

---

[12] Eliasson, J., 'Humanitarian action and peacekeeping', eds O. A. Otunnu and M. W. Doyle, *Peacemaking and Peacekeeping for the New Century* (Rowman & Littlefield: Lanham, Md., 1998), p. 210.
[13] *Sydney Morning Herald*, 9 Apr. 1993, p. 5.
[14] UNTAC Electoral Component, Phnom Penh, *Free Choice: Electoral Component Newsletter*, no. 11 (15 Jan. 1993), pp. 12–14; and Schear, J. A., 'The case of Cambodia', eds D. C. F. Daniel and B. Hayes, *Beyond Traditional Peacekeeping* (Macmillan: London, 1995), pp. 294, 298.
[15] Sanderson (note 9), p. 12.
[16] Schear (note 14), p. 294.
[17] Sanderson (note 9), p. 12.

1993 the MMWG reached agreement with these parties on cooperative arrangements for the use of minimum force and proportionate response in providing such security,[18] thus binding them to the UN peacekeepers' use-of-force norms. In return, UNTAC was obliged to return some of the parties' cantoned weapons. This initiative allowed UNTAC to 'use the armed elements of three factions against the fourth in a way that did not jeopardize [the UN's] impartiality'.[19]

In February 1993 SOC forces launched an offensive against the KR in at least 10 provinces. UNTAC described it as the largest ceasefire violation it had registered, going 'beyond the SOC's right to defend itself against any hostile action' by the KR. Akashi reportedly proposed to UN Headquarters that UNTAC troops be stationed in a buffer zone between the two sides to end the fighting.[20] Sanderson apparently responded that it was impossible for his troops to fulfil such a role.[21] The USA also failed to react positively.[22] A situation which might have involved the use of force by UNTAC was thus avoided.

In March and April 1993 the KR stepped up its attacks on UNTAC troops.[23] In late March a Bangladeshi soldier became the first UN peacekeeper to die in Cambodia from enemy fire, when the KR launched a three-hour attack on his unit in the Angkor Chum district in the north-west. On 2 April the KR murdered three Bulgarian peacekeepers and wounded six others in Kompong Speu. UNTAC refused to be drawn into a military response.

The most politically sensitive casualty of the entire UNTAC mission occurred on 8 April, one day into the official election campaign, when the Japanese volunteer and his Khmer interpreter were killed, allegedly by the KR, in Kompong Thom province.[24] Japan had endured an agonizing constitutional debate over the dispatch of its peacekeepers to Cambodia—the first time Japanese troops had been abroad since World War II. Under public pressure, the Japanese Defence Minister threatened to withdraw all Japanese personnel from Cambodia if any more were harmed.

Australian Foreign Minister Gareth Evans made matters worse by declaring that Australia would consider withdrawing its troops—who, critically, provided UNTAC's communications system—if there were a 'major, systematic, full-frontal assault on the UN peacekeepers or on other parties to the peace accords'.[25] This, along with Japanese withdrawal, could have caused UNTAC's collapse. Evans later 'clarified' his statement, saying that there was 'no question of Australia taking any unilateral action to withdraw, however much the situation might deteriorate'.[26] However, the damage had been done. Evans had

---

[18] Akashi, Y., 'The challenges faced by UNTAC', *Japan Review of International Affairs*, summer 1993, p. 197.

[19] Farris, K., 'UN peacekeeping in Cambodia: on balance, a success', *Parameters*, vol. 24, no. 1 (1994), p. 47.

[20] *The Australian*, 4 Feb. 1993, p. 8.

[21] *The Age* (Melbourne), 5 Feb. 1993, p. 8.

[22] *Weekend Australian*, 6 Feb. 1993, p. 15.

[23] Findlay (note 2), p. 48.

[24] It later transpired that he had been killed by an SOC soldier over the issue of electoral jobs.

[25] *The Age* (Melbourne), 12 Apr. 1993, p. 1.

[26] *Canberra Times*, 22 Apr. 1993, p. 12.

violated one of the first precepts of deterrence (in this case the presence of an armed peacekeeping force): do not advertise in advance the conditions that would cause your bluff to be called.

The incident indicated the fragility of even relatively large peace operations when faced with the prospect of casualties, which in turn constrains their ability to use force, even in self-defence, with its attendant risks of creating even more casualties. As the experience of Somalia was to demonstrate, in these circumstances the pressures for withdrawal, rather than use of force, are considerable.

In the event, the elections proceeded smoothly. This relieved UNTAC of the extraordinarily difficult decision about how to respond to an all-out armed KR attack on the electoral process and on its personnel. Some of the painful dilemmas that were to face UNOSOM II in Somalia were thus avoided. Sanderson has intimated that this was due as much to luck as to good management.[27]

## Should UNTAC have moved to peace enforcement?

To turn UNTAC into an enforcement mechanism would have required a considerable change of mandate. Neither the participating states nor the Security Council were likely to countenance it; China would almost certainly have vetoed it. Moreover, more rigorous enforcement was not deemed strictly necessary and could have been provocative and counterproductive. The KR had neither renounced the Paris Peace Accords nor demanded UNTAC's removal. Total breakdown of the peace process, as was to happen repeatedly in Angola, was not in prospect.

Even if the political problems of giving UNTAC an enforcement role had been overcome, daunting military ones would have remained. UNTAC was not equipped or deployed to use force except in self-defence, and an aggressive reaction risked igniting a widespread military confrontation. Gerald Segal and Mats Berdal cite UNTAC's lack of interoperable equipment, the absence of close air support, the dearth of adequate tactical communications and tracking equipment, and the effective absence of logistical support.[28] The mission had, for instance, only 26 helicopters. On the other hand, a larger military presence and a more resolute military posture from the outset, including not necessarily the use of force but certainly the implicit threat of force, might have cowed the KR and the government of Hun Sen into greater compliance at an early stage. Initially because it was deployed so late, and then because of an apparent unwillingness to use its powers to the limit, UNTAC failed to take advantage of its greatest assets—its international character and its Security Council mandate. More specifically, it failed to capitalize on the element of surprise, the combatants' unfamiliarity with the UN and the deterrent effect of its modern military capabilities (especially its mobility and communications), however unsuited they were to peace enforcement.

---

[27] Findlay (note 2), p. 134.
[28] Segal, G. and Berdal, M., 'The Cambodian dilemma', *Jane's Intelligence Review*, vol. 5, no. 3 (Mar. 1993), p. 132.

As Nick Warner puts it, there is an element of 'theatre or symbolism' involved in a UN force asserting its visibility and legitimacy.[29] In situations where the consent of the parties is fragile or tentative it is even more important that visibility and legitimacy be established as soon as possible. Akashi himself concedes that the deterioration of the security situation in early 1993 might have been avoided through a 'timely request for a few more infantry battalions and the addition of more APCs and helicopters, which gave mobility, and through a clearer definition of UNTAC's right of self-defense'.[30] However, overall, the UNTAC leadership knew the mission's limits: both Akashi and Sanderson believed that 'political pressure applied by external patrons would do far more to influence the behavior of various Khmer factions than ill-advised excursions by UNTAC into the realm of peace enforcement'.[31]

## The UN Protection Force (1992–95)

Just as it was mounting one of its largest missions ever, in Cambodia, the UN was required to turn its attention to the collapse of the former Yugoslavia. While Slovenia was left to go its own way after a brief war, the Yugoslav National Army (JNA) attempted to carve out Serb-only areas in Croatia, while at the same time defending itself against Croatian irregulars seeking to drive it from the country. When the UN brokered a ceasefire in Croatia on 23 November 1991, most of the JNA moved to Bosnia, which itself soon erupted in an even more complex war than that in Croatia. After the Bosnian Government declared its sovereignty in October 1991 a three-way conflict began between the Muslim-dominated government, the Bosnian Serbs, inspired and supported by Serbia, and the Bosnian Croats, supported by Croatia.

Into this nationalist and ethnic cauldron the UN Security Council deployed UNPROFOR, which was to evolve over the coming three years into a complex mix of humanitarian intervention, peacekeeping and peace enforcement. It was established by the Security Council in February 1992 for an initial period of 12 months as 'an interim arrangement to create conditions of peace and security required for the negotiation of an overall settlement of the Yugoslav crisis'.[32] Its mandate at first related only to Croatia, but in June 1992 was extended to include Bosnia[33] and in December 1992 to include the Former Yugoslav Republic of Macedonia (although its personnel there initially comprised only civilian police monitors rather than troops).[34]

---

[29] Warner, N., 'Cambodia: lessons of UNTAC for future peacekeeping operations', Paper presented to an international seminar on UN Peacekeeping at the Crossroads, Canberra, 21–24 Mar. 1993, p. 3.

[30] Akashi, Y., 'The challenges of peacekeeping in Cambodia: lessons to be learned', Paper presented to the School of International and Public Affairs, Columbia University, New York, Nov. 1993, p. 24.

[31] Schear (note 6), p. 174.

[32] UN Security Council Resolution 743, 21 Feb. 1992.

[33] UN Security Council Resolution 758, 5 June 1992.

[34] UN Security Council Resolution 795, 11 Dec. 1992.

In terms of their use of force, the UN operations in the three parts of the former Yugoslavia were completely different.[35] While that in Macedonia used practically no force, either in self-defence or otherwise, the operation in Bosnia used substantial force, both in self-defence and beyond. The mission in Croatia lay somewhere between the two, mostly adhering to traditional UN use-of-force norms but straying beyond them occasionally, including on one notable occasion. The Bosnia mission after 1993 is largely dealt with in chapter 7, while that in Macedonia is considered in relation to the issue of preventive deployment in chapter 8, section III. As the launching in 1992 and the early performance in 1992–93 of UNPROFOR in Croatia and Bosnia had a crucial impact on early UN reconsideration of the use-of-force issue, and on the feverish activity in the Security Council and the Secretariat in dealing with multiple missions simultaneously, they are initially considered here.

## UNPROFOR in Croatia

Following its establishment in February 1992, UNPROFOR was deployed in parts of Croatia designated as United Nations Protected Areas (UNPAs), where Serbs constituted the majority or a substantial minority of the population and where inter-ethnic tensions had led to armed conflict. UNPROFOR's mandate was to ensure that the UNPAs were demilitarized through the withdrawal or disbandment of all armed forces in them and that UNPA residents were protected from armed attack. UNPROFOR was authorized to control access to the UNPAs, ensure that they remained demilitarized and monitor the local police to ensure non-discrimination and protection of human rights. Outside the UNPAs, UNPROFOR's military observers were to verify the withdrawal of all JNA and irregular forces from Croatia, other than those disbanded and demobilized.

In June 1992 the mandate was enlarged by authorizing UNPROFOR to monitor 'pink zones'—areas of Croatia previously controlled by the JNA and populated largely by Serbs, but which were outside the UNPAs and where the authority of the Croatian Government was now to be inserted.[36] In August 1992 UNPROFOR was further authorized to control the entry of civilians into the UNPAs and perform immigration and customs functions at UNPA borders which coincided with international frontiers.[37] The mandate in Croatia was enlarged for the third time in October 1992, when UNPROFOR was authorized to monitor the demilitarization of the Prevlaka Peninsula near Dubrovnik and assume control of the strategic Peruca dam in one of the pink zones.[38]

---

[35] In Mar. 1995 the 3 operations—in Croatia, Bosnia and Macedonia—acquired 3 different names and were grouped under an umbrella mission, the UN Peace Forces (UNPF). UN Security Council resolutions 981, 982 and 983, 31 Mar. 1995. The Croatia mission was titled the UN Confidence Restoration Operation in Croatia (UNCRO), while that in Macedonia was known as the UN Preventive Deployment Force (UNPREDEP). The operation in Bosnia retained the name UNPROFOR.

[36] UN Security Council Resolution 762, 30 June 1992.

[37] UN Security Council Resolution 769, 7 Aug. 1992.

[38] UN Security Council Resolution 779, 6 Oct. 1992.

UNPROFOR was, at least in Croatia, intended to be a substantial military force. It was originally authorized to deploy 12 enlarged infantry battalions (10 400, all ranks); headquarters, logistics and other support elements totalling approximately 2480 (all ranks); and 100 military observers.[39] It was also to have 530 CivPols. By April 1992 it had an actual strength of 8332, including 7975 military personnel and a fully operational headquarters in the Bosnian capital, Sarajevo.[40]

Force Commander Jean Cot of France issued UNPROFOR's first ROE (applicable in both Croatia and, later, Bosnia) on 24 March 1992. He revised them on 19 July 1993 to give more precise definitions and to expand Annex D on cordon and search operations,[41] but basically his initial ROE remained operative until the end of the mission.[42] Intended to apply to all nations con-tributing to UNPROFOR, they authorized the use of force '*normally* [emphasis added] only in self-defence'. UNPROFOR troops could defend themselves and other UN personnel and, as in the UNTAC case, 'persons and areas under their protection against direct attack, acting always under the order of the senior officer/soldier at the scene'. Self-defence included resistance to attempts by forceful means to prevent UNPROFOR from discharging its duties under its mandate. UNPROFOR could also 'resist deliberate military or para-military incursions into the United Nations Protected Areas (UNPAs) or Safe Areas', although apparently this was only in the context of defending itself.

Beyond this, the use-of-force instructions were extremely complex, com-prising a general introduction and four annexes—annex A, 'Definitions'; annex B, ROE; annex C, 'Instructions to military personnel'; and annex D, 'Principles of cordon and search operations'. They set out alternative actions that might be taken when encountering different scenarios in the 'normal, daily situation'. Annex C was essentially a complex 'decision tree' which is difficult to fathom even after prolonged study, let alone in an emergency. For example, in response to a hostile act involving the use of fire, sequential options were offered. Option A was to take immediate protection measures, observe, report and warn the aggressor of intent to use force, 'while demonstrating resolve with appropriate means, including warning shots'. Option B, to be taken if firing did not cease and life was threatened, allowed fire to be opened on order. Within options A and B, the force could withdraw, stay in place and defend, or 'move through to escape'. Warning shots were permitted as part of 'challenging' pro-cedures. The only circumstance in which it was permissible to open fire without challenging was in self-defence, 'when an attack by an aggressor comes so unexpectedly that even a moment's delay' could lead to death or injury. Rule

---

[39] United Nations, *The Blue Helmets: A Review of United Nations Peace-keeping*, 3rd edn (UN Department of Public Information: New York, 1996), p. 514.

[40] Its headquarters was later moved to Zagreb, Croatia.

[41] UNPROFOR, Rules of engagement, Force Commander's Policy Directive no. 13, issued 24 Mar. 1992, rev. 19 July 1993, reproduced in appendix 2 in this volume; and UNPROFOR, Outgoing fax, from Force Commander Gen. Jean Cot, UNPROFOR HQ, to all UN personnel, 19 July 1993.

[42] William Durch has established that they were used in Bosnia at least up to Dec. 1994. Durch, W. J. and Schear, J. A., 'Faultlines: UN operations in the former Yugoslavia', ed. Durch (note 6), p. 262, fn. 57.

no. 5, however, seemed to sweep away these niceties by asserting that: 'Anytime, in self-defence situations', the force 'could take immediate protection measures and/or return fire without challenging'. 'Minimum necessary and proportional force up to and including use of fire' could be used to disarm paramilitaries, civilians and soldiers if failure to disarm them would prevent UNPROFOR from carrying out its tasks, if a hostile act was committed, or even (as later in Somalia) 'if hostile *intent* [emphasis added] so warrants'. 'Hostile intent' was defined as an action which 'appears to be preparatory to an aggressive action'.

The UNPROFOR ROE seemed unnecessarily complicated—a reflection presumably of their origins as a compromise between mostly British and French practices. Bruce Berkowitz notes that they were much more complicated than typical US ROE, which are approximately one page in length and do not use the 'option' approach. US military commanders, 'familiar with the micromanagement problems encountered in Viet Nam and the disasters caused in part by the ambiguous orders issued in the 1983 Lebanon peacekeeping operation', tend, he records, to insist on simple and concise ROE.[43]

The language used was also quite different from that of previous UN ROE, indicating that yet again a UN mission drew up its own rules without reference to previous UN templates. William Durch and James Schear claim that the ROE for cordon and search operations in annex D were the only part of UNPROFOR's ROE that allowed more 'latitude' than the peacekeeping norm.[44] For Berkowitz that was the main problem: while the ROE might work in a true peacekeeping operation, they were being used in a situation in which there was no peace to keep and thereby left the UN vulnerable: 'UN forces cannot carry out offensive operations without specific approval; must use the minimum force necessary; can use their weapons only as a last resort; cannot retaliate; and must cease fire when an opponent ceases fire. Thus, hostile forces (usually Bosnian Serbs in this case) can ratchet up their provocation just under the threshold beyond which UNPROFOR can use force'.[45] Overall, the UNPROFOR ROE appeared more flexible than any other UN ROE previously issued. They were clearly inappropriate in a situation in which the local parties refused to accept the basic premises of peacekeeping and in effect only respected peace enforcement.

In spite of its name, UNPROFOR's troops were not authorized to provide protection to the civilian population. This was a cause of much subsequent misunderstanding in Croatia and Bosnia on the part of the local population and international public opinion.

In contrast to its behaviour in Bosnia, UNPROFOR in Croatia by and large adopted a conservative interpretation of its ROE and the UN's standard use-of-force norms. Although in 1992–93 it was able to help ensure the complete

---

[43] Berkowitz, B. D., 'Rules of engagement for UN peacekeeping forces in Bosnia', *Orbis*, vol. 38, no. 3 (fall 1994), p. 636.
[44] Durch and Schear (note 42), p. 210.
[45] Berkowitz (note 43), p. 636.

withdrawal of the JNA from the country, and until January 1993 help prevent a recurrence of hostilities in the UNPAs and pink zones, the 'uncooperative attitude'[46] of the local Serb authorities stopped it demilitarizing the UNPAs and disarming the Serb irregulars. Despite the possibility of using force to achieve the latter objectives, UNPROFOR refrained from doing so. It was too weak militarily and too thinly deployed to apply force successfully.[47]

In January 1993 the Croatian Army launched an offensive in the southern part of UNPROFOR's Sector South and adjacent pink zones, broke into several UN weapon storage areas under joint control in the UNPAs and removed heavy weapons, and captured the Peruca dam. Despite being attacked in the process, UNPROFOR by and large acted as a traditional peacekeeping force in declining to use force to resist such moves, except *in extremis*, in self-defence. One exception was the Princess Patricia's Canadian Light Infantry battalion, which reportedly dealt 'forcibly' with Croatian incursions along the Zagreb–Belgrade highway and was subsequently cited as an example of 'offensive action' in peace operations.[48]

Croatian President Franjo Tudjman, attempting to use UNPROFOR for his own ends, demanded that it be given an enforcement mandate in order to end the Serbs' refusal to demilitarize and disarm. For their part the Serbs accused UNPROFOR of betrayal for being unwilling to protect them, and began rearming and remobilizing in response to the Croatian military moves. The new UN Secretary-General, Boutros Boutros-Ghali, rejected calls for a more robust UN presence, arguing that an enforcement capability would be a 'fundamental contradiction of the nature and purpose of UNPROFOR's deployment in Croatia, as a peace-keeping force entrusted with the implementation of a plan agreed by all the parties'.[49] He also opposed withdrawing UNPROFOR, instead opting for strengthening its military capability but, paradoxically, only when a more secure peace agreement had been reached.[50]

On 9 September, after several serious incidents in the UNPAs and pink zones, the Croatian Army once again carried out a military incursion into the Medak area, where three Serb villages were seized. In this case Canadian and French peacekeepers used force to interpose themselves between Croat and Serb forces.[51] Billed subsequently by the press as Canada's 'biggest battle since the Korean War', it left four Canadian and seven French soldiers wounded, but reportedly 50 Croat casualties. Largely kept secret from the Canadian public by a nervous government, it earned the Princess Patricia's Canadian Light Infantry

---

[46] *The Blue Helmets*, 3rd edn (note 39), p. 515.

[47] Cervenak, C. M., 'Lessons of the past: experiences in peace operations', eds A. H. Chayes and G. T. Raach, *Peace Operations: Developing an American Strategy* (National Defense University Press: Washington, DC, 1995), p. 46.

[48] Bergstrand, B. M. (Maj.), 'Operations other than war: the Canadian perspective', eds A. Woodcock and D. David, *Analytic Approaches to the Study of Conflict* (Canadian Peacekeeping Press: Clementsport, 1996), p. 109.

[49] Quoted in *The Blue Helmets*, 3rd edn (note 39), p. 515.

[50] *The Blue Helmets*, 3rd edn (note 39), p. 517.

[51] Last, D., *Theory, Doctrine and Practice of Conflict De-Escalation in Peacekeeping Operations* (Canadian Peacekeeping Press: Clementsport, 1997), pp. 105–107.

a unit citation from the UN force commander.[52] Far from simply using force in self-defence when attacked, on this occasion the French and Canadian 'peacckeepers' 'virtually attacked through the Serb lines, rolled up to the Croat lines and physically pushed both sides back to establish a buffer zone'.[53]

In October 1993 the Security Council extended the mandate of UNPROFOR in Croatia, this time under Chapter VII of the UN Charter, not to permit it to engage in peace enforcement but to ensure its 'security' and 'freedom of movement'.[54] In September 1994 the close air support which NATO had been providing to UNPROFOR in Bosnia was extended to Croatia, in theory to enhance the peacekeepers' security.[55]

In March 1995 UNPROFOR in Croatia became the UN Confidence Restoration Operation (UNCRO),[56] but it had no more success than its predecessor in restoring peace to the country. Its fate was sealed in August of that year when Croatian Government forces simply seized the remaining Serb areas supposedly under UN protection in the Krajina, a large area of southern Croatia. Over 100 UN observation posts were overrun and destroyed. Croatian troops and Serb irregulars fired directly and indirectly on such posts, used peacekeepers as human shields, arrested and temporarily disarmed them, and stole UN equipment. Four peacekeepers were killed and others wounded. The force commander called in a NATO air presence to 'deter' hostile action against UNCRO, but to no avail.

## UNPROFOR in Bosnia

As war broke out in Bosnia, UNPROFOR found itself scrambling to deal with that conflict too. This was partly because Sarajevo, where UNPROFOR was headquartered, was soon besieged by Serb forces and subject to incessant mortar attack and shelling, and partly because international public opinion demanded that something be done to relieve the increasingly appalling humanitarian situation. UNPROFOR began by trying to protect and provide humanitarian relief to the suffering civilian population and to provide a modicum of assistance to the belligerents in implementing their erratic and inadequate peace efforts. Thereafter its role was expanded piecemeal in response to events on the ground through a relentless series of Security Council resolutions that Boutros-Ghali himself described as 'mission creep'.[57] It ended up, in league with NATO, engaging in peace enforcement.

Unlike other peacekeeping operations, it was not deployed fully formed and en masse, but was continuously enlarged, at least on paper, by the Security Council. It began with 50 military observers, a Canadian mechanized battalion

[52] 'Canada's secret battle', *Ottawa Citizen*, 7 Oct. 1996.
[53] Maloney, S. M., 'Insights into Canadian peacekeeping doctrine', *Military Review*, Mar./Apr. 1996, p. 22.
[54] UN Security Council Resolution 871, 4 Oct. 1993.
[55] UN Security Council Resolution 908, 31 Mar. 1994.
[56] See note 35.
[57] Boutros-Ghali, B., *Unvanquished: A US–UN Saga* (I. B. Tauris: New York, 1999), p. 40.

and a company of French marines poached from the Croatia mission. In early July 1992 the authorized strength of UNPROFOR in Bosnia was only a reinforced battalion of some 1000 personnel, 60 military observers, additional military and civilian staff at the Sarajevo headquarters, 40 CivPols, and a number of technical personnel, engineers and airport staff.[58]

Bosnian President Alija Izetbegovic originally requested a 'preventive' deployment of 2000–3000 peacekeepers and then, as conditions deteriorated, a UN enforcement operation of 10 000–15 000, supported by air power, to 'restore order'.[59] Boutros-Ghali was reluctant to consider either. One of his principal advisers, Marrack Goulding, UN Under Secretary-General for Political Affairs, warned that: 'The peacekeepers will come back in body bags'.[60] In April and again in May 1992 Boutros-Ghali reported to the Security Council that the Bosnian conflict was not 'susceptible to the peacekeeping treatment'.[61] He pointed to the lack of agreement among the hostile parties on a workable mandate and warned that disrespect for the UN was already at such a level that: 'These are not conditions which permit a United Nations peace-keeping operation to make an effective contribution'.[62] Presciently, he privately told the European Union's negotiator, Lord Carrington, that he feared the UN becoming involved in a contradiction in terms—'peacekeeping requiring complete impartiality toward the parties and peace enforcement against one party' (which he— incorrectly—assumed would be a 'first' for the UN). He admits fearing that what the Congo had done to Hammarskjöld, Yugoslavia would do to him.[63]

The reluctance of the Secretary-General and several key members of the Security Council to become involved in Bosnia was reflected in the first Council resolution on the Bosnian situation. Resolution 752 of 15 May 1992, while quixotically calling on the non-Bosnian Government forces to withdraw and/or disband, asked only that the Secretary-General keep under review the possible deployment of a UN peacekeeping force to assist in disarmament and in the placing of heavy weapons under international monitoring, and to protect humanitarian relief efforts. Boutros-Ghali noted that this was only likely to be possible in the context of an overall peace settlement and advocated instead that a non-UN force, presumably led by NATO, be deployed.[64] Neither the USA nor the European countries were prepared to contemplate such a move at this stage.

Yet the Security Council needed to be seen to be doing something as a vicious ethnic civil war, characterized by an age-old activity with a new

---

[58] *The Blue Helmets*, 3rd edn (note 39), p. 522.

[59] Leurdijk, D. A., *The United Nations and NATO in Former Yugoslavia, 1991–1996: Limits to Diplomacy and Force* (Netherlands Atlantic Commission: The Hague, 1996), p. 22.

[60] Boutros-Ghali (note 57), p. 38.

[61] Boutros-Ghali (note 57), p. 40. Indeed, 40 military observers deployed in the Mostar region were withdrawn by the UN in May when their position became untenable. *The Blue Helmets*, 3rd edn (note 39), p. 522.

[62] United Nations, Report of the Secretary-General pursuant to Security Council Resolution 749 (1992), UN document S/23836, 24 Apr. 1992; and Further report of the Secretary-General pursuant to Security Council Resolution 749 (1992), UN document S/23900, 12 May 1992.

[63] Boutros-Ghali (note 57), pp. 42, 38.

[64] Boutros-Ghali (note 57), p. 41.

moniker—ethnic cleansing—engulfed the country. On 5 June UNPROFOR managed to negotiate a limited ceasefire around Sarajevo. Despite widely held misgivings, in Resolution 758 of 8 June the Security Council tasked the UN force with ensuring the security and functioning of Sarajevo Airport, assisting in the delivery of humanitarian assistance to Sarajevo and its environs, verifying the agreed withdrawal of anti-aircraft weapons from within range of the airport and monitoring the agreed concentration of heavy weapons in specified areas. On 17 July 1992 Lord Carrington managed to negotiate a Bosnia-wide ceasefire and agreement by the three sides to place all heavy weapons under international supervision, but the minuscule UNPROFOR could not handle such a task and UN member states were unwilling to boost its size to the 10 000 military observers that Boutros-Ghali estimated would be required. Nothing eventuated, as the ceasefire collapsed almost immediately—the first of many to do so.

In response to further fighting around Sarajevo, the Security Council tried to signal its determination to the parties, giving the first hint that the use of force beyond peacekeeping norms might be necessary. In Resolution 770 of 13 August 1992 it invoked Chapter VII of the UN Charter for the first time in relation to Bosnia, calling on states to 'take nationally or through regional agencies or arrangements *all measures necessary* [emphasis added] to facilitate delivery of humanitarian assistance to Sarajevo and other parts of Bosnia'. This language, which had been used to authorize activity by Coalition forces during the 1991 Persian Gulf War, and which implied that NATO or some other 'sheriff's posse' would now appear, was the first of many empty threats by the Security Council to use force in Bosnia. 'For a brief 30-day period . . . no legal constraints prevented any state in the world from taking action to break the siege of Sarajevo'.[65] Notably, the resolution had not authorized UNPROFOR itself to use force beyond self-defence for any purpose.

In the event NATO proved unwilling either to deploy ground forces under its command or to use air power to 'facilitate' humanitarian aid deliveries, especially since it was at that stage not operationally able to do so. The USA also backed away from the use of force, instead supporting British and French proposals to deploy NATO units to UNPROFOR.[66]

The Security Council, in Resolution 776 of 14 September, retreated from the enforcement operation implied in Resolution 770, deciding that the 'facilitation' of humanitarian aid should be entrusted to UNPROFOR,[67] not an international posse, but without using the phrase 'all measures necessary' or the backing of Chapter VI.[68] UNPROFOR in Bosnia would be expanded by up to five infantry battalions and a transport battalion, to a total of approximately 7000 troops, and acquire a separate sub-command under a major-general. The force was to be lightly armed, although Major-General Lewis MacKenzie, the Canadian first

[65] Caplan, R., *Post-Mortem on UNPROFOR*, London Defence Studies no. 33 (Brassey's for the Centre for Defence Studies, King's College, London: London, Feb. 1996), pp. 10–11.
[66] Durch and Schear (note 42), p. 228.
[67] United Nations, Report of the Secretary-General, UN document S/24540, 10 Sep. 1992.
[68] Berkowitz (note 43), p. 636.

chief of staff in Bosnia, did acquire TOW anti-tank missiles, without UN approval, to match the firepower of Serbian tanks surrounding Sarajevo Airport.[69] When Ottawa tried to foist more firepower on him he demurred: 'They didn't understand that too much force dooms you to confrontation and failure in a peacekeeping operation. We would have just enough if they approved what I'd requested; risk is unfortunately part of the game'.[70]

UNPROFOR's command and control arrangements were as makeshift as its composition.[71] In September 1992 a separate Bosnia and Herzegovina Command (BHC) was established which reported to the UNPROFOR military commander for all the UN missions in the former Yugoslavia and through him to the UN Secretary-General. One advantage that UNPROFOR in Bosnia had over other peace operations was that BHC headquarters was provided ready-made by NATO's Northern Army Group headquarters in Rheindahlen, Germany, so that all the staff were familiar with each other from the outset. NATO also provided all its initial equipment, although initially it had to scrape by with voluntary funding contributions. Command and control was, however, hindered throughout 1993 by the fact that the BHC operated from a small forward headquarters in Sarajevo in order to allow political consultations with local leaders and to be nearer the 'centre of gravity' of the conflict.[72] Much of the day-to-day control fell to the chief of staff, British Brigadier Roderick Cordy-Simpson, at the main UNPROFOR base at Kiseljak, 24 km from Sarajevo. Command and control was also hindered by the lack of a secure real-time communications system linking UNPROFOR's forces throughout Bosnia. In March 1995 UNPROFOR in Bosnia acquired its own force commander, but still reported through what was now called UN Peace Forces (UNPF)[73] headquarters in Zagreb, Croatia. A second chain of command was added when NATO air power became involved.[74]

Initially, unlike other UN peace operations, UNPROFOR had no civilian head of mission, apparently because the Secretary-General wished to keep his peacemaking and peacekeeping efforts separate.[75] The few UN civilians in the field had no authority to make decisions on behalf of the Secretary-General. Nor were there large civilian components as there were in other 'second-generation' UN missions. Hence there was no theatre political–military interface and no joint civil–military strategic plan.[76] In September 1992 UNPROFOR Director of

[69] MacKenzie, L. (Maj.-Gen.), *Peacekeeper: The Road to Sarajevo* (HarperCollins: London, 1994), p. 310.

[70] MacKenzie (note 69), p. 311.

[71] For a detailed discussion of the early arrangements see Berdal, M., 'United Nations peacekeeping in the former Yugoslavia', eds Daniel and Hayes (note 14), pp. 236–39.

[72] Ripley, T., 'Bosnia mission forces UN to grow with the times', *International Defence Review*, no. 5 (1994), p. 64.

[73] See note 35.

[74] See chapter 7 in this volume.

[75] Cyrus Vance, personal envoy of the Secretary-General from Oct. 1991 to Apr. 1993, was tasked with seeking a negotiated settlement to the conflict, while the first SRSG, Thorvald Stoltenberg, also UN envoy to the International Conference on the Former Yugoslavia, was based in Geneva.

[76] Ripley (note 72), p. 65; and Speech by Maj.-Gen. R. A. Cordy-Simpson, Chief of Staff, HQ, British Army on the Rhine, former Chief of Staff, United Nations, Bosnia (date and place unknown), p. 10.

Civil Affairs Cedric Thornberry acquired a second 'hat' as deputy chief of mission, but it was only in January 1994 that the situation was regularized with the appointment of Yasushi Akashi, former SRSG in Cambodia, as resident SRSG and head of mission. The normal peacekeeping chain of command applied from then on.

Boutros-Ghali's proposed concept of operation for UNPROFOR in Bosnia, approved by the Security Council, was to provide 'protective support' to humanitarian convoys, but only those run by the UN High Commissioner for Refugees (UNHCR), the lead humanitarian agency. It could also protect convoys of released civilian detainees if the International Committee of the Red Cross (ICRC) so requested. UNPROFOR would be deployed in four or five new zones in Bosnia, each with an infantry battalion group, whose headquarters would include civilian staff to undertake political and information functions and liaison with the UNHCR.[77] Typically for UN operations, no further detail was supplied.

Colonel Alistair Duncan, who commanded a British battalion in Bosnia for six months in 1993, saw his task as simply to 'provide an escort to the convoys from the UNHCR through our area of operations at their request. In addition we were to provide assistance to endangered people as required. That was all. There was no further close direction either from the UN or from the British Government or military'. He reflects that UNPROFOR's situation and tasks were unique and that there was no template from his experience or any other military commander's to use. Duncan thus devised his own concept of operations, which was to 'create the conditions whereby aid could be delivered into and through our area of responsibility'.[78] Although the use of force was part of his armoury, he was aware that in UN operations it was important to be 'particularly careful on how and when force is to be applied to meet a situation. Military force is a very blunt instrument. Before it is used, those who have to use it have to be very clear as to exactly what is to be achieved . . . Once used, force cannot be taken back and there are always ramifications'.[79]

As to ROE, UNPROFOR in Bosnia was supposed to use those promulgated for the Croatia operation by Cot in March 1992. Although they were apparently intended to cover every contingency, Cordy-Simpson found them too 'loose': 'It was probably as a direct reflection of our years of experience in Northern Ireland where we have had every last "i" dotted and "t" crossed in the rules of engagement'.[80] He was concerned that battalion commanders would use too much force. The power to give permission for the use of heavy mortars and anti-tank weapons was retained by the force commander, despite constant pleas from the battalion commanders to be allowed to use them. Cordy-Simpson says that he made it quite clear to them that: 'We were geared for a peacekeeping

---

[77] *The Blue Helmets*, 3rd edn (note 39), p. 523.
[78] Duncan, A. D. (Col), 'Operating in Bosnia', *IBRU Boundary and Security Bulletin*, vol. 2, no. 3 (Oct. 1994), pp. 47–48.
[79] Duncan (note 78), p. 53.
[80] Cordy-Simpson, R. A. (Maj.-Gen.), 'Keynote address', ed. A. Morrison, *The New Peacekeeping Partnership* (Canadian Peacekeeping Press: Clementsport, 1994), pp. 51–52.

mission whose function was to ensure that humanitarian aid was delivered, and that our forces had been structured for that task. We were not structured for war fighting, and had we used mortars against any side we would have been moving towards war fighting and away from peacekeeping'.[81]

The British issued an Orange Card to their troops which specified that fire could be returned in self-defence 'if the source can be identified; in doing so, they must attempt to minimize collateral damage and be mindful of the principle of proportionality. These rules apply equally to attacks by direct fire or indirect fire. Thus the 81-mm mortars, where deployed, could be used in self defence as a last resort to return indirect fire if the attacking weapons could be located'.[82] It was implicit in this British notion of self-defence that a soldier need not wait until he was attacked directly before acting to defend himself and others. The British Minister of State for the Armed Forces confirmed to the Parliamentary Defence Committee that the British soldier 'may as a last resort open fire in order to anticipate and prevent an act likely to endanger his life'.[83] Moreover, according to the British Government, in some cases a soldier may be justified in responding to a sniper's rifle fire by use of a 'superior' weapon, such as a cannon mounted on a Warrior armoured vehicle.[84]

From the outset, UNPROFOR's mission in Bosnia was quixotic. The Security Council had inserted a relatively lightly armed, purportedly impartial UN force with a limited humanitarian mandate but an increasingly intrusive presence into a vicious civil war in which populations and the means of sustaining them were either targets or tools of warfare. MacKenzie recalls sitting in his bunker under fire reading a Security Council resolution and saying: 'Are these people out of their minds? What do they want me to do?'[85] Then, he says, 'you finally figured out what they wanted you to do, but they didn't provide the resources'.

Governments were reluctant to mandate a normal peacekeeping force since key elements of a normal peacekeeping scenario were missing. Notably, there was no peace to keep. Fighting continued to rage unchecked. No comprehensive ceasefire was ever adhered to by all the parties all of the time. Unlike most peacekeeping operations, UNPROFOR had to create the conditions for its own success by negotiating ceasefires with the parties, often repeatedly, simply in order to operate.

Consent to UNPROFOR's presence and activities varied from shaky to non-existent. It was obtained from some of the parties (or elements of some of the parties) for the UN's humanitarian activities, but it was frequently withdrawn. Consent for UNPROFOR's initial deployments and activities thus did not necessarily extend to all the tasks it cumulatively acquired through successive

[81] Cordy-Simpson (note 80), pp. 51–52.

[82] British House of Commons, *Government Reply to the Fourth Report from the Defence Committee, Session 1992-93*, HC 1992/93 988 (Her Majesty's Stationery Office: London, 3 Nov. 1993), para. 55, cited in Warbrick, C. (ed.), 'Current developments: public international law', *International and Comparative Law Quarterly*, vol. 43 (Oct. 1994), p. 948.

[83] *Government Reply to the Fourth Report from the Defence Committee* (note 82), p. 119.

[84] *Government Reply to the Fourth Report from the Defence Committee* (note 82), para. 55.

[85] Quoted in Prager, K., 'The limits of peacekeeping', *Time*, 23 Oct. 1995, p. 35.

Security Council resolutions. Even in Sarajevo, while the Bosnian Government had consented to UNPROFOR's presence, the consent of the Serbs and Bosnian Croats was tacit rather than explicit. Although all sides benefited from the UN presence in one way or another and all had given at least de facto 'strategic consent', at the very least by not waging outright war on them, the safety of UN personnel and the continuity of UN operations were bound to be minor considerations to the factions, especially their more ruthless elements, and particularly to the Bosnian Serbs, who had begun the conflict and stood to gain most by its continuation.

Maintaining the perception of UNPROFOR's impartiality in these circumstances was virtually impossible. UN forces were seen by one or other party, at different times and in different places, as at best a nuisance, at worst collaborators with the enemy. Usually they were treated as pawns to be used to achieve the parties' strategic or tactical objectives. UNPROFOR was even portrayed by some observers as sustaining the conflict by feeding the factions and their populations, thus allowing them to divert precious funds and resources to their military effort.

UNPROFOR valiantly attempted a range of peacekeeping activities in this non-peacekeeping environment. It used its good offices to assist the parties in conflict prevention, management and resolution; supervised and operated Sarajevo Airport (which led to the longest airlift in history); protected humanitarian convoys; deployed border monitors to help implement the arms embargo; monitored ceasefires; monitored and guarded heavy weapons at collection points; and helped normalize life in Sarajevo;[86] but without a lasting ceasefire or peace settlement, and unable to affect the outcome of the war raging around it, it came to be seen as a largely humanitarian operation, providing what Rosalyn Higgins has called 'ancillary relief' to civilians suffering from a vicious war.[87]

Boutros-Ghali warned the Security Council in July 1992:

The situation on the ground was drawing the UN forces into functions and conflicts far beyond normal peacekeeping practice . . . They had been sent there to help those who were providing humanitarian aid, and both the Serb and Bosnian forces knew that they were not allowed to use force if challenged. A pattern of checkpoints and extortion benefited the fighters and progressively humiliated the UN troops. For the first time in memory, Blue Helmet peacekeepers, who formerly had been welcomed, were threatened and treated with contempt by those they had come to help.[88]

By the same token the Security Council was reluctant to authorize a UN peace enforcement operation, whether by a UN or a non-UN force. The Bosnian war seemed too bitter and too vicious to allow a peace imposed from outside.

---

[86] Leurdijk (note 59), pp. 22–23. Since UNPROFOR did not use force to oppose attempts by the factions to remove their heavy weapons from designated storage areas, and since the arrangement was based on agreement by the parties, this activity could be regarded as a traditional peacekeeping activity, rather than enforcement as Leurdijk would classify it.

[87] Higgins, R., 'The new United Nations and the former Yugoslavia', *International Affairs*, vol. 69, no. 3 (1973), p. 469.

[88] Boutros-Ghali (note 57), pp. 44–45.

The Serbs' historic resistance to invaders, most recently by the anti-Nazi Partisans during World War II, and the rugged nature of much of Bosnian territory were cited as reasons for staying out of the conflict. The US Joint Chiefs of Staff estimated that 400 000 troops would be required to quell the fighting and occupy the country.[89] In order to implement a peace agreement, Boutros-Ghali estimated that a combat force of 50 000, ready and willing to take military action to enforce peace should it meet with violent resistance, would be needed.[90] NATO estimated that 100 000 would be needed just for humanitarian tasks.[91] UN member states were unwilling to provide sufficient forces for any of these assignments. The USA, whose forces would be essential for any effective 'peace enforcement', was unwilling to risk ground troops, either as part of UNPROFOR or in any other type of Bosnian operation.

Although UNPROFOR never came near its estimated requirements, it gradually expanded. By the end of its mission in December 1995 it was the largest UN mission in the field. At its maximum strength, on 31 August 1995, it comprised 30 574 troops, 278 military observers and 17 civilian police. Although they varied in number and capability over time, the most important contingents, both politically and militarily, were provided by France and the UK. Other important contributors were Canada, Malaysia, the Netherlands, Pakistan, Spain, Sweden and Turkey. UNPROFOR also gained a Nordic armoured infantry battalion (Nordbat), deployed jointly by Denmark, Finland, Norway and Sweden, equipped with tanks, APCs and such special equipment as night-vision devices (although the tanks only arrived after Nordic governments pressed the UN command for better means of protecting their troops).[92] A Rapid Reaction Force comprising 15 000 troops (2000 of them already in-theatre) was provided by France, the Netherlands and the UK in late 1995.[93]

With all these contradictions UNPROFOR ended up using significant force in self-defence, in protecting humanitarian deliveries and, in a limited number of cases, in protecting civilian populations at risk. Eventually, it was drawn into peace enforcement. This is considered in detail in chapter 7.

### The UN Operation in Somalia I (1992–93)

In 1992 the UN also dispatched a peacekeeping mission to Somalia, again not in response to a peace agreement being reached but to help deal with a famine, induced by drought and prolonged by warfare, that portended a major humanitarian catastrophe.[94] After the repressive regime of President Siad Barre col-

[89] Durch and Schear (note 42), p. 228.

[90] Boutros-Ghali (note 57), p. 74.

[91] Durch and Schear (note 42), p. 228.

[92] Dalsjö, R., 'Sweden and Balkan Blue Helmet operations', ed. L. Ericson, *Solidarity and Defence: Sweden's Armed Forces in International Peace-keeping Operations During the 19th and 20th Centuries* (Swedish Military History Commission: Stockholm, 1995), pp. 105, 108.

[93] United Nations, *The Blue Helmets: A Review of United Nations Peace-keeping*, 2nd edn (UN Department of Public Information: New York, 1990), p. 558.

[94] The UN estimated that almost 4.5 million people, half the population, faced starvation. *The Blue Helmets*, 3rd edn (note 39), p. 287.

lapsed in early 1991, clans and sub-clans had battled for control of a country from which civil society, law and order and government services had almost entirely disappeared.[95] Somalia was the archetypal 'failed state'. Media coverage, even more than in Bosnia, produced worldwide pressure for the international community to respond.

On 3 March 1992 a ceasefire was brokered by the SRSG for Somalia, Algerian Mohammed Sahnoun, between the two main opposing warlords in the capital, Mogadishu—General Mohamed Farah Aideed, who led the United Somali Congress/Somali National Alliance (USC/SNA) which controlled south Mogadishu, and Ali Mahdi Mohamed, who led the USC faction which controlled the north.[96] Seizing the opportunity of the ceasefire, Boutros-Ghali asked the Security Council to dispatch a small military detachment to monitor the ceasefire and provide security for humanitarian agencies. In response, on 24 April 1992, the Security Council established the UN Operation in Somalia (later known as UNOSOM I).[97] Initially it would comprise just 50 unarmed, although uniformed, military observers to monitor the ceasefire. The Security Council also agreed in principle to deploy a 'security force', a 500-strong but lightly armed infantry unit. It would supposedly provide UN relief convoys with a 'sufficiently strong military escort to deter attack and to fire effectively in self-defence if deterrence should not prove effective'.[98] According to the Secretary-General's plan, designated corridors and 'zones of peace' were to be established to facilitate the delivery of aid. As in Bosnia, there was a supposition that the use of force in self-defence could deter local belligerents determined to disrupt a UN operation.

No chapter of the UN Charter was cited, although the preamble to the resolution did express the Security Council's concern that the 'continuation of the situation in Somalia constitutes a threat to international peace and security'—the phrase which clears the way for a Chapter VII operation. So far, however, the mission was to be traditional Chapter VI peacekeeping, with the traditional self-defence concept applicable. A January 1996 report by Boutros-Ghali gave a coherent description of UNOSOM's concept of operations, although it was not as clearly expressed at the time. As he described it retrospectively, UNOSOM's original concept of operations reflected the classic view, which was soon to change dramatically, of the UN's role in using force:

UNOSOM I was conceived as a peace-keeping mission even though, for the first time in the history of United Nations peace-keeping, one of its primary purposes was to make possible the delivery of emergency assistance to a civilian population. Peace-keeping, in contrast with peace enforcement, is not intended to achieve its objectives

[95] For an explanation of the Somali tribal structure see Sahnoun, M., *Somalia: The Missed Opportunities* (United States Institute of Peace: Washington, DC, 1994), annex A, pp. 58–59.

[96] Both had been part of the USC which had opposed Siad Barre and both were members of the Hawiye clan. Along with other clan- and sub-clan-based factions, they began an armed struggle for dominance in Mogadishu and, by extension, all of Somalia.

[97] UN Security Council Resolution 751, 24 Apr. 1992.

[98] United Nations, Report of the Secretary-General on the situation in Somalia, UN document S/23829, 21 Apr. 1992.

through the use of force. When peace-keepers are deployed, they make every effort, by peaceful persuasion, to stop the fighting between warring parties or to carry out other aspects of their mandates; they do not force belligerents to cease their hostilities. Indeed, peace-keeping operations use weapons only in self-defence, which is defined to include defence of their mandate as well as of their personnel and property. The rationale for the neutrality of United Nations peace-keeping forces is that it will serve to defuse tensions, deter violence and build confidence among the parties to a conflict. The security force to be sent to Somalia . . . was intended to help deter armed attacks on humanitarian relief operations and was to use its weapons only in self-defence if deterrence failed.[99]

Although the Security Council resolution referred to a ceasefire in Somalia as a whole, when the observers finally arrived on 23 July they were deployed only in Mogadishu, since that was the only place where a ceasefire had actually been agreed. They had no logistical support or protection and thus had a 'tendency to observe from their hotel rooms'.[100]

As conditions in Somalia continued to deteriorate, the Secretary-General proposed a comprehensive effort to restore all aspects of Somali life, rather than simply coping with the famine. The UN, he suggested, should establish a presence in all regions of the country and facilitate humanitarian relief and recovery, the cessation of hostilities, the provision of security, promotion of the peace process and of national reconciliation and demobilization, and disarmament of the factional forces.[101] The Security Council approved such a plan on 27 July in Resolution 767. On 12 August 1992 the Secretary-General announced that agreement had been reached with the warring parties on deploying the 500-strong 'security force' that the Security Council had envisaged and which Pakistan had agreed to provide.[102] No Somali government approval for the mission was obtained, since there was no Somali government.[103]

For the more ambitious plans of the Secretary-General to be carried out, a larger and militarily more capable force would be required. On 28 August the Security Council authorized the deployment of 3500 troops, including the 500 Pakistani soldiers who were on their way and the 50 military observers already there.[104] Again, no mention was made of any particular chapter of the UN Charter or of any concept of operation. On 8 September the Security Council agreed to add three logistics units, bringing the total authorized force to 4219.[105] Unfortunately, while months had been spent in delicate negotiations to

---

[99] Boutros-Ghali, B., 'Introduction' in United Nations, *The United Nations and Somalia 1992–1996* (UN Department of Public Information: New York, 1996), section 1, p. 24.

[100] Chopra, J., Eknes, Å and Nordbø, T., *Fighting for Hope in Somalia*, Peacekeeping and Multinational Operations no. 6 (Norwegian Institute of International Affairs (NUPI): Oslo, 1995), p. 35.

[101] United Nations, Report of the Secretary-General on the situation in Somalia, UN document S/24343, 22 July 1992.

[102] *The Blue Helmets*, 3rd edn (note 39), p. 292.

[103] Boutros-Ghali (note 57), p. 55.

[104] UN Security Council Resolution 775, 28 Aug. 1992.

[105] United Nations, Letter dated 8 September 1992 from the President of the Security Council to the Secretary-General informing the Secretary-General of the Council's agreement with the proposed deployment of logistic units, UN document S/24532, 8 Sep. 1992.

convince the Somalis, especially Aideed, to accept the small Pakistani force, no consultations were held about the much larger UN force now authorized.[106] This lack of consent from one of the most important factions made armed opposition to the presence of UN troops much more likely.

By this stage, Boutros-Ghali had presented his *Agenda for Peace* to the Security Council.[107] It envisaged a more expansive role for peacekeepers, including the possible use of force for peace enforcement. The 'peace enforcement units' he mentioned in *An Agenda for Peace* were supposed to be more heavily armed than peacekeepers and be available to enforce a ceasefire; these were not the type of units sent to Somalia as part of UNOSOM.

In any event, UN member states, despite the urging of aid organizations and the media, were reluctant to contribute any additional troops to UNOSOM, however the force was characterized, because of the dangerous conditions and the absence of a peace to be kept. No additional troops ever materialized, although Belgian and Canadian contingents were mobilized as a non-UN mission was being authorized in December 1992 to supplement the UN mission.

It became clear soon after the Pakistani troops began arriving on 14–15 September that they were unable to carry out their intended 'security' functions. Largely confined to Mogadishu Airport, they were harassed and humiliated by armed looters and factional gangs from all sides, some of whom demanded 'protection money'. As a light infantry unit, they had no artillery, heavy weapons or air support. Although authorized to defend themselves if attacked, they were, the Secretary-General later admitted, 'ill-equipped to do so and had to proceed in their tasks with great caution'.[108] John Hirsch and Robert Oakley contend that the Pakistani peacekeepers were also 'hobbled by stringent rules of engagement that allowed them to shoot only in rigidly defined cases of self-defense and to move only when granted permission'.[109]

On 28 October 1992 Aideed announced that the Pakistani troops would no longer be tolerated on the streets of Mogadishu and rejected their deployment to Berbera or Kismayo. Ironically, in view of subsequent developments, local faction leaders were apparently spreading rumours that the UN was abandoning its policy of cooperation with the factions and would 'resort to forcible action' in an effort to 'invade' the country.[110] Boutros-Ghali tried unsuccessfully to counter such misapprehensions. On 12 November Aideed's forces shelled and shot at the Pakistani troops at Mogadishu Airport, demanding that they with-

---

[106] Durch, W. J., 'Introduction to anarchy: humanitarian intervention and "state building" in Somalia', ed. Durch (note 6), p. 316. As Durch notes, in a pattern that was to be repeated many times in the next 3 years, Ali Mahdi Mohamed and his relatively weak faction 'were basically delighted to see further foreign intervention, while Aideed was outraged', especially at not having been consulted.

[107] United Nations, *An Agenda for Peace: Preventive Diplomacy, Peacemaking and Peace-keeping. Report of the Secretary-General Pursuant to the Statement Adopted by the Summit Meeting of the Security Council on 31 January 1992* (UN Department of Public Information: New York, 1992). See also section IV in this chapter.

[108] Boutros-Ghali (note 99), p. 26.

[109] Hirsch, J. L. and Oakley, R. B., *Somalia and Operation Restore Hope: Reflections on Peacemaking and Peacekeeping* (United States Institute of Peace Press: Washington, DC, 1995), p. 27.

[110] *The Blue Helmets*, 3rd edn (note 39), p. 293.

draw from the facility just two days after taking up positions there. Aideed's forces also shelled relief supply ships trying to enter Mogadishu harbour. On 13 November, after enduring being fired at with machine guns, rifles and mortars, the Pakistani troops returned fire in self-defence.[111] Although they were able to remain in control of the airport, their situation was impossible. Outside the fortified UN compound, relief organizations' vehicles were hijacked, their convoys and warehouses looted and expatriate staff harassed, detained and in some cases killed. Anarchy and factional fighting continued unabated.

This half-hearted attempt at traditional peacekeeping in an anarchic civil war threatened to undermine the world's confidence in the UN's perceived new role. Far from being able to use force as a 'deterrent' to prevent attacks on the delivery of humanitarian supplies to Somalia's starving millions, UNOSOM I could barely defend itself. A 1995 Norwegian study argued that the application of the traditional peacekeeping model to Somalia at this time was also flawed because it led to UN officials treating the factions and warlords as if they were sovereign entities, thereby affording them status, legitimacy and leverage.[112] Yet it was difficult to see what the alternative was, given that it was the factions which had signed a ceasefire and which were preparing, apparently, to engage in a peace process. Walter Clarke argues that if 'political doctrine' on humanitarian intervention had been available at the time it would probably have indicated that in mid-1992 the situation was ripe for inserting a substantial military force into Somalia, presumably for peace enforcement, rather than a small peacekeeping presence, since opposition to international intervention was weaker then than it later became.[113]

Deciding that the situation was intolerable, the Security Council on 25 November 1992 expressed strong support for the Secretary-General's view that it was necessary to move to Chapter VII of the UN Charter.[114] This was the first time the Security Council had openly reached this conclusion with regard to an internal conflict. It asked Boutros-Ghali for specific recommendations as to how the UN should proceed.

Meanwhile, US President George Bush, coming towards the end of his presidency and under strong international and domestic pressure to act, also asked for options from his advisers. State Department officials had begun arguing for the dispatch of a major UN military force, including US troops, to distribute humanitarian assistance directly.[115] At a National Security Council meeting on 25 November, aides outlined three alternatives: (*a*) expanded UN peacekeeping, with 3500 US troops joining the Pakistani troops in a supporting role; (*b*) a larger, Chapter VII UN peace enforcement operation, to which the USA would supply airlift and other support but no ground troops; and (*c*) deployment of a

---

[111] *The Blue Helmets*, 3rd edn (note 39), p. 293.

[112] Chopra, Eknes and Nordbø (note 100), p. 34.

[113] Clarke, W., 'Failed visions and uncertain mandates in Somalia', eds W. Clarke and J. Herbst, *Learning from Somalia: The Lessons of Armed Humanitarian Intervention* (Lynne Rienner: Boulder, Colo., 1996), p. 8.

[114] *The Blue Helmets*, 3rd edn (note 39), p. 293.

[115] Bolton, J. R., 'Wrong turn in Somalia', *Foreign Affairs*, vol. 73, no. 1 (Jan./Feb. 1994).

US division with Security Council authorization but under US command and control.[116] Although many in the Department of Defense reportedly viewed Somalia as a 'bottomless pit' or potentially another Viet Nam,[117] it apparently proposed this last option as a way of establishing its own relevance in the face of calls for post-Gulf War budget cuts. Bush surprised everyone by immediately choosing it.

On 25 November Boutros-Ghali received a visit from Lawrence Eagleburger, Acting US Secretary of State, who indicated that, should the Security Council decide to authorize the use of force by member states to deliver humanitarian aid to Somalia, the USA would be ready to organize and command the operation.[118] This was an unprecedented offer which the Secretary-General and Security Council could hardly refuse. In view of what transpired, it is significant that no consideration was given to disarming the Somali factions, deploying US troops in the northern secessionist region of Somaliland or nation-building.[119]

In reporting to the Security Council, Boutros-Ghali laid out the following options, more numerous than the Pentagon's, but obviously heavily influenced by its thinking: (*a*) continued efforts to reach agreement with the factions on deploying the full complement of 4300 peacekeepers already authorized; (*b*) abandoning the idea of using peacekeepers to protect humanitarian work, withdraw the military elements of UNOSOM and leave the humanitarian agencies to negotiate the best protection deals they could with local leaders (Boutros-Ghali was lukewarm about this option since the problem was not the presence of international personnel but insufficient numbers and the wrong mandate); (*c*) a show of force by UNOSOM in Mogadishu to create the conditions for safe delivery of humanitarian relief and deter the factions both there and elsewhere from withholding cooperation; (*d*) a country-wide enforcement operation authorized by the Security Council, presumably under Chapter VII but undertaken by member states (which the USA had already offered to lead), to 'resolve' the immediate security problems, including disarming the irregular armed bands and bringing their heavy weapons under international control (the operation would then be replaced by a conventional UN peacekeeping operation); and (*e*) the deployment of a country-wide UN enforcement mission, with troops provided by member states and under UN command and control; crucially, unlike traditional UN peacekeepers, these troops would have the authority to use force to accomplish their mission—presumably also under Chapter VII.[120]

---

[116] '"How did this happen?" Clinton demanded of Les Aspin', *Time*, 18 Oct. 1993.

[117] Stevenson reports that there is 'substantial evidence' that the US military resisted any deployment of ground forces during repeated inter-agency meetings until mid-Nov. 1992, and Gen. Colin Powell, Chairman of the Joint Chiefs of Staff, reportedly stressed the 'downsides of intervention' up to the moment President Bush made his decision on 25 Nov. Stevenson, C. A., 'The evolving Clinton doctrine on the use of force', *Armed Forces and Society*, vol. 22, no. 4 (summer 1996), p. 523.

[118] *The Blue Helmets*, 3rd edn (note 39), p. 293; and Boutros-Ghali (note 57), p. 58.

[119] Bolton (note 115), p. 59.

[120] Boutros-Ghali (note 99), pp. 30–32.

For Boutros-Ghali an enforcement operation under UN command and control would have been 'consistent with the expansion of the Organization's role in the maintenance of international peace and security made possible by the end of the cold war'.[121] He recognized, however, that the UN would have great difficulty mounting such an operation. By now it had 13 peacekeeping missions in the field, with some 55 000 troops and a peacekeeping budget three times that of a year earlier. In 1992 it had launched two large and expensive new operations, in Cambodia and the former Yugoslavia, and it was about to establish another in Mozambique. Already struggling to service its existing and planned missions, the UN had almost no permanent logistical and contingency planning capability and no command and control structure to permit it to conduct peace enforcement in a hostile environment. That would only be possible if member states provided personnel for a headquarters in the field as well as in New York. In addition, such a mission would require an agreed concept of operations, robust ROE, and interoperable military forces and equipment, all of which the UN lacked. In any event, it was apparent that UN member states were not yet prepared to entrust the command of a peace enforcement operation to a UN Secretary-General, especially one as untested as Boutros-Ghali.

Thus it was that, after considerable lobbying of heads of state by President Bush, the Security Council took the historic step of authorizing, for the first time, a non-UN multilateral military mission, a 'coalition of the willing', for humanitarian purposes. This was followed by a renewed UN effort in the shape of the second UN Operation in Somalia (UNOSOM II).[122] Both missions are considered in detail in chapter 6. The UN's initial humiliation in Somalia was to be a significant factor in triggering debate about the new type of peacekeeping that seemed to be required in the civil war situations of the post-cold war era.

## II. Use-of-force norms under strain

As the cold war era receded, the UN use-of-force norm, grounded in the concept of self-defence and latterly in that of defence of the mission, began to show increasing signs of strain. The new conditions that were causing this were becoming all too apparent.

### Deployment in situations of anarchy and disorder

One of the most obvious factors was that peacekeepers were increasingly being deployed in conditions of civil war—intra-state or internal conflicts. Such conflicts tend to be anarchical, disorderly or 'messy'.[123] They usually involve multiple parties, the territory held by each party may be unclear and subject to rapid change, rogue elements within factions may adopt independent positions

[121] Boutros-Ghali (note 99), p. 32.
[122] UN Security Council Resolution 794, 3 Dec. 1992.
[123] Zinni, A. (Lt-Gen.), 'It's not nice and neat', *Proceedings, US Naval Institute*, vol. 121, no. 8 (Aug. 1995).

and take independent action, and outside states may be involved in supporting one side or other. Civil wars tend to be life-or-death struggles in which the alternative to total control of state power is usually political or physical oblivion. In such circumstances parties are less likely to comply with the agreements they sign and more likely to see peacekeepers as obstacles to their goals or as pawns with which to achieve them. This puts peacekeepers at greater risk since the impartiality and international identity of the peacekeeping troops will not be universally recognized. Interpositional techniques are often impossible because of constant ceasefire violations, the lack of front lines and the denial of peacekeepers' right of freedom of movement.[124]

Instead of being deployed along a more or less clear demarcation line, facing more or less recognizable erstwhile belligerents, and with relatively safe staging areas out of the potential conflict zone, in civil war situations peacekeepers are deliberately deployed in the middle of the actual or former contested areas. As Colonel Duncan in Bosnia noted: 'We were effectively sitting in the middle of somebody else's war'.[125] Instead of facing a potential resumption of conflict from just one or perhaps two directions, peacekeepers were now surrounded by potential violence and were required to help change such an environment. As Alan James observed, while a traditional UN border-monitoring operation can proceed with its duties relatively unaffected by internal instability, a peacekeeping force in the middle of an intra-state conflict is invariably caught up in events and may through its actions pivotally affect their outcome.[126]

Also posing danger to peacekeepers is the fact that civil war belligerents tend be better armed than they were in the past.[127] Small ragtag armies may have more firepower than is available to the peacekeepers, even those from developed countries. All these factors may lead to the greater use of force by UN peacekeepers in self-defence or beyond.

## The number, size and complexity of missions

Another factor that could lead peacekeepers into using more force than customarily envisaged was the supplementation of traditional peacekeeping with a broad range of new activities. Steven Ratner describes 'second-generation' UN missions as combining the three roles of administrator (or executor), mediator and guarantor.[128] The first and third roles, in particular, could lead to an increased need for more forceful measures. Expanded new missions often had, as in Cambodia, large civilian components, sometimes larger than the military, whose security and safety was the responsibility of the military component.

---

[124] Berdal, M., International Institute for Strategic Studies, *Whither UN Peace-keeping?*, Adelphi Paper no. 281 (Brassey's: London, 1993), p. 31.

[125] Duncan (note 78), p. 47.

[126] James, A., 'A review of UN peacekeeping', *Internationale Spectator*, vol. 18, no. 11 (Nov. 1993), p. 632.

[127] Martin, L., 'Peacekeeping as a growth industry', *The National Interest*, summer 1993, p. 7.

[128] Ratner, S., *The New UN Peacekeeping* (Macmillan: London, 1995), pp. 44, 50.

The Security Council seemed increasingly willing to give the military component of such missions almost any task, however unrealistic or provocative to the warring parties, and assume that it could be successfully accomplished using the tried and true methods of traditional peacekeeping. Such tasks might include: (a) disarmament, demilitarization and cantonment of factions' military forces; (b) military assistance to an interim civilian authority, including assistance with election monitoring or organization; (c) protection of civilian populations and their human rights; and (d) protection and delivery of humanitarian relief. These could bring peacekeepers into contact with a whole new range of interlocutors, many of them armed, some of whom might not be familiar with foreign armed personnel or approve of the involvement of foreign armed personnel in their own activities or their own country.

The large-scale protection, delivery and distribution of humanitarian aid and the management of huge refugee movements involved particular dilemmas concerning the use of force. Sometimes civilian populations receiving aid and assistance, and the aid and assistance themselves, were targets of the fighting. In some cases civilians became hostile to the presence of the peacekeepers, or alternatively so dependent on them as to threaten obstruction or violence against them if they tried to depart. Although the UN had experience of some of the challenges of internal conflicts, such as crowd control and inter-communal violence, in the Congo, Cyprus and Lebanon, as previous chapters have shown, it was not prepared for the scale and ferocity of many of the post-cold war scenarios. Although the best militaries are by training well disciplined, organized and resourceful, few had the flexibility and sensitivity (not to mention training and equipment) to handle such delicate situations in a foreign, often hostile environment. Resort to the use of force was, in some cases, more likely.

More prosaically but just as importantly, the operations mandated immediately after the end of the cold war could not be prepared properly. Facing mission overload, the UN Secretariat was unable to draft the proper planning and operational documents, including concepts of operation and ROE; recruit the best and most appropriate force commanders, other senior military staff and military contingents; or provide operations in the field with the equipment, logistical support and communications they needed. UN member states increasingly found themselves hard pressed to provide the necessary funding, military capability and other support to the growing number of peace operations. In these conditions corners were cut and operations became less sturdy, more vulnerable, and thus easier targets for warring factions which were willing to engage them militarily.

**Poor political foundations for deployment of missions**

The involvement of peacekeepers in the use of force was also made more likely by the poor political foundations laid for mission deployments. At the strategic level, as hubris overcame the Security Council it tended to lose sight of some of the fundamental requirements for effective peacekeeping, in particular a sturdy political settlement or framework within which peacekeepers could operate and the consent of the parties. Making the situation even worse were the surprisingly limited attention the Security Council paid to each mission (until it got into serious trouble, which then often led to it attempting to micromanage the mission) and the lack of clarity of mission mandates (sometimes intentional) emerging from the Security Council's inevitably highly political drafting processes.

The effort put into preparing the political foundations, internationally and in-country, for the dispatch of peace operations varied enormously, ranging from the carefully considered and negotiated political framework and mission plans for UNTAC and UNTAG to the flimsy ceasefires or hollow political settlements and unclear mission statements that attended the deployment of the missions in Somalia and the former Yugoslavia. The flimsier the political settlement the stronger the peacekeepers' military capability needed to be, both for self-protection and for effective implementation of their mission. As John Mackinlay and Jarat Chopra note:

Although success in cold war peacekeeping was largely dictated by the effectiveness of the preceding political agreement between the parties and not by the capabilities of the military force, in a second generation continuum this immutable principle becomes less steadfast. The requirement that sound political decisions precede or underwrite a successful UN mandate is still paramount, but in the execution of tasks the importance of military effectiveness grows as the intensity of the operation increases until, at the threshold of collective enforcement, it becomes the overriding key to success.[129]

## Deployment in situations of tenuous consent

The Security Council, in its new interventionist mode, appeared increasingly willing to override a strict interpretation of the consent rule. In these circumstances the traditional peacekeeping norms—consent, impartiality and the use of force in self-defence—came under increasing strain. As consent was only partially secured or was overlooked completely in the rush to deploy new missions, the appearance and reality of impartiality became more difficult to maintain and the self-defence norm inevitably came under increasing pressure.

The failure of the Security Council to seek the complete consent of the parties could be due to the political or strategic importance of a particular conflict or the scale of the threat it posed to international security, a calculation that the conflict was ripe for settlement despite the absence of appropriate levels of consent, or the need to be seen to be acting in an emergency.

Security Council members seemed to take for granted that 'defence of the mission' could cover all possible contingencies. Such an assumption increased the possibility either of peacekeepers appearing ineffectual in the face of more complex scenarios, such as mass violations of human rights, if they declined to

[129] Mackinlay, J. and Chopra, J., 'Second generation multinational operations', *Washington Quarterly*, summer 1992, p. 118.

use force, or, more dangerously, of their using force beyond any reasonable interpretation of 'defence of the mission'. The latter possibility ran the risk of a militarily weak UN force being dragged into armed conflict with one or other belligerent party. Such dangers were compounded by wishful thinking on the part of Security Council members about the extent to which warring factions would be impressed by their demands for compliance and threats of the use of force under the Council's Chapter VII enforcement authority.

Whatever the reason, once many of the new missions were deployed the Security Council soon discovered the transient nature of whatever consent it had assumed existed. Many of the new operations were to experience gradual or sudden erosion of the consent of the parties to either the very presence or at least some of the activities of UN peacekeepers. As Christine Cervenak notes: 'Consent is more of a dynamic process than a condition or end state, and it will change over time'.[130] Consent even to the mere arrival of peacekeepers could be shaky, perhaps because the parties had been inveigled against their will into a peace process or into agreeing to a UN presence, or because the extent of consent had been misjudged in the first place.

Consent might degrade after the arrival of the peacekeepers because of the activities of the mission itself or factors beyond its control. Unfortunately, even when fully restored, it might only be a 'consent of convenience', to be withdrawn as opportunities were presented to one opponent or other.[131] If consent is tenuous, the maintenance of an impartial, non-discriminatory stance towards all the parties to a conflict becomes more difficult. Safeguarding both impartiality and the appearance of impartiality becomes a constant preoccupation, requiring fine judgement on the part of the heads of mission. If, for instance, only one party violates a ceasefire or peace agreement, the appearance of impartiality becomes more difficult to maintain because the UN must adopt punitive and defensive measures only against that party. Even though a warring party has brought such 'discrimination' on itself, it invariably accuses the UN of bias.

The most feared scenario is a complete loss of consent leading to organized violence against peacekeepers. This is most likely to occur after the UN has tried to take punitive or retaliatory action against one of the parties as a result of non-cooperation or violation of agreements or of international law. In these circumstances all elements of the mission need to become more vigilant and security-conscious, and this restricts their movement, complicates their tasks, especially those of the more vulnerable civilian components, and gives the UN presence a garrison appearance and mentality. Peacekeeping missions in these situations become surprisingly fragile. They are especially vulnerable to the understandable intolerance that public opinion in troop-contributing countries has for rising numbers of casualties in remote and little-understood conflicts. The stark choices for the peacekeepers are to withdraw, soldier on or move to peace enforcement.

[130] Cervenak (note 47), p. 54.
[131] Cervenak (note 47), p. 57.

Having invested scarce human and financial resources in such complex missions, and eager to avoid embarrassment, the UN is noticeably reluctant to abandon an operation when serious danger or failure threaten. When it is concluded that withdrawal would simply reward rather than punish a recalcitrant party, or when the momentum of a mission is so great that withdrawal is inconceivable, the question of coercing the parties, including through the use of force, invariably arises. As soon as the UN begins to invest money and resources in a peace mission, the bargaining relationship with the local parties alters dramatically, as the success of the UN's intervention becomes increasingly dependent on their cooperation.[132] This could lead either to appeasement of the local parties or to the temptation to enforce their cooperation.

**Pressures to use force**

The simplest solution for the UN immediately after the end of the cold war would have been to avoid peacekeeping in situations which might call for greater use of force than traditional norms allowed, but this proved impossible. Led by the media, international public opinion clamoured for the UN to respond proactively to actual or threatened genocide, mass carnage, humanitarian distress, gross human rights violations and non-compliance with peace settlements. The Security Council, especially the three Western permanent members—France, the UK and the USA—responded to and helped create such pressure by giving the impression that peacekeeping was the solution to all the intra-state conflicts that now confronted it. Once peacekeepers were deployed, pressures to respond with military force (or the threat of its use) in such situations came not only from international opinion and some governments, but from local parties (usually those who were abiding by or claiming to abide by the peace agreement in question), human rights groups, and aid and other non-governmental organizations (NGOs), and from within the UN system itself. On the other hand, troop-contributing countries, elements of the UN Secretariat, peace organizations and other voices often, although perhaps surprisingly not always, urged caution over the use of force.

At the mission level, too, pressures developed to use greater force. Although in general both civilian and military commanders were only too aware of the dangers, the self-defence norm was sometimes pushed to its limits. This was done for well-intentioned reasons, such as extending the categories of those to whom the UN would afford protection, for instance, to local UN officials. It was also done for political reasons—to preserve the perception that the UN peacekeeping model was effective and relevant, and conversely to avoid engaging the UN overtly in peace enforcement or, even worse, all-out armed conflict. The thinking seemed to be that it was better to stretch the self-defence norm to illogicality than to declare war.

---

[132] Doyle, M. W., 'UNTAC: sources of success and failure', ed. H. Smith, *International Peacekeeping: Building on the Cambodian Experience* (Australian Defence Studies Centre: Canberra, 1994), p. 97.

After the cold war ended, UN peace operations almost routinely began to include military personnel, often at the highest levels, from the most militarily capable states, including France, Russia, the UK and the USA.[133] Often these states' policies towards the use of force were quite different from the traditions of the neutral and non-aligned states and medium powers. In some cases this was to lead to increased use of force, in others to a reluctance to risk it, even when it was appropriate and authorized by higher authority. Perhaps contrary to what might be expected, it was not necessarily the 'new peacekeepers' who invariably wished to be more robust: sometimes it was the traditional peacekeeping contributors, such as the Scandinavian countries, who were inclined to use more force when confronted with obstruction on the ground, perhaps because they were better equipped and protected.

The policies of the states with the greatest influence on the UN's use-of-force policies and practices after the end of the cold war—France, the UK and the USA—were quite different in respect of their experience of and attitudes to the use of force.[134] Invariably, as the danger that force would be used, either by the parties themselves or by peacekeepers, increased, the tendency of all national contingents to seek instructions from home and to follow their national predilections towards the use of force increased.

## III. The peace enforcement debate

By early 1992 it was being recognized that UN operations were developing beyond the conventional parameters of traditional peacekeeping. Calls were increasingly heard for a third option between traditional peacekeeping and full-scale enforcement. The participants in the ensuing debate divided roughly into three camps—traditionalists, 'wider peacekeepers' and 'peace enforcers'. However, the debate was disorderly, and the differences between the camps were not stark and often not clear even to those advocating a particular argument. Part of the confusion was semantic. Whereas many observers used 'peace enforcement' to mean a new category of operations occupying the supposed 'grey zone' between traditional peacekeeping and Gulf War-style Chapter VII enforcement, others took it to be synonymous with the latter type of operation.

**The traditionalists**

Traditional exponents of peacekeeping and many military personnel opposed tampering with the tried and tested norms of peacekeeping—impartiality, consent and the use of force only in self-defence. They opposed the use of force by peacekeepers beyond defending themselves and their mission (some even opposed the use of force beyond maintaining the individual personal and collective safety of peacekeepers themselves), arguing that such action inevitably

---

[133] Exceptions included the UN missions in Angola, the UN Mission for the Referendum in Western Sahara (MINURSO) and the UN Observer Mission in Liberia (UNOMIL).
[134] See appendix 1 in this volume.

destroys consent and impartiality and draws a peacekeeping force into armed conflict with the local parties. Even small tactical incidents in which force was used beyond self-defence were seen as 'going to war' or 'war-fighting'. They apparently favoured deployment only in situations where consent was to all intents and purposes assured and the desire for peace practically guaranteed (although such criteria would have ruled out several traditional missions, such as those in Cyprus and Lebanon).

For the traditionalists peace enforcement was simply war by another name. Sanderson, force commander in Cambodia, argued that: 'Any reasoned debate about transition from peacekeeping to enforcement operations will very quickly lead to the conclusion that it is beyond the practical scope of a neutral peacekeeping force and would be to its political detriment. Enforcement action is war!'[135] For Major-General John Archibald MacInnis: 'Peace enforcement, except in some rare circumstances . . . is another name for war-fighting, pure and simple'.[136] The traditionalists also dismissed the notion that the use of force in a peace operation could wax and wane depending on the need for it and saw escalation as inevitable once it was used beyond self-defence. Having crossed the 'peace enforcement Rubicon', they argued, the UN is invariably perceived as having become a party to the conflict and from that there is no going back. As one UN official put it, going back to peacekeeping after conducting peace enforcement was 'like giving first-aid to a wounded rattlesnake'.[137]

For this camp there was no grey area between peacekeeping and peace enforcement. James saw no 'viable halfway house between peacekeeping and enforcement', since impartiality must govern the use of force by an operation which claims to be engaged in peacekeeping.[138] Although he contended that 'the proactive use of force could meet the peacekeeping criterion of impartiality provided it was seen, *by the parties*, as an entirely apolitical act' (emphasis in the original), he seemed to think this implausible. Inis Claude warned that it was essential to retain a clear distinction between 'those approaches that involve evenhanded treatment of the parties engaged in conflict and those that involve tilting to one side or the other'.[139]

Traditionalists also opposed 'stretching' the concept of peacekeeping. According to Claude there was nothing to be gained and much to be lost 'by stretching the concept of peace-keeping to cover missions that must engage in full-scale military operations to frustrate governments or other armed entities that are determined to fight for their objectives'.[140]

---

[135] Sanderson, J. M. (Lt-Gen.), 'Australia, the United Nations and the emerging world order', the 28th Alfred Deakin Lecture, Melbourne, 5 Sep. 1994, p. 10.

[136] MacInnis, J. A. (Maj.-Gen.), 'Lessons from UNPROFOR: peacekeeping from a force commander's perspective', ed. Morrison (note 80), pp. 181–82.

[137] Quoted in 'UK, US agree on keeping the peace', *The Independent*, 29 Mar. 1995, p. 14.

[138] James, A., 'Peacekeeping in the post-cold war era', *International Journal*, vol. 30, no. 2 (spring 1995), p. 252.

[139] Claude, I. L., Jr, 'The new international security order: changing concepts', *Naval War College Review*, vol. 47, no. 1 (winter 1994), p. 17.

[140] Claude (note 139), p. 17.

## 'Wider' peacekeepers

Although the differences between this group and the 'traditionalists' were often unclear or too subtle to be noticed by many observers, the 'wider' peacekeepers apparently believed that peacekeepers could use somewhat more force than they had traditionally used and still retain the essential characteristics of peace-keepers.

Some advocates of 'wider peacekeeping' were well aware that peacekeepers historically had often been much more passive, even in strict self-defence, than they needed to be. On the other hand, the use of force in self-defence to the maximum degree permitted, for instance, by interpositioning, could achieve a great deal without moving (at least officially) into peace enforcement. Others were aware (many were apparently not) that the self-defence norm had been expanded in 1973 to encompass 'defence of the mission' but, again, that such additional powers had rarely been used. Much more could be done under this rubric, they believed, without harming the essential character of peacekeeping. So long as consent was maintained (or restored when lost) at the strategic level, considerable force could, they argued, be used tactically in self-defence and defence of the mission.

Major-General Indar Jit Rikhye, former commander of UNEF I and military adviser to past UN secretaries-general, whose musings on peacekeeping over the years had been seen by some as representing de facto UN peacekeeping doctrine, advocated broadening peacekeeping mandates and capabilities to enable peacekeeping forces to protect themselves better.[141] This did not, he cautioned, mean that peacekeeping should evolve into 'enforcement actions', but rather that 'self-defence' should be redefined to include *effective* defence of the mission. It may also be possible to use limited force, he said, when all significant parties agree on a ceasefire or settlement, or when unauthorized groups such as renegade units or bandits create security problems. Unusually, Cordy-Simpson countenanced, with qualifications, the use of force by peacekeepers to prevent human rights abuses: 'We must never hesitate to use appropriate force, within the framework of the rules of engagement . . . in certain circumstances, when faced with blatant human rights abuses'.[142]

The British Army—relatively new to UN peacekeeping, with the major exception of Cyprus—invented the term 'wider peacekeeping' to describe the expanded tasks now being undertaken by peacekeepers. Its view was that, since these tasks fell within the philosophical framework of traditional peacekeeping, a term to distinguish these new types of operations could be simply achieved by adding the adjective 'wider'. Its field manual, *Wider Peacekeeping*, issued in 1994, saw wider peacekeeping as being carried out 'with the general consent of

---

[141] Rikhye, I. J. (Maj.-Gen.), 'Lessons of experience', *Soldiers for Peace*, Supplement to *Military History Quarterly*, vol. 5, no. 1 (autumn 1992), p. 60.
[142] Cordy-Simpson (note 80), p. 184.

the belligerent parties but in an environment that may be highly volatile'.[143] While this pushed the boundaries of traditional peacekeeping, and could involve more robust military activity, it thus retained the notion of consent and the need for impartiality to be maintained. The presence or absence of consent was seen as the dividing line between wider peacekeeping and peace enforcement. Peace enforcement operations were seen as being mounted 'to restore peace between belligerent parties who do not at all consent to intervention and who may be engaged in combat activities'. For the UK, the consent divide between wider peacekeeping and peace enforcement was the real Rubicon: 'Once on the other side, there is very little chance of getting back and the only way out is likely to be by leaving the theatre'.[144]

Yet another group seemed to want to permit peacekeepers to use more force by further stretching the definition of peacekeeping without actually calling it peace enforcement—presumably on the basis that if it were so labelled the UN would not be permitted to do it. Some argued that, while it might be possible intellectually to draw a sharp distinction between peacekeeping and peace enforcement, there is in practice a continuum along which the one merges into the other.[145] For them the difference between 'defending the mandate' and 'enforcing the peace' was not readily apparent in situations on the ground. Some in this group argued for leaving things doctrinally as they were and apparently doing whatever worked in practice—which is what the UN had been doing, with such mixed results.

### The peace enforcers

A third group saw the need for and the actual existence of a 'third way' between peacekeeping (whether traditional or wider) and all-out enforcement. Mackinlay and Chopra argued that: 'Peacekeeping cannot be stretched any further to meet second generation contingencies. There is a pressing need for a new category of international military operations somewhere between peacekeeping and large-scale enforcement'.[146] Olara Otunnu, President of the IPA, noted that: 'Situations encountered in the "gray zone" required responses that were neither traditional peacekeeping nor enforcement action, but something in

---

[143] British Army, *Army Field Manual, Vol. 5. Operations Other than War, Part 2: Wider Peacekeeping*, 1D/HQDT/18/34/30 (Her Majesty's Stationery Office: London, 1994), para. 8, p. 2-5. See appendix 1 in this volume.
[144] *Wider Peacekeeping*, para. 25, p. 2-12.
[145] See, e.g., Wurmser, D. and Dyke, N. B., *The Professionalization of Peacekeeping* (United States Institute of Peace: Washington, DC, Aug. 1993); Daniel, D. C. F., 'Issues and considerations in UN gray area and enforcement operations', Center for Naval War Studies, Strategic Research Department Research Memorandum 4-94, US Naval War College, Newport, R.I., 1994; and Mackinlay, J., 'Defining a role beyond peacekeeping', ed. W. H. Lewis, *Military Implications of United Nations Peacekeeping Operations* (National Defense University, Institute for National Strategic Studies: Washington, DC, June 1993), pp. 32–38.
[146] Mackinlay and Chopra (note 129), p. 118.

between'.[147] Mackinlay pointed to the growing list of expanded tasks faced by the UN in second-generation missions which were incorrectly described as peacekeeping because 'UN forces involved do not necessarily enjoy the support of all the parties involved locally and consequently will have to take much more vigorous steps to achieve a standard of military effectiveness that ensures their personnel safety and achieves the conditions required in the mandate'.[148] Swedish defence analyst Robert Dalsjö put it less delicately: 'In spite of oft-repeated claims to the contrary, there probably is a middle ground in Blue Helmet operations between always giving in to confrontation and habitually responding with overwhelming force, between the extremes of "bray and pray" and "slay and spray"'.[149]

Those arguing for the need for or existence of a third way claimed that the UN could not simply ignore violations of agreements, often painstakingly arrived at, by recalcitrant parties, often small in size and venal in nature, simply because of fear of becoming involved militarily. They asserted that as long as overall consent was maintained or restored, and as long as force was proportionately and discretely used, a peace enforcement operation would not necessarily be drawn into full-scale combat.

Those advocating a new peace enforcement doctrine argued that the conservative military notion that all military action beyond traditional (or wider) peacekeeping involves going to war or war-fighting was absurd. Good military strategy, they noted, has always tried to distinguish between different types of military operations, from deterrence to the threat of force to pitched battles. War is never unlimited (indeed, nuclear strategists have long talked of 'limited nuclear war') and a good military campaign is always geared to political objectives. To dismiss out of hand the need to contemplate a new type of military operation because it would amount to war-fighting seemed to run counter both to common sense and to the evolution of military strategy. Most alarmingly, it seemed reminiscent of the refusal of Western military strategists in the 1950s and 1960s to recognize that a new type of military strategy was required to deal with guerrilla warfare.

To its proponents, peace enforcement had recognizable characteristics that distinguished it from both peacekeeping and war-fighting. For John Ruggie, while peacekeeping was essentially an attempt to overcome a 'coordination problem between two adversaries', enforcement was akin to a game of 'chicken': 'The international community, through escalating measures that ultimately threaten war-making and military defeat, attempts to force an aggressor off its track'. Peace enforcement, in contrast to both, was a 'suasion game' in which UN forces, by presenting a credible military threat, 'seek to convince all conflictual parties that violence will not succeed'. The military

---

[147] Otunnu, O. A., 'The peace-and-security agenda of the United Nations: some critical issues for the next century', IPA Seminar Report, International Peace Academy Seminar on Peacemaking and Peacekeeping, New York, 3–8 Sep. 1996, p. 10.

[148] Mackinlay (note 145), p. 32.

[149] Dalsjö (note 92), pp. 111–12.

objective of the strategy was thus to 'deter, dissuade and deny'.[150] Don Daniel defines peace enforcement as 'the judicious resort to coercive diplomacy or forceful persuasion by the international community in the interest of furthering the implementation of community norms or mandates'.[151] He explains that: 'It must form part of a concerted campaign involving a variety of means—politico-diplomatic, economic, hortatory, as well as military—to influence behavior'. Ultimately, the successful conclusion of any kind of peace operation must entail some form of political settlement.[152]

Peace enforcement, then, was seen to involve, if necessary, the use of force to coerce parties to comply with obligations previously agreed to, either in a peace agreement or less formally. The goal of peace enforcement was not to punish an aggressor, bring about the humiliation or defeat of one party, or roll back its forces from illegally acquired territory, as would be the case with a 'pure' enforcement operation, but a just and lasting peace between the parties. Most advocates of peace enforcement believed that, as in peacekeeping, such a force would attempt to act impartially in the manner of an umpire, making rulings in disputes between parties and providing incentives and disincentives (including the threat and use of force) for the parties to comply. Describing the aim of peace enforcement as 'conflict suppression', the Washington DC-based Henry L. Stimson Center identified its principal characteristics as follows:

By comparison to traditional combat, its rules of engagement will seek to minimize casualties, both its own and local (whether combatant or civilian). In consequence, it may place much greater reliance than a traditional combat force on non-lethal weaponry. An enforcement operation may also attempt to maintain an appearance of impartiality, using necessary force against any faction violating a cease-fire. Implementing such a mandate generally requires clear superiority over combined local forces. In practice, although such superiority may suppress organized, formed-unit combat, it requires accompanying diplomatic action to resolve underlying disputes, lest fighting reemerge at lower levels in the form of guerrilla or terrorist activities.[153]

Proponents of peace enforcement recognized that an effective military presence was a prerequisite. 'At the high end of the spectrum, [peace enforcement] would be virtually indistinguishable from warfighting units in all respects *except* their political and military objectives.'[154] There would also have to be greater flexibility in the use of force and a greater range of options than peacekeepers traditionally had. This did not mean lowering the threshold for the use of force or aggressively fighting for peace. On the contrary, the flexibility

[150] Ruggie, J. G., 'Wandering in the void: charting the UN's new strategic role', *Foreign Affairs*, vol. 72, no. 6 (Nov./Dec. 1993), p. 29.

[151] Daniel, D. C. F., 'Wandering out of the void? Conceptualizing practicable peace enforcement', eds A. Morrison, D. A. Fraser and J. D. Kiras, *Peacekeeping with Muscle: The Use of Force in International Conflict Resolution* (Canadian Peacekeeping Press: Clementsport, 1997), p. 3.

[152] Henry L. Stimson Center, *Handbook on United Nations Peace Operations*, Handbook no. 3 (Henry L. Stimson Center: Washington, DC, Apr. 1995), p. 5.

[153] *Handbook on United Nations Peace Operations* (note 152). p. 5.

[154] Ruggie, J. G., 'The UN and the collective use of force: whither or whether?', ed. M. Pugh, *The UN, Peace and Force* (Frank Cass: London, 1997), p. 14. Emphasis in original.

available to an effective military force might help avoid the use of force rather than increase its likelihood by ensuring more rigorously policed, monitored and verified peace agreements.

## IV. The UN reconsiders the use-of-force issue

The first official evidence that the UN itself was beginning to take into account the new potentialities and challenges of peace operations came from the Security Council. Basking in the euphoria of the successful Security Council-authorized Gulf War operation, the USA became enthusiastic about using the UN to uphold, in President Bush's words, a 'new world order'. At an unprecedented summit meeting of the heads of state of the five permanent members of the Security Council in January 1992, the USA suggested that they ask the new Secretary-General, Boutros-Ghali, to prepare a blueprint for enhancing the UN's role in the maintenance of peace and security, including ways of strengthening UN peacekeeping.[155] Never since the UN came into existence had the USA been so enthusiastic about giving it a proactive role. It even urged member states to negotiate special agreements with the UN to make military forces available to the Security Council on a permanent basis for peace enforcement and other military purposes, as called for under Article 43 of the Charter.[156]

### An Agenda for Peace

Drafted by Boutros-Ghali, with the assistance of his Secretariat, his report to the Security Council was issued in June 1992 as *An Agenda for Peace: Preventive Diplomacy, Peacemaking and Peace-keeping*.[157] It expanded the previous tacit understandings about when the UN might use force and touched off a long-overdue debate, but also caused considerable conceptual confusion. The document divided UN involvement in securing the peace into preventive diplomacy, peacemaking, peacekeeping and peace-building.

It was with regard to the new category of 'peacemaking' that the Secretary-General first broached the use-of-force issue in his document. Although he defined peacemaking as 'action to bring hostile parties to agreement, essentially through such peaceful means as those foreseen in Chapter VI of the Charter of the United Nations',[158] he muddied the waters by including in his peacemaking repertoire the use of military force, including by 'peace enforcement units'. These would only be used in 'clearly defined circumstances and with their terms of reference defined in advance'. They would be provided by member states, be available on call and consist of troops 'that have volunteered

---

[155] 'Security Council summit declaration: "New risks for stability and security"', *New York Times*, 1 Feb. 1992, p. 4.

[156] *National Security of the United States* (The White House: Washington DC, Aug. 1991), p. 13; and *National Security of the United States* (The White House: Washington DC, Jan 1993), p. 7.

[157] *An Agenda for Peace* (note 107).

[158] *An Agenda for Peace* (note 107), para. 20.

for such service'. They would be more heavily armed than peacekeeping forces and would undergo extensive preparatory training within their home forces. The deployment and operation of such forces would be authorized by the Security Council and they would be under the command of the Secretary-General, as in traditional peacekeeping. Echoing Hammarskjöld 30 years previously, Boutros-Ghali said he considered these units to be warranted as a 'provisional measure under Article 40 of the Charter'.

The Secretary-General seemed, however, to envisage that such forces would only be used when 'ceasefires had been agreed but not complied with', when the task—presumably the use of force to compel the parties to comply—exceeded both the mission of a peacekeeping force and 'the expectations of peace-keeping contributors'. Boutros-Ghali distinguished between such units and the use of full-scale military forces under Chapter VII, Article 43 of the UN Charter for responding to 'outright aggression, imminent or actual', as well as with standby arrangements under which states would pledge military and other capabilities for peacekeeping only.

In addition to these perplexing characterizations, Boutros-Ghali defined peacekeeping as 'the deployment of a United Nations presence in the field, *hitherto with the consent of all the parties concerned*, normally involving United Nations military and/or police personnel and frequently civilians as well'.[159] He subsequently compounded the confusion in his 1993 annual report by declaring that peace enforcement should be regarded as peacekeeping activities which 'do not necessarily involve the consent of all the parties concerned'.[160]

Both statements, coming before prolonged long international debate in diplomatic, military and academic circles over how to characterize 'muscular' peacekeeping operations, alarmed those who wished to preserve the sanctity of traditional peacekeeping. A British parliamentary committee believed that *An Agenda for Peace* 'appeared to confuse military operations under Chapter VII of the UN Charter, designed to enforce peace, with so-called "Chapter 6 1/2" peacekeeping operations, which have traditionally scrupulously avoided using force, evinced impartiality and relied on consent of the parties'.[161] Adam Roberts noted that the 'hitherto' in Boutros-Ghali's definition became the subject of much comment, on two grounds: 'First, tried-and-true principles of UN peacekeeping were being changed and, perhaps, fatally weakened without a full discussion of all the implications. Second, many individuals and states (mainly small and/or developing) feared a new interventionist peacekeeping'.[162]

[159] *An Agenda for Peace* (note 107), para. 20. Emphasis added.
[160] United Nations, Report on the work of the organization from the 47th to the 48th session of the General Assembly, New York, Sep. 1993, p. 96.
[161] British House of Commons, Foreign Affairs Committee, *The Expanding Role of the United Nations and its Implications for United Kingdom Policy, Third Report*, vol. I, HC 1992/93 235-1 (Her Majesty's Stationery Office: London, 23 June 1993), p. ix.
[162] Roberts, A., 'The crisis in UN peacekeeping', *Survival*, vol. 36, no. 3 (autumn 1994), p. 100.

Indeed, closer examination of the document in various UN forums[163] and in national capitals produced misgivings on the part of some states. The developing countries, led most vocally by Brazil, India, Malaysia, Mexico and Pakistan, were fearful of the implications of the concept of peace enforcement for their sovereignty, even though several of them not only supported UN peacekeeping missions involving elements of enforcement, as in Somalia and the former Yugoslavia, but contributed substantial numbers of troops.[164] Western reactions combined enthusiasm for the UN finally engaging in fundamental reform with caution about the envisaged increased use of force by the UN. With regard to the idea of peace-enforcement units, only France was completely supportive, having already offered the UN 1000 troops on 48 hours' notice. The USA was initially cautious in its response, but in September 1992 President Bush acknowledged the need for states to train soldiers for 'establishing ceasefires and protecting humanitarian aid' and make them available to the UN for dispatch to places like Somalia at short notice, and said he was directing the Pentagon to establish such training for US forces.[165] The traditional providers of peacekeeping contingents were wary of the Secretary-General's idea of peace enforcement, although quick to volunteer proposals for streamlining and bolstering the UN's traditional peacekeeping efforts. France criticized the typology as being based 'on ends ("to keep the peace", "to make peace", "to reinforce peace") rather than on means, and not therefore operational [*sic*]'.[166]

In one of its few collective responses to *An Agenda for Peace*, the Security Council in May 1993 announced criteria for establishing peacekeeping operations which contained several actual and implied references to the use of force. The document reiterated the notion that the UN should not deploy peacekeeping missions without 'the consent of the government and, where appropriate, the parties concerned, *save in exceptional circumstances*' (emphasis added). Hence the Security Council was on the same track as Boutros-Ghali in this respect. It also proclaimed its readiness to take 'appropriate measures' against parties which did not observe its decisions and reserved the right to authorize 'all means necessary for United Nations forces to carry out their mandate'. This seemed to suggest that Chapter VII might be used to reinforce peacekeeping operations. Finally, the Security Council reiterated 'the inherent right of peacekeepers to use force in self-defence'.[167]

[163] For the views of the General Assembly's Special Committee on Peace-keeping Operations see United Nations, Comprehensive review of the whole question of peace-keeping operations in all their aspects, UN document A/48/173, 25 May 1993. For General Assembly resolutions on the subject see resolutions 47/120A, 18 Dec. 1992 and 47/120 B, 8 Oct. 1993. For public reactions of the Security Council see United Nations, Notes by the President of the Security Council, 30 Nov. 1992 (UN document S/24872), 30 Dec. 1992 (UN document S/25036), 29 Jan. 1993 (UN document S/25184), 26 Feb. 1993 (UN document S/25344), 31 Mar. 1993 (UN document S/25493), 30 Apr. 1993 (UN document S/25696) and 28 May 1993 (UN document S/25859).

[164] Malaysia had troops in Somalia and Bosnia, while India and Pakistan had troops in Somalia.

[165] Boutros-Ghali (note 57), p. 56.

[166] Chilton, P., 'French policy on peacekeeping', *Brassey's Defence Yearbook* (Brassey's for the Centre for Defence Studies, King's College, London: London, 1995), p. 140.

[167] United Nations, Note by the President of the Security Council, UN document S/25859, 28 May 1993, p. 1. Emphasis added.

In the press and among outside observers Boutros-Ghali's proposal for 'peace-enforcement units', combined with experience in several missions, touched off debate about the UN acquiring its own military force.[168] Former US President Ronald Reagan called for a standing UN force supported by the USA. The task of this 'Army of Conscience', as he called it, would be to carve out humanitarian sanctuaries in failed or oppressive states, by force if necessary.[169] A 1993 report on the UN by a US commission headed by Congressman James Leach endorsed a 5000–10 000-strong force to 'contain conflicts before they get out of control or to deter them altogether'.[170] At least one observer suggested using the Ghurkas as a UN force.[171] Veteran peacekeeper Brian Urquhart reversed his previous long-standing position by advocating, in an article in the New York Review of Books, a 'highly trained international volunteer force, willing, if necessary, to fight hard to break the cycle of violence at an early stage in low-level but dangerous conflicts, especially ones involving irregular militias and groups'.[172] He argued later that:

Experience of recent UN operations shows that even a small, highly trained group with high morale and dedication, arriving at the scene of action immediately after a Security Council decision, would in most cases have far greater effect than a larger and less well prepared force arriving weeks, or even months, later. The failure to come to grips with a situation before it gets completely out of hand usually necessitates a far larger, more expensive, and less effective operation later on.[173]

The rules of engagement for such a force would be different from both peace-keeping and peace enforcement:

The rapid-reaction group will never initiate the use of force but will be highly trained so that it can take care of its own security and mobility and have the ability and equipment to maintain its operations in the face of harassment and even opposition. It will in no circumstances have military objectives or be required to take sides in a civil war. It will be trained in peacekeeping and problem-solving techniques but will also have the training, military expertise, and esprit de corps to pursue those tasks in difficult, and even violent, circumstances.[174]

---

[168] E.g., the Trilateral Commission, an independent, non-governmental body formed in 1973 by citizens of Europe, Japan and North America to foster cooperation between the 3 regions, supported the idea of a peace enforcement force. Trilateral Commission, *Keeping the Peace in the Post-Cold War Era: Strengthening Multilateral Peacekeeping* (Trilateral Commission: New York, Mar. 1993).

[169] Sokolsky, J. J., 'Great ideals and uneasy compromises: the United States approach to peacekeeping', *International Journal*, vol. 50, no. 2 (spring 1995), p. 277.

[170] Longworth, R. C., 'Phantom forces, diminished dreams', *Bulletin of the Atomic Scientists*, Mar./Apr. 1995, p. 25.

[171] 'Ghurkas as the UN peace-keepers', *Times of India*, 26 Nov. 1993, p. 12.

[172] Urquhart, B., 'For a UN volunteer military force', *New York Review of Books*, 10 June 1993, p. 3.

[173] Urquhart, B., 'Prospects for a rapid response capability', eds O. A. Otunnu and M. W. Doyle, *Peacemaking and Peacekeeping for the New Century* (Rowman & Littlefield: Lanham, Md., 1998), p. 190. Former US Secretary of State John Foster Dulles, according to Urquhart, favoured a UN standing army, but it was opposed by Hammarskjöld because of the 'legal restrictions' imposed on the UN by national sovereignty. Longworth (note 170), p. 25.

[174] Urquhart (note 173), p. 194.

In subsequent editions of the *New York Review of Books* and elsewhere critics pointed to the costs and political difficulties associated with such an idea and the danger that it would lead to escalation requiring deployment of a much larger force.[175] A rapid reaction force was a step too far for most UN members at this stage. Consensus eventually emerged around a much less risky option—which the UN began trying to implement, with limited success—of governments earmarking standby military capabilities of all types for rapid assignment to the UN when needed. However, this UN Standby Forces Arrangements System (UNSAS) was to be more a 'data bank than a force'.[176] Contributors could refuse to agree to the use of their pledged contributions in any particular mission.

**Institutional reforms with implications for the use of force**

Meanwhile, in response to heightened expectations and demands, problems in the field and widespread criticism, the UN began a series of reforms of its peacekeeping operations, especially focused on its headquarters in New York. In March 1992 the Department of Peace-keeping Operations (DPKO) was established, gathering all peacekeeping expertise in one department, including the Field Operations Division. Headed after March 1993 by then Under Secretary-General Kofi Annan, the department's expertise grew rapidly, mostly as a result of secondments from governments. The military advice available to UN Headquarters was substantially boosted by the expansion of the Office of the Military Advisor (MILAD) in the DPKO to more than 40 officers, including secondment of de-mining experts, civilian police advisers and officers responsible for training and coordination. To facilitate long-range planning for its operations, a Policy and Analysis Cell was also established. Another much-needed reform was the establishment of a Situation Centre to keep in touch with missions in the field 24 hours a day, seven days a week. While none of these reforms addressed the question of the use of force per se, they could, in contributing to more effective and efficient peace operations, pave the way for more considered and appropriate use of force.

One activity of the Secretariat that did have direct implications for the future handling of use-of-force issues was the attempt to fashion guidance on conducting and managing peace operations and for the training of peace operations personnel. In June 1993 the DPKO established a Training Unit (previously the Training and Coordination Office, later the Training and Evaluation Service) which began writing manuals, training guidelines and other materials to assist member states in preparing their military, CivPol and civilian personnel for peacekeeping assignments, with the assistance of the UN Institute for Training and Research (UNITAR) in Geneva and the International Training Centre of

---

[175] E.g., 'A UN volunteer military force: four views', *New York Review of Books*, 24 June 1993, pp. 58–60; 'A UN volunteer force: the prospects', *New York Review of Books*, 15 July 1993, pp. 52–56; and 'For the UN, a volunteer peace force', *International Herald Tribune*, 12 July 1993, p. 8.

[176] Longworth (note 170), p. 26.

the International Labour Organization (ILO) in Turin.[177] In early 1994 the DPKO established a Mission Planning Service (MPS). Its activities were to include: preparing generic guidelines and procedures to streamline the process of mission planning; preparing generic guidelines for troop-contributing countries, from which mission-specific guidelines are formulated; preparation of standard operating procedures for essential functions;[178] and in-house studies pertaining to important issues such as command and control, coordination, rules of engagement and the structure of missions.[179]

Taken together, these documents might have been expected to give glimmers of at least an implicit peace operations doctrine. However, this was not to be the case. None of the documents was produced in time to provide guidance to traumatized peacekeepers in Somalia, Bosnia or Rwanda, and when finally released they revealed a UN that was keeping close to its traditional peace-keeping line on the use of force.

Doctrinally, as in so many other ways, peacekeepers were tragically unprepared for what was to come. Using an expression that stuck, Ruggie in an article in *Foreign Affairs* charged that the UN had entered a 'vaguely defined no-man's land lying somewhere between traditional peacekeeping and enforce-ment—for which it lacks any guiding operational concept. It has merely ratcheted up the traditional peacekeeping mechanism in an attempt to respond to wholly new security challenges', bringing itself to the point of 'strategic failure'.[180] The UN was thus forced onto a steep learning curve in its handling of use-of-force issues.

---

[177] United Nations, Comprehensive report on lessons learned from United Nations Operation in Somalia April 1992–March 1995, Dec. 1995, p. 32. For lists of publications produced see United Nations, Department of Peace-keeping Operations, Military Division, Training and Evaluation Service (TES), 'Peacekeeping publications 2001', UN, New York, 2001 (on CD-ROM). Prior to the establishment of the Training Unit, 1 training document existed: United Nations, Department of Peace-keeping Operations, 'Training guidelines for national or regional training operations', New York, 1991.

[178] United Nations, Department of Peace-keeping Operations, Mission Planning Service, 'Guideline standard operationg procedures' (GSOP-PKO), 1992.

[179] Comprehensive report on lessons learned (note 177), p. 28.

[180] Ruggie (note 150), p. 26.

# 6. Somalia: crossing the Mogadishu Line

When UNOSOM I failed to protect the delivery and distribution of humanitarian aid, it was massively augmented, indeed swamped, by the United Task Force (UNITAF), a non-UN multinational 'coalition of the willing' led by the USA. UNOSOM I and UNITAF were in turn succeeded by the second UN Operation in Somalia (UNOSOM II). While UNITAF was regarded at the time as a successful mission which skilfully employed the threat and use of force to bring a measure of normality to Somalia, UNOSOM II, like another UN operation 30 years before, became embroiled in an African intra-state conflict. It is alleged to have succumbed to 'mission creep', crossed the line from peace-keeping to peace enforcement, and lost its impartiality and legitimacy, and it was forced to withdraw ignominiously.

This chapter deals with both UNITAF and UNOSOM II, since the former is indispensable to an understanding of the use of force by the latter. Moreover, since UNITAF had Chapter VII authorization, it is relevant to the whole question of peace enforcement by multinational forces, whether UN or non-UN. UNITAF was at the time viewed as a possible model for future UN operations.

## I. The United Task Force (1993–94)

The United Task Force, known as Operation Restore Hope by the US military, arrived in a blaze of publicity, in full view of the world's press, on the beaches of Mogadishu on 9 December 1992. It quickly secured the port, meeting no resistance. 'UNITAF made its entrance with a show of force. Warships patrolled the coast, and planes and helicopters flew over Mogadishu as soldiers fanned out across the city. As a consequence, Somali militiamen disappeared from the streets of Mogadishu, taking their weapons with them . . . On the first day Mogadishu airport was secured and a WFP [World Food Program] aircraft landed with food aid'.[1]

### Mandate and concept of operations

On 3 December 1992 the UN Security Council had unanimously adopted Resolution 794, determining that the situation in Somalia constituted a 'threat to international peace and security' and authorizing action under Chapter VII of the UN Charter. It mandated the Secretary-General and UN member states to use 'all necessary means to establish as soon as possible a secure environment for humanitarian relief operations in Somalia'. 'All means necessary' was, of

---

[1] Boutros-Ghali, B., 'Introduction' in United Nations, *The United Nations and Somalia 1992–1996* (UN Department of Public Information: New York, 1996), p. 34.

course, the Security Council's euphemism for force. The Council had never before explicitly authorized action under Chapter VII in relation to an internal armed conflict or a humanitarian situation.[2]

Although the Chapter VII authorization made it seem that UNITAF would engage in peace enforcement, US President George Bush, undoubtedly influenced by the US military, insisted from the outset that the mission would have a limited objective—to 'open the supply routes, to get the food moving, and to prepare the way for a UN peacekeeping force . . . We will not stay one day longer than is absolutely necessary'.[3] The day after the UN resolution was passed he wrote to Boutros-Ghali to that effect. Obsessed with having clear exit strategies for military adventures abroad, the US Department of Defense insisted that UNITAF be a 'surgical humanitarian strike' without additional tasks. Unfortunately, as William Durch notes, this 'signalled clearly to Somali factions that any of them temporarily inconvenienced by the intervention could probably afford to wait it out, and that the USA was not proposing to fix what was broken in Somalia'.[4]

Despite Bush's statement, Boutros-Ghali wrote to him on 8 December, the day before the first UNITAF troops arrived in Somalia, urging that UNITAF undertake disarmament of the factions as a necessary condition for the achievement of a 'secure environment' in Somalia and that it be extended throughout the country.[5] The USA declined. Chairman of the Joint Chiefs of Staff General Colin Powell declared that: 'Disarmament is not possible in a country where everyone has a weapon and, while it might be successful for a while, would only serve to make money for arms dealers in neighbouring states'.[6] Former US Ambassador to Somalia Robert Oakley, who later became US Special Envoy, asked how 'house-to-house, hut-to-hut searches' could be carried out in the conditions prevailing in Somalia.[7] Complete disarmament would have generated much greater friction with the population and the militia, pulling the USA into a morass from which it would have difficulty extricating itself. Some senior US officers also believed that to pursue disarmament would have meant diverting resources at the cost of another 100 000 civilian lives to famine.[8]

---

[2] It had only explicitly authorized such enforcement action 4 times previously: in 1950 in relation to Korea; in 1966 in authorizing the interception of tankers carrying oil to Rhodesia; and in 1990 and 1991 concerning the Iraq–Kuwait conflict.

[3] 'Bush's talk on Somalia: US must "do it right"', *New York Times*, 5 Dec. 1992, p. 4.

[4] Durch, W. J., 'Introduction to anarchy: humanitarian intervention and "state building" in Somalia', ed. W. J. Durch, *UN Peacekeeping, American Policy, and the Uncivil Wars of the 1990s* (St Martin's Press: New York, 1996), p. 321.

[5] United Nations, Letter dated 8 December 1992 from the Secretary-General to President Bush of the United States discussing the establishment of a secure environment in Somalia and the need for continuous consultations, published in *The United Nations and Somalia 1992–1996* (note 1), pp. 216–17.

[6] US Senate, Committee on Armed Services, 'Review of the circumstances surrounding the Ranger raid on October 3–4, 1993 in Mogadishu, Somalia', Memorandum for Senator Thurmond and Senator Nunn from Senator Warner and Senator Levin, Washington, DC, 29 Sep. 1995, p. 19.

[7] Hirsch, J. L. and Oakley, R. B., *Somalia and Operation Restore Hope: Reflections on Peacemaking and Peacekeeping* (United States Institute of Peace Press: Washington, DC, 1995), p. 105.

[8] Cited in Chopra, J., Eknes, Å and Nordbø, T., *Fighting for Hope in Somalia*, Peacekeeping and Multinational Operations no. 6 (Norwegian Institute of International Affairs (NUPI): Oslo, 1995), p. 44.

Not only was disarmament abjured; so were civil affairs activities and, at least initially, the re-establishment of the Somali police.[9] According to Walter Clarke, the reasons for this included: the naive expectation that the mission would be over in weeks; the fact that the US Marine Corps, which would spearhead the mission, specializes in expeditionary, short-term, high-intensity operations rather than 'nation-building'; and concern on the part of the US Central Command (CENTCOM) that no 'encumbering requirements' should be placed on the mission.[10] The Marines' experience in Beirut in 1982–84 was also presumably a factor.

UNITAF's operational plan was oriented to its key humanitarian mission. It divided southern Somalia into eight humanitarian relief sectors constituting the famine belt. The aim was to establish food distribution centres in each and guarantee the delivery of large quantities of food in order to eliminate looting, hoarding and the use of food as a weapon, thereby weakening the power of the warlords.[11] The north-east and Somaliland, less affected by the disaster, were not included in UNITAF's area of operations, which at its height covered less than one-third of the country.

UNITAF was thus to be primarily a military mission with a strictly limited humanitarian role. This had major implications for its successor mission, which was forced to deal with the issues that UNITAF had not tackled, in particular disarmament, deployment throughout Somalia and the wider nation-building agenda.

## The force

The multinational force was considerably larger than any UN peacekeeping operation had ever been. At its peak it numbered 37 000 troops, including approximately 8000 on ships offshore. The largest contingent by far was from the USA, with about 28 000 Marines and infantry. They were joined by some 9000 troops from more than 23 other countries. Several elite units were provided, including the French Foreign Legion, Belgian paratroop commandos and Italian paratroopers. Australia and Canada also sent highly capable forces.

Meanwhile, UNOSOM I remained in place, with its 500 troops and 50 observers. In a typical conceit, the UN pretended (despite pressing the USA for greater involvement in Somalia) that it remained 'fully responsible' for providing humanitarian relief and promoting national reconciliation and economic reconstruction.[12] UNITAF was supposedly to take the lead only in creating a

---

[9] CENTCOM, which was charged with translating into military terms the political guidance for the mission agreed by the appropriate agencies and approved by President Bush, removed the critical civil affairs and police training components from the original package, in effect changing the political guidance. In fact, the UN and UNITAF did later agree to establish an interim Somali police force of retired Somali police officers.

[10] Clarke, W., 'Failed visions and uncertain mandates in Somalia', eds W. Clarke and J. Herbst, *Learning from Somalia: The Lessons of Armed Humanitarian Intervention* (Lynne Rienner: Boulder, Colo., 1996), p. 9.

[11] Chopra, Eknes and Nordbø (note 8), p. 41.

[12] Letter dated 8 December 1992 from the Secretary-General to President Bush (note 5).

'secure environment' for these UN activities. Oakley notes that in fact UNOSOM 'generated little action on the ground' during UNITAF's tenure.[13]

## Command and control

According to its mandate UNITAF was to have 'unified' command and control. It was to be commanded by Lieutenant-General Robert P. Johnston of the US Marine Corps, who would report direct to Commander-in-Chief, CENTCOM, General Joseph P. Hoar, and thence through the US Department of Defense and Joint Chiefs of Staff to the president. Within UNITAF, all participating contingents reported to Johnston, although the command relationship was based on voluntary coordination and cooperation rather than strict command, as in NATO. Ironically, this was a looser arrangement than that which, at least in theory, is required for UN peace operations. Outside this chain of command, but playing a political/diplomatic role described as that of a 'proconsul', was Special Envoy Oakley, who headed the US Liaison Office in Mogadishu.

UNOSOM I retained its own chain of command headed by SRSG Ismat Kittani of Iraq, with Brigadier-General Imtiaz Shaheen of Pakistan as force commander. There were to be 'appropriate mechanisms' for coordination between UNITAF and UNOSOM, including a small UNOSOM liaison staff attached to UNITAF field headquarters. While Oakley reports that this worked well, Admiral Jonathan Howe, later head of UNOSOM II, notes that the coexistence of two missions in the same theatre 'made for an awkward relationship'.[14] The most effective relationship was reportedly that between Washington, including its operational command, and the UN Secretary-General.[15]

## Use of force concept and ROE

Beyond the mission mandate, no guidance was provided by the Security Council on the use of force. The matter was left entirely to the USA which, being inexperienced in UN peacekeeping, had at that time no peacekeeping doctrine.[16] 'Much of what had to be done in Somalia was without established doctrine or precedent, and priority was given to adaptability, initiative and good judgement.'[17]

Broad US policy for the mission was enunciated by Powell. The goal was to deploy a large force capable of controlling the violence and making it clear to the faction leaders that order would be restored with or without their cooperation. This was a reconceptualization of peacekeeping along the lines of the 'Weinberger–Powell doctrine', which advocated that US forces should only go

[13] Hirsch and Oakley (note 7), p. 51.
[14] Hirsch and Oakley (note 7), p. 51; and Howe, J., 'Relations between the United States and United Nations in dealing with Somalia', eds Clarke and Herbst (note 10), p. 184.
[15] Chopra, Eknes and Nordbø (note 8), p. 41.
[16] Allard, K., *Somalia Operations: Lessons Learned* (National Defense University, Institute for National Strategic Studies: Washington, DC, 1995), p. 6.
[17] Hirsch and Oakley (note 7), p. 50.

to war if they had a clear, finite mission and overwhelming, efficient force, with ROE that allowed the expeditious use of force when necessary.[18] CENTCOM, in cooperation with the Joint Chiefs of Staff, produced the UNITAF mission statement and concept of operations, including force structure and ROE, according to these precepts.[19] Recognizing that operations would take place in a situation of near-anarchy, Hoar proposed using UNITAF's Chapter VII mandate to use 'all necessary means' to give the commander maximum flexibility to determine what constituted a threat and the appropriate response, 'including first use of deadly force'.[20]

All this appeared diametrically opposed to traditional UN peacekeeping doctrine, but it was in fact only declaratory. The USA in reality hoped that an impressive show of force would cow the factions into submission without the use of force, which might result in US casualties and the return of its soldiers home in body bags, which was presumed to be political suicide. Both Johnston and Oakley were 'determined to avoid any confrontations with the Somali factions so long as UNITAF's mission was not compromised, and to ensure that if force were used it would not lead to permanent hostilities'.[21]

## The ROE

UNITAF's ROE reflected the USA's hesitancy over its mission. Jonathan T. Dworken notes that the humanitarian nature of the operation meant a tension between two competing objectives:

If the ROE [were] too restrictive, [they] would not allow soldiers to protect themselves and could hamper operational effectiveness. It was necessary to allow sufficient force to be used to deter warlords or bandits and demonstrate US resolve in delivering relief supplies. If the ROE [were] too permissive, US forces might have been perceived as using excessive force. If that happened, the mission might no longer have appeared humanitarian in nature, and the military could have lost support at home and abroad and faced conflict escalation on the ground.[22]

Ultimately CENTCOM decided to base UNITAF's ROE on standing US peacetime rather than wartime models: hence, they would not identify any force as hostile.[23] Clarke claims that the ROE amounted to little more than those for a Chapter VI UN peacekeeping operation.[24] Yet on several counts they were tougher, particularly regarding their treatment of hostile intent, the use of

[18] Hirsch and Oakley (note 7), p. 47. On the Weinberger–Powell doctrine see also appendix 1, section I, in this volume.

[19] Hirsch and Oakley (note 7), p. 43.

[20] Hoar, J. P. (Gen.), 'Humanitarian assistance operations challenges: the CENTCOM perspective on Somalia', *Joint Forces Quarterly*, vol. 1, no. 2 (Nov. 1993).

[21] Hirsch and Oakley (note 7), p. xviii.

[22] Dworken, J. T., 'Rules of engagement: lessons from Restore Hope', *Military Review*, vol. 74, no. 5 (Sep. 1994), p. 29.

[23] The ROE for Operation Restore Hope are detailed in US Department of the Army, 'Sample rules of engagement: rules of engagement for Operation Restore Hope' in *Peace Operations*, FM 100-23 (Department of the Army: Washington, DC, Dec. 1994), appendix D.

[24] Clarke (note 10), p. 8.

deadly force and the enforced disarmament of 'technicals'—the four-wheel drive vehicles mounted with an array of weapons which were terrorizing the Somali capital. They essentially dealt with three issues: the proper use of force, including in self-defence; the confiscation and disposition of weapons; and the handling of civilians. Kenneth Allard summarizes them as comprising, with 'admirable simplicity', four basic 'noes': no 'technicals'; no banditry; no road-blocks; and no visible weapons.[25]

Unlike typical UN ROE, they authorized troops to use not just 'force' but 'deadly force' to protect themselves, other soldiers or persons in areas under US control from 'threats of death or serious bodily harm'. Also unlike UN ROE, they authorized the use of deadly force not only when troops were fired on or human life was threatened but also when there was 'a clear demonstration of hostile intent'—defined as 'the threat of imminent use of force'.[26] Deadly force was also authorized in protecting relief supplies, when armed elements, mobs, and/or rioters threatened human life, sensitive equipment and aircraft or the free passage of relief supplies. An entire section of the ROE was devoted to 'crew-served weapons' or technicals, defined as 'any weapon system that requires more than one individual to operate', including tanks, artillery pieces, anti-aircraft guns, mortars and machine guns. Such weapons were to be considered a threat 'whether or not the crew demonstrates hostile intent'.[27] Armed Somalis not manning technicals who were neither attacking nor threatening UNITAF forces were also defined as 'threats'. Dworken places this designation some-where between 'friendly' and 'hostile',[28] the standard distinctions in wartime ROE. If a weapon crew or armed individual demonstrated hostile intent they could be engaged with 'deadly force'.

Closer to traditional peacekeeping was the stipulation that in situations where deadly force was not appropriate the 'minimum force necessary' to accomplish the mission was to be used.[29] When confronted by unarmed hostile elements, mobs or rioters, soldiers were to use a graduated response, including verbal warnings to demonstrators 'in their native language', shows of force (including the use of riot control formations), warning shots fired over the heads of the hostile elements, and other 'reasonable uses of force . . . which are necessary and proportional to the threat'. Use of riot control agents could only be authorized by the commander.

Surprisingly, despite the USA's opposition to becoming involved in disarm-ament, in areas under its control (as opposed to the streets of Mogadishu) 'all necessary force' was authorized to disarm and demilitarize groups or indi-

---

[25] Allard (note 16), p. 36.

[26] 'Rules of engagement for Operation Restore Hope' (note 23), p. 90. Factors to be considered included: '(a) Weapons—Are they present? What types?; (b) Size of the opposing force; (c) If weapons are present, the manner in which they are displayed; that is, are they being aimed? Are the weapons part of a firing position?; (d) How did the opposing force respond to the US forces?; (e) How does the force act toward unarmed civilians?; (f) Other aggressive actions'.

[27] 'Rules of engagement for Operation Restore Hope' (note 23), p. 93.

[28] Dworken (note 22), p. 28.

[29] 'Rules of engagement for Operation Restore Hope' (note 23), p. 92.

viduals. Detained Somalis were to be treated 'with respect and dignity and turned over to military police'. Indicating that the US military had done its cultural homework to a certain extent, the ROE declared that: 'Troops should understand that any use of the feet in detaining, handling or searching Somali civilians is one of the most insulting forms of provocation'.[30] Altogether, the ROE appeared well calibrated to the self-imposed restrictions on UNITAF's role and its mandate—which, although authorized under Chapter VII, hardly amounted to peace enforcement.

Normally US ROE would remain classified, but Johnston wished to release them to all forces under his command to ensure that they would be operating on the same basis. Classified ROE were seen not only as detracting from the mission's objectives but as making 'little sense in a multinational coalition with the native population closely observing and taking advantage of every move'.[31] CENTCOM thus took the unprecedented step of developing declassified 'operating rules' similar to the ROE (although confusingly often described as ROE) which were printed on plastic cards and distributed to the entire force.[32] Although these were no more restrictive than the ROE, they contained some additional elements to help soldiers understand the mission, such as: 'The United States is not at war'.[33] They also stressed the right of self-defence and the traditional peacekeeping notion of minimum proportionate force.

Most contingent commanders appear to have adopted the US ROE, some with minor, mostly grammatical, changes.[34] However, the Canadian troops, preoccupied in their area of operations, Beledweyne, with Somali fighters infiltrating their compounds, adopted a strong 'force protection' stance (described as a 'don't mess with me' attitude).[35] The ROE were 'adjusted' to permit the use of deadly force against any Somali, armed or unarmed, caught inside the UNITAF compounds or escaping with goods. This turned out to be ill-advised.

## UNITAF's use of force

Overall, compared with its successor, UNITAF used very little force and was spared the violence that UNOSOM II experienced. The casualty rate on both sides was relatively low. During its five-month deployment, 8 UNITAF troops

---

[30] 'Rules of engagement for Operation Restore Hope' (note 23), p. 94.

[31] Allard (note 16), p. 38.

[32] Ord, R. L. (Lt-Gen.), 'Rules of engagement: a template for interoperability', ed. H. Smith, *The Force of Law: International Law and the Land Commander* (Australian Defence Studies Centre: Canberra, 1994), p. 210. The ROE card is reproduced in appendix 2 in this volume.

[33] Dworken (note 22), pp. 28–29.

[34] Mellor, W. J. A. (Col), 'Somalia a catalyst for change in the command and control of UN operations', ed. H. Smith, *International Peacekeeping: Building on the Cambodian Experience* (Australian Defence Studies Centre: Canberra, 1994), p. 162. The Australians, who were deployed in and around Baidoa, adapted the ROE by adding authorization to use tent poles and pickaxe handles as non-lethal options and ruling out the use of full-strength riot control agents because of the threat to Somalis' health, which in many cases was poor. Cayenne and pepper spray were used as alternatives and separate ROE devised for their use.

[35] Klep, C. and Winslow, D., 'Learning lessons the hard way: Somalia and Srebrenica compared', ed. E. A. Schmidl, *Peace Operations: Between War and Peace* (Frank Cass: London, 2000), pp. 104–105.

were killed in action and 24 wounded. Although the number of Somali civilians killed cannot be accurately determined because of the custom of immediately spiriting bodies away, there were probably 50–100 deaths.[36]

As in the Congo, it was difficult to differentiate between UNITAF's ways of using force to accomplish different aspects of its mandate. The full deployment of the force and simultaneous start of operations to protect humanitarian relief deliveries spilled over rapidly into protecting the relief agencies and NGOs themselves, which in turn was closely connected with establishing law and order and ultimately attempting limited enforced disarmament. One of the failures of UNITAF's concept of operations was in fact that it did not sufficiently appreciate the interconnectedness of these elements and their relationship to the ultimate achievement of a political settlement and nation-building in Somalia.

By and large, UNITAF used force only in self-defence. Attacks came mostly from gangs and criminals. The aspect of UNITAF's mandate which was most successfully achieved, the protection and delivery of humanitarian relief supplies, also involved the least use of force. Creating a more secure environment, particularly in urban areas, especially Mogadishu, involved more force, but again usually only in self-defence. The disarmament of the factions, into which UNITAF was drawn haphazardly, also led to some use of force, but again relatively minor. The most substantial battle that UNITAF troops engaged in— in Kismayo—was both an act of self-defence, since a substantial premeditated attack had been launched against them, and a form of peace enforcement, in the sense that UNITAF's intention was to enforce a ceasefire in the area.

Occasionally UNITAF used force in ways that UN peacekeepers would be reluctant to countenance, such as destroying arms dumps in retaliation for attacks. Overall, however, it hardly used much more force than a UN peacekeeping operation would have, and certainly less than the 1960s Congo mission. In many respects it was a paper tiger, albeit a heavily armed one.

*Full deployment and protection of humanitarian relief deliveries*

After Mogadishu's port and airport were secured, UNITAF continued to deploy slowly throughout December 1992 without meeting armed resistance. Humanitarian agencies and NGOs, reporting intimidation and violence by gangs of looters eager to seize what they could before UNITAF arrived, pressed for more haste. Johnston, concerned about overstretch, refused to accelerate the deployment, extending it only when conditions and forces permitted.[37] By 13 December US forces had secured the former Soviet airfield at Baledogle without the use of force, and by 16 December they had seized Baidoa in the centre of southern Somalia. Advance elements of the US Army's 10th Moun-

---

[36] Hirsch and Oakley (note 7), p. 82.
[37] Daniel, D. C. F. and Hayes, B. D. (eds) with Chantal de Jonge Oudraat, *Coercive Inducement and the Containment of International Crises* (United States Institute of Peace Press: Washington, DC, 1999), p. 92.

tain Division received a warm welcome in Baledogle, including a symbolic handover of weapons. Thereafter UNITAF forces moved inland into the areas worst affected by famine. Full deployment was completed by 28 December, a month ahead of schedule, reportedly facilitated by 'the near absence of organized resistance, advanced political preparation in each of the sectors, the formidable military reputation established by UNITAF, and tactical intelligence provided by a special field intelligence detachment assigned to UNITAF, combining civilian and military capabilities'.[38]

There were some relatively minor incidents in Mogadishu as various militias tried to test UNITAF's resolve. In mid-December three technicals opened fire on patrolling US Marine helicopters on the outskirts of the city and were immediately eliminated by Cobra helicopter gunships.[39] Just after Christmas helicopter gunships eliminated the weapons of the Murasade sub-clan which had been shelling the north-eastern suburbs. On 7 January 1993 UNITAF acted with substantial force for the first time, destroying a weapon storage compound from which forces of Mohamed Farah Aideed (leader of the USC/SNA), despite repeated warnings, had fired on Marine Corps patrols. Tanks, artillery and Cobra helicopters were involved in a firefight lasting an hour, after which the defenders fled.[40] This temporarily put a stop to the widespread view that UNITAF favoured the Aideed faction (caused in part by the collocation of UN, US and Aideed headquarters in south Mogadishu).

Notwithstanding these incidents, UNITAF was able to fully deploy and begin establishing a secure environment for the delivery of humanitarian supplies, essentially without the use of force. It successfully escorted hundreds of long- and short-haul convoys, accompanied food distribution and humanitarian activities, undertook engineering works to improve roads and airports and dig wells, provided management for ports and airfields, and supplied technical and support services to the humanitarian community.[41] Its overwhelming military presence quickly broke the stranglehold that rival militias had over supply routes, and ended the looting of humanitarian supplies and protection rackets.[42]

*Protection of humanitarian agencies and NGOs*

One issue which was never entirely resolved by UNITAF was the protection, including through the use of force, of humanitarian relief organizations. Paradoxically, in the first three months of UNITAF's tenure, more aid agency staff—both foreign and Somali—were killed than in the previous two years.[43] In Mogadishu UNITAF was reluctant to respond to requests for site security or emergency assistance. While relief organizations generally understood that

[38] Hirsch and Oakley (note 7), p. 67.
[39] Hirsch and Oakley (note 7), p. 81.
[40] Durch (note 4), p. 324.
[41] Kennedy, K. M., 'The relationship between the military and humanitarian organizations in Operation Restore Hope', *International Peacekeeping*, vol. 3, no. 1 (spring 1996), pp. 101–102.
[42] Patman, R. G., 'The UN Operation in Somalia', eds R. Thakur and C. A. Thayer, *A Crisis of Expectations: UN Peacekeeping in the 1990s* (Westview Press: Boulder, Colo., 1995), p. 94.
[43] Bryden, M., 'Somalia: the wages of failure', *Current History*, vol. 94, no. 591 (Apr. 1995), p. 148.

permanent site security was impossible because of their number and because of UNITAF's other responsibilities, they were, as in Cambodia, 'incredulous at the reluctance of the military to respond when they were in trouble'.[44] They saw this as a natural part of the military's mission to establish a 'secure environment'. Oakley describes it as an 'extremely complicated' and 'dangerous' problem which UNITAF never resolved.[45]

UNITAF was particularly troubled about what to do about the heavily armed private guards retained by most of the relief organizations before UNITAF's arrival. The military viewed them as unreliable and likely to complicate any emergency response. In a number of cases UNITAF forcibly disarmed them, making the agencies feel even more vulnerable and leading to protests from NGOs and multilateral aid agencies about the effects on their security and the inconsistencies in the policy.[46] Eventually, in March 1993, UNITAF decided to routinely respond to NGO emergency calls in Mogadishu after a major incident at the headquarters of CARE (Cooperative for Assistance and Relief Everywhere) USA and the WFP, which had been blockaded and threatened by Somalis claiming back wages.[47] In contrast to Mogadishu, in the interior UNITAF's 'security umbrella' was routinely extended to humanitarian organizations, including by dispatching emergency response units if they were threatened and providing military guards for residences and warehouses. In Baidoa Australian troops provided permanent security to 10 NGO or UN agency locations, while in Jilib and Kismayo Belgian troops guarded 12 sites.[48]

### Re-establishing law and order

UNITAF troops were also faced with the problem of using force in establishing law and order more generally. This would normally be termed aid to the civil power—except that in this case there was no established civil power. Initially, despite rampant crime, UNITAF avoided adopting the role of a police force in Mogadishu, recognizing the risk this posed to its relationship with the Somali populace and the danger of becoming enmeshed in intra-Somalia conflicts. The military focused rather on asserting its presence, providing convoy escorts and force protection, reducing the level of violence generally, and preparing the transition to the UN follow-on force.[49]

---

[44] Kennedy (note 41), p. 105.
[45] Hirsch and Oakley (note 7), p. 68.
[46] United Nations Institute for Disarmament Research, *Managing Arms in Peace Processes: Somalia* (UNIDIR: Geneva, 1995), p. 78. In mid-Jan. 1993 UNITAF responded by returning confiscated weapons to the relief organizations pending the standardization of rules governing weapon confiscation. In Apr. it issued a standard weapon policy card in English and Somali which 'spelled out clearly in words and pictures the few rules that governed who could possess a weapon, what weapons were prohibited, how weapons could be carried, and what acts would result in confiscation of a weapon'. This cleared up most of the confusion. Lorenz, F. M. (Col), 'Law and anarchy in Somalia', *Parameters: US Army War College Quarterly*, vol. 23, no. 4 (winter 1993/94), p. 32.
[47] Kennedy (note 41), p. 105.
[48] Kennedy (note 41), p. 104.
[49] Kennedy (note 41), p. 104.

One of the most challenging problems in maintaining law and order concerned the use of proportionate force, short of deadly force, against low-level threats. Somalis quickly learned that, despite giving verbal warnings and making shows of force, US soldiers would not shoot at children throwing rocks or swarming over vehicles to steal equipment. This led to injuries to soldiers, frustration and inappropriate actions such as throwing rocks back.[50] Although the use of riot control agents was considered several times, it was never authorized. Soldiers eventually discovered alternatives, including tent pegs, batons, sticks and cayenne pepper spray to repel unarmed Somalis who harassed them. Cayenne pepper became such an effective tool that by the end of the operation the troops found that simply waving a can in the air was enough to warn Somalis off.[51] There were two problems with this: first, the troops' fear of inappropriate use led to delay in requesting permission to obtain and use it; and, second, some soldiers became even more hesitant to use force in appropriate circumstances because cayenne pepper was available. Marines perceived cayenne as a substitute for, rather than a complement to, the use of deadly force.

After much delay, the UN and UNITAF agreed to establish an interim Somali police force of retired Somali police officers in an attempt to establish a modicum of law and order. They were issued with light weapons for protection of police stations and use in joint patrols with UNITAF in dangerous areas. A UNITAF unit was stationed at each police station in Mogadishu to provide communications, logistics, psychological and, if necessary, military support. John Hirsch and Robert Oakley report, somewhat optimistically, that this enabled the Somali police to 'stand up to' the factions.[52]

Outside Mogadishu, non-US troops took a more proactive role in re-establishing law and order, using vastly different methods. Unlike US troops, who moved around only in trucks, usually surrounded by an impressive show of force, the French troops in Bakool province gave the impression of being at ease in their environment, which was similar to that of their previous assignment in Djibouti, and 'ready to fight on the enemy's terms if the need arose but friendly enough to be open to verbal contact if fighting could be avoided'.[53] Gérard Prunier claims that the French Foreign Legionnaires' 'authoritarian and yet "nativist" flavor' corresponded more closely to Somali expectations than 'the mixture of subsidized democratization offered by the UN—which was supported by massive US overkill capacity and involved little rapport with the natives'.[54] Ironically, the French troops were dubbed 'trigger-happy' by the US command after they killed two Somali fighters and wounded seven on a truck which tried to break through a roadblock.

In Baidoa the Australian troops, from the moment they arrived in January 1993, reportedly established 'a furious pace of aggressive patrolling and asser-

[50] Dworken (note 22), p. 30.
[51] Dworken (note 22), p. 30.
[52] Hirsch and Oakley (note 7), p. 90, fn. 4.
[53] Prunier, G., 'The experience of the European armies in Operation Restore Hope', eds Clarke and Herbst (note 10), p. 140.
[54] Prunier (note 53), p. 141.

tion', assisted by APCs.[55] They appear to have had no problem 'disposing of' or arresting 'bandits' in their area of operation, and they also re-established the local police force and legal system, including jails and courts. They described their mission as 'applying the military strategy appropriate in a low intensity conflict or peace enforcement environment with long term national rehabilitation in mind'.[56] This was said to draw on 'a rich vein of received wisdom' in the Australian Army deriving from involvement in counter-insurgency or guerrilla warfare in Viet Nam and Malaya, which Australia felt 'bore a close relationship to the situation in Somalia'.[57] An *International Herald Tribune* editorial claimed that: 'By comparison [with US troops], Australian peacekeepers operating with more restraint and impartiality were notably more successful in pacifying Baidoa'.[58] While this may be unfair, given that Mogadishu was the centre of power in Somalia while Baidoa was a backwater, there is an element of truth in it. Martin Ganzglass contrasts the Australian contingent's fully-fledged civil affairs programme, which it regarded as essential for restoring security in its area, with the US view of such efforts as mission creep.[59]

*Enforced disarmament*

Inextricably linked to the law-and-order problem was the question of disarmament. Despite continual urging by Boutros-Ghali, the pressure of humanitarian NGOs and the expectations of many Somalis, including clan leaders, UNITAF did not attempt systematic and comprehensive disarmament using force or the threat of force. As Boutros-Ghali pointedly noted, the US command interpreted the establishment of a 'secure environment' to mean the securing of ports, airports, warehouses, feeding centres and roads in order to ensure the unimpeded delivery of relief supplies, not the disarmament of armed gangs or the confiscation of heavy weapons.

The US forces made 'extraordinary efforts' to avoid involvement in disarmament of any kind.[60] Initially, they focused on reducing the visibility of weapons, especially technicals, on the streets of Mogadishu by attempting to stop them being brandished or used when US troops were present and if necessary confiscating them—although soldiers were permitted to exercise per-

---

[55] 'Report by Australia to the Comprehensive Seminar on Lessons-Learned from United Nations Operation in Somalia (UNOSOM)', Plainsboro, N.J., 13–15 Sep. 1995, p. 5.

[56] 'Report by Australia' (note 55), p. 4.

[57] 'Report by Australia' (note 55). Differences in approach to the law-and-order issue stemmed partly from different assessments of UNITAF's rights and obligations under international law. Australia argued that the presence of foreign troops in Somalia was governed by the 1949 Fourth Geneva Convention, which implied that they should restore and maintain public order, since there was no Somali government. The view of the UNITAF command was that, since UNITAF was a humanitarian rather than a military operation, it could not be considered an army of occupation and therefore could not be held legally responsible for the health, safety and welfare of the Somali people. Lorenz (note 46), p. 35.

[58] 'Learn how to peacekeep', editorial, *International Herald Tribune*, 25 Oct. 1994, p. 4.

[59] Martin R. Ganzglass, comments in *World View*, vol. 8, no. 2 (spring 1995), p. 3. Attorney Ganzglass prepared a report for UNOSOM on the Somali Penal Code.

[60] Lyons, T. and Samatur, A. I., *Somalia: State Collapse, Multilateral Intervention, and Strategies for Political Reconstruction*, Brookings Occasional Papers (Brookings Institution: Washington, DC, 1995), p. 41.

sonal judgement in each case. Normally no use of force was necessary, the threat of the heavily armed US troops being sufficient. Such efforts began as part of attempts to create security zones around US facilities, but invariably spread beyond them. While small arms were initially ignored, they too were increasingly confiscated when necessary.

There was some confusion between the weapon confiscation policy and the ROE, especially since the former changed during the mission, while the latter did not. While the ROE stated that armed individuals 'could' be challenged, the mission's disarmament policy at times said they 'should'.[61] Moreover, the right to use 'all necessary force' in relation to confiscating weapons and demilitarizing militias was confusing. Johnston decided that it did not mean 'shoot on sight' and directed commanders rather to challenge and approach the technicals to seek their voluntary surrender, using all necessary force only if this did not work.[62] Paradoxically, UNITAF probably initially disarmed more merchants and private guards of relief agencies than militiamen, who simply hid their weapons or moved them temporarily out of town.

Increasingly and inevitably, however, UNITAF became involved in what can only be described as enforced disarmament in Mogadishu, albeit limited and piecemeal. While its forces seized arms caches reported or discovered in their area of operations, relying on tips and random sweeps, they did not conduct systematic searches of houses or vehicles. Even this policy was not applied consistently. On one occasion US Marines withdrew on finding an arms cache of heavy weapons belonging to a close ally of Aideed.

Outside Mogadishu non-US contingents developed their own approach to disarmament, but none except the Belgian troops used much force. The French troops, deployed in the relatively safe Bakool province that they had requested, took a 'very minimal, close-to-the-ground, down-to-earth approach', albeit somewhat improvised, 'without bothering too much to check it with the UN'.[63] Patrolling at night in small groups on foot, they conducted surprise confiscations before the locals realized that disarmament was not official policy. After initially rebuking the French troops for exceeding their mandate,[64] the UNITAF command later reportedly let them know that it would look the other way 'provided they did not boast too much about it'.[65] The Belgian troops were the most successful at disarmament and managed to create a 'weapon-free' environment in Kismayo, but this was heavily dependent on intimidation rather than cooperation and it collapsed as soon as they withdrew.[66] The Australian and Canadian troops also conducted extensive patrolling in their sectors in order to seize technicals and arms caches in remote locations.[67]

---

[61] Dworken (note 22), p. 32.
[62] Allard (note 16), pp. 36–37.
[63] Prunier (note 53), p. 139.
[64] Patman (note 42), p. 95.
[65] Prunier (note 53), p. 139.
[66] Chopra, Eknes and Nordbø (note 8), pp. 44–45.
[67] Hirsch and Oakley (note 7), p. 74.

Despite its reluctance to enforce disarmament without agreement with the factions, UNITAF announced at an early stage that it would enforce any voluntary agreement by the factions to canton their heavy weapons.[68] Presumably this meant using force to prevent cantoned weapons being removed, rather than using force to achieve cantonment in the first place. Negotiations conducted by Oakley succeeded in producing, only days after UNITAF's arrival, the 11 December Seven-Point Agreement between Ali Mahdi Mohamed and Aideed which provided for the withdrawal of heavy weapons from city streets into designated cantons.[69] However, it took until 26 December for both sides to begin the process and even then it was only patchily implemented. UNITAF declined to use force to achieve implementation.

There were two further efforts at negotiated disarmament of heavy weapons which were equally unsuccessful. First, on 8 January 1993, in Addis Ababa, Ethiopia, 15 Somali factions signed an Agreement on Implementing the Cease-fire and on Modalities of Disarmament.[70] The process was to begin immediately and, totally unrealistically, was expected to be completed in March. In mid-February 1993 Ali Mahdi Mohamed did in fact turn over all his cantoned technicals to UNITAF. Aideed's technicals, however, quietly disappeared from their cantons to points unknown, outside Mogadishu. Hirsch and Oakley explain that it seemed unnecessary to confront Aideed over this so long as the weapons posed no threat to UNITAF or humanitarian operations and UNITAF was able to confiscate weapons found in the course of its operations without setting off a firefight.[71] This happened occasionally in Mogadishu, Baidoa and elsewhere, but Aideed always disowned those involved as 'bandits'. By late February, as more of his weapons caches were discovered and either removed or placed under guard in accordance with the Addis Ababa Agreement, Aideed was complaining that UNITAF was favouring Ali Mahdi Mohamed.

Second, on 27 March the same 15 Somali factions which had signed the Addis Ababa Agreement met there again in the Conference on National Reconciliation in Somalia.[72] They reaffirmed their commitment to disarmament under UN supervision and declared that June would now be the target date. Ironically, in view of what was to follow, they practically invited peace enforcement against themselves by urging UNITAF/UNOSOM to 'apply strong and effect-

---

[68] Hirsch and Oakley (note 7), p. 105.

[69] *Africa Watch*, vol. 5, no. 2 (7 Mar. 1993), p. 6; and Hirsch and Oakley (note 7), p. 58.

[70] United Nations, Progress report of the Secretary-General on the situation in Somalia, including annexes containing the texts of the agreements reached by the Somali factions in Addis Ababa from 4 to 15 January 1993, UN document S/25168, 26 Jan. 1993, annex III, Agreement on implementing the cease-fire and on modalities of disarmament (supplement to the General Agreement signed in Addis Ababa on 8 January 1993). It called for a verifiable, country-wide ceasefire supervised by a UNITAF/UNOSOM monitoring group; the surrender of all heavy weapons to the group; the encampment of militias at 'appropriate areas outside major towns where they would 'not pose difficulties for peace'; the simultaneous disarmament of all factions throughout Somalia; and the disarming and reintegration into society of all other 'armed elements'.

[71] Hirsch and Oakley (note 7), p. 59.

[72] The Addis Ababa Agreement, concluded at the first session of the Conference on National Reconciliation in Somalia, 27 Mar. 1993, reproduced in *The United Nations and Somalia 1992–1996* (note 1), pp. 264–66.

ive sanctions against those responsible for any violations of the January 1993 ceasefire'.[73] Ironically, too, UNITAF's leadership and staff had by now come to see disarmament as an important, if unmandated, component of their mission in Somalia.[74]

While UNITAF for the most part avoided using force to achieve what little disarmament occurred, it also failed to achieve a truly secure environment. Essentially the policy occupied a middle ground between doing nothing about disarmament and expending too much political and military capital on it.[75] Somalis 'naturally hedged their bets and hid guns until they could feel secure without them', with enormous consequences for the follow-on UN force.[76]

## Use of force for peace enforcement

On 24 January 1993 UNITAF used its peace enforcement powers on a signifi-cant scale for the first and only time when US helicopter gunships and Belgian armour attacked the forces of General Mohamed Siad Hersi (known as Morgan), leader of the Somali National Front (SNF), near Kismayo. His forces had ignored warnings by the local UNITAF commander and broken the Addis Ababa ceasefire agreement by attacking forces of Aideed's ally Colonel Omar Jess. UNITAF destroyed technicals and artillery pieces and forced the SNF to withdraw into the bush. When Morgan's forces managed to infiltrate past UNITAF back into Kismayo, collusion between UNITAF and Morgan against Jess was suspected. This led to an attack by Aideed forces against Nigerian troops in Mogadishu at the Kilometre Four (KM4) traffic circle, apparently because they were perceived to be the weakest contingent and the easiest to terrorize. Forewarned by US intelligence and supported by US Marines, the Nigerian troops beat off the attack, with only two wounded, 'but in four hours they expended a great deal of ammunition, leaving the widespread impression that a large battle had occurred'.[77] Despite exaggerated press reports and panicky reactions on the part of the UN and some NGOs, the violence was con-fined to several city blocks and died out as UNITAF waited the crisis out. No further violence against UNITAF occurred after Oakley and Marine Brigadier Anthony Zinni (Johnston's deputy for operations) warned Aideed that he would be held personally responsible.[78]

[73] Hirsch and Oakley (note 7), p. 99.

[74] Interviews conducted by UNIDIR researcher Clement Adibe with military personnel. *Managing Arms in Peace Processes: Somalia* (note 46), p. 82.

[75] *Managing Arms in Peace Processes: Somalia* (note 46), p. 77.

[76] Lyons and Samatur (note 60), p. 41. Boutros-Ghali reported to the Security Council that in Mar. and Apr. 1993 UNITAF had confiscated about 150 handguns; more than 750 rifles; more than 200 machine guns and an equal number of other heavy weapons such as rocket launchers and mortars; nearly 50 armoured vehicles including tanks, APCs and self-propelled guns; more than 400 artillery pieces; almost 700 other weapons; and close to 79 000 items of ordnance. United Nations, Further report of the Secretary-General submitted in pursuance of paragraph 18 of Resolution 814 (1993), UN document S/26317, 17 Aug. 1993, para. 18. Impressive as this sounds, it merely scratched the surface of the problem.

[77] Hirsch and Oakley (note 7), p. 77.

[78] Hirsch and Oakley (note 7), pp. 78–79.

## Factors in the avoidance of use of force

UNITAF was widely judged as having been highly successful in fulfilling its mandate, albeit using a narrow interpretation, without using significant force. It certainly succeeded in creating the conditions for the safe delivery of humanitarian assistance to Somalis in need. By January 1993 a measure of normalcy had even returned to Mogadishu. By March the number of deaths from famine had dropped dramatically and the rudiments of civil society were being reconstructed, especially outside the capital.

The reasons why UNITAF was able to accomplish its mission successfully without using much force are complex. At the strategic level, UNITAF's deployment in force, its overwhelming military capability and its robust posture overawed the factions. For Hirsch and Oakley at least:

At the height of UNITAF's success it became clear that a severely minimalist approach to the use of force was far more likely to hamper a peacekeeping operation, inviting challenge by appearing weak, rather than inspiring cooperation by demonstrating both strength and peaceful intent . . . The will and ability to use overwhelming force to back a peacekeeping operation—as the Weinberger-Powell doctrine recommends—offers the greatest possibility of successfully completing a peacekeeping mission and minimizing casualties on all sides.[79]

Unlike most UN peacekeeping operations, whose military capabilities are far less impressive, UNITAF also sought, both from the outset and throughout its mission, deliberately to employ the deterrent effect of the explicit threat of force. On 11 December, along with Force Commander Johnston and SRSG Kittani, Oakley held a meeting with the faction leaders. Reminding them of the massive firepower the USA had used in the Persian Gulf War, he warned them of the potential disaster should they 'unintentionally' clash with US forces.[80]

Like a classic UN peacekeeping operation, UNITAF sought to lessen the chances of armed opposition by obtaining the consent of the parties to its arrival and presence. Oakley, who as former US Ambassador to Somalia knew most of the major local players, arrived ahead of the force to 'clear a political path' for the intervention.[81] However, consent was hardly rock solid: Aideed reportedly acquiesced only at the last minute in the face of overwhelming odds and because he saw UNITAF as an alternative to 'his perceived nemesis', the UN.[82] Ali Mahdi Mohamed welcomed UNITAF as a counterweight to Aideed. As is common in peace operations, each side sought to use the intervention to its own advantage.

This threat of the use of force was combined with continuing dialogue with the factions throughout the deployment. Oakley says that he hoped to create a peaceful environment by 'dialogue and cooption, using the implicit threat of coercion to encourage the faction leaders to gain prestige by showing leadership

[79] Hirsch and Oakley (note 7), p. 162.
[80] Hirsch and Oakley (note 7), p. 55.
[81] Durch (note 4), p. 323.
[82] Durch (note 4), p. 320.

at home and to the international community'.[83] The establishment of a 'joint security committee', a Somali-language newspaper and a radio station to promote UNITAF's objectives, and the eventual resurrection of the rudiments of a Somali police force were all elements of the strategy. Remarkably, the main factions also established a security committee, sometimes with US military and civilian officials present, which met almost daily between January and April 1993 to discuss weapons and other issues.[84] Don Daniel and Brad Hayes claim that Oakley 'demonstrated time and time again that skilful diplomacy backed by political will and credible force can be used to achieve desired objectives'.[85] By such means UNITAF was relatively successful in treating the parties impartially.

At the tactical level, the use of force was avoided because of the relatively tight command and control and discipline of the coalition forces. Hirsch and Oakley claim that the low number of Somali casualties demonstrates the success of the UNITAF command in instilling restraint and discipline in all the contingents.[86] The Somalis, they say, responded similarly. The high degree of discipline and restraint shown by the US forces as the lead contingent was a key factor. Although in a number of cases the ROE would clearly have permitted the use of deadly force, US troops often held fire or relied on less violent means. Lorenz notes that his had the positive effect, at least during the first few months, of maintaining good relations with the community and saving many lives.[87] Nonetheless Zinni wished he had had more non-lethal options, particularly to deal with orchestrated demonstrations: 'The Somalis knew we could not use deadly force; if we were provoked into using deadly force, it would just serve the ends of one or more of the warlords orchestrating the violence'.[88]

During the mission there were only four cases where US soldiers were suspected of using inappropriate force (called 'Article 32' cases in US military parlance) and two courts martial.[89] Only after the mission was over was it publicly revealed that a small group of Canadian soldiers in Beledweyne had been involved in the torture and murder of a Somali and mistreatment of others.[90]

---

[83] Hirsch and Oakley (note 7), p. 56.

[84] Hirsch and Oakley (note 7), p. 58.

[85] Daniel and Hayes with de Jonge Oudraat (note 37), p. 109.

[86] Hirsch and Oakley (note 7), p. 82. However, neither UNITAF nor UNOSOM kept records of Somali casualties. Chopra, Eknes and Nordbø (note 8), p. 46.

[87] Lorenz (note 46), p. 25.

[88] Zinni, A. (Lt-Gen.), 'It's not nice and neat', *Proceedings, US Naval Institute*, vol. 121, no. 8 (Aug. 1995), p. 30.

[89] Dworken (note 22), p. 26. Lorenz records that during the UNITAF operation all reported shooting incidents were followed by a command review to determine if there had been excessive use of force. Lorenz (note 46), p. 33.

[90] 'The killing of a Somali jars Canada', *New York Times*, 11 Feb. 1996; and *Financial Times*, 4 July 1997, p. 5. The soldiers involved were tried and 1 was convicted. On 16 Mar. 1993, the commanding officer of Canada's 2 Command had ordered his troops 'to capture and abuse prisoners'. For these and other transgressions their unit, the Canadian Airborne Regiment, was disbanded in disgrace in 1995, ultimately forcing a rethinking of Canadian military and peacekeeping training. For a detailed discussion of the factors that resulted in this tragedy see Klep and Winslow (note 35), pp. 93–137.

Similar accusations were made against the Belgian contingent.[91]

In contrast to the case of UNOSOM II, there were few command and control problems between the various national contingents. This was due to the use of liaison officers, who provided continuous communication with headquarters. Moreover, national commanders were allowed considerable discretion in carrying out mission objectives, taking into account differences in doctrine, training and equipment, the extent of their area of responsibility and the degree of threat. An additional factor, Hirsch and Oakley claim, was 'the prestige enjoyed by the well prepared, equipped, and commanded US forces'.[92] Yet not all contingents could be swayed into doing what the UNITAF command wanted them to do:

We had the forces of eight nations defending the airport. Was that because that airfield was so big or so threatened? No. It was because the forces of those eight nations could go no farther than the airfield when they got off the airplane. For either political or military reasons, that was about it. But they got participation points; and obviously the sense of international legitimacy that is given to you is important to someone. It shouldn't be discounted. So as a commander you've got to take all that into account.[93]

Allard attributes UNITAF's success in avoiding widespread violence to its ROE,[94] which its leadership had concluded early on would be critical. Indeed, much more attention was devoted by UNITAF to achieving appropriate ROE, applicable across the entire mission, than was normal for a UN mission. There were claims, however, that the ROE were 'too technical, incomplete and ambiguous to be easily understood . . . and appeared too late to be integrated into pre-deployment training'.[95] There was also confusion over which rules took precedence in a particular area of operations—the unclassified cards given to soldiers or the actual, classified ROE.

Several US units asked for tailored ROE explanations and clarification after the Article 32 incidents.[96] A significant point of confusion was whether the use of deadly force was authorized to prevent theft of weapons or vital equipment. The best known case, highlighted by the press, involved the theft of a soldier's night-vision goggles.[97] A Fragmentary Order was given stating that deadly force could be used.[98] Colonel W. J. A. (Bill) Mellor notes that there were some 'delicate' issues between the contingents relating to ROE, notably the use of riot control agents, but these were 'generally resolved to everyone's satisfaction'.[99]

[91] Some Belgian troops were accused of brutality against Somalis and of beating and shooting violators of their disarmament regulations, but were acquitted. Chopra, Eknes and Nordbø (note 8), p. 45.

[92] Hirsch and Oakley (note 7), p. 76.

[93] Zinni (note 88), p. 30.

[94] Allard (note 16), p. 37.

[95] Klep and Winslow (note 35), p. 105.

[96] Dworken (note 22), p. 30.

[97] Hardesty, J. M. (Col) and Ellis, J. D., 'Training for peace operations: the US Army adapts to the post-cold war world', *Peaceworks* (United States Institute of Peace, Washington, DC), no. 12 (Feb. 1997), p. 11.

[98] Dworken (note 22), p. 31.

[99] Mellor (note 34), p. 162.

At least before its successor mission began to go seriously wrong, UNITAF was being promoted as a model to which UN peace operations should aspire. Some saw it as an example, perhaps the first, of multilateral peace enforcement. In the view of one observer: 'Uniquely in the history of peace operations, UNITAF maintained consent by making the parties believe that opposition would be futile'.[100] Certainly the US component had arrived decisively and adopted a tough, albeit defensive, posture. It was also successful in achieving its mission, in not being drawn into the conflict itself, in using minimal force and in safely withdrawing. Yet not only did US forces fail to forcibly disarm the warlords when they were militarily able to do so, but they 'compounded their error by telegraphing their departure and creating a dozen other reinforcements for negative behavior'.[101] The warlords cooperated with UNITAF, undoubtedly in the expectation that the UN follow-on peacekeeping force would be militarily weaker. Had UNITAF stayed longer it might have encountered exactly the same challenges to its authority as UNOSOM II did—and behaved in exactly the same way.

## II. The second UN Operation in Somalia (1993–95)

On 26 March 1993 the Security Council unanimously adopted Resolution 814, authorizing the second UN Operation in Somalia (UNOSOM II) to succeed UNITAF. It was to be the first mission organized and commanded by the UN to be *explicitly* mandated under Chapter VII of the UN Charter and the first since the Congo to be specifically mandated to use force beyond self-defence. Like UNOSOM I and UNITAF before it, it was to be deployed without the consent of a host government, since Somalia still did not have one.

The original intention had been that UNITAF would be succeeded by a traditional UN peacekeeping mission which would inherit a secure and peaceable theatre of operations. As it became increasingly clear that UNITAF was both unwilling and unable to achieve this, pressure mounted on the UN to prepare to deploy a follow-on peace enforcement operation. The Bush administration, eager for the US forces to leave Somalia as soon as possible, argued as early as 18 December 1992 for a more 'muscular' approach by the UN.[102] The administration of President Bill Clinton, inaugurated in January 1993, shared Bush's fears about the USA becoming bogged down in a quagmire or suffering politically unacceptable casualties if it stayed too long. It too supported a robust UN operation, in line with its policy of 'assertive multilateralism'.

Boutros-Ghali, however, arguing that his conditions for a smooth transition—disarmament and the deployment of UNITAF throughout Somalia—had not been met, hoped that he could use public pressure and the power of inertia to

---

[100] RAND Project Memorandum, May 1995, cited in Cervenak, C. M., 'Lessons of the past: experiences in peace operations', eds A. H. Chayes and G. T. Raach, *Peace Operations: Developing an American Strategy* (National Defense University Press: Washington, DC, 1995), pp. 55–56.

[101] Rotberg, R., 'The lessons of Somalia for the future of US foreign policy', eds Clarke and Herbst (note 10), p. 235.

[102] Boutros-Ghali (note 1), p. 41.

prolong UNITAF's stay.[103] Despite his ground-breaking *Agenda for Peace* and his brave references to the need for UN 'peace enforcement units', the Secretary-General was extremely hesitant to launch the UN into anything beyond peacekeeping. He and his senior officials—Under Secretary-General for Peace-keeping Marrack Goulding and Under Secretary-General for Political Affairs James Jonah—considered that the UN was not yet prepared for such a challenge as peace enforcement, especially because it was barely coping with its burgeoning peacekeeping commitments. Moreover, the ethos of traditional peacekeeping remained strong in UN thinking. Boutros-Ghali and his top officials had insisted from the earliest discussions on UNITAF that the coalition force itself should not become the follow-on UN operation, since it was seen as a 'corruption of traditional peacekeeping involving too much emphasis on use of force and too great a role for the United States'.[104]

The dispute was resolved by the USA drafting and pushing through a resolution that reflected its own vision. As the Secretary-General noted: 'This implied a return to the fifth option I had presented to the Security Council in November 1992'—a country-wide UN enforcement operation.[105]

## The mandate

UNOSOM II's mandate, unlike UNITAF's, was widely perceived to be nation-building. Madeleine Albright, the US Ambassador to the UN, called it 'an unprecedented enterprise aimed at nothing less than the restoration of an entire country as a proud, functioning and viable member of the community of nations'[106] but, belying her enthusiasm, the mandating resolution asked the UN only to provide 'assistance' to the Somalis, rather than take charge of rebuilding the country for them.[107]

The first part of the resolution, which was not linked to Chapter VII, enjoined UNOSOM and all other UN agencies to assist in famine relief, economic rehabilitation, the repatriation of refugees and displaced persons, the re-establishment of national and regional institutions, the re-establishment of the Somali police, the investigation and facilitation of the prosecution of serious violations of international law, the development of a de-mining programme, the monitoring of the arms embargo, disarmament, and the creation of conditions for political reconciliation, rehabilitation and reconstruction. The second part of the resolution, which did fall under Chapter VII, in addition to demanding greater cooperation from the Somali factions, mandated the most ambitious military tasks of any UN peace operation ever:

---

[103] By Mar. 1993 only 40% of Somalia was under UNITAF control. Boutros-Ghali (note 1), p. 41. There were no UNITAF forces in the north-east (Somaliland), the north-west or the extreme south near the Kenyan border, where the security situation was particularly unstable. In addition, in the central area around Galcaio there was a 'security hole' where UNITAF did not penetrate.

[104] Hirsch and Oakley (note 7), p. 45.

[105] Boutros-Ghali (note 1), p. 42.

[106] Quoted in Boutros-Ghali (note 1), p. 44.

[107] UN Security Council Resolution 814, 26 Mar. 1993.

(*a*) to monitor that all factions continue to respect the cessation of hostilities and other agreements to which they have agreed, particularly the Addis Ababa agreements of January 1993; (*b*) to prevent any resumption of violence and, if necessary, take appropriate action against any faction that violates or threatens to violate the cessation of hostilities; (*c*) to maintain control of the heavy weapons of the organized factions which will have been brought under international control pending their eventual destruction or transfer to a newly constituted national army; (*d*) to seize the small arms of unauthorized armed elements and to assist in the registration and security of such arms; (*e*) to secure or maintain security at all ports, airports and lines of communications required for the delivery of humanitarian assistance; (*f*) to protect, as required, the personnel, installations and equipment of the United Nations and its agencies, ICRC as well as NGOs and to take such forceful action as may be required to neutralize armed elements that attack, or threaten to attack, such facilities and personnel, pending the establishment of a new Somali police force which can assume this responsibility; (*g*) to continue the programme for mine-clearing in the most afflicted areas; (*h*) to assist in the repatriation of refugees and displaced persons within Somalia; (*i*) to carry out such other functions as might be authorized by the Security Council.[108]

The resolution clearly envisaged the use of force beyond self-defence in carrying out these tasks. The factions were to be forcibly disarmed if they failed to comply with agreed timetables and modalities. Armed elements were to be 'neutralized' if they even threatened to attack UN personnel or facilities, the ICRC or NGOs. To prevent any resumption of violence, 'appropriate action' could be taken against any faction. Despite Colin Powell's retrospective claim that 'I always said that disarming the factions was stupid',[109] this wide-ranging mandate was approved in US inter-agency forums, where there was no resistance from the Department of Defense.[110]

The Secretary-General himself seemed to have an expansive view of the use of force, recommending that the force commander be permitted to draw up ROE to permit him to take 'any action needed to implement UNOSOM II's mandate'.[111] He also requested the following capabilities for UNOSOM II: (*a*) patrolling and close combat; (*b*) information-gathering and interpretation; (*c*) indirect fire; (*d*) anti-armour fire; (*e*) all-weather night and day operations; (*f*) casualty evacuation; (*g*) tactical communications; and (*h*) air support (firepower and transport).[112] Such capabilities were unheard of in a UN operation, with the exception of the Congo. Boutros-Ghali warned, however, that:

Notwithstanding the compelling necessity for authority to use enforcement measures as appropriate, I continue to hold to my conviction that the political will to achieve security, reconciliation and peace must spring from the Somalis themselves. Even if it is

---

[108] United Nations, Further report of the Secretary-General submitted in pursuance of paragraphs 18 and 19 of Resolution 794 (1992), UN document S/25354, 3 Mar. 1993, and addenda S/25354/Add. 1, 11 Mar. 1993, and S/25354/Add.2, 22 Mar. 1993, reproduced in *The United Nations and Somalia 1992–1996* (note 1), pp. 244–57.

[109] Memorandum for Senator Thurmond and Senator Nunn (note 6), p. 19.

[110] Memorandum for Senator Thurmond and Senator Nunn (note 6), p. 19.

[111] Further report of the Secretary-General (note 108), para. 88.

[112] Further report of the Secretary-General (note 108), para. 77.

authorized to resort to forceful action in certain circumstances, UNOSOM II cannot and must not be expected to substitute itself for the Somali people. Nor can or should it use its authority to impose one or another system of governmental organization.[113]

Presciently, he wondered whether the troop-contributing countries would 'follow through on an enforcement mission if hostile action by one or more of the factions led to casualties among their troops'.[114]

## The force

Despite its more ambitious mandate, UNOSOM II had a smaller, less capable and less coherent military force than UNITAF.[115] Its authorized strength was just 28 000, including 20 000 troops and 8000 civilian and logistics personnel. Along with major contingents from Belgium, France and Italy, a 4000-strong Pakistani brigade was pledged. Eventually 30 countries contributed troops.

The USA provided 4000 troops, the bulk of UNOSOM's logistical units, which were simply transferred from UNITAF, thereby ensuring at least some continuity. While this was the first time the USA had ever contributed troops to UN peacekeeping, and was therefore a ground-breaking venture into multi-lateral cooperation, the USA aimed to keep its contribution as small as possible while not allowing the UN operation to fail.[116]

To this end, for use in emergencies the USA positioned a Joint Task Force (JTF) off the Somali coast, and on land provided a small tactical Quick Reaction Force (QRF). Consisting of a light battalion from the 10th Mountain Division, with helicopter support, the QRF would be available for immediate combat deployment 'for a limited period or for show-of-force operations' at the request of the UNOSOM II commander 'to counter specific threats that exceed the capability of UNOSOM II units'.[117] It was expressly barred from spear-heading routine operations, escorting convoys or conducting other longer-term security tasks.[118] The plan was for it to move offshore as soon as conditions improved and return to the USA as soon as possible. In August 1993 the USA deployed a third force to Somalia, the US Army Task Force Ranger and Delta Force commandos.

The Secretary-General explained to the Security Council why he felt UNOSOM II could manage with just 28 000 troops for the whole of Somalia (excluding the JTF and QRF), while UNITAF had had 37 000 in only part of the country for less ambitious tasks. First, UNITAF had managed to largely end organized fighting with heavy weapons. The current challenge, to contain sporadic and localized fighting, could be met with fewer troops. Second,

---

[113] Boutros-Ghali (note 1), p. 254.
[114] Boutros-Ghali (note 1), p. 44.
[115] Although 28 000 was the scaled-down size of UNITAF after the initial large-scale landing.
[116] Memorandum for Senator Thurmond and Senator Nunn (note 6), p. 17.
[117] 'Terms of reference for US Forces Somalia, United Nations Operation in Somalia' in *Peace Operations*, FM 100-23 (note 23), appendix A, annex A, p. 70.
[118] 'Terms of reference for US Forces Somalia' (note 117), p. 70.

intelligence-gathering capabilities developed by UNITAF could provide early warning of violent situations and allow the force commander to deploy troops in timely fashion. Third, the re-establishment of a Somali police force should help improve law and order and release UNOSOM troops from guard duties for more demanding tasks. Finally, the QRF was available on call. Appearing not entirely convinced of his own reasoning, Boutros-Ghali warned that reinforcements might be needed and emphasized the crucial importance of US logistic and other support.[119]

By the 4 May 1993 handover date UNOSOM II was nowhere near its authorized strength. It comprised barely 18 000 troops. Two of the most capable UNITAF contingents, the Australian and the Canadian, were leaving their deployment areas without being replaced. The troops who had arrived lacked adequate equipment. The Pakistani troops, due to take over from the US Marines in south Mogadishu, and who were just starting to arrive as the Marines left, had no armour or vehicles (which were still on the high seas) and, 'somewhat pathetically', no flak jackets.[120] Neither the Pakistani nor the Italian contingents, who were deployed in north Mogadishu, had body armour or riot control agents, nor were they trained in military operations in urban areas, night operations or riot control, deficiencies that were to prove fatal as the situation turned violent.[121] Helicopters were in short supply and tanks non-existent. Logistical, engineering, intelligence and psychological warfare resources were inadequate. Ominously, small but vital parts of UNITAF were not replicated, notably the psychological operations (PsyOps) unit which ran the mission radio station and newspaper, the engineers, the civil affairs unit (which UNITAF had eventually acquired) and other 'force multipliers'.[122]

Surprisingly, Hirsch and Oakley argue that UNOSOM II's military was in 'relatively sound condition' in the sense that it had enough troops to take over from UNITAF in Mogadishu and in the nine humanitarian relief sectors, and had more troops than Johnston had had in the preceding month.[123] The largest gap was in the Bardera–Kismayo corridor and towards the Kenyan border, where the expected Indian brigade had yet to deploy.

On the civilian side the situation was much bleaker. The civilian component was 'minimalist', fashioned ad hoc from the remnants of UNITAF and UNOSOM I and overwhelmed by the powerful military command. At the time of the handover it comprised a 'small, exhausted, and demoralized staff at UNOSOM headquarters and an even skimpier, equally demoralized staff in the interior',[124] only 25 per cent of its authorized level of 2800, with no computers

[119] Further report of the Secretary-General and addenda (note 108), p. 252.

[120] Clarke, W. and Herbst, J., 'Somalia and the future of humanitarian intervention', eds Clarke and Herbst (note 10), p. 244.

[121] Anderson, G., 'UNOSOM II: not failure, not success', eds D. C. F. Daniel and B. C. Hayes, *Beyond Traditional Peacekeeping* (Macmillan: London, 1995), p. 274.

[122] Hirsch and Oakley (note 7), p. 153.

[123] Hirsch and Oakley (note 7), p. 112.

[124] Hirsch and Oakley (note 7), p. 113; and Chopra, Eknes and Nordbø (note 8), p. 73.

and a 'low level of organization'.[125] By May little more than half of its staff had materialized. The SRSG asked for US and UN assistance, and staff were seconded from US government agencies, further Americanizing the mission. UNOSOM II's inauspicious beginnings 'magnified every administrative and operational problem that it faced'[126] and left it 'in a state of disarray at precisely the time that it most needed to resemble a united, coherent initiative'.[127]

## Command and control

As in traditional UN peacekeeping, the head of UNOSOM II was the SRSG, to whom UNOSOM II's civilian hierarchy and the military force commander reported. In this case, however, the SRSG was a military man, retired US submarine commander Admiral Jonathan Howe. The USA thus retained a key position in the follow-on operation. It also provided the deputy military commander, Major-General Thomas Montgomery. The force commander was General Çevik Bir of Turkey, a NATO ally. Despite this US influence, Howe and Bir tended to look to UN Headquarters for decisions and Boutros-Ghali's style (like that of Hammarskjöld in the Congo) was to retain close control.[128]

The most significant departure from the normal UN command structure was the fact that all the US forces except its logistics troops were under US, not UN, command. This included the QRF, the JTF and the Intelligence Support Element. The QRF was under the command of the CENTCOM commander-in-chief, based in the USA (although for each of the series of raids on Aideed's clan in 1993 it came under the temporary tactical control of Deputy Commander Montgomery in his US role). The US Rangers deployed in October 1993 came with their own commanding general and remained under US Special Operations Command in Florida, bypassing both the UN command and Montgomery, even in his US role.[129] These arrangements reflected three fundamental US objectives designed to satisfy military and congressional concerns: 'to keep US forces firmly under US operational control, to reduce the visibility of US combat forces in the operation, and to eliminate any misperception that those forces were under the command of the United Nations'.[130]

Montgomery claimed that these unusual formal arrangements were offset by close working relationships between UNOSOM II and all the US commanders tasked with supporting it.[131] Nonetheless, while it had been relatively easy for UNITAF's single force commander to make rapid decisions by himself, maintain operational security regarding the use of force and obtain a high degree of

[125] Chopra, Eknes and Nordbø (note 8), p. 67.
[126] Durch (note 4), p. 335.
[127] Boulden, J., *The United Nations and Mandate Enforcement: Congo, Somalia, and Bosnia*, Martello Papers no. 20 (Centre for International Relations, Queen's University: Kingston, Ont., 1999), p. 67.
[128] Hirsch and Oakley (note 7), p. 113.
[129] Ruggie, J. G., 'Peacekeeping and US interests', *Washington Quarterly*, vol. 17, no. 4 (autumn 1994), pp. 181–82.
[130] Allard (note 16), p. 57.
[131] Allard (note 16), pp. 59–60.

cohesion between the various national contingents,[132] it was clear that Howe, Bir and Montgomery collectively could not 'provide the kind of glue or create the centre of gravity that the US provided in UNITAF'.[133]

UNOSOM II's civilian command relationships were even weaker. The SRSG's operational authority did not extend to the other UN agencies in the country. Nor did it extend to the NGO community, close contact with which was lost when UNITAF's successful Civilian–Military Operations Center (CMOC) was not reconstituted.[134] When Oakley was sent back to Somalia as US Special Representative after the killing of US troops on 3 October 1993, the civilian line of authority became even less clear.[135] Boutros-Ghali himself described UNOSOM II as a 'strange and fragmented mission'.[136]

## The military concept of operations

In striking contrast to most previous UN peace operations, with their makeshift arrangements and ad hoc operational concepts, UNOSOM II from the outset actually had both a 'military concept of operations' and a 'cease-fire and disarmament concept'. Proposed by the Secretary-General and approved by the Security Council, they displayed strong US influence, since most of the initiative in drawing them up had come from UNITAF.

Military operations were to be conducted in four phases—I: transition from UNITAF; II: consolidation and expansion of security; III: transfer to civilian administration; and IV: redeployment.[137] The phases were not meant to be applied rigidly or uniformly throughout Somalia but to describe a general sequence. Military support to relief operations and disarmament would thus continue throughout the transition until it was no longer necessary. In phase III, major efforts would be made to help civil authorities exercise greater responsibility, permitting the military presence to be scaled down and the tempo of military operations to be reduced. Phase III would end when a Somali national police force was operating and major UN military operations were no longer required. At an appropriate stage UNOSOM II would be redeployed or reduced.

A key accompaniment to the military concept of operations was the disarmament strategy, worked out jointly by UNITAF and UNOSOM II prior to the handover and presented by the Secretary-General to the Security Council for approval in March 1993.[138] Deriving from the factions' 27 March disarmament agreement, the plan involved the establishment of 'transition sites', open to verification by UNOSOM, where factional forces would be given temporary accommodation while they turned in their small arms, registered for

---

[132] Hirsch and Oakley (note 7), p. 114, fn. 21.
[133] Chopra, Eknes and Nordbø (note 8), p. 48.
[134] Gary Anderson appears to believe that it continued to operate under UNOSOM II. Anderson (note 121), p. 271.
[135] Howe (note 14), p. 185.
[136] Boutros-Ghali, B., *Unvanquished: A US–UN Saga* (I. B. Tauris: New York, 1999), p. 93.
[137] Further report of the Secretary-General and addenda (note 108), pp. 252–53.
[138] Further report of the Secretary-General and addenda (note 108).

future government and NGO support, and received guidance and training for their reintegration into civilian life. Factions or personnel who failed to comply would have their weapons and equipment confiscated and/or destroyed. The plan called for a phased approach, beginning in the south and moving north. By May 1993, in order to prevent the ceasefire and disarmament agreement from total collapse[139] and pending the arrival of the necessary resources for fulfilling the original plan, a new four-stage plan was devised with different tiers of disarmament in different regions. One of the stages called, optimistically, for 'commencement of overt military action within selected zones to effect disarmament',[140] including cordon and search missions. This would undoubtedly involve the use of force if resistance were encountered.

Despite having enforcement powers, UNOSOM headquarters was divided over using force to achieve disarmament.[141] Seasoned UN officials with traditional UN peacekeeping experience favoured negotiated disarmament only. The opposing, predominant, view was held by other UN civilian officials, the many US advisers from the Department of Defense and the National Security Council, the UNOSOM military and Boutros-Ghali.

## Use of force policy and ROE

Although this was the first UN peace operation to be mandated from the outset to use force beyond self-defence, neither the Security Council nor the Secretary-General provided guidance on the use of force. The ROE for UNOSOM II were, typically for a UN operation, to be devised by the force commander without assistance from the Security Council, the Secretary-General or the UN Secretariat. In what may have been one of the first references ever in a UN document to the term 'rules of engagement' (undoubtedly reflecting US influence on UNOSOM II planning), the Secretary-General simply noted that the ROE would 'authorize and direct commanders to take certain specific actions if they were judged necessary to fulfil the mandate'.[142] There were no prior consultations with or agreements among the troop contributors on ROE or command and control.[143]

The UNOSOM II ROE were, in these circumstances, modelled closely on UNITAF's.[144] Like UNITAF's they were based on the concepts of 'perceived threat and proportional response'.[145] Hirsch and Oakley claim that there was, at least initially, 'a fair amount of conceptual carryover from traditional peacekeeping'.[146] Given that so little of UN experience had been conceptualized, this

[139] Adibe, C., 'Part I: case study' in *Managing Arms in Peace Processes: Somalia* (note 46), p. 90.

[140] *Managing Arms in Peace Processes: Somalia* (note 46), pp. 88–91.

[141] Chopra, Eknes and Nordbø (note 8), p. 63.

[142] Further report of the Secretary-General and addenda (note 108), p. 254.

[143] Hirsch and Oakley (note 7), p. 113. UNOSOM's ROE are reproduced in appendix 2 in this volume.

[144] Lorenz (note 46), p. 29. In Apr. 1993, as UNITAF Staff Judge Advocate, Lorenz assisted UNOSOM staff in developing the UNOSOM II ROE.

[145] Harrell, M. C. and Howe, R., 'Military issues in multinational operations', eds Daniel and Hayes (note 121), p. 198.

[146] Hirsch and Oakley (note 7), p. 113.

was itself worrying. Even more worrying was that UN staff responsibility for UNOSOM II's ROE fell to a Belgian lieutenant-colonel in the operations section who had no prior experience of ROE.[147]

When the confrontation with Aideed began, the ROE were strengthened. In May 1993 the force commander issued Fragmentary Order 39 (FO 39), which stated that: 'Organized, armed militias, technicals, and other crew served weapons are considered a threat to UNOSOM Forces *and may be engaged without provocation*'.[148] This entitled UN forces to act more preventively in potentially dangerous situations and gave them virtually a blank cheque with regard to coercive weapons control. Allard suggests that: 'There is a direct line of continuity between [FO 39] and the increasing involvement of US forces in combat operations' in UNOSOM II.[149] A new fragmentary order on 8 July 1993 replaced the term 'hostile forces' with 'enemy forces'.[150] In January 1994, after a marine sniper team engaged a machine gunner atop a bus, the ROE were again amended to exclude targets where collateral damage could not be controlled.[151]

## The use of force by UNOSOM II

Although the immediate transitional period was relatively quiet, force was increasingly used by UNOSOM in self-defence as the factions began testing the mission's resolve through random sniping and harassment. UNOSOM also began using force in defence of its mission and in enforcing disarmament. After June 1993 it used substantial military force in attempting to capture or kill General Aideed and his senior lieutenants. The most violent of these military engagements were, however, initiated and conducted not by UNOSOM forces but by US troops acting outside the UN chain of command. Since UNOSOM used very little force in carrying out the humanitarian and other non-disarmament aspects of its mandate, the following account deals principally with the use of force to ensure disarmament and the consequences of doing so.

### The events of 5 June: an inspection goes wrong

With UNOSOM II's arrival, the USC/SNA began to infiltrate its heavy weapons back into Mogadishu. Since UNOSOM II was relatively well resourced and militarily strong in the capital, it was here that it first attempted systematic disarmament. In early June UNOSOM command decided to re-inspect five of the USC/SNA's authorized weapon storage sites in south Mogadishu which had

---

[147] Lorenz (note 46), p. 38.

[148] Allard (note 16), p. 37. Emphasis added.

[149] Allard (note 16), p. 37.

[150] United Nations, Report of the commission of inquiry established pursuant to Security Council Resolution 885 (1993) to investigate armed attacks on UNOSOM II personnel which led to casualties among them, appended to United Nations, Note by Secretary-General, UN document S/1994/653, 1 June 1994, para. 152.

[151] Allard (note 16), p. 37.

been inspected by UNITAF in February 1993. The action, planned for 5 June, was backed by the USA.

Relations with the Aideed faction had already begun to deteriorate, leading to military clashes. On 6–7 May 1993 Belgian troops barred Jess from retaking Kismayo by force. Howe contends that UNOSOM II met this first military test successfully.[152] However, this incident and UNOSOM's attempts to establish police and judicial authorities across Somalia led to virulent criticism of the UN by Aideed's Radio Mogadishu.

One of the sites chosen for the inspection was co-located with the radio station. Opinions differ even among UNOSOM officials as to whether the inspection was merely a cover for reconnaissance for subsequent seizure of the station.[153] In any event, the commission of inquiry appointed by the Security Council later concluded that the size and military strength of the inspection teams left no doubt that UNOSOM had decided to use force if cooperation during the inspection was not forthcoming.[154] Nonetheless, to ensure that there would be no misunderstanding, the day before the operation UNOSOM sent two US Army officers to formally notify the USC/SNA that the inspection was imminent. One of the faction's officers objected strenuously and warned that there would be 'war'.[155]

The operation was conducted on 5 June, the inspectors being escorted by Pakistani troops in unarmoured, so-called soft-skin vehicles. They had not been told of the threat against them and were not expecting trouble. The patrol completed its inspection, including that of Radio Mogadishu, and successfully withdrew. However, angry crowds of civilians, among them women and children, confronted UN troops elsewhere in the city. Using the crowds as cover, militiamen ambushed and attacked the peacekeepers. A firefight near a cigarette factory lasted 2–3 hours. QRF attack helicopters and Italian tanks were deployed, but too late to be effective. Twenty-four Pakistani peacekeepers were killed and 57 wounded—the highest toll for a single day in UN peacekeeping history.[156] Six were also missing, one of whom died in captivity. One Italian and three US soldiers were injured.[157] A UN investigation conducted by Professor Tom Farer and the later UN commission of inquiry implicated the Aideed faction in the attacks.[158]

UNOSOM II had been caught unprepared. Some members of its Cease-fire and Disarmament Committee were unaware of the inspection; the majority of

[152] Howe, J., 'The United States and United Nations in Somalia: the limits of involvement', *Washington Quarterly*, vol. 18, no. 3 (summer 1995), p. 53.

[153] Report of the commission of inquiry (note 150), para. 94. The Pakistani contingent had been asked to draw up a plan to shut down or silence it and this had been leaked to the USC/SNA. Suspiciously, the inspection team included a US radio technician.

[154] Report of the commission of inquiry (note 150), para. 211.

[155] Boutros-Ghali (note 1), p. 50; and Durch (note 4), p. 342.

[156] Boutros-Ghali (note 1), p. 50.

[157] Report of the commission of inquiry (note 150), para. 117.

[158] United Nations, Executive summary of the report prepared by Professor Tom Farer of American University, Washington, DC, on the 5 June 1993 attack on United Nations forces in Somalia, UN document S/26351, 24 Aug. 1993, reproduced in *The United Nations and Somalia 1992–1996* (note 1), pp. 296–300; and Report of the commission of inquiry (note 150), para. 184.

the QRF were in Kismayo; secondary reserves had not been alerted to help the Pakistani escort if needed; and the Pakistanis themselves were not suitably armed and protected.[159] The commission of inquiry concluded that the inspection had been unwise and probably went beyond UNOSOM's mandate in that it suggested peace enforcement.[160] The incident demonstrated UNOSOM's naivety, poor organization and military weakness.

*Military action against Aideed authorized*

The Security Council reacted furiously and, in retrospect, peremptorily. Fearing that a dangerous precedent would be set for other UN operations, especially in the former Yugoslavia, if it failed to act, in Resolution 837 it quickly and unanimously authorized the Secretary-General to take 'all necessary measures against all those responsible', including 'their arrest and detention for prosecution, trial and punishment'. It re-emphasized the crucial importance of early disarmament of all Somali factions and of 'neutralizing' radio stations which contributed to the violence against UNOSOM, and sought significant reinforcement of UNOSOM's capabilities to 'confront and deter armed attacks directed against it' by calling on member states to contribute, on an emergency basis, military support and transport, including APCs, tanks and attack helicopters.[161]

Notably, in view of later criticism of the UN, the USA played a prominent role in crafting the resolution. Albright asserted that: 'It would have been extraordinary if we had not responded to the ambush of UN peacekeepers this way'.[162] Although Pakistan, which had produced the first draft, had wanted to name Aideed, the USA resisted this on the grounds that his guilt was not proven. It did, however, press for the USC/SNA to be named. Other Security Council members also exerted strong pressure for tough tactics, including the UK. According to the UN's chief military adviser, Canadian General Maurice Baril: 'There was a lot of war paint in the Council—a feeling that enough is enough. Nobody ever stood up and said, "This peace enforcement is bull. It won't fly"'.[163] In contrast, the Canadian UN commander in Sarajevo, Major-General Lewis MacKenzie, argued publicly that the UN should resort to military action in retaliation because its credibility in the new world order had to be established somewhere—and Somalia was the right place.[164]

Hirsch and Oakley claim, on the basis of extensive interviews, that there was no real appreciation among Security Council members or UN personnel of how much of a change of policy and mission this was.[165] Boutros-Ghali called it a 'crucial moment in UN history': 'For the first time since the 1950 Korean War,

---

[159] Report of the commission of inquiry (note 150), paras 214–15.
[160] Report of the commission of inquiry (note 150), paras 204, 211, 212.
[161] UN Security Council Resolution 837, 6 June 1993.
[162] Albright, M. K. (US Permanent Representative to the United Nations), 'Building a consensus on international peace-keeping', Statement before the Senate Foreign Relations Committee, Washington, DC, 20 Oct. 1993, *US Department of State Dispatch*, vol. 4, no. 46 (15 Nov. 1993), p. 789.
[163] *European Wall Street Journal*, 29 Dec. 1993, p. 5.
[164] Quoted in *Maclean's* (Toronto), 28 June 1993, p. 18.
[165] Hirsch and Oakley (note 7), p. 118, fn. 8.

UN forces had been mandated to engage in military operations against an adversary specified by the Security Council. This came as something of a shock to those who identified the United Nations with impartial peacekeeping under a cease-fire agreement'.[166]

It appears that the UNOSOM leadership was not consulted. Jarat Chopra *et al.* report that Howe opposed the military option and was only persuaded at a marathon meeting of UNOSOM's leadership in Mogadishu on 8 June.[167] This does not, however, tally with a report of the US Senate Armed Services Committee, which recorded that the day after the ambush of the Pakistani escort, supported by Bir and Montgomery, Howe began a 'persistent effort to obtain the deployment of US special operations forces to attempt to seize Aideed'.[168] Howe subsequently warned that: 'Ducking inevitable conflicts associated with carrying out a UN mandate . . . will quickly make a chapter VII force ineffectual'.[169] On 17 June Howe compounded the naming of the USC/SNA as UNOSOM's enemy by calling for Aideed's detention and advertising a $25 000 reward.

Boutros-Ghali was strongly in favour of action against Aideed, reportedly out of personal animus: unwisely, he publicly declared that Aideed's 'physical elimination' would help the situation.[170] Also supportive were the US State Department and most members of the US Congress, as reflected in their approval of a supplemental appropriation for Department of Defense costs in Somalia on 23 June.[171] The only people opposed seemed to be the senior command at the Pentagon. Secretary of Defense Les Aspin opposed the hunt for Aideed because it could make the latter a hero in local opinion and because of the difficulty of acquiring the intelligence to determine where he was. For General Hoar, 'The UN decision to go after Aideed was a dumb thing to do'. 'I thought there was a 50 per cent chance of getting the required intelligence, and, once gotten, only a 50 per cent chance that we would get Aideed. So it was a 25 per cent chance of success and it would be high risk'.[172]

## UNOSOM goes to war

UNOSOM thus became further militarized and was enjoined to become more aggressive at the very time when it had acquired an enemy. Since in Somalia an attack on an individual is an attack on his clan, UNOSOM's actions were tanta-

---

[166] Boutros-Ghali (note 136), p. 97.

[167] Chopra, Eknes and Nordbø (note 8), pp. 97–98. Notably, no one from the Political Division of UNOSOM II or from Howe's civilian staff was present except April Gillespie (formerly US Ambassador to Iraq but by then a UN adviser), who supported the military option.

[168] Memorandum for Senator Thurmond and Senator Nunn (note 6), p. 24.

[169] Howe (note 152), p. 54.

[170] *La Repubblica*, 15 July 1993, quoted in Prunier (note 53), p. 147, fn. 31. Boutros-Ghali denies any personal animosity, claiming that there was a misinformation campaign alleging, *inter alia*, that he once had a farm in Somalia which Aideed had confiscated. Boutros-Ghali (note 136), p. 121.

[171] 'Glaspie faulted over Somali role', *The Independent*, 22 Sep. 1993, p. 12; and Memorandum for Senator Thurmond and Senator Nunn (note 6), p. 11.

[172] Memorandum for Senator Thurmond and Senator Nunn (note 6), pp. 23, 25, 27.

mount to a declaration of war against the USC/SNA. It responded with classic urban guerrilla tactics, resulting in a 'virtual war situation' over the next four months.[173] As UNOSOM's regular forces did not have the capabilities to capture Aideed forcefully, there was an immediate expansion in the use of the QRF, beyond its original purpose, now backed by armed helicopters from the 10th Mountain Division and US Air Force AC-130 helicopter gunships.

The commission of inquiry later noted three distinct phases of the 'war': the first characterized by UN offensive operations, where the UN had the upper hand; the second where the USC/SNA seized the initiative; and the third when US special forces took up the offensive on behalf of UNOSOM II. By mid-June 1993, however, Pakistani troops had lost control of much of south Mogadishu and by early July Aideed's forces were making a concerted effort to close the main line of communications between UN Headquarters and the ports and airfield. Thereafter the USC/SNA gradually took the initiative, increasing its attacks dramatically from 6 July onwards. As in the Congo, the feeling of being at war was heightened by the change in UNOSOM's fragmentary orders after 8 July to include reference to 'enemy forces'.[174] By mid-July UN forces in Mogadishu were under siege in their compounds and at the port and airport, moving safely only in armoured convoys through selected streets.

The 'war' began on 12 June when UNOSOM began what Boutros-Ghali described retrospectively as a 'systematic' drive to restore law and order in south Mogadishu by destroying or confiscating the USC/SNA's weapon stocks and neutralizing its broadcasting stations.[175] The offensive continued for several days, with aerial bombardments (the first such UN action since the Congo) and ground assaults by UNOSOM and QRF troops. On 14 June the Security Council endorsed these actions.[176] However, as Boutros-Ghali noted ruefully afterwards:

Although [USC/SNA] forces were small in comparison with UNOSOM II, they were well armed, battle-hardened, apparently willing to suffer casualties and willing as well to use civilians as 'screens' for military attacks. The faction possessed another advantage in that its strongholds were located in built-up urban areas of south Mogadishu. Military engagements between UNOSOM II and the USC/SNA thus risked additional civilian casualties, which could possibly have the effect of consolidating, rather than weakening, General Aideed's political support . . . There was, finally, a risk of the United Nations becoming deeply involved in Somalia's civil war.[177]

A favoured tactic was for gunmen to mingle with crowds of women and children and fire from their midst, making it exceedingly difficult for the UN and QRF troops to defend themselves. On 17 June, five Moroccan soldiers were

---

[173] Report of the commission of inquiry (note 150), para. 125. The report appends a comprehensive list of the military engagements between UNOSOM II and the SNA at annexes 4 and 5.

[174] United Nations, Report of the commission of inquiry (note 150), para. 152.

[175] Boutros-Ghali (note 1), p. 51.

[176] United Nations, 'Statement by the President of the Security Council endorsing the actions of UNOSOM II', UN Press release SC/5647-SOM/24, 14 June 1993.

[177] Boutros-Ghali (note 1), p. 52.

killed in such an incident. Two Pakistani soldiers were killed on 28 June and three Italian soldiers on 2 July. Attacks on and ambushes of UN personnel and facilities also increased, leading to the deaths of several Somali UN employees. On 2 July Italian forces carrying out a search operation in Heliuaa were ambushed, resulting in three deaths and the wounding of 30.[178] Although the UNOSOM force commander wanted to use the occasion to 'teach the SNA a lesson', the Italian troops broke off the engagement and abandoned their check-point, UN Strong Point 42, minutes before UN air support could be deployed.[179]

### The 12 July raid on USC/SNA headquarters

On 12 July the QRF attacked the house of a Habr-Gedir clan elder which was believed to be USC/SNA operational headquarters, using TOW anti-tank miss-iles fired by helicopter gunships. It was understood that a meeting of clan elders, including Aideed, would be taking place there. Unlike in previous raids, no advance warning was given. The attack had been planned and recommended by UNOSOM but approved in advance through the entire US chain of com-mand to the White House, as well as by UN Headquarters.[180] According to the ICRC, at least 54 Habr-Gedir clan members, mainly civilians, were killed.[181] After a sweep through the area by UNOSOM forces, four journalists were murdered by a Somali crowd and their bodies displayed for television cameras. Hirsch and Oakley and Durch all claim that this pre-emptive attack was a turning point for UNOSOM, changing the atmosphere irrevocably.[182] Ameen Jan notes that UNOSOM II became known thereafter us the '16th Somali fac-tion'.[183] Italy threatened to withdraw from the mission. By August the threat of surface-to-air missiles (SAMs) had closed Mogadishu to all except military helicopters and Aideed's forces were actively trying to shoot down even these with small-arms fire.[184]

### Reinforcement of US forces

On 8 August the omens for the mission worsened when four US soldiers were killed by a remote-controlled landmine—the first US casualties. This finally convinced the US administration to agree to Howe's persistent request for the deployment of Task Force Ranger. Powell and Hoar opposed the idea but reportedly bowed to pressure from Montgomery, US Ambassador Robert

---

[178] Report of the commission of inquiry (note 150), paras 143–49.

[179] Durch (note 4), p. 346. The Italian contingent commander, Gen. Bruno Loi, blamed this on a previous QRF sweep in the Italian sector which had been conducted without him being informed. This is corroborated by Boutros-Ghali (note 136), pp. 96–97.

[180] Hirsch and Oakley (note 7), p. 121.

[181] Jan, A., 'Peacebuilding in Somalia', IPA Policy Briefing Series, International Peace Academy, New York, July 1996, p. 15.

[182] Hirsch and Oakley (note 7), p. 121; and Durch (note 4), p. 346.

[183] Jan (note 181), p. 15.

[184] Anderson (note 121), p. 272.

Gosende, Howe and Boutros-Ghali.[185] National Security Advisor Anthony Lake, Under Secretary of Defense for Policy Frank Wisner and Secretary of Defense Aspin made the decision to proceed, but with the greatest reluctance and as 'the least objectionable of a series of options'.[186]

With UNOSOM still not at its full authorized strength, the USA thus reinforced its presence with 400 Rangers and a handful of Delta Force commandos. In effect, 'they became a posse with standing authority to go after Aideed and his outlaw band'.[187] Howe claims, rather implausibly, that the presence of the Rangers 'appeared to open up the possibility for a negotiated resolution of the conflict and a halting dialogue began between UNOSOM and the SNA'.[188]

A debate then ensued about whether the task force should include AC-130 helicopter gunships. It painfully illustrated the dilemmas of peace enforcement, especially in urban areas. Task Force Commander Major-General William Garrison claimed that they were the only 'machine' Somalis were 'petrified of'.[189] Powell and Hoar refused to countenance their deployment despite the fact that they were part of the 'force package' the Rangers had trained with.[190] Although aware of the gunships' 'tremendous psychological impact', Hoar was concerned about 'collateral damage', since this weapon system was never designed to be fired in populated areas.[191] Claims of such damage had been made after AC-130 strikes in Mogadishu in June, Powell remarking that: 'They wrecked a few buildings and it wasn't the greatest imagery on CNN'.[192] The Senate Armed Services Committee later concluded that it was difficult to understand the decision to omit the AC-130s, claiming that concerns about collateral damage, while appropriate, could have been met with carefully crafted ROE that would have precluded their use in the city except in extreme circumstances.[193]

Operating solely under US command, the Rangers conducted several raids in August and September and succeeded in seizing a number of Aideed's aides.[194] The first raid, on 24 August, turned to embarrassment when they mistakenly surrounded the Mogadishu headquarters of the United Nations Development Programme (UNDP). Garrison's motivation for launching this fiasco was suspect, as he later inadvertently revealed to the Senate Armed Services Committee: 'Because the mortar attacks were the first time that the majority of our

---

[185] Memorandum for Senator Thurmond and Senator Nunn (note 6), p. 25; and Hirsch and Oakley (note 7), pp. 124–25.

[186] Memorandum for Senator Thurmond and Senator Nunn (note 6), pp. 25–26.

[187] Hirsch and Oakley (note 7), p. 122.

[188] Howe (note 152), p. 58.

[189] Memorandum for Senator Thurmond and Senator Nunn (note 6), p. 30.

[190] 'Study faults Powell aides on Somalia', New York Times, 1 Oct. 1995.

[191] Memorandum for Senator Thurmond and Senator Nunn (note 6), p. 28.

[192] Memorandum for Senator Thurmond and Senator Nunn (note 6), p. 31.

[193] Memorandum for Senator Thurmond and Senator Nunn (note 6), p. 49. The US Senate Armed Services Committee later criticized them for the decision, saying that it could have saved US lives in the Oct. 1993 attack on US troops. 'Study faults Powell aides on Somalia' (note 190).

[194] Report of the commission of inquiry (note 150), para. 169. Task Force Ranger carried out 7 raids during its deployment, 3 at night and 4 in the daytime. The ill-fated 3 Oct. raid was their last. Memorandum for Senator Thurmond and Senator Nunn (note 6), p. 15.

troops were ever in combat. I didn't want them to develop a "bunker mentality" and I knew how important it was to get my guys up and operating. So I went to UNOSOM headquarters and said give me your number one target that Aideed has reportedly been at within the last 24 hours . . . We launched on that target'.[195]

The committee described this reasoning as 'invalid' since it served to announce the presence, the mission and some of the tactics of the task force. It proposed greater oversight through the chain of command. In what may be interpreted as a reprimand, General Hoar subsequently gave Garrison 'specific guidance' for raids on suspected Aideed hideouts. Before launching them he had to have 'current, actionable intelligence, i.e. I had to know the guy was actually at the target—it had to be verified'.[196] Garrison also 'provoked a fire-storm' when he sought to expand the Rangers' mission to active patrolling, conducting ambushes and force protection. The Joint Chiefs of Staff reportedly 'went ballistic', Powell expressing increasing concern about mission creep.[197]

The Security Council nonetheless appeared to be firmly behind the general strategy, unanimously affirming on 22 September that those who committed or ordered attacks against UNOSOM personnel would be held individually res-ponsible.[198] However, in the hunt for Aideed hundreds of Somalis were being killed and wounded in the heavily populated areas of south Mogadishu and there were more casualties among the Italian, Nigerian and Pakistani troops. Between 2 July and 3 October 1993, the international forces suffered 21 fatal-ities.[199] Mortar attacks against and ambushes of UN personnel were increasing, as was firing on helicopters. Skilful SNA propaganda turned Aideed into a national hero.

Aspin publicly refused Montgomery's request for tanks and APCs, apparently because he feared US troops were becoming too involved in offensive opera-tions, even though Montgomery wanted them for self-protection.[200] Howe later argued that it might have made a significant difference if the USA had been more resolute during this period and more willing to augment its residual mil-itary force substantially 'once it recognized how dependent the UN had become'.[201]

Demonstrating the confused state of US policy, Aspin acknowledged on 27 August that significant disarmament of the clans was now necessary for peace.[202] Simultaneously, US Secretary of State Warren Christopher, respond-ing to growing public anxiety, was approaching Boutros-Ghali with a 'non-

---

[195] Memorandum for Senator Thurmond and Senator Nunn (note 6), pp. 37–38.
[196] Memorandum for Senator Thurmond and Senator Nunn (note 6), p. 38.
[197] Memorandum for Senator Thurmond and Senator Nunn (note 6), pp. 29–30.
[198] UN Security Council Resolution 865, 22 Sep. 1993.
[199] Boutros-Ghali (note 1), p. 53.
[200] Allard (note 16), p. 58; and Hirsch and Oakley (note 7), p. 125, fn. 27.
[201] Howe (note 152), p. 58.
[202] Aspin, L., 'Remarks prepared for delivery by Secretary of Defense Les Aspin at the Center for Strategic and International Studies, Washington DC, August 27, 1993', News Release, Office of the Assistant Secretary of Defense, Washington, DC, 27 Aug. 1993, p. 5.

paper' suggesting a switch from a militarized approach to a political one.[203] Boutros-Ghali strongly rebuffed him. A US inter-agency team which visited Somalia between 20 and 27 July concluded that UNOSOM seemed to have no political strategy beyond seeking Aideed's death.[204] Its recommendation that an attempt be made to place him under house arrest in a third country was ignored. Hirsch and Oakley agree that the hunt for Aideed had become an obsession and that UNOSOM's humanitarian and nation-building efforts in Mogadishu were being neglected as the security situation worsened.[205] The mission's Civilian–Military Affairs Branch was reduced and its Operations Branch expanded, 'diminishing further the critical means of fostering popular support and forcing greater reliance on military force'.[206] Between 4 May 1993 and 6 January 1994 there was no disarmament of any kind.[207] Virtually no action was being taken to re-establish a Somali police force and judiciary.[208] Howe denies that UN strategy was ever single-mindedly focused on the arrest of Aideed, but contends, rather unconvincingly, that the concept was to 'isolate him and those few considered responsible for the 5 June massacres while instituting a well-integrated political, humanitarian, and security program countrywide'.[209] In early September, Belgium, France and Sweden announced that they would withdraw.

## The 3 October denouement

On 3 October the US Rangers raided the Olympia Hotel in central Mogadishu where USC/SNA leaders were meeting, hoping to catch Aideed. Bir and Montgomery were not informed until shortly before the raid got under way, while Howe did not learn of it until after it had begun. Although the Rangers succeeded in apprehending 24 leaders, they were trapped in a huge firefight when two of their helicopters were shot down. With no advance warning, let alone joint planning or interoperable communications equipment, it took several hours of fighting before Malaysian and Pakistani forces and the QRF, under heavy fire from militiamen, got through to the Rangers' assistance.[210] Eighteen US troops and one Malaysian were killed, while 90 US, Malaysian and Pakistani troops were wounded. A US pilot was captured but later released. Estimates of the numbers of Somalis killed and wounded, both civilians and factional fighters, ranged between 300 and 1000.

The ferocious, chaotic battle, a shocking juxtaposition of high-technology weaponry and visceral, hand-to-hand fighting, was a defining moment in the UN's Somalia venture, thoroughly turning Somali public opinion, to the extent

[203] Hirsch and Oakley (note 7), p. 127.

[204] Hirsch and Oakley (note 7), p. 122, fn. 20.

[205] Hirsch and Oakley (note 7), pp. 122–23.

[206] Chopra, Eknes and Nordbø (note 8), p. 81.

[207] Hirsch and Oakley (note 7), p. 106, fn. 8.

[208] Clarke and Herbst (note 120), p. 245. Funds and attention were devoted to rebuilding the Somali police after Oct. 1993, but by then it was too late.

[209] Howe (note 152), p. 57.

[210] 'US expedition in Somalia: the making of a disaster' and 'Somalia: the battle that changed US policy', *International Herald Tribune*, 1 and 2 Feb. 1994.

that it could be gauged, against UNOSOM and its US backers.[211] By far the greatest impact was on the USA itself. Public and congressional outrage, especially at the televised sight of a dead and mutilated US soldier being dragged through the streets of Mogadishu, led the administration to quickly reconsider its Somalia strategy and eventually its entire peacekeeping and peace enforcement policy. Although resisting almost intolerable pressure for an immediate withdrawal, President Clinton announced on 7 October that US troops would pull out by 31 March 1994 regardless of the situation on the ground.

This signalled to the factions that they now need only wait out that period before reasserting themselves. Implying that the UN was to blame for the debacle, the president announced that US forces would only be under US command, 'as if that were a change in status', Boutros-Ghali notes.[212]

The main US objective in Somalia now became self-protection until departure. Additional forces were to be sent immediately to ensure such protection, including AC-130 gunships, a light infantry battalion, an armoured battalion task force and two marine expeditionary units. Boutros-Ghali notes wearily that: 'As a cover for the American withdrawal, another US task force, under another US general, would be sent in as a show—but only a show—of strength'.[213] US forces ended their hunt for Aideed and their attempted forcible disarmament of the factions, entrenched themselves in fortified areas and sharply curtailed their presence on the streets of Mogadishu. UNOSOM followed suit. US policy, and consequently UN policy, was to be 'depersonalized' and a political solution again given priority. Aideed reacted by announcing a unilateral ceasefire. Oakley returned as US Special Envoy, reverting, according to Daniel *et al.*, to the 'coercive inducement tactics he had used so successfully during UNITAF'.[214] He told SNA representatives that the USA would not make hostage deals but would prefer to mount a rescue operation and that south Mogadishu would suffer badly if the US reinforcements on their way to Somalia had to use force.[215]

Following the US lead, European troop contributors which had not already signalled their departure—including Germany, Italy and Spain—now announced that they too would withdraw by March 1994. Boutros-Ghali notes, with barely concealed bitterness, that governments which had strongly supported the peace enforcement strategy in Somalia and had voted in the Security Council for the UN to take 'all necessary measures' now spoke of the need to place greater emphasis on negotiations.[216] One UN official notes that the UN

[211] Makinda, S., *Seeking Peace from Chaos: Humanitarian Intervention in Somalia*, Occasional Paper (International Peace Academy: New York, 1993), p. 81.

[212] Boutros-Ghali (note 136), p. 105.

[213] Boutros-Ghali (note 136), p. 105.

[214] Daniel and Hayes with de Jonge Oudraat (note 37), p. 105.

[215] Yet both he and the UN facilitated Aideed's participation in peace talks sponsored by Eritrea and Ethiopia, thereby reinstating the status and credibility of the warlords generally and Aideed in particular. After holding several key Aideed supporters in custody for several months without charge and without legal proceedings being instituted, the UN released them in Jan. 1994 to facilitate the peace talks.

[216] Boutros-Ghali (note 1), p. 62.

had been seduced and then abandoned by the USA.[217] Ironically, all this occurred shortly before UNOSOM II reached its authorized strength of 30 000 troops. Even more ironically, US commanders in Somalia believed that the attacks on Aideed's forces had significantly weakened him. Montgomery later told the Senate Armed Services Committee that: 'October 3rd was a bad day for Aideed. He sustained lots of casualties. I think that the US [by withdrawing] gave Aideed a victory he didn't win'.[218]

## Retreat to peacekeeping and withdrawal

On 16 November the Security Council suspended the call for Aideed's arrest and established an international commission of inquiry into the attacks on UNOSOM II personnel.[219] The Secretary-General, widely and unfairly blamed for the fiasco, was asked by the Council for new options.[220] His first option was to continue the current course, assisting with voluntary disarmament but retaining the capability to resort to coercive disarmament and initiate counter-measures if factions attacked UN forces. The second was to rely entirely on the cooperation of the Somalis, using force in self-defence in accordance with traditional peacekeeping doctrine. The third was a scaled-down version of the second, requiring only 5000 troops—essentially a return to UNOSOM I. The Security Council, however, declined to consider the options at that stage and asked for a progress report in January, including an updated strategic plan for UNOSOM II's future. By January, Boutros-Ghali realized that there was no chance of support for the first option—staying the course. Short of an even more humiliating UN retreat, in which Somalia would be totally abandoned, the second option, back to peacekeeping, became the only one possible.

On 4 February 1994 the Security Council took the long-awaited decision to withdraw UNOSOM II by March 1995, whatever the situation on the ground at the time, and adopted a scaled-down mandate.[221] Although still authorized under Chapter VII, the operation would abandon coercive means and revert to reliance on the cooperation of the Somali parties. UNOSOM II would retain the right to defend itself and be mandated to protect the ports, airports and essential infrastructure of Somalia, and keep main supply routes between Mogadishu and outside areas open. It would continue to pursue reorganization of the Somali police and judicial systems. While the Security Council had intended to pressure the factions to reach a political settlement by signalling that it did not see the UN presence in Somalia as open-ended, the effect of the resolution was the opposite: the factions now simply had to wait out the UN presence, as they were waiting out that of the USA.[222]

---

[217] Quoted in Clarke and Herbst (note 120), p. 241.

[218] Memorandum for Senator Thurmond and Senator Nunn (note 6), p. 44.

[219] UN Security Council Resolution 885, 16 Nov. 1993.

[220] Boutros-Ghali (note 1), p. 64.

[221] UN Security Council Resolution 897, 4 Feb. 1994.

[222] On 8 Mar. Adm. Howe completed his tour of duty as SRSG and was replaced first by his deputy as acting SRSG, Guinean Ambassador Lansana Kouyate, and in July 1994 by James Victor Ghebo of Ghana.

US troops began their staged withdrawal from Somalia in mid-December 1993. By March 1994 only a token Western presence remained.[223] Fortunately, two of the remaining large troop contributors, India and Pakistan, decided to stay. For the rest of the scaled-down force of only 15 000, troops were obtained from Bangladesh, Egypt, India, Malaysia, Nepal, Pakistan and Zimbabwe. Some, like Egypt and Pakistan, had to be induced to stay by the provision of extra equipment. The USA leased some 30 M-603A tanks, 80 M-113 APCs and 8 AH-15 Cobra anti-tank helicopter gunships to the UN to bolster its shrunken force. On paper UNOSOM II continued to look aggressive, its ROE having remained virtually the same as when upgraded by Fragmentary Order 39. But the force had lost the will and the capacity to implement them: it was essentially in defensive mode and would only use deadly force in response to an immediate and direct attack.[224]

Somalia did not revert instantly to complete anarchy, as had been feared.[225] In the former famine areas conditions continued by and large to improve. However, violence and clan warfare increased in Mogadishu, and law and order began to deteriorate again, with international aid agencies once more under attack. Inter-factional skirmishes resumed, including in Kismayo. UNOSOM II continued to suffer unacceptably high numbers of deaths, other casualties and material losses. Five Nepalese soldiers were killed in May 1994 when their convoy was attacked in south Mogadishu, while two Malaysian soldiers were killed and four others wounded in a similar ambush, also in May.[226] In August seven Indian soldiers were killed,[227] the highest loss in a single incident since the pitched battles of 1993. A political settlement to produce a national government or even a lasting ceasefire continued to elude the Somali factions.

A Security Council mission in October 1994, led by New Zealand Ambassador Colin Keating, reported that 'nobody, but nobody, asked the UNOSOM military component to stay any longer'.[228] The mission confirmed that March 1995 was the appropriate date for UNOSOM's withdrawal, but warned that despite assurances from the factions their cooperation could not be taken for granted.[229]

As the deadline for the complete withdrawal approached, UNOSOM II began to shrink its area of operations and pull its contingents either out of Somalia altogether or back to Mogadishu. On 6 December Bangladeshi troops had to

Gen. Aboo Samah Bin Aboo Bakar of Malaysia had become force commander in Jan. 1994 and Gen. Michael Nayumbua of Zimbabwe deputy commander. Thus was UNOSOM II de-Americanized.

[223] Australia had 66 military personnel, Ireland 99 and New Zealand 50. *Jane's Intelligence Review*, Sep. 1994, pp. 410–11.

[224] Lorenz (note 46), p. 22.

[225] United Nations, Report of the Secretary-General on the work of the organization, UN document A/49/1, 2 Sep. 1994, p. 86.

[226] Durch (note 4), p. 349.

[227] United Nations, Press Release DH/1716, Geneva, 25 Aug. 1994, p. 2.

[228] *Wireless File* (US Information Service, US Embassy, Stockholm), 1 Nov. 1994, p. 4. See also United Nations, Report of the Security Council mission to Somalia (26–27 October 1994), UN document S/1994/1245, 3 Nov. 1994, para. 27.

[229] The Security Council promptly confirmed its earlier decision to end UNOSOM II's agony on 31 Mar. 1995. UN Security Council Resolution 954, 4 Nov. 1994.

fight their way out of Afgoye, west of Mogadishu, under cover of UN armoured vehicles and helicopter gunships, after militiamen blocked their withdrawal, demanding 'back rent' for the two years of the UN presence.[230] The UN asked the UK, the USA and others for military assistance in ensuring the safe removal of UNOSOM II and its property from Somalia, raising the unprecedented prospect that a UN operation might have to fight its way out of its mission area. The USA agreed to provide some 1800 Marines, along with US Special Forces soldiers. On 28 February 1995 troops from France, India, Italy, Malaysia, Pakistan, the UK and the USA landed at Mogadishu to provide cover for the withdrawal of the approximately 2500 Bangladeshi and Pakistani troops who remained at the airport and port. Although there were 27 incidents involving weapon fire, from snipers to rocket-propelled grenades fired by bandits, the entire force was withdrawn well ahead of schedule, in 73 hours instead of 7–10 days.[231] No lives were lost. UNOSOM II was gone by 3 March.

## III. Somalia and the use-of-force issue

In Somalia the UN moved from traditional peacekeeping in UNOSOM I to quasi-peace enforcement in UNOSOM II and back again to peacekeeping, punctuated by the presence of a non-UN multilateral coalition force. For the first time since the Congo in the 1960s, a UN force was drawn into sustained armed conflict with one of the parties to a civil war, abandoning its impartiality and irretrievably damaging consent to its presence. An estimated 800 largely urban guerrillas were able to frustrate and severely harass 28 000 UN troops and outwit highly capable US support units. The mission cost the lives of 136 UN and associated soldiers and thousands of Somali lives, both combatants and civilians.

UNOSOM II's experience, especially in contrast to that of UNITAF, raised a plethora of issues about the use of force, some of which are still being debated. They include questions about: (*a*) whether it had fallen prey to mission creep: (*b*) whether and how it had lost its impartiality and crossed the 'Mogadishu Line'—a term attributed to Lieutenant-General Sir Michael Rose, then force commander of UNPROFOR in Bosnia; and (*c*) to what extent the use of force had been appropriate and proportionate.

### Mission creep or deliberate escalation?

To many observers Somalia was infamous above all for mission creep. This was alleged to have occurred both in relation to the mission as a whole, including the UNITAF and UNOSOM II phases, and in relation to the use of force. The implication was that the mission had gradually increased the scale and type of its activities beyond its original mission through a series of incremental, ill-considered steps, without anyone considering the strategic goals being sought.

[230] Durch (note 4), p. 350.
[231] Zinni (note 88), p. 27.

Although the press seized on the term as a useful sound bite for all that was wrong with the Somalia operation, the thesis is difficult to sustain. In the case of UNITAF, although it was charged with straying into forcible disarmament, this was well within its mandate to create a secure environment. In the case of UNOSOM II, the only activity it undertook that had not been anticipated in the original mandate was the hunt for Aideed, but that was added to the mandate not through mission creep but by a unanimous decision of the Security Council. In fact there is a case for arguing that, far from engaging in mission creep, UNOSOM II had shirked its clearly mandated responsibilities by not, for instance, moving more quickly to initiate comprehensive, systematic disarmament or to re-establish the Somali police force.

Specifically in relation to the use of force, UNOSOM II only ever used force within its mandate, both its original mandate and Resolution 837 authorizing the hunt for Aideed. Even the assignment of US forces to help UNOSOM hunt Aideed can hardly be cited as a case of mission creep, given that they were deliberately assigned that role with UNOSOM II approval. As Allard contends, US military operations 'clearly resulted from specific decisions reached by the national command authorities'.[232]

Mission creep did undoubtedly occur, however, in respect of the role of US forces. First, they acted outside the UN chain of command in several of their operations and used force in ways that were unauthorized by the UN and were inappropriate and disproportionate, particularly in terms of UN peacekeeping practice. The UN commission of inquiry questioned whether the Security Council 'really initially envisaged bombing of houses, garages, radio stations and meetings'.[233] Mission creep was also seen (*a*) in the assumption by the USA of increasing responsibility for critical UNOSOM II activities as it became clear that the UN could not replicate UNITAF, (*b*) in the increasing numbers and types of US forces assigned to Somalia, and (*c*) in the steady militarization of UNOSOM II. The QRF itself suffered from mission creep: although intended as an emergency back-up force, it ended up destroying weapon caches and initiating the hunt for Aideed.

None of this amounts to a very strong case for the UN itself having engaged in mission creep. Far from being a case of mission creep, UNOSOM II was both a deliberate experiment in 'assertive multilateralism' and a case of 'mission cringe'.

## Impartiality: crossing the Mogadishu Line

General Rose argued that peace operations should maintain absolute impartiality in the face of any provocation in order to avoid being drawn into civil war.[234] Yet impartiality does not require passivity. While maintaining impartiality between the local parties has been a byword of traditional peace-

[232] Allard (note 16), pp. 31–32.
[233] Report of the commission of inquiry (note 150), para. 231.
[234] Rose, M. (Lt-Gen.), *Fighting for Peace: Bosnia 1994* (Harvill Press: London, 1998), p. 241.

keeping, even in that type of operation UN troops have never been expected to ignore all provocation. Indeed, the self-defence rule, as has been shown above, allows considerable latitude in responding to attacks on UN troops, facilities, associated personnel and 'the mission'.

There are always difficult choices to be made between maintaining the credibility of the mission by not allowing it to be harassed and intimidated, and using force in response to provocation in a way that risks making the situation worse. The use of force does not, however, necessarily mean being drawn into civil war, nor does it preclude a return to the *status quo ante* afterwards so long as all the parties hold the same view, including the notion that the UN is genuinely trying to act impartially. Successful military action taken against Aideed's forces by UNITAF demonstrates the point.

There are also alternatives to the use of force in dealing with provocation. Jan argues that, while UNOSOM was obliged to react to the killing of its Pakistani peacekeepers, its response should have been preceded by a thorough and impartial investigation of the event, followed by the use of 'softer' tools.[235]

The debate over impartiality in the Somalia case was confused by the fact, already noted, that there was at that stage no consensus as to whether peace enforcement operations, as they were beginning to be conceived, should, like peacekeeping operations, try to maintain impartiality.

Although UNOSOM II may be considered to have been at least a quasi-peace enforcement operation, it always purported to be acting in accordance with the standard UN peacekeeping norms, including impartiality. It seemed not to realize, however, that impartiality was lost with the hunt for Aideed. Such action was too suggestive of knee-jerk revenge for UN losses, was too directly personal and was led by the USA in heavy-handed style without an attempt at more peaceable means.

Behind this blatant loss of impartiality was a more subtle one which was to be perceived in the UN's political strategy. After failing to win the factions' cooperation in a negotiated peace process, the UN switched to trying to bypass them by establishing an alternative authority on the basis of the 'Somali people', particularly elders, women and clan-based social institutions not involved in factional competition.[236] Durch argues that in choosing to function as an arbiter of Somali politics and champion of the disempowered Somali people, a 'kind of super-clan',[237] it damaged its impartiality. Farer charges more baldly that:

With the enthusiastic backing, indeed apparently at the urging of US diplomats in Mogadishu, Washington and New York, the main strategists and operational directors of the mission . . . chose to make it the mentor and disciplinarian, the main creative force. They chose an active tutelary role, one in which they would hand out white and black hands respectively to favored and disfavored politicians. Thus they made the UN

---

[235] Jan (note 181), p. 15.
[236] Chopra, Eknes and Nordbø (note 8), p. 64.
[237] Durch (note 4), p. 351.

a player rather than an honest broker in the country's unruly political life, and thus they set the stage for confrontation.[238]

When the factions refused to accept its political strategy UNOSOM was left with military force as its only response. This further damaged the perception of the UN's impartiality and made it even less plausible as a peace broker.

A fundamental problem was that from the very advent of UNOSOM I Aideed had regarded the UN as partial, suspecting Boutros-Ghali of personal animosity towards himself and believing that the UN's hidden agenda was to deprive him of supreme power in Somalia. The UN therefore began the mission with an 'impartiality deficit'. Hirsch and Oakley go so far as to claim that the clash with Aideed was 'virtually inevitable', not only because of Somali perceptions that UNOSOM II was weaker than UNITAF but because of Aideed's perception that the UN was biased against his faction.[239] This need not necessarily be fatal: the Cambodia mission had also started with an impartiality deficit, but impartiality was carefully restored and nurtured. UNOSOM II's attempt at enforced disarmament, directed against Aideed first, alienated him further, while its use of force against Aideed personally after June 1993 simply confirmed his perception. Worst of all, it made his claims of UN bias look credible to his factional members, to Somalis generally and to international opinion.

The commission of inquiry also implied that the clash with the factions was inevitable since UNOSOM's mandate to use force if the militias refused to disarm was the first direct challenge to their military power.[240] The 1995 lessons-learned report warned that in collapsed states there usually exist 'conflict constituencies' with a vested interest in continued instability, communal tension and an 'economy of plunder'.[241] Marginalizing them, whether intentionally or not, entails the risk of a backlash. In such situations the UN cannot simply rely on its authority, prestige and purported impartiality but must have a proper political and military strategy that takes the possibility of a backlash into account. Decisions to deliberately abandon UN impartiality must also be taken in full cognizance of the political and military consequences, rather than impetuously, as occurred in the Somalia case. Moreover, recent claims that the al-Qaeda Islamist terrorist network had a crucial role in fomenting the clashes in Mogadishu raise the question whether UNOSOM II could have done anything to avoid a conflict that was designed to drive the USA and the UN from Somalia at all costs.[242] It is possible that UNOSOM II had a determined, shadowy enemy of which it was completely oblivious.

[238] Farer, T., 'United States military participation in UN operations in Somalia: roots of conflict with General Mohamed Farah Aideed and a basis for accommodation and renewed progress', Testimony for submission to the Committee on Armed Services, US House of Representatives, US Congress, US Government Printing Office, Washington DC, 14 Oct. 1993, p. 21.

[239] Hirsch and Oakley (note 7), p. 115.

[240] Report of the commission of inquiry (note 150), para. 45. For an explanation of the roots of the UN's conflict with Aideed see Farer (note 238).

[241] United Nations, Comprehensive report on lessons learned from United Nations Operation in Somalia April 1992–March 1995, Dec. 1995, p. 13.

[242] Bodansky, Y., Bin Laden: The Man Who Declared War on America (Random House: New York, 1999), chapter 3.

## The lessons of Somalia for the use of force

Unlike the Congo mission, the Somalia debacle gave rise to a wave of soul-searching by the UN, the USA and other contributors to the mission. All identified the use and misuse of force as a major concern, both in its own right and because it was closely related to so many other factors that contributed to the failure of the mission.

### The paramountcy of political solutions

One of the principal lessons drawn from Somalia was that purely military solutions are unlikely to succeed in 'failed states'; a political strategy, in which the use or threat of force is well integrated and calibrated, is more likely to succeed. Political negotiations and inducements, along with institution building, must be the principal tool, with force taking only a supporting role. If force is to be used judiciously, there must be a proper understanding of the local political situation and the likely impact that the use of force will have.[243]

To be fair, Boutros-Ghali was fully conscious, from the outset, of the primacy of political over military means. He pinned his hopes on two approaches to reconstituting Somalia—disarmament and political reconciliation—with the re-establishment of the civilian police thrown in for good measure. However, these were not integrated into a holistic vision and comprehensive strategy. Chopra *et al.* claim that they were 'very much a vestige of the diplomatic activity of UNOSOM I that approached reconciliation through negotiation rather than by institution-building'.[244]

Under Secretary of Defense Wisner surely exaggerates in claiming that: 'The single most serious flaw in our policy was that we tried to accomplish political objectives solely by military means'.[245] Yet what is notable about UNOSOM II is the vagueness of its non-military gaols compared with the specificity of its military ones. There was no political operational plan comparable to the military one. Indeed, 'surprisingly little energy seems to have been devoted to the concepts actually needed to make peace . . . Instead, the US and the UN seem to have been left with the hope that the warlords would somehow become peacelords'.[246] Alarmingly, Bir told the US Senate Armed Services Committee that he had encountered neither a political nor a military plan: 'We were not given broad political guidance, so there was *no* military plan'.[247] In an open letter to Boutros-Ghali he pleaded for one.[248]

There was also a mismatch of responsibility between the military mandate, where the UN was, at least in theory, in charge, and the non-military aspects, where it was not. Chopra *et al.* also argue that the military concept of opera-

---

[243] Hirsch and Oakley (note 7), p. 163.
[244] Chopra, Eknes and Nordbø (note 8), p. 68.
[245] Quoted in Memorandum for Senator Thurmond and Senator Nunn (note 6), p. 10.
[246] Clarke and Herbst (note 120), p. 249.
[247] Quoted in Memorandum for Senator Thurmond and Senator Nunn (note 6), p. 18. Emphasis added.
[248] *Jane's Defence Weekly*, 29 Jan. 1994, p. 6.

tions was itself flawed since the stages were defined by the degree of military activity involved, without criteria for judging the political progress necessary before each successive stage could be entered into.[249]

## Mission transition

A poor transition from one mission to another has serious implications for the use of force, since it is likely to be perceived by the warring parties as an opportunity to take advantage of a power vacuum and to test the resolve of the incoming mission's leadership and military forces. Since UNOSOM I was such a small mission, the transition to UNITAF had not been problematic. The subsequent transition from a large, militarily powerful coalition force to a substantial UN peace operation was at the time unique—although much emulated in subsequent years. With UNITAF only just holding the lid on violence and a more intrusive, quasi-enforcement operation but with less military strength now envisaged, it was vital that there be a seamless transition.

Regrettably, transition planning was delayed by dispute between the UN and the USA over two key issues, both with major implications for the use of force—the date when UNOSOM II would take over, and the type of operation (peacekeeping or peace enforcement) it should be. In effect, Boutros-Ghali refused to present the plan for a follow-on mission as requested by the Security Council in the hope that UNITAF could be induced to carry out disarmament and deploy throughout the country before the UN deployed its own force.[250] The Secretary-General also refrained from deploying the 3500 UN troops to Somalia that he was authorized to under UNOSOM's pre-UNITAF mandate, thereby making the transitional shortfall that much greater.

Once the arbitrary date of 4 May 1993 was set for the handover, UNITAF naturally refrained from undertaking new initiatives, especially those that might have involved the use of force. Howe explains that a handover date has 'major psychological ramifications and a significant influence on decisions such as whether to undertake military operations'.[251] So suddenly did the last UNITAF units withdraw that UNOSOM II's fledgling command was left scrambling to organize itself, bargaining desperately with the departing force to leave behind essential equipment and personnel. The withdrawal itself was so complete that when the last units left for the airport they did so in a single truck.[252]

## Mission planning

When planning for the transition did finally begin, most of it was done in the field and most of the initiative came from UNITAF. UNITAF's planning tended to assume that it would hand over to an organization not unlike itself, with

[249] Chopra, Eknes and Nordbø (note 8), p. 57.
[250] United Nations, Report of the Secretary-General submitted in pursuance of paragraphs 18 and 19 of Security Council Resolution 794 (1992), UN document S/24992, 19 Dec. 1992.
[251] Howe (note 14), p. 178.
[252] Clarke and Herbst (note 120), p. 249.

instant access to experienced people, adequate resources and operational doctrine. The plans were thus not necessarily appropriate for a UN force and,
perhaps more importantly, had not been collectively devised and were therefore
not collectively 'owned'. 'Many aspects of the transition, from logistics, to
infantry battalion handoffs, to intelligence, operations, and psychological warfare ("Psyops") posed problems for a UN uncomfortable with the operational
tasks and aggressive nomenclature of a military mission.'[253] The US reliance on
a UN-based exit strategy, says Durch, 'reflected US domestic political requirements and wishful thinking much more than a realistic appraisal of UN capabilities'.[254] Hoar admitted in retrospect that his expectations of the UN were too
high.[255]

The lack of UN preparedness and involvement in planning until very late led
to a 'tardy, half-realized operation with a double dose of problems', namely, a
more ambitious mandate with fewer resources.[256] It is only possible to speculate
as to whether a month's extension of UNITAF's stay would have made a difference regarding the attacks against Pakistani peacekeepers in June. The difficulties of the transition would have been known to the Somalis.[257] Anticipating
the arrival of a less well organized, less robust UN force, Aideed in particular,
and other Somali leaders, would have seen the opportunity for advantage. This
in turn would have led to a need for coercion to implement the new mandate.

The lack of mission planning also resulted in confusion among the military
about the authorizing resolution and mandate. There was no prior consultation
and agreement among troop contributors to UNOSOM II on the political and
military functions of the mission.[258] Many contingents did not appear to
appreciate what Resolution 814 meant or what it would take to implement.
Some considered themselves bound by Chapter VI rather than Chapter VII and
accordingly restricted themselves to self-defence.[259] This included several
Middle Eastern countries—Kuwait, Saudi Arabia and the United Arab Emirates
(UAE)—whose troops were new to peace operations.[260] Citing Germany's constitutional limitations, the German troops interpreted Chapter VI as meaning
that they should protect their own camp at Beledweyne but nothing outside it.
Other contingents, such as those from Bangladesh, Malaysia, Nigeria and
Pakistan, signed up without any apparent initial restrictions on their activities.[261]
Although the Italian force was assumed to be a Chapter VII contingent, there
was later controversy as to whether they had ever agreed to this.[262]

One result, with major implications for the use of force, was the adoption of
different military postures by different contingents. Prunier argues that the very

[253] Durch (note 4), p. 335.
[254] Durch (note 4), pp. 325–26.
[255] Memorandum for Senator Thurmond and Senator Nunn (note 6), p. 18.
[256] Durch (note 4), p. 326.
[257] Howe (note 152), p. 53.
[258] Hirsch and Oakley (note 7), p. 113.
[259] Mellor (note 34), p. 163.
[260] Chopra, Eknes and Nordbø (note 8), p. 88.
[261] Anderson (note 121), p. 271.
[262] Anderson (note 121), p. 270.

appearance and demeanour of the US troops helped to provoke fear and loath-ing on the part of the Somali population. US troops always appeared in flak jackets and helmets, were heavily armed and were guarded by helicopters or other protection forces. The Somalis joked about this, calling the US troops 'human tanks'. Without the latter realizing it, Prunier says, 'this was a constant irritant and a definite factor in the Somali aggressiveness toward them during Summer 1993'.[263] The French troops, by contrast, only wore helmets or flak jackets when fighting was a strong possibility and when off duty wore the native *futah* (skirt).

The Somali lessons-learned report mused that, had planning been done before UNOSOM II, 'perhaps the different national perceptions and agendas which resulted in unity of command problems . . . would have been exposed sooner rather than during the operation itself'.[264] It might also have prevented over-militarization of the mission and thereby reduced the likelihood of force being used ill-advisedly or at all.

*Providing the appropriate means*

It was ironic that UNITAF, a non-UN mission with a limited, humanitarian mandate covering only part of southern Somalia, was given generous military and civilian resources while UNOSOM II, a UN operation with a much more ambitious mandate and nationwide coverage, was given vastly fewer resources.

UNOSOM II's strategy was derailed not only by an over-reliance on military means but also by a lack of resources to support non-military means. The Humanitarian Division had neither the money nor the resources to support voluntary disarmament and the Justice Division had no resources to train or equip police forces. UN Under Secretary-General for Humanitarian Affairs Jan Eliasson has pointed out that, for every dollar spent on the humanitarian operation, 10 were spent on the military.[265]

UNOSOM II's military component was itself not adequate for the ambitious military tasks envisaged. Military resources arrived piecemeal and were often inadequate to the task. Whatever their intentions, the Bangladeshi, Malaysian, Nigerian and Pakistani troops did not adapt well to peace enforcement. Defi-ciencies in marksmanship and urban warfare training, as well as a lack of aggressiveness in patrolling, rapidly contributed to the UN losing control of the streets of Mogadishu.[266] Critically, the Pakistani troops who replaced the US Marines in south Mogadishu sharply curtailed day and night patrolling, partly because of lack of equipment and personnel, but also because their doctrine and training were different.[267] Some countries had apparently 'volunteered' only after the USA had promised their troops protection.[268] This limited their

[263] Prunier (note 53), pp. 146–47, fn. 18.
[264] Comprehensive report on lessons learned (note 241), p. 7.
[265] *The Independent*, 24 Nov. 1993, p. 13.
[266] Anderson (note 121), p. 274.
[267] Hirsch and Oakley (note 7), p. 116.
[268] Chopra, Eknes and Nordbø (note 8), p. 88.

usefulness and in some instances necessitated additional forces to assist them. Hence Mogadishu Airport continued to be over-defended, as some contingents restricted their deployment to guarding that facility.

A British parliamentary committee investigation concluded that: 'Given the chaotic circumstances prevailing in parts of Somalia, only a force both more heavily armed than conventional UN peacekeepers, and with the rules of engagement that allowed them to use arms aggressively where necessary, could achieve the aims of the UN'.[269] The US Senate Armed Services Committee charged that the Clinton administration's policy of reducing the US military presence in Somalia to a minimum, while at the same time agreeing to UN requests (via Admiral Howe) to perform a variety of high-risk military operations, had 'stretched the capability of US forces'.[270]

*Intra-mission coordination*

Along with proper planning, there must be close intra-mission coordination if an operation in which military force is contemplated or used is to be successful. The Pakistani commander, Brigadier-General Ikram Ul Hassan, records that on his arrival in April 1993, before the handover to UNOSOM II, he had expected a 'substantive meeting' to integrate the military, humanitarian and diplomatic plans, but none occurred.[271] Of greater concern, the interpretation of the UNOSOM II mandate was apparently never formally discussed between the political and military wings of the mission. Policy guidelines and interpretation of the mandate fell to the respective contingents, who operated according to their own perspectives and understanding.

Political decisions were kept separate from military considerations and military commanders, and vice versa.[272] An official of the Political Division reported that when UNOSOM II replaced UNOSOM I the division was 'left completely in the dark'.[273] Between 7 May and 9 October 1993, he alleges, there were 'no relations between the political and military side of UNOSOM'. For its part the Political Division was occupied in the countryside trying to establish regional and district councils, while the military component was involved in fighting a war. Only after 9 October did the two sides begin to cooperate, with the Political Division negotiating between the SNA and the UNOSOM II military regarding such issues as troop deployments. Although the Political Division was in touch with Howe, there were no round tables convened between the components until 9 October 1993.

---

[269] British House of Commons, Foreign Affairs Committee, *The Expanding Role of the United Nations and its Implications for United Kingdom Policy, Third Report*, vol. I, HC 1992/93 235-1 (Her Majesty's Stationery Office: London, 23 June 1993), para. 134, cited in Warbrick, C., 'Current developments: public international law', *International and Comparative Law Quarterly*, vol. 43 (Oct. 1994).

[270] Memorandum for Senator Thurmond and Senator Nunn (note 6), p. 5.

[271] Based on discussions at the off-the-record Comprehensive Seminar on Lessons Learned from UNOSOM, New Jersey, 13–15 Sep. 1995.

[272] Hirsch and Oakley (note 7), p. 114.

[273] Chopra, Eknes and Nordbø (note 8), pp. 91–92.

*Command and control*

One of the most painful lessons for the use of force in peace operations that can be derived from the Somalia experience is the paramountcy of strong command and control. Boutros-Ghali himself acknowledged that the Somalia tragedy 'exposed weaknesses in UNOSOM II's complicated operational structure'.[274] Somalia illustrated two major types of problem to be avoided—first, the operation of allied military forces outside UN command structure, and, second, insubordination within the UN command structure.

The most egregious flaw was the separation of the US support forces from the UN command and control structure. By keeping the QRF and the Rangers under its own command, the USA was able to unilaterally militarize the operation and propel the UN towards trying to capture Aideed. Jane Boulden contends that UNOSOM II's command and control problems were 'symptomatic of the UN decision to subcontract the UNITAF operation, and then to accept heavy US involvement and control in UNOSOM II in order to keep American assets involved'.[275]

Within the UN command structure there were also major difficulties from the outset. Although all national contingents except the US support units were in theory under the operational control of the force commander, the reality was quite different. Indian and Pakistani troops, for instance, would not serve under each other's control. On numerous occasions national contingents sent operational and tactical orders issued by Bir or Montgomery to their governments for approval, and in some instances they were countermanded. In August 1993, for example, Saudi troops were ordered to protect a certain perimeter, but replied that this was outside their understanding of Chapter VI. Montgomery complained about the 'timid behavior of the coalition with which our security rests'.[276] Chopra *et al.* argue that UNITAF contingents which transferred to UNOSOM II found it especially difficult to adapt to the tighter control demanded of UN operations.[277]

It is a truism of peacekeeping that, as the level of violence rises, so do command and control difficulties. This was certainly the case in Somalia. Following the 5 June ambush, the deficiencies in UNOSOM's internal command and control became worse. While the US military leadership demanded greater use of force, contingents which claimed that they were limited to a Chapter VI mandate entrenched their positions against participating. Howe notes that, paradoxically, just as UNOSOM II was becoming more militarily capable, its ability to implement a coherent strategy was waning because of such constraints.[278] According to Bir: 'Nations were here for a humanitarian mission and when forces started to take casualties, they stopped cooperating, with negative

[274] Boutros-Ghali (note 1), p. 55.
[275] Boulden (note 127), p. 67.
[276] Memorandum for Senator Thurmond and Senator Nunn (note 6), p. 32.
[277] Chopra, Eknes and Nordbø (note 8), p. 85.
[278] Howe (note 152), p. 58.

consequences'.[279] US planners felt that Bir was not forceful enough in demanding compliance with the UN mandate from his assorted contingents.[280]

The Italian contingent, convinced that as the heirs of the former colonial power they understood the Somali people better than anyone else, caused the greatest command and control difficulties. They actively opposed the anti-Aideed policy and contended that a softer, negotiated approach would work better. Their commander, General Bruno Loi, began to insist on clearing instructions with Rome and conducted what Durch describes as 'his own operation-within-an-operation, intended to show UNOSOM how experts deal with Somalis'.[281] Boutros-Ghali bluntly describes the Italians as pursuing 'their own agenda at the expense of the common UN effort', accusing Loi of uni-laterally negotiating with Aideed and, even more alarming, giving him warning of UN military movements.[282] US and UN officials also accused the Italian troops of deliberately refusing to come to the aid of other peacekeepers, includ-ing Nigerian and Pakistani troops.[283] The Under Secretary-General for Peace-keeping Operations, Kofi Annan, publicly rebuked Loi and on instruction from Boutros-Ghali called for him to be replaced. Italy in turn accused the UN of incompetence and blamed it for not seeking its advice in dealing with the Somalis.[284] The French contingent, too, began to check UN orders with Paris, returning to Baidoa after an operation against a USC/SNA enclave in Moga-dishu in June despite being told by Bir to remain in Mogadishu.[285]

## Rules of engagement

Although UNOSOM II's ROE were very similar to UNITAF's, the UNOSOM command was much less successful than UNITAF's in imposing common ROE on participating contingents. Zinni noted of some contingents that: 'They come with different rules of engagement—which makes life interesting when the shooting begins'.[286] Every country which contributed troops to UNOSOM II placed restrictions on the way in which its forces could use force, and this was reflected either in their own ROE or in how they interpreted the supposedly

---

[279] Quoted in Memorandum for Senator Thurmond and Senator Nunn (note 6), p. 18.

[280] Chopra, Eknes and Nordbø (note 8), p. 49.

[281] *The Independent*, 17 July 1993, p. 10; and Durch (note 4), pp. 345–56. Italian disenchantment with the international mission in Somalia had begun in the early days of Operation Restore Hope when Robert Oakley said it might be better to delay the Italian troops' arrival 'because they had left a pretty bad image'—a reference to their arms dealing and corrupt economic aid programmes with the Siad Barre dictatorship. Prunier (note 53), p. 137.

[282] Boutros-Ghali (note 136), pp. 96–97.

[283] When 7 Nigerians were killed in an ambush on 5 Sep., the Italians charged that a Nigerian soldier had lost his nerve when confronted by protesters and had begun firing, whereas the Italians had started negotiating. The Nigerians accused the Italians of refusing to come to their aid. Report of the commission of inquiry (note 150), paras 164–66.

[284] Clapham, C., 'Problems of peace enforcement: some lessons from operations in Africa', eds J. Cilliers and G. Mills, *Peacekeeping in Africa*, vol. 2 (Institute for Defence Policy and South African Institute of International Affairs: Braamfontein, 1995), p. 143.

[285] Prunier claimed that the French 'consulted' the US command. Prunier (note 53), p. 143.

[286] Zinni (note 88), p. 30.

common ROE.[287] Chopra *et al.* speculate that the force commander did not even have a collection of all national ROE, discovering them only by 'trial and error'.[288] Daniel and Hayes conclude that: 'In the end, each contingent used whatever rules with which it felt most comfortable'.[289] Without agreed ROE, different contingents used different levels of force. This increased tensions between contingents and put UNOSOM at risk.

Certain of the contingents were reportedly notorious for lack of discipline in firing. On several occasions they opened up with full protective fire, using weapons of all calibres, including heavy machine guns, when the situation did not warrant it.[290] Allard contends that there was a noticeable difference in the way US troops interpreted the ROE, stressing aggressive enforcement, while other national contingents emphasized more graduated responses before using deadly force.[291] Contrary to this view, Margaret C. Harrell and Jonathan Howe claim that training vignettes and anecdotes indicate that US forces in UNOSOM II 'possibly used excessive restraint—more than required by the ROE or recommended for personal safety by higher command'.[292] They found that the lower echelons in particular frequently interpreted ROE more restrictively than intended.

## Intelligence

Although the USA provided UNOSOM II with a 60-person Intelligence Support Element (ISE),[293] it remained under US command and its products were not shared between all contingents, mission headquarters and UN Headquarters according to standard procedures. This was clearly unsatisfactory and put lives at risk. Noting that a well-managed intelligence programme can have a dramatic effect on the success of any military mission, the 1995 lessons-learned report urged the UN to continue to move beyond its traditional nervousness about the propriety of 'intelligence' and its role in UN peace operations.[294] Had the presence of al-Qaeda operatives in Mogadishu been more widely known, there might have been a different assessment of the problems facing the mission.

## Enforced disarmament

One of the enduring arguments about peace operations, which first arose in the Congo case, is whether they can and should use force to achieve the disarmament of warring parties. In the Somalia case Durch accuses the UN Secretariat

---

[287] The German troops had probably the most restrictive ROE of all. Their pink ROE card permitted them to protect themselves, other Germans and German facilities or those under German protection. Even in self-defence the use of a firearm was only permitted if milder forms of defence, such as pushing or hitting with a stick, fists or rifle butts, were unsuccessful. Chopra, Eknes and Nordbø (note 8), p. 90.

[288] Chopra, Eknes and Nordbø (note 8), p. 88.

[289] Daniel and Hayes with de Jonge Oudraat (note 37), p. 107.

[290] Anderson (note 121), p. 75.

[291] Allard (note 16), p. 37.

[292] Harrell and Howe (note 145), p. 198.

[293] Durch (note 4), p. 335.

[294] Comprehensive report on lessons learned (note 241), p. 22.

of engaging in wishful thinking about UNITAF's chances of disarming a 'hypertrophied Somali gun culture, in the process neutralizing Somalia's rapacious faction leaders and making them suitably respectful of traditional peacekeepers'.[295] Yet enforcement of disarmament would surely have signalled to the factions that attempts to maintain or seize political power by force of arms would no longer be permitted, that military prowess would not confer legitimacy, and that the USA and the UN were serious about restoring law and order.[296] Early enforced disarmament would also have avoided the later loss of life during UNOSOM II's belated attempts at enforced disarmament in a more hostile environment. Boulden notes that most observers agree in retrospect that the UNITAF period provided the only window of opportunity for disarmament to be carried out.[297]

Using the momentum of its deployment, its impressive show of force and the initial disarray of the factions, UNITAF could have made substantial inroads into the disarmament problem. Heavy weapons could have been systematically seized and destroyed, major light-arms caches uncovered and impounded, and bandit activity brought under control. This could probably have been done with minimal resort to the use of force, although it would certainly have required a more determined military posture and perhaps stronger ROE (although, as seen above, these were already reasonably robust). It would also have had to start immediately a sufficient number of troops had arrived. Hirsch and Oakley retrospectively concede that: 'There is little doubt that most heavy weapons could have been removed from control of the factional militias and organized "bandits" throughout Somalia by UNITAF, probably with minimal combat, had it maintained momentum'.[298]

Complete enforced disarmament throughout Somalia would, however, have required a substantial increase in military and financial resources, an indefinite time commitment, expansion of the original mandate, and a willingness to confront and overcome armed resistance.[299] For its long-term success it would have required the sealing of air, sea and land borders,[300] presumably through the usual system of UN military observers.

Whether force was used to compel disarmament or not, its long-term sustainability would have required a plan which included demobilization and reintegration components, so that those who were disarmed did not simply rearm immediately, as well as the resuscitation of the Somali national police. The 1995 lessons-learned report concluded that what was required was an integrated strategy aimed at supporting the judiciary, the police, local government, the economy, reconciliation, disarmament and demobilization.[301] Finally,

---

[295] Durch (note 4), p. 326.
[296] Clarke and Herbst (note 120), p. 243.
[297] Boulden (note 127), p. 61.
[298] Hirsch and Oakley (note 7), p. 154.
[299] Hirsch and Oakley (note 7), p. 154.
[300] Gen. Hoar records that resupply of arms into south Mogadishu from Ethiopia, Sudan and northern Somalia was continuous. Memorandum for Senator Thurmond and Senator Nunn (note 6), p. 41.
[301] Comprehensive report on lessons learned (note 241), p. 12.

progress in political reconciliation would ultimately have been necessary to sustain disarmament over the longer term. Such a strategy would, however, have taken UNITAF well into the nation-building it was so keen to avoid.

The UN commission of inquiry placed some blame for the Somalia debacle on the fact that there were no seasoned peacekeepers among the UNOSOM military leadership to advise on and teach 'the modalities of UN disarmament inspections and other useful practices learned during 45 years of UN peace-keeping'.[302] It argued, for instance, that a 'non-confrontational typical UN peacekeeping approach' to disarming the factions would have obliged UNOSOM II to draw the SNA's attention to its disarmament obligations, and if the SNA persisted in breaching them more forceful action would have been appropriate.[303] This is in fact exactly what UNOSOM had done—although this can hardly be described as typical peacekeeping behaviour.

*Humanitarian intervention and the use of force*

A further lesson of Somalia with implications for the use of force was the difficulty of conducting humanitarian and nation-building activities while the UN is also engaged in military operations. Not only are those involved in humanitarian activities often uncomfortable with the use of any force, but military operations can stop, severely disrupt or distract attention and resources from humanitarian ones and, conversely, the proximity of humanitarian operations can hamper military operations. Since it may be difficult for the local population to distinguish between the different parts of the UN involved in the peace enforcement and non-enforcement aspects of the mission, all international actors may be 'tarred with the same brush' by local belligerents and the local populace generally. Sometimes this is deliberately encouraged by the belligerents, who are aware that the civilian parts of UN operations are the most vulnerable to attack.

Paradoxically, in Somalia the security situation was so bad that humanitarian organizations and NGOs called on both UNITAF and UNOSOM II to provide them with military protection. Ironically, in some cases, the enforced disarmament of their hired guards had left them vulnerable. When offensive military operations began, however, the humanitarian organizations once more felt the need to distance themselves from the international military presence. Chester Crocker, former US Assistant Secretary of State, argued that the humanitarian purist cannot have it both ways: 'If there is an appeal for outside force, it must be accompanied by an outside strategy for leashing the dogs—while healing the wounds—of war'.[304]

The effects of the mix of humanitarian activities and the use of force were to be felt even more keenly in Bosnia, and it was from that mission that more far-reaching lessons would be learned.

[302] Report of the commission of inquiry (note 150), para. 223.
[303] Report of the commission of inquiry (note 150), paras 195–211.
[304] Crocker, C., 'Foreword' in Hirsch and Oakley (note 7), p. xvi.

It may be argued that the UN used both too little and too much force in Somalia—too little in the early days when a show of force combined with a well-designed and well-resourced disarmament plan might have hastened disarmament, and too much indiscriminate force when pursuing General Aideed. Without a strategy that would marry both non-coercive and coercive tools with a coherent vision for Somalia's future, and faced with the intransigence of various Somali factions and their insistence on advancing their own interests to the detriment of peace and reconciliation, the use of force in the Somalia case was ultimately self-defeating. Somalia should, however, be seen not as a failure of peace enforcement doctrine but as a failure to conceive of one properly and then apply it effectively.

# 7. Bosnia: from white-painted tanks to air strikes

Coincident with its painful experiences in Somalia, the UN became involved in the substantial use of force, ranging from the tactical to the strategic, in Bosnia. Ultimately, the Security Council authorized two organizations to use force on its behalf, in different circumstances, at different levels of intensity and in different environments, and obliged them to try to cooperate and coordinate in doing so. The first, UNPROFOR, was its own creation. The second, not named specifically in any Security Council resolution but nonetheless clearly intended, was NATO, tasked with using air power provided by its member states.

This chapter examines how force was used in Bosnia by and on behalf of the UN between 1993 and 1995. For analytical purposes the discussion has been artificially divided. While the first section of this chapter deals with the use of force on the ground, the second deals largely with the use of force from the air. The third section deals with the move to peace enforcement by both UNPROFOR and NATO. This approach necessarily distorts the chronology of the conflict and simplifies the intricate interplay between the two organizations and events on the ground. However, such was the complexity of the Bosnia conflict that this seems the only feasible approach.

## I. The use of force by UNPROFOR

UNPROFOR used force on the ground in Bosnia in fulfilling its humanitarian mission, in self-defence and to protect civilian populations. As in other missions, it is often difficult to disentangle the precise role of the use of force in any one situation. Force might be used to protect a humanitarian convoy but only when the accompanying troops were fired on and they responded in self-defence. Similarly, the use of force by UNPROFOR to protect itself in situations not involving convoy escort could be seen as furthering its right of freedom of movement which in turn would facilitate the fulfilment of its humanitarian mission. UNPROFOR also used force to protect civilians at risk, both in situations where it happened to encounter incidents or potential incidents during its other operations and in respect of the 'safe areas' progressively established from April 1993 onwards.

### The use of force in self-defence

From the outset UNPROFOR troops were harassed, obstructed and manhandled. They faced such incidents mostly with great forbearance and using patient negotiating techniques to permit them to proceed with their business.

Sniping by hidden assailants was also common, but again handled with appropriate levels of response. On occasions UNPROFOR troops used considerable force in self-defence when attacked, especially after repeated provocation.

The first reported occasion was in November 1992, when British soldiers on reconnaissance in central Bosnia returned fire after they drove into a gun battle near Tuzla. British Lieutenant-Colonel Alistair Duncan records that during his tour of duty his unit opened fire on 69 separate occasions against all factions.[1] Unofficial estimates put at 18 the number of Croats and Muslims shot dead by British troops on the 'fault line' between Bosnian Government troops and the Bosnian Croats between May and August 1993.[2] Duncan claims that the parties all apparently understood the rules, since there was no backlash from the local commanders: 'Indeed, they had told me that on a number of occasions they were quite happy if I shot who I liked'.[3] In February 1994, for instance, British Coldstream Guards, reportedly with the tacit approval of the local Croat commander, attacked 'freelance' Croat fighters after they fired at a UN convoy.[4]

The Nordic Battalion (Nordbat) had major confrontations with the Bosnian Serb fighters in the Tuzla area, which was their area of responsibility. These incidents tended to occur after the rotation of units—a familiar pattern in peace-keeping. One of the most substantial battles of the entire UNPROFOR mission occurred in 1994 when Serb gunners fired on Danish peacekeepers outside Tuzla. The Danish contingent reportedly 'didn't hunker down, they shot back, letting loose more than 70 rounds'.[5] Robert Dalsjö reports that: 'This probably earned them the respect of the Bosnian Serbs, but also their wrath, as communications and contacts across the line of confrontation were subsequently cut'.[6] The brief battle reportedly had two consequences: UN officials moved to restrain the Danish soldiers from overstepping the theoretical line between peacekeeping and peace enforcement; and the Serbs began severely harassing the Danish troops.[7]

The skirmishing between UNPROFOR and factional forces could usually only be prevented from escalating through local negotiations. Duncan cites the example of Gornji Vakuf, where:

Every time we were fired at we fired back and things began to escalate violently. Shootings by either side, UN and locals, were happening more and more often until at one stage the Croats fired back with a wire-guided anti-tank missile. This was clearly upping the ante a touch and besides which, what were we going to do in response?

---

[1] Duncan, A. D. (Col), 'Operating in Bosnia', *IBRU Boundary and Security Bulletin* (International Boundaries Research Unit, University of Durham), vol. 2, no. 3 (Oct. 1994), p. 54.

[2] '18 fighters killed by British', *The Independent*, 28 Aug. 1993, p. 8.

[3] Duncan (note 1), p. 54.

[4] 'British troops get tough with Croat attackers', *The Independent*, 25 Feb. 1994, p. 12.

[5] Wren, C., *New York Times* International Section, 14 June 1995, cited by Senator William Cohen during US Senate Armed Services Committee hearings, reported in *Wireless File* (US Information Service, US Embassy, Stockholm), 14 June 1995, p. 26.

[6] Dalsjö, R., 'Sweden and Balkan Blue Helmet operations', ed. L. Ericson, *Solidarity and Defence: Sweden's Armed Forces in International Peace-keeping Operations During the 19th and 20th Centuries* (Swedish Military History Commission: Stockholm, 1995), p. 111.

[7] Wren (note 5).

Well, the response was that we went back to first principles and asked the question 'Are we achieving our aim? Are we creating the conditions to get the aid through?' We weren't. So we talked to the local commanders, and we managed to de-escalate the situation and get the convoys moving again.[8]

This suggests that the use of force can be effective in some cases at the tactical level, when local consent is not damaged or is easily restored and when strategic consent is not affected.

Sometimes UNPROFOR was averse to using the self-defence capacity it had. Around Sarajevo, in particular, it was reluctant to engage in duels with the Serbs because of the danger of escalation, with its attendant local and international political implications, and because of the danger of civilian casualties and 'collateral damage' in an urban environment. As French reinforcements arrived in Sarajevo in July 1993 they were subjected to a 45-minute Serb barrage as they set up positions and before they had unpacked their weaponry, including anti-tank weapons. They declined to respond to the firing. Belgian Lieutenant-General Francis Briquemont, second force commander of the Bosnia and Herzegovina Command (BHC) from September 1992 to December 1993, warned the Serbs that such attacks would in future face immediate retaliation: 'I am angry at this betrayal. I have told my commanders they must reply immediately, within the next few seconds . . . That is the last time that we restrain ourselves from exercising our right to self-defence'.[9]

Dismayed by escalating attacks on and hostility towards UNPROFOR in both Bosnia and Croatia, the Security Council, in Resolution 807 of 19 February 1993, explicitly put the operation under Chapter VII for the first time, for the protection of UNPROFOR and its activities, but without using the term 'all necessary means'. This invocation of the enforcement chapter of the UN Charter for the purpose of protecting a peacekeeping force rather than imposing the Council's will on warring parties was a case of the Security Council wishing to appear tough without actually being so, hinting at peace enforcement without actually moving into that feared domain. UNPROFOR already had the authority and the ROE to use as much force as was necessary to protect itself. What it lacked was the capability.

## The use of force in UNPROFOR's humanitarian operations

By March 1993 UNHCR convoys, assisted and protected by UNPROFOR, were delivering aid to some 2.28 million people, half the population of the country. UNPROFOR also played a critical role in maintaining routes to the safe areas successively declared after March 1993. Many of the best roads and bridges used for humanitarian traffic were opened as a result of a combination of UNPROFOR's engineering and negotiation skills.[10]

[8] Duncan (note 1), p. 54.
[9] *Canberra Times*, 27 and 28 July 1993.
[10] Prutsalis, M., 'Too little, too late', eds M. Cohen and G. Stamkoski, *With No Peace to Keep: United Nations Peacekeeping and the War in the Former Yugoslavia* (Grainpress Ltd: London, 1995), p. 81.

Yet from the outset UNPROFOR's humanitarian mission was thwarted by physical obstruction, mine laying, hostile fire and the refusal of the parties, particularly but not exclusively the Bosnian Serbs, to cooperate. Undertakings by the three political leaderships to give unimpeded access to humanitarian deliveries, including one made at a special meeting called by the UNHCR in Geneva in November 1993 after the killing of a Danish lorry driver, were widely disregarded at lower levels. Access to populations in need was repeatedly denied for political or military purposes, especially by the Bosnian Serbs and Bosnian Croats. Infuriatingly to outside critics, lone individuals with a single weapon on occasions held up convoys for days as negotiations took place. Air drops were sometimes used in such cases. All three sides frequently threatened the security of UNPROFOR, UNHCR and other humanitarian personnel. Convoy operations were suspended altogether on occasions.

The reasons for the harassment were complex. Suspicion of the UN's motives, and especially suspicion that its humanitarian aid was designed to favour one side or the other, was widespread. Harassment might also be designed to manipulate the aid for political purposes, to divert it to one ethnic stronghold or another, or to permit some of it to be diverted for factional or personal profit. The warring parties' command and control structures were often incomplete, unclear and unreliable. Communications and transport in the often mountainous terrain were difficult. Many of the forces, trained in the former communist Yugoslav National Army, were inflexible and overzealous.[11] New recruits were poorly trained, led, managed and disciplined. Alcohol often clouded judgement. Extremist elements, gangs of bandits and criminals operated uncontrolled.

The use of force in these circumstances would often have been at best ineffective and at worst counterproductive. Mostly the methods of traditional peacekeeping were employed and worked. Constant negotiation and renegotiation, patience, perseverance and guile (and even non-traditional methods, such as bribery) were used to ensure that aid deliveries got through, albeit often in reduced amounts. Some peacekeepers used either implicit or explicit threats of the use of force to achieve tactical breakthroughs. 'Over a number of days, a contest of wills took place where the determination, armour and firepower of Nordbat, as well as the traditional blue and white flag, were used as means of persuasion. Nordbat's activities were not always appreciated by local "soldiers", who tried to intimidate or kill the Blue Helmets.'[12]

The commander of the second Nordic Battalion, Ulf Henricsson, himself led the first Nordic convoy across the conflict line. At a Bosnian Serb roadblock he was confronted by an aggressive soldier who told him he had orders to stop him passing. Henricsson put a loaded pistol to the soldier's head and informed him that he had just received a new set of orders.[13] The more robust Nordic policy

---

[11] Morillon, P. (Lt-Gen.), 'UN operations in Bosnia: lessons and realities', *RUSI Journal*, Dec. 1993, p. 34.
[12] Dalsjö (note 6), p. 108.
[13] Rose, M. (Lt-Gen.), *Fighting for Peace: Bosnia 1994* (Harvill Press: London, 1998), p. 34.

emanated from the Danish troops' experience in Croatia and, Henricsson notes, showed great similarities to that applied by Swedish Colonel Jonas Waern in the Congo and Cyprus decades before. General Sir Michael Rose, the third BHC force commander after January 1994, says that the Swedish troops 'could be extremely bloody-minded and always returned fire immediately with their heavy weapons if they were fired upon'.[14] On one occasion the UNPROFOR staff commander wrote to Henricsson 'wondering if we really had to be so forceful and robust'.[15] Nordbat was also criticized in some quarters for taking too much heavy armour with it, but, as Swedish Major Daniel Ekberg noted: 'A tank as back-up gives you an entirely different bargaining position. It's like flexing your muscles, but not hitting'.[16] Duncan noted the same phenomenon: 'Very sadly the rule of the gun is what matters . . . the man with the AK-47 is a big man. I had clout because with 56 Warriors I was considered to be the most powerful man in Central Bosnia'.[17]

William Durch and James Schear claim that a broad interpretation of the UNPROFOR ROE would have allowed UN convoys to push their way through roadblocks and other obstacles without waiting to be fired on.[18] UNPROFOR did not attempt to do so—for very practical reasons.[19] The UNHCR's civilian truck crews were vulnerable to retaliation. The use of force risked igniting running battles with factional forces, made subsequent deliveries more difficult or impossible, and could rebound on peacekeepers in other areas doing other tasks. Major-General Roderick Cordy-Simpson noted that the methods for getting humanitarian convoys through successfully were dictated by 'a realisation that most of your drivers are civilians and are not protected, the rules of engagement where we may only engage in self defence against an identified target and a realisation that the United Nations has to remain impartial and must pass the same way again with another convoy'.[20] 'No doubt United Nations troops might be able to destroy the first roadblock they encounter, or deal with the first threatening soldiers or irregulars they meet, but thereafter they are likely to become the targets of violence.'[21]

UNPROFOR could not have withstood a concerted attack on its humanitarian operations by one or more of the Bosnian parties, and both it and all the parties knew this. Nor did it have the political backing to do so. Declaring that he no longer read Security Council resolutions, Briquemont said they contained

[14] Rose (note 13), p. 34.

[15] Torstensson, J., 'Pioneers in Bosnia', *Försvarets forum* [Defence forum] (Stockholm), special edn, 1996, p. 11.

[16] Torstensson (note 15), p. 10.

[17] Duncan (note 1), p. 54. A Warrior is a tracked mechanized infantry combat vehicle.

[18] Durch, W. J. and Schear, J. A., 'Faultlines: UN operations in the former Yugoslavia', ed. W. J. Durch, *UN Peacekeeping, American Policy, and the Uncivil Wars of the 1990s* (St Martin's Press: New York, 1996), p. 267, fn. 128.

[19] MacInnis, J. A. (Maj.-Gen.), 'Peacekeeping and postmodern conflict: a soldier's view', *Mediterranean Quarterly*, vol. 6, no. 2 (spring 1995), p. 39.

[20] Speech by Maj.-Gen. R. A. Cordy-Simpson, Chief of Staff, HQ, British Army on the Rhine, former Chief of Staff, United Nations, Bosnia (date and place unknown), p. 9.

[21] Stewart, B. (Lt-Col), *Broken Lives: A Personal View of the Bosnian Conflict* (HarperCollins: London, 1993), p. 317.

'beautiful words' but: 'There is a fantastic gap between the resolutions of the Security Council, the will to execute those resolutions and the means available to commanders in the field'.[22] Threats by commanders, usually soon after their arrival, to act more aggressively fell away as the realization of the implications of doing so for vulnerable humanitarian convoys and peacekeepers sank in.

On becoming BHC force commander in January 1994, Rose announced just such a 'more robust approach' by UNPROFOR, particularly in delivering humanitarian aid: 'If they shoot at us, we'll shoot back, and I have no hesitation about that whatsoever'.[23] Henceforth, UNPROFOR would no longer request permission of the parties to traverse their territory but would simply inform them of its intentions. It would also attempt to open up two new convoy routes closed by fighting, using a platoon of Danish Leopard tanks. Rose's chief of staff was horrified. Rose had already been told that the use of tanks for peacekeeping was politically sensitive and that he would need permission from UNPROFOR and UN Headquarters.[24] The commander of Sector Sarajevo, Brigadier-General André Soubirou, welcomed the new approach but warned that only France, other NATO countries and the Scandinavian countries (by implication not others, such as Bangladesh and Egypt) would implement it.[25] A French lieutenant shortly after Rose's arrival ordered his unit to smash through a Serb checkpoint outside Pale with armoured cars, telling the Serbs that this represented UNPROFOR's new muscular approach.[26]

After checking with the Danish troops, but without seeking permission from UN Headquarters, Rose ordered Danish tanks to relieve the besieged town of Tuzla, which they did without firing a shot. Although there was criticism from some Security Council members about his failure to consult them, Rose says that he detected that Kofi Annan, then UN Under Secretary-General for Peace-keeping Operations, was glad that a problem had been solved. As many a peacekeeper before him, Rose says: 'I learned from this episode that the Secretariat often secretly welcomed independent action from the field, as long as it proved successful, and I was to repeat the manoeuvre many times in the coming year'.[27] After the Tuzla breakthrough Rose gave a firm direction that, as long as clearances had been obtained in the correct manner for the passage of a convoy, any illegal obstacles were, after due warning, to be forcibly dealt with.

The new tough strategy seemed to work for a time. In early February 1994 Rose used the threat of a platoon of British Coldstream Guards in Warrior APCs, accompanied by NATO A10 aircraft overhead, to break through, without actually using force, a Serb control point that had blocked UN traffic for two days between Kiseljak and Sarajevo.[28] Later he sent French Foreign Legion

---

[22] *New York Times*, 31 Dec. 1993.
[23] *International Herald Tribune*, 4 Feb. 1994, p. 2.
[24] Rose (note 13), p. 36.
[25] Rose (note 13), p. 27.
[26] Rose (note 13), p. 36.
[27] Rose (note 13), p. 36.
[28] Rose reports that so fearsome was the reputation of the British UNPROFOR troops that they were known as 'Shootbat' rather than Britbat. Rose (note 13), p. 40.

commandos across Sarajevo's Brotherhood and Unity bridge into Serb-held suburbs in a calculated show of strength.

However, the new policy eventually collapsed as UNPROFOR's bluff was repeatedly called. It failed its first major test when the Serbs rejected the entry of a convoy into Maglaj, the last Muslim pocket in Bosnia cut off from outside aid.[29] On 20 March the Serbs, after being buzzed by NATO aircraft and under the renewed threat of the use of force, finally permitted a convoy to enter the town for the first time in six months.[30] However, a second convoy, which left for the town almost immediately with a Serb police escort, was looted by the Serb military at a new checkpoint on the way.[31] This demonstrated the Serbs' determination to constantly test the resolve of the UN in its threats to use force.

Rose was eventually forced to backtrack, partly because of opposition within UNPROFOR and nervousness at UN Headquarters, but principally because the Serbs did not always back down. Worse still, they soon discovered the strategy of taking UN peacekeepers and others hostage to stave off military action. Rose's mantra now suddenly became: 'Patience, persistence and pressure is how you conduct a peacekeeping mission. Bombing is a last resort because then you cross the Mogadishu line . . . and I'm not going to fight a war in white-painted tanks'.[32] He described his initial hope that UNPROFOR could concentrate on what he saw as its main role—humanitarian relief—as 'hopelessly naive'.[33] In September 1994 he wrote to Bosnian Serb military commander General Ratko Mladic a letter, later leaked to *The Times*, to explain his view of UNPROFOR's role: 'I fully agree with you that we must, in the future, avoid all situations which necessitate the use of force, whether it be applied from the ground or the air. We can only do this through closer liaison and cooperation . . . it is not part of our mission to impose any solution by force of arms. We are neither mandated nor deployed for such a mission'.[34]

UNPROFOR's unwillingness and inability to act more forcefully provoked harsh criticism from local people, the media and international commentators and governments. Opinion in the USA was especially critical. Rose, trying to act even-handedly as a traditional impartial peacekeeper, soon came to be seen by the Bosnian Government as an agent of British 'appeasement' policies, more concerned with preventing NATO action than with protecting Bosnians. Nevertheless (and although Somalia was the only comparable UN mission to date), Rose claims that UNPROFOR used a level of force never before seen in any 'humanitarian-based peacekeeping mission'.[35]

---

[29] 'Serbs rebuff an aid request as UN backs off on new policy', *International Herald Tribune*, 4 Mar. 1994, p. 4.

[30] 'UN finds heavy weapons Serbs hid near Sarajevo', *International Herald Tribune*, 22 Mar. 1994, p. 1.

[31] 'After 2 years, Muslim and Serb Sarajevo are linked', *International Herald Tribune*, 24 Mar. 1994.

[32] *International Herald Tribune*, 30 Sep. 1994, p. 2.

[33] Rose (note 13), p. 15.

[34] Cited in Bryant, L. and Loza, T., 'Expectations and realities', eds Cohen and Stamkoski (note 10), p. 59.

[35] Rose (note 13), p. 242.

## The use of force to protect civilians

Although it was not part of their mandate, some UNPROFOR contingents did intervene to protect civilians at risk and prevent massacres and other gross violations of human rights. In central Bosnia, British troops occasionally protected civilians under threat, but it was left to the local commander to decide how far he should go. Lieutenant-Colonel Stewart explains that: 'I took the mandate we were given and examined in detail what it implied . . . I felt strongly that the main reason we had been sent to Bosnia was to support the operation to save lives—anyone's life, for that matter. Moreover, any action taken with that intention was not simply defendable, it was an imperative'.[36] However, the British were unable to prevent Croat atrocities such as the April 1993 massacre at Ahmici and other incidents in the Lasva Valley area.[37]

The commander of Nordbat-2, Henricsson, also decided not just to 'observe and report' as instructed, but as far as possible to act to protect civilians and prevent atrocities. Dalsjö notes that this was an important departure from traditional UN peacekeeping and from that of other battalions in Bosnia, 'which at times had stood idly by as atrocities took place'.[38]

Other UNPROFOR troops did indeed ignore human rights violations as being outside their mandate or beyond their ability to control. In Mostar the Spanish contingent simply withdrew when ordered to do so by the Bosnian Croat military, leaving the latter free to continue expelling Muslims from west Mostar to the ghetto on the east side of the Neretva River.[39] This was less than would be expected of UN troops even under the traditional peacekeeping norms.

Despite calls by successive commanders for reinforcements and better protective capability, UNPROFOR was never given the explicit mandate or the requisite forces or firepower to comprehensively and robustly protect the civilian population.

## The use of force to enforce demilitarized or exclusion zones

Despite numerous threats to do so, UNPROFOR used very little ground-based force in attempting to coerce the parties to comply with their agreements to withdraw and canton heavy weapons or to demilitarize particular areas. One exception occurred in early October 1994, when UNPROFOR used armoured vehicles, rockets and cannon fire to clear hundreds of Bosnian Government troops off the Mount Igman demilitarized zone south-west of Sarajevo. This was the greatest use of UN firepower against the Muslim-led government since the start of the Bosnian war.[40] A Swedish unit, trained to fight in deep snow, had after due warning opened fire on newly dug Bosnian trenches, forcing the

[36] Stewart (note 21), p. 316.
[37] Hedl, D. and Magas, B., 'The unfulfilled mandate', eds Cohen and Stamkoski (note 10), p. 56.
[38] Dalsjö (note 6), pp. 108–109.
[39] Hedl and Magas (note 37), p. 56.
[40] *The Guardian*, 8 Oct. 1994, p. 4.

Bosnian Army to withdraw.[41] This was at least a demonstration that UNPROFOR was trying to treat all sides even-handedly—a signal that Rose, in particular, was determined to send. Greater consideration was given to the use of air power for enforcing such exclusion zones (see the sub-section on air power below).

### The use of force to 'protect' the safe areas

The most controversial use-of-force issue during the UN's involvement in Bosnia came in relation to the so-called safe areas. These were declared in 1993 around several towns that were being besieged by Bosnian Serb forces. The move drastically increased UNPROFOR's responsibilities, plunging it into what many perceived as the 'grey zone' between peacekeeping and enforcement (or what other observers now describe as peace enforcement).

The idea arose following a visit by the first BHC force commander, Lieutenant-General Philippe Morillon, in March 1993 to the besieged city of Srebrenica, and his declaration that the safety of the population would be guaranteed. In response, on 16 April the Security Council, acting explicitly under Chapter VII, declared the city a safe area, free from armed attack and other hostile acts.[42] The term 'safe haven' was avoided, since it has a specific meaning and requires specific obligations under international law which go beyond the safe area concept.[43] The resolution demanded the withdrawal of the Bosnian Serb paramilitary units from the area and the ending of armed attacks on the town. UNPROFOR and humanitarian agencies were to be allowed free access to Srebrenica and to all other areas of Bosnia. UNPROFOR was ordered to increase its presence there, which it did after negotiating a demilitarization agreement with the parties. After an investigative mission to Bosnia, the Security Council declared additional safe areas around Sarajevo, Tuzla, Zepa, Gorazde and Bihac.[44] However, it authorized the strengthening of UNPROFOR's presence in each of these by only 50 military observers.

In response to continued attacks on the safe areas, the Security Council, although refraining from mandating UNPROFOR to 'protect' them, mandated it in Resolution 836 of 4 June 1993 to 'ensure respect' for them. To achieve this it would: (a) 'deter' attacks against the safe areas; (b) monitor the ceasefires reached around them; (c) 'promote' the withdrawal of military or paramilitary units other than those of the Bosnian Government; and (d) occupy 'key points' on the ground. UNPROFOR was authorized, 'acting in self-defence, to take the necessary measures, including the use of force, in reply to bombardments against the safe areas by any of the parties, or to armed incursion into them or in the event of any deliberate obstruction in and around those areas to the freedom of movement of UNPROFOR or of protected humanitarian convoys'.

[41] Rose (note 13), p. 185.
[42] UN Security Council Resolution 819, 16 Apr. 1993.
[43] Hedl and Magas (note 37), p. 56.
[44] UN Security Council Resolution 824, 6 May 1993.

The resolution also authorized member states to take, 'subject to close coordination with the Secretary-General and UNPROFOR, all necessary measures,
through the use of air power, in and around the safe areas . . . to support
UNPROFOR in the performance of its mandate'. NATO's capabilities were to
be unleashed.

Clearly, UNPROFOR would require additional military capabilities to carry
out such a resolution. UN Secretary-General Boutros-Ghali estimated that
approximately 34 000 additional troops would be needed to obtain 'deterrence
through strength' to ensure full respect for the safe areas.[45] However, taking
into account what could realistically be expected from member states, and
under strong pressure from British Ambassador Sir David Hannay,[46] he declared that it would be possible to start implementing the resolution with a 'light
option' of approximately 7600 troops, relying on the threat of NATO air action.
UNPROFOR would thus 'protect the civilian populations of the designated safe
areas against armed attacks and other hostile acts, through the presence of its
troops and, if necessary, through the application of air power, in accordance
with agreed procedures'.[47] Boutros-Ghali argued that successful implementation
of this concept required three overriding principles:

(a) that the intention of the safe areas was primarily to protect people and not to defend
territory and that UNPROFOR's protection of these areas was not intended to make it a
party to the conflict; (b) that the method of execution of the safe-areas task should not,
if possible, detract from, but rather enhance, UNPROFOR's original mandates in
Bosnia and Herzegovina, namely supporting humanitarian assistance operations and
contributing to the overall peace process through implementation of cease-fires and
local disengagements; (c) that the mandate must take into account UNPROFOR's
resource limitations and the conflicting priorities that inevitably arise from unfolding
events.[48]

Boutros-Ghali urged that the safe areas be clearly defined and delineated, as
proposed by UNPROFOR, but, strangely, not that they be demilitarized
(although clearly he recognized this as necessary in the long run).[49]

The Security Council, struggling to identify additional troop contributors,
chose the light option in Resolution 844 of 18 June 1993. Contradictions
abounded. The intention of the major powers which oversaw the drafting of the
resolution was that UNPROFOR should not be perceived as having entered the
realm of peace enforcement (no doubt to ensure that China and Russia would
not veto the resolution), that existing troop contributors would not withdraw in
fright and that a concerned Secretary-General would be reassured that this

---

[45] United Nations, Report of the Secretary-General pursuant to Security Council Resolution 836 (1993),
UN document S/25939, 14 June 1993.
[46] Boutros-Ghali, B., *Unvanquished: A US–UN Saga* (I. B. Tauris: New York, 1999), p. 86.
[47] United Nations, Report of the Secretary-General pursuant to Resolution 844 (1993), UN document
S/1994/555, 9 May 1994.
[48] Report of the Secretary-General (note 47).
[49] See his report to the Security Council of 17 Sep. 1994, reported in United Nations, *The United
Nations and the Situation in the Former Yugoslavia*, Reference paper, Department of Public Information,
DPI/1312/Rev. 4, July 1995, p. 32.

peacekeeping operation was not drifting into the same situation as that in Somalia. At the same time it was intended, in response to strong US pressure for punitive action against the Bosnian Serbs, to signal greater resolve by 'threatening' to protect the safe areas' populations (but not the safe areas themselves) by using force in self-defence, assisted by NATO air power.

Despite these niceties, UNPROFOR's actions were to have the unintended consequence of interfering in a war by depriving one side of a strategic outcome, namely the seizure of several urban areas, without that side's consent. Moreover, the light option purported to assume the 'consent and cooperation of the parties'; had this been forthcoming, the threat or use of force to deter attacks would have been unnecessary in the first place.

Although Resolution 844 proposed to double the size of UNPROFOR in Bosnia, it provided only a basic level of deterrence. Except for Sarajevo, just 900 troops would be assigned to each safe area. UNPROFOR never received the forces necessary even for implementing the light option. By February 1994 only some 3400 additional troops had been deployed, most of them in Sarajevo and Tuzla, while in Zepa a UN advance party consisted of only 10 soldiers. The offer by a group of Muslim states (Bangladesh, Iran, Malaysia, Pakistan, Tunisia and Turkey, plus the Palestinians) to provide more than 17 000 troops to protect the safe areas was rejected by the Bosnian Serbs and ignored by the UN because of the political implications.[50] By March 1994, a year after the safe areas had been declared, only 5000 extra troops had arrived.[51] Only the Netherlands volunteered to send troops to a safe area, and then in the hope that this would encourage others to do so.

Surprisingly, in view of all its shortcomings, the safe areas concept initially had some success. The Serb advance on such areas halted and the level of violence declined. However, artillery bombardment continued, humanitarian supplies were frequently interrupted and the conditions pertaining in most of the safe areas were appalling. What little deterrence existed was gradually whittled away as the Security Council's bluff was repeatedly called by all the parties. On occasions Bosnian Government forces deliberately tried to trigger UNPROFOR intervention by firing at the Serb forces from within the safe areas to invite a response, or even more cynically by attacking their own safe area in the hope that the Serbs would be blamed.[52]

UNPROFOR commanders, concerned that they had not been allocated the forces needed to protect the safe areas, interpreted their mandate extremely narrowly. They took refuge, Rosemary Righter says, 'in the militarily nonsensical pretence that their task was to deter attacks against the "safe areas", but not to defend them, if necessary, if deterrence failed'.[53] As it became increasingly clear that UNPROFOR could protect neither the people in the safe areas

---

[50] *International Herald Tribune*, 16 July 1993, p. 2.
[51] United Nations, Report of the Secretary-General pursuant to Resolution 871 (1993), UN document S/1994/300, 16 Mar. 1994, pp. 8–9.
[52] Honig, J. W. and Both, N., *Srebrenica: Record of a War Crime* (Penguin: London, 1996), p. 116.
[53] Righter, R., 'A marriage made in hell', eds Cohen and Stamkoski (note 10), p. 39.

nor the safe areas themselves, Western public opinion began to regard the policy as morally iniquitous, as did the peoples and governments of Muslim countries—who suspected the UN of failing to act because these were not Christian communities at risk. The policy seemed particularly immoral to the populations trapped in the towns, especially when peacekeepers themselves seemed well protected and provided for. UNPROFOR became known by the cynics as 'UNSPROFOR'—the UN Self-Protection Force.

By March 1994 mounting criticism of the effectiveness of UNPROFOR, which was never able to ensure compliance with the various ceasefires or other aspects of a peace settlement, and increasing threats to UN personnel in Croatia led the Secretary-General once more to contemplate withdrawal, especially since UN member states had not provided the authorized force levels or assessed financial contributions for UNPROFOR. There was, as always, great pressure for the force to remain, lest its withdrawal trigger even greater catastrophes. In May 1994, in response to a Security Council request for further working papers on the safe areas, the UN Secretariat proposed an 'oil slick' strategy for the safe areas, proposing the use of force to enlarge them gradually. The USA opposed the idea, apparently because it feared being pressured to provide ground troops for such a strategy.[54]

A particularly Byzantine problem presented itself in the Bihac safe area, in north-western Bosnia, against which attacks were launched periodically by Muslim forces loyal to local leader Fikret Abdic and by Krajina Serbs from Croatia. It was unclear whether UNPROFOR had a mandate to 'deter' such attacks, since they were not being carried out by the Bosnian Serbs. This illustrates the complications attending peace enforcement in a multiparty civil war. Bihac also illustrated the problems of the safe areas more generally. After initially being popular for helping deliver humanitarian aid and for their mere presence in the enclave, the French UN troops there became increasingly unpopular as they appeared unable to prevent Serb attacks. While they deployed in the town, returned fire when fired on and promised to defend Bihac against a Serb advance, they were unable to prevent constant shelling. According to the President of the Regional Assembly, Hamdija Kabiljagic: 'They're not defending us because they're either scared or on the Serb side. They brought in huge quantities of weapons. It's abnormal that they've not used them to protect civilians from shelling'.[55]

On 14 April 1994 Bosnian Serb fighters took 150 UN soldiers and aid workers hostage and attacked Tuzla. Rose ordered Danish tanks to advance towards the Serb guns. As they did so, the shelling ceased, indicating, according to Rose, that: 'The UN was not completely reliant on NATO for its deterrence capability'.[56] On 29 April a major battle took place between the UN and the Serbs near the town. Five Serb T55 tanks were destroyed by the Danish tank company, which fired nearly 100 rounds—more, says Rose, than in any battle

[54] Boutros-Ghali (note 46), pp. 84–85.
[55] 'Cursed are the peacekeepers in Bosnia's last besieged town', *The Guardian*, 29 Mar. 1994, p. 4.
[56] Rose (note 13), p. 111.

the unit had been involved in during World War II. 'Delighted' with this outcome, Rose says that once again UNPROFOR had 'demonstrated to the Serbs
and to the world that the UN was prepared to use *extreme* levels of force, so
long as that use remained within the constraints of peacekeeping'.[57]

However, the safe areas remained untenable, with UN threats and use of force
working sometimes, but not often enough. In a further attempt to refine the
failing concept, Boutros-Ghali in November 1994 again proposed the clear
delineation and complete demilitarization of the safe areas, recognizing what
had been apparent from the outset—that allowing the Bosnian Government to
retain troops, weapons and military installations within a safe area created an
unstable situation and drew attacks from the Bosnian Serbs.[58] 'The efforts of
UNPROFOR to defend the safe areas make it necessary to obstruct only one of
the hostile forces, which considers itself to be merely reacting to offensives
launched by the other. In such circumstances, the impartiality of UNPROFOR
becomes difficult to maintain and there is a risk of the Force being seen as a
party to the conflict.'[59]

Boutros-Ghali again resisted the idea that UNPROFOR should be given a
mandate to enforce compliance with the safe area regime since: (*a*) there would
be a greatly increased level of risk for the forces to be deployed compared with
normal peacekeeping forces; (*b*) a drastic increase in UNPROFOR military and
civilian support units would be needed; (*c*) UNPROFOR would no longer be
able to function as an impartial peacekeeping force elsewhere in Bosnia; and
(*d*) the delivery of humanitarian assistance would become virtually impossible.
His report was studiously ignored as former US President Jimmy Carter prepared the way for SRSG Yasushi Akashi to negotiate a four-month ceasefire,
beginning on 1 January 1995, including guarantees for humanitarian assistance
and access to Sarajevo.

## II. The use of force by NATO on behalf of UNPROFOR

In view of the apparent success of air power in the 1991 Persian Gulf War and
the reluctance of the USA and most of its NATO allies to commit ground troops
to Bosnia, the possibility of using air power there was raised at an early stage.
General Lewis MacKenzie, the Canadian UNPROFOR chief of staff in Bosnia,
records that as early as July 1992, as the siege of Sarajevo tightened, he began
to receive hints from both UN and non-UN sources that 'certain nations' were
standing by with air power to assist UNPROFOR if necessary. He warned
against it, telling the UNPROFOR commander, Indian Lieutenant-General
Satish Nambiar, that: 'The use of air power on our behalf would clearly asso-
ciate us with the side *not* being attacked, and thereafter we would very quickly
be branded an intervention force, as opposed to an impartial peacekeeping

[57] Rose (note 13), p. 127. Emphasis added.
[58] *The United Nations and the Situation in the Former Yugoslavia*, rev. 4 (note 49), p. 37.
[59] United Nations, Report of the Secretary-General pursuant to Security Council Resolution 959, UN
document S/1994/1389, 1 Dec. 1994, para. 37.

force . . . this was a vital issue, much misunderstood by non-military types, and I wanted to make my point before someone came to our "rescue" and got us all killed'.[60]

Despite MacKenzie's misgivings, the initial uses envisaged for air power in Bosnia included enforcement of the no-fly zone,[61] the protection of UNPROFOR, 'facilitation' of the delivery of humanitarian aid and the breaking of the siege of Sarajevo. Ambitions soon graduated to the deterrence of attacks on safe areas, the protection of safe areas, the enforcement of weapon exclusion zones, the punishment of one or more of the parties for transgressions of agreements and ultimately the bombing of the parties to the negotiating table.[62]

As UNPROFOR lacked its own air capability, members of NATO—mainly France, the Netherlands, the UK and the USA—were to provide air power using aircraft based at Aviano, Italy, and on aircraft carriers in the Adriatic.[63] While the UN had been directly involved in the use of air power in both the Congo in the 1960s and Somalia more recently, this was the first time an alliance of member states was 'subcontracted' to support a UN peace operation.[64]

### Concept of operations

For such an unprecedented UN/NATO collaboration there was no joint concept of operations, and no command and control arrangements or agreed ROE.[65] It took some time for the two organizations to establish the necessary framework. For both the UN and NATO 'solutions were ad hoc, and revolutionary'.[66]

Essentially, the use of air power in Bosnia was considered in three categories. The first, 'close air support', meant the tactical use of air power to protect UN forces under attack or threat of attack.[67] This could involve overflights to demonstrate NATO's presence, a 'show of force' to intimidate the parties, or an actual attack. The targets would be the belligerents and the weaponry directly involved in attacking UN peacekeepers. The second category, air strikes, meant

---

[60] MacKenzie, L. (Maj.-Gen.), *Peacekeeper: The Road to Sarajevo* (HarperCollins: London, 1994), p. 428.

[61] In Resolution 781 of 9 Oct. 1992 the Security Council had mandated UNPROFOR to monitor, with ground-based observers, a ban on military flights by the Bosnian parties—a 'no-fly zone'—with the 'technical assistance' of member states, namely NATO air surveillance.

[62] For a comprehensive study of the use of air power by NATO in Bosnia see Solli, P.-E., *UN and NATO Air Power in the Former Yugoslavia*, NUPI Report no. 209 (Norwegian Institute of International Affairs (NUPI): Oslo, Oct. 1996).

[63] For a comprehensive account of the NATO air power capabilities and command and control structures see Leurdijk, D. A., *The United Nations and NATO in Former Yugoslavia: Partners in International Cooperation* (Netherlands Atlantic Commission and Netherlands Institute of International Relations 'Clingendael': The Hague, 1994).

[64] Air power was provided by some NATO members to enforce no-fly zones over Iraq after the Persian Gulf War but, despite the presence of UN guards undertaking humanitarian assistance efforts in northern Iraq, this was not a case of air power being used in conjunction with a UN peacekeeping operation.

[65] Righter (note 53), p. 23.

[66] Solli, P.-E., 'In Bosnia, deterrence failed and coercion worked', eds C. F. Rønnfeldt and P.-E. Solli, *Use of Air Power in Peace Operations*, Peacekeeping and Multinational Operations no. 7 (Norwegian Institute of International Affairs (NUPI): Oslo, 1997), p. 97.

[67] Defined as 'the application of air power in direct support of the land battle'. Sweetman, A. D. (Group Capt.), 'Close air support over Bosnia-Hercegovina', *RUSI Journal*, Aug. 1994, p. 34.

the use of air power to send a warning signal to one or more of the parties in retaliation for its breaking an agreement, such as a weapon exclusion zone, or advancing militarily against a safe area. Favoured targets were heavy weapons such as tanks being removed from cantonment or into weapon exclusion zones, command and control facilities, ammunition dumps and, from NATO's perspective, anti-aircraft radars and weaponry which threatened its aircraft. The third category was large-scale 'strategic' air strikes, which were in effect a type of peace enforcement, designed to coerce the parties into compliance more generally or into agreeing to peace talks.

These categories may appear distinct in theory. In practice they were constantly conflated, including by politicians, diplomats, UN officials, the press and, perhaps most surprisingly, the military.

The debate over the use of 'air strikes' was particularly confused, since the term was often used to mean all use of air power. It could also be used to refer to close air support for UNPROFOR troops which involved strikes on targets not directly and immediately involved in attacking the peacekeepers.

Contrary to what might be expected, the determination of a concept of operations for the use of air power in Bosnia was a bottom–up process. First, tactical capability in theatre, both ground and air assets, was established; then operational systems were constructed; finally the military (and political) strategy was determined.[68] The most important UN ground tactical asset that had to be established was the forward air controllers deployed to guide aircraft to their targets in close proximity to UN troops, humanitarian workers or local civilians.[69] A list of standing operating procedures (SOP) and terminology was issued and refined over a period of several months. It was not until mid-August 1993 that Boutros-Ghali was able to inform the Security Council that the UN had the 'initial operational capability for the use of air power in support of UNPROFOR in Bosnia-Herzegovina'.[70]

Since the degree of escalation—from lightly armed infantry to modern jet fighters—was substantial, the UN and NATO first developed a mechanism for shows of force. 'If a tense situation developed on the ground . . . the ground commander could request a NATO air *presence*. The show-of-force effect was created by NATO jet fighters present overhead, flying medium-level. To escalate one step further the aircraft could stage a *demonstration*, low-altitude "fly-bys" or simulated attacks.'[71]

UN air staff in the force commander's headquarters in Zagreb issued the first close air support operational order in late July 1993 regarding tactical-level procedures. The ROE at this stage limited the use of air power to proportionate retaliatory responses to attacks on UN peacekeepers. An operational order in October 1993 covered issues such as requesting, authorizing and notifying the

[68] Solli (note 62), p. 42.
[69] Solli (note 62), p. 43.
[70] United Nations, *The United Nations and the Situation in the Former Yugoslavia*, Reference paper, Department of Public Information, DPI/1312/Rev. 2, 15 Mar 1994, reprint; and Add. 1, 23 Jan. 1995, p. 16.
[71] Solli (note 66), pp. 105–106. Emphasis in original.

use of air power, the escalation of its use and coordination with civilian agencies more comprehensively. These were refined through joint training and exercising. In early 1994, once air strikes, as opposed to close air support, were envisaged, common targeting procedures were agreed by NATO and the UN.[72]

## Command and control and coordination

The NATO chain of command for the use of its aircraft went from its supreme decision-making body, the North Atlantic Council (NAC), through the military officers at NATO's Strategic Air Command Europe (SACEUR), to NATO's commander of Allied Forces Southern Europe (AFSOUTH) in Italy, Commander-in-Chief South (CINCSOUTH).

The relationship between NATO and the UN commands had to be established from scratch. This was to be the source of the worst command and control problems of the Bosnia operation. Initially, the arrangements were predicated on the idea that air power would mainly be used to support UNPROFOR in the field. A request for close air support by the local UNPROFOR commander on the ground would be forwarded to the BHC in Sarajevo and thence to UNPROFOR headquarters in Zagreb, where it needed the approval of both the military and the civilian heads of mission before being transmitted to the UN Secretary-General. If he agreed, the request for action would go to CINCSOUTH, who would then attempt to meet it.

The question of 'air strikes' was further complicated in that both NATO and UNPROFOR could, and did, have views on when and where they might be used. A 'dual-key' system was established: NATO and UNPROFOR could each propose the use of air strikes but could veto each other's requests and proposed targets. This system exposed fundamental disagreements between the USA, its NATO allies with ground troops in Bosnia and the UN over the use of force in Bosnia. It also became a proxy for the broader debate over strategic goals in the former Yugoslav state.

The problem was that, while UNPROFOR wished to be able to call on NATO for close air support when needed, it also wanted to be able to veto NATO air strikes that might endanger its forces. The UN also had to consider the wider international implications of any use of force. NATO, on the other hand, was impatient to demonstrate resolve against what it perceived to be threats to its own and the UN's credibility, particularly from the Bosnian Serbs. On 26 April 1994, for instance, in a meeting with General Bertrand de Lapresle (the overall UNPROFOR force commander) and Rose, NATO Supreme Commander General George Joulwan repeatedly demanded that UNPROFOR improve its 'credibility, clarity and unity of command'.[73] He seemed to have difficulty accepting that NATO was in a supporting role to UNPROFOR and that 'both were engaged in a mission in where there were no enemies or victories'. There

[72] Solli (note 62), pp. 45–46.

[73] Leurdijk, D. A., *The United Nations and NATO in Former Yugoslavia, 1991–1996: Limits to Diplomacy and Force* (Netherlands Atlantic Commission: The Hague, 1996), p. 50; and Rose (note 13), p. 122.

were also genuine differences over how rigorously to deal with Serb non-compliance with Security Council decisions and negotiated agreements. One regular argument was over whether 'technical violations' were sufficient to invoke air strikes or whether such action was only justified by major violations.

Air strikes were also at times stymied by disagreements within UNPROFOR—between its commanders on the ground (who often had their requests for air strikes turned down by their military or civilian superiors), its military commanders (who had the wider military situation to consider) and Akashi (who was by inclination uncomfortable with the use of force, cautious to the point of indecision, and required to consider a wider range of political factors). Even if Akashi agreed he could be overruled by UN Headquarters in New York or by the Secretary-General. Akashi also insisted on giving the parties warning of air strikes in order to reduce the dangers of misunderstanding and collateral damage, but this only reduced their military effectiveness. UNPROFOR's military command eventually concluded that for ease and speed of execution a request for air power, especially close air support, should be able to be made direct to NATO, bypassing the civilian leadership.

In July 1993 Lieutenant-General Jean Cot, overall UNPROFOR force commander before de Lapresle, tried unsuccessfully to convince Akashi that he alone should be authorized to request close air support.[74] As an alternative Akashi tried to clarify the position by setting out the following considerations to be taken into account by the UNPROFOR command in approving close air support:

1. Is the request within the UNPROFOR mandate?
2. Does the use of close air support in the particular instance contribute to fulfilment of the objectives of the Security Council?
3. Is the use of close air support in the particular instance related to the support of humanitarian relief?
4. Is there a clearly defined military target?
5. Is the response proposed proportional?
6. What are the implications for the safety of UN personnel, and has sufficient time been allowed for precautionary action to protect UN personnel?
7. Is the use of close air support likely to be successful?
8. Is the proposed use of close air support compatible with international humanitarian norms?
9. How is the reputation of the UN likely to be affected by the use of close air support?
10. What will be the impact of the use of close air support on peacemaking efforts?[75]

[74] Conversation reproduced verbatim in de Rossanet, B., *Peacemaking and Peacekeeping in Yugoslavia* (Kluwer Law International: The Hague, 1996), pp. 89–90.
[75] Reported in de Rossanet (note 74), pp. 92–93. Boutros-Ghali later sought the opinion of the UN Legal Counsel, but it was singularly unhelpful, simply reciting the usual precedents and noting that the exercise of such a right 'is to be adapted to the framework of each operation in accordance with its mandate'. de Rossanet (note 74), pp. 90–91.

The problem with these criteria was that they would almost invariably rule out the use of close air support when it was requested.

There was also almost constant tampering with the dual-key system in an attempt to satisfy NATO's increasing frustration with its inability to use force effectively. The NAC at one stage proposed to Boutros-Ghali that, while retaining the dual-key system, and having NATO's Southern Command and the UNPROFOR force commander together choose a minimum of four targets for each occasion, NATO alone should be allowed to choose which was actually hit.[76] Boutros-Ghali insisted that UNPROFOR needed to be consulted about the target, so that reprisals could be avoided, and about the number of attacks, so that the UN principle of proportionality could be maintained. Increasingly, NATO pressed for an end to the dual-key arrangement in order to give it the freedom to choose both timing and targets for the use of air power, which was more and more seen as a means to force the Bosnian Serbs to sue for peace.

**Enforcing the no-fly zone**

NATO's first authorization to use force in Bosnia came with Resolution 816 of 31 March 1993 by which the Security Council, acting explicitly under Chapter VII, authorized NATO to enforce, rather than simply monitor, the 'no-fly zone' over Bosnia that it had declared in October 1992.[77] Designed to help protect humanitarian deliveries from attack by Bosnian Serb aircraft, it had been repeatedly violated. The authorization of Operation Deny Flight was the Security Council's first real foray into peace enforcement in Bosnia in the sense of imposing terms and conditions on the parties through the use or threat of the use of force. The term 'all necessary measures' was used and the ban extended to all flights by fixed- or rotary-wing aircraft. NATO action was to be taken in 'close coordination' with the UN Secretary-General and UNPROFOR. NATO aircraft were also permitted to use force in self-defence, including if they were fired on or had radars locked onto them. NATO ROE would be used and the operation would be under the command of NATO's CINCSOUTH. Although they are classified, it is known that the ROE stressed the need for 'minimum collateral damage and positive target identification'.[78]

Despite the call for close cooperation with the UN, the decision to attack any aircraft violating the zone was NATO's alone.

In March 1994 NATO used force for the first time in its 45-year history when US aircraft enforcing the no-fly zone shot down three Bosnian Serb aircraft engaged in bombing Muslim towns—the only time aircraft were shot down by NATO over Bosnia.[79] It was also the first use of force by a military alliance directly on behalf of the UN.

---

[76] Boutros-Ghali (note 46), p. 213.
[77] See note 61.
[78] Sweetman (note 67), pp. 34–35.
[79] *Time*, 14 Mar. 1994, pp. 26–27.

## Defence of UNPROFOR through close air support

Close air support was seen as the easiest and most likely use of NATO air power in Bosnia, but it was also viewed as a potentially powerful deterrent to attacks on UNPROFOR, whether force was actually used or not. Indeed, in the early stages, overflights and shows of force were enough to end particular attacks on peacekeepers, stop localized fighting between the parties or halt the advance of one party or another. On 18 August 1993 NATO aircraft engaged in a show of force to threaten Bosnian Serb forces attacking Bosnian Government forces on Mount Igman. The attacks stopped and French UNPROFOR troops deployed to the area, intermingling with Serb units. (The proximity of French forces had the unfortunate consequence of forestalling future air strikes against the Serbs.[80]) It was the first time the UN had seriously threatened the use of NATO air power for such purposes and it had worked.

Indeed, initially, every time NATO seriously threatened to use air power the Bosnian Serbs backed down. It helped induce them, for instance, to sign a temporary ceasefire agreement in January 1994 and to comply with NATO's ultimata to establish exclusion zones around Sarajevo and Gorazde in February and April 1994. The utility of threats declined, however, the longer NATO waited to actually attack. As NATO and UNPROFOR showed continuing reluctance to use the weapons with which the aircraft were armed, even when UNPROFOR was directly under fire, the factions became emboldened. After a year of operating under constantly buzzing Western jets which failed to use force, the Bosnian Serbs became blasé about the devastating potential of air power.[81] Overflights and shows of force were increasingly ignored.

Suspicion about the responsibility for this situation fell increasingly, and unfairly, on Akashi and Boutros-Ghali, both of whom were accused of vetoing each proposed use of air power. Boutros-Ghali tried to absolve himself: 'I want it to be clear that so far I have never received a request to use the air force. The day I receive such a request and that I have the support of those responsible . . . I will be the first to support its use'.[82] Boutros-Ghali later, disingenuously, denied that he had refused the use of air strikes in Bosnia. He told a press conference in December 1995 that: 'The discussion of bombing or not bombing was undertaken by the people on the ground. I am not a military specialist. My decision, or the decision of my Special Representative, was taken according to the point of view of the military people on the ground. The military people on the ground were saying, "Don't bomb, because this will represent a risk for our soldiers", or "Bomb, because we are ready to take that risk"'.[83]

In July 1995 Akashi made up a list for reporters entitled 'SRSG approval of employment of air power' which showed that he had approved 11 air operations

---

[80] Durch and Schear (note 18), p. 237.
[81] Durch and Schear (note 18), p. 242.
[82] Quoted in Leurdijk (note 73), p. 41, fn. 49.
[83] United Nations, Press Conference, UN Secretary-General Boutros Boutros-Ghali, UN Headquarters, 18 Dec. 1995, UN document SG/SM/95/331, 18 Dec. 1995, p. 8.

since being assigned to Bosnia, agreeing to virtually every request made by field commanders.[84] Per-Erik Solli estimates that 98 per cent of requests for air strikes were turned down by the military, not by UN civilians.[85]

Part of the problem was the scepticism of UNPROFOR's military personnel, both at headquarters and in the field, about the efficacy of air power. UNPROFOR spokesman Commander Barry Frewer cautioned in July 1993 that air strikes were a last resort to be considered 'very, very carefully. We hope [they] will never have to be used'.[86] Briquemont declared that: 'To make threats is easy, to carry them out is more difficult. Those who want to carry out air strikes should come to Sarajevo and study the map with me'.[87]

Such statements tended to undermine the deterrent effect of NATO air power even before it was used, but they reflected a genuine concern that the use of air power could endanger UNPROFOR forces on the ground, risked escalating conflict between the UN and the local belligerents, and would jeopardize the UN's attempt to remain impartial.

Notwithstanding these considerations, Rose was 'determined to engineer a situation in which I could legitimately employ NATO air strikes in order to demonstrate a more robust UN approach to peacekeeping'.[88] He decided soon after arriving in January 1994 to confront Bosnian Croat forces who had been firing on Canadian convoys resupplying a hospital for mentally handicapped children by sending in British Coldstream Guards to lead the next convoy. The troops would be accompanied by a NATO forward air controller, who could call in air power if necessary. Rose wanted to target the local command structure, not just their firing trenches, to send a tough message to all the factions that UNPROFOR was not to be toyed with. He says that he chose the Bosnian Croats rather than the Bosnian Serbs in order to demonstrate his even-handed 'peacekeeping' approach. UNPROFOR headquarters opposed the mission on the grounds that carefully nurtured relationships with the Croats would be destroyed. As it turned out, with four A10 'tank-busting' aircraft flying overhead, the convoy was not fired on, nor was it ever fired on again. Rose was disappointed: 'Although a tactical advantage had been gained by opening up the route, the overall strategic impact of carrying out an early air strike was lost'.[89] The plan, to spring a trap as a means of signalling resolve, was an unusual departure from the normal peacekeeping ethos from someone who professed to be adhering to it.

Thereafter, successive incidents illustrated the difficulties involved in attempting close air support in defence of peacekeepers in a volatile environment. On 22 February 1994, after five of their number were wounded in a mortar attack on a Nordbat convoy near Tuzla, Swedish troops called for air cover. While two Harrier jets flew over, neither the troops nor the jets could identify a

[84] Boutros-Ghali (note 46), p. 241.
[85] Personal conversation with the author.
[86] *Sydney Morning Herald*, 31 July 1993.
[87] 'Sarajevo's besiegers sneer at international disarray', *Sunday Times*, 8 Aug. 1993, p. 13.
[88] Rose (note 13), p. 36.
[89] Rose (note 13), p. 37.

target. Nor was it clear whether the Serbs or Bosnian Government forces had carried out the attack. An official at UNPROFOR headquarters was reported as claiming: 'We came very, very close to using air power'.[90] Rose had supported the request, but Cot was opposed, 'only because there was no absolute means of determining the origin of the shell'.[91]

On 13 March 1994, when two tank shells were fired at a UN observation post and the French base at Bihac came under heavy machine-gun and anti-aircraft fire, the French forces requested close air support. Akashi approved the request but bad weather prevented NATO jets from taking off immediately. By the time they arrived, the offending tank had withdrawn. According to a French officer in Bihac: 'It was a joke; the planes took five hours to turn up. If the UN wants us to carry out this mission, we have to be able to strike back. We're all very angry with our chiefs'.[92]

In mid-May 1994 the Nordbat commander at Tuzla Airport asked, for the fifth time, for close air support. The source of shelling—Serb tanks—had this time been clearly identified. Akashi refused authorization.[93] An UNPROFOR spokesperson explained that by the time headquarters learned of the 20-minute tank attack the firing had stopped, adding that: 'The procedure is very clear—the attack has to be in progress for us to strike'.[94] The following day another spokesperson added: 'Close air support from NATO is a last resort for UN troops under attack and when loss of life is at stake. This request did not meet those standards'.[95] Clearly, as regards close air support, troops in the field and their commanders had different views of the ROE.

In June 1994 British troops being attacked by Serb artillery in Bugojno in Central Bosnia requested close air support. Akashi and de Lapresle approved it and passed the request to NATO, but the attack was cancelled when the shelling stopped.[96]

## The use of air power in respect of the safe areas

NATO's most challenging and complex involvement in the use of force in Bosnia came in connection with the safe areas. Resolution 836 of 4 June 1993, which mandated UNPROFOR to act in self-defence to deter attacks on these areas, also authorized NATO, 'with all necessary measures, through the use of air power' and in 'close coordination with the Secretary-General and UNPROFOR', to support UNPROFOR in carrying out its mandate. What this meant in practice was left unspecified, although it was generally interpreted as meaning that NATO was not mandated to protect the safe areas or their popula-

---

[90] *International Herald Tribune*, 23 Feb. 1994, p. 1.
[91] *The Independent*, 23 Feb. 1994, p. 1.
[92] 'Weather thwarts UN air strikes', *The Independent*, 14 Mar. 1994, p. 8.
[93] Zucconi, M., 'The former Yugoslavia: lessons of war and diplomacy', *SIPRI Yearbook 1995: Armaments, Disarmament and International Security* (Oxford University Press: Oxford, 1995), p. 226.
[94] *International Herald Tribune*, 18 May 1994.
[95] *International Herald Tribune*, 18 May 1994.
[96] Recounted in Leurdijk (note 73), p. 53.

tions directly, but only indirectly by giving UNPROFOR close air support. US Secretary of State Warren Christopher at one stage explicitly declared that NATO air cover would not be used to protect civilian populations under attack.[97] Boutros-Ghali seemed to have a different view, arguing that: 'Since it is assumed that UNPROFOR ground troops will not be sufficient to resist a concentrated assault on any of the safe areas, particular emphasis must be placed on the availability of a credible air-strike capability provided by Member States'.[98]

The first concerted attempt to expand NATO operations to include air attacks, as opposed to close air support to UNPROFOR, came in August 1993. On 2 August, in response to the continuing siege of Sarajevo and the seizure by the Bosnian Serbs of two strategic positions overlooking the city, the NAC convened an emergency session at the USA's request to consider two pressing issues—the command and control controversy, and stronger use of air power in the form of air strikes. On the first, the USA had already been lobbying to exclude both Boutros-Ghali and Akashi from the dual key with regard to air strikes—although so loosely was the latter word bandied about that it is difficult to tell whether it referred to all use of air power or only air power beyond close air support. Christopher presented the Secretary-General with a 'non-paper' proposing this, but Boutros-Ghali, determined not to let NATO take over the Bosnia operation or use the UN flag as 'a flag of convenience', insisted in his own 'non-paper' that he retain the power to approve air strikes.[99] He reached agreement with NATO Secretary General Manfred Woerner on 1 September that the decision to call air strikes still belonged with the UN.[100]

On the second issue the US delegation sought an 'extensive interpretation' of Resolution 836 to allow NATO, on its own initiative, to conduct air attacks on a wide range of targets in Bosnia (and even outside it) in order to secure Serb compliance (with what exactly was never quite clarified).[101] Criticized by Congress, the press and other observers for not adopting a 'lift and strike' policy (lifting sanctions and hitting the Serbs with massive air strikes), the US administration hoped that NATO air power could not only defend the safe areas but also punish the Bosnian Serbs for violating agreements, drive them to the negotiating table and force them to agree a peace settlement.

Canada, France, Spain and the UK, now with thousands of troops in the field, would not agree to a proposal for a major bombing campaign. Not only would their forces be endangered, but they risked being drawn into a shooting war with the Bosnian Serbs for which they were ill-equipped. They argued that troops do not surrender to aircraft and that therefore large numbers of ground troops would be needed if peace enforcement were to be seriously undertaken.

---

[97] Leurdijk (note 73), p. 37, fn. 41, citing *Atlantic News*, no. 2534 (12 June 1993).
[98] United Nations, Report of the Secretary-General to the Security Council, UN document S/25939, 14 June 1993.
[99] *Nouvelles Atlantiques*, no. 2550 (3 Sep. 1993), p. 2; 'UN commander proposes limited Bosnia air strikes', *The Times*, 5 Aug. 1993, p. 9; and Boutros-Ghali (note 46), pp. 88–90.
[100] Zucconi (note 93), p. 226.
[101] Leurdijk (note 73), p. 38; and 'We must bomb now', *The Times*, 8 Aug. 1993, p. 12.

The USA, which had no troops in Bosnia, was unwilling to provide such forces in the absence of a peace settlement.

The compromise, agreed on 9 August 1993, was to expand the target options beyond ground forces directly involved in attacks on UNPROFOR to artillery positions, ammunition storage areas, command posts and similar facilities.[102] However, the ROE would still limit air strikes to proportionate retaliatory responses to attacks on UN peacekeepers. The deterrent effect was weakened by NATO's surreal declaration that air strikes 'must not be interpreted as a decision to intervene militarily in the conflict'.[103]

A year later, on 11 September 1994, Admiral Leighton Smith (CINCSOUTH) wrote to de Lapresle stating that the Bosnian Serbs' ceasefire violations were undermining the collective credibility of NATO and the UN, and suggesting that NATO attack significant targets within the next 48 hours.[104] Rose says that the letter provoked shock in Zagreb and Brussels given the low level of military activity in Bosnia that summer, as well as the decision of the international community to give peace another chance. Rose suspects that Joulwan drafted the letter and Smith sent it against his better judgement. De Lapresle, in what Rose calls a 'tough reply', restated that force should only be used in relation to confirmed violations of the ceasefire and should be proportional to the event.

## The use of air power to enforce heavy weapon exclusion zones

When it became clear that simply creating safe areas and threatening retaliation for attacks on UNPROFOR would not end the threat to the besieged cities of Bosnia, NATO added the concept of heavy weapon exclusion zones. Established first around Sarajevo in February 1994, they were extended in April 1994 to Gorazde and all other safe areas. The idea arose following the mortar attack on a Sarajevo marketplace of 5 February 1994, widely assumed to be the work of the Bosnian Serbs, which killed at least 58 civilians and wounded 142 others. The next day Boutros-Ghali wrote to Woerner, suggesting that preparations be made to use air strikes to 'deter further such attacks' and asking NATO to prepare to launch strikes at his request against artillery or mortar positions in and around Sarajevo which were determined by UNPROFOR to be responsible for attacks against civilian targets.[105]

The mood in favour of the use of force had by now shifted somewhat, with Belgium, France, Germany, Italy and the USA supportive. The UK remained cautious, calling for unspecified 'immediate and strong pressure' by the UN to halt attacks on Sarajevo, as well as stronger ROE, but not generalized air strikes.[106] Canada and Ukraine both opposed military intervention, fearing that

---

[102] *Atlantic News*, no. 2547 (Aug. 1993); and Rader, S., 'NATO', ed. T. Findlay, *Challenges for the New Peacekeepers*, SIPRI Research Report no. 12 (Oxford University Press: Oxford, 1996), p. 149.

[103] *Atlantic News*, no. 2547 (Aug. 1993).

[104] The following account is from Rose (note 13), p. 170.

[105] Boutros-Ghali (note 46), p. 144. He acted under Security Council Resolution 836 of 4 June 1993.

[106] *Financial Times*, 9 Feb. 1994, p. 16; and 'British troops with UN set to stay in Bosnia', *The Guardian*, 17 Feb. 1994, p. 20.

it might endanger their peacekeepers. Russia, reluctant for historical and domestic political reasons to countenance the bombing of the Bosnian Serbs, accused Boutros-Ghali of overstepping his mandate and strongly warned the West that air strikes could lead to 'all-out war'.[107]

NATO nonetheless accepted the Secretary-General's request, putting approximately 170 fighter aircraft, bombers and ground attack aircraft as well as approximately 30 reconnaissance, communication and refuelling aircraft on standby—the largest concentration of air power since the Gulf War.[108] The NAC first issued an ultimatum to the parties to establish within 10 days a 20-km heavy weapon exclusion zone around Sarajevo (and a 2-km zone around Pale, the Bosnian Serb capital) and either withdraw such weapons or canton them under UNPROFOR supervision. Bosnian Government forces within the Sarajevo exclusion zone were also required to place their heavy weapons under UNPROFOR supervision and refrain from launching attacks from the city. Heavy weapons of either party found within the zone after 10 days (by 21 February) would be subject to NATO air strikes conducted in 'close coordination' with the UN.

Boutros-Ghali, determined that the UN should retain the initiative in requesting such air strikes, responded to the NATO communiqué by declaring that: 'We have no difficulty. All that is required is for those responsible for military, humanitarian and political operations to ask, decide to use the air force, and we would immediately ask NATO to use it'.[109] The Secretary-General did, however, delegate to Akashi the right to approve a request from the UNPROFOR force commander for close air support for the defence of UNPROFOR anywhere in Bosnia.[110]

In fact there was no use of air power at this time in response to violations of the heavy weapon exclusion zones. Rose, fearing that they would endanger his troops and plunge UNPROFOR into further difficulties, apparently convinced British Defence Minister Malcolm Rifkind to resist pressure from the USA and NATO for air strikes[111] and managed to negotiate a withdrawal of the heavy weapons from Sarajevo and surrounding areas. Russia agreed to dispatch 400 troops to help create a buffer zone separating predominantly Serb neighbourhoods from the rest of the city.[112] Additional reasons for avoiding air strikes at this time included the facts that the Vance–Owen Peace Plan[113] was close to being accepted by the parties and that there was continuing uncertainty

---

[107] *The Guardian*, 19 Feb. 1994, p. 1.

[108] Leurdijk (note 73), pp. 42–43.

[109] Quoted in Leurdijk (note 73), p. 43.

[110] Zucconi (note 93), p. 226, quoting *Atlantic News*, no. 2597 (16 Feb. 1994), p. 3.

[111] Rose (note 13), p. 46.

[112] Lagunina, I., 'Learning from Bosnia: new modes of cooperation complicate the future of peace-keeping', *Moscow News*, 18–24 Mar. 1994, p. 5. Ironically, this was the closest UNPROFOR had yet come in Bosnia to engaging in a traditional peacekeeping activity—separating combatants along a ceasefire line—although using the forces of a country sympathetic to one of the parties was unusual and, in the view of some, violated classic peacekeeping norms.

[113] Zucconi (note 93), p. 214.

about who was responsible for the marketplace massacre.[114] Akashi weakened the UN's credibility by agreeing with Bosnian Serb leader Radovan Karadzic, on 30 April, to allow seven Serb tanks through the Sarajevo exclusion zone.[115] Although the French forces tried to block their departure from Sarajevo in a cat-and-mouse game over several nights, this was unsuccessful.

While compliance with the exclusion zone was far from complete, and the sieges of Sarajevo and other towns continued, Sarajevo gained a respite from major attack until May 1995. Both Akashi and Rose felt that substantial compliance with the spirit of the ultimatum was more important than total compliance with the letter.[116] UNPROFOR, NATO and the USA all settled in the end for non-use of the heavy weapons, rather than their strict cantonment, in the realization that this was the real issue and could be verified as soon as a weapon was used.

On 24 May 1994 the US Embassy in Sarajevo reported the presence of Bosnian Serb tanks near the city, a clear violation of the exclusion zone, amid continued shelling. UNPROFOR reportedly refused to call in air strikes, this time because the exchanges of fire were evenly matched and not directed against civilians.[117] The USA rejected this and called for air strikes to enforce UN resolutions. Akashi's continuing reluctance to call in air strikes brought criticism from President Clinton himself.[118]

On 2 August 1994 Rose received intelligence that the Serbs were about to seize weapons from two sites guarded by French and Ukrainian troops.[119] He warned publicly that force would be used against the Serbs if they did so and immediately put NATO air power on standby to destroy the weapons as they left the site. When two days later the Serbs did seize weapons from the Ukrainian troops, de Lapresle came under great pressure from Smith to ask for attacks on strategic targets, including ammunition bunkers and communication sites, but he and Rose resisted. On 5 August NATO aircraft destroyed a Bosnian Serb self-propelled artillery piece. A second target was chosen but bad weather prevented an attack. Later the Serbs began returning all the heavy weapons they had taken. Rose claims that, although NATO was accused of carrying out 'pinprick attacks', this was a textbook example of 'the precise use of force in a peacekeeping mission'.[120]

On 22 September 1994 a Bosnian Serb anti-tank weapon was destroyed by a NATO bomb near Sarajevo. Also in September British fighter aircraft tried to attack a tank that was violating the weapons exclusion zone, but demolished a

---

[114] It was rumoured that the Bosnian Government had itself been the culprit, apparently in an effort to attract world sympathy for its plight. The result was the establishment of a UN enquiry into the bombing, which allowed the Geneva peace talks to proceed. *The Independent*, 7 Feb. 1994, p. 1.

[115] Rose (note 13), p. 127. The Bosnian leadership accused Akashi of complicity with the Serbs and said they would never speak to him again. According to Rose, this was the moment when Akashi's influence as chief negotiator in Bosnia began to decline. Rose (note 13), p. 127.

[116] Durch and Schear (note 18), p. 241.

[117] *Wireless File* (US Information Service, US Embassy, Stockholm), 24 May 1995, pp. 1–2.

[118] *Wireless File* (US Information Service, US Embassy, Stockholm), 23 May 1995, p. 1.

[119] Rose (note 13), pp. 159–61.

[120] Rose (note 13), p. 161.

pigsty instead, allegedly missing the target because the sun was in the pilots' eyes. Rose concedes that the UN was becoming sceptical about the capabilities of NATO aircraft.[121] More worryingly, he reports the chaos that engulfed the entire chain of command on this occasion as it tried to agree on the type of target that should be attacked (attacks on ammunition dumps near Pale had been suggested) and whether or not warning of the impending attack should be given.

In practice the weapon exclusion zones, like the safe areas, were unverifiable and unenforceable. Weapons could be hidden and camouflaged, and even the parties themselves were probably unaware how much weaponry they had within the zones. The whole episode demonstrated both a lack of forethought in establishing the ultimatum and a weakening of resolve, and therefore of the deterrent effect of NATO air strikes, when strict enforcement was not pursued.

Talks were held in New York in October 1994, resulting in detailed procedures for 'stricter, swifter, more effective air strikes in response to exclusion zone violations'.[122] NATO would carry out the strikes with 'appropriate speed' and be able to choose among several targets—three or four compared with just one in the past—because of the difficulties of identification, risk of collateral casualties, weather conditions and other reasons. While violators could be given a generic warning, tactical warning of imminent air strikes would no longer be given. Requests for air strikes would still have to come from the UN and be subject to the dual key, but decisions concerning the target and the execution of the mission would be taken jointly by UN and NATO military commanders. This was the beginning of the devolution of authority for authorizing air strikes away from the UN civilian command to the military.

### The case of Gorazde: air power used

In March 1994 the safe area of Gorazde came under a sustained infantry and artillery offensive by the Bosnian Serbs. NATO jets 'buzzed' the town on 13 March 1994, allowing 10 UN military observers to enter. Plans were also approved to deploy 800 Ukrainian troops to the safe area, almost a year after it had been declared.[123]

On 1 April the Serbs began attacking Gorazde in large numbers, using tanks to bombard the town. The government forces retreated in disarray. The UN had only four military observers present.[124] Rose initially played down reports of the attacks, apparently suspecting that the Bosnian Government was trying to goad UNPROFOR into action.[125] In traditional peacekeeping fashion, he also tried to

---

[121] Rose (note 13), p. 177.
[122] Wireless File (US Information Service, US Embassy, Stockholm), 28 Oct. 1994, p. 1.
[123] The Guardian, 2 Apr. 1994, p. 3.
[124] Zucconi (note 93), p. 225.
[125] Despite the horrific nature of the attacks on a town packed with refugees, Rose refuted claims that the Serbs had deliberately targeted civilians and insisted that it was correct for the UN not to respond to 'propaganda designed to ensnare the West in a war in Bosnia'. He later claimed that it was discovered that

balance reports of Serb misdemeanours with reports of alleged Bosnian Government infringements.[126] On 9 April Boutros-Ghali instructed UNPROFOR to use 'all available means' to force the Serbs to pull back to positions held before this latest offensive—which would require much more than close air support. Although he had delegated to Akashi his authority to request air strikes, he issued the instruction himself, he says, 'because I was engaged in a regularly scheduled discussion with Akashi when the moment for decision arrived'.[127]

After UN military observers were endangered by Serb shelling, on 10 April Rose finally requested close air support. He records that he 'found himself back in the familiar business of war-fighting' and that it did not cross his mind that the UN should refrain from using force if the lives of his soldiers and civilians were being threatened.[128] He signed the relevant request forms to initiate the Blue Sword procedure which was needed to obtain political clearance for air strikes, first from Akashi, and then, he says, from New York. He seems to have been unaware that authority had been delegated to Akashi—another example of confusion over the dual-key procedure. Two A-10 aircraft called in to give close air support had to return to base after running out of fuel. However, two US F-16s did destroy an artillery command post, killing nine Serbs and ending the firing. This was the first time NATO air power had been used to defend UNPROFOR. The following day, 11 April, a Bosnian Serb T-55 tank and two APCs were destroyed on Rose's orders when the vehicles were seen heading towards Gorazde. The remaining vehicles withdrew. Rose warned Mladic that: 'UN soldiers were non-combatants in the war, but . . . we had the right of self-defence and we would not hesitate to exercise that right again'.[129]

In two days six bombs were dropped, two of which failed to detonate. Although no doubt intended to demonstrate resolve and enhance deterrence, such 'pinpricks' had no effect on the battlefield and merely succeeded in making NATO look ineffectual and incompetent. Ill-judged remarks by US Defense Secretary William J. Perry further weakened the deterrent effect of NATO's air power. When asked if the USA would 'do nothing' if Gorazde fell to the Serbs, he said: 'We will not enter the war to stop that from happening'.[130] Gorazde had highlighted the muddled thinking about the use of force to protect the safe areas.

In subsequent meetings between Rose, Akashi, de Lapresle, US Ambassador Charles Redman and Vitaliy Churkin (Russian President Boris Yeltsin's special representative to Bosnia), Rose reports that there was 'general agreement that

---

UN military observers in the town, on whom he had relied, had ceased to function as a disciplined unit and had cowered in a bank building, obtaining most of their information from local sources. Rose (note 13), p. 121.

[126] Durch and Schear note that, because he tended to assume that no one believed the Serbs and their 'reflexive political hyperbole', Rose devoted most of his public statements to debunking what he considered the inflated claims of the Bosnian Government, thus earning himself no friends in government or among its US supporters. Durch and Schear (note 18), p. 240.

[127] Boutros-Ghali (note 46), p. 147.

[128] Rose (note 13), p. 106.

[129] Rose (note 13), p. 109.

[130] *Defense and Foreign Policy*, 16 Apr. 1994, p. 906.

an appropriate level of force was being applied against the Serbs in accordance with the UN mandate and that any attempt to raise significantly the level of bombing would risk changing the nature of the mission from peacekeeping to war-fighting'.[131] Rose had privately decided, however, that if they were wrong about Serb intentions towards Gorazde and the Serbs did attempt to overrun it, he would have no choice but to 'call down massive air strikes against them'.[132] This would, he warned, 'spell the end of the peacekeeping mission'.

Karadzic responded to the NATO attacks by refusing further cooperation with UNPROFOR, which from then on he would regard as 'a potentially hostile force'.[133] While Akashi was negotiating with Karadzic in Pale on 12 April, Rose contacted Karadzic to seek approval for close air support in Gorazde because British soldiers had been injured and were under fire.[134] Instead of ordering close air support, on which Rose was insisting, Akashi asked Karadzic for an immediate ceasefire to permit the wounded to be evacuated and Karadzic agreed. Rose concedes that it is impossible to say whether the threat of the use of air power had had any effect.[135]

The Serbs launched a new assault on Gorazde on 15 April. A lone Sea Harrier aircraft attempted to identify suitable tank targets but was shot down by the Serbs. Smith responded by saying that he would no longer agree to requests for air strikes on tactical-level targets as it was too risky, but would in future only accept strategic targets, such as major headquarters or communications sites, or logistic installations such as ammunition bunkers.[136] Akashi, de Lapresle and Rose all believed that an escalation in the air campaign would spell disaster. Rose told Smith that neither NATO nor the UN had the authority to escalate the use of air power in this manner. In the end Smith agreed to consider further requests, but no air strikes ever took place over Gorazde.

Meanwhile Russian envoy Churkin managed to negotiate a ceasefire around Gorazde. When Rose and Akashi conveyed the news to Bosnian President Alija Izetbegovic and Prime Minister Haris Silajdzic, they accused Rose of failing his mission and called on the UN Secretary-General to resign. When Silajdzic asked if it was only Karadzic's words that were stopping Gorazde from being overrun—implying that the UN could and would not defend Gorazde—Akashi replied in the affirmative. Rose says that 'at last the truth had been spoken'.[137] That night Rose withdrew the forward air controllers from Gorazde by helicopter, rendering close air support impossible.

Surprisingly, without consulting UNPROFOR, Boutros-Ghali now asked NATO on 18 April to conduct air strikes, at UNPROFOR's request, against any artillery, mortar positions or tanks attacking civilian targets in Gorazde, as well

[131] Rose (note 13), p. 110.
[132] Rose (note 13), p. 110.
[133] Leurdijk (note 73), p. 47.
[134] Bryant and Loza (note 34), p. 58.
[135] Rose (note 13), p. 113.
[136] Rose (note 13), p. 114.
[137] Rose (note 13), p. 115.

as the safe areas of Tuzla, Zepa, Bihac and Srebrenica.[138] As in the case of Sarajevo, the UN had apparently finally decided that civilians within the safe areas must be protected, regardless of the niceties of the mandate. The NAC responded on 22 April. Ignoring the negotiations going on in Belgrade between Akashi and de Lapresle, it issued an ultimatum authorizing air strikes around Gorazde if the Serbs did not end their attacks immediately, pull their forces back 3 km from the city centre by 24 April, and allow UN forces and humanitarian relief convoys freedom of movement.[139] A 'military exclusion zone' was to be established for 20 km, from which all Serb heavy weaponry was to be withdrawn by 27 April.[140] Extraordinarily, Rose claims that the initiative 'seemed to be a tactic by the hawks in NATO to push the peacekeeping force towards war' rather than a negotiated settlement.[141] When the Bosnian Serbs failed to comply with NATO's ultimata and shelled Gorazde throughout 23 April, NATO's Southern Command called for air strikes. Akashi, supported by de Lapresle and Rose, called Woerner to ask that air strikes be held off lest they jeopardize progress being made in his negotiations with Karadzic, imperil the prospects for eventual Serb compliance, risk the lives of UN personnel and delay the arrival of desperately needed medical units and other UNPROFOR reinforcements in Gorazde.[142] Boutros-Ghali and Woerner consulted by telephone and agreed to authorize air strikes if the Serbs did not comply with the withdrawal deadline of 1600 GMT, just two hours away. Boutros-Ghali then telephoned Akashi and ordered him to approve air strikes.[143] When Karadzic signed an agreement to end the siege of Gorazde, air strikes became unnecessary.[144] The 24 April deadline was not fully met by the Bosnian Serbs, but a ceasefire agreement was reached and de Lapresle decided that sufficient progress had been made to make air strikes unnecessary.[145]

### The case of Bihac

Ironically, one of the most decisive air strikes came not in Bosnia but in Croatia, in retaliation for an attack on Bihac. After Krajina Serb aircraft flying from the Udbina airstrip in Croatia dropped napalm and cluster bombs in the

[138] Boutros-Ghali (note 46), p. 147; and Rose (note 13), p. 116.

[139] Quoted in Leurdijk (note 73), pp. 48–49.

[140] Unfortunately, Akashi had already negotiated a later deadline than the NAC's. In the end the earlier deadline was ignored, including by Adm. Smith. The NAC agreed on similar arrangements for 4 other safe areas if they were attacked by heavy weapons from any range or if there was concentration or movement of heavy weapons within a 20-km radius. Leurdijk (note 73), p. 49.

[141] Rose (note 13), p. 118.

[142] Leurdijk (note 73), p. 49.

[143] Boutros-Ghali (note 46), p. 148.

[144] UNPROFOR convoys were permitted to enter the city on 23 and 24 Apr.

[145] The Bosnian Serbs did 'withdraw' but left behind an estimated 65 soldiers as 'policemen'. Akashi appeared to have conceded too much by permitting such a 'transitional' presence. UNPROFOR further damaged its reputation by first denying the presence of the Serbian militia, then saying that there were no more than a handful, then describing them as police, and finally conceding that there were 100 of them and that they constituted a 'problem'. Cohen, R., 'UN admits Serb pullout is "unresolved"', *International Herald Tribune*, 4 May 1994, p. 2.

Bihac pocket on 28 February 1994, the Security Council hurriedly extended NATO air support to include targets in Croatia.[146] On 21 November 1994, 39 aircraft from France, the Netherlands, the UK and the USA bombed the airstrip—the largest military operation ever conducted by NATO to that point.

De Lapresle was 'extremely unhappy' with the idea and only gave his approval after hearing that Russia supported it and that Boutros-Ghali and Akashi had accepted its inevitability. UNPROFOR officials argued that it went beyond peacekeeping norms because it was retrospective punitive action, not self-defence.[147] De Lapresle taunted Rose: 'So, we have finally crossed the Mogadishu Line'.[148] At de Lapresle's request the aircraft carefully targeted only the airstrip, not aircraft operating from it, in order to limit collateral damage and casualties. The main runway and taxi-ways were damaged (but were easily repaired and back in operation within days) and anti-aircraft guns and SAMs destroyed. The attack was a further humiliating example of NATO's apparent powerlessness in the face of Bosnian complexities.

On 22 November 1994, after the Bosnian Serbs fired two SAMs at two British Harrier jets patrolling the Bihac area and locked their radar onto reconnaissance aircraft, NATO sought agreement to carry out air strikes in reprisal against other Serb targets, since it had not been possible to identify the firing point of the missiles. De Lapresle and Akashi were dissuaded from this by Rose and others on the grounds that there were many aid convoys in Serb territory at that time and that NATO's proposed strikes were outside the peacekeeping norm.[149] The following day, without seeking UN consent, NATO conducted the air strikes against the SAMs anyway, Smith describing this as 'legitimate defence'.[150] Smith told Rose that he intended to clear all air defence systems from Bosnia before responding to any further calls from the UN for close air support. Moreover, NATO would respond to every hostile action by the Serbs with greater use of force. Rose notes that he feared that responsibility for Bosnia was slowly but surely drifting out of UNPROFOR's hands.[151]

On 25 November 1994, after Bosnian Serb forces began shelling the Bihac township, NATO aircraft were again called in by UNPROFOR to protect UN troops. They flew for 60 minutes but could not initiate any attack without endangering both UNPROFOR troops and civilians. In retaliation for NATO air strikes on their anti-missile defences the Bosnian Serbs took Canadian, French and Ukrainian peacekeepers hostage at weapon collection sites around Sarajevo, as well as a British convoy en route to Gorazde, and refused to allow UNPROFOR to resupply the 1000-strong Bangladeshi battalion in Bihac. Western resolve to use force quickly disappeared as the situation deteriorated for UNPROFOR troops on the ground. The Bosnian Serbs detained another

[146] UN Security Council Resolution 908, 31 Mar. 1994. The self-declared Republic of Serbian Krajina was a part of Croatia.
[147] Rose (note 13), p. 202.
[148] Rose (note 13), p. 201.
[149] Rose (note 13), p. 203.
[150] *Atlantic News*, no. 2673 (25 Nov. 1994).
[151] Rose (note 13), p. 204.

50 Canadian peacekeepers, made UN military observers lie bound on an airfield and held other UN troops hostage by blockading them in weapon collection centres around Sarajevo.

However, Rose had publicly committed himself to ordering air strikes if the Serbs started shelling Bihac. On 24 November he requested NATO strikes against all Serb tanks and artillery firing on the town, couching his request in terms of needing close air support for UNPROFOR troops in self-defence.[152] Although the NATO command seemed to favour only strategic strikes, Rose felt that a request to assist peacekeepers could not be ignored. The strikes were authorized, but after two hours the aircraft were forced to return to base, having failed to locate any targets.

Late that night General Wesley Clark called Rose from the US Department of Defense to inform him that the dual key had effectively been taken out of his hands because NATO now regarded UNPROFOR as being held hostage and unable to make decisions for itself. Rose responded that UNPROFOR could not operate without the dual key and that if air strikes took place in Bosnia without UN permission UNPROFOR would have to withdraw, which would require US military assistance. Admiral Smith later also tried to persuade Rose to agree to a strategic air campaign against the Serbs.[153]

However, no strategic bombings took place at this time. Indeed, worried that its detained peacekeepers might be used as human shields against further air attacks, the UNPROFOR command even asked NATO to stop patrolling the no-fly zone over Bosnia in order to avoid possible incidents. They were halted until March 1995. The new leader of the US Senate, Republican Bob Dole, reflected US frustration by declaring that 'we have a complete breakdown of NATO'.[154] Ironically, Rose himself threatened Mladic with strategic air strikes in December when the Serbs began once again to remove heavy weapons from UN storage sites around Sarajevo, although he did so in full recognition that this could be the end of UNPROFOR's mission in Bosnia.[155] NATO did not undertake another attack in defence of a safe area until Srebrenica was being overrun in July 1995.

On 7 May 1995, after a mortar attack on the Sarajevo suburb of Butmir, in which 10 people were killed, Lieutenant-General Rupert Smith, the new BHC force commander, requested air strikes. Akashi, UNPF[156] Force Commander General Bernard Janvier and Thorvald Stoltenberg, the UN mediator, opposed them for fear of inflaming the situation in both Bosnia and Croatia (where Croatian forces had just seized Eastern Slavonia from rebel Serbs in a blitzkrieg attack, isolating UN peacekeepers in the process).[157] Another reason was that

---

[152] Rose (note 13), p. 209.

[153] Rose (note 13), pp. 209, 210.

[154] 'Serbs cannot be stopped, US and UN concede: diplomatic effort called a failure', *International Herald Tribune*, 28 Nov. 1994, p. 1.

[155] Rose (note 13), p. 218.

[156] On the UN Peace Forces (UNPF) see chapter 5, note 35, in this volume.

[157] 'Wary UN rules out air raids on Serbs', *The Independent*, 9 May 1995, p. 12; and 'UN failure to call air raids boosts Serbs', *The Guardian*, 9 May 1995, p. 6.

the UNHCR was keen to escort Serb refugees from Eastern Slavonia to Serb-held parts of Bosnia. Instead of air strikes, the UN sent the Bosnian Serbs a protest letter. Madeleine Albright, US Ambassador to the UN, said that she failed to understand the logic.[158]

## The cases of Srebrenica and Zepa

The humiliation of UNPROFOR and NATO was crowned by the fall of the eastern enclaves of Srebrenica and then Zepa in July 1995, despite the Serbs being warned of dire consequences by the Security Council, UNPROFOR and NATO.

In Srebrenica the UN deployment comprised 300 Dutch troops equipped very much like a traditional peacekeeping unit, with 'just enough to manage the situation' and, as the Dutch Government reassured the Dutch Parliament, with traditional peacekeeping ROE.[159] While they had mortars, long-range TOW and anti-tank missiles, and machine gun-equipped APCs, they had no tanks and the Serbs refused to allow them to bring in light helicopters. As the Serbs began their onslaught on the enclave, NATO was put on standby, at UN request, with a plan for attacks on 40 Serb artillery positions around the city.

The Dutch commander's repeated pleas for air support (he made at least six) were turned down either by Akashi or by Janvier until it was too late. Boutros-Ghali records that Akashi 'agonized over whether close air support would fend off the Serbs or drive them to seize the areas with greater ferocity'.[160] Indeed, it was not clear what the Serbs' intentions were since they had not seized a safe area before. Admiral Smith said that he had telephoned UN commanders on several occasions suggesting rapid NATO action but was rebuffed by the UNPF command.[161] The reasons given included a belief that the Serb attack was not serious and, on one occasion, that they were not actually attacking at that exact time.

On 11 July, after repeated requests from the besieged Dutch peacekeepers, Janvier and Akashi finally approved an attack, but limited it to tanks in the safe area and artillery seen firing—conditions NATO described as 'corseting' and which made their pilots' jobs impossible.[162] Its aircraft attacked two tanks and withdrew. The Dutch Defence Minister, Joris Voorhoeve, learned that an air operation was under way and immediately telephoned Akashi to warn that Dutch troops were so close to the Serb gunners that air attacks were endangering their lives.[163] He asked Akashi to suspend the attacks, despite US pressure on the Dutch Government to permit them to continue.[164] By then the safe area

---

[158] 'UN failure to call air raids boosts Serbs' (note 157), p. 6.
[159] Honig and Both (note 52), pp. 123–25.
[160] Boutros-Ghali (note 46), p. 238.
[161] Leurdijk (note 73), p. 74, fn. 98.
[162] '"I have to get rid of these enclaves"—UN chief', *The Independent*, 30 Oct. 1995, p. 3.
[163] Boutros-Ghali (note 46), p. 238.
[164] Holbrooke, R., *To End A War* (Random House: New York, 1998) , p. 70. The Apr. 2002 report to the Dutch Government (discussed below) accuses Akashi of blaming Voorhoeve's request for his failure to act, when in fact he had already decided not to. Nederlands Instituut voor Oorlogsdocumentatie

was lost. Faced with overwhelming odds, far from using 'all necessary means' to respond to the attack, the Dutch troops surrendered to the Serbs, were taken captive or staged tactical retreats from their posts. They then assisted the Bosnian Serbs in removing the terrified Muslim population from the town, including the separation of men and boys, more than 5000 of whom were later massacred.[165] Zepa, notionally protected by 79 Ukrainian peacekeepers, fell to the Serbs on 25 July with even less resistance.[166]

Following the fall of Srebrenica the Security Council authorized Boutros-Ghali, completely unrealistically, to 'use all resources available to him' to restore the safe area to UN control.[167] This, according to former Swedish Prime Minister Carl Bildt, the European Union (EU) negotiator for the former Yugoslavia, would have required approximately two mechanized divisions, something no country voting for the resolution was prepared to provide.[168] Akashi later confirmed that no attempt would be made by UNPROFOR to restore Srebrenica to UN control.[169]

An initial Dutch Government enquiry exonerated its forces, blaming the situation on inadequate troop and supply levels (due to the Serbs' refusal to allow normal rotation of troops, the entry of heavy weapons and the supply of adequate fuel, ammunition and other essentials), a limited mandate (deterring aggression by means of a largely symbolic presence), the intransigence of Bosnian Government troops (who had threatened to attack retreating Dutch troops and actually killed one) and the UN's failure to provide adequate and timely air support.[170] The Netherlands had in January 1994 pressed Boutros-Ghali, during a visit to The Hague, to devolve responsibility for calling in close air support to the commander on the ground, but he demurred, claiming alternately that this was his prerogative and the Security Council's.[171] The Netherlands later sought clarification from the UN Secretariat, but it felt unable to provide it lest it impinge on the prerogatives of the Security Council.

In April 2002 the Netherlands Institute for War Documentation (NIOD) released a report on the Srebrenica episode commissioned by the Dutch Government.[172] It blamed the Dutch officers themselves for failing to obtain information on the situation in Srebrenica from the Canadian troops before taking over and prepare the Dutch contingent accordingly; for overestimating the likelihood of close air support and air strikes by NATO, by failing to obtain

(Netherlands Institute for War Documentation), 'Summary for the press', available on the institute's Internet site at URL <http://www.srebrenica.nl/en/perssamenvatting.htm>.

[165] For a detailed account see Honig and Both (note 52).
[166] *International Herald Tribune*, 31 Oct. 1995.
[167] UN Security Council Resolution 1004, 12 July 1995.
[168] Bildt, C., 'We cannot walk away', *Financial Times*, 21 July 1995, p. 14.
[169] 'Impotent UN insists that it still has a role', *The Guardian*, 13 July 1995, p. 6.
[170] Dutch Ministry of Defence, 'Debriefing report on Srebrenica to the Speaker of the Lower House of the States-General', The Hague, 30 Oct. 1995. The report also blames UN member states which failed to provide troops to protect Srebrenica and Zepa.
[171] Honig and Both (note 52), p. 126.
[172] Nederlands Instituut voor Oorlogsdocumentatie, 'Srebrenica: a "safe area". Reconstruction, background, consequences and analysis of the fall of a safe area', Apr. 2002, available on the institute's Internet site at URL <http://www.srebrenica.nl/en/start.htm>.

and use intelligence information once the Dutch Battalion (Dutchbat) had been deployed; and for failing to properly record and report the military and humanitarian situation in the enclave. However, on the use-of-force question, it concluded that Dutchbat had 'few grounds for mounting a counterattack [against the Bosnian Serbs] on its own initiative' because:

– active defence of the enclave by military means was not in accordance with the mandate, the UN policy (the maintenance of impartiality) or the rules of engagement
– the instruction ('to deter by presence') was for military reaction to be above all reticent
– the military balance of power was such that, without outside support, Dutchbat would have been defenceless in a serious confrontation as a result of the 'stranglehold strategy' (the blockade policy of the [Bosnian Serbs]), Dutchbat III was no longer a fully operational battalion in terms of manpower, supplies or morale
– military means could only be deployed if the safety of the battalion was in danger and if it was the target of direct fire—the 'smoking gun' requirement—which the [Bosnian Serbs] deliberately avoided
– the circumstances, such as the failure of air support to materialise and the death of the Dutchbat member Van Renssen through an action by a Bosnian Muslim, hardly encouraged the mood for a counterattack on its own initiative.[173]

The report concluded that it was impossible to say whether another battalion in a different condition or more heavily armed could have acted differently. It did note, however, that Mladic's decision to seize Srebrenica was 'primarily motivated by the lack of any significant armed resistance'. Since action by Dutchbat on its own initiative, contrary to its instructions, was not an option, the initiative would have had to have come from the higher UN echelons—and this was not forthcoming.

## III. The use of force by UNPROFOR and NATO for peace enforcement

As the frustrations of the Bosnia operation deepened and the use of force for various purposes proved useless or counterproductive, several apparently uncoordinated changes were made in strategy which would eventually permit UNPROFOR and NATO to use force strategically for peace enforcement purposes—to drive the Bosnian Serbs to the negotiating table.

### Demonstration of the futility of the existing 'strategy'

In mid-1995 General Rupert Smith decided to use air strikes to demonstrate once and for all the dilemma the UN and NATO faced over the use of force, given the vulnerability of UN peacekeepers. He hoped to provoke the Security Council and troop contributors into deciding whether the operation was

---

[173] 'Summary for the press' (note 164).

peacekeeping or peace enforcement and to take the necessary steps. Smith is 'credited with having played a pivotal role in forcing the UN to grasp the nettle of peace enforcement when it was evident that peacekeeping was at a dead end'.[174]

When the Serbs refused to return four heavy weapons, taken in violation of the Sarajevo exclusion zone agreement, to a UN collection point, Smith ordered air strikes on ammunition dumps near Pale on two separate occasions over two days, 25 and 26 May. This was the first time retaliation had been carried out on a target not directly connected with an attack.[175] The Bosnian Serbs reacted, as predicted, with fury, coming close to declaring war on UNPROFOR—a peace-keepers' nightmare—by describing it as the enemy, annulling all agreements with it and threatening the life of a UN spokesperson. They surrounded or took hostage approximately 400 peacekeepers and observers in various locations, chaining some in humiliating situations, as human shields, near presumed targets of further NATO attacks. They also shelled Sarajevo, Tuzla (killing at least 71 people) and other safe areas. Although General Smith wished to continue the strikes until the Serbs handed back the weapons, Janvier and Akashi were opposed, as negotiations to secure the release of the hostages had already commenced.[176] Boutros-Ghali ordered the strikes to end.[177]

On 26 May, at his weekly lunch with the Security Council, Boutros-Ghali had been 'bluntly confrontational', telling members that he and they had known this would happen, but that there had been no option but to order the strikes.[178] The next morning in the Security Council chamber, in what Boutros-Ghali describes as a 'unique moment', not a single member was willing to respond when he asked whether he should order a third air strike. Unfortunately, the Security Council and NATO were not to draw the appropriate conclusions from the Pale bombings until after the fall of Srebrenica and Zepa.

UNPROFOR decided in the meantime to lie low, reverting to peacekeeping, quietly withdrawing troops that would be vulnerable to hostage-taking into protected positions (despite US opposition),[179] effectively abandoning the weapon storage areas and avoiding air strikes. On 9 June, at a meeting in Split, Croatia, Akashi, Janvier and Smith agreed that UNPROFOR should abide by 'strictly peacekeeping principles'.[180] Force could be used in self-defence, but not to ensure delivery of humanitarian aid or to protect Bosnian civilians. UN spokesman Alex Ivanko admitted on 22 June that the weapon exclusion zones no longer existed.[181]

[174] 'Nato comes to the fore on day of the generals', *The Guardian*, 20 Dec. 1995, p. 7.

[175] The new NATO Secretary General, Willy Claes, said the action was in response to 'persistent and flagrant violations' by the Bosnian Serbs of the 6 safe areas, as well as attacks against UNPROFOR, blind shelling and the systematic blocking of humanitarian aid. Quoted in Leurdijk (note 73), p. 63.

[176] Janvier and de Lapresle held secret talks with Mladic to secure their release on 4 June.

[177] 'British general defined the solution to peacekeeping in Bosnia', *International Herald Tribune*, 22 Dec. 1995, p. 7.

[178] Boutros-Ghali (note 46), p. 235.

[179] Boutros-Ghali (note 46), p. 241.

[180] 'France "took lead in UN hostage deal"', *Guardian Weekly*, 2 July 1995, p. 3.

[181] Cited in Leurdijk (note 73), p. 77; and *Guardian Weekly*, 25 June 1995, p. 3.

Even NATO seemed to be lying low. It had scaled down its patrols to enforce the no-fly zone, apparently because of increasing concern at the Bosnian Serbs' advanced ground-to-surface missile capability, presumably supplied by Serbia. In any event, on 21 June Janvier refused a NATO request for air strikes after fixed-wing Serb aircraft were seen flying over Banja Luka.[182] The aircraft landed after two NATO F-18s were dispatched to the area.[183]

NATO officials and others were concerned that a deal had been done by the UN with the Bosnian Serbs involving an end to air strikes in return for the release of hostages.[184] Boutros-Ghali, however, assured NATO that: 'Neither I, nor my Special Representative, nor the Theatre Force Commander, have given assurances to the Bosnian Serbs that the use of air power is no longer being considered'.[185] Confirming once again that he had delegated to Akashi the authority to request close air support, but was retaining for himself the authority to approve air strikes,[186] he assured the new NATO Secretary General, Willy Claes, that: 'I will not hesitate to authorize air strikes if I consider that they are warranted by serious transgressions' and that they would further the Security Council's objectives.[187]

## Deployment of the Rapid Reaction Force

The second piece of the puzzle to fall into place was the establishment of an UNPROFOR Rapid Reaction Force (RRF). On 27 May 1995 the most serious ground confrontation so far between French UN troops and the Bosnian Serbs occurred when, disguised as UN peacekeepers, Bosnian Serbs took control of a French observation post at the Vbranja Bridge in Sarajevo. The French contingent commander sent reinforcements and retook the position by force.[188] Tired of the continuing humiliation of French troops, French Prime Minister Jacques Chirac convinced the Netherlands and the UK to join France in establishing a 12 500-strong, brigade-size RRF, backed by artillery and attack helicopters. This addition to UNPROFOR, endorsed by the Security Council in Resolution 998 on 16 June, was expected to become operational by 15 July.

The new force would be a strategic ground reserve that would operate around and south of Sarajevo. Although it would not wear the UN colours, it would be

[182] *Financial Times*, 22 June 1995, p. 2.

[183] *Wireless File* (US Information Service, US Embassy, Stockholm), 22 June 1995, p. 3.

[184] 'NATO anger at hostage "trade-off"', *The Guardian*, 23 June 1995, p. 7. The Apr. 2002 report by the Netherlands Institute for War Documentation claims that the available evidence does not support this interpretation. 'Summary for the press' (note 164). Holbrooke, however, claims that there was substantial, if circumstantial, evidence for this. Holbrooke (note 164), p. 64.

[185] Boutros-Ghali (note 46), p. 237.

[186] Holbrooke claims that Boutros-Ghali thus removed Gen. Smith's authority to approve air strikes, whereas in fact he had not, to that point, had such authority. Holbrooke (note 164), p. 65.

[187] Claes meanwhile declared that NATO would only take part in future peace operations where it had sole command. He described as 'tragic' the conflict between NATO and the UN over command and control and stated, rather intemperately, that: 'If we, ourselves, cannot set the rules of the game for our military operations, then we shall have to seek other madmen to go and support these peace-keeping operations'. Quoted in Leurdijk (note 73), p. 66.

[188] 'Game of lethal Balkan roulette', *Sunday Times*, 28 May 1995, p. 15.

an integral part of UNPROFOR, under its regular chain of command, and follow peacekeeping ROE. NATO would give it close air support. It would help to protect and if necessary rescue UNPROFOR troops, strengthen deterrence against Serb attacks and give the UNPROFOR commander 'tactical flexibility', somewhere 'between protests and air strikes'.[189] It would also be available to help UNPROFOR consolidate its forces prior to withdrawal should that become necessary. General Smith also reportedly hoped to use it to open and secure a land corridor from the sea to Sarajevo and to 'secure' Sarajevo Airport.[190]

Boutros-Ghali now seemed to have at least part of what he had called his 'missing option' realized. A UN official in Sarajevo was reported as saying that: 'Until now the next level of escalation available to us has been a 1000 lb bomb. The artillery will present us with another rung. It allows us to escalate the response, without having to immediately respond with air strikes'.[191] Solli describes it as a significant addition to UNPROFOR, since it would give the ground commander an 'internal heavy-weapon and air-mobile capability'.[192] To others it seemed too 'thin', lacking engineering support and having too many support personnel.[193]

There was also widespread confusion about its role. Richard Holbrooke, the new US negotiator for Bosnia, noted that it was not clear, perhaps even to its creators, whether it was designed to keep the UN in Bosnia or help it get out.[194] Shashi Tharoor, an adviser to the DPKO, also cautioned that it might drag the UN into peace enforcement:

The United Nations is blurring the distinction between peacekeeping, which requires consent, and peace-enforcement, an ill-defined concept practically indistinguishable from war-fighting. But wars are not, and cannot be, fought effectively in blue helmets from white-painted armoured personnel carriers; so, in its new-found capacity to be forceful, UNPROFOR has to be constantly careful not to trip over the line that separates peace from war, and peacekeeping from disaster.[195]

The British were even reluctant to call it a rapid reaction force, seeing it more as a theatre reserve for protecting UN troops. 'The theatre reserve force is designed to do one thing and one thing only, and that is to protect the troops of UNPROFOR . . . and to enable them to carry out their humanitarian and peacekeeping mission . . . Talk of rapid reaction forces, to be frank, goes a little bit further than we would like . . . We are not there to war-fight. They are there to keep the peace.'[196]

[189] Leurdijk, D. A., 'The Rapid Reaction Force', *International Peacekeeping*, Oct./Nov. 1995, p. 133.

[190] 'Paris talks will set seal on tough new military policy', *The Guardian*, 1 June 1995, p. 7.

[191] 'Serbs kept at bay in fight for ground near Gorazde', *The Guardian*, 2 June 1995, p. 7.

[192] Solli (note 66), p. 101.

[193] Collins, J. M., 'Military options in Bosnia', *US Naval Institute Proceedings*, vol. 121, no. 8 (Aug. 1995), p. 38.

[194] Holbrooke (note 164), p. 65.

[195] Tharoor, S., 'United Nations peacekeeping in Europe', *Survival*, vol. 37, no. 2 (summer 1995), pp. 126–27.

[196] Nicholas Soames, British Armed Forces Minister, on Newsnight, BBC2, 13 June 1995, cited in Almond, M., 'A faraway country . . . ', eds Cohen and Stamkoski (note 10), p. 131.

The deterrent effect of the RRF was weakened further by Akashi, who informed Karadzic that it would abide by the same peacekeeping principles as the rest of UNPROFOR. Albright called Akashi's letter 'highly inappropriate', declaring: 'We would be concerned if the letter were taken to mean that the rapid reaction force is more of the same for the United Nations in Bosnia'.[197]

In the end, the RRF was not needed to evacuate UNPROFOR but played a key role in the military action which broke the Bosnian impasse. Using the initial RRF deployments, UNPROFOR began for the first time to deliver aid over the perilous Mount Igman road into Sarajevo without Serb permission and despite Serb attacks.[198] In early July French troops fired back against the Serbs over three consecutive days as aid convoys came under fire along the route.[199]

## A new strategy: regroup and strike

The third peace of the puzzle was agreement on a new strategy. In the second week of May 1995 Boutros-Ghali called a meeting in Paris of top UN officials involved in the former Yugoslavia to help him prepare options for the future of UNPROFOR, as requested by the Security Council.[200] Janvier and General Smith presented him with two stark alternatives—the use of force or peacekeeping. Since peacekeeping was problematic, UNPROFOR's effectiveness and security had to be improved so that force could be used. This would involve asserting its freedom of movement, if necessary by force, and making UN personnel less vulnerable through redeployment.

Janvier and Smith proposed concentrating their troops in central Bosnia by withdrawing their most vulnerable personnel from weapon collection points in Bosnian Serb territory and greatly reducing the UN presence in the safe areas in order to allow renewed air strikes. It was preferable, they suggested, to have just a few observers and forward air controllers in the safe areas who could call in air power when they were violated. This would have at least as much credibility as, if not more than, the 'mini-battalions' currently deployed there. The two generals also proposed the emergency supply of the eastern enclaves by helicopter, the creation of a ground corridor to Sarajevo and expansion of the target list for NATO air attacks beyond just 'smoking guns' and air-defence systems.[201] Boutros-Ghali strongly supported the plan and asked them to discuss it with NATO and then present it to the Security Council.[202]

At an informal secret meeting in the Netherlands on 19 May, NATO chiefs of defence staff reportedly baulked at the ideas.[203] Janvier briefed the Security Council on his proposals on 24 May.[204] Germany, the Netherlands and the USA

[197] 'France "took lead in UN hostage deal"', *Guardian Weekly*, 2 July 1995, p. 3.
[198] Durch and Schear (note 18), p. 245.
[199] 'Bosnia backing for extra peacekeepers', *Financial Times*, 5 July 1995, p. 2.
[200] The following account is based on Honig and Both (note 52), pp. 151–52.
[201] Honig and Both (note 52), p. 152.
[202] Boutros-Ghali (note 46), p. 233.
[203] Honig and Both (note 52), p. 152.
[204] Minear, L. *et al.*, 'Caught in a vice', eds Cohen and Stamkoski (note 10), p. 94.

were totally opposed to what they perceived as abandonment of the enclaves. Janvier was 'vehemently attacked' by US Ambassador Albright and Dutch Ambassador Niek Biegman, while even France and the UK expressed reservations.[205] Albright and Biegman 'failed to see that the chances of more robust action could only be enhanced if the vulnerability of UNPROFOR to hostage-taking was reduced. By having it both ways, these ambassadors did much to ensure that UNPROFOR remained in its quagmire'.[206] Boutros-Ghali describes the situation as 'a bizarre paradox': 'The United States was singularly outspoken in its demands for air strikes, but, by opposing UN redeployment, the United States was now making a major NATO air assault impossible'.[207]

After the bombing of Pale and the taking of UN hostages had dramatically demonstrated his point, Boutros-Ghali, on 30 May, put new options to the Security Council, telling it that UNPROFOR had become 'mission impossible', that the UN now faced a 'truly defining moment' in Bosnia and that 'nothing is more dangerous for a peacekeeping operation than to ask it to use force when its composition, armament, logistic support, and deployment deny it the capacity to do so'.[208] The first option was withdrawal, but he rejected this as a last resort that would signal the abandonment of the Bosnian people. The second, maintaining the status quo, was untenable, since it would further damage UN credibility. His third option was to turn the Bosnia operation over to a militarily more capable coalition of member states, authorized by the Security Council but under the command of a leading member state (as had occurred in Haiti and Somalia), which would use force to carry out its mandate. A final option was to revise UNPROFOR's mandate to include 'only those tasks that a peace-keeping operation can realistically be expected to perform in the circumstances currently prevailing in Bosnia-Herzegovina' and to return to the use of force, including air power, only in self-defence. A presence in the safe areas would be maintained after 'negotiating appropriate regimes for them but without any actual or implied commitment to use force to deter attacks against them'. This would 'probably' require some redeployment and could eventually lead to a reduction in UNPROFOR's strength.[209]

Yet Boutros-Ghali failed to advocate the most viable alternative, which he himself described as the 'missing option'—the Janvier–Smith plan to redeploy UNPROFOR into more defensible positions so that greater force could be used against the Bosnian Serbs. He says that he omitted it because: 'It seemed to promise only an aggravation of the existing situation, portending even more

[205] Boutros-Ghali (note 46), p. 235.

[206] Honig and Both (note 52), p. 153.

[207] Boutros-Ghali (note 46), p. 234. Honig and Both note that US support for a continuing UN presence in the enclaves also gave hope to the Bosnian Government that the USA might fight politically, if not militarily, to prevent them falling to the Serbs. However, senior figures in the US administration, such as Secretary of State Warren Christopher, had already given up on the enclaves, even though the US Government never explicitly told the Bosnian Government so. Honig and Both (note 52), p. 184. Even senior members of the Bosnian Government acknowledged that holding on to them was untenable. Honig and Both (note 52), pp. 161–62.

[208] United Nations, Report of the Secretary-General, UN document S/1995/444, 30 May 1995.

[209] Report of the Secretary-General (note 208).

forceful action against the Bosnian Serbs and more retaliation'.[210] Moreover, he doubted whether the idea was compatible with the impartial peacekeeping and humanitarian role that UNPROFOR was supposed to be playing. The real reason was US opposition.

In any event the Security Council declined to take a decision on Boutros-Ghali's options and during the following weeks the initiative was seized by the Contact Group for the former Yugoslavia (France, Germany, Russia, the UK and the USA). At an emergency meeting of defence ministers in The Hague on 30 May, the group finally endorsed a French proposal that UNPROFOR regroup its forces into larger, more easily defended contingents—but without evacuating the safe areas. It was agreed that UNPROFOR should be given a 'military capacity to respond rapidly' and more aggressive ROE.[211] The group also deemed it essential that UNPROFOR should enjoy full freedom of movement, including to and from the safe areas.

Agreement on a new strategy and deployment of the RRF was not enough to save Gorazde and Zepa. After the fall of the two enclaves, the Contact Group and UNPROFOR troop contributors, while refusing a French offer to retake Srebrenica by force (with US air support), agreed at the London Conference on 21 July that any attack on the next enclave under threat, Gorazde, would be 'met by a substantial and decisive response'. NATO alone would make the decision as to where and when to do so. Thus a 'line was drawn in the sand'—a deliberate evocation of US President George Bush's language in relation to Iraq in 1990.[212] On 1 August 1995, after 'tumultuous' negotiations in the NAC, driven by Joulwan and US Ambassador to NATO Robert Hunter, NATO extended its threat to all remaining safe areas, including Sarajevo and Bihac.[213] A precondition would be the reduction of the UN forces' vulnerability to an 'acceptable minimum'. No new Security Council resolutions were passed on these matters: the initiative had essentially passed to NATO.

It followed from this that UN civilians had to be removed from the dual key.

### Removing UN civilians from the dual-key arrangement

On 23 July the British, French and US ambassadors visited Boutros-Ghali to ask him to delegate his dual-key authority to authorize air strikes. He responded that he had already decided to delegate his authority to Janvier but insisted that he first receive a letter from NATO reaffirming the principle of the dual key, so that: 'I would be able to take back the authority delegated whenever I considered it necessary to do so'.[214] In reality he appeared to have little choice but to acquiesce in a decision that had already been made by NATO.

---

[210] Boutros-Ghali (note 46), pp. 236–37.
[211] *New York Times* (Internet edn), 30 May 1995, p. 1; *International Peacekeeping*, vol. 2, no. 6 (Oct./Nov. 1995), p. 132; and Leurdijk (note 189), p. 132.
[212] Holbrooke (note 164), p. 72.
[213] *Atlantic News*, no. 2739 (28 July 1995); Leurdijk (note 73), p. 10; and Holbrooke (note 164), p. 72.
[214] Boutros-Ghali (note 46), p. 240.

On 26 July 1995 the NAC announced that NATO air strikes for both close air support and wider purposes would in future be authorized by Janvier, who could delegate authority further down the chain of command if required. Akashi also delegated his authority to authorize close air support to Janvier, who was authorized to delegate it to the UNPROFOR commander when operational circumstances required.[215]

On 10 August a secret memorandum of understanding (MOU) was signed by Janvier and Admiral Smith setting out the new arrangements for NATO air strikes.[216] Either party could request NATO action. If both agreed, the attacks could proceed. If one were opposed, the decision would be referred higher up the chain of command. Attacks might be made against troop concentrations, command and control facilities, supporting lines of communication, and direct and essential military support, including air defence systems. The type of threat to the safe areas that might trigger an attack would include concentrations of military forces and/or heavy weapons, the conduct of threatening military operations and direct military attacks. The MOU noted, however, that in the event of a 'provocation' (presumably by Bosnian Government forces within the enclaves) a limited response by 'an opposing faction' (i.e., the Serbs) might not constitute a condition for a NATO attack.[217]

Richard Holbrooke welcomed the end of the dual-key system, noting that it was 'a terrible idea to begin with and never should have been put into place'.[218] However, even the new system still involved, necessarily, a type of dual key, since it involved reconciling the interests of different parties—NATO and UNPROFOR—which, although represented now by military commanders, could never be identical. Moreover, any dispute between them over a particular air strike could ultimately only be resolved at the level of their superior commanders, the NAC and Boutros-Ghali, respectively.

## Operation Deliberate Force

The final act in the Bosnian war was now ready to be played out, with UNPROFOR and NATO combining forces in a military operation—a peace enforcement operation—to induce Serb compliance. On 28 August 1995 a mortar round was fired into Sarajevo, killing 43 people in a busy street near the site of the previous marketplace massacre. This was the final straw for the USA, which lobbied the UN and NATO intensively to approve US air strikes in res-

---

[215] United Nations, Report of the Secretary-General, UN document S/1995/623, 27 July 1995.

[216] Memorandum of understanding (MOU) between CINCSOUTH and FC UNPF pursuant to the North Atlantic Council (NAC) decisions of 25 July 1995 and 1 August 1995 and the direction of the UN Secretary-General, Camp Pleso, Croatia, 19 Aug. 1995.

[217] Boutros-Ghali records that the air strikes issue was still not settled completely. On 11 Aug. he received a communication from NATO protesting that Janvier would not agree to pre-emptive strikes against Bosnian Serb air defence installations on the grounds that Security Council Resolution 816 had not authorized such attacks. Boutros-Ghali, demonstrating a degree of flexibility (and realism), interpreted the resolution as doing so, thus providing 'a more expansive interpretation for Janvier to work with'. Boutros-Ghali (note 46), p. 242.

[218] *Wireless File* (US Information Service, US Embassy, Stockholm), 28 July 1995, p. 12.

ponse. Since Boutros-Ghali was unreachable on a commercial aircraft, Albright dealt with Kofi Annan, who on 29 August agreed to instruct UNPROFOR's military command to relinquish, for a limited period, their authority to veto air strikes. On the NATO side, Claes simply informed his NATO colleagues that he had authorized Joulwan and Admiral Smith to take military action.[219] The strikes were authorized by Admiral Smith, but, despite all the talk about the end of the dual key, were necessarily decided in consultation with UNPROFOR's General Rupert Smith, who helped establish that the attack came from Bosnian Serb positions.

NATO waited only until the last British troops were out of Gorazde before launching the largest military operation in its history to that point, appropriately called Operation Deliberate Force. Its stated intention was to deter further attacks on Sarajevo and other safe areas.[220] Beginning on 30 August, successive waves of bombing targeted air defence radars, SAMs, communications facilities, ammunition plants, command posts and artillery batteries. It was strictly a NATO operation, with guidance from the NAC, under NATO command and according to NATO ROE.[221] The RRF meanwhile reopened Sarajevo Airport, the Mount Igman route and the route to Kiseljak, north-west of Sarajevo. UNPROFOR thus became 'militarily engaged', in the UN's own words, and lost its impartiality. Durch and Schear note that fortunately the engagement was brief; had the fighting continued much longer the political stresses of the operation might have taken an increasing toll on the UN and NATO.[222]

The air raids were suspended on 1 September, partly to allow peace talks to proceed and partly to give NATO and the UN time to assess whether the Serbs were complying with demands that they restore the exclusion zones, respect the safe areas and give UNPROFOR freedom of movement in the air and on land. Janvier was to try to negotiate an end to the siege of Sarajevo with Mladic. Some UN and NATO commanders, including Janvier and, more surprisingly, Admiral Smith, who was concerned about the well-being of his forces, hoped to avoid a resumption of bombing no matter what the outcome of the talks.[223] Joulwan and Wesley Clark, representing the US Joint Chiefs of Staff, advocated strongly that the bombing resume.[224] At a NATO meeting in Brussels, Holbrooke noted that they now confronted 'in its purest form a classic dilemma in political–military relations, one we faced but never solved in Vietnam: the relationship between the use of force and diplomacy'.[225]

The Janvier–Mladic talks went badly. According to Holbrooke, Janvier received an 'insolent' proposal from Mladic but publicly deemed it to be

[219] Holbrooke (note 164), p. 99.
[220] United Nations, Statement by the Secretary-General, UN document SG/SM/5712, 29 Aug. 1995.
[221] Leurdijk (note 73), p. 79. On the same day Albright reportedly called Kofi Annan to ask when the bombing would end, apparently unaware that authority had been delegated to the field weeks before. Boutros-Ghali (note 46), p. 245.
[222] Durch and Schear (note 18), p. 252.
[223] Holbrooke (note 164), pp. 113, 118.
[224] Holbrooke (note 164), pp. 118–19.
[225] Holbrooke (note 164), p. 119.

acceptable and was immediately supported by Admiral Smith.[226] Both Joulwan and Claes seemed convinced. When a token withdrawal of Bosnian Serb heavy weapons from around Sarajevo began, even General Smith recommended that bombing should not resume.[227] Ultimately, they were all talked round through persistent lobbying by various US officials. Faced with NATO's indecision, Claes ruled on his own authority that a new NAC decision was not necessary to resume bombing.[228] After determining that the Bosnian Serbs had not fully complied with their undertaking to end the siege of Sarajevo, a further two weeks of air raids were launched on 5 September, including, for the first time in Europe, the use of cruise missiles. NATO also attacked military targets near the largest Serb city in Bosnia, Banja Luka.[229]

On 14 September the bombing campaign was 'suspended' for 72 hours after Holbrooke's negotiations in Belgrade with Serbian President Slobodan Milosevic and Karadzic, in which they agreed once more to end the siege of Sarajevo. This came just as Russian patience over the bombing was wearing thin. Russia was urging Boutros-Ghali to retrieve his dual-key authority, but the USA was telling Serbia that henceforth the USA and NATO, not the UN, would decide if the Bosnian Serbs were in compliance, and by implication whether bombing should resume.[230] On 17 September Holbrooke flew to Sarajevo to observe for himself that the siege was indeed ending. He tried to convince Smith to take a firmer line on the ground with the Bosnian Serbs in order to take advantage of the situation. Smith, however, still feared retaliation against UN troops and noted command and control problems, specifically with the French contingent.

One more UN–NATO dispute ensued, as Boutros-Ghali and Claes argued over whether the halt to the bombing was temporary or permanent. On 22 September Boutros-Ghali wrote to NATO to confirm his view that the military operations 'initiated with the agreement of the United Nations on August 30 had terminated' and that UN commanders in the field were agreed that the objectives had been met.[231] He argued that, if a similar situation requiring bombing arose, a new decision would have to be made. Indeed, the USA itself had realized that, if a wider set of targets were to be used in a third round of bombing, not only NATO but Security Council authorization would have to be sought.[232]

This demonstration of NATO resolve, coming after many years of indecision, clearly paid off. While there were initial questions about the actual damage done to the Bosnian Serbs' capacity to wage war, the bombing gave them a psychological jolt which led them to back down. As Boutros-Ghali put it: 'With

[226] Holbrooke (note 164), p. 120.
[227] Holbrooke (note 164), p. 132.
[228] Holbrooke (note 164), p. 120.
[229] At an NAC meeting on 11 Sep., Canada, France, Greece and Spain criticized the attacks in western Bosnia as an unauthorized escalation.
[230] Boutros-Ghali (note 46), p. 245; and Holbrooke (note 164), p. 157.
[231] Boutros-Ghali (note 46), p. 246.
[232] Holbrooke (note 164), p. 146.

strength at last joined to diplomacy, serious negotiations could take place'.[233] Holbrooke notes, tellingly, that the bombing was not linked to any negotiating strategy and that only in retrospect did the outcome look pre-planned: 'It took an outrageous Bosnian Serb action to trigger Operation Deliberate Force—but once launched it made a huge difference'.[234]

Other factors facilitated the Bosnian Serb retreat, including pressure from a Serbian Government that was increasingly eager to have UN sanctions lifted, and Russian agreement to deploy troops to reassure the Bosnian Serbs that Bosnian Government troops would not seize their positions. The bombing campaign pushed the Bosnian Serbs further into a peace process already induced by war-weariness among all the parties, by the loss of 'Serbian Krajina' and Eastern Slavonia to Croatia, ending Serb ambitions for a greater Serbia; by signs that Bosnian Government forces were beginning to gain the initiative on the battlefield in cooperation with Croatian forces; and by increased US diplomatic activism and pressure represented in the formidable person of Richard Holbrooke.[235]

As in the Congo, a military operation undertaken for other purposes had ended up bringing a conflict to a conclusion. On 5 October Holbrooke brokered a Bosnia-wide ceasefire that took effect on 12 October; the reopening of supply routes to relief convoys; the restoration of public utilities to Sarajevo and reopening of the city's airport; and commitments to attend proximity peace talks in the USA (at Dayton, Ohio), to be followed by a peace conference in Europe. One final NATO air raid took place on a Bosnian Serb command bunker after the Serbs shelled the Nordbat base south-east of Tuzla, killing a Norwegian peacekeeper. Thereafter, the guns fell silent.

## IV. The lessons of the use of force in Bosnia

The lessons of Bosnia include some that were relearned after previous experiences in the Congo and Somalia, while others were new. They were lessons not just for the UN and its peacekeeping bureaucracy but for the UN Security Council, NATO and UNPROFOR troop-contributing countries.

### Linking the use of force to strategic and political objectives

One lesson of Somalia that was strongly reinforced by the Bosnia experience was that the use of force should never become a substitute or palliative for a

---

[233] Boutros-Ghali (note 46), p. 247.

[234] Holbrooke (note 164), p. 104.

[235] The independent International Commission on the Balkans identified 3 factors which had changed the situation. The most important was the hubris of the Bosnian Serbs in their offensive against the enclaves, the mass slaughter at Srebrenica, the bombing of Tuzla and the taking of UN hostages. The 2nd was US congressional pressure for the arms embargo against the Bosnian Government to be lifted. The 3rd was the successful Bosnian–Croatian offensive in Western Slavonia. International Commission on the Balkans, *Unfinished Peace* (Brookings Institution Press for the Aspen Institute, Berlin, and the Carnegie Endowment for International Peace: Washington, DC, 1996), p. 73.

coherent strategic plan for tackling an international crisis. Without a clear game plan other than a halt to the fighting, the UN Security Council and NATO both threatened and authorized the use of force in ways that bore no relation to political realities or the situation on the ground and contained subliminal and confused messages. 'The reluctance to use military force . . . remained a cover for major disagreements among the major powers about their objectives in the Balkan peninsula and the continuing absence of a policy toward the conflict itself'.[236] The USA was unwilling to commit any ground troops until a peace settlement had been reached, while the other NATO members already on the ground in Bosnia were fearful of becoming bogged down in a Balkan war. In the Security Council, China, worried about future UN intervention in Tibet or over Taiwan, and Russia, concerned about pro-Serb sentiment among the Russian people, constantly urged caution.

A peace process was in fact being pursued in Geneva, London and elsewhere throughout UNPROFOR's tenure, but UNPROFOR's use-of-force policy and practice were entirely divorced from it, except when Akashi, Rose or some other UNPROFOR official sought to prevent the use of force on any particular occasion from adversely affecting the talks. No thought seemed to be given to the possibility that force might actually be used to assist the peace process. However, responsibility for the failure systematically to link the use of force to the peace process lay not with UNPROFOR but with those responsible for the overall peace strategy, namely, the Security Council and the Contact Group. When resolve to finally settle the conflict, principally on the part of France, the UK and the USA, was backed by a clear strategy and the credible threat and use of force, the problem was solved.

## Mixing peacekeeping and peace enforcement

The Security Council, responding in improvised fashion to events on the ground with a continuous stream of resolutions, entrusted UNPROFOR with increasingly complex and dangerous tasks that suggested a mix of traditional peacekeeping, 'wider peacekeeping' and peace enforcement, and mixed Chapter VI and Chapter VII authorizations.[237] This produced a confusing operational environment for peacekeepers on the ground, where consent was present one day and not the next, in one situation and not another. It also led to relationships with the parties that bordered on the surreal. As Tharoor put it: 'It is extremely difficult to make war and peace with the same people on the same territory at the same time'.[238]

The addition of an outside organization subcontracted to use air power made the situation worse. The Bosnian Serbs increasingly refused to accept the

---

[236] Woodward, S. L., *Balkan Tragedy: Chaos and Dissolution after the Cold War* (Brookings Institution: Washington, DC, 1995), p. 378.

[237] Between Feb. 1992 and Dec. 1995 there were 32 Security Council resolutions relating to UNPROFOR's role in Croatia and Bosnia. United Nations, *The Blue Helmets: A Review of United Nations Peace-keeping*, 3rd edn (UN Department of Public Information: New York, 1996), pp. 744, 750.

[238] Quoted in Prager, K., 'The limits of peacekeeping', *Time*, 23 Oct. 1995, p. 36.

Security Council's pretence that the roles of its two agents in Bosnia could be hermetically sealed from each other—UNPROFOR as non-threatening peace-keeper and NATO as protector, punisher and enforcer. They also refused to accept the Security Council's notion that UNPROFOR was acting impartially, simply responding to bad behaviour from either side. In any event, the Serbs from the outset had perceived the UN as being biased against them, not least because the Bosnian Government had a seat at the UN and UNPROFOR had its main presence in Sarajevo.

However, the lesson that many drew—that peacekeeping and peace enforce-ment can never be conducted in the same theatre of operations at the same time—ultimately proved to be mistaken. UNPROFOR's successor, the Imple-mentation Force (IFOR) in Bosnia, had a clear peace enforcement mandate authorized by the Security Council under Chapter VII, a strong military capa-bility and peace enforcement posture, and much stronger ROE than any UN force had ever been given.[239] Holbrooke recalls how he convinced Clark to add a 'silver bullet' to IFOR's mandate, giving it the freedom to use force whenever it felt it was necessary, without recourse to civilian authorities.[240] Ironically, however, thanks to a Bosnia-wide ceasefire, the 1995 Dayton Peace Agree-ment[241] and the threat of the use of force both before and during IFOR's deployment, IFOR ended up essentially carrying out peacekeeping duties in a peacekeeping environment. UNPROFOR had suffered from the opposite set of circumstances—a vacillating mandate and a peacekeeping capability, posture and ROE in a non-peacekeeping environment.

Since IFOR was deployed with the explicit consent of the parties (like a peacekeeping force), the parties to the Dayton accord in effect consented to the use of force against themselves. Hence, if any party reneged on its obligation to give up territory under the peace accord, force would be used to 'roll' that party back. The parties were to be held equally responsible for compliance and to be equally subject to enforcement action by IFOR as it considered necessary. In addition to being mandated to use 'all necessary measures' to implement the peace agreement, IFOR was authorized to use force to defend itself and to prevent others from obstructing the carrying out of its mandate.[242] It was also much more militarily capable than UNPROFOR had been, numbering 60 000 at its peak (not including forces on standby in Hungary). This included more than

---

[239] UN Security Council Resolution 1031, 15 Dec. 1995. IFOR took over from UNPROFOR on 20 Dec. 1995. Several elements that had been part of UNPROFOR simply transferred to NATO command, swapping UN blue berets for their normal military uniforms. General Janvier became deputy to IFOR Commander Adm. Leighton Smith.

[240] Holbrooke (note 164), p. 223.

[241] General Framework Agreement for Peace in Bosnia and Herzegovina, Dayton, Ohio, 21 Nov. 1995. The text is reproduced in *SIPRI Yearbook 1996: Armaments, Disarmament and International Security* (Oxford University Press: Oxford, 1996), pp. 22–33.

[242] President Clinton told personnel of the 1st US Armored Division that 'If you are threatened with attack you may respond immediately and with decisive force' (*Jane's Defence Weekly*, 7 Feb. 1996, p. 22), while the Chairman of the Joint Chiefs of Staff, Gen. John Shalikashvili, said: 'I am very well satisfied that the catalog of rules of engagement [is] very well suited to ensure not only the protection of the forces from any hostile act, but also when someone exhibits hostile intent' (*International Herald Tribune*, 28 Nov. 1995, p. 1).

20 000 US troops and smaller forces from 32 other countries. It was equipped for substantial military operations, unlike UNPROFOR, and had full protective equipment on the ground, in addition to support from NATO air power.

NATO's first peace operation proved, in military terms, highly successful. It quickly secured the Bosnia-wide ceasefire and began implementing the various stages of the Dayton plan. Its tasks included establishing a zone of separation between the parties; supervising the withdrawal of forces to barracks, cantonments or other areas; monitoring the withdrawal of heavy weapons to holding areas; contributing to the provision of a 'security environment' for other elements of the international presence; and assisting the civilian elements in their tasks, including the holding of elections. Once it had deployed military force sufficient to cow the belligerents into compliance it turned essentially to peacekeeping. While shows of force were occasionally necessary, no actual use of force was required.

### Safe areas and exclusion zones

While the idea of attempting to protect thousands of vulnerable Bosnian Muslims trapped in besieged towns was an admirable one, the concept of safe areas and its execution were fatally flawed from the outset.

1. The first problem was the authorizing resolution and its contradictory juxtaposition of the call for the taking of 'all necessary measures', which usually means Chapter VII peace enforcement, with the restriction of the use of force to 'self-defence', the traditional Chapter VI norm of peacekeeping. This was a carefully worded compromise between those who wished to use force to protect the safe areas (mostly the non-aligned members of the Security Council), on the one hand, and France, Spain and the UK, on the other hand, who were concerned for the well-being of their troops and believed that real protection was impossible. It was designed to give the impression of protecting the safe areas without actually doing so. In reality attacks on the safe areas were unlikely to be deterred only by the use of force in self-defence.

Some blamed the Secretary-General for misinterpreting the resolution and taking a minimalist view of what it implied.[243] Certainly a broader interpretation could have been sustained, based on the reference to the use of 'all necessary means', to argue the case for using force to defend the enclaves. However, Boutros-Ghali did not misinterpret it: he was just more aware than most of the nuances of Security Council opinion and of the impossibility of truly defending the enclaves with the small and weak military forces at UNPROFOR's command.[244] Tharoor confirms that the resolution 'carefully avoided asking the peacekeepers to "defend" or "protect" the safe areas': 'It was a masterpiece of diplomatic drafting, but largely unimplementable as an operational directive'.[245]

---

[243] E.g., Williams, P. and Scharf, M., 'The letter of the law', eds Cohen and Stamkoski (note 10), p. 39.

[244] Honig and Both (note 52), p. 113.

[245] Tharoor, S., 'Should UN peacekeeping go back to basics?', *Survival*, vol. 37, no. 4 (winter 1995/96), p. 60.

2. The safe areas were never defined or delineated, despite the urging of UNPROFOR and the Secretary-General. This made accurate verification of compliance impossible (and would have done so even if UNPROFOR had had enough observers and equipment to do so), and led to genuine (as well as contrived) confusion on the ground.

3. The safe areas were not actively demilitarized: this was only to be 'promoted' by UNPROFOR. The wording of the authorizing resolution was again a compromise between the non-aligned Security Council members, on the one hand, led by Pakistan and Venezuela, which had wanted UNPROFOR to defend the safe areas, and France and the UK, on the other hand, which did not want it involved in such a role.[246] The Bosnian Government correctly surmised, in any event, that UNPROFOR would never have the will or the ability to protect the areas, and was thus reluctant to demilitarize them even if it could convince its forces on the spot to do so. Bosnian Government forces thus remained in the safe areas and used them to regroup and launch attacks from.

4. By responding to Bosnian Serb attacks on the safe areas and seeking their withdrawal, but not that of government forces, UNPROFOR was bound to be perceived as having taken sides, despite UN protestations that it was continuing to act impartially and was primarily motivated by humanitarian concerns. This jeopardized both the purported peacekeeper status of UNPROFOR and the consent and cooperation of the Bosnian Serbs for other vital aspects of its mandate, particularly the delivery of humanitarian aid. UNPROFOR inevitably suffered increased obstruction and harassment by the Bosnian Serbs.

The lesson of Bosnia is that safe areas should not be declared unless they are properly defined, delineated, demilitarized, verifiable and protected. Similarly, exclusion zones should not be declared unless they have been properly characterized and verification of compliance is physically and politically possible. Otherwise the use of force to defend and enforce such areas and zones will be arbitrary and ineffective, lack deterrent effect and even be self-deterred.

## Deterrence and peace operations

Much of the political posturing and activity of UNPROFOR and NATO seemed to be based on an implicit theory of deterrence that was poorly and only spasmodically enunciated, which lacked inherent credibility and which was constantly undermined by those who should have been upholding it.

The most egregious misuse of deterrent strategy occurred in regard to the safe areas. Since most of them were militarily indefensible and no UN member state would provide troops for such purposes, the Security Council was obliged to rest all its hopes on deterrence. The hope seemed to be that for safe areas without a UN presence on the ground, such as Gorazde, the moral authority of the

[246] Honig and Both (note 52), p. 114. Cited in Caplan, R., *Post-Mortem on UNPROFOR*, London Defence Studies no. 33 (Brassey's for the Centre for Defence Studies, King's College, London: London, Feb. 1996), p. 8.

UN would be sufficient deterrent. As Antonio Pedauye, head of UN civilian operations in Bosnia, said: 'We thought deterrence could be based on the moral authority of the United Nations, but we learned that moral authority is not enough. When the Serbs realized there was a 155-millimetre cannon on top of Mount Igman, they understood the language'.[247]

Yet, as noted, the effectiveness of deterrence depends on the credibility and size of the threatened response. A riposte by a small, lightly armed group of peacekeepers was laughable. Moreover, the peacekeeping ROE under which UNPROFOR was operating allowed only for a proportionate response to attack, while the essence of good deterrence is the threat of disproportionate response. As long as the Serbs avoided directly attacking peacekeepers, they could presumably overrun any safe area without fear of counterattack from UNPROFOR in 'self-defence'. Presumably the Security Council thought that the risk of global moral opprobrium and wider international intervention, or at the very least air strikes, would itself constitute such a disproportionate response.

In any event, in the middle of a vicious civil war characterized by gross violations of human rights and the laws of war, and conducted in pursuit of 'ethnic cleansing', no moral authority was likely to be heeded. The Serbs were reasonably certain that wider international intervention would not occur, having snubbed the international community so often with impunity and having seen the divisions over policy towards Bosnia that divided even the Western allies, not to mention the Security Council. So contemptuous of such possibilities were the Serbs that they deliberately attacked UN troops in the belief that they would be self-deterred from fighting back. Somalia had by this stage demonstrated that the staying-power of peacekeepers under sustained attack was fleeting.

### The use of air power

The attempt to contract out the use of air power to NATO proved too riven with contradictions to succeed. The fact that NATO was only authorized to protect UNPROFOR and that it could only do so at UNPROFOR's request, combined with the mission's reluctance to actually use air power and the operational difficulties of doing so effectively and safely, produced confusion, resentment and eventually disgust among the populations of the safe areas, the Bosnian Government, outside observers, foreign governments, especially the US administration, and peacekeepers on the ground.

It might have been expected that having three of the permanent members of the Security Council—France, the UK and the USA—as the main shapers of Council resolutions and as key members of NATO would be an advantage. In fact it proved to be the opposite. Once France and the UK had contributed sizeable contingents to UNPROFOR they had a vested interest in preventing decisive air or ground action because their troops would be at risk (from 'collateral' damage, retaliatory attacks by Serb forces and, increasingly, hostage-

---

[247] 'NATO's turn in Bosnia as UN flags come down', *International Herald Tribune*, 21 Dec. 1995, p. 1.

taking). They thus objected to, stalled and weakened every resolution pressed by the USA that envisaged greater use of force.[248] This in turn made agreement within NATO on a firm use-of-force policy almost impossible to achieve. Even more extraordinarily, British and French UNPROFOR commanders found themselves at times at odds both with their governments and with NATO over the use of air power.

The reluctance of the UN to request air strikes was a combination of traditional UN disinclination to use force, a quixotic attempt to retain its vaunted impartiality (in the sense of never disadvantaging one party over another, whether it deserved it or not), a dread of mission creep into peace enforcement and fears for the safety of its troops on the ground. The UN was not just historically and culturally reluctant to see force used, but it had absorbed the lessons of Cambodia, Somalia and other UN missions better than most. As Boutros-Ghali has noted, UN forces on the ground had no hesitation in calling for close air support when a specific attack was under way against them. What UN commanders could not readily accept were requests for air strikes against targets that were not threatening the UN operation: 'The difference was, in essence, between defense and offense. The United Nations had to defend itself, of course, but to go on the offensive through air strikes would be regarded as a belligerent act in an international war against the Serbs'.[249] An UNPROFOR spokesperson was reported as saying: 'We do not want carpet-bombing by B52s. Ideally, we want to get the guy who triggered the artillery piece that smashed our armoured personnel carrier'.[250]

The use of air power seemed inherently incompatible with peacekeeping. Slow to be activated unless aircraft happen to be overhead, air strikes do not permit direct and ready retaliation—one of the requirements of the use of force in defence of peacekeepers. Actually finding clearly identifiable targets for easy and proportionate retaliation (another traditional requirement of UN use-of-force doctrine) was difficult. Other practical problems included the proximity of civilians or 'friendly forces' (of the Bosnian Government); physical constraints such as poor weather, rough terrain and darkness; the increasing presence of Serb SAM sites; the fact that control teams on the ground were entirely under UN control, while the aircraft were under NATO command; and the ground controllers' extremely limited freedom of movement.[251] While all these factors are present to some degree in normal war-fighting scenarios, in a peacekeeping context they are exacerbated by the stricter rules of engagement designed to avoid collateral damage to peacekeepers, non-hostile warring parties and civilians, and proportionality of response.

The political implications of some types of air strike were also so great—for instance, the effects that a major strike might have on the peace process or

---

[248] Woodward (note 236), p. 297.
[249] Boutros-Ghali (note 46), p. 87.
[250] 'UN commander proposes limited Bosnia air strikes', *The Times*, 5 Aug. 1993, p. 9.
[251] United Nations, Report of the Secretary-General pursuant to Security Council Resolution 959, UN document S/1994/1389, 1 Dec. 1994; and Righter (note 53), pp. 23–24.

delicate matters on which UNPROFOR was dealing with the warring factions—that political input into the decision-making process over air strikes could not simply be cast aside. Military personnel were not always best placed to make such judgements. Even the use of air power for close air support, strictly in self-defence, was sometimes precluded by the need to avoid harming the peace process.

Nor can air power be an effective deterrent, either to attacks on peacekeepers or to broader purposes, if the chain of command for authorizing it is too long, complicated and transparent. In Bosnia too many players were involved, the chain of command was too long and all the world, including the warring parties, could see the political and military disagreements, personal machinations and outside interference involved in the decision-making process which made a go-ahead for strikes improbable.

The vulnerability of UN peacekeepers to Serb hostage-taking was eventually the biggest obstacle to the effective use of air power in Bosnia. The awful dilemma that the UN found itself in was that the presence of its peacekeepers was deterring not the Bosnian Serbs, but NATO. Moreover, UNPROFOR could not withdraw its troops from vulnerable positions or from Bosnia altogether without Bosnian Serb cooperation. Only when this Gordian knot was broken did air power come into its own.

The conclusion can only be that air power is unsuitable for assisting peace-keepers acting in self-defence since it is difficult to use directly, discretely, proportionately, reliably and accurately. It is constrained by too many physical limitations, including the danger of collateral damage to peacekeepers and other innocent parties. Moreover, air strikes are too politically charged to be used routinely, even if peacekeepers were to have their own air power rather than employing that of an outside alliance. On the other hand, air power did prove its effectiveness in helping coerce the parties to the negotiating table, despite widespread scepticism that it could do so.[252]

## Command and control

The greatest difficulty in command and control in the Bosnia operation related to air power. Effective use of air power, especially for close air support, requires rapid decision making, and this was effectively stymied by a dual-key arrangement involving two very different organizations with different priorities and perspectives. Even when there is unquestioned unity of command a degree of tension must be expected between land and air forces about how air power should be used. Although the dual-key system was much derided, it was impossible for NATO air power to be used in such a complex theatre of operations without consulting commanders on the ground (who were in any case mostly from NATO member states). Boutros-Ghali notes that the dual-key controversy was in reality a clash between NATO military commanders on the

[252] Solli (note 66), p. 94.

ground and NATO political leaders in their national capitals—'a confrontation conducted through, and, as usual blamed on, the United Nations'.[253]

What is most extraordinary about the dual-key system is the confusion over exactly who held the keys at any time: almost all the major players, as we have seen, made mistakes about where the authority to call in air power had been vested. If subcontracted air power is ever to be used by the UN again this type of confusion needs to be avoided, not only because it portrays incompetence but because it weakens the deterrent effect of air power.

With regard to command and control of its ground troops, UNPROFOR often had the appearance of 'an assortment of national contingents rather than that of an integrated United Nations Command'.[254] Since France, the UK and their NATO allies provided the most militarily capable forces, the headquarters staff and most of the funding, they dominated the command and control structure. Nonetheless there were still strains among allied military commanders. General Smith reportedly told Holbrooke that: 'I cannot control the French commander of Sector Sarajevo [General René Bachelet]. He gets his guidance directly from Janvier, and you know what that means'.[255] De Lapresle in October 1994 said he included NATO among the threats he had to confront in the former Yugoslavia.[256] As in other peace operations, there was much checking of orders with national capitals, especially as the violence escalated.

There were also strains between the military leadership of UNPROFOR and its civilian masters. The most public incident occurred when Force Commander Cot publicly challenged Boutros-Ghali's authority, accusing him of repeatedly rejecting requests for air support and criticizing the need for 'time-consuming approvals from civilians in the UN hierarchy'.[257] Boutros-Ghali asked France to recall Cot after he reportedly tried to bypass him and communicate directly with the Security Council.[258] Holbrooke claims that another French force commander, Janvier, 'virtually ignored' the authority of SRSG Akashi.[259]

### Rules of engagement

Charles Thomas, the US representative on the Contact Group, described UNPROFOR's 'very conservative' ROE as leading the warring parties, particularly the Serbs, to believe that force was unlikely to be used.[260] They thus had little incentive to negotiate and presented a greater threat to the UN aid convoys

[253] Boutros-Ghali (note 46), p. 148.
[254] de Rossanet (note 74), p. 87.
[255] Holbrooke (note 164), pp. 163–64. This seems odd in view of the record that the French had of acting robustly towards both the Bosnian Serbs and Bosnian Government forces. See, e.g., Rose (note 13), pp. 187–88.
[256] Zucconi (note 93), p. 227.
[257] Righter (note 53), p. 24; and Durch and Schear (note 18), p. 271, fn. 161.
[258] Reuters, 9 Oct. 1993, reproduced in de Rossanet (note 74), pp. 93–94.
[259] Holbrooke (note 164), p. 200.
[260] Dixon, A. M. and Wigge, M. A., *Military Support to Complex Humanitarian Emergencies: From Practice to Policy. Annual Conference Proceedings 1995* (Center for Naval Analyses: Alexandria, Va., 1995), p. 29.

than they otherwise might have. However, as Durch and Schear note: 'It was the consensus of the UN's leadership (both political and military), as well as UNPROFOR's major troop contributors, that the force could not sustain a tougher ROE given its equipment, physical disposition, and increasingly variegated nationality'.[261] It is clear, moreover, that those contingents that were inclined to take a tougher stand with the factions were able to do so within the UNPROFOR ROE. As a respondent to a 1996 questionnaire by the UN Institute for Disarmament Research remarked: 'The numerous contingents who do not want to take risks are those who most criticize the rules of engagement, which they do not make full use of in the realm of legitimate defense'.[262] Out of 44 respondents only 8 described the ROE as inadequate.

The lesson seems to be that, as in other cases, while the ROE could have been improved, it was their full implementation, rather than their inadequacy, that was the main problem.

## V. Conclusions

The most egregious and fundamental failing of UNPROFOR was the attempt to use force in a supposedly peacekeeping context—in which moral and political equivalence had been accorded to all parties according to traditional UN principles of impartiality—in order surreptitiously to punish and coerce one party, the Bosnian Serbs. The alternative was the mounting of a proper peace enforcement operation, appropriately mandated and equipped but still impartial in its treatment of the parties, in which agreements reached between them would have been enforced by military means, including if necessary the use of force against violators. Such an operation would have been much more effective at the outset of the conflict, when the UN's authority was unsullied by the ineffectiveness of its attempted 'peacekeeping'. Another, more drastic alternative, on which there probably would not have been agreement in the UN Security Council, was an enforcement operation in which the Bosnian Serbs were openly declared the principal aggressor and violator of international law, and appropriate and transparent military steps were taken to deal with them.

Just as no one suggested a peacekeeping force when Hitler invaded Poland, so no one should have expected that the Bosnian Serbs, determined to seize as much of Bosnia and expel as many Muslims as they could in the cause of a Greater Serbia, would have been deterred by the sweet reason of the 'Blue Helmets'. As Warren Zimmerman, the last US Ambassador to the former Yugoslavia, said: 'Diplomacy without force against an adversary without scruples is useless'.[263] The International Commission on the Balkans concurred: 'Diplomacy not backed by power is tantamount to hollow gesturing. It is the punch of power that lends conviction to the suasion of diplomats. Where it is

---

[261] Durch and Schear (note 18), p. 227.
[262] United Nations Institute for Disarmament Research, *Managing Arms in Peace Processes: Croatia and Bosnia-Herzegovina* (UNIDIR: Geneva, 1996), p. 298.
[263] Cited in Graff, J. A., 'A good season for war', *Time*, 15 May 1995, p. 29.

lacking, the well-meaning are left to the mercy of the reckless, and brute force rather than reason sustained by might determines the outcome of conflict'.[264] The mounting of a joint NATO–UNPROFOR peace enforcement bombing campaign against the Bosnian Serbs in August 1995 indicated that lessons were belatedly learned, but at enormous cost.

---

[264] International Commission on the Balkans (note 235), p. 7.

# 8. From Haiti to Rwanda to Sierra Leone: new missions, old dilemmas

While the UN was licking its wounds and reconsidering its attitudes and policy towards the use of force after Somalia and Bosnia, new missions continued to be established, some of which, particularly that in Rwanda, threw old issues into stark relief. Some of them, most notably those in Haiti, Eastern Slavonia and East Timor, exhibited heartening evidence that lessons had been learned and applied, but others, such as that in Sierra Leone, suggested that the lesson-learning had been partial and fleeting. Some missions were slow to use force, even in self-defence. Others established precedents which seemed to call into question the caution which pervaded UN discussion of the use of force. The missions most relevant to the use-of-force issue, most of them with explicit or assumed Chapter VII authorization (with the notable exception of the mission in Rwanda), are considered in this chapter.

## I. The UN Mission in Haiti (1993–96)

A relatively modest UN Mission in Haiti (UNMIH), with normal UN self-defence authorization, was scheduled for deployment in October 1993 to help monitor human rights and retrain the Haitian military and police in anticipation of the return of ousted President Jean-Bertrand Aristide, as agreed in the 1993 Governors Island Agreement and related Pact of New York.[1] However, armed thugs, gathered at the docks at Port-au-Prince, the capital, succeeded in turning away the *Harlaan County*, a ship carrying the military and police component of the mission. Although there was no question that the small force on the ship could have fought its way ashore, this appeared to be yet another example of UN humiliation in the face of the threat of force by renegade elements.

In response the Security Council authorized the deployment of a Multi-national Force (MNF), led by the USA and supported by a small number of Caribbean troops. Resolution 940 of 31 July 1994 cited Chapter VII, authorized the use of 'all necessary means' and gave as justification for the deployment the Haitian regime's violation of the Governors Island Agreement and various Security Council resolutions. This operation could be considered an enforcement, rather than a peace enforcement, operation, as its aim was to overthrow ('facilitate the departure from Haiti of') the regime, rather than impartially implement a peace accord between erstwhile combatants. On the other hand, it was also intended to implement a peace agreement, and should therefore per-

---

[1] Governors Island Agreement and Pact of New York, July 1993, UN documents S/26063, 3 July 1993, and S/26297, 16 July 1993.

haps be considered a hybrid enforcement/peace enforcement operation, as was IFOR in Bosnia. Indeed, the Security Council itself described the situation as having an 'extraordinary nature, requiring an exceptional response'.[2] This again indicates the Council's tendency to ignore the niceties of UN Charter distinctions and to approve whatever seems practicable and able to produce consensus among its members.

In the end the threat of a US-led invasion proved sufficient (but only after former US President Jimmy Carter intervened with the Haitian regime and the US invasion force on its way to the island was recalled at the last minute). The 21 000-strong MNF occupied Haiti peacefully on 19 and 20 September 1994 in Operation Uphold Democracy. They pacified the country, to the extent that such a lawless country could be pacified, and oversaw the reconvening of the Haitian Parliament, the departure of the military junta and the return of Aristide. As Robert Oakley and David Bentley put it: 'In both Somalia and Haiti, the US use of force concept was to deploy overwhelming force; to use political dialogue to persuade potential adversaries to avoid conflict; and be ready either to apply decisive force against opposition or to exercise maximum restraint when the mission could be successfully achieved without force'.[3]

No serious opposition was encountered. One US serviceman was killed in action.[4] The most significant issue with regard to the use of force concerned the ROE. The rapid collapse of the Haitian security forces and confusion among US forces about their role in maintaining law and order led to several incidents. Ten Haitians died after a firefight on 24 September in Cap-Haïtien, where the US Marine Corps, last deployed in Somalia, focused on self-protection from hostile fire and adopted an aggressive interpretation of the ROE.[5]

The ROE also caused difficulties because they were interpreted as leaving law enforcement to indigenous forces, the Forces Armées d'Haïti (FAd'H). However, it was soon realized that this was the very force that had terrorized the population for decades. There was a public outcry after the media televised US troops standing by while FAd'H members beat pro-Aristide protesters; a Haitian woman died as a result of the beating. The interpretation of the ROE (but not the ROE themselves[6]) was quickly changed to permit troops to use both non-lethal and 'deadly' force to prevent the loss of human life. Altogether five sets of ROE were issued during the mission.[7]

In March 1995 a reinforced UNMIH succeeded the MNF, with a mandate which matched the MNF's but without Chapter VII authorization (which presumably was not considered necessary in view of the improved security situa-

[2] UN Security Council Resolution 940, 31 July 1994, para. 2.

[3] Oakley, R. and Bentley, D., 'Peace operations: a comparison of Somalia and Haiti', *Strategic Forum* (National Defense University, Institute for National Strategic Studies, Washington, DC), no. 30 (May 1995), p. 3.

[4] Oakley, R. and Dziedzic, M., 'Sustaining success in Haiti', *Strategic Forum*, no. 77 (June 1996), p. 2.

[5] Hayes, M. D. and Wheatley, G. F. (eds), *Peace Operations: Haiti—A Case Study* (National Defense University, Institute for National Strategic Studies: Washington, DC, Feb. 1996), p. 47.

[6] Hayes and Wheatley (note 5), p. 48.

[7] US Army, 'Operation Uphold Democracy: initial impressions', D-20 to D-40, Center for Army Lessons Learned, Fort Leavenworth, Kans., Dec. 1994, pp. 119–20.

tion).[8] With the Somalia experience in mind, both the UN and the USA were determined to ensure that the handover would be 'seamless' and only take place when both the parties and the situation on the ground permitted. To this end a US commander, Major-General Joseph Kinzer, was appointed to lead the UNMIH military component—the first time a serving US military commander had led a UN operation. Approximately one-half of UNMIH's authorized force of 6000 consisted of US troops from the MNF with several months' experience in Haiti—indicating that another lesson had been learned from Somalia.

The UNMIH ROE were the first UN ROE to benefit from the lessons of Somalia. Although they preserved the essence and spirit of traditional UN ROE, they contained new phraseology and somewhat different emphases. One innovation was the reference to 'collateral damage': it was to be minimized, 'consistent with mission accomplishment and the security of UNMIH personnel'. Rule 5 provided that in the event of an attack or threat of imminent attack UNMIH could use 'necessary force up to and including deadly force' in self-defence and defence of UNMIH personnel, international personnel and installations designated as 'key' by the force commander. Rule 6 was perhaps the most strikingly different from the usual UN rules and those used by US forces in Somalia: 'UNMIH forces may intervene to prevent death or grievous bodily harm of innocent civilians at the hands of an armed person or group'. However, force was not authorized to prevent criminal activity which did not involve violence. Rule 8 authorized 'search, apprehension, and disarmament' when acting in self-defence; those arrested were to be handed to the Haitian authorities as soon as possible. The use of chemical riot control agents, presumably tear gas, was authorized as a form of force.[9]

UNMIH in its new incarnation performed well. Unlike Somalia, Haiti demonstrated a successful transition from a non-UN to a UN mission without the outbreak of violence. The transition was based, according to US Lieutenant-Colonel Mike Bailey, on three key documents drawn up for the UN mission—the Conditions for Transition, the ROE and the standardized Force Training Program.[10] The latter comprised a 75-page ROE training component, including definitions, terminology and scenario training.[11] This was the first time in UN history that a comprehensive training document for a specific UN operation had been produced. The training package drew on Nordic peacekeeping manuals, national regulations and previous experience, and was written from a UN perspective as a UN document. It ensured standardized ROE across the UN force, which helped play a role in ensuring that the use of force was avoided.

In addition, CivPols—quite a large component of UNMIH, at 900 as compared with 5000 troops—were completely integrated into the mission and had their own standardized ROE. Special ROE were also devised for the election

[8] UN Security Council Resolution 975, 30 Jan. 1995.

[9] UN Mission in Haiti, 'Rules of engagement, United Nations Mission in Haiti', in 'United Nations Forces in Haiti Force Training Program', Port-au-Prince, 3 Mar. 1995.

[10] Bailey, M. (Lt-Col), personal communication with the author, Washington, DC, 18 June 1996.

[11] 'United Nations Forces in Haiti Force Training Program' (note 9).

period. However, problems were encountered in delineating the roles of the military and the CivPols in providing a 'secure and stable environment' for the local population, a major task of the mission.[12]

According to Bailey, other factors that helped UNMIH avoid the use of force and ensure its success were the training undertaken by all participating forces, the use of psychological operations (PsyOps),[13] the availability of a US-led Quick Reaction Force, and civic education and civic action programmes (including so-called Quick Impact Projects). Clarke and Herbst contend that the Haiti intervention demonstrated that another lesson of Somalia—the need for humanitarian intervention to be accompanied by nation-building if violence was to be avoided—had been learned.[14]

UNMIH's mission ended in June 1996, after which it was replaced by a series of UN operations with different acronyms, fewer personnel and less encompassing mandates, none of which envisaged or involved the use of force.[15]

## II. The UN Assistance Mission for Rwanda (1993–94)

The mission after Somalia that had the greatest impact on the use-of-force debate was that in Rwanda. Essentially it was a nil return in the ledger of the use of force by UN missions, since it declined to use force. Nonetheless the experience of Rwanda was a powerful counterweight to the post-Somalia and post-Bosnia conventional wisdom that the UN could not or should not attempt to use force to impose peace or prevent gross violations of human rights.

Envisaged as a traditional Chapter VI peacekeeping operation, the UN Assistance Mission for Rwanda (UNAMIR) was deployed in October 1993.[16] Its mandate was: to monitor observance of the Arusha Peace Agreement of August 1993, including the cantonment, demobilization and integration of the armed forces of the parties;[17] to establish a weapons-secure area in the capital, Kigali, and monitor the security situation until elections could be held; to help in mine clearance, the repatriation of Rwandan refugees and the coordination of human-

---

[12] Ahlquist, L. (ed.), *Co-operation, Command and Control in UN Peace Support Operations: A Case Study on Haiti from the National Defence College* (Försvarshögskolan, Operativa Institutionen [Swedish National Defence College, Department of Operations]: Stockholm, 1988), pp. 128–29.

[13] Brown, S. D., 'Psyop in Operation Uphold Democracy', *Military Review*, Sep./Oct. 1996, pp. 57–73.

[14] Clarke, W. and Herbst, J., 'Somalia and the future of humanitarian intervention', eds W. Clarke and J. Herbst, *Learning from Somalia: The Lessons of Armed Humanitarian Intervention* (Lynne Rienner: Boulder, Colo., 1996), p. 245.

[15] UNMIH was replaced by the UN Support Mission in Haiti (UNSMIH) in July 1996, followed by the UN Transitional Mission in Haiti (UNTMIH) in Aug. 1997 and by the entirely CivPol mission, the UN Civilian Police Mission in Haiti (MIPONUH), in Jan. 1998.

[16] UN Security Council Resolution 872, 5 Oct. 1993. For a summary account of the mission see Karhilo, J., 'Case study on peacekeeping: Rwanda', *SIPRI Yearbook 1995: Armaments, Disarmament and International Security* (Oxford University Press: Oxford, 1995), appendix 2C, pp. 100–16. See also Findlay, T., 'UNAMIR and the Rwandan humanitarian catastrophe: marginalization in the midst of mayhem', ed. N. Azimi, *Humanitarian Action and Peacekeeping Operations: Debriefing and Lessons* (Kluwer Law: The Hague, 1997).

[17] For the text of the Arusha Agreement see United Nations, Letter dated 93/12/23 from the Permanent Representative of the United Republic of Tanzania to the United Nations addressed to the Secretary-General, UN document A/48/824–S/26915, 23 Dec. 1993.

itarian assistance; and to investigate incidents involving the gendarmerie and police.

UNAMIR had the misfortune to be established in the wake of the Somalia debacle and during the continuing traumas of Bosnia. The US administration, driven by concern that the US public and Congress were suffering from 'peace-keeping fatigue', was reluctant to involve the UN and the USA in yet another messy intra-state conflict in Africa for fear of painful political and military entanglements and—most dreaded of all—their military personnel coming home in body bags. France and the UK shared at least some of these concerns. It was also a period of increasing financial strictures on the UN peacekeeping budget, imposed largely by a US administration that was in turn goaded by an increasingly anti-UN Congress unwilling to pay the USA's assessed share of UN dues. Hard-pressed and short-staffed as a result of the unforeseen explosion in the number, size and complexity of peacekeeping operations, the UN Secretariat, in planning for the Rwanda mission, fell back on a traditional peace-keeping model which was geared largely to the international aspects of the problem, was dependent on the goodwill of the parties, and had only a symbolic presence and capabilities. In proposing a minimalist commitment it opted for what it believed the 'traffic would bear', rather than what the situation required.[18]

UNAMIR was headed by SRSG Jacques-Roger Booh-Booh of Cameroon (who proved singularly unsuitable), while the force commander was Canadian General Roméo Dallaire (who proved the hero of the mission). Its authorized strength was only 2548, including 2217 troops (compared with the 4500 sought by the force commander) and 331 military observers, plus 60 CivPols, but even these numbers were not quickly achievable. The Belgian battalion in Kigali, formerly deployed in Somalia, numbered only 450, rather than the 800 originally envisaged. In addition, there was a poorly equipped, inexperienced and below-strength Bangladeshi battalion.[19] By March 1994 a Ghanaian contingent had brought the force to its authorized level.

UNAMIR was authorized to use force only in self-defence. Its interim ROE, drafted by Dallaire but never approved, also permitted the use of force to defend 'persons under [UN] protection against direct attack' and against armed persons 'when other lives are in mortal danger'—presumably meaning those of non-UN personnel.[20] Dallaire also included a highly unusual provision stating that, with or without the support of local authorities, 'UNAMIR will take the necessary action to prevent any crime against humanity'.[21] On the other hand, he also included a provision that the firing of weapons by individual troops required higher authorization, while the use of heavier weapons or light and

[18] Joint Evaluation of Emergency Assistance to Rwanda, 'The international response to conflict and genocide: lessons from the Rwanda experience', Study 2, Copenhagen, 1996, p. 68, available at URL <http://www.reliefweb.int/library/nordic>.

[19] Suhrke, A., 'Facing genocide: the record of the Belgian battalion in Rwanda', Security Dialogue, vol. 29, no. 1 (1998), p. 38.

[20] Suhrke (note 19).

[21] UNAMIR Interim ROE, 19 Nov. 1993, cited in Surkhe (note 19), p. 44 and fn. 17.

medium machine guns had to be authorized at the sector commander and force commander levels, respectively.

From the outset UNAMIR was an inappropriate instrument for dealing with the violent challenges it was to face. Established to help implement a peace agreement between two sides in what was presumed to be a 'classic' civil war, in reality it faced conflict within and between Rwanda's highly fractured coalition government, its 'loyal' opposition and its mixed Tutsi/Hutu society. An August 1993 report of a UN special rapporteur on extrajudicial, summary or arbitrary executions in Rwanda proposed quite different measures for dealing with the situation, including a mechanism for the protection of civilian populations against massacres, support for Rwandan NGOs involved in protecting human rights and a national reconciliation campaign.[22] UNAMIR was not even provided with human rights or public information components—a critical lapse given the role in the coming holocaust of genocidal propaganda from the notorious Radio Milles Collines.

In April 1994, with the small UN force barely in place, Rwanda plunged into crisis when an aircraft carrying the presidents of Rwanda and Burundi back to Kigali after peace talks in Tanzania was shot down on its approach to the airport. The death of the Rwandan President, Juvénal Habyarimana, 'unleashed two parallel processes of violence which continued unabated for the next three months—massacres of the civilian population and a resumption of the civil war'.[23] Within hours of the crash, government troops, the Presidential Guard and armed militias attacked and killed opposition politicians and Tutsi, and then moved on to the general Tutsi population. There is strong evidence that the massacres proceeded according to a preconceived plan.[24] The worst were carried out by the Interahamwe and Impuzamugambi militias, Hutu supremacists both inside and outside the fragile transitional governing coalition.

Adding to the complexity of the situation, the civil war resumed shortly after the massacres began, ending the ceasefire that had been in effect since August 1993. Troops of the opposition Rwanda Patriotic Front (RPF), stationed in Kigali under UN protection, broke out of their barracks and engaged government forces, while RPF units from the demilitarized zone in the north advanced rapidly towards the capital, gaining control of the north-east of the country by the end of the month.

While Belgium, France and the USA sent aircraft to evacuate their nationals, UNAMIR was unable to control the situation as roadblocks were set up, its headquarters in Kigali was shelled and UN vehicles were shot at. The mission did what it could to protect tens of thousands of foreign and Rwandan civilians who sought protection in hotels, hospitals and the Amahoro stadium. It also helped evacuate foreign nationals, protected UN civilian personnel, rescued

[22] United Nations, Report on the situation of human rights in Rwanda submitted by Mr R. Degni-Ségui, Special Rapporteur of the Commission on Human Rights, 25 May 1993, UN document E/CN.4/1994/7/Add.1, Aug. 1993.

[23] Karhilo (note 16), p. 103.

[24] Adams, G., 'Rwanda: an agenda for international action', Oxfam, Oxford, 1994; and Human Rights Watch Africa, 'Genocide in Rwanda April–May 1994', London, May 1994.

individuals and groups trapped in the fighting and provided humanitarian assistance to those under its protection. Although facing increasing difficulties within Kigali, UNAMIR carried out daily patrols through areas in which no resident UN presence was possible, to attempt to deter killings by the militias.[25] It was forced, however, to withdraw its troops and observers stationed outside the capital, thereby reducing its capacity to monitor events there. While some UN troops risked their lives and acted bravely in seeking to protect Rwandans, others turned a blind eye to massacres taking place in front of them.[26] Dallaire believed that the Belgian contingent, at least, had serious misconceptions about the ROE, making them unnecessarily passive.[27]

The Rwanda mission would trigger a passionate debate about the incapacity of the UN not only for peacekeeping but also for 'early warning'. As early as 11 January 1994 Dallaire had sent to the DPKO 'unequivocal warnings' from a Hutu informant that weapons were being stockpiled in preparation for mass killings of Tutsi, that lists of Tutsi to be eliminated were being compiled and that there were plans to provoke the Belgian troops into retaliation and kill some of them in order to bring about Belgium's withdrawal (and presumably the collapse of UNAMIR).[28] UN Secretariat officials questioned the veracity of the information and made no plans for the worst-case scenario it predicted. Secretary-General Boutros-Ghali, who was travelling extensively at the time, says he did not learn of the cable until three years later.[29] Dallaire also informed the Belgian, French and US ambassadors in Kigali of the situation, but again nothing was done. When Dallaire requested authorization to seize the weapons caches using 'overwhelming force', this was refused on the grounds that the UN mandate did not permit it. While UNAMIR could assist in arms recovery operations, the Secretariat said, this could only be done to assist the Rwandan parties in establishing the agreed weapon-free zone in Kigali, and UNAMIR should avoid 'a course of action that might lead to the use of force and to unanticipated repercussions'.[30] UNAMIR was compelled to return seized weapons to their owners.[31] Extraordinarily, Boutros-Ghali says that he was not involved in this decision, again claiming that he only learned of it three years later.[32]

Once the massacres began, Dallaire pleaded with the UN Secretariat for a new mandate and forces to allow him to protect civilians, but the request was

[25] Minear L. and Guillot, P., *Soldiers to the Rescue: Humanitarian Lessons from Rwanda* (Organisation for Economic Co-operation and Development (OECD) Development Centre: Paris, 1996), p. 78.

[26] Minear and Guillot (note 25), pp. 78–79.

[27] He had tried, apparently unsuccessfully, to correct these deficiencies before the massacres began. Windsor, L., 'Rwanda 1994: historian rebuts *Saturday Night* view', *Vanguard*, vol. 2, no. 6 (1996), p. 23.

[28] Joint Evaluation of Emergency Assistance to Rwanda, 'The international response to conflict and genocide: lessons from the Rwanda experience', Synthesis report, Copenhagen, 1996, p. 19, URL <http://www.reliefweb.int/library/nordic/book5/pb025.html>; and InterPress Service International News, 29 Nov. 1996, cited in *International Peacekeeping News*, vol. 2, no. 5 (Nov./Dec. 1996), p. 9.

[29] Boutros-Ghali, B., *Unvanquished: A US–UN Saga* (I. B. Tauris: New York, 1999), p. 130.

[30] United Nations, *The United Nations and Rwanda 1993–1996* (UN Department of Public Information: New York, 1996), p. 32.

[31] Minear and Guillot (note 25), pp. 77–78.

[32] Boutros-Ghali (note 29), p. 130.

again refused. UNAMIR troops in APCs were unable, under the ROE, to fight through roadblocks to rescue the interim president, Agathe Uwilingiyimana, who had sought refuge in the UNDP compound. She was later murdered, along with 10 Belgian peacekeepers who had tried to protect her. As the Hutus had planned all along, Belgium panicked and announced, despite Boutros-Ghali's pleading with the Belgian Government at a meeting in Brussels, that it was withdrawing its contingent. When a Belgian platoon withdrew its protection from several thousand people at the École Technique Officielle on 11 April, they were massacred.[33] The platoon even withdrew its heavy weaponry, despite appeals from the Secretary-General that it be left for other contingents.[34]

With the imminent departure of the most militarily capable element of the force, the Security Council had to face the prospect that UNAMIR would collapse altogether. Bangladesh and Ghana also indicated that they intended to withdraw their troops.

Boutros-Ghali told the Security Council on 20 April that there were three options—withdrawal, a drawing-down of the mission to a small group under the force commander to mediate a ceasefire, or immediate and massive reinforcement of the operation with an authorization to coerce the parties into a ceasefire and restore law and order. Boutros-Ghali favoured what he has called 'peace enforcement'.[35] Yet he failed to portray correctly the organized and systematic nature of the violence against civilians and saw the most urgent task as being to secure a ceasefire between the government and the RPF. Again, the formalistic and apolitical approach of the Secretariat was evident in his briefing. As the Joint Evaluation Report initiated by Denmark in 1994 (involving 19 countries and similar numbers of international organizations and NGOs) put it: 'With limited experience in protecting civilians, and doctrinal poverty, the Secretariat's response was framed by the conventional dichotomy of Chapter VI versus Chapter VII'.[36] No option that would have allowed UNAMIR to deal with the genocidal war against civilians was ever presented to the Security Council.

The Security Council was in any event deeply divided. France, New Zealand, Nigeria (on behalf of the non-aligned nations), Russia, Rwanda and the Organization of African Unity (OAU) were in favour of expanding UNAMIR and switching its mandate to Chapter VII.[37] However, no volunteers for sending troops, either among Council members or among the UN membership at large, came forward. Invoking its new conservative peace operations policy, Presidential Directive 25 (PDD 25),[38] for the first time, the USA, supported by the

---

[33] Joint Evaluation of Emergency Assistance to Rwanda, Synthesis report (note 28), p. 32.
[34] *The United Nations and Rwanda 1993–1996* (note 30), pp. 40–41.
[35] Boutros-Ghali (note 29), p. 133.
[36] Joint Evaluation of Emergency Assistance to Rwanda, Study 2 (note 18), pp. 42–43.
[37] Minear and Guillot (note 25), pp. 75–76.
[38] US Department of State, *The Clinton Administration's Policy on Reforming Multilateral Peace Operations*, Department of State Publication 10161 (Department of State, Bureau of International Organization Affairs: Washington, DC, May 1994). Excerpts are reproduced in *SIPRI Yearbook 1995* (note 16), appendix 2B, pp. 97–99. For an analysis of its origins see Daniel, D. C. F., 'The United States', ed. T.

UK, opposed the deployment of a sizeable intervention force. Scandalously, the USA declined to label the situation 'genocide' lest it be obliged to act in compliance with the 1948 Convention on the Prevention and Punishment of Genocide. The Security Council therefore decided, in the only compromise possible, to reduce UNAMIR's strength from 2500 to a pathetic 270 and downgrade its mandate. It would now only act as an intermediary in securing a ceasefire, help in the resumption of humanitarian assistance and monitor developments.[39]

Faced with the unfolding of genocide as Rwanda descended into barbarism, Boutros-Ghali, within a week of the new mandate being authorized, called on the Security Council to reverse its decision and deploy a substantial force to end the massacres. The Council, unable to withstand public outrage at the unfolding situation, agreed on 17 May to expand UNAMIR to 5500 in a phased plan which depended, absurdly, on the cooperation of the parties. It would now be mandated to protect civilians and provide security to humanitarian relief operations.[40] However, although it obtained an expanded right of self-defence, to be used to protect particular 'sites and populations', UNAMIR did not receive a Chapter VII mandate, that chapter being referred to only in relation to the arms embargo imposed on the country. The resolution was an attempt to use humanitarianism as a substitute for political and military action; it did not address the issue of prime importance—stopping the massacres.

In any event the UN member states proved unwilling to provide troops immediately. Not one of the 19 countries that had signed up to the UN's new Standby Arrangements System (UNSAS) honoured its pledge when asked to do so, for the first time ever, by the Secretary-General.[41] Ghana offered 800 troops, but these did not have the necessary equipment, such as APCs, to give them the required protection and mobility.[42] Eventually Australia, Canada, Ethiopia and the UK provided small numbers of troops and support personnel. Ethiopian and Malawian troops came with only their rifles (the latter completely 'out of the clear blue sky'), while the Tunisians arrived with no equipment at all.[43] All this made a mockery of the standby arrangements and demonstrated dramatically once more the need for a rapid reaction force. Boutros-Ghali, in frustration, lamented: 'It is a genocide which has been committed . . . and the international community is still discussing what ought to be done. I have tried. I was in contact with different heads of State and I begged them to send troops. I was in contact with different organizations and tried my best to help them find a

Findlay, *Challenges for the New Peacekeepers*, SIPRI Research Report no. 12 (Oxford University Press: Oxford, 1996), pp. 85–98. See also chapter 9, section I, in this volume.

[39] UN Security Council Resolution 912, 21 Apr. 1994.

[40] UN Security Council Resolution 918, 17 May 1994.

[41] Findlay, T., 'Conflict prevention, management and resolution', *SIPRI Yearbook 1995* (note 16), p. 64.

[42] The USA agreed to provide the vehicles but insisted they be rented, not donated. They would be taken out of mothballs, which would take 4 weeks, rather being taken from working stocks. *The United Nations and Rwanda 1993–1996* (note 30), p. 51.

[43] Minear and Guillot (note 25), p. 79.

solution to the problem. Unfortunately, let me say with great humility, I failed. It is a scandal. I am the first one to say it . . . '.[44]

Meanwhile the RPF advanced rapidly to capture, by July, sizeable parts of the country, including the capital, largely ending the massacres as it did so. France proposed a 'humanitarian mission' of limited duration, under UN authorization, to carve out a safe area in the south-west of the country. After intensive diplomacy, France was authorized by the Security Council to lead such a multinational mission 'under national command and control', to act in 'an impartial and neutral' fashion for strictly humanitarian purposes.[45] It would not constitute an interpositional force between the Rwandan parties and would be limited to two months until the expanded UNAMIR could take over, but it was given Chapter VII authorization to use 'all necessary means' to achieve its humanitarian objectives. Many Security Council members had reservations about France's motives (it had supported the Rwandan Government against the RPF), the absence of direct UN control over the force, the possibility that it would permanently divide the country into two opposing zones and the practicability of the idea.

Opération Turquoise began on 23 June, deploying from neighbouring Zaire with a force of over 3000.[46] It had over 100 armoured vehicles, a battery of heavy 120-mm marine mortars, 2 light Gazelle and 8 heavy Super Puma helicopters, and air cover provided by 4 Jaguar fighter bombers, 4 Mirage ground-attack aircraft and 4 Mirages for reconnaissance. The French zone soon filled with thousands of internally displaced persons and members of the rump government, the army and Hutu militia. French troops used some force to disarm militia members. France withdrew according to plan in August and its zone was occupied by new UNAMIR contingents finally received from African countries.

By this time millions of Rwandans had been killed, wounded, internally displaced or made refugees. The whole saga had been a sorry one for the Security Council, UN member states and the UN Secretariat. It had been marked by ignorance, incompetence, timidity and even cowardice.[47] Despite the force commander's bravery in staying in Kigali and pleading for more troops and the authorization to use force, this had been denied by both the UN Secretariat and the Security Council. Clearly, UNAMIR could not have mounted a military campaign to stop the killing altogether once it had gathered momentum. With an extremely weak logistics base, it was rapidly running out of food, medical supplies and even sandbags for its own protection. It had no ambulances and mainly soft-skin vehicles for transport of its troops. Gérard Prunier records, somewhat unfairly, that: 'Militiamen quickly understood that they had nothing

---

[44] *The United Nations and Rwanda 1993–1996* (note 30), p. 51.

[45] UN Security Council Resolution 929, 22 June 1994.

[46] The USA also launched a rapid-reaction humanitarian mission, Operation Support Hope, but was even more constrained in its objectives, permitting US troops to remain in the country only long enough to unload supplies. Other countries, such as Australia, mounted their own limited relief operations.

[47] Melvern, L., *The Ultimate Crime: Who Betrayed the UN and Why* (Allison & Busby: London, 1995), pp. 16–19.

to fear from these toy soldiers and that the worst atrocities could be committed in their presence with total freedom from interference'.[48]

The question arises whether UNAMIR would have been able to prevent the genocide if at an early stage it had been given an appropriate mandate and extra forces to intervene to provide humanitarian assistance and protection to those at risk. General Dallaire believed that the mission should carry on as long as possible as 'a matter of moral concern'.[49] In his view, a fully equipped brigade of 5000 (approximately five battalions) or even the original authorized force of 2600 troops with 'sustainment capability' could have contained the killings in April if it had been mandated to intervene for humanitarian protection purposes—although as each week elapsed another battalion would have been needed.[50] He noted that only the original Belgian contingent, 'the best equipped in UNAMIR and with significant operational experience from Somalia could have become an effective deterrent force had we been given the appropriate mandate and backing'.[51]

Even the reduced UNAMIR force of 450 had been able to protect over 25 000 people in Kigali and to move tens of thousands to safety. Unarmed Red Cross personnel had been able to protect civilians in danger simply by their presence. The 3000 troops of Opération Turquoise had, moreover, managed to stabilize a displaced population of 1.4 million in a vast safe area. Since the 'enemy' was not a conventional, well-armed military force but poorly armed and trained paramilitary and civilian gangs, a relatively modestly armed and sized force could have had a substantial deterrent effect, perhaps even without significant actual use of force. Jonathan Howe, former SRSG for Somalia, concurred that a 'well-organized and immediately available force in Rwanda might have saved many lives'.[52]

In 1997 General Dallaire's contention that a suitably mandated and equipped force of 5000 could have prevented genocide in Rwanda was studied by a workshop involving senior UN and US military officers, and subsequent research. The resulting report concluded that: 'A modern force of 5,000 troops, drawn primarily from one country and sent to Rwanda between April 7 and 21, 1994, could have significantly altered the outcome of the conflict'. Although such an operation would have entailed significant risk, it would have 'thrown a wet blanket over an emerging fire'. 'Forces appropriately trained, equipped, and commanded, and introduced in a timely manner, could have stemmed the violence in and around the capital, prevented its spread to the countryside, and

---

[48] Prunier, G., *The Rwanda Crisis: History of a Genocide 1959–1994* (Hurst: London, 1995), p. 274.

[49] Joint Evaluation of Emergency Assistance to Rwanda, Synthesis report (note 28), p. 44.

[50] Dallaire, R. A. (Gen.), personal communication with Jaana Karhilo, 16 Dec. 1994, quoted in Karhilo (note 16), p. 115.

[51] Dallaire, R. A. (Maj.-Gen.), 'The changing role of UN peacekeeping forces: the relationship between UN peacekeepers and NGOs in Rwanda', eds J. Whitman and D. Pocock, *After Rwanda: The Coordination of United Nations Humanitarian Assistance* (Macmillan: London, 1996), quoted in Minear and Guillot (note 25), p. 78.

[52] Howe, J., 'Relations between the United States and United Nations in dealing with Somalia', eds Clarke and Herbst (note 14), p. 187.

created conditions conducive to the cessation of the civil war'.[53] The force would have needed to deploy quickly and decisively, be mandated under Chapter VII and have robust ROE.[54]

A panellist who had witnessed both the evacuation of UNAMIR and Opération Turquoise argued that a 'determined, modern force that advertised its mission and its robust ROE had no difficulty in controlling the level of violence. It was only when the extremist perpetrators sensed that the world was not going to address the crisis and that UNAMIR's contingents were in self-protection mode that the genocide began in earnest'.[55] The panel agreed that the window of opportunity for intervening with such a force was small and that after the last week of April massive amounts of force would have been necessary because the violence had spread beyond Kigali to the countryside.[56] The report concluded that the UN itself would have been unable to come to its own rescue in April, and an intervention force would have had to be organized and transported to Rwanda by the USA.

Quite apart from the shortcomings of the peacekeeping model itself, the Rwanda tragedy illustrated once more the continuing lacuna in UN peace operations doctrine regarding the use of force for the protection of innocent civilians from organized violence and genocide, whether connected or not with armed conflict. It also demonstrated the need for a genuine ready-response capability.

## III. New missions in the Balkans

Despite the UN's bitter experiences in the Balkans, two new missions were deployed there which would have had implications for the use of force had they gone badly wrong.

### The UN Preventive Deployment Force (1995–99)

Amid all the hand-wringing about definitional issues arising from *An Agenda for Peace*,[57] one innovative addition to the UN arsenal of conflict prevention techniques mentioned in that document was quietly inaugurated by the Security Council in 1992—the 'preventive deployment' of 1000 UN troops to the Former Yugoslav Republic of Macedonia.[58] Originally established as an off-shoot of UNPROFOR, it can be presumed to have inherited the Chapter VII authorization of its parent body, although that was never made clear. In March 1995 it became a 'distinct operating entity', the UN Preventive Deployment Force (UNPREDEP), under the umbrella UNPF structure, along with the UN

---

[53] Feil, S. R., 'Preventing genocide: how the early use of force might have succeeded in Rwanda', A report to the Carnegie Commission on Preventing Deadly Conflict, Carnegie Corporation of New York, New York, Apr. 1998, p. 4, URL <http://www.ccpdc.org/pubs/rwanda/rwanda.htm>.

[54] A Canadian 'after-action analysis' apparently concluded that the ROE had been 'quite adequate' for the mission, both before 6 Apr. and afterwards. Windsor (note 27), p. 23.

[55] Feil (note 53), p. 11.

[56] Feil (note 53), p. 14.

[57] See chapter 5, section IV, in this volume.

[58] UN Security Council Resolution 795, 11 Dec. 1992.

commands in Croatia and Bosnia.[59] Again, no mention was made of Chapter VII.

The aim of the deployment was to deter the spread of the Balkans war to Macedonia, which presumably would come in the form of an attack by Serbia. (The permission of Serbia was not obtained for the deployment. It would in any case have been unlikely to be given.) The name of the force, the involvement of armed troops, including militarily capable Nordic and especially US contingents rather than unarmed military observers, and its deployment only on the Macedonian side of the border were undoubtedly intended to signal to Serbia that UNPREDEP might use force to stop a Serbian invasion or incursions.

What was left unanswered in regard to this novel deployment was under what circumstances UNPREDEP would use force. Was it meant to be simply a 'trip wire', designed to signal a military incursion to UN Headquarters and, if the incursion were not directly targeted at itself, step aside as UNEF had done in Sinai? If only a 'trip wire' effect had been intended, would not unarmed observers have sufficed? Alternatively, would UNPREDEP fight back, using force in self-defence if directly attacked, either in its original positions or after having redeployed itself in time-honoured peacekeeping fashion between the Serbs and any counterattacking Macedonian forces? Would it ignore the niceties of its mandate and simply use force anyway to stop the Serb advance, thereby instantaneously transforming itself into a peace enforcement operation? The use of force by UNPREDEP against Serb forces beyond self-defence would have been a much more serious matter, especially as US forces would have been involved. On the other hand, UNPREDEP was tiny, its observers were strung out in vulnerable positions on hilltops along the border and it had no defensive depth. It would not have been able to mount much resistance without NATO air support and simultaneous reinforcement by capable fighting forces.

The precise deterrent or 'preventive' effect that UNPREDEP was intended to have therefore remained uncertain. Perhaps this very uncertainty constituted the deterrent. In the event, the invasion never came and UNPREDEP was not required to use any force whatsoever. Although widely judged to have been successful, it was withdrawn in 1999 as a result of a Chinese veto in the Security Council completely unrelated to the Macedonia issue. Ironically, the withdrawal took place just months before serious border incursions by Albanian separatists into Macedonia began.

### The UN Transitional Administration for Eastern Slavonia (1996–98)

Bizarrely, at the same time as the Western allies were taking responsibility for Bosnia away from the UN because of its alleged inability to run a peace enforcement operation, the same powers were demanding that it assume res-

---

[59] UN Security Council Resolution 983, 31 Mar. 1995. On the UNPF, see chapter 5, note 35, in this volume.

ponsibility for the contested areas of Croatia for which the Dayton Agreement[60] had not found a solution. The proposal was for a UN Transitional Administration for Eastern Slavonia, Baranja and Western Sirmium (UNTAES) with complex responsibilities for supervising and assisting in the demilitarization of the region and its transfer from local Serbian control to Croatian Government control in accordance with their 1995 Basic Agreement, a part of the Dayton Agreement.

The UN Secretary-General and Secretariat were naturally reluctant to take on the task because of their experience with peace enforcement in Bosnia, because the compliance of the parties could not be assumed, and because the Basic Agreement was worryingly imprecise. Indicating that he had learned important lessons, Boutros-Ghali demanded that the force have a Chapter VII mandate and the capacity to take action necessary to maintain peace and security, be sufficiently credible to deter attack from any side and be capable of defending itself. Estimating that 11 300 troops were required, he expressed concern that:

Anything less than a well-armed division-sized force would only risk repeating the failures of the recent past. The concept of deterrence by mere presence, as attempted in the 'safe areas' in Bosnia and Herzegovina, would be no likelier to succeed on this occasion. Should there be a mismatch between the international force's mandate and its resources, there would be a risk of failure, of international casualties, and of undermined credibility for those who had put the force there.[61]

The Secretariat was eventually placated by a NATO commitment to provide close air support to defend the UN force or help it withdraw (although this had proved problematic in Bosnia). UNTAES was also to be afforded substantial military capability, including attack helicopters, tanks and artillery, and robust ROE.[62] Jacques Klein of the USA was appointed transitional administrator and a US Major-General, Jozef Schoups, force commander, ensuring that cooperation and coordination with IFOR in neighbouring Bosnia would be more likely. As a further indication that lessons had been learned, the use of 'all necessary measures', including close air support, to defend or help the force withdraw would be at UNTAES' request, based on its own procedures and communicated to UN Headquarters, not directly to NATO.

Established in January 1996,[63] UNTAES was a full-scale UN operation, subtly combining Chapter VI and Chapter VII elements, with Chapter VII elements being particularly notable at the tactical level, but with an authorized force of only 5000, plus 100 military observers and 600 CivPols, it was hardly

---

[60] General Framework Agreement for Peace in Bosnia and Herzegovina, Dayton, Ohio, 21 Nov. 1995. The text is reproduced in *SIPRI Yearbook 1996: Armaments, Disarmament and International Security* (Oxford University Press: Oxford, 1996), pp. 22–33.

[61] United Nations, *The Blue Helmets: A Review of United Nations Peace-keeping*, 2nd edn (UN Department of Public Information: New York, 1990), p. 554.

[62] Information from a workshop on Implementation of the Dayton–Paris Peace Agreement and Options for Follow-on Forces to IFOR, organized by the Centre for Defence Studies, King's College, London, the Swedish Defence Research Organization (FOA) and the Swedish Ministry of Foreign Affairs, Stockholm, 28–29 Oct. 1996.

[63] UN Security Council Resolution 1037, 15 Jan. 1996.

equipped for a peace enforcement role in its own right. Nevertheless it performed well, using its military capability to good effect in bringing about demilitarization and ensuring steady progress towards eventual Croatian control. The military side of the mission ended in October 1997 when the bulk of the military component was withdrawn. It had used the threat of force on occasions but had not actually had to use force.

## IV. The East Timor operations[64]

In June 1999 the UN Security Council voted to deploy the UN Mission in East Timor (UNAMET), a tiny civilian mission with fewer than 1000 international personnel, intended to be deployed for just a year, to conduct and certify a referendum on whether East Timor should have autonomy within, or independence from, Indonesia.[65] When the referendum did not go their way, pro-Indonesian elements began killing supporters of independence, burning the capital, Dili, and attacking the UN mission.[66] Most of UNAMET was evacuated to Darwin, Australia, leaving the East Timorese to their fate. 'In a scene hauntingly reminiscent of what had happened in Rwanda in 1994 and Srebrenica in 1995, the UN was forced to abandon large numbers of those whom it had committed to protect.'[67] The UN had, once again, been caught unprepared for the possibility of violence, despite early warning signs. It had meekly accepted Jakarta's assurances that an international force was unnecessary because Indonesia would provide security before and after the referendum.

The new Secretary-General, Kofi Annan,[68] sought to bind the UN and its member states by declaring that the UN would not fail in guiding the territory to independence. 'We cannot stand by and allow the people of East Timor to be killed', he said on 8 September, even though it was clear that the Security Council would not authorize the deployment of a UN force, whether peacekeeping or peace enforcement, without Indonesia's permission.[69] He pressed for a Security Council mission to go quickly to East Timor to assess the situation and for a UN force to be deployed once it became clear that Indonesia could not or would not provide security for the East Timorese and the UN mission. The Council delegation secured from the Indonesian Government its unconditional acceptance of 'international peacekeeping forces through the United Nations from friendly nations to restore peace and security in East Timor, to protect the

---

[64] The author is grateful to Doug Dyer for his assistance in researching this section.

[65] UN Security Council Resolution 1246, 11 June 1999. The mission plan provided for 242 international staff, 271 CivPols, 50 military liaison officers, 425 UN volunteers and over 600 local staff, with a further 3600 to be recruited for the election itself.

[66] The vote had already been postponed once, for 2 weeks, because of UN unpreparedness and intimidation of voters by anti-independence militias. 'Vote delay seen aiding UN in Timor', *International Herald Tribune*, 24 June 1999, p. 5.

[67] Maley, W., 'The UN and East Timor', *Pacific Review*, vol. 12, no. 1 (Feb. 2000), p. 74.

[68] Annan became Secretary-General in Jan. 1997.

[69] 'Annan showed what one leader can achieve', *International Herald Tribune*, 31 Aug. 2000, p. 7.

people and to implement the results of the direct ballot of 30 August 1999'.[70] In a classic case of 'coerced consent', the USA had told Indonesia that if it did not permit the deployment of a peace operation it would lose all financial support from the World Bank and the International Monetary Fund.[71]

## The International Force in East Timor (1999–2000)

When it became clear that only a non-UN multinational force could be deployed in time to make any difference, and that Indonesia would not countenance a UN operation because it suspected the UN's impartiality, the Security Council authorized the deployment of a multinational coalition operation, the International Force for East Timor (INTERFET). Australia, despite procrastinating for days about the need for an international peace operation, volunteered to lead it, but only if it was deployed with Indonesia's consent.

INTERFET was mandated under Chapter VII to 'restore peace and security in East Timor, to protect and support UNAMET in carrying out its tasks and, within its force capabilities, to facilitate humanitarian assistance operations'.[72] The states participating in the mission were authorized to 'take all necessary measures to fulfil this mandate'. Australian Foreign Minister Alexander Downer urged the UN to approve ROE for a peace enforcement operation that would allow the disarmament and pacification of hostile elements.[73] The UK, which drafted the resolution, was only able to secure the support of non-aligned Security Council members for such a use-of-force authorization by dropping a provision for preparations to be made for possible war crimes trials for those responsible for the violence.[74]

The mission eventually consisted of 9400 troops from 19 countries commanded by Australian Viet Nam War veteran Major-General Peter Cosgrove. While Australia provided the bulk of the force (4500 troops), given the sensitivities of the relationship between Australia and Indonesia over many decades, the member states of the Association of South-East Asian Nations (ASEAN) also provided substantial numbers to offset the Australian presence.[75] The robust ROE would be the same for the entire force, but individual contingents would be able to use their own combination of firepower and protective equipment.

[70] United Nations, Report of the Security Council mission to Jakarta and Dili, 8–12 September 1999, UN document S/1999/976, 14 Sep. 1999, para. 12.

[71] Martinkus, J., *A Dirty Little War: An Eyewitness Account of East Timor's Descent into Hell, 1997–2000* (Random House Australia: Sydney, 2001), p. 349.

[72] UN Security Council Resolution 1264, 15 Sep. 1999.

[73] *The Australian*, 15 Sep. 1999.

[74] 'UN clash on fate of Indonesia troops', *The Times*, 16 Sep. 1999, p. 21.

[75] Malaysia, the Philippines, Singapore and Thailand provided contingents. Malaysia initially declined to participate because of Australia's leadership but changed its mind after a plea by Kofi Annan. 'The nations contributing to UN force', *International Herald Tribune*, 18–19 Sep. 1999, p. 4. The members of ASEAN in 1999 were Brunei, Cambodia, Indonesia, Laos, Malaysia, Myanmar (Burma), the Philippines, Singapore, Thailand and Viet Nam.

INTERFET's concept of operations involved first taking control of Dili and establishing 'safe corridors' to gain access to internally displaced persons hiding in the surrounding hills. Cosgrove described it as 'a very quick build-up of combat power ashore so that we could both secure the heart of the problem, that being Dili, very rapidly and provide sufficient space behind ourselves in which to continue to build up and introduce logistics'.[76] The force would then deploy to other areas, including the border with Indonesian West Timor. Cosgrove flew to Dili prior to INTERFET's arrival for talks with Indonesian Major-General Kiki Shahnakri, head of the martial law administration of the province, in an attempt to head off any military confrontation with Indonesian troops and militia.[77] The Indonesian Armed Forces undertook to cooperate with INTERFET through a Joint Consultative Security Group established in Dili, with the participation of UNAMET.[78]

The USA was to deploy 1800 marines and sailors to provide logistics, communications, intelligence and heavy lift support for the mission. The commander in chief of US forces in the Pacific, Admiral Dennis Blair, unambiguously signalled that the USA and its allies were prepared to use 'overwhelming force' if threatened by the Indonesian Army.[79] Australian Prime Minister John Howard also warned that any attacks by Indonesian troops on INTERFET would 'provoke a massive reaction from other parts of the world'.[80] Preparing the Australian public for the worst, he cautioned that: 'Although the goal of our forces will be the restoration of peace and stability, the conditions they encounter could well be violent and disruptive. Any operation of this kind is dangerous. There is a risk of casualties'.[81] Cosgrove declared that, despite the 'first class' cooperation he had received from Kiki, he was prepared for violence: 'We will be ready to respond robustly if violence is used against us'.[82] Although there were reported to be as many as 30 000 militiamen in East Timor, armed with weapons ranging from modern assault rifles to home-made guns and long-bladed knives, many had fled to West Timor and other parts of Indonesia when word spread that an international force was arriving.[83]

INTERFET began deploying from Darwin by air and sea on 20 September 1999. The initial landing went smoothly and unopposed. The advance troops, including British Ghurkas, flew into Dili to secure the airport and harbour, discovering a largely destroyed, looted and empty town. There was no use of force, although four men were disarmed and arrested at the airport and shots

[76] 'Interview: Major General Peter Cosgrove, Commander International Force East Timor', *Jane's Defence Weekly*, 23 Feb. 2000, p. 32.

[77] 'Grim risks for Timor force', *International Herald Tribune*, 20 Sep. 1999, p. 6; and Australian Defense Public Affairs Organisation, Media advisory, 9 Oct. 1999.

[78] United Nations, Report of the Secretary-General on the situation in East Timor, UN document S/1999/1024, 4 Oct. 1999, para. 8.

[79] 'US promises to back allied force', *The Age* (Melbourne), 20 Sep. 1999.

[80] 'With a warning to Jakarta, UN force prepares to land in East Timor', *International Herald Tribune*, 18–19 Sep. 1999, p. 4.

[81] 'Grim risks for Timor force' (note 77), p. 1.

[82] 'Grim risks for Timor force' (note 77), p. 6.

[83] The militias had access to 20 000 weapons of varying sophistication, according to Australian intelligence. 'ADF: forewarned is forearmed', *The Age* (Melbourne), 15 Sep. 1999.

were fired at a helicopter. By the second day 2000 troops had been deployed. In the following days, as Indonesia withdrew its uniformed forces, INTERFET staged a show of force, sealing off and searching the city centre for hours, with helicopters providing cover. The commander of the operation, Lieutenant-Colonel Nick Welch, said it was intended to send a clear message, to both frightened civilians and potential troublemakers, that 'Dili belongs to us now'.[84] There were reports of dissent in the Thai contingent over the readiness of the Australians to confront the militias, but this was promptly denied by an Australian Army spokesman.[85] The Ghurkas were also reportedly critical of the Australians' 'aggressive' stance, their wearing of full protective gear when patrolling (compared with the Ghurkas' berets) and their alleged excessive concern with their own security (reminiscent of US peacekeeping practice).[86]

With growing food shortages in the province and concern that massacres of civilians might still be occurring away from Dili, INTERFET was under great pressure to deploy more quickly into the countryside and towards the border with West Timor. Australian Defence Minister John Moore announced at the end of September that the Security Council had given INTERFET a 'limited right' to pursue any hostile forces into West Timor.[87] Several hundred Australian soldiers deployed to the town of Bilibo near the border in early October, backed by armoured vehicles and helicopters, but encountered no resistance.[88] The UN mission, UNAMET, now began to redeploy to East Timor.

The first INTERFET casualties occurred on 6 October when two militiamen were killed and two Australian soldiers wounded during an ambush of an Australian military convoy in Suai, the first gun battle experienced by the mission. Earlier in the day Australian, British and New Zealand troops had occupied the town, a notorious militia stronghold, in a surprise airborne operation, and had thrown a cordon around it to search for weapons and militiamen. In every previous instance the militia had simply fled INTERFET deployments. Subsequently, INTERFET tried to seal the border with West Timor, with mixed results. Cosgrove rebuffed criticism, including from resistance leader Xanana Gusmao and independence campaigner José Ramos-Horta, that INTERFET was moving too slowly.[89]

There were several incidents along the East Timor–West Timor border in October. In the most serious, on 10 October, shots were fired at a 60-strong INTERFET patrol in APCs. Australian troops returned fire, killing one policeman and wounding another. After the incident, the first between INTERFET and Indonesian forces, the two sides compared maps and discovered that the Indonesian patrol had mistakenly believed that the INTERFET soldiers had

[84] 'Peacekeepers stage show of force', *International Herald Tribune*, 25–26 Sep. 1999, p. 5.
[85] 'A longer stay in Timor looms for Australians', *International Herald Tribune*, 25–26 Sep. 1999, p. 5.
[86] *The Times*, 25 Sep. 1999, p. 13.
[87] 'Disarm Timor militias, US warns Indonesia', *International Herald Tribune*, 1 Oct. 1999, p. 8.
[88] 'Arson attacks in Dili expose security risks', *International Herald Tribune*, 2–3 Oct. 1999, p. 2.
[89] 'Timor peacekeeper dismisses critics', *International Herald Tribune*, 8 Oct. 1999, p. 5.

crossed into West Timor.[90] On 17 October Australian soldiers shot dead three militiamen after they were ambushed near the West Timor border.[91] Further incidents occurred during INTERFET's deployment, although none involved the substantial use of force, either in self-defence or otherwise.

Overall INTERFET did a creditable job in securing the territory, ensuring the departure of Indonesian troops, restoring law and order, disarming the anti-independence militia, preventing them from infiltrating back to East Timor from across the border and paving the way for the follow-on UN peacekeeping force. The only part of its mandate that it did not fulfil was the disarming, forcefully or otherwise, of the pro-independence militia, the Forças Armadas de Libertação Nacional de Timor Leste (Armed Forces of Liberation of East Timor, FALINTIL).[92] INTERFET and the UN, undoubtedly at the urging of the East Timor leadership, apparently reached agreement that this would not be necessary.

Although, or probably because, a forceful posture had been adopted, very little actual force had been used. No INTERFET troops were killed in military action, while six militiamen and one Indonesian policeman were killed, and 11 militiamen wounded.[93] Ramos-Horta lauded the operation as 'almost flawless': 'I haven't heard of a single peacekeeping operation in the world that matches Interfet in the way it conducts itself. All the contingents remain extremely popular with everybody'.[94]

The Australian troops had employed, for the first time, their peace enforcement doctrine, the drafting of which had begun as early as 1994 at the Australian Defence Forces Peacekeeping Training Centre.[95] The success of the mission appeared to be a validation of the Australians' doctrine, training and operational conduct.[96] Cosgrove attributed the success of INTERFET to 'a very powerful force that was able to meet and overwhelm the threat', combined with Indonesia's decision to withdraw from East Timor and end its assistance to the militias once they had fled into West Timor. The key to the early and continuing suppression of militia groups, he noted, was the deployment of infantry units, supported by armoured and combat support elements and tasked with the

---

[90] 'Timor peacekeepers clash with Jakarta troops', *International Herald Tribune*, 11 Oct. 1999, pp. 1, 11.

[91] *The Times*, 18 Oct. 1999, p. 13. Indonesia proposed joint border patrols, while Gen. Cosgrove suggested a demilitarized buffer zone. In the meantime, INTERFET deployed military observer liaison teams to West Timor for cross-border liaison and confidence building. On 25 Nov. INTERFET and the Indonesian Armed Forces signed the Motaain Agreement on border management, establishing a joint border commission, regular coordination by the parties and secure checkpoints for refugee border crossings. United Nations, Report of the Secretary-General on the United Nations Transitional Administration in East Timor, UN document S/2000/53, 26 Jan. 2000, para. 19.

[92] FALINTIL was the armed wing of the Frente Revolucionaria de Timor Leste Independente (Revolutionary Front for an Independent East Timor, FRETILIN).

[93] 'East Timor peace force is held up as model', *International Herald Tribune*, 28 Feb. 2000, p. 4.

[94] 'Timorese praise the Australians', *International Herald Tribune*, 3 Feb. 2000, p. 5.

[95] Waddell, J. G. (Maj.), 'Legal aspects of UN peacekeeping', ed. H. Smith, *The Force of Law: International Law and the Land Commander* (Australian Defence Studies Centre: Canberra, 1994), p. 48. On Australian peace operations doctrine see appendix 1, section IV, in this volume.

[96] Bostock, I., 'By the book: East Timor: an operational evaluation', *Jane's Defence Weekly*, 3 May 2000, p. 24.

most demanding assignments. On the ROE, he reported that: 'We still applied fairly rigid and rigorous rules of engagement to ensure that any shooting incident was righteous in terms of a lethal threat being prosecuted'.[97] The psychological effect of professional fighting forces aligned against them had, Cosgrove claims, a telling effect on the overall scope and nature of militia activities: 'I think we presented a hugely capable, credible adversary to the militia who had armed, gone through some level of training and were certainly espousing a protracted violent struggle'.

Cosgrove also argued for clear mandates for peace enforcement operations: 'You want to be crystal clear about what it is you're asking your people to do, especially when it involves danger'. Finally, in terms of training requirements for such missions he concluded that: 'You learn to warfight and you adapt down for challenges for which outcomes are rendered more credible by your high-end skills'.[98]

The operation also confirmed several operational capabilities, techniques and technologies for consideration in future peace enforcement missions. According to Ian Bostock, they included the high quality of junior non-commissioned officers, who 'adhered to battle-proven infantry minor tactics, strict observance of the rules of engagement and a high degree of fire discipline'.[99] Since it is at the level of the infantry soldier that peace operations may be 'lost or won', this is a significant finding. One lesson that was learned was that the local populace were more reassured by four-man patrols, alert but with weapons held casually, than larger units on high alert with weapons trained. Another was that night-fighting equipment and night-vision devices had enabled INTERFET troops to 'own the night'—a time when the militia were not inclined to operate. Finally, although it had previously been thought that the use of armoured vehicles would probably escalate conflict, in East Timor they enabled the force to protect itself better, project power more convincingly and avoid the actual use of force.

The INTERFET operation could be seen as a model for future UN peace operations. Kofi Annan, on a tour of inspection, praised the professionalism and leadership of the Australian Army, agreeing that there was a need to build on the rapid response model used in East Timor: 'Speedy deployment is an absolute necessity if a cease-fire is to hold or a conflict is to be contained. Yet the average time from decision to deployment can be three or four months. The United Nations needs rapid-response capability'.[100] Speedy deployment had been possible in this case only because a lead nation had stepped forward to command the operation and take the considerable risks of being involved in the use of force. It was fortuitous that that nation happened to be situated close to the theatre of operations and militarily sophisticated enough to lead an operation, and that the territory itself was relatively small and accessible by sea.

[97] 'Interview: Major General Peter Cosgrove' (note 76), p. 32.
[98] 'Interview: Major General Peter Cosgrove' (note 76), p. 32.
[99] Bostock (note 96), pp. 24–27.
[100] 'East Timor peace force is held up as model' (note 93), p. 4.

While these conditions did pertain in other cases, for example, Operation Alba in Albania in 1997,[101] they were not always replicated, as Canada had discovered in its unsupported bid to lead a mission to Zaire in 1996 to carve out 'humanitarian corridors' as escape routes from the civil war there.[102]

The military threat posed to the peace enforcement operation was also far less than the threats in Somalia or Bosnia. As Bostock notes, there were no 'technicals', no proliferation of semi-automatic assault rifles, rocket-propelled grenade infantry assault weapons, main battle tanks, armoured fighting vehicles, air defence systems or long-range sniper fire.[103] Although some of the militia had modern Indonesian Army semi-automatic assault rifles and hand grenades, most carried ageing bolt-action rifles, shotguns, pistols, home-made pipe guns and knives. Similarly, INTERFET did not face the three-way violence of Bosnia or the machinations of Somali warlords in their internecine warfare. However, the East Timorese militia were reputedly vicious and determined, and the Indonesian Army would have been a formidable threat to the international force had it decided to support the anti-independence side whole-heartedly. As usual it is only after the event that the real extent of the threat can be properly gauged. In this case it was relatively containable.

### The UN Transitional Authority in East Timor (2000 to the present)

On 25 October 1999 the Security Council established the UN Transitional Administration in East Timor (UNTAET) under Chapter VII and, as with INTERFET, authorized it to use 'all necessary measures to fulfil its mandate'.[104] Unlike INTERFET, which was principally a military operation, UNTAET would attempt nation-building in the most comprehensive way since UNTAC in Cambodia, eventually, it was hoped, shepherding East Timor to independence. It was to be established immediately and coexist with INTERFET until it was ready to assume the latter's military responsibilities. The mission would reconstitute and administer almost all public services in the territory—the Indonesian civil servants having departed as East Timor descended into chaos. The

---

[101] Operation Alba was the short-lived Multinational Protection Force (MPF) led by Italy in Albania in 1997, authorized by the Security Council under Chapter VII, to provide humanitarian assistance and security after anarchic conditions threatened to engulf the country and cause massive refugee flows towards the Italian coast and into other neighbouring states. Greco, E., 'New trends in peace-keeping: the experience of Operation Alba', *Security Dialogue*, vol. 29, no. 2 (June 1998). In retrospect the operation appears to have been an oddity—an Italian conceit designed more to enhance Italy's bid for a permanent seat on the UN Security Council and to demonstrate that, like France, it could lead a coalition force than as a serious attempt at resolving a dangerous crisis. The force was fired on and used lethal force in self-defence, but sustained no fatalities. The ROE for the mission were drawn directly from those of IFOR and SFOR (the Stabilization Force in Bosnia). Greco, p. 207. However, the mission was not permitted to engage in peace enforcement in the sense of dealing with the causes of the unrest and restricted itself to protecting humanitarian deliveries, international and NGO aid agencies, and itself. Findlay, T., 'Conflict prevention, management and resolution', *SIPRI Yearbook 1998: Armaments, Disarmament and International Security* (Oxford University Press: Oxford, 1998), p. 57.

[102] UN Security Council Resolution 1080, 15 Nov. 1996; and *Wireless File* (US Information Service, US Embassy, Stockholm), 14 Nov. 1996.

[103] Bostock (note 96), p. 23.

[104] UN Security Council Resolution 1272, 25 Oct. 1999.

experienced UN Under Secretary-General for Humanitarian Affairs, Brazilian Sergio Vieira de Mello, was appointed SRSG.

### The military component and transition

The military component of UNTAET would comprise 8950 troops, of which approximately 80 per cent would transfer from INTERFET. It would also have 200 military observers and 1640 CivPols. Kofi Annan told the Security Council that: 'The military capability of the United Nations force will be close to that of INTERFET and it will adopt *a firm posture* in maintaining security throughout the Territory'.[105] The military tasks of UNTAET would be to 'maintain a secure environment throughout the territory of East Timor, to provide direct security for United Nations personnel and property, to monitor the prompt and complete withdrawal of any remaining Indonesian military and security personnel, to take measures to disarm and demobilize armed groups and to assist humanitarian activities as appropriate, including the safe return of refugees and internally displaced persons'.[106] Annan recommended to the Security Council that the force have 'robust rules of engagement and a rapid reaction capability in order to carry out its responsibilities'.[107]

The Australians, conscious of the financial and political costs (the latter in terms of their relationship with Indonesia and other ASEAN states) of being the lead nation for INTERFET, had pressed for a UN follow-on peacekeeping force, led by a South-East Asian nation, to take over as soon as possible. The USA, on the other hand, was concerned that such a mission would not act sufficiently robustly. A senior US official was quoted as saying that:

Right now, with an Australian-led force and some very tough troops that are willing, where necessary to use force, considerable order has been imposed, even along the border area. The question is, if you have a change in the force, will it still carry out the duties: being neutral, enforcing security along the border with West Timor, disarming the militias, and if, necessary, confronting them if they try to attack. Would Asian forces hold their ground if there were military incidents, or would they just retreat?[108]

These were the same doubts as had been expressed about the transitions in Haiti and Somalia. East Timorese independence supporters had the same concerns, believing that the ASEAN nations were too close to Indonesia to be impartial peacekeepers. Indeed, Malaysian Prime Minister Mahathir bin Mohamed had publicly criticized Australia for 'the rather heavy-handed' way in which it had led INTERFET, suggesting that Malaysia would take a less robust approach.[109] The East Timorese foreign minister-designate, José Ramos-Horta,

---

[105] Report of the Secretary-General on the United Nations Transitional Administration in East Timor (note 91), para. 27. Emphasis added.
[106] United Nations, Report of the Secretary-General on the situation in East Timor, UN document S/1999/1024, 4 Oct. 1999, para. 75.
[107] Report of the Secretary-General on the situation in East Timor' (note 106), para. 77.
[108] 'New Timor force raises questions', *International Herald Tribune*, 20 Oct. 1999, p. 7.
[109] 'New Timor force raises questions' (note 108), p. 7; and 'East Timor leaders oppose a Malaysian-led force', *International Herald Tribune*, 3 Nov. 1999, p. 5.

promptly vetoed Malaysia's bid to command the UN force because of its 'extremely poor record in upholding human rights in East Timor' and warned of 'total civil disobedience' if a Malaysian were appointed.[110] This unprecedented public interference in the Secretary-General's prerogative of appointing the force commander of a UN operation succeeded: Lieutenant-General Jaimé de los Santos of the Philippines was appointed. An Australian, Major-General Geoffrey Smith, who oversaw East Timor matters in the Australian Department of Defence, was appointed deputy commander, helping to ensure a smooth transition.

UNTAET inherited a territory with security largely restored but with a still tenuous situation along the border with Indonesia, marked by occasional clashes between INTERFET patrols and militia forces from across the border. However, a small local police force and judiciary were now in place and a number of militia leaders alleged to have committed atrocities had been arrested and were awaiting trial.

The UN force took over security responsibilities from INTERFET from the beginning of February 2000 in several stages. Troops from the Philippines, South Korea and Thailand were first assigned responsibility for security in the eastern districts of the territory. The final transfer of responsibility came in the sensitive districts closest to the Indonesian border. UNTAET took over completely from INTERFET on 28 February.

Only a week later UNTAET began to experience increased infiltration and incidents across the border—16 raids in as many days.[111] The familiar pattern of belligerents testing a UN follow-on force was being played out once more. At least one East Timorese was killed and shots were fired at an Australian helicopter. Indonesia's first democratically elected leader, President Abdurrahman Wahid, promised stern action, including disarming the rebels sheltering in West Timor. On 20 March a Jordanian UN officer fired two warning shots after he was kicked and stabbed while walking along Dili's waterfront—the first deliberate attack on an individual peacekeeper since UNTAET's deployment.[112]

In July 2000 anti-independence militia launched a new series of raids from West Timor. Clashes along the border with UNTAET troops resulted in several UN troops being injured and two killed—the first deaths incurred by UNTAET in military operations.[113] Plans to reduce UNTAET's military component were halted and a renewed debate took place over whether FALINTIL, numbering

[110] 'East Timor leaders oppose a Malaysian-led force' (note 109), p. 5.
[111] 'East Timor in transition', Radio Australia Online, 10 Mar. 2000, URL <http://www.abc.net.au/etimor>.
[112] 'East Timor in transition', Radio Australia Online, 20 Mar. 2000, URL <http://www.abc.net.au/etimor>.
[113] United Nations, Report of the Secretary-General on the United Nations Transitional Administration in East Timor, UN document S/2000/738, 26 July 2000; United Nations, Statement by the President of the Security Council, UN document S/PRST/2000/26, 3 Aug. 2000; and United Nations, Press Release SC/6915, 29 Aug. 2000.

approximately 1000, should be allowed to become a national security force or at least cooperate with UNTAET in maintaining security in the territory.[114]

Since mid-2000 the security situation has improved dramatically, border incursions from the West have to all intents and purposes ended, and there have been no major uses of force. UNTAET successfully guided East Timor to independence on 20 May 2002.

## V. The UN Mission in Sierra Leone (1999 to the present)

Of all the peace operations authorized under Kofi Annan's tenure to date, the UN Mission in Sierra Leone (UNAMSIL) illustrates most graphically the continuing failings of the UN—especially in relation to the use of force.[115] For Renata Dwan it offered 'a textbook example of the weaknesses of UN peacekeeping'.[116] While peace enforcement was apparently expected of it—although this was never entirely clear—its willingness to appease one party which had violated the peace agreement led to the near-collapse of the mission. Only when strengthened by the deployment of a separate British force did the UN operation begin to act robustly and restore some of its lost credibility.

UNAMSIL was designed to first supplement and then supplant the failing regional peace operation deployed by the Economic Community of West African States (ECOWAS). The 15 000-strong ECOWAS Military Observer Group (ECOMOG) had become the main bulwark against the defeat of the Sierra Leonean Government by the Revolutionary United Front (RUF), led by Foday Sankoh. Despite its innocuous name, ECOMOG had in effect engaged in peace enforcement, pushing the RUF back from its siege of the capital, Freetown, in 1998 and into a few strongholds in the north and east of the country. However, ECOMOG was now facing collapse as a result of the withdrawal of the largest and dominant Nigerian contingent. The Lomé Peace Agreement, signed by the government and the RUF in July 1999, was meant to end the war.[117] At the urging of the British and US governments, Sierra Leone's demo-

---

[114] Haseman, J., 'Falintil unit to bolster UN peace operation in East Timor', *Jane's Defence Weekly*, 30 Aug. 2000, p. 15.

[115] Other UN missions established during Kofi Annan's first term in office are not considered in detail here as they reveal no new lessons for the use-of-force question. The UN Mission in the Central African Republic (MINURCA), established in Apr. 1998, was given a Chapter VI mandate even though it replaced a non-UN but Security Council-authorized multinational mission, the Inter-African Mission to Monitor the Implementation of the Bangui Agreements (MISAB), established in 1997. However, MISAB had Chapter VII authorization only to ensure the security and freedom of movement of its own personnel. Karhilo, J., 'Conflict prevention, management and resolution', *SIPRI Yearbook 1999: Armaments, Disarmament and International Security* (Oxford University Press: Oxford, 1999), pp. 91–92. The MPF for Albania, also established in 1997 (see note 101), received the same authorization as MISAB. The UN Mission in the Democratic Republic of the Congo (MONUC), established in Nov. 1999, was given a Chapter VII mandate in Feb. 2000 but could only use force to protect UN and Joint Military Commission personnel and 'civilians under imminent threat of violence'. UN Security Council Resolution 1291, 24 Feb. 2000.

[116] Dwan, R., 'Armed conflict prevention, management and resolution', *SIPRI Yearbook 2001: Armaments, Disarmament and International Security* (Oxford University Press: Oxford, 2001), p. 82.

[117] Peace Agreement between the Government of Sierra Leone and the Revolutionary United Front of Sierra Leone, 7 July 1999, available at URL <http://www.sierra-leone.org/lomeaccord>.

cratically elected president, Ahmad Tejan Kabbah, gave Sankoh an amnesty for war crimes and eight cabinet posts, one of which ensured his control of the diamond mines which provided the main source of income for his rebels. In return, he was expected to disarm his forces and participate in free and fair elections.

It was into this unpromising situation that UNAMSIL was to be deployed.

## The mission

UNAMSIL was established by the Security Council in October 1999[118] to monitor compliance with the Lomé Peace Agreement, encourage the parties to establish confidence-building mechanisms, support the anticipated elections and ensure the security and freedom of movement of UN personnel.[119] The mission was also mandated to 'assist' the government in implementing a disarmament, demobilization and reintegration plan by establishing a presence at key locations throughout the country, including at disarmament, reception and demobilization centres. Although predicated on the 'cooperation of the parties and a generally permissive environment', the mission acquired a Chapter VII mandate authorizing 'necessary action to ensure the security and freedom of movement of its personnel'.

It was also mandated 'within its capabilities and areas of deployment' to 'afford protection to civilians under imminent threat of physical violence, taking into account the responsibilities of the Government'.[120] Secretary-General Annan, having absorbed the lessons of Rwanda, clearly favoured such a mandate and suggested that 'robust rules of engagement' would be needed.[121] However, the mandate was carefully worded so as not to raise expectations that UNAMSIL could provide comprehensive protection in the event of outbreaks of mass violence that were beyond its ability to control.

With UNAMSIL's deployment, ECOMOG was left responsible for protecting Freetown and the government. UNAMSIL would also absorb the tiny UN Observer Mission in Sierra Leone (UNOMSIL). Its 105 military observers had since July 1998 been monitoring the behaviour of ECOMOG, whose contingents, especially the Nigerian, had been widely accused of human rights violations, corruption, and ill-judged and undisciplined use of force.

## The force

UNAMSIL was to have an authorized strength of 4500 troops, mostly from Ghana, India, Jordan, Kenya and Nigeria. The Nigerian troops simply transferred from ECOMOG to UN command. The mission also had 220 military

---

[118] UN Security Council Resolution 1270, 22 Oct. 1999.
[119] United Nations, Second report of the Secretary-General pursuant to Security Council Resolution 1270 (1999) on the United Nations Mission in Sierra Leone, UN document S/2000/13, 11 Jan. 2000.
[120] UN Security Council Resolution 1270, 22 Oct. 1999.
[121] Second report of the Secretary-General (note 119).

observers and four CivPols. Nigerian diplomat Oluyemi Adeniji was appointed SRSG; the force commander was to be Indian Major-General Vijay Kumar Jetley.

Even before it had achieved its authorized strength, the Secretary-General feared that UNAMSIL would be too small and militarily weak to fulfil its mandate, especially as the new Nigerian President, Olusegun Obasanjo, had decided on an even earlier Nigerian withdrawal from ECOMOG. After failing to convince Nigeria to stay, Annan urged the Security Council as early as December 1999 to reinforce UNAMSIL quickly, if possible by air, with four infantry battalions and necessary military support elements, to bring it to 10 000 troops. He also recommended that the mandate be expanded to permit UNAMSIL to provide security to key installations in Freetown. This would require 'more robust rules of engagement for the entire force' and additional battalions 'robustly equipped', including with the 'necessary force multipliers'.[122] It was important, Annan said, that UNAMSIL, 'through its military capabilities and posture, be able to deter any attempt to derail the Sierra Leonean peace process'.

On 7 February 2000 the Security Council agreed to double the size of UNAMSIL to 11 100 troops, making it the UN's largest peace operation at that time.[123] UNAMSIL was now mandated to take over completely the tasks of the departing ECOMOG, including providing security at key locations and government buildings, facilitating humanitarian assistance along 'specified thoroughfares', providing security at all disarmament, demobilization and reintegration sites, assisting the government in law enforcement and guarding weapons surrendered in the disarmament process. Its use-of-force instructions remained the same. While there was continued pressure from West African states to turn the mission into a peace enforcement operation, the Secretary-General and permanent members of the Security Council such as the UK stressed that UNAMSIL remained a peacekeeping operation, but one that was required to adopt a robust stance against threats to its security and mission.

The deployment of UNAMSIL was painfully slow. More than half the troops arrived without the required weapons, communications equipment or logistical support. In particular they lacked sufficient transport, resulting in their slow movement into the interior of the country, and radios to permit communication between isolated units. Nor were the troops well trained in peacekeeping or even, it seems, in basic military techniques. There were different views among the contingents as to the meaning of their mandate and many were not briefed on the ROE or, apparently, misunderstood them. The Brussels-based International Crisis Group reported that an informal poll of various contingents revealed that they would return fire if attacked but considered themselves under

[122] United Nations, Letter dated 23 December 1999 from the Secretary-General addressed to the President of the Security Council, UN document S/1999/1285, 28 Dec. 1999.

[123] UN Security Council Resolution 1289, 7 Feb. 2000. Annan lamented, however, that UNAMSIL had only 5 UN officials at Headquarters in New York to manage the mission—something a national government would 'never dream of' doing. United Nations, Report of the Secretary-General on the work of the organization, UN document A/55/1, 30 Aug. 2000, pp. 1–2.

no obligation to rescue other contingents' soldiers.[124] The slow arrival of the authorized troops, their military weakness and the unwillingness of Western states, especially the USA, to contribute troops, finance and resources to the mission left it dangerously vulnerable. It was a classic case of the willing being unable and the able being unwilling.

By early 2000 the Lomé agreement was being implemented fitfully, but the overall security situation had begun to improve as UNAMSIL troops stepped up their patrols and deployed out of Freetown to new areas.[125] Disarmament was slow, but humanitarian access was gradually improving in some areas. There were, however, early warning signs that UNAMSIL was failing to perform. In February, Guinean and Kenyan peacekeepers allowed themselves to be disarmed by RUF soldiers without any resistance.[126] Substantial amounts of UN *matériel* were surrendered in at least three ambushes, including assault rifles, rocket-propelled grenade launchers, four APCs and communications equipment. UN officials explained, in their defence, that in two of the ambushes the Kenyans were severely outnumbered, while in the third the Guineans had not yet come under UN command. There were also incidents in March and April in which UNAMSIL was obliged to return fire in self-defence.

### The crisis of May–June 2000: UNAMSIL fails to defend itself and its mission

In May the peacekeeper's worst nightmare began to unfold as the RUF challenged UNAMSIL militarily and it failed to use force in defence of its mission, to preserve its freedom of movement or even in self-defence. The entire mission teetered on the verge of collapse as the emboldened RUF took advantage of the situation to advance on Freetown in the hope of bringing the government down.

The crisis began with an error of judgement: just as the remaining elements of ECOMOG were finally departing on 2 May, UNAMSIL attempted to deploy to the Koidu area, the centre of RUF diamond mining, to begin the disarmament process there.[127] The rebels, clearly unnerved by this prospect, began to test UNAMSIL's resolve by detaining and disarming UN troops, beginning with the detention of four Kenyan soldiers and three military observers on 1 May. Jetley immediately met Sankoh to demand the release of his troops, but Sankoh accused UNAMSIL of trying to start a war by forcibly disarming the RUF. Sankoh was in fact encouraging his troops to challenge UNAMSIL and march on the capital.

The UN had not seen the signs of trouble brewing. Kofi Annan later acknowledged that: 'We were completely sleeping on the issue of intelligence. The way

---

[124] International Crisis Group, 'Sierra Leone: time for a new military and political strategy', ICG Africa Report no. 28, Freetown, London and Brussels, 11 Apr. 2001, p. 20.

[125] United Nations, Fourth report of the Secretary-General pursuant to Security Council Resolution 1270 (1999) on the United Nations Mission in Sierra Leone, UN document S/2000/455, 19 May 2000, para. 14.

[126] 'In Sierra Leone, UN forces robbed of guns', *International Herald Tribune*, 8 Feb. 2000, p. 3.

[127] The following account is from Fourth report of the Secretary-General (note 125), paras 56–70.

things happened, [the rebel attacks] must have been reasonably well coordinated. We should have had a sense of what was going on'.[128] George Tenet,
Director of the US Central Intelligence Agency (CIA), had warned the US
Congress (but apparently not the UN) in February 2000 that the RUF was
'poised to break a tenuous cease-fire and resume a campaign of terror'.[129]

On 2 May the situation deteriorated sharply when the RUF tried to forcibly
disarm Kenyan troops at Magburaka. This time they resisted and exchanges of
fire continued throughout the day, the RUF using small arms, rocket-propelled
grenades and mortars, and wounding three Kenyans. The RUF also attacked
Kenyan troops at Makeni, wounding two in one location, and attacking and
overrunning a 60-strong Kenyan unit at the disarmament, demobilization and
reintegration camp. Thereafter, as the UN force displayed little effective opposition, mass detentions of UNAMSIL troops took place, often, it appears,
without any resistance. Almost 500 UN troops, as well as elements of the
Kenyan sector headquarters, fell into RUF hands, some being relocated to the
RUF stronghold in Kono. UNAMSIL headquarters seemed unable to obtain
accurate information on the total number or their exact status.[130] Poor communications not only left the force unsure of the true situation, but led to more
peacekeepers being taken hostage as endangered units could not call for
reinforcements and troops sent to find those missing could not communicate
with them and were captured as well.[131]

Meanwhile, a Zambian battalion, instructed to move from Lungi to Makeni to
reinforce the town, was stopped at a 'strong roadblock' and 'presumably
ambushed and detained by a large group of RUF fighters' (the fact that the
Secretary-General apparently still did not know what had happened more than
two weeks later is symptomatic of the confused situation).[132] Jetley later conceded that some of the obstacles placed in the way of his troops by the RUF had
been militarily insignificant, although 'others were strong, involving a lot of
firepower'.[133] President Kabbah said on national radio that he was 'disappointed' by the way some UN troops had capitulated to the RUF.[134]

With RUF units advancing on Freetown and refugees streaming into it, panic
began to grip the city. The UN prepared to evacuate its civilian and non-
essential personnel, mistakenly announcing on 7 May that the rebels were
poised to attack.[135] UN spokesman Fred Eckhard declared that: 'We'll do what

[128] 'With US loath to send troops, UN seeks peacekeeping change', *International Herald Tribune*,
12 May 2000, p. 1.
[129] Quoted in 'In Sierra Leone, UN forces robbed of guns' (note 126).
[130] The total number of UNAMSIL personnel 'presumed' to be in the hands of the RUF on 19 May was
352 (297 Zambians, 29 Kenyans, 23 Indians and 3 military observers). Fourth report of the Secretary-
General (note 125), para. 69.
[131] 'Old problems, and split in command, hamper UN in Sierra Leone', *International Herald Tribune*,
12 June 2000, p. 6.
[132] Fourth report of the Secretary-General (note 125), para. 62. The Zambians were later released as a
result of the negotiating efforts of Liberian President Charles Taylor.
[133] 'Interview: Maj.-Gen. Vijay Kumar Jetley, Commander United Nations Mission in Sierra Leone',
*Jane's Defence Weekly*, 12 July 2000, p. 32.
[134] 'Sierra Leone in grip of panic and chaos', *The Times*, 8 May 2000, p. 15.
[135] 'Sierra Leone in grip of panic and chaos' (note 134).

we have to do to defend ourselves and the government. We hope it won't come to a pitched battle, but we are preparing for one'.[136] Jetley attempted to redeploy his forces to protect the capital, as well as Port Loko and Masiaka.[137] The Jordanians, however, refused to remain at the 'front line', even in defensive positions, and retreated towards Freetown. A Jordanian officer was quoted as saying: 'No Jordanians should die here. This is a British problem. It was their colony'.[138] The Guineans were rumoured to have said the same.[139]

## British reinforcements arrive

Kofi Annan appealed to militarily capable states to quickly provide a rapid reaction force to UNAMSIL for 'deterrent purposes'. Alarmed by the deteriorating situation in its former colony, the UK was alone in rapidly deploying. A so-called Joint Force, involving troops, aircraft and a substantial naval presence, started arriving on 9 May. It consisted of 1st Parachute Group, an Amphibious Readiness Group comprising 42 Commando Royal Marines, a combat air group of 13 Harrier jump-jets, two frigate gunships with a logistic support group of three Royal Fleet Auxiliaries, and support helicopters. It was reportedly given 'robust' ROE to act in self-defence, but not offensively.[140]

While ostensibly having as its objective the safe evacuation of British and other foreign nationals, the force was soon involved in helping organize and train UN troops, establishing fortified positions, manning roadblocks, securing Freetown and its airport, conducting joint patrols with UNAMSIL, and coming under fire and returning it robustly in self-defence.[141] This enabled UNAMSIL to redeploy much-needed troops to threatened areas east of Freetown. Although not under UN command and control, the British forces worked in close cooperation with UNAMSIL and attended UN planning meetings.[142] Their Harriers, based on an aircraft carrier off the coast, were used to collect invaluable intelligence information on rebel troop movements to pass to the UN force.[143]

The British presence proved crucial in steeling the UN's nerve. According to Annan, it was 'a pivotal factor in restoring stability' and 'boosted the confidence of the Sierra Leoneans'.[144] Jetley stated: 'They helped very effectively to stiffen my defences'.[145] According to Lieutenant-Colonel Philip Wilkinson:

---

[136] 'UN troops prepare to defend Freetown', *International Herald Tribune*, 11 May 2000, p. 1.

[137] Fourth report of the Secretary-General (note 125), para. 62.

[138] 'Battle-hardened troops stiffen UN morale in Sierra Leone', *Independent on Sunday*, 4 June 2000, p. 21.

[139] 'Interview: Maj.-Gen. Vijay Kumar Jetley' (note 133).

[140] 'Paratroops dig in to secure key peninsula', *The Times*, 12 May 2000, p. 18.

[141] 'Paras put rebels to flight after brief battle', *The Times*, 18 May 2000, p. 16.

[142] 'Hoodwinked by rebel leader: UN's misreading of Sankoh hastened Sierra Leone fiasco', *International Herald Tribune*, 15 May 2000, p. 11.

[143] 'Jets track Sierra Leone's rebels', *The Times*, 30 May 2000, p. 18. The first combat involving British troops came on 17 May after a joint patrol with Nigerian UN troops was attacked by RUF rebels north of Freetown's airport.

[144] Fourth report of the Secretary-General (note 125), para. 69.

[145] 'Interview: Maj.-Gen. Vijay Kumar Jetley ' (note 133).

'The deployment of UK forces arguably rescued the UN mission and certainly played a significant part in averting a full-scale humanitarian catastrophe'.[146]

## The threat averted

As the British were deploying, counter-attacks by UNAMSIL troops (mainly the Nigerian contingent), government forces and revived pro-government militia (including the Kamajors and the so-called West Side Boyz[147]) succeeded in staving off the rebel assault on Freetown.[148] On 9 May the Indian quick-reaction company and a Kenyan company, which had been surrounded at Magburaka, successfully broke through RUF lines (whether by using force or not is unclear), as did Kenyan troops detained at Makeni. Praising their military courage and determination, Annan noted that: 'Before their breakout, these units stood their ground and did not surrender in spite of continuing threats and attacks by [the] RUF, which had encircled their positions'.[149] On the same day, however, UNAMSIL troops withdrew from the strategic crossroads town of Masiaka, a UN spokesman admitted, after running out of ammunition following exchanges of fire with the RUF.[150] In an hour-long battle on 11 May, government helicopter gunships pounded rebel forces at Waterloo, 33 km south-east of Freetown, while Nigerian troops used anti-aircraft guns, rocket-propelled grenade launchers and automatic weapons to capture territory from the RUF.[151]

By 15 May the threat to Freetown had receded significantly. Government forces and pro-government militia retook Masiaka and pressed on to Makeni. Adeniji, bizarrely, proposed a ceasefire, apparently fearing that continued fighting would jeopardize the safety of the remaining UN hostages.[152] By late May government and pro-government forces had slowly pushed the RUF out of other important towns. The situation was also helped by the capture and gaoling of Foday Sankoh by government security forces on 17 May.[153]

On 5 June, urged on by the British and helped by their involvement in operations planning, Jetley sent two companies of battle-hardened Indian troops, newly arrived from Kashmir, to retake by force a strategic crossroads at Rogberi Junction, approximately 60 km north-east of Freetown. (The Nigerians, in what has been described as 'direct insubordination', had refused Jetley's order to do so.[154]) The Indians broke through RUF roadblocks and, although

[146] Wilkinson, P. R. (Lt-Col), 'Peace support under fire: lessons from Sierra Leone', International Security Information Service (ISIS) Briefing Paper on Humanitarian Intervention no. 2, London, June 2000, p. 8.

[147] Some of their members had previously committed atrocities and later turned their weapons on government forces.

[148] 'In panic, thousands flee to Freetown', International Herald Tribune, 12 May 2000, p. 1.

[149] Fourth report of the Secretary-General (note 125), para. 64.

[150] 'Annan struggling on Sierra Leone aid', International Herald Tribune, 10 May 2000, p. 1. See also Fourth report of the Secretary-General (note 125), para. 62.

[151] International Herald Tribune, 12 May 2000, p. 5.

[152] '157 UN peacekeepers freed in Sierra Leone', International Herald Tribune, 16 May 2000, p. 4.

[153] 'How Scorpion captured the ruthless lion', The Times, 18 May 2000, p. 16.

[154] 'Battle-hardened troops stiffen UN morale in Sierra Leone' (note 138), p. 21; and 'Old problems, and split in command' (note 131), p. 6.

encountering little opposition, responded robustly to machine-gun fire.[155] An Indian helicopter gunship was also involved in a brief exchange of fire. The operation, despite its military insignificance, was widely seen as a sea change in UNAMSIL's approach.

UNAMSIL was now reported to be planning 'daily aggressive patrols' on a key route from Freetown to Lunsar and on to Lungi Airport. However, on 30 June RUF fighters ambushed a unit escorting the Jordanian contingent, killing one peacekeeper and wounding four others. Most of the attackers were killed in the 'robust response' by UNAMSIL troops.[156] The RUF also staged a series of attacks on the Jordanian company deployed at Rokel Bridge as well as on the Nigerian positions at Port Loko. On 4 July, a day after RUF forces attempted to seize Masiaka from pro-government forces, UNAMSIL swiftly dislodged them after a brief exchange of fire. On 16 July a Nigerian soldier was killed in an ambush on his patrol. On 22 July a group of West Side Boyz ambushed an UNAMSIL convoy, injuring a Guinean peacekeeper.

On 15 July, in cooperation with British troops, UNAMSIL partly redeemed its reputation by successfully mounting an operation, planned for months, to rescue the remaining hostages held by the RUF at Kailahun. As British commandos rescued several British and other hostages in a daring helicopter raid, without shots being fired,[157] UNAMSIL troops freed 222 Indian peacekeepers.[158] One thousand mostly Indian but also Ghanaian and Nigerian UN troops in APCs, backed by helicopter gunships and commanded by Jetley himself, carried out the operation. While the force met no initial resistance, a convoy carrying the soldiers and observers to freedom was later ambushed, leaving six UN soldiers wounded and one dead, and many RUF casualties. In what sounded like a throwback to the Congo, the UN described the operation as follows: 'Since intensive diplomatic and political efforts, at all levels, to seek a solution by peaceful means were unsuccessful, UNAMSIL decided to launch a robust military operation to ensure the security of United Nations personnel and to restore their freedom of movement, in accordance with its mandate and rules of engagement'.[159] It was reported, however, that Jetley had originally opposed a forcible rescue, arguing that negotiations were preferable.[160] He apparently only agreed when the hostages appeared to be running short of food.

On 22 July, having learned of plans for an attack on its troops, UNAMSIL launched a pre-emptive operation to remove illegal checkpoints and clear the Occra Hills area of the by now anti-government West Side Boyz. This was achieved without UNAMSIL casualties and led effectively to the demise of this

---

[155] United Nations, Daily press briefing of the Office of the Spokesman for the Secretary-General, UN, New York, 5 June 2000.
[156] United Nations, Fifth report of the Secretary-General on the United Nations Mission in Sierra Leone, UN document S/2000/455, 31 July 2000, p. 4.
[157] The Times, 17 July 2000, p. 6.
[158] 'Peacekeepers are freed in Sierra Leone by UN force', International Herald Tribune, 17 July 2000, p. 6.
[159] Fifth report of the Secretary-General (note 156), p. 5.
[160] The Times, 17 July 2000, p. 6.

militia group. The crisis cost the lives of nine UN peacekeepers, seven from Nigeria, one from India and one from Jordan.[161] The number of RUF casualties was unknown, although there were indications that it was high. Some of the UN troops who had been abducted were later found dead, while others escaped or were released after negotiations. The whole episode was deeply disturbing to those who had been attempting to reform UN peacekeeping and who had envisaged a peace enforcement role for the UN in post-civil war situations.

**Efforts to strengthen and improve UNAMSIL's performance**

Both during and after the May 2000 crisis efforts were made by the Secretary-General to strengthen UNAMSIL and improve its performance, particularly with regard to the use of force. New Security Council resolutions authorized an increase in its size and a heightening of its military posture, several investigations conducted into the mission recommended sweeping changes, and UNAMSIL became the guinea pig for several recommendations of the Brahimi Report on peacekeeping reform.[162] The impact of all these initiatives was slow and in many instances negligible.

*Emergency measures*

Immediate attempts to reinforce UNAMSIL militarily during the crisis, except for the British deployment, came to nought. At a meeting of the Security Council on 11 May, as the crisis was unfolding, many members, especially Nigeria on behalf of the African countries, advocated giving UNAMSIL a strong Chapter VII peace enforcement mandate. Annan responded that, while he was not opposed in principle, UNAMSIL had to obtain the necessary resources from member states with 'ready capacity'. He warned that, unless the international community demonstrated the necessary resolve to impose peace on Sierra Leone, any effort to strengthen UNAMSIL's mandate would 'unduly raise expectations, increase the risk of loss of life, and undermine the credibility of the Organization'.[163]

On 19 May the Security Council approved the immediate reinforcement of UNAMSIL to a strength of 13 000 to enhance its capability to defend its positions at Lungi Airport, on the Freetown Peninsula and at other strategic locations in the western and southern parts of the country.[164] Because it was possible that the RUF would adopt 'guerrilla tactics', it would be necessary, Annan said, to deploy with 'due care and preparation, in sufficient numbers and backed up by adequate military means to deter attacks and, if necessary, respond decisively to any hostile action or intent'.[165]

---

[161] Fifth report of the Secretary-General (note 156), p. 12.
[162] United Nations, Report of the Panel on United Nations Peace Operations, UN document A/55/305, S/2000/809, 21 Aug. 2000. On the Brahimi Report see also chapter 9, section IV, in this volume.
[163] Fourth report of the Secretary-General (note 125), para. 100.
[164] UN Security Council Resolution 1299, 19 May 2000.
[165] Fourth report of the Secretary-General (note 125), para. 85.

UNAMSIL's existing robust ROE enabled it to 'use force, including deadly force, in self-defence against any hostile act or intent'. Annan declared that: 'The use of force against all elements *that continue to display a hostile intent* toward the United Nations would be warranted and justified'.[166] This was probably the first time a UN Secretary-General had so openly warned the Security Council of a guerrilla threat to UN forces and the first time since Somalia that it had been suggested that they respond decisively to hostile 'intent' rather than when fired on. It sounded very much like peace enforcement and the type of declaration made by U Thant in instructing ONUC to engage the Katangans in the 1960s.

Once UNAMSIL had reached its new authorized strength and stabilized the situation, it should, the Secretary-General proposed, be expanded further, to 16 500 troops, to enable it gradually to increase its presence, with sufficient military strength, in all of Sierra Leone. This would require two additional infantry battalions (a mechanized one and one air-transportable battalion for rapid reinforcement), a logistics battalion, a light artillery unit, additional air transport assets and armed helicopters, a maritime unit of six armed patrol boats, and the necessary medical, communications, intelligence and command personnel.[167] The Secretary-General was at last telling the Security Council bluntly what the military requirements for a mission would realistically be, rather than what it wanted to hear.

None of these ambitious plans was to be realized. No Western states offered forces, although several offered to fly in Bangladeshi troops.[168] In desperation Annan proposed bringing forward planned additional deployments of troops from two existing contributors, India and Jordan.[169] The 4th Nigerian battalion, which was to have been repatriated by the end of May, would now stay on. Regular meetings were held with troop-contributing countries to address command and control issues and shortfalls in equipment. Most delegations stressed, however, that their contingents could not be expected to take part in peace enforcement.[170] On 18 May the ECOWAS defence ministers agreed to contribute 3000 extra West African troops but demanded logistical support.[171] (An ECOWAS summit meeting at the end of the month also demanded that UNAMSIL's mandate be changed to peace enforcement and that a West African be appointed force commander.[172]) Meanwhile, an emergency airlift of communications equipment from the UN Logistics Base at Brindisi, Italy, was

---

[166] Fourth report of the Secretary-General (note 125), para. 89. Emphasis added.

[167] Fourth report of the Secretary-General (note 125), para. 86.

[168] 'With US loath to send troops, UN seeks peacekeeping change', *International Herald Tribune*, 12 May 2000, p. 1.

[169] 'Annan struggling on Sierra Leone aid' (note 150), p. 8.

[170] United Nations, Sixth report of the Secretary-General on the United Nations Mission in Sierra Leone, UN document S/2000/832, 24 Aug. 2000, p. 6.

[171] 'Foday Sankoh's fate: a government is torn', *International Herald Tribune*, 19 May 2000, p. 8.

[172] 'West Africans set to return peace force to Sierra Leone', *International Herald Tribune*, 30 May 2000, p. 2.

undertaken and new military equipment, including vehicles, provided to replace that seized by the RUF.[173]

*The crisis assessment team report*

Annan also dispatched to Sierra Leone a crisis assessment team from UN Head-quarters, led by General Manfred Eisele of Germany. The team, which visited from 31 May to 8 June, reportedly focused on command and control arrange-ments and Jetley's reluctance to forward-deploy UNAMSIL troops behind government troops as they recaptured territory—the strategy recommended by the British. The team also examined whether UNAMSIL's mandate and ROE should be made more robust.[174]

The team reported 'a serious lack of cohesion within the Mission', including 'no commonly shared understanding of the mandate and rules of engagement' and other command and control problems, 'in spite of extensive briefings at Headquarters'. There were serious problems in internal communication and coordination between the civilian and military components (presumably between Adeniji and Jetley) as well as within each component. This was due in part to a lack of communications equipment, but also to the fact that at the time of the May crisis UNAMSIL was moving headquarters, while also being asked to support an unanticipated and massive air deployment of reinforcements. Disappointingly, in view of all the work that had been done since the end of the cold war to improve the planning and coordination of complex peace opera-tions, Eisele's team noted 'a lack of integrated planning and logistic support as well as insufficient coordination and sharing of information with UN agencies, NGOs and diplomatic missions in Freetown'.[175]

Having come under intense criticism for not acting more forcefully, Jetley had earlier lamely explained that: 'We have been provoked as a peacekeeping force on several occasions since we deployed in Sierra Leone, but we have tried to resist such provocation. We are not in Sierra Leone to fight, but I am appealing to the combatants not to continuously push us into a corner'.[176]

He now defended UNAMSIL's record, saying that his original concept of not using any force had initially worked quite well. He had tried to move slowly and methodically, partly because he was unsure of his force's capabilities. He said, for instance, that he had cautioned the Zambian troops about carrying out reconnaissance patrols shortly before some of them were taken hostage, but admits that: 'At that time we were all sort of feeling our way'. He now claimed to have changed strategy: 'While we would always try to negotiate our way, for instance, through a roadblock or a stoppage, we have had to resort to force on occasion. When this happened, we reacted aggressively. That would leave nobody in any doubt of our intentions'.[177]

---

[173] Fifth report of the Secretary-General (note 156), p. 10.
[174] 'Old problems, and split in command' (note 131), p. 6.
[175] Fifth report of the Secretary-General (note 156), pp. 9–10.
[176] *Jane's Defence Weekly*, 10 May 2000, p. 6.
[177] 'Interview: Maj.-Gen. Vijay Kumar Jetley' (note 133).

Jetley said that his instructions to UNAMSIL were now clear: 'If threatened, they have been told to comply with very robust rules of engagement'. Jetley said he would not hesitate to use the three Indian Mi-24 attack helicopters which he had just acquired: 'They are very effective force multipliers, but I don't want to bring any speculation into what the UN will or won't do'.[178]

## The Secretary-General's report

The Secretary-General quickly did his own assessment of the operation, identifying multiple problems, including command and control, force cohesiveness, the flow of information, the equipment and preparedness of the troops, and coordination between and within the various military and non-military components.[179] He told the Security Council that during the worst of the fighting UNAMSIL had 'experienced serious difficulties in obtaining accurate information about the situation on the ground' and had been 'forced' to conduct frequent aerial reconnaissance missions to gather information on RUF movements.[180] To improve command and control he recommended, belatedly, that all international forces in Sierra Leone, 'with the exception of those sent for a brief period for strictly national purposes' (that is, the British), should be integrated into UNAMSIL and that military liaison officers be appointed to the various Sierra Leonean Government and militia forces 'to avoid misunderstandings which could lead to incidents'.[181]

He now, in August 2000, also proposed a new concept of operations to establish a 'robust and credible international presence':

(a) To maintain the security of the Lungi and Freetown peninsulas and their major approach routes;

(b) To deter and, where necessary, decisively counter the threat of RUF attack by responding robustly to any hostile actions or threat of imminent and direct use of force;

(c) To deploy progressively in a coherent operational structure and in sufficient numbers and density at key strategic locations and main population centres;

(d) To assist, in coordination with the Government of Sierra Leone, through the presence of UNAMSIL and within the framework of its mandate, the efforts of the Government of Sierra Leone to extend State authority, restore law and order and further stabilize the situation progressively throughout the entire country;

(e) Within its capabilities and areas of deployment, to afford protection to civilians under threat of imminent physical violence;

(f) To patrol actively on strategic lines of communication, specifically main access routes to the capital, in order to dominate ground, ensure freedom of movement and facilitate the provision of humanitarian assistance; [and]

(g) To assist in the promotion of the political process leading to a renewed disarmament, demobilization and reintegration programme where possible.[182]

---

[178] 'Interview: Maj.-Gen. Vijay Kumar Jetley' (note 133).
[179] Fourth report of the Secretary-General (note 125), para. 105.
[180] Fourth report of the Secretary-General (note 125), para. 63.
[181] Fourth report of the Secretary-General (note 125), para. 90.
[182] Sixth report of the Secretary-General (note 170), pp. 1–2, 11.

The Security Council did not move immediately to adopt this new strategy, despite the fact that UNAMSIL essentially began to carry it out. Again, it seems that the Council, as it had often done throughout the history of peacekeeping, preferred to back away from explicitly mandating peace enforcement, while turning a blind eye to its actual conduct in the field. Presumably it was concerned about proclaiming a mandate that could not be fulfilled because of constraints on resources and military capability.

The Secretary-General reported that his priority tasks could be 'largely achieved' under the existing February 2000 mandate and 'robust rules of engagement' but he proposed an even larger force of 20 500, to achieve forward deployment into RUF areas and to create a 'robust and determined peacekeeping force' (something of a contradiction in terms). He suggested that part of its strategy, not mentioned in the 'priority tasks' previously outlined, would be to 'induce armed groups to disarm'.[183] He had obviously been strongly influenced by the Brahimi Report, which had just been released.[184]

*The Security Council mission*

In October 2000 the Security Council dispatched its own mission to Sierra Leone to investigate. In a closed briefing to the Council on its return, the mission's leader, British Ambassador Sir Jeremy Greenstock, described the situation as 'a mess and deteriorating'.[185] The force was still not deploying behind RUF lines as the British had urged. Both India and Jordan had announced in September that they were withdrawing. There had been a damaging public rift between Jetley and Major-General Gabriel Kpamber, former head of ECOMOG. In a leaked memorandum Jetley accused Kpamber, Adeniji and Jetley's immediate subordinate, Nigerian Brigadier-General Mohamed Garba, of colluding with the RUF in its diamond-mining ventures.[186] General Victor Malu, the Nigerian Chief of Staff, demanded Jetley's immediate removal, declaring that: 'We are not going to serve under that man in whatever circumstances'.[187] India's withdrawal was reportedly due both to this dispute and to the number of casualties Indian troops had sustained. Jordan cited as its reason the continuing conspicuous absence of Western contingents.[188]

While praising UNAMSIL's contingents for their civic action programmes, the Security Council mission largely concurred in Eisele's criticisms.[189] It admitted that the mandate was imprecise and that there were still differences between contingents over it. The mission lamented the departure of the 'very

---

[183] Sixth report of the Secretary-General (note 170), p. 7.

[184] See note 162.

[185] 'Crisis in Sierra Leone: the failure of UN peacekeeping', *Strategic Comments* (International Institute for Strategic Studies, London), vol. 6, no. 9 (Nov. 2000), p. 2.

[186] 'Crisis in Sierra Leone' (note 185), p. 1.

[187] 'UN to bolster peacekeeping force by 7000', *The Guardian*, 13 Sep. 2000, p. 10.

[188] United States Institute of Peace (USIP), *Peacekeeping in Africa*, Special Report (USIP: Washington, DC, 13 Feb. 2001), p. 7.

[189] United Nations, Report of the Security Council mission to Sierra Leone, UN document S/2000/992, 16 Oct. 2000. It comprised the ambassadors to the UN of Canada, China, France, Jamaica, Mali, the Netherlands, Russia, Ukraine and the USA.

professional' Indian battalion, describing it as a 'serious loss'.[190] It concluded that UNAMSIL should be strengthened as recommended by Kofi Annan. In what sounded more like advocacy of peace enforcement than peacekeeping (although the mission adhered faithfully to the latter term), it concluded that:

Only a sustained and effective military instrument, with the capability to extend its reach throughout the country and following clear political and military objectives, can *maintain pressure* on [the] RUF and create incentives for dialogue and disarmament . . . The combination of *firm, proactive peacekeeping*, within the flexibility authorized by the resolutions, and the implementation of our broader recommendations can exert a significant impact on a rebellion, many members of which are looking for a road to a life without conflict.[191]

### The mission turns around

By late 2000 there were signs that the situation in Sierra Leone was turning around. This was due to a combination of political and military factors.

Attempting the negotiations route, UNAMSIL and ECOWAS induced the Sierra Leonean Government and the RUF to sign the Abuja Ceasefire Agreement on 10 November 2000.[192] The two sides agreed inter alia that UNAMSIL could deploy behind RUF lines in order to supervise the ceasefire and the resumption of disarmament and have full freedom of movement throughout the country. The RUF agreed to return all seized UN weapons and equipment. The RUF was beginning to lose the support of Liberia, in particular as the latter began to face its own insurgency. In May 2001 the Security Council finally imposed economic sanctions—a form of non-military peace enforcement under Chapter VII—on Liberia for aiding the RUF.[193]

The continuing British military presence acted as a deterrent, a confidence-building measure, and a source of moral and actual support to UNAMSIL and government forces. The British Government, still sceptical of UNAMSIL's capabilities, especially since it had still not reached its authorized strength, announced on 1 January 2001 that its troops would remain 'until the RUF has been defeated by war or diplomacy'.[194] The original British force had departed in mid-June 2000, being replaced by a 200-strong training unit, although two British warships remained stationed off the coast. The UK subsequently announced the provision of a 'rapid reaction capability', up to brigade strength,

---

[190] Report of the Security Council mission to Sierra Leone (note 189), p. 3.

[191] Report of the Security Council mission to Sierra Leone (note 189), p. 13. Emphasis added.

[192] Ceasefire Agreement between the Government of Sierra Leone and the Revolutionary United Front, Abuja, 10 Nov. 2000, reproduced in United Nations, Identical letters dated 2000/11/13 from the permanent representative of Mali to the United Nations addressed to the Secretary-General and the President of the Security Council, UN document S/2000/1091, 14 Nov. 2000, annex.

[193] These had been foreshadowed in Security Council Resolution 1343, 7 Mar. 2001. Sanctions were actually imposed on 7 May 2001 when Liberia failed to comply with the Council's demand that it stop supporting the RUF by that date.

[194] Quoted in International Crisis Group (note 124), appendix C.

for deployment in support of the UN.[195] The British personnel remained separate from UNAMSIL, although the appointment of a British chief of staff, Brigadier-General Alistair Duncan, to the UN force helped to maintain close coordination.[196] British training teams meanwhile trained a new 8000-strong Republic of Sierra Leone Army, which soon began to show its capabilities.

## New leadership and forces for UNAMSIL

On 30 March 2001 the Security Council extended UNAMSIL's mandate to 30 September 2001 and expanded its strength to 17 500.[197] New troop contributions were promised from Bangladesh, Nepal, Pakistan, Ukraine and some West African countries, which would bring UNAMSIL near to its newly authorized strength. This was not in fact reached until September 2001, when Pakistani reinforcements arrived. Meanwhile Jetley was essentially dismissed, both because of his leadership shortcomings and to appease the Nigerians. He was replaced by Lieutenant-General Daniel Opande of Kenya, who promptly helped negotiate the return of the remaining weapons and vehicles seized from UNAMSIL in May 2000.

With the Secretariat's help UNAMSIL had already, under Jetley, attempted some reforms.[198] It established a joint operations cell, including officers from all contingents, and mixed civilian–military coordination mechanisms, including mechanisms to handle logistic support. Meetings were held in the field between the mission leadership and contingent commanders to discuss the mandate, explain the ROE and improve internal communication. An intra-mission training programme on the ROE was launched. The mission also prepared pocket-sized cards with information on the peacekeeper's code of conduct and ROE in all the languages used by UNAMSIL's contingents.[199] The fact that these steps were being treated as praiseworthy developments shows how badly UNAMSIL had previously been handled.

## UNAMSIL implements its new concept of operations

It was not until March 2001 that the Security Council adopted the concept of operations recommended by the Secretary-General in August 2000, telling him to 'proceed to its completion'.[200] The document had by now been revised to take into account the Abuja Ceasefire Agreement, changes in the mission's structure and circumstances on the ground.[201] It purportedly integrated the military and civilian aspects of the mission (which, surprisingly, had never been done) and

---

[195] United Nations, Seventh report of the Secretary-General on the United Nations Mission in Sierra Leone, UN document S/2000/1055, 31 Oct. 2000, p. 8.
[196] International Crisis Group (note 124), p. 24.
[197] UN Security Council Resolution 1346, 30 Mar. 2001.
[198] Fifth report of the Secretary-General (note 156), p. 10.
[199] Sixth report of the Secretary-General (note 170), p. 6.
[200] UN Security Council Resolution 1346, 30 Mar. 2001.
[201] United Nations, Ninth report of the Secretary-General on the situation in Sierra Leone, UN document S/2001/228, 14 Mar. 2001.

envisaged the phased deployment of UNAMSIL into RUF-controlled areas by means of 'robust' patrols. UNAMSIL would thereafter establish a permanent presence in Lunsar, Magburaka, Makeni, Mano Junction and Yele. Then, subject to the availability of troops, it would deploy to the diamond-producing regions—a move which had previously almost derailed the mission—and some border areas. Finally, the force 'might need to' deploy to major towns to create the conditions necessary for elections to be held.

In its movement and forward deployment, Annan pledged that UNAMSIL would 'continue to project the necessary military strength and determination to deter any attempt to use force against the United Nations and its mandate in Sierra Leone'. The mission's ROE, he confirmed, allowed it to 'respond robustly to any attack or threat of attack, including, if necessary, in a pre-emptive manner'.[202] This was probably the first time a UN Secretary-General had ever explicitly and publicly extended the peacekeeping self-defence rule to pre-emption.

On 14 March 2001 UNAMSIL finally deployed some of its troops behind RUF lines for the first time since the May 2000 crisis. Nigerian troops travelled to the northern town of Lunsar, which the RUF had guaranteed would be free of weapons and roadblocks. Further deployments were subsequently made to other towns. By May UN control extended to the Kailahun region. Both UNAMSIL and the new Sierra Leonean Army were succeeding in forward-deploying and in conducting long-range 'robust patrols' to assert UNAMSIL's freedom of movement, although usually retreating to base by nightfall. Disarmament proceeded slowly but steadily, with negotiations being conducted with the RUF when difficulties were encountered. By December 2001, 37 000 combatants had given up their arms, including in the Tongo diamond-mining area. Government troops and British advisers were deployed along the Liberian and Guinean borders. By January 2002, 45 000 rebels had been disarmed and demobilized, and the programme was declared completed with the symbolic closure of the last disarmament reception camp in Kailahun.[203] On 2 March 2002 President Kabbah announced the end of the four-year state of emergency.[204]

UNAMSIL's remaining challenge was to help monitor and provide logistical support for the general elections on 14 May 2002, which saw Kabbah re-elected. Sine then peace has largely returned to Sierra Leone.

## UNAMSIL: back to the future

Contrasted particularly with the effective and efficient performance of the multinational force in East Timor and its UN follow-on force, the performance of UNAMSIL was a major embarrassment to the UN. It revealed that all the presumed improvements since the early 1990s in the UN's ability to plan,

---

[202] Ninth report of the Secretary-General on the situation in Sierra Leone (note 201), p. 9.
[203] *Jane's Defence Weekly*, 23 Jan. 2002; and BBC News, 13 Jan. 2002, available at URL <http://www.news.bbc.co.uk>.
[204] BBC News, 2 Mar. 2002, available at URL <http://www.news.bbc.co.uk>.

deploy and manage peace operations had, at least in this test case, amounted to very little. In terms of the use of force it revealed that absolutely nothing had been learned: the original concept of operations, such as it was, proved farcical, the force's so-called robust ROE had proved illusory and even the self-defence norm evaporated under the slightest pressure. UNAMSIL had been timid in deploying to RUF areas both before and after the May 2000 crisis, even when the RUF pledged its cooperation. At the very least the force should have tested the RUF's word.

To make matters worse, neither the Security Council nor the UN Secretariat had decided whether UNAMSIL was engaging in peacekeeping or peace enforcement. As its force commander had inadvertently revealed, UNAMSIL was 'feeling its way'.[205] Despite talk of robust ROE there was no clear indication of what purposes force could be used for, other than self-defence. It was never entirely clear, for instance, whether UNAMSIL could use force to implement the peace agreement by attempting to coerce the RUF to comply, use it only to prevent the RUF from stopping the UN carrying out its mission (that is, 'defence of the mission'), actively join with government forces in offensive or defensive operations to protect the government and the capital city, or interpose itself between the RUF and government forces and then use force in self-defence.

Nor did the Security Council ensure that the composition and military capabilities of the force matched the allegedly robust ROE (although the Secretary-General and the Secretariat made strenuous efforts to get it to do so). The five permanent members of the Security Council (except the UK) notably failed to deploy any troops, even token forces, as a symbol of their determination to see the Lomé agreement implemented. The USA attempted to overcharge the UN for airlift support, although it did begin a crash (if belated) training programme for West African troop contributors. Other key Western states also declined to contribute. UNSAS again proved virtually useless in providing the troops and support personnel required. DPKO planning and post-deployment support for UNAMSIL was less than optimal, partly as a result of the General Assembly's ill-judged decision in 1999 to remove seconded military officers from the DPKO, and partly because of the demands of several other new peacekeeping missions.[206] An under-equipped, underfunded and motley UNAMSIL was the result.

The scourge of peacekeeping—poorly equipped and poorly trained troops— was wearyingly evident once again. This was doubly shocking in view of the fact that some of the contributors, notably Ghana, India and Kenya, had contributed troops to the Congo mission four decades earlier. With the exception of the Indians, none of the contingents seems to have even been prepared for peacekeeping in terms of having weapons for self-defence, protective gear and

---

[205] 'Interview: Maj.-Gen. Vijay Kumar Jetley' (note 133).
[206] There were 4 new peace operations in 1999 and 1 more in 2000—UNAMET and UNTAET in East Timor, MONUC in the Democratic Republic of the Congo, the UN Mission in Kosovo (UNMIK), and the UN Mission in Ethiopia and Eritrea (UNMEE).

an understanding of peacekeeping procedures and doctrine. Not surprisingly, since few of the contingents were properly prepared for peacekeeping, none was militarily prepared or trained for peace enforcement—even though the Chapter VII mandate implied that possibility. As of November 2001 UNAMSIL had incurred 57 fatalities, 36 of them in 2001.[207] As Wilkinson noted:

Unfortunately, UNAMSIL is a disparate group of over 30 national contingents, without a coherent operational infrastructure. These contingents arrived and are still arriving in Sierra Leone in an unstructured manner. There is no common doctrine or approach that differentiates peacekeeping and peace enforcement, no common operating procedures or training standards and several of the national contingents are not trained or equipped for the demands of peace enforcement.[208]

The blame for this certainly could not, however, be placed entirely to the participating contingents. As Jonathan Eyal comments:

There was no serious attempt to evaluate the future of the operation immediately after Nigeria announced the withdrawal of its forces from the mission [except by the Secretary-General and the Secretariat] and no effort to help with the costs of the mission. Nor was there any thought given to an accelerated programme of training for the troops dispatched to Sierra Leone. In essence, the Africans were left to repeat all the mistakes which Western governments themselves committed in previous peace-keeping operations.[209]

Even considering the dilemmas and handicaps facing UNAMSIL which were not of its own making, poor organization and leadership in the field com-pounded the problem. Kofi Annan had little choice but to publicly support UNAMSIL's embattled leadership, but it was obvious from the list of the mission's shortcomings that he himself drew up that both Adeniji and Jetley were ultimately responsible for at least some of them, notably command and control and intra-mission coordination.[210] It was clear that their personal relationship was poor. Their inability and/or unwillingness to ensure that relevant intelligence information was obtained and passed to the UN Secretariat in timely fashion was one of their most serious failings. The mission even seemed ignorant of developments occurring under its nose in Freetown, where UNAMSIL, the government and the RUF were all based.

The real root of the problem lay, however, as so often in past peace opera-tions, in a flawed peace agreement which treated the belligerent parties as equally culpable for the civil war and equally honourable in attempting to end it. By bringing the demonstrably untrustworthy Sankoh into a coalition govern-

[207] United Nations, Department of Public Information, The year in review: UN peace operations in 2001, UN document DPI/2240, Dec. 2001.

[208] Wilkinson (note 146), p. 6.

[209] Eyal, J., 'Sierra Leone: saving Africa from another disaster?', RUSI Newsbrief, vol. 20, no. 40 (June 2000), p. 2.

[210] Clare Short, British Minister for International Development, called for the sacking of Adeniji for allegedly refusing to permit the use of force by UN troops to restore government authority throughout the country. The Times, 23 Apr. 2001, p. 14.

ment, without democratic elections, the Lomé Peace Agreement sowed the seeds of catastrophe. The UN was, as usual, left with little choice but to deploy a peacekeeping operation to oversee this shaky deal. When Sankoh reneged on his agreement by refusing to disarm his forces or allow UN troops into his territory, the UN was left with three options—to attempt to enforce compliance, which UNAMSIL was unable and unwilling to do; to withdraw, also a difficult option while peacekeepers were being held hostage; or to appeal for diplomatic assistance from the RUF's unpalatable political and military backers, in particular Liberia. As former US Ambassador to Mozambique Dennis Jett bluntly put it: 'Mr Sankoh has dared to break the flawed peace pact because of the flawed UN peacekeeping force, which he does not fear'.[211]

Again, as in Somalia, Rwanda and East Timor, the UN had completely misread the intentions of a rebel group, was acting as if both sides in a civil conflict were morally equivalent and assumed that the UN's role was simply to keep or restore the peace. Both SRSG Adeniji and Force Commander Jetley were apparently convinced of Sankoh's reasonableness, despite his long history of broken promises to the UN and others. Bernard Myet, UN Under Secretary-General for Peace-keeping Operations, on a supposedly morale-boosting visit during the May crisis had demonstrated how the old UN peacekeeping mentality prevailed, even after the mission had gone so terribly wrong. Instead of offering strong UN support for the embattled government, he used traditional UN language in declaring that: 'It is now the goal of our force to preserve the stability and peace in Freetown. It is our immediate priority'.[212]

Overall the Sierra Leone operation seemed to plunge the UN back into the Congo era. Every dilemma and difficulty faced by the UN in the Congo in the 1960s in contemplating or using force was revisited, often with less favourable outcomes. Even the minimalist demands of traditional peacekeeping, the use of force in self-defence, were not met, still less the more demanding requirements of post-cold war missions. Clearly, a drastic overhaul of UN peace operations was still required.

[211] Quoted in 'West African fiasco renews doubts on UN missions', *International Herald Tribune*, 9 May 2000, p. 1.
[212] 'In panic, thousands flee to Freetown' (note 148), p. 1.

# 9. Retreat, resurgence and reform: rethinking the use of force by the United Nations

Just as the UN had begun tentatively to cast off its cold war shackles and envisage a more expansive role for itself, the Somalia and Bosnia debacles caused it to pull 'back to basics' in its thinking about the use of force. Only with a series of reports on and deeper thinking about the implications of the Rwanda and Srebrenica cases, and the advent of a new UN Secretary-General in January 1997, did new thinking begin to emerge, especially with regard to the use of force for protecting civilians from massacres. This chapter traces the UN's reaction to its post-cold war missions, its attempts to learn lessons and implement reforms, and its tentative steps towards a new conceptualization of the use of force in peace operations.

## I. Back to basics?

The experiences of Somalia and Bosnia appeared to produce a consensus that the UN was incapable of conducting peace enforcement operations and should therefore retreat to doing what it did best—peacekeeping. As *The New York Times* thundered in early 1995: 'Rethinking and retrenchment are in order . . . There should be a shift back toward more limited objectives like policing cease-fires. UN peacekeeping does what it can do very well. It makes no sense to continue eroding its credibility by asking it to do what it cannot'.[1] Multinational 'coalitions of the willing' were seen to be the preferable model for peace enforcement operations. The US Senate Armed Services Committee concluded that: 'The United Nations was not and is not now the best organization to direct the conduct of large-scale Chapter VII peace enforcement operations that may involve substantial risk of combat'.[2] Commanders Çevik Bir and Thomas Montgomery concurred, the latter declaring that: 'Desert Storm is the correct model for Chapter VII operations'.[3] Then Under Secretary-General for Peace-keeping Operations Kofi Annan predicted in 1994 that it would 'be a very long time before the United Nations as an organization takes on a peace enforcement mission and manages it itself'.[4]

The UN Commission of Inquiry into Somalia, too, recommended that the UN 'refrain from undertaking further peace enforcement actions within the internal

---

[1] 'The future of peacekeeping', editorial, *New York Times*, 8 Jan. 1995.
[2] US Senate, Committee on Armed Services, 'Review of the circumstances surrounding the Ranger Raid on October 3–4, 1993 in Mogadishu, Somalia', Memorandum for Senator Thurmond and Senator Nunn from Senator Warner and Senator Levin, Washington, DC, 29 Sep. 1995, p. 47.
[3] Memorandum for Senator Thurmond and Senator Nunn (note 2), p. 18.
[4] 'Kofi Annan: the soft-spoken economist who runs UN peacekeeping forces', *Los Angeles Times*, 21 June 1994.

conflicts of states'. However, the commission displayed an awareness that abstention from using force altogether was unlikely to be possible, particularly given the UN's continuing involvement in Bosnia. It suggested that if peace enforcement was undertaken the mandate 'should be limited to specific objectives and the use of force should be applied as the ultimate means after all peaceful remedies have been exhausted'.[5]

A significant player seeking a UN retreat to peacekeeping was the USA. As by far the most militarily capable state, the single most important country in the shaping of Security Council resolutions, a veto-wielding permanent member of the Security Council and the provider of more than one-quarter of the funding for UN peace operations, the USA had seminal influence. The humiliation it suffered in Mogadishu caused a hasty retreat from its earlier support for an expansive UN role in peace operations.[6] Boutros Boutros-Ghali reports that in October 1993 the director of the US State Department policy planning staff telephoned him to say that the hopes he and many others in Washington had had for close UN–US cooperation in peace operations over the next years 'blew up in our faces' in Mogadishu.[7] More publicly, Assistant Secretary of Defense Ted Warner declared that: 'We have come to believe that the United Nations is not the best organization to direct . . . large-sized Chapter VII peace enforcement operations that may involve substantial risk of combat. We believe such operations are best carried out by coalitions or capable regional organizations'.[8]

The controversy over authorization of NATO air power in Bosnia took a further toll on relations between the USA and the UN. Madeleine Albright, former US Ambassador to the UN and now US Secretary of State, told Boutros-Ghali: 'You are blamed for trying to control American military power. You used the "dual key" to oppose NATO air strikes against the Serbs. Your stance was very badly perceived by military circles in Washington'.[9] Albright partly attributed widespread US opposition to Boutros-Ghali's having a second four-year term as Secretary-General to his handling of the air power issue.

More formal US strictures on the UN's role in peace operations came with Presidential Decision Directive 25 (PDD 25) on 'Reforming multilateral peace operations', released in May 1994.[10] Originally intended to support and encour-

---

[5] United Nations, Report of the Commission of Inquiry established pursuant to Security Council Resolution 885 (1993) to investigate armed attacks on UNOSOM II personnel which led to casualties among them, appended to United Nations, Note by Secretary-General, UN document S/1994/653, 1 June 1994, p. 48.

[6] Don Daniel also notes the influence on US policy of the perennial US ambivalence between Jeffersonian/Wilsonian internationalism and Adamsian dislike of foreign entanglements. Daniel, D. C. F., 'The United States', ed. T. Findlay, *Challenges for the New Peacekeepers*, SIPRI Research Report no. 12 (Oxford University Press: Oxford, 1996), p. 86.

[7] Boutros-Ghali, B., *Unvanquished: A US–UN Saga* (I. B. Tauris: New York, 1999), p. 116.

[8] Quoted in Memorandum for Senator Thurmond and Senator Nunn (note 2), p. 9.

[9] Boutros-Ghali (note 7), p. 333.

[10] US Department of State, *The Clinton Administration's Policy on Reforming Multilateral Peace Operations*, Department of State Publication 10161 (Department of State, Bureau of International Organization Affairs: Washington, DC, May 1994). Excerpts are reproduced in *SIPRI Yearbook 1995: Armaments, Disarmament and International Security* (Oxford University Press, Oxford, 1995), appendix 2B, pp. 97–99. For an analysis of its origins see Daniel (note 6), pp. 85–98.

age an expansive UN role, it now set out, post-Somalia, strangulating criteria for US support for UN peace operations. When deciding whether to even vote for the establishment of a UN peace operation, the administration would consider not only the nature of the threat to international peace and security but also whether there were clear objectives and an understanding of where the mission fitted on the 'spectrum between traditional peacekeeping and peace enforcement'.[11] For the USA to support peace enforcement the threat would need to be 'significant', the means to accomplish the mission would have to be available, including the forces, financing and appropriate mandate, and the operation's anticipated duration would have to be tied to clear objectives and realistic criteria for ending it. Even more rigorous criteria were to be applied when there was the possibility of 'significant' US participation in Chapter VII operations 'likely to involve combat'. There needed to be *inter alia* 'a determination to commit sufficient forces to achieve clearly defined objectives', 'a plan to achieve those objectives decisively' and 'a commitment to reassess and adjust, as necessary, the size, composition, and disposition of our forces'.

As it turned out, the impact of PDD-25 was not long-lasting. The first test case, the peace enforcement operation in Haiti, was supported (and led by) the USA, its desire to resolve a serious problem in its own backyard overruling its qualms about the dangers of such operations. The first and only victim of PDD-25 was Rwanda, after which little was heard of it. The USA's failure to pay in full its assessed financial contributions because of congressional opposition, incited by the anti-UN animus of Senator Jesse Helms, had a far greater impact on UN peace operations.[12]

The British *Wider Peacekeeping* document, the British Army's initial attempt at a peace operations doctrine, also had unfortunate consequences on UN thinking.[13] Touted internationally as the definitive peace operations doctrine (despite being described at home as simply a generator of debate), it was influential both at UN Headquarters (where many British military personnel were seconded) and in national defence establishments worldwide. British doctrine was also used as the basis for the training and preparation of contingents from a wide variety of countries which were destined for UN peace operations in Africa and Europe.[14] Unfortunately, it drew heavily on traditional peacekeeping doctrine,[15] simply stretching the old concept to fit new circumstances. It thus reinforced the general impression that peace enforcement was impossible and implausible, providing 'an overwhelming reason not to search for a new approach to the dynamic and crucially important aspects of the problem'.[16] It undoubtedly

---

[11] *The Clinton Administration's Policy on Reforming Multilateral Peace Operations* (note 10), p. 4.

[12] By 1995 the total US debt to the UN was $3.24 billion.

[13] British Army, *Army Field Manual, Vol. 5. Operations Other than War, Part 2: Wider Peacekeeping*, D/HQDT/18/34/30 (Her Majesty's Stationery Office: London, 1994). See appendix 1 in this volume for further details of British and other national peace operations doctrines.

[14] Mackinlay, J., 'International responses to complex emergencies: why a new approach is needed', *International Peacekeeping News*, vol. 2, no. 5 (Nov./Dec. 1996), p. 36.

[15] Mackinlay, J. and Kent, R., 'Complex emergencies doctrine: the British are still the best', *RUSI Journal*, vol. 142, no. 2 (Apr. 1997), p. 40.

[16] Mackinlay and Kent (note 15).

steeled those at UN Headquarters who feared involvement in peace enforce-ment and argued that the UN should stick to traditional peacekeeping.

**Retreat from *An Agenda for Peace***

In this environment the UN had little choice but to retreat. Evidence came in March 1994, when Boutros-Ghali retracted some of the more radical innova-tions of his 1992 *Agenda for Peace*.[17] In a report on improving the UN's peace-keeping capacity he quietly reverted to the traditional definition of peace-keeping as requiring 'the consent of the parties'.[18]

In his January 1995 *Supplement to An Agenda for Peace*, which drew heavily on the lessons of Somalia and Bosnia, he noted that three types of activity had led such operations to forfeit the consent of the parties. These were: protecting humanitarian operations during continuing warfare; protecting civilian popula-tions in designated safe areas; and pressing parties to achieve national recon-ciliation at a faster pace than they were ready for. Such missions had, he said, dangerously blurred the distinction between peacekeeping and peace enforce-ment. The Secretary-General suggested that: 'Peacekeeping and the use of force (other than in self-defence) should be seen as alternative techniques and not as adjacent points on a continuum, permitting each transition from one to the other'.[19] Although he did not say so explicitly, he seemed to be suggesting that the UN should only be involved in peacekeeping, not peace enforcement. He failed to mention the idea of peace enforcement units again, although he did support the establishment of a UN rapid reaction force as a strategic reserve for use in emergencies.[20]

**Secretariat views**

Opinion in the UN Secretariat over a future UN role beyond traditional peace-keeping was divided: generally, those previously involved in peacekeeping were opposed to peace enforcement, while new staff were in favour.[21] One of the most erudite commentators on the use-of-force issue in the UN Secretariat,

[17] United Nations, *An Agenda for Peace: Preventive Diplomacy, Peacemaking and Peace-keeping. Report of the Secretary-General Pursuant to the Statement Adopted by the Summit Meeting of the Security Council on 31 January 1992* (UN Department of Public Information: New York, 1992).

[18] United Nations, Improving the capacity of the United Nations for peace-keeping: report of the Secretary-General, UN document A/48/403, S/26450, 14 Mar. 1994, p. 2.

[19] United Nations, Supplement to *An Agenda for Peace*: position paper of the Secretary-General on the occasion of the 50th anniversary of the United Nations, UN document A/50/60, S/19951, 3 Jan. 1995, p. 9.

[20] In 1996 the Secretary-General made further changes to the terminology used in *An Agenda for Peace* by sensibly conceding that 'preventive diplomacy', which had previously been taken to include such patently non-diplomatic approaches as the preventive deployment of military forces, should now be known as 'preventive action'. He also attempted to disperse some of the confusion surrounding the term 'peace-making' by reserving it for diplomatic means used to persuade parties to cease hostilities and negotiate a peaceful settlement. Peacemaking thus excludes peace enforcement. United Nations, *The 50th Anniversary Report of the Secretary-General on the Work of the Organization* (UN Department of Public Information: New York, 1996), pp. 193–94.

[21] According to Marrack Goulding, at seminar to launch his book, *Peacemonger* (John Murray: London, 2002) held at the International Institute for Strategic Studies, London, 3 July 2002.

Shashi Tharoor, Special Assistant to Kofi Annan, argued that the UN should essentially go back to the basics of peacekeeping. If one chooses the 'logic of peace' then one opts, Tharoor said, for peacekeeping, 'with all its limitations: the requirement for consent and cooperation, the indispensability of impartiality, a sensible reluctance to use force; one abjures victories, disclaims enemies, treats all the parties as partners in a common endeavour to attain peace'.[22] If one opts for the 'logic of war', which he equated with peace enforcement, 'one commits the necessary political will and the military and financial resources required to obtain victory; one identifies an enemy and devotes the means required to destroy it'. 'Enforcement action', he said, 'proceeds from different premises and is not merely one more stage in a 'peacekeeping continuum'.[23]

Marrack Goulding, who was Under Secretary-General for Peacekeeping from 1986 to 1992 and subsequently Under Secretary-General for Political Affairs, was also conservative on the use-of-force issue. He did not oppose 'enforcement' operations by the UN in internal conflicts, but characterized them as full-scale Chapter VII operations, cautioning that UN members must take a clear decision about whether the UN should intervene as 'an impartial peacekeeper or as an avenging angel to punish the wicked and protect the righteous'. If a mission is changed from peacekeeping to enforcement, 'the change must be clearly signalled to all the parties concerned, there must be convincing evidence of a real political will to use force to achieve a strategic objective and deployments must be adjusted in advance to ensure that those who have been working in impartial mode with the party which is now to be struck are not exposed to retaliation'.[24] Goulding rightly criticized the attempt to use force in self-defence to accomplish broader enforcement goals as an 'illusion' with dangerous political consequences, but was sceptical about the possibility of a 'halfway house' between peacekeeping and enforcement.

Nonetheless Goulding did not rule out the possibility of peace enforcement entirely (although he abjured the term), citing two possible purposes—protection of humanitarian aid delivery in a civil war and enforcement of an agreed ceasefire. He warned, however, that success was contingent on the fulfilment of four conditions: (a) the Security Council should make a clear political commitment to the countries contributing troops to a peace operation that it was determined to prevail against any opposition; (b) the force should have evident military superiority over any known protagonist: reinforcements must be provided if required; (c) the force should be absolutely impartial and ready to use force against any party which obstructed it; and (d) the force should have no other mandate in relation to the conflict in question, since this would sooner or later inhibit the impartial use of force against the recalcitrant party.[25] After retiring from the UN Secretariat to Oxford University, Goulding changed his

[22] Tharoor, S., 'Should UN peacekeeping go "back to basics"?', *Survival*, vol. 37, no. 4 (winter 1995/96), p. 60.
[23] Tharoor (note 22), p. 56.
[24] Goulding, M., 'The use of force by the United Nations', *International Peacekeeping*, vol. 3, no. 1 (spring 1996), pp. 15, 16.
[25] Goulding (note 24), pp. 16–17.

mind, admitting that 'we in the Secretariat adjusted too slowly to the demands of the new types of conflict which proliferated after the end of the Cold War'.[26] By the second half of the 1990s it had become clear, he concedes, that there was a 'need to revise peacekeeping doctrine'. He now regrets that this was not done sooner.

Annan was one of those in the Secretariat who resisted going 'back to basics'. *Time* quoted him in October 1995 as saying that: 'Classical peacekeeping would be a neat solution, but if you restrict yourself to it, you're excluding the main new sources of threat'.[27] He had been an original enthusiast of an expanded UN role in peace operations, writing in late 1993 that:

Today's conflicts in Somalia and Bosnia have fundamentally redrawn the parameters. It is no longer enough to implement agreements or separate antagonists; the international community now wants the United Nations to demarcate boundaries, control and eliminate heavy weapons, quell anarchy, and guarantee the delivery of humanitarian aid in war zones. These are clearly tasks that call for 'teeth' and 'muscle', in addition to less tangible qualities that we have not sought in the past. In other words, there are increasing demands that the United Nations now enforce the peace, as originally envisaged in the charter.[28]

## II. The UN struggles to learn lessons

Unlike during the cold war, the UN made efforts to draw lessons from its most recent experiences, including with regard to the use-of-force issue. In early 1995 the DPKO established a Lessons Learned Unit in the Office of Planning and Support. The unit produced a series of reports, in cooperation with troop-contributing countries, academic institutions and NGOs. Unfortunately, the process was so slow that by the time the reports were published there were new lessons to be absorbed. Moreover, none of them was entirely satisfactory. It was also difficult for the UN to engage in totally honest lessons-learned exercises on its own missions, not only because any organization finds it difficult to admit its own failings, but because the contributing states involved in each mission invariably attempted to blame the UN and the Secretariat for any failings, while Secretariat officials in turn tended to blame the Security Council and member states for not providing enough support for their efforts.

### The lessons-learned report on Somalia

In December 1995 a lessons-learned report on the Somalia operation, based largely on the findings of two seminars, and drafted with the involvement of German, Norwegian and Swedish institutes and the Lessons Learned Unit, was

[26] Goulding, M., *Peacemonger* (note 21), p. 17. Goulding was apparently convinced by exposure to the thinking of Adam Roberts on the issue and by the experiences of the UN in such missions as Sierra Leone and East Timor.

[27] Prager, K., 'The limits of peacekeeping', *Time*, 23 Oct. 1995, p. 33.

[28] Annan, K. A., 'UN peacekeeping operations and cooperation with NATO', *NATO Review*, vol. 41, no. 5 (Oct. 1993), p. 4.

published by the Swedish Government.[29] The implementation of many of its recommendations would enhance the UN's ability to use force appropriately and effectively. These include clearer mandates, adequate means, an integrated plan, improved coordination, reconciliation and institution-building strategies, a humanitarian assistance strategy, unity of command and control, standard operating procedures (SOP) for logistics and administration, and improved accountability, public information campaigns and intelligence-gathering.[30]

The report, however, completely ducked the questions whether the UN should engage in peace enforcement, whether there was such a category of operations and even whether peacekeepers in their expanded roles should be permitted to use greater force. The working assumption appeared to be that the report was dealing only with peacekeeping. Indeed, 'peacekeeping' was the preferred term throughout and the introduction to the report quoted Boutros-Ghali as acknowledging that the years since the cold war had confirmed that respect for certain principles of peacekeeping—consent, impartiality and use of force only in self-defence—were essential to its success.[31]

The fact that the report writers were sharply divided over the use-of-force issue is indicated only in the section on 'Disarmament and a secure environment'. It records that some participants believed that the experience of disarmament in Somalia had demonstrated that force 'judiciously deployed at the tactical level, is an important and viable tool in the context of peace-keeping, as long as care is taken to maintain strategic-level consent'.[32] An alternative view held that peacekeeping and enforcement were incompatible and are 'carried out simultaneously in the same mission area at great risk'. A third opinion was that generalizations were impossible and that each case is *sui generis* and must be judged on its own merits.

The second half of the report, a paper by the DPKO itself on the 'Application of lessons learned from the United Nations Operation in Somalia', written after new lessons had been learned in Haiti, Rwanda and Bosnia, provides a unique snapshot of Secretariat thinking on peace operations at the time. It confirmed that the DPKO had largely retreated to the traditional peacekeeping ethos and parroted the line that peace enforcement operations could only be undertaken by coalitions of the willing or single states. There were, however, ambiguities. One lesson it drew from the Haiti operation, for instance, was that, while a peacekeeping operation should not be deployed at all if there was no political will among the parties towards reconciliation, 'since a peacekeeping force has

[29] Friedrich Ebert Stiftung (Germany), Life and Peace Institute (Sweden), Norwegian Institute of International Affairs (NUPI) and United Nations Department of Peace-keeping Operations, Lessons Learned Unit, 'Comprehensive report on lessons-learned from United Nations Operation in Somalia April 1992–March 1995', Swedish Government, Stockholm, Dec. 1995. The first seminar in New York in June 1995 involved UNOSOM commanders and officials, NGOs, experts and UN officials, and was held with the assistance of the Norwegian Government and NUPI. A 2nd seminar, more widely attended by troop-contributing countries, was held in Plainsboro, N.J., in Sep. 1995. In addition, troop-contributing countries and NGOs were asked to provide the DPKO with detailed notes of their experiences.

[30] 'Comprehensive report on lessons-learned . . . Somalia' (note 29), p. 7.

[31] 'Comprehensive report on lessons-learned . . . Somalia' (note 29), p. 3.

[32] 'Comprehensive report on lessons-learned . . . Somalia' (note 29), p. 24.

no enforcement powers', on the other hand it should be given 'robust' ROE to ensure that no party took advantage of the changeover from a peace enforcement operation.[33] This seemed to be stating a truism that had applied to peacekeeping for decades, but it avoided the question what to do if such a mission faced a decline in parties' willingness to achieve reconciliation after it was deployed and whether it should then revert to a peace enforcement operation.

### The lessons-learned report on Rwanda

In December 1996 the Lessons Learned Unit released a report on Rwanda.[34] Like the Somalia report, it was biased towards improving peacekeeping in the traditional sense rather than considering any new peace operations paradigm. It proffered 43 lessons, most of them eminently sensible, which would undoubtedly improve all types of peace operations. Not one of them related to the use of force, even in self-defence. The possibility of peace enforcement was not even mentioned, much less entertained.

Even the strong case made by Force Commander Roméo Dallaire that UNAMIR could have done more if it had been reinforced and given a stronger, Chapter VII, mandate once the massacres began was dismissed: 'There are those who feel that many more lives could have been saved if the peacekeeping operation had been reinforced at that critical juncture. However, the speed with which the massacres were carried out and the organized control of their commission suggests that in the time it would have taken for an expanded force to be deployed, much of the damage might still have been done'.[35] The report went on to exaggerate the difficulties of deploying reinforcements to Rwanda, claiming (wrongly) that: 'Never before in the history of peacekeeping had the United Nations deployed such a large number of troops and logistics to a land-locked country'.[36] In the 1960s ONUC had been a much larger force and its advance units had deployed within days of authorization to a land-locked African country several times the size of Rwanda and in the much more basic conditions of the time.

The report also dismissed the argument that UNAMIR should have been able to use force to protect civilians at risk and to secure human rights. Senior military officials had apparently agreed at the lessons-learned seminar that UNAMIR had neither the mandate nor the means to take effective military action to protect the victims of the slaughter, even in self-defence, and that 'the force had not been put together with this in mind'.[37] This seemed to ignore the military capability of the Belgian troops and the fact that all peacekeepers have

---

[33] 'Comprehensive report on lessons-learned . . . Somalia' (note 29), p. 27.

[34] United Nations, Department of Peace-keeping Operations, Lessons Learned Unit, Comprehensive report on lessons learned from United Nations Assistance Mission for Rwanda (UNAMIR), October 1993–April 1996, New York, Dec. 1996. It was based on consultations with external experts in New York on 28 Mar. 1996, an 'internal consultation' at UN headquarters on 15–16 May 1996 and a Comprehensive Seminar held at Plainsboro, N.J., on 12–14 June 1996.

[35] 'Comprehensive report on lessons learned . . . Rwanda' (note 34), p. 32.

[36] 'Comprehensive report on lessons learned . . . Rwanda' (note 34), p. 27.

[37] 'Comprehensive report on lessons learned . . . Rwanda' (note 34), p. 23.

the right to self-defence. The report remarked that: 'Some people have advanced the argument that UNAMIR could have resorted to its rules of engagement, one paragraph of which was interpreted as authorizing the operation to take any action, including the use of force, to protect civilians',[38] while others countered that the authority of the Security Council should not be so usurped. The legal argument for ignoring the massacre of thousands of people seemed both tendentious and immoral.

Demonstrating the continuing naivety of the UN, the report suggested that the inclusion of a human rights component in the mission from the outset would have taken care of the problem of protecting civilians from 'political violence'. While it mentioned that participants at the seminar argued that 'the case of genocide is so compelling that the United Nations must act expeditiously under one conceptual umbrella',[39] it contained no recognition that the UN, for both moral and international legal reasons, must not allow its peace operations to be silent witness to such events but must act, including by using force. No mention was made of the need for doctrinal development to anticipate such action, nor of the possibility that UN preparedness to act might deter future outrages.

The paucity of thinking at UN Headquarters about use-of-force issues was graphically illustrated the same month with the release of a purportedly comprehensive report on 'Lessons learned from recent experience' of what was called 'multidisciplinary peacekeeping'. Presumably intended to collate and expound all the lessons learned in UN operations since the beginning of the cold war, it almost totally avoided the use-of-force issue. Its sole reference was a plea that ROE should be 'sufficiently detailed to eliminate doubts as to individual and unit behaviour under various contingencies, and should include guidance concerning mutual support by personnel and units of the force as a whole'.[40] This might as well have been a lessons-learned report from UNEF I, so little did it advance thinking about modern peace operations.

## UN guidelines on and training for the use of force in peace operations

Meanwhile in other parts of the DPKO new documents were being produced to give peacekeepers, for the first time, reasonably comprehensive guidelines for conducting their mission, as well as furnishing national militaries with guidance on how their troops should be trained for UN missions. The use of force was mentioned in these unprecedented documents, although hardly comprehensively.

In 1995 the UN published its *General Guidelines for Peace-keeping Operations*.[41] While they are a realistic reflection of past UN experience, they remain

[38] 'Comprehensive report on lessons learned . . . Rwanda' (note 34), p. 23.

[39] 'Comprehensive report on lessons learned . . . Rwanda' (note 34), p. 49.

[40] United Nations, Department of Peace-keeping Operations, Lessons Learned Unit, *Multidisciplinary Peacekeeping: Lessons from Recent Experience* (United Nations: New York, Dec. 1996), p. 17.

[41] United Nations, Department of Peace-keeping Operations, *General Guidelines for Peace-keeping Operations*, UN document 95-38147 (United Nations: New York, 1995).

restricted to traditional peacekeeping rather than incorporating any wider concepts. The document does at least give a well-rounded account of the responsibilities of peacekeepers in using force in self-defence, something which has not always been the case in UN formulations: 'The peace-keeper's right to self-defence does not end with the defence of his/her own life. It includes defending one's comrades and any persons entrusted in one's care, as well as defending one's post, convoy, vehicle, or rifle. Each peace-keeping operation is expected to function as a single, integrated unit and an attack on any one of its members or subunits engages the right to self-defence of the operation as a whole'.[42]

The guidelines mention that since 1973 UN peacekeepers have been permitted to use force to resist attempts to prevent them from carrying out their mandate. However, the document also bluntly observes that, while 'this is a broad conception of "self-defence" which might be interpreted as entitling United Nations personnel to open fire in a wide variety of situations', in practice 'commanders in the field have been reluctant to use their authority in this way, for well-founded reasons relating to the need for a peace-keeping operation to maintain the active cooperation of the parties to a conflict'.[43]

The guidelines enjoined commanders to 'develop a range of options, appropriate to the specific operation and short of the actual use of force, for dealing with threats . . . for example, negotiation, raising a matter to a higher political level, employment of a variety of defensive measures and the concentration of sufficient armed force to act as a deterrent'. Acknowledging the reality of modern peacekeeping operations, the guidelines nonetheless concede that:

While peace-keeping is incompatible with enforcement, in exceptional circumstances a United Nations operation may be mandated by the Security Council to carry out, concurrently, aspects of both in a single mission area. This is an inherently problematic situation and must be handled with utmost caution and care. Experience has shown that it is dangerous for a peace-keeping operation to be asked to use force when its existing composition, armament, logistics support and deployment deny it the capacity to do so. In general in such a situation, decisions regarding the use of force or any escalation in the use of force should be highly centralized, since decisions made at the tactical level could have extreme consequences for the entire operation.[44]

A final admonition is delivered about the difficulty of resolving conflicts through peace operations, reflecting the conservative military view that there is a sharp divide between peacekeeping and peace enforcement: 'Peace-keeping and the use of force (other than in self-defence) should be seen as alternative techniques and not as adjacent points on a continuum. There is no easy transition from one to the other'.[45]

---

[42] *General Guidelines for Peace-keeping Operations* (note 41), p. 20.
[43] *General Guidelines for Peace-keeping Operations* (note 41), p. 20.
[44] *General Guidelines for Peace-keeping Operations* (note 41), p. 21.
[45] *General Guidelines for Peace-keeping Operations* (note 41), pp. 21–22. The only other reference to the use of force in the guidelines is in relation to crowd control, where it notes that: 'The use of crowd control techniques and equipment designed to avoid inflicting casualties is essential' (p. 30).

In addition to producing guidance for peacekeepers, the UN embarked on an attempt to improve the training of peacekeepers before deployment. The training documents also reveal a conservative view of peacekeeping. The UN's *Peacekeeping Training Manual*, prepared by the DPKO with the help of the International Training Centre of the International Labour Organization in Turin, Italy, relied heavily on the Nordic peacekeeping training manual, including in its sections on the use of force.[46] It therefore contains the flaws of that model, including a lack of clarity and rudimentary characterization of complex issues.

It stresses the importance of training in relation to use-of-force issues for various reasons: 'an integral part' of peacekeeping is now its 'non-enforcement nature'; soldiers from contributing countries 'will have been conditioned to an "automatic return of fire" philosophy'; contingents with wide experience of 'aid to the civil power at home' will still find differences in the application of 'UN doctrine'; and troops with previous UN experience may find the doctrine slightly changed 'as part of the ongoing evolutionary process'. This seems odd: far from 'non-enforcement' being an integral part of peacekeeping, there has been more debate about it than ever since the cold war ended; and the document never explains what the 'slight' changes to UN doctrine have actually been.

The basic principle of the use of force in peacekeeping, it says, remains that established by the UN Secretary-General for UNIFIL: 'The Force will be provided with weapons of a defensive character and shall not use force except in self-defence. Self-defence would include resistance to attempts by forceful means to prevent it from discharging its duties under the mandate of the Security Council'.[47] (In fact, these were the principles established for UNEF-II.) No explanation is given of what using force to protect the peacekeepers' mission means in practice. The guidelines completely ignore the possibility that non-UN civilians might be protected through the use of force, for instance, in cases of massacre or threatening genocide. Nor do the guidelines mention what should happen if the use of force escalates, or new tasks for peacekeepers, such as escorting delivery of humanitarian aid or protecting an electoral process. There is also no mention of the fact that different contingents in an operation will have been trained to use different ROE and that the escalatory steps envisaged, such as use of warning shots, might be unfamiliar to some contingents and might not even be included in the UN ROE for a particular mission. Finally, the distinction between unarmed force and armed force is not matched to the various scenarios that might be envisaged.

Taken together, these documents, insofar as they can be said to reflect UN thinking, provide a glimpse of the state of UN 'doctrine' on the use of force in peace operations by the mid-1990s. What is astounding is how little their drafting was influenced by the traumatic failures, or even the successes, of the UN over the previous half-decade. Also missing was any hint that outside the UN

---

[46] United Nations, Department of Peace-keeping Operations, *A Peace-keeping Training Manual*, 2nd edn (United Nations: New York, [1997]); and Joint Nordic Committee for Military UN Matters (NORDSAMFN), *Nordic UN Tactical Manual* (Gummerus Kirjapaino Oy: Jyväskylä, 1992), vols 1 and 2.

[47] *Peace-keeping Training Manual*, 2nd edn (note 46), p. 60.

considerable developments were occurring in respect of peace operations doctrine, especially in the UK and the USA. UN peace operations 'doctrine' was still essentially locked in the mindset of traditional peacekeeping, was timid and unimaginative, and failed to cater for the range of challenges being faced by UN forces, even in conditions of 'wider peacekeeping'—much less peace enforcement.

## III. The Annan era

On 1 January 1997, Kofi Annan, a Ghanaian, became UN Secretary-General. He was to adopt a view of the UN's obligations and role in peace operations that was much more expansive than those of any previous secretary-general. This was partly based on a more coherent analysis of the nature of peace operations inspired by a new cadre of advisers, such as John Ruggie, Andrew Mack and chief speech-writer Edward Mortimer,[48] but the most telling factor seems to have been the fact that as Under Secretary-General for Peacekeeping Operations he was partly responsible for the Bosnia and Rwanda tragedies which, in his view, had so tarnished the UN's credibility and moral standing.

Annan, as Secretary-General, would later argue that the UN needed to develop a 'new paradigm' for peace operations that would include measures for 'inducing consent', along with appropriate capabilities for deployment and a serious capacity for the lawful gathering and analysis of intelligence.[49] Controversially, he would contend that the old dictum of consent of the parties would be 'neither right nor wrong; it will be, quite simply, irrelevant'. While much of the peacekeeping literature, he said, treated consent as an independent variable, in fact the decision of the parties to grant consent is never taken in a vacuum but is a function of alternatives: 'If consent carries with it certain rewards and the failure of consent carries certain costs, this obviously affects the decision as to whether or not consent will be granted'.[50] Hence a UN mission must, as well as having the support of the great powers, be able to have a mix of costs and rewards at its disposal in the mission area. He used the terms 'coercive inducement', to include the use of force and other types of sanctions, and 'positive inducement',[51] which would include 'civic action' and 'peace incentives'.[52] However, he warned against bluffing: 'It follows that inducement operations should be deployed with the mandate and capacity to conduct, if necessary, offensive operations against recalcitrants'.[53]

---

[48] Ruggie, J. G., 'The UN and the collective use of force: whither or whether?', ed. M. Pugh, *The UN, Peace and Force* (Frank Cass: London, 1997); and Daniel, D. C. F. and Hayes, B. D. (eds) with Chantal de Jonge Oudraat, *Coercive Inducement and the Containment of International Crises* (United States Institute of Peace Press: Washington, DC, 1999), p. 200.

[49] Annan, K. A., 'Challenges of the new peacekeeping', eds O. A. Otunnu and M. W. Doyle, *Peacemaking and Peacekeeping for the New Century* (Rowman & Littlefield: Lanham, Md., 1998), p. 172.

[50] Annan (note 49), pp. 172–73.

[51] Don Daniel and Brad Hayes claim to have been the first to use the term 'inducement', which Annan then allegedly 'built on'. Daniel and Hayes with de Jonge Oudraat (note 48), p. 4.

[52] Annan (note 49), p. 175.

[53] Annan (note 49), p. 174.

Since becoming Secretary-General Annan has apparently deepened his conviction that such a strategy is necessary and possible. He has clearly identified himself with what has been called the emerging norm of humanitarian intervention. In a landmark address to the General Assembly in September 1999—just hours after INTERFET arrived in East Timor—he called on member states and the Security Council to confront the 'core challenge' in the next century: 'to forge unity behind the principle that massive and systematic violations of human rights—*wherever* they may take place—should not be allowed to stand'.[54] He challenged those who opposed NATO's intervention in Kosovo on the grounds that it did not have Security Council authorization to ask themselves whether in the Rwanda case a coalition of states ready to act but without Security Council authorization should have 'stood aside as the horror unfolded'. Similarly, he challenged those who supported military action for humanitarian purposes outside the established mechanisms for enforcing international law to consider whether such actions risked setting dangerous precedents which muddied the criteria for deciding by whom and when such interventions should be made.

Annan posited four aspects of intervention which he believed held important lessons for the future. First, intervention should be defined as broadly as possible, 'to include actions along a wide continuum from the most pacific to the most coercive', while also recognizing that armed intervention is a result of the failure of prevention. Second, not only sovereignty but also member states' definition of their national interest stood in the way of effective action in human rights or humanitarian crises: states should therefore broaden their definition of national interest. Third, in the event of forceful intervention becoming necessary, the Security Council should be permitted to rise to the challenge: its credibility depended on its enforcement and deterrent power. Finally, after a conflict is over, it is vitally important that the commitment to peace be as strong as the commitment to war. Explicitly recognizing a 'developing international norm in favor of intervention to protect civilians from wholesale slaughter', he argued that there was nothing in the UN Charter that 'precludes a recognition that there are rights beyond borders'. He called for the Security Council to collectively assert itself 'where the cause is just and the means available'.[55]

What is remarkable about Kofi Annan's interventionist stance is that it flew in the face of the views of at least one permanent member of the Security Council—China—and of key developing countries such as Algeria, Cuba, India and Malaysia.[56] According to Gareth Evans, former Australian foreign minister,

[54] United Nations, Secretary-General, Address to the United Nations General Assembly, New York, 20 Sep. 1999, reproduced in United Nations, 'Secretary-General presents his annual report to General Assembly', Press release SG/SM/7136, GA/95920, 20 Sep. 1999.

[55] 'Secretary-General presents his annual report to General Assembly' (note 54).

[56] For the subtleties of the Chinese position, however, see Gill, B. and Reilly, J., 'Sovereignty, intervention and peacekeeping: the view from Beijing', *Survival*, vol. 42, no. 3 (autumn 2000), pp. 41–59. In 1995, as a result of Malaysia's involvement in UNPROFOR, Malaysian Prime Minister Mahathir Mohamed called for a UN Peace Enforcement Force to be established to stop the occurrence of atrocities in armed conflicts. He described UNPROFOR's failure to stop atrocities in Bosnia as 'a massive slap in

and Mohamed Sahnoun, who had been SRSG in Somalia, the response to the Secretary-General's speech revealed more division than emerging consensus: 'Those delegates who chose to emphasize the virtues of either humanitarian intervention, on the one hand, or the protection of state sovereignty on the other, far outnumbered those seeking to find a workable accommodation between the two concepts'.[57] Algerian President Abdelaziz Bouteflika said that at least three questions would need to be resolved before debate on intervention, or 'interference' as he called it, could be closed: 'First, where does aid stop and interference begin? Second, where are the lines to be drawn between the humanitarian, the political and the economic? Third, is interference valid only in weak or weakened states or for all states without distinction?'[58]

The Security Council as a body was apparently not ready to tackle the Secretary-General's challenge. In September 1999 it held a thematic discussion on the protection of civilians in armed conflict, but most of its recommendations focused on long-term prevention, rather than considering the implications for UN peace operations faced with dealing with crimes against humanity.[59] A year later Annan expressed frustration at UN members' lack of willingness to confront the difficult issue of forcible humanitarian intervention: 'If the reaction to my address last year to the General Assembly is any guide, I fear we may still prove unable to give a credible answer to the question of what happens next time we are faced with a comparable crime against humanity'. He was even more blunt in posing the question again:

Recognition that many States have serious and legitimate concerns about intervention does not answer the question I posed in my report, namely, if humanitarian intervention is, indeed, an unacceptable assault on sovereignty, how should we respond to a Rwanda, to a Srebrenica—to gross and systematic violations of human rights that offend every precept of our common humanity? In essence the problem is one of responsibility: in circumstances in which universally accepted human rights are being violated on a massive scale we have a responsibility to act.[60]

## The Srebrenica report

In November 1999 Kofi Annan released a comprehensive report on the tragedy of Srebrenica of July 1995.[61] Unusually frank and detailed, it not only covered Srebrenica itself but traced the entire history of the 'safe areas' in the Bosnian

the face for the UN peacekeeping operations'. Danapal, G., 'PM: time to set-up a UN peace enforcement force', *New Straits Times*, 27 Oct. 1995, p. 2.

[57] Evans, G. and Sahnoun, M., 'Intervention and state sovereignty: breaking new ground', *Global Governance*, vol. 7, no. 2 (Apr./June 2001), p. 120.

[58] United Nations, General Assembly, Verbatim records (provisional), UN document A/54/PV.4, 20 Sep. 1999, p. 14.

[59] UN Security Council Resolution 1265, 17 Sep. 1999.

[60] United Nations, Report of the Secretary-General on the work of the organization, UN document A/55/1, 30 Aug. 2000, p. 5.

[61] United Nations, Report of the Secretary-General pursuant to General Assembly Resolution 53/35: the fall of Srebrenica, UN document A/54/549, 15 Nov. 1999, available on the UN Internet site at URL <http://www.un.org/peace/srebrenica.pdf>.

war. The 155-page report, compiled by two young officials in the UN Secretariat, and based on a review of classified UN cables and interviews with more than 100 officials, concluded that: 'Through error, misjudgement and inability to recognize the scope of evil confronting us, we failed to do our part to save the people of Srebrenica from the Serb campaign of mass murder'.[62]

The lessons the report drew with regard to the use of force were many. Noting that the Dutch UNPROFOR troops in Srebrenica had never shot at the attacking Serbs, but had only fired flares and warning shots over their heads, it said that if they had engaged the Serbs it was possible that events would have unfolded differently.[63] Yet the report recognized that the 150 men of Dutchbat were lightly armed and in indefensible positions, and were faced with 2000 Serbs advancing with the support of armour and artillery. It concluded that it was impossible to say with certainty that stronger action would have saved lives, and it might even have done more harm than good. The UN Secretariat, it said, had not helped the situation:

Rather than attempting to mobilize the international community, we gave the Security Council the impression that the situation was under control, and many of us believed that to be the case. The day before Srebrenica fell, we reported that the Serbs were not attacking when they were. We reported that the Bosnians had fired on UNPROFOR blocking positions when it was the Serbs. We failed to mention urgent requests for air power.[64]

The report conceded that, even according to the most restrictive interpretation of the mandate, the use of close air support against attacking Serb targets was 'clearly warranted' since the Serbs were directly firing at Dutch command posts with tank rounds as early as five days before the enclave fell.[65] In one of the report's most revealing passages, the Secretary-General explained that there were four main reasons why almost the entire UNPROFOR and UN leadership were 'deeply reluctant to use air power against the Serbs'. First, they believed the UN would be perceived as having entered the war against the Serbs, a potentially fatal step for a 'peacekeeping' operation. Second, they feared losing control over the process: 'Once the key was turned we did not know if we would be able to turn it back'. Third, they believed that air power would disrupt the primary, humanitarian, mission of UNPROFOR. Finally, they feared Serb reprisals against UN peacekeepers.

Nonetheless Annan concluded, in retrospect, that it was incumbent on the UN, its concerns notwithstanding, to make full use of air power as a deterrent. It was wrong to declare repeatedly and publicly that the UN did not want to use air power against the Serbs except as a last resort and to accept the daily shelling of the safe areas. He quotes the UNPROFOR force commander in

---

[62] Report of the Secretary-General (note 61), para. 503.
[63] Report of the Secretary-General (note 61), para. 472.
[64] Report of the Secretary-General (note 61), para. 496.
[65] Report of the Secretary-General (note 61), para. 480.

Sarajevo at the time as saying that the UN's reluctance to 'escalate the use of force' meant that the UN would then always be 'stared down by the Serbs'.[66]

The Secretary-General noted that many of the errors of the UN in Bosnia flowed from a 'single and no doubt well-intentioned effort: we tried to keep the peace and apply the rules of peacekeeping when there was no peace to keep':

Knowing that any other course of action would jeopardize the lives of our troops, we tried to create—or imagine—an environment in which the tenets of peacekeeping— agreement between the parties, deployment by consent and impartiality—could be upheld. We tried to stabilize the situation on the ground through ceasefire agreements, which brought us close to the Serbs, who controlled the larger portion of the land. We tried to eschew the use of force except in self-defence, which brought us into conflict with the defenders of the safe areas, whose safety depended on our use of force.[67]

An arms embargo, humanitarian aid and a peacekeeping force were, he said, poor substitutes for 'more decisive and forceful action to prevent the unfolding horror'. He conceded that when, in June 1995, the international community provided UNPROFOR with a heavily armed rapid reaction force, the UN Secretariat argued against using it robustly to implement the mandate.[68]

On the future use of safe areas, the Secretary-General urged that they must be truly safe and 'fully defended by a credible military deterrent'.[69] The safe areas were established by the Security Council without the consent of the parties and were neither protected areas nor safe havens in the sense of international humanitarian law, nor safe areas in any militarily meaningful sense.

On the use of force more generally, Annan concluded that the international community as a whole must accept responsibility for the prolonged refusal to use force in the early stages of the war. The Security Council, the Contact Group and other governments contributed to the delay in the use of force, as did the UN Secretariat and UNPROFOR.[70] In the case of the Secretariat, the delay was at least partly due to a failure to fully comprehend the true nature of the Serb war aims and a tendency to accord all the parties moral equivalence.

Acknowledging his own role as Under Secretary-General for Peace-keeping Operations at the time, Annan apologized for the UN's failures, concluding that: 'The cardinal lesson of Srebrenica is that a deliberate and systematic attempt to terrorize, expel or murder an entire people must be met decisively with all necessary means, and with the political will to carry the policy through to its logical conclusion'. He ended his report with a challenge to UN member states to clarify and improve the capacity of the UN to respond to such conflicts:

[66] Report of the Secretary-General (note 61), para. 483.
[67] Report of the Secretary-General (note 61), para. 488.
[68] Report of the Secretary-General (note 61), paras 490, 497.
[69] Report of the Secretary-General (note 61), para. 499.
[70] Report of the Secretary-General (note 61), para. 501. The Contact Group consisted of Russia and the USA, together with France, Germany and the UK, the 3 latter representing the European Union.

I have in mind addressing such issues as the gulf between mandate and means; the inadequacy of symbolic deterrence in the face of a systematic campaign of violence; the pervasive ambivalence within the United Nations regarding the role of force in the pursuit of peace; an institutional ideology of impartiality when confronted with attempted genocide; and a range of doctrinal and institutional issues that go to the heart of the United Nations ability to keep the peace and help protect civilian populations from armed conflict.[71]

## The UN and Organization of African Unity reports on Rwanda

In April 2000 yet another soul-searching exercise by the UN was revealed with the publication of the report of the Independent Inquiry into United Nations Actions during the 1994 Genocide in Rwanda.[72] Submitted to the Security Council by the chairman of the inquiry, former Swedish Prime Minister Ingvar Carlsson, the report blamed the UN system as a whole for the calamity, but described the lack of political will in the Security Council as the most dangerous obstacle to the UN's work in maintaining peace. It concluded that: 'Rwanda was to prove a turning point in United Nations peacekeeping, and came to symbolize a lack of political will to commit to peacekeeping, and above all, to take risks in the field'.[73]

With regard to the performance of UNAMIR and the possibility that it might have used force, the panel concluded that the mission:

was not planned, dimensioned, deployed or instructed in a way which provided for a proactive and assertive role in dealing with a peace process in serious trouble. The mission was smaller than the original recommendations from the field suggested. It was slow in being set up, and was beset by debilitating administrative difficulties. It lacked well-trained troops and functioning materiel. The mission's mandate was based on an analysis of the peace process which proved erroneous, and which was never corrected despite the significant warning signs that the original mandate had become inadequate. By the time the genocide started, the mission was not functioning as a cohesive whole; in the real hours and days of deepest crisis, consistent testimony points to a lack of political leadership, lack of military capacity, severe problems of command and control and lack of coordination and discipline.[74]

The report agreed with Dallaire and other observers that a properly constituted and mandated force of 2500 'should have been able to stop or at least limit' the massacres'.[75] It asserted that, faced with genocide, the UN had 'an obligation to act which transcended traditional principles of peacekeeping'.[76] In its most notable break with past thinking, it enunciated what previously had

---

[71] Report of the Secretary-General (note 61), paras 502, 506.

[72] United Nations, Report of the Independent Inquiry into the Actions of the United Nations during the 1994 Genocide in Rwanda, UN document S/1999/1257, 15 Dec. 1999, p. 17 (published in Apr. 2000). The other members of the inquiry were Han Sung-Joo, former foreign minister of South Korea, and Lt-Gen. Rufus M. Kupolati of Nigeria.

[73] Report of the Independent Inquiry (note 72), p. 26.

[74] Report of the Independent Inquiry (note 72), p. 22.

[75] Report of the Independent Inquiry (note 72), p. 22.

[76] Report of the Independent Inquiry (note 72), p. 38.

only been implied—that, regardless of its mandate, a UN peacekeeping operation must be prepared to 'respond to the perception and the expectation of protection created by its very presence'.

The inquiry recommended a range of reforms to improve UN peacekeeping, most of which had been made countless times before. The most important relating to the use of force were: improved protection of civilians in conflict situations; clearer rules of engagement; a more effective flow of information within the UN system and to the Security Council; and coordination of national evacuation operations with UN missions on the ground.

In July 2000 an International Panel of Eminent Personalities to Investigate the 1994 Genocide in Rwanda and the Surrounding Events, mandated by the Organization of African Unity (OAU) rather than the UN, reported on its findings. It concluded that for genocide to be avoided, 'all that was required was a reasonable-sized international military force with a strong mandate to enforce the Arusha agreement'.[77] Yet, while claiming that the Security Council, 'led unremittingly by the United States, simply did not care enough about Rwanda to intervene appropriately', it was vague in its recommendations about how to prevent such tragedies in future. Far from endorsing peace enforcement or humanitarian intervention, it focused on the UN Secretary-General's role in promoting early conflict resolution, undoubtedly reflecting African states' concerns about their sovereignty and interference by outside powers.

As a result of the UN report Kofi Annan apologized for the second time in a year for the UN's actions, including his own personal role: 'There was a United Nations force in [Rwanda] at the time, but it was neither mandated nor equipped for the kind of forceful action which would have been needed to prevent or halt the genocide'. In a revealing conclusion he stated that: 'Both reports—my own on Srebrenica and that of the Independent Inquiry on Rwanda—reflect a profound determination to present the truth about these calamities. Of all my aims as Secretary-General, there is none to which I feel more deeply committed than that of enabling the United Nations never again to fail in protecting a civilian population from genocide or mass slaughter'.[78]

## IV. The Brahimi Report

As the Sierra Leone mission was beginning to unravel, revealing again how little progress had been made, Kofi Annan promised in his Millennial Report of March 2000 that he would establish a high-level panel to review all aspects of

---

[77] Organization of African Unity, Executive Summary, Report of the International Panel of Eminent Personalities to Investigate the 1994 Genocide in Rwanda and the Surrounding Events, Addis Ababa, 11 July 2000, para. E.S.33, available on the OAU Internet site, URL <http://www.oau-oua.org/ipip/report/rwanda-e>.

[78] United Nations, Secretary-General, 'Statement on receiving the report of the Independent Inquiry into the Actions of the United Nations during the 1994 genocide in Rwanda', New York, 16 Dec. 1999, available on the United Nations Internet site at URL <http://www.un.org/news/ossg/sgsm_rwanda.htm>.

peace operations, from the doctrinal to the logistical.[79] Highlighting the 'structural weakness' of UN peacekeeping, he said that comparing it to a volunteer fire department was 'too generous': 'Every time there is a fire, we must first find fire engines and the funds to run them before we can start dousing any flames'.[80] While Annan did not call for a UN peace enforcement doctrine to emerge from this review, Under Secretary-General for Peace-keeping Operations Bernard Myet in the same month told the General Assembly's Special Committee on Peacekeeping Operations that there was a need for 'clarity as to whether peacekeeping or *peace enforcement* was needed in a specific situation' and—implying that the UN could do either—'the provision of commensurate resources for each'.[81]

The Panel on United Nations Peace Operations was convened in March 2000. Headed by former Algerian Foreign Minister Lakhdar Brahimi, it undertook 200 interviews, visited the latest UN operation (the UN Mission in Kosovo, UNMIK), and held discussions with every UN department.[82] Its findings, popularly known as the Brahimi Report, presented in August 2000, constituted the most far-reaching examination of UN peacekeeping in its history.[83] Reinforcing the conclusions of the Rwanda and Srebrenica reports, it set about demolishing some of the long-cherished UN notions about peacekeeping.

While conceding that 'there are many tasks which United Nations peacekeeping forces should not be asked to undertake and many places they should not go', it declared that when the UN does send its forces to uphold the peace 'they must be prepared to confront the lingering forces of war and violence, with the ability and determination to defeat them'. Although force alone could only create the space in which peace may be built, no amount of good intentions could substitute, it said, for the 'fundamental ability to project credible force if complex peacekeeping, in particular, is to succeed'.[84]

While Brahimi adhered throughout his report to the safe term 'peacekeeping', his use of the adjectives 'robust' and 'complex' could be read as a euphemism for peace enforcement—a term he was keen to avoid lest the controversies surrounding it detract from his essential message that peace operations of all types needed a substantial overhauling.

Brahimi reiterated that the traditional principles of consent, impartiality and the use of force only in self-defence should remain the 'bedrock' of peace operations. However, since experience showed that in intra-state conflicts consent

[79] United Nations, 'We the peoples: the role of the United Nations in the twenty-first century', Report of the Secretary-General, UN document A/54/2000, 27 Mar. 2000, para. 227.

[80] 'We the peoples' (note 79), para. 224.

[81] Quoted in United Nations, Comprehensive review of the whole question of peacekeeping operations in all their aspects: report of the Special Committee on Peacekeeping Operations, UN document A/54/839, 20 Mar. 2000, p. 2. Emphasis added.

[82] Its members were international experts in peacekeeping, peace-building, development and humanitarian assistance: Brian Atwood, Colin Granderson, Ann Hercus, Richard Monk, Laus Naumann, Hisako Shimura, Vladimir Shustov, Philip Sibanda and Cornelio Sommaruga.

[83] United Nations, Report of the Panel on United Nations Peace Operations, UN document A/55/305, S/2000/809, 21 Aug. 2000 (the Brahimi Report).

[84] Report of the Panel on United Nations Peace Operations (note 83), p. viii.

could be manipulated, the other two principles had to be adapted accordingly. Impartiality had to mean adherence to the principles of the UN Charter, rather than continuing to treat all parties as if they were morally equivalent: to do otherwise 'can in the best case result in ineffectiveness and in the worst may amount to complicity with evil'. The report concluded that: 'No failure did more to damage the standing and credibility of United Nations peacekeeping in the 1990s than its reluctance to distinguish victim from aggressor'.[85] The Secretariat must tell the Security Council what it needed to hear, not what it wanted to hear, and the Council must anticipate worst-case scenarios and plan accordingly.

## The use of force

The panel urged that, once deployed, UN military units must be capable of defending themselves, other mission components and the mission's mandate. ROE should be 'sufficiently robust and not force UN contingents to cede the initiative to their attackers'. Mandates should specify an operation's authority to use force. ROE should not limit contingents to 'stroke-for-stroke' responses but allow 'ripostes sufficient to silence a source of deadly fire'. UN forces should be bigger and better equipped and become 'a credible deterrent threat, in contrast to the symbolic and non-threatening presence that characterizes traditional peacekeeping'. Brahimi advocated that: 'UN forces for complex operations should be sized and configured so as to leave no doubt in the minds of would-be spoilers as to which of the two approaches [traditional or complex] the Organization has adopted'.[86]

With Rwanda and Srebrenica obviously in mind, the report proposed that UN peacekeepers, whether troops or police, who witness violence against civilians should be presumed to be authorized, within their means, to stop it. Hence the conclusion that Dag Hammarskjöld had reached four decades previously was finally becoming mainstream thinking. The panel reiterated the Rwanda report's conclusion that such action should be consistent with 'the perception and the expectation of protection created by [an operation's] very presence'.[87]

## Reforms to enhance military effectiveness

Among the many sensible reform proposals that the panel made, which would improve all aspects of UN peace operations, several would enhance the UN's ability to use force. To ensure more 'robust' peacekeeping forces the report recommended that the existing limited UNSAS be augmented by incorporating several coherent, multinational, brigade-sized forces, created jointly by member states. Minimum training, equipment and other standards should be enforced for contingents offered and unsatisfactory offers rejected. To ensure more rapid

---

[85] Report of the Panel on United Nations Peace Operations (note 83), p. ix.
[86] Report of the Panel on United Nations Peace Operations (note 83), paras 50, 49, 51.
[87] Report of the Panel on United Nations Peace Operations (note 83), para. 62.

deployment of a capable headquarters to the field, an Integrated Mission Task Force (IMTF) should be established to coordinate planning and support for each new mission, involving all relevant parts of the UN Secretariat and other UN agencies; UNSAS should include lists of well-qualified military officers available for duty on seven days' notice to translate broad 'strategic-level' mission concepts developed at UN Headquarters into concrete operational and tactical plans in advance of troop deployments; rosters of potential SRSGs and other senior civilian staff should be established; and the mission leadership should be assembled in New York for planning, briefing and training prior to deployment.

To ensure better availability of timely intelligence information, there should be established, under the Secretary-General's Executive Committee on Peace and Security (ECPS), an ECPS Information and Strategic Analysis Secretariat (EISAS). It would enable peace operations to exchange strategic information within the entire UN system.[88]

## Defining rapid deployment

For the first time in UN history the Brahimi Report attempted to define what 'rapid and effective deployment' of UN peace operations would realistically entail. Arguing that the first 6–12 weeks after a ceasefire or peace accord are 'often the most critical period for establishing both a stable peace and the credibility of the peacekeepers', it proposed that the UN develop the operational capabilities to fully deploy 'traditional' peacekeeping operations within 30 days of the adoption of a Security Council resolution, and 'complex' peacekeeping operations within 90 days.[89] In the case of the latter, the mission headquarters should be fully installed and functioning within 15 days (this would amount to implementation of the 'vanguard' headquarters deployment concept long advocated by Canada[90]).

However, the panel recognized the obstacles to meeting even these relatively long lead times. Ironically, its call for stricter standards for peacekeepers, including better-selected and better-prepared force commanders and SRSGs, might mean slower rather than faster deployment, as the UN would be likely to struggle even more than it does now to enlist suitable personnel. According to

---

[88] The ECPS, which was meant to coordinate UN agencies involved in peace operations, is chaired by the Under Secretary-General for Political Affairs and consists of: the departments of peace-keeping operations and disarmament affairs; the offices of the Coordinator for Humanitarian Affairs, the Special Representative for Children and Armed Conflict, and the Legal Counsel (OLA); the UN high commissioners for human rights and refugees; the UN Development Programme (UNDP); and the UN Children's Fund (UNICEF). The World Food Programme (WFP) is considering joining. United Nations, Implementation of the recommendations of the Special Committee on Peacekeeping Operations and the Panel on United Nations Peace Operations, Report of the Secretary-General, UN document A/55/977, 1 June 2001, p. 52. It has reportedly not been working as well as intended.

[89] Report of the Panel on United Nations Peace Operations (note 83), paras 87–88.

[90] Government of Canada, *Towards a Rapid Reaction Capability for the United Nations* (Government of Canada: Ottawa, Sep. 1995). For background see Cox, D. and Legault, A. (eds), *UN Rapid Reaction Capabilities: Requirements and Prospects* (Lester B. Pearson Canadian International Peacekeeping Training Centre: Clementsport, 1995). For analysis of the Canadian proposal's fate see Fergusson, J. and Levesque, B., 'The best laid plans: Canada's proposal for a United Nations rapid reaction capability', *International Journal*, vol. 52, no. 1 (winter 1996/97).

one Secretariat official, the assumption was that in dire emergencies a 'coalition of the willing' would be deployed first, to be followed by a UN force once it was organized.[91]

## Headquarters planning and support

The Brahimi Report recognized, too, the need for a major upgrading of the UN Secretariat's capacity to plan and support peace operations. To be fair, this had been improving for some time. The US General Accounting Office (GAO) reported in May 2000 that reforms in the structure and management of UN Headquarters had resulted in better operational plans for new peace operations. The plan for East Timor, which included 'all anticipated activities' and 'considered overall logistical needs', had, the GAO concluded, 'resulted in deploying the mission more quickly and with fewer problems than past operations of comparable size and complexity'.[92]

Despite the undoubted improvements that had already been made, Brahimi realized that the DPKO would have to acquire the capabilities of at least a medium-sized country's national military headquarters if it were to have any chance of deploying and managing more 'complex' missions. It was plainly not sufficient to have just 32 officers providing military planning and guidance for 27 000 troops in the field; 9 civilian police staff to identify, vet and provide guidance for up to 8000 police; and 15 political desk officers for 14 current operations and 2 new ones. Nor was it realistic to allocate just 1.25 per cent of the total costs of peacekeeping to Headquarters administrative and logistics staff.[93] Noting that the DPKO and related Headquarters staff were expected in 2001 to administer more than $2 billion-worth of peacekeeping with an administrative budget of just $50 million, the report asked the Secretary-General to submit a budget proposal to the General Assembly estimating fully the organization's requirements: a historical review would suggest that there needed to be a near-doubling of the resources allocated to UN Headquarters—$70 million as a baseline and up to $24 million extra to permit 'surge' activity.[94]

## The need for a peace enforcement doctrine sidestepped

Notwithstanding all the eminently practical suggestions in the report, it did not explicitly recommend a new type of UN operation, whether called 'peace enforcement' or not. Although its list of contents indicated that it would discuss the implications of its recommendations for UN peacekeeping 'doctrine', the

[91] Discussion with DPKO official, UN Headquarters, New York, 5 Feb. 2001.

[92] US General Accounting Office (GAO), 'United Nations: reform initiatives have strengthened operations, but overall objectives have not yet been achieved', Report to Congressional requesters, GAO/NSIAD-00-150, Washington, DC, 10 May 2000, p. 9. The success of the East Timor mission may also have been the result of the prior deployment of INTERFET, which bequeathed much of its experience and capacity to the UN follow-on operation.

[93] Report of the Panel on United Nations Peace Operations (note 83), p. xiii.

[94] Report of the Panel on United Nations Peace Operations (note 83), paras 194–95.

report in fact did not do so. It did recommend a long-overdue 'new doctrinal approach to civilian police operations' that would emphasize protection and promotion of human rights,[95] but nowhere did it recommend the development of a comprehensive new peace operations doctrine.

Instead it fudged the issue of doctrine, preferring to focus on capabilities and readiness, presumably in anticipation of opposition from some developing countries to any doctrinal excursions or even to the expression 'peace enforcement'. John Mackinlay was among those who criticized the report for this alleged 'lack of vision', comparing it unfavourably to the doctrinal development that has taken place in national militaries.[96]

Reading between the lines, however, Brahimi's advocacy of more robust, rapidly deployable forces with deterrent capabilities amounted to a call for a UN peace enforcement capability in all but name. While his report said that the UN 'does not wage war' (which was to be left to 'coalitions of willing states' authorized by the Security Council under Chapter VII),[97] he was deliberately vague as to whether the UN could be made capable of 'waging' peace enforcement—but his report suggested that it might.

## V. Beyond Brahimi

After Annan presented the Brahimi Report to the General Assembly and the Security Council on 21 August 2000, various parts of the UN system began digesting, commenting on and implementing parts of the recommendations, albeit not without controversy and delay.

### The Security Council

The Security Council welcomed the report, expressed broad support and pledged to deal expeditiously with the matters that fell within its area of responsibility.[98] It established a Working Group on Peacekeeping Operations, which began by examining the Security Council's relationship with troop-contributing countries in mandating, deploying and managing peace operations.[99] In June 2001 the Security Council announced a new format for involving the Secretariat in the planning of peace operations,[100] and this was inaugurated on 10 September 2001 with a meeting between the Security Council, the UN Secretariat and troop contributors to the UN Mission in Ethiopia and Eritrea (UNMEE).[101]

---

[95] Report of the Panel on United Nations Peace Operations (note 83), para. 119.

[96] Mackinlay, J., 'Mission failure', *World Today*, vol. 56, no. 11 (Nov. 2000), p. 9.

[97] Report of the Panel on United Nations Peace Operations (note 83), para. 5.3.

[98] UN Security Council Resolution 1318, 7 Sep. 2000.

[99] Ambassador Curtis Ward, Representative of Jamaica to the UN Security Council, presentation at the Joint FCO-UNA Seminar on Steps towards Implementation of Conflict Prevention and the Brahimi Report, Lancaster House, London, 28 Mar. 2001.

[100] UN Security Council Resolution 1353, 13 June 2001.

[101] United Nations, Implementation of the recommendations of the Special Committee on Peacekeeping Operations and the Panel on United Nations Peace Operations: report of the Secretary-General, UN document A/56/732, 21 Dec. 2001, p. 4. In Jan. 2002 the Council announced that it would inaugurate periodic joint meetings of its working group and troop-contributing countries to discuss specific aspects of

Other Security Council initiatives included a resolution on 13 November 2000 agreeing to give future missions clear, credible and achievable mandates, including when necessary 'deterrent credibility'.[102] It also discussed the issue of the closure of operations and the importance of ensuring a smooth transition from the conflict phase of peace operations to the post-conflict phase.[103] The Security Council's support for Brahimi no doubt reflected its own sobering experiences in attempting conflict prevention, management and resolution.[104]

### The Secretary-General

Describing the Brahimi Report as 'far-reaching yet sensible and practical',[105] Kofi Annan quickly asked the UN Secretariat to consider how the recommendations might be implemented. On 20 October 2000 he presented a report on the steps taken so far and the additional steps needed.[106] In his opening remarks he noted that the Brahimi Report did not address the question whether the UN should become involved in specific situations, but rather how it could improve its performance once a decision to undertake an operation had been taken. He stressed that Brahimi's recommendations regarding the use of force applied only to operations in which armed UN peacekeepers had deployed with the consent of the parties concerned. He added:

I . . . do not interpret any portions of the Panel's report as a recommendation to turn the United Nations into a fighting machine or to fundamentally change the principles according to which peacekeepers use force. The Panel's recommendations for clear mandates, 'robust' rules of engagement, and bigger and better equipped forces must be seen in that light. They are practical measures to achieve deterrence through strength, with the ultimate purpose of diminishing, not increasing, the likelihood for the need to use force, which should always be seen as a measure of last resort.[107]

Notably, he skirted the issue of whether the UN should explicitly engage in peace enforcement.

Annan seemed to agree with almost all the Brahimi Report's recommendations. The one subject on which he appeared sceptical was that of defining 'rapid and effective deployment capacities'. While noting that the 30- and 90-day standards proposed by Brahimi were 'ambitious', he recalled that the Security Council had asked the Secretariat to fully deploy the UN Mission in the Central African Republic (MINURCA) in less than three weeks and had

peacekeeping, in addition to its normal meetings with troop-contributing countries. United Nations, Note by President of the Security Council, UN document S/2002/56, 14 Jan. 2002.

[102] UN Security Council Resolution 1327, 13 Nov. 2000.

[103] UN Press release SC/6951, 15 Nov. 2000.

[104] Ambassador Curtis Ward (note 99).

[105] United Nations, Identical letters dated 21 August 2000 from the Secretary-General to the President of the General Assembly and the President of the Security Council, UN document A/55/305, S/2000/809, 21 Aug. 2000, p. 1.

[106] United Nations, Report of the Secretary-General on the implementation of the report of the Panel on United Nations Peace Operations, UN document A/55/502, 20 Oct. 2000.

[107] Report of the Secretary-General (note 106), p. 3.

applied similar time pressures to the deployment of UNAMET in East Timor. Peace processes, he noted, were often most fragile in the initial phases and the UN should be able to deploy operations when they can make the greatest contribution. Pointing out that many of Brahimi's proposals could not be implemented because of staff and resource limitations, the Secretary-General requested emergency funding for the UN Secretariat for 2000–2001.

In his only explicit reference to the development of doctrine, Annan suggested enhanced capacity for the Lessons Learned Unit (which had been criticized as ineffective and whose name was promptly changed to the Peacekeeping Best Practices Unit) to enable 'development of multidimensional doctrine, guidelines, and standard operating procedures, as well as sharing of "best practices" between missions'.[108] Having been himself a victim of the absence of timely information in making life-and-death decisions over Bosnia, Rwanda and Sierra Leone, including in relation to the use of force, he strongly supported Brahimi's recommendation to establish an Information and Strategic Analysis Secretariat, proposing to do so as early as January 2001. In what proved to be a vain attempt to head off non-aligned opposition to the idea, he denied that it would constitute an 'intelligence-gathering capacity'.[109]

### The commissioned management report on implementing Brahimi

In June 2001 Annan presented the first ever 'in-depth and comprehensive managerial examination of the way in which the Organization plans, deploys, conducts and supports peacekeeping operations'.[110] Marking a significant departure for the UN, it was prepared with the help of external management consultants. In an attempt to ensure that the views of developing countries were considered, or at least to avoid accusations that they had not been consulted, an External Review Board was formed to review the report made up of experts from Argentina, Canada, Egypt, Finland, Germany, Ghana, India, Iran, Jordan, Mali, Pakistan and Switzerland, all of them with current or past close involvement in UN peacekeeping either at Headquarters or in the field. Even though it was essentially a management report, it held significant implications for the use-of-force issue.

Its most important findings in this respect related to rapid and effective deployment capacities (see figure 9.1). The report described the challenge of deploying UN peace operations within 30–90 days as 'considerable'.[111] In assessing the feasibility of various options it assumed that most contingents would require all of their strategic lift and most of their service support to be provided by the UN, while civilian and CivPol components would require all their support from the UN. In order to generate comparative analyses, two different types of missions were hypothesized—traditional and complex.

---

[108] Report of the Secretary-General (note 106), p. 26.
[109] Report of the Secretary-General (note 106), p. 10.
[110] Implementation of the recommendations (note 88).
[111] Implementation of the recommendations (note 88), p. 22.

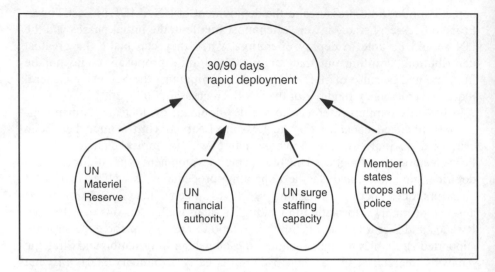

**Figure 9.1.** Rapid deployment

*Source*: United Nations, Implementation of the recommendations of the Special Committee on Peacekeeping Operations and the Panel on United Nations Peace Operations, report of the Secretary-General, UN document A/55/977, 1 June 2001, annex D, p. 23.

A traditional mission was assumed to consist of approximately 5000 troops (50 per cent self-sustaining), 100 'substantive' staff, 200 military observers and CivPols and 200 administrative staff (international and local). A complex mission was hypothesized to consist of 10 000 troops (25 per cent self-sustaining), 300 substantive staff, 1000 military observers and CivPols, and 1000 administrative staff (international and local). It was also assumed that these missions would be deployed in areas with limited local infrastructure and launched at a frequency of one traditional and one complex mission per year.

On the basis of these assumptions, the report set out three options for achieving the 30-to-90-day deployment goal. This was based almost entirely on the establishment of strategic reserves of equipment and *matériel* at the UN Logistics Base at Brindisi, Italy. Option 1 was a heavy strategic reserve: the UN would acquire and store all its *matériel* for a complex mission. Option 2 was a light strategic reserve, supported by sustained annual funding of extensive retainer servicing agreements and 'letters of assist'.[112] Option 3 was a medium strategic reserve which would combine the two first. The third option was recommended, costing $170 million 'up front' and $40 million annually in recurring costs. In addition, the report recommended prearranged contracts and letters of assist for key services; increased reliability of standby arrangements with member states, especially for support units; improved personnel 'surge' capacity, especially for administrative support staff; and pre-commitment

---

[112] These are letters to the UN from member states or groups of states which promise in advance to provide certain types of assistance and/or equipment at the time required in order to help contingents from other countries to deploy.

**Table 9.1.** Mission support requirements for effective deployment

| Types of support | Materials/services | Personnel |
| --- | --- | --- |
| Requirements | Strategic air/sea lift<br>Vehicles, tracked and wheeled<br>Communications, IT services<br>Power generators<br>General engineering services<br>Office equipment<br>Water, fuel, rations | Formed units (infantry, support)<br>Military observers<br>Police contingents<br>Political and related 'substantive' staff<br>Administrative staff<br>  – logistics, communications, procure-<br>  ment, contracts management, recruit-<br>  ment, personnel administration |
| Means of<br>delivery | Strategic Reserve (UNLB Brindisi)<br>LOAs<br>Service contracts (logcap)<br>Fast track acquisition/procurement<br>Pre-mission commitment authority<br>Post-mission financial authorities | Standby arrangements for troops and<br>  support units<br>Standby arrangements for police<br>Core surge rosters for staff (DPKO,<br>  field missions)<br>Expanded surge rosters (agencies)<br>Member states and other sources |

*Note*: UNLB = UN Logistics Base. LOA = Letter of assist.

*Source*: United Nations, Implementation of the recommendations of the Special Committee on Peacekeeping Operations and the Panel on United Nations Peace Operations, report of the Secretary-General, UN document A/55/977, 1 June 2001, annex D, p. 23.

spending authority before the adoption of a resolution establishing an operation. These measures would enable the UN, the report said, to 'go a long way' in ensuring not only that the military component of an operation could be rapidly deployed but that there would be an effective civilian and police structure established in parallel. However, the report cautioned that none of the options would guarantee 30-to-90-day deployment, as this could only be achieved by 'fully self-sustaining and completely self-sufficient troops provided by Member States with the means to do so'.[113]

Other proposed reforms that would affect the ability of a UN force to use force, at least in self-defence and the defence of its mission, included: the completion of the 'myriad' of policies, SOP, systems and training programmes 'which are critical for efficient and effective performance in the field'; additional resources to permit better interaction between the DPKO and member states, especially troop, CivPol and financial contributors; and enhancement of public information efforts in the field (which could help avoid misunderstandings about the UN's intentions and thus avoid dangerous incidents leading to the use of force). For the UN Secretariat itself, the report recommended the addition of 150 posts to the DPKO and others on a case-by-case basis, many of which would enhance the UN's ability to act as a military headquarters. Major structural reorganization of the DPKO was also proposed, including expansion

---

[113] Implementation of the recommendations (note 88), p. 26.

of the management structure for CivPol operations. In response to the Special Committee on Peacekeeping Operations' opposition to the establishment of a large strategic information analysis unit, the report, clearly regretfully, proposed a small, multidisciplinary policy and analysis unit, half the size of the proposed EISAS.[114] Absurdly, it would not absorb the information technology, cartographic and media monitoring capabilities of the Department of Information as originally planned.

The report was a major advance in the history of UN peacekeeping reports in openly and honestly assessing, for the first time, the managerial and logistical difficulties facing the UN in rapidly deploying peace operations—whatever their mandate. It brought into stark relief the fact that member states would have not only to contribute more financially to expand the UN's own capacity but also to provide better-quality and self-sustaining military forces themselves if they expected peace operations to work better.

The report did not, however, directly address the question of the ability of UN peace operations to use force. Clearly, a 'complex' operation of at least 10 000 troops, supplied with the 'heavy strategic reserve', would have the greatest chance of being effective in deploying quickly and robustly and in acting as a deterrent once it began arriving in force. However, the report did not consider military capability per se, only the deployment and maintenance of an operational military force in the field. This could presumably be the foundation on which both defensive and offensive capabilities would be built. Heavy weaponry, including tanks, attack helicopters, artillery and fighter aircraft, would have to be provided by the more militarily sophisticated member states, as it had been in the past, and so would the necessarily specialized communications, command and control personnel, and structures to permit the use of such weapons.

One of the report's flaws was that its definition of 'effective deployment'—minimum operational capability required for a mission to begin implementing its mandate—begged too many questions to be helpful. How 'complex' was the mandate? What was the size of the territory to be covered? How many and how well armed were the belligerent parties? Perhaps most importantly, how likely was it that force might have to be used beyond self-defence?

The report concluded by pointing out that the past 50 years of UN peacekeeping had demonstrated that the instrument was not 'a temporary aberration'. It was necessary therefore to invest in future capability and leave behind the days of 'gifted amateurism', so that 'the likelihood of peacekeeping success substantially increases'.[115]

## The General Assembly

To consider the Brahimi Report the General Assembly convened an extraordinary session of the Special Committee on Peacekeeping Operations from

---

[114] Implementation of the recommendations (note 88), p. 51.
[115] Implementation of the recommendations (note 88), p. 4.

30 October to 4 December 2001, during which a working group chaired by Canada dissected the report in detail.[116] There were sharp differences of opinion over several use-of-force issues. Non-aligned members, for instance, rejected the idea of creating a unit in the DPKO with the word 'doctrine' in its title.[117] At the behest of these members the committee also asked the UN Secretariat to provide clarification of its intention to develop a 'military doctrine', a term it said was 'open to several interpretations, thus causing concern'.[118] There was also 'extreme opposition' by developing countries to the Secretariat's being allowed to establish EISAS, on the predictable grounds that this would necessitate intelligence-gathering.[119]

A number of the Brahimi Report's recommendations were, however, accepted—including, perhaps surprisingly, the need to set and enforce standards for contributing countries, the non-aligned countries demanding only that Western contributions be subject to the same scrutiny as theirs. The committee also approved 93 new posts in the DPKO 'to give the Secretariat the oxygen it needed'[120] and agreed that troop-contributing countries would be involved in formulating mandates and concepts of operation and in changing them when necessary, especially when increased use of force was envisaged.[121]

## Political opposition to the Brahimi recommendations

The developing countries' resistance to key Brahimi recommendations appears to be due to several factors. They include: (*a*) a concern that the attention being given to peacekeeping reform might distract the UN from other high-priority issues, especially economic and social development, and more specifically a fear that the UN's general and development budgets might be affected by the costs of peacekeeping reform (peacekeeping being seen, paradoxically, as the agenda of the 'North', while development is the agenda of the 'South'); (*b*) resentment at perceived Western dominance of the peacekeeping reform process; (*c*) a fear that changes in UN peacekeeping might facilitate the establishment of a 'UN army' and a more interventionist norm; (*d*) a concern that Western peace enforcement doctrine might be imposed on the UN, leading to greater use of force, in which troops from developing countries would be used as 'cannon fodder'; and (*e*) more cynically, a calculation that non-aligned approval of or acquiescence in Western countries' demands for peacekeeping reform might be traded for concessions in other areas.[122]

---

[116] United Nations, Comprehensive review of the whole question of peacekeeping operations in all their aspects, Report of the Special Committee on Peacekeeping Operations, UN document A/C.4/55/6, 4 Dec. 2000.

[117] Personal communication with a DPKO official, UN Headquarters, New York, 5 Feb. 2001.

[118] Comprehensive review of the whole question of peacekeeping operations (note 116), para. 45.

[119] Ambassador Curtis Ward (note 99).

[120] 'Peacekeeping reform soldiers on', *UN Chronicle*, no. 4 (2000/2001), p. 46.

[121] Comprehensive review of the whole question of peacekeeping operations (note 116), p. 2.

[122] Some of these are suggested in Dwan, R., 'Armed conflict prevention, management and resolution', *SIPRI Yearbook 2001: Armaments, Disarmament and International Security* (Oxford University Press: Oxford, 2001), p. 74. Even the NGO community was divided, reflecting the divisions between states. The

There also seems to be a fear that higher professional standards for peace-keeping leadership positions and troops contributed might lead to developing countries' forces being excluded from even traditional peacekeeping. For many developing countries the provision of abundant military manpower to peace-keeping is one of the few substantive contributions they can afford to make to international affairs. It increases their influence and involvement and, as in the case of countries like Bangladesh and Fiji, it can be financially profitable.

Finally, there seems to be a lack of familiarity among developing country delegations with modern, 'best practice' planning and management concepts—invariably Western—which are increasingly being applied to peacekeeping reform. This may be viewed as threatening the influence on peace operations policy of the 'legislative' organs of the UN, where the developing countries have a majority (including in the Special Committee and the General Assembly itself) in favour of what is seen as a Western-dominated Secretariat.

Canadian Ambassador Michael Duval, Chairman of the Special Committee on Peacekeeping Operations, bluntly described non-aligned fears about the process as 'illogical'.[123] Indeed, some key self-appointed spokespersons for the non-aligned countries, such as Algeria, Cuba, India, Malaysia and Pakistan, are among the states which participate most often in peace operations and would benefit most from greater effectiveness and efficiency, including in the areas of improved doctrine, ROE, training, planning and management. Malaysia and Pakistan, for instance, had several peacekeepers killed in Somalia as a result of bad management of the use of force. Those states which might experience a peace enforcement operation on their own territory—the African countries—seem by and large to be most keen on improving the UN's ability to deploy them. This was certainly true in the Democratic Republic of the Congo (DRC), Rwanda and Sierra Leone cases.

There are undoubtedly unspoken fears on the part of a number of the non-aligned countries that they might one day be 'victims' of a UN peace enforce-ment operation. India, for instance, tends to view any issue of foreign inter-ventionism through the prism of Kashmir and its outright opposition to any foreign involvement there. China, which is also wary of radical peace opera-tions reform, regularly abstains in votes on Security Council resolutions that mandate the use of force beyond self-defence 'in any conflict that could be construed as having an internal dimension', but has not vetoed them.[124] Being extremely sensitive about the possibility of external interference in its own internal affairs, especially in relation to Tibet, and over Taiwan, China is

Millennial Forum for NGOs, held in New York on 22–26 May 2000, reflected these divisions between states, partly as a result of the presence of non-independent NGOs which are essentially a front for their governments. While declaring that national sovereignty and the prohibition on the use of force, as set out in the UN Charter, must be respected, the forum recommended that the General Assembly 'set up a broad commission to analyse standards for forceful action in cases where crimes or genocide are committed'. United Nations, 'We the peoples: Millennium Forum declaration and agenda for action. Strengthening the United Nations for the twenty-first century', in UN document A/54/959, 8 Aug. 2000, para. B.7.

[123] 'Peacekeeping reform soldiers on' (note 120), p. 46.

[124] Ruggie (note 48), pp. 15–16.

worried that any UN peace operations doctrine, including one that envisaged peace enforcement, would legitimize UN action against it. Even though this could never happen because of China's Security Council veto, China undoubtedly wants to avoid the humiliation of international pressure to permit such an operation on its territory on the basis of precedents set elsewhere.

On the other hand, while keen to make peace operations more effective and efficient and to expand the UN repertoire to encompass peace enforcement, the Western states (with the exception of the UK) exhibit the greatest reluctance to become involved themselves in 'complex' UN peace operations, especially in Africa, and especially if there is a possibility of peace enforcement being involved. The debates over the size and nature of the UN missions in Sierra Leone and the DRC in 2000 are evidence of this.[125] Western states are even reluctant to support multinational operations led by developing states which they believe are incapable of such leadership, presumably on the grounds that they may be forced to bail out a failing mission that they originally sanctioned. Such concern was evident in Western unwillingness to support an offer by Senegal to lead an operation in Congo-Brazzaville in 1997.[126]

## Current developments

By early 2002 there was further heartening progress towards implementation of the Brahimi Report, although also some continuing difficulties. The new Under Secretary-General for Peace-keeping Operations, Jean-Marie Guéhenno, told the Special Committee in February that, while a DPKO Change Management Group had begun work on projects to implement the recommendations, the process was 'still too slow and not always smooth'.[127]

Among the most important developments for the use-of-force issue were continuing attempts to strengthen the UN's rapid deployment capability. Consultations were continuing on the proposed Strategic Deployment Stock (SDS) of military equipment at Brindisi, but there were continuing disagreements over its size, equipment lists and the attendant financial requirements and methodologies; nonetheless the DPKO announced that once the budget was approved it would begin immediately to assemble the SDS with the aim of having it fully deployable by the end of 2002 or early 2003. A generic mission headquarters structure has been created in the DPKO requiring approximately 100 military officers deployable on seven days' notice.[128] A 'surge roster' of key administrative staff essential for the rapid and effective start-up of new missions has

---

[125] Rwanda, South Africa and Uganda were all pressing the Security Council to permit the UN Observer Force in the Democratic Republic of Congo (MONUC) to engage in forcible disarmament if necessary. 'Africans ask UN to disarm rebel groups in Congo', *International Herald Tribune*, 14 Feb. 2000, p. 6.

[126] Findlay, T., 'Armed conflict prevention, management and resolution', *SIPRI Yearbook 1998: Armaments, Disarmament and International Security* (Oxford University Press: Oxford, 1998), p. 36.

[127] United Nations, 'Under-Secretary-General for Peacekeeping Operations tells Special Committee operations must deploy credibly, rapidly to succeed', Press release GA/PK/174, 11 Feb. 2002, p. 1.

[128] Implementation of the recommendations (note 101), p. 6.

been established. The DPKO is in the process of establishing a standby arrange-ment for strategic airlift capacity in the form of letters of assist from member states which possess such aircraft, which could be activated on an 'as required' basis (this method was chosen after the aircraft industry confirmed that it was the quickest option).[129] Finally, with regard to strategic sea lift, the DPKO was once again proposing a memorandum of understanding with the World Food Programme which could respond quickly as necessary.

Improvements were also under way to mission planning processes. The Office of Mission Support has developed a mission planning template which outlines the planning and preparation process for mission deployment at both Headquarters and field level. A Strategic Manual for Multidimensional Peace-keeping Operations is being developed, comprising a volume on policy in a number of critical areas and a companion volume on guidelines and SOP.

Other positive developments included the following. First, the capacity of the DPKO itself has been significantly supplemented, exceeding the Brahimi rec-ommendations: in addition to the 92 new posts in the DPKO created in 2000, another 91 were approved in 2001, with an additional 30 posts in other depart-ments at UN Headquarters dealing with peace operations. Second, a Mission Orientation Programme (MOP) was devised in 2001 and the first MOP course was scheduled (although postponed because of 'operational constraints'). Third, a project is under way to update the methodology used by the DPKO for learning lessons and applying them in the planning and management of opera-tions.[130] Fourth, pre-deployment training assessment standards are being developed in consultation with member states in a series of workshops being held in 2002, after which initial assessment of contingents prior to deployment (to improve standards) will begin.[131] Finally, Standardised Generic Training Modules (SGTMs) for use by member states in training their prospective peacekeepers have been issued in 2002 by the DPKO's Training and Evaluation Service (TES).[132] The modules include sections on ROE and the use of force. Finally, Guideline Standard Operating Procedures for Peace-keeping Opera-tions (GSOP-PKO) have been issued.[133]

Strong differences persist over the establishment of an EISAS, including its purpose and location; the size of the SDS; and the granting of 'pre-mandate commitment authority' to the Secretary-General to permit him to authorize significant spending on peace operations before mandates are agreed. Perhaps the most troubling development has been the decline in size, instead of augmen-tation, of UNSAS. As of 31 January 2002 only 21 member states had provided personnel updates as recommended by the Secretary-General. Worse still, the

[129] Statement of Jean-Marie Guéhenno, Under Secretary-General for Peacekeeping Operations to the Special Committee on Peacekeeping Operations, in United Nations, 'Special Committee on Peacekeeping Operations ends two-day debate on need for rapid deployment of peace operations', Press release GA/PK/175, 12 Feb. 2002, p. 16.
[130] Implementation of the recommendations (note 101), p. 5.
[131] Implementation of the recommendations (note 101), p. 13.
[132] See the DPKO Internet site at URL <http://www.un.org/Depts/dpko/training>.
[133] See note 132.

44 000 troops available at that date constituted a significant decrease from the 147 000 previously declared available.[134] In addition, only 25 member states had responded to the 'on call' list for key mission personnel, with only nine providing nominations, although this would enable the DPKO to fill 134 of the 154 positions on the list.

## Model rules of engagement

Sadly emblematic of the tortuous process of reform of UN peace operations and of its 'one step forward, two steps back' quality was the fate of the model ROE which the Secretariat had been trying for three years to draft. These were intended to help the UN quickly produce mission-specific ROE for future missions and for training purposes. The result was a prolonged tussle between the Secretariat and members of the Special Committee, notably the developing-country troop-contributors and China, over the content of the sample ROE, presumably because they feared they would become a 'Trojan horse' for Western doctrine.

A three-member Secretariat Working Group was established in 1998, involving the DPKO and the Office of Legal Affairs, to produce the first draft,[135] and there was extensive consultation with various UN member states. The resulting draft apparently covered the spectrum of UN operations from Chapter VI to Chapter VII and all weapons and weapon systems except artillery and aircraft. However, the draft was restricted to the use of force in self-defence and defence of the mission, and did not contemplate the use of force for large-scale protection of civilian populations at risk or for peace enforcement.

Following approval by the Under Secretary-General for Peace-keeping Operations, the draft was sent to all member states in February 2001 for comment. Twenty-two submissions from member states and the International Committee of the Red Cross (ICRC), containing more than 320 observations and proposals, were received.[136] The DPKO formed another working group in July, comprising officers from the Military Division, the Office of Operations and the Office of Legal Affairs, to prepare a revised document.

Clearly deciding that the consultation process could not go on for ever, especially given fundamental disagreements over the content, the Secretary-General simply announced in December 2001 that the document, now known as Guidelines for the Development of Rules of Engagement (ROE) for United Nations Peace-keeping Operations,[137] was being used provisionally by military planning staff in the Military Division of the DPKO to guide them in preparing mission-

---

[134] 'Under-Secretary-General for Peacekeeping Operations tells Special Committee operations must deploy credibly, rapidly to succeed' (note 127), p. 3.

[135] Personal communications with UN Secretariat staff, New York, May 1998 and Feb. 2001.

[136] Implementation of the recommendations (note 101), p. 13; and Statement of Mr Jean-Marie Guéhenno (note 129), p. 16.

[137] United Nations, Department of Peace-keeping Operations, Military Division, Guidelines for the development of rules of engagement (ROE) for United Nations peace-keeping operations, UN document MD/FGS/0220.0001, May 2002.

specific ROE. The document is also being issued to troop-contributing countries for training purposes. Avoiding the issue of when the sample ROE would be finalized, and hoping thereby to elude demands from developing countries to keep commenting on them, the Secretary-General noted that: 'Given the changing nature of peacekeeping, the sample Rules of Engagement are considered a continuous work in progress, and will be subject to periodic reviews'.[138] This sounds rather like peace operations reform writ large.

Nonetheless the existence even of a working document should improve the future formulation and implementation of UN ROE. The document clearly states for the first time that the purpose of UN ROE is to 'provide the parameters within which armed military personnel assigned to United Nations Peacekeeping Operations may use force'. They are intended to ensure that the use of force is undertaken in accordance with the UN Charter, relevant Security Council mandates and the relevant principles of international law, including the laws of armed conflict. They aim to assist the force commander in implementing the military objectives of a peacekeeping force's mandate.

The guidelines consist of general instructions for the drafting, approval and implementation of ROE, along with a master list of numbered ROE for insertion into actual ROE depending on the mission's mandate and field requirements.[139] They also include, in attachment 2, a single 'sample ROE', which consists of a general section with several annexes—the authorized numbered ROE for the putative mission, UN definitions for use with the ROE, supporting directions and procedures, and a list of alternative 'weapon states' options (whether weapons may be loaded, cocked, concealed or displayed). This odd arrangement of the material makes the detailed sample ROE appear to be as authoritative as the brief general guidance to which it is attached.

Despite attempts by some UN members to assert the right of troop-contributing states to be involved in determining the ROE for specific missions, and despite the past practice whereby force commanders drafted and sought approval for ROE, the guidelines clearly state that responsibility for preparing the ROE for new missions now rests with the Military Division of the DPKO and that they are to be issued only on the authority of the Under Secretary-General for Peacekeeping Operations. During existing peacekeeping operations the force commander may propose changes to the ROE, but these must be reviewed by the Military Division and be subject to approval by the Under Secretary-General. The only mention of a role for troop-contributing countries comes in relation to the annual review of the sample ROE that is envisaged. Any suggestions for amendment of the document will be 'taken into account' in the review, along with '*all* [emphasis added] comments and observations' of the DPKO's Office of Operations and the Office of Legal Affairs.

Several principles are set out for future ROE which have not been clearly enunciated by the UN in previous documents. One of the most significant is the

---

[138] Implementation of the recommendations (note 101), p. 13.
[139] The list is reproduced as appendix 3 in this volume.

principle that no UN guidelines or directives in any way restrict an individual's right to self-defence. Naturally, the principle of minimum necessary force is given pride of place in the introductory material. Most of the other principles are spelled out in the 'execution of ROE' part of the introduction to the sample ROE. Here there are admonitions to force commanders to abide by the principle of military necessity ('the use of only that force which is required to accomplish the mission), try alternatives to the use of force first, challenge and warn before resorting to force, use 'minimum and proportional force' (commensurate with the level of threat) and avoid collateral damage.

Despite these principles, UN forces are not expected to be quite as reactive as they have traditionally been: while the use of force should be commensurate with the threat, the guidelines intimate that the 'level of response may have to be higher in order to minimise the cost in terms of UN casualties and civilian casualties'. This is probably a coded reference to the difficulties encountered in Bosnia, where factions harassed peacekeepers just below the level at which they judged the ROE would permit deadly or significant force to be used against them. The implication of the sample ROE is that a greater degree of force can be used to pre-empt escalation or to cow those attacking UN forces into desisting.

The master list of numbered ROE, from which specific rules are to be selected for each mission's ROE package, encompasses all the contingencies that have confronted UN peacekeeping operations since the Congo mission, with the exception of peace enforcement. Even the right to respond with the use of force to hostile intent, rather than only to hostile acts, is now included, as is the concept of 'deadly force'. These innovations clearly show the impact of the lessons of Somalia. A further innovation is the definition of 'other international personnel' to which protection may be afforded, including through the use of force. It now encompasses members of authorized charitable, humanitarian or monitoring organizations and other individuals or groups specifically desig-nated by the head of mission (but excluding foreign nationals such as business-men and journalists).

The guidelines also clarify for the first time that force commanders must not exceed the ROE without permission, but if the situation demands it they may recommend tighter restrictions on the use of force than the authorized ROE would indicate. Commanders are also now obliged to seek clarification of the authorized ROE if they are unclear or seem inappropriate to the military situa-tion. Any contravention is to be reported to UN Headquarters as quickly as possible and be formally investigated. The troop-contributing country may also undertake its own investigation.

It is the responsibility of the contingent commanders to ensure that all under their command understand the ROE. They must be translated into the languages of all the troop-contributing countries. UN Headquarters will in future issue an ROE aide-memoire (Blue Card) to all troops in the field in their own language. This must be done 'before the contingent can be considered effective'. Training in ROE is to be considered the responsibility of commanders at all levels and must be conducted on a regular basis, at a minimum once a month and whenever replacement troops are deployed.

These are all long-overdue and admirable innovations. What the guidelines do not do, however, is explicitly to take the UN beyond peacekeeping towards peace enforcement. The term 'peacekeeping operations' is used throughout and the list of ROE reflects the evolution of peacekeeping practice rather than doctrinal development that would encompass peace enforcement.

This does not indicate that the guidelines exclude the use of force beyond self-defence. Indeed, the master list of numbered ROE is 'not deemed to be exhaustive and may be subject to subsequent adjustments as required'. More-over, a careful examination of some of the rules indicates some intriguing possibilities. Rule 1.8, for instance, permits 'use of force, up to, and including deadly force, to defend any civilian person who is in need of protection against a hostile act or hostile intent, when competent local authorities are not in a position to render immediate assistance'. This would have been sufficient in Rwanda to stop atrocities. The freedom of movement rule, 1.10, is also redolent of possibilities in authorizing 'use of force, up to, and including deadly force, against any person and/or group that limits or intends to limit freedom of movement'. Action to counter civil unrest may be authorized in cases where the local civil authority is unable to operate effectively. Cordon operations may be conducted, although only if the force commander 'judges that the situation warrants isolation of the area'.

The strongest evidence that the ROE have been designed to permit more than traditional peacekeeping if required comes discreetly in point j(1) of the 'execution of ROE' part of the sample ROE. Headed 'The use of force beyond self-defence', it provides that: 'The use of force beyond self-defence may be applied only in the circumstances listed below, consistent with the relevant provisions of Security Council resolution . . . of [month/year] and subject to the conditions set out in these ROE'. It then invites a list of all relevant provisions of the Security Council resolution to be inserted. This ensures that if the Security Council decides, for example, that violations of a ceasefire are to be responded to with deadly force, or that force is to be used to stop widespread human rights abuses, such elements can be readily accommodated in the UN peacekeeping ROE template.

The guidelines and sample ROE, on close inspection, represent a significant advance for the conduct of UN peace operations, at least in so far as the con-sistent and logical drafting and application of ROE are concerned. It will now be much clearer to force commanders exactly what their instructions are and what they need to request in addition if they are to fulfil their mandates. Although the original concept of model ROE for various types of UN missions has not eventuated because of political obstacles, the alternative may prove to be just as efficacious. The document also provides some pointers to how a UN peace operations doctrine, freed of its political shackles, might look.

# 10. Conclusions

As the preceding chapters have shown, the use-of-force issue is the most vexing of all the challenges that face UN peace operations, since it has the greatest potential to derail or destroy a mission entirely. All the other weaknesses of UN peace operations are amplified when the use of force is badly handled. This concluding chapter summarizes how the UN has handled the use-of-force issue since the inception of peace operations and considers how its capacity to use (and avoid using) force might be enhanced. It also considers whether there is such a phenomenon as peace enforcement as it is defined here, whether the UN might be capable of conducting it, and what a UN peace enforcement doctrine might look like.

## I. The use of force and the UN: a reckoning

On the whole, the way in which the UN has dealt with the use-of-force issue has been unimpressive. Neither the Security Council, successive secretaries-general nor the Secretariat, nor indeed peacekeepers themselves (despite their 1988 Nobel Peace Prize), can be given high marks. Although there have been some successes, in general the use of force by UN peacekeepers has been marked by political controversy, doctrinal vacuousness, conceptual confusion and failure in the field.

### The Security Council

The Security Council, which has prime responsibility for the proper use of force in UN peace operations, has seriously abdicated this responsibility on several counts.

First, the Council has repeatedly issued unclear and unimplementable mandates which have failed to mention what chapter of the UN Charter an operation was being authorized under, resorted to euphemisms such as 'all necessary means' to convey the possibility that force might be used and abused the concept of deterrence. Ranging from the plainly undeliverable—in the Congo and Bosnia—to the outright irresponsible—in the case of Security Council Resolution 837 aimed against the faction of Mohamed Farah Aideed in Somalia—the Security Council's mandates have left force commanders and their peacekeepers bewildered, vulnerable and in some cases mortally endangered, Rwanda being the worst example. Unclear mandates have resulted not only from the need for political compromise, but because the Council has pinned its hopes on the goodwill of the belligerent parties and the moral authority of the UN, and refused to face the facts of the situation lest it feel obliged to act more robustly.

Second, the Security Council has failed to provide sufficient military and other resources to allow peace operations to carry out their mandate, however limited in terms of the use of force they may have been. Its debates on proposed operations have tended to focus more on financial costs and how the requisite raw numbers of troops might be obtained than on the military requirements of the intended force for carrying out its various responsibilities. The permanent members have been unwilling to authorize the necessary military forces because they themselves would be among the few states capable of providing them at short notice and transporting them to their destination quickly.

Third, the Security Council, at least until recently, has paid scant attention to the appropriate concept of operations or rules of engagement for its peace operations. Usually the standard wording, authorizing the mission to use force only in self-defence and (after 1973) in defence of the mission, was repeated, but hidden deep in the Secretary-General's mission plan which was referred to only in passing in the authorizing resolution. Until the operation in Sierra Leone, no mention was ever made in a Security Council resolution of the right of a UN peace operation to use force to protect civilians at risk of genocide or other gross violations of human rights, even in the darkest days of Rwanda or Bosnia.

Finally, the Security Council has allowed itself to remain dangerously amateurish in military matters. Since initial planning talks on a Military Staff Committee (provided for in Chapter VII of the UN Charter[1]) collapsed in 1948, it has not attempted to establish its own independent source of military advice within the UN system. Instead it has relied on the advice of the Secretary-General and the Secretariat, continuing in the 'leave it to Dag' mode that characterized Hammarskjöld's period in office. Hence, for example, the Security Council has never examined comprehensively the qualifications or suitability of UN force commanders or SRSGs, or the state of readiness or capability of troop contributions. The Secretariat and secretaries-general have lacked military expertise and been reluctant to present the Security Council with worst-case scenarios and estimates of the real cost of the most difficult options. Luckily, individual delegations have relied to a certain extent on their national military advisers and defence departments, and some of this advice has been shared with other Security Council members, but because of the constant turnover in its membership and in the delegations of even its permanent members the Security Council lacks a collective memory and has a tendency to reinvent the wheel every time a crisis arises. This should not, of course, prevent it from trying to institutionalize its memory.

## The secretaries-general

Although they are the commanders-in-chief of UN military forces, successive secretaries-general, with the notable exceptions of Dag Hammarskjöld and

---

[1] Chapter VII of the UN Charter is reproduced in appendix 4 in this volume.

possibly Kofi Annan, have been essentially militarily illiterate. Some have even been suspicious of the military on principle. Others have been dismissive of the importance of military matters until a crisis, such as that in the Congo or Bosnia, brought such issues to the fore. Some, notably Hammarskjöld and Boutros-Ghali, have then resorted to micromanagement of the use of force, especially in the Congo, Somalia and Bosnia. While some have made courageous decisions regarding the use of force, they have mostly, like the Security Council itself, failed to ensure that they were provided with a range of military advice, instead acting on instinct and the advice of a select few. Not all of them have even retained a senior military adviser.

## The UN Secretariat

The UN Secretariat is not set up, financed, resourced or mandated to plan, manage, control and support military expeditions. Indeed, UN member states have at times resisted giving it the necessary capacity to manage traditional peacekeeping operations, let alone operations that might be expected to use more force. In the cold war years it relied on a handful of skilled officers, such as Ralph Bunche and Brian Urquhart, who brought wisdom and experience to the handling of sensitive peacekeeping issues such as the use of force. However, this seemed more like good fortune than good management. With the explosion of the number of peace operations after the end of the cold war this 'gifted amateurism' was unsustainable. Many of the reforms adopted by the DPKO since the end of the cold war have enhanced the department's planning and management capacity, but this has rarely been seen in the context of improving the UN's ability to deal with the use-of-force issue.

The Secretariat's lack of capacity has often been seen most clearly in the planning of operations. In drawing up options for the Secretary-General and Security Council, the Secretariat, overburdened simply with organizing an operation from scratch, has seldom had time to give consideration to the use of force. Its plans have, until recently, considered only the raw numbers of troops required to perform various tasks. They have not provided comprehensive assessments of the risk that force might be used against peacekeepers and/or UN civilians or the defensive weaponry, protective equipment or other capabilities that might be needed. Worst-case scenarios that might imply a need to be prepared to use significant force either in self-defence or beyond have traditionally been avoided in order not to scare potential troop contributors away. Assessments of risk were usually made only after missions got into difficulties. Most disastrously, the planning for Rwanda exhibited this tendency, although it has been evident in the planning for almost every UN peace operation.

After a mission plan has been approved the Secretariat has traditionally focused on finding, as quickly as possible, the requisite numbers of troops to meet the authorized strength of the mission, organizing transport to the mission area as soon as possible, and thereafter (rarely before) ensuring that the troops deployed had basic equipment and logistical support. The possibility that the mission might have to use force has been the Secretariat's last consideration: the problem is devolved to the force commander.

## Mission leadership

As has been seen in the preceding chapters, great reliance for the proper functioning of UN missions in the field has been placed on the force commander. Until relatively recently, the regulations for the use of force were determined almost entirely in the field by the force commander and/or the SRSG. Characteristically, the concepts of operation, SOP and ROE were drafted in the field and sometimes, but not always, cleared with the UN Secretariat. Occasionally they were approved by the Secretary-General himself. Sometimes they were submitted to the Secretariat by the force commander but ignored, as in the cases of the Congo and Rwanda. At other times such documents remained entirely in the field, the Secretariat being left ignorant and oblivious of them.

During actual military engagements, especially in the days before rapid communications with UN Headquarters in New York, the UN was entirely dependent on the judgement of the force commander in respect of the use of force. This could be useful, at times, to both sides in providing 'deniability'. At other times it clearly hindered the proper conduct of military operations. Even today, as the Somalia, Bosnia and Sierra Leone cases have shown, the force commander's attitude and behaviour can make or break a mission that is engaged in using substantial force.

While there have been some excellent force commanders, there have also been appointments based purely on the grounds of nationality without any consideration of military competence (which the Secretariat and Secretary-General can only judge indirectly, by reputation, usually on the basis of a glowing recommendation by the appointee's government); some have been militarily incompetent and/or had a poor understanding of peace operations; and in almost all cases they have been poorly briefed about their mission, and most probably never briefed at all on use-of-force issues.

Similarly, while there have been some excellent SRSGs, there have been some notable disasters in respect of their understanding of and attitude towards the use of force.[2] SRSGs have not been subjected to rigorous selection procedures, much less training. In almost all cases they have had no military expertise whatsoever. Some have been directly antipathetic to the military.

The relationship between the SRSG and the force commander has turned out to be more critical to the success of peace operations which are faced with using

---

[2] A 1999 Norwegian report, while recommending numerous ways in which the performance of SRSGs could be improved, failed to recommend improvements in the way they are selected (except for examining carefully any previous relationships with the warring parties in their mission area) or trained (although it did recommend that the UN Secretariat provide them with written terms of reference to clarify their role). Fafo Institute for Applied Science, Programme for Co-operation and Conflict Resolution, Peace Implementation Network, 'Command from the saddle: managing United Nations peace-building missions. Recommendations. Report of the Forum on the Special Representative of the Secretary-General: shaping the UN's role in peace implementation', Fafo Report no. 266, Oslo, 1999.

force than might have been expected. Given that SRSGs represent the Secretary-General in the field and are superior in command to the force commander, the possibility of misunderstandings and outright disagreements over the use of force is high. Sometimes this has had a benign result: the SRSG has been able to temper the inclination of a force commander to act more 'robustly' than was warranted or wise. More common, however, is the phenomenon of an SRSG, unschooled in military matters and imbued with the UN's pacifist and conciliatory tendencies, misunderstanding the role military force can play in deterrence and compliance, and inadvertently or deliberately undermining it. There have also been occasions when SRSGs were keener to use force than their force commander, most notably in UNOSOM II.

## The peacekeepers

As the preceding chapters have shown, the actual use of force by UN peace operations has for the most part been inconsistent and incoherent, in both political and military terms. Lacking a clear mandate and strong backing from the Security Council, a coherent doctrine, proper military training and equipment, and the requisite ROE, UN forces have by and large been extremely reluctant to use any force at all.

Looked at in the most favourable light, this is completely understandable. The chief concern and duty of commanders at all levels is to avoid exacerbating a situation and damaging consent, both at the tactical and, more dangerously, at the strategic level. Marrack Goulding has also pointed out good operational reasons for peacekeepers to avoid the use of force: they are widely deployed in small groups and vulnerable to retaliation, hostage-taking or worse; they are often outgunned by local factions; they cannot therefore be sure of military superiority if self-defence should lead to escalation; their ability to carry out their peacekeeping functions depends critically on the cooperation of the parties, which will be withheld if their use of force in self-defence causes casualties, especially among civilians; and they know that neither the Security Council nor their own governments want them to become combatants in someone else's war.[3] There are, however, other, less laudable reasons why UN peacekeepers have failed to use force when it has been justified:

1. There has been widespread confusion, both real and contrived, about whether peacekeepers are entitled to use force at all, at a minimum, or strictly in defence of themselves and their own national contingents. Even today references are still made to the non-use of force as one of the inherent characteristics of UN peacekeeping.

2. Many states send peacekeepers to missions for reasons of national prestige and as a symbol of their contribution to an international enterprise, without any conception of the level of risk involved.

[3] Goulding, M., 'The use of force by the United Nations', *International Peacekeeping*, vol. 3, no. 1 (spring 1996), p. 9.

3. Most militaries do not train for the more subtle application of force envisaged in UN operations, compared with traditional warfare, and arrive in the mission area quite ignorant of the role expected of them as peacekeepers.

4. Many contingents arrive unequipped even to defend themselves, much less any other UN personnel or 'the mission'; some arrive even without basic provisions, weaponry in working order or sufficient ammunition.

### The use of force in self-defence

Peacekeepers have continued to fail to use force in self-defence, even in life-and-death situations where it would be universally perceived as legitimate and warranted under the self-defence rule. They have been fired at for hours without retaliating, permitted themselves to be disarmed and arrested, allowed their posts and vehicles to be seized, and suffered all manner of humiliation without resorting to force in self-defence. Far from being the result of some considered strategy for avoiding loss of consent, this has often been the result of other factors—a failure of nerve or an over-conciliatory attitude on the part of local commanders, force commanders or SRSGs (in some cases amounting to appeasement); poor ROE or poor understanding of the ROE; deficiencies in the equipment, training and briefing of troop contingents; inadequate command, control and communications; and lax or non-existent intelligence-gathering.

While it is essential that any threat or use of force in a UN peace operation is carefully considered, the failure of UN troops to use force even to defend themselves leads to a loss of credibility both for the UN and for its peace operations, and contributes to the widespread view that peacekeepers are paper tigers who can be pushed around and manipulated. Particularly in civil wars, faction leaders will have no respect for a military force that fails even to defend itself. Despite Goulding's fears, in practice the robust use of force in self-defence by peacekeepers has not led to their becoming embroiled in escalating violence. It has mostly had the opposite effect, of reducing the harassment of peacekeepers, particularly when they react after a sustained period of provocation and when that is followed up by negotiations to calm the situation.

If on the whole the self-defence rule has not been taken advantage of, at other times it has been stretched beyond credulity. The norm has been stretched and ultimately broken, both inadvertently and deliberately, and at three levels: (a) strategically, by the Security Council; (b) operationally, by SRSGs and/or force commanders; and (c) tactically, by national contingents and troops in the field. It was stretched most spectacularly in the Congo, where it was used by U Thant as practically the sole justification for bringing down the Katangan regime. In other cases it was invoked to permit UN peacekeepers to use force when they had been deliberately interposed between warring forces. In Cyprus it was used to justify cordoning off and protecting a strategic facility. In Bosnia the 'safe areas' were a by-product of protecting the peacekeepers. Often, when the bounds of self-defence are about to be or have been breached, there has been an implicit understanding on the part of the force commander that his superiors did not want to be asked for permission or even to be informed until after the operation had succeeded. This attempt to preserve deniability until success is achieved occurred on occasions in the Congo, Cyprus, Lebanon and Bosnia.

The deterrent effect of self-defence has been shown to be largely illusory. Sometimes uncertainty as to how peacekeepers might use their weapons appears to have had some deterrent effect. This seems to have occurred in Cambodia. It also appeared to happen in Bosnia on occasions, usually because hard-bitten belligerents could not believe that UN ROE could possibly be so constraining. However, the Bosnian case illustrated perfectly the deterrence dilemma which UN peacekeepers, acting under the self-defence rule, have always faced: UNPROFOR could not threaten the Bosnian Serbs with unacceptable consequences because it, and the UN civilians and unarmed military observers under its protection, were too vulnerable to retaliation. UN peacekeepers were self-deterred from taking robust military action. The taking of UN hostages in Cambodia, Bosnia and Sierra Leone effectively stymied the use of force by the UN and weakened any deterrent effect. The classic case of a mission whose deployment used an implicit threat of the use of force as part of its *raison d'être* was UNPREDEP in Macedonia, but the bluff was never called. Finally, the failure of NATO air power to deter Serb attacks on the Bosnian safe areas provided further tragic evidence of widespread misunderstanding about the purported deterrent role of the use of force in self-defence.

None of this history of failed deterrence seems to stop the Security Council, the Secretary-General and the Secretariat blithely talking of the deterrent capabilities of UN peace operations. The language reappeared most recently in the case of Sierra Leone.

### The use of force to assert the right of freedom of movement

The right of freedom of movement has proved difficult to understand and apply consistently ever since it was first asserted for UNEF I. In the Congo, the right of freedom of movement was taken to its logical extreme and used to justify a pre-emptive military operation against the Katangan Government. In Cambodia the force commander and SRSG retreated humiliated from a Khmer Rouge roadblock rather than try to push through. In the later stages of the Bosnia operation the freedom of movement principle was used to justify breaking the siege of Sarajevo by opening supply routes across Mount Igman. In Rwanda and Sierra Leone, simple roadblocks halted the UN in its tracks. In general no one has understood how far the right could be asserted or whether it could be used to achieve other mission goals. In theory, in combination with the right of self-defence, it could be used to achieve almost any military goal. The UN has never provided proper guidance on how the right to freedom of movement was to be implemented in practice.

Connected with the freedom of movement issue is the question of freedom of deployment and withdrawal. No UN peace operation has ever had to fight its way in (the original ship-borne deployment of UNMIH sailed away after local thugs brandished weapons at them from the quay). Usually, armed opposition during the deployment and establishment phase has been quite minor, the belligerents and local populace normally being surprised and nonplussed by the sudden arrival of UN 'Blue Helmets', rather than opposed. Normally incidents involving the use of force begin only after a 'honeymoon' period has elapsed, as local belligerents test the force's tolerance and capability, and disillusionment at the lack of progress begins to set in. Similarly, no UN mission has ever had to fight its way out, although UNEF I was withdrawn under fire (some of it directed at the mission itself), fire was exchanged with Somalis during the withdrawal of UNOSOM II, and UNPROFOR in Bosnia began serious preparations for withdrawal under fire (including by deploying the RRF).

## Defence of the mission

The use of force 'in defence of the mission' has also remained problematic ever since it was first promulgated as a right. The closest any force commander has come to publicly using the 'defence of the mission' justification was General John Sanderson in Cambodia in redeploying his forces to 'protect the electoral process' and, in addition, any person going about UN business. General Roméo Dallaire proposed using the 'defence of the mission' justification in Rwanda by authorizing in his draft ROE the use of force to prevent crimes against humanity—presumably on the grounds that if his troops were prevented from protecting civilians at risk they could at least use force to defend their mission.

As the 1995 UN *General Guidelines for Peacekeeping Operations* coyly note, the wider definition of self-defence used by the UN since 1973 has not been fully utilized: 'Peace-keeping forces have gone to great lengths in order not to be drawn into cycles of attack and retaliation, which would turn them into enemies rather than peace-keepers who are above the fray'.[4] Indeed, using force in 'defence of the mission' is potentially open-ended and could, if not properly regulated, lead inadvertently from peacekeeping to peace enforcement. Force commanders have never been properly briefed on what it means in practice and there have been no comprehensive guides, concepts of operation or ROE for 'defence of the mission'. It is also difficult to operationalize. While soldiers have an ingrained sense of what self-defence means, few have any idea of what 'defence of the mission' means in a peace operations context, especially since they are often unclear as to exactly what the mission is.

## Mandated uses of force beyond self-defence and defence of the mission

In other cases, as has been seen, the Security Council has given peacekeepers authority to use force beyond self-defence for particular purposes. These have invariably been controversial and have not been very successful ventures.

---

[4] United Nations, Department of Peace-keeping Operations, *General Guidelines for Peace-keeping Operations*, UN document 95-38147 (United Nations: New York, 1995), p. 14.

ONUC was authorized (under Chapter VII) to use force to prevent civil war, prevent inter-tribal warfare and expel mercenaries. Most of these tasks were accomplished, paradoxically, by the use of force in self-defence after the interposition of peacekeepers between the belligerents, but the expulsion of mercenaries did engage the UN in substantial, offensive use of force. The first two 'rounds' of the campaign were poorly executed, while the third, even though ultimately successful, suffered from severe command and control problems. Although military 'victory' was achieved, it was at enormous cost to the UN.

UNOSOM II was authorized (also under Chapter VII) to use force, if necessary, to enforce disarmament and, later, to apprehend General Aideed and his cohorts. The offensive actions taken by UNOSOM II in Somalia to track and apprehend Aideed ended in military and political disaster (although great damage was done to Aideed's forces in the meantime).

More recently, UNAMSIL and the UN Observer Force in the Democratic Republic of Congo (MONUC) were authorized under Chapter VII to use force to protect civilians at risk, but no reported use of force has yet occurred in this respect. Hammarskjöld authorized ONUC to use force for such purposes, but without consulting the Security Council, which would undoubtedly have opposed it. While the Security Council has been reluctant to mandate such use of force, peacekeepers have, as a matter of simple humanity or as a 'duty of care', often offered shelter and protection to those at risk (including in the Congo, Rwanda and Bosnia). Sometimes this has involved the use of force. However, there has been no consistent policy and force commanders, contingent commanders and lower ranks have often simply taken matters into their own hands as required. In other cases, most notably in Rwanda, Haiti, Somalia, Bosnia and Sierra Leone, peacekeepers have stood by and observed or withdrawn from the scene.

The few offensive UN military operations that the UN has undertaken have been fundamentally hampered by a lack of intelligence-gathering capability, weak command and control, low levels of interoperability and varying degrees of commitment by contributing states to military action. With the possible exceptions of ONUC towards the end of its tenure, UNPROFOR's RRF, UNTAES and UNTAET, UN peace operations have not been geared for military engagements beyond self-defence.

On the other hand, some of the military disasters that have befallen UN operations have not been of the UN's making. US hubris and military incompetence played a significant role in the Mogadishu catastrophe. The 'dual-key' controversy in Bosnia was as much a product of intra-NATO disunity as it was of UN reluctance to use air power. The Rwanda and Srebrenica episodes were, as has been seen, as much a result of the Security Council's pusillanimity, ineptness and wishful thinking as of UN peacekeepers' reluctance to use force.

## II. Improving the ability of UN peace operations to use (and avoid using) force

In an ideal peace operations world, the UN would have a well-established doctrine, model concepts of operation for various missions, strategic and operational planning documents, SOP and model ROE. The UN Secretariat would have a department of peace operations which resembled the national defence department of at least a middle-ranking UN member state, such as Argentina, Australia, Canada, India, the Netherlands, South Africa or Sweden. An intelligence unit would provide the department with timely and pertinent information on likely political, military and humanitarian 'trouble spots' in which UN forces were or might be deployed. It would have the capability to deploy a vanguard military headquarters within 24 hours and a militarily capable rapid reaction force within days, to be followed by a self-sustainable, sizeable military force within weeks. Airlift, logistics and basic military equipment would be pre-arranged. Civilian, civilian police, humanitarian, human rights and peace-building capabilities would also be available for rapid deployment. Trained and experienced civilian and military leadership would be available on call. Round-the-clock, secure communications between UN Headquarters and the UN force in the field and the necessary chain of command and control would be readily establishable. Perhaps most utopian of all, the Security Council would draft clear mandates that established realistic goals for each mission and would guarantee to provide the means of carrying out the mandate, whether involving the use of force beyond self-defence or not.

Clearly this ideal world is some way off. Many of the reforms proposed for UN peacekeeping by the plethora of studies conducted since the end of the cold war—by military academies, universities and other research centres and the UN itself, and especially the Brahimi Report[5]—would, by improving the capability of the UN to deploy and manage peace operations in general, automatically improve its ability to deploy militarily capable forces and to use them effectively. This would include the use of force where necessary and appropriate.

### Mandates

Security Council mandates are beginning to improve as more realistic assessments are made of mission requirements and of the situation on the ground. Both worst-case and best-case scenarios are being factored in. Recent mandates have been less open-ended, more nuanced and more carefully drafted.

One reform which might be considered in order to end the confusion over whether to mandate operations under Chapter VI or Chapter VII would be to authorize all missions involving armed military personnel under Chapter VII regardless of their mandate. Chapter VI would be reserved for unarmed

---

[5] United Nations, Report of the Panel on United Nations Peace Operations, UN document A/55/305, S/2000/809, 21 Aug. 2000 (the Brahimi Report).

observer missions or peacemaking and peace-building missions with no uniformed personnel. This reform would end the artificial distinction between Chapter VI and Chapter VII operations, which no longer signifies whether a mission is peacekeeping or something more expansive. It would accord all missions and their mandates and functions the same degree of seriousness and determination; make it obligatory for all states and non-state actors to cooperate with every UN peace mission and refrain from frustrating its objectives, including by attacking it; establish the basis for punitive action under Article 39 of the UN Charter for any attack on a UN peace operation; and, for troop-contributing countries, confirm the serious view the Security Council takes of attacks on their personnel, while at the same time serving notice to contributors that the dispatch of their forces is not necessarily a risk-free undertaking, even if the mission is labelled 'peacekeeping'.

As is the case now, giving all armed missions Chapter VII authorization would not signify that all would necessarily be involved in peace enforcement. Furthermore, since compliance with all Security Council resolutions is compulsory, establishing peace operations under Chapter VII would hardly be revolutionary.

In addition, all resolutions establishing armed peace operations should explicitly state that they have the right to use force in self-defence and to defend their right of freedom of movement. Freedom of movement should be understood to mean the right of the mission to deploy to, from and within the theatre of operations and to resupply itself. All mandates should also make it explicit that the UN is obliged to protect civilians at risk of human rights abuses or other forms of attack. If there are constraints on the mission's ability to do so, such as geographical constraints, these should be made explicit.

The Security Council should also stop using the euphemism 'all necessary means' and instead state its intentions explicitly by specifying in what circumstances and in what areas force may be used. Such an effort to be more specific should at least focus the minds of Security Council members which seek to use the cloak of ambiguity to absolve themselves of responsibility for any use of force. It should also remove ambiguity for those states and parties which either are ignorant of the subtleties of Security Council resolutions or pretend to be. References to 'deterrence' or the alleged deterrent capabilities of a force should also be dropped from resolutions except where the Council is absolutely certain that the threat of the use of force inherent in the language of deterrence can be successfully carried out. Mandates should explicitly state which elements of the mandate are subject to peace enforcement action. If disarmament is to be enforced, for example, that should be mentioned. If humanitarian aid is to be protected and its distribution enforced if necessary, that should be made clear.

It should be recognized, however, that total clarity is unlikely to be achieved in Security Council mandates, given the difficulties of reaching consensus or a veto-free vote without using obscure language to hide major disagreements. Obfuscation in a mandate is sometimes preferable to no mandate at all, especially if it can be translated by the Secretariat and mission leadership into a workable operational plan.

## Mission planning and management

While at first glance mission planning would seem to be at some remove from the use-of-force issue, in fact poor planning can be the underlying cause of poor decisions being made about the use of force, as UNOSOM II, UNAMIR and UNAMSIL all demonstrated. The Somalia lessons-learned report concluded that a coordinated overall mission plan should be prepared in advance of every mission, in consultation with troop contributors. It should include, but not be limited to, clear mission statements, command relations, rules of engagement, coordination procedures, SOP, intelligence management, and administrative and logistics policy and procedures.[6]

Both before a mission is launched and while it is in the field, military planning must be an integral part of overall UN mission planning to ensure that military goals are subordinate to, not independent of, the overall mission mandate and objectives.

When the use of force is contemplated it is even more vital than usual that there be tight coordination and cooperation within the mission, as well as between the mission and other UN agencies in the country, as well as with non-UN bodies, such as the Red Cross and NGOs. The Civil–Military Cooperation Committee model used by UNITAF and the later stages of UNAMIR should be built into planning for all missions, but particularly robust or complex ones. Aid agencies and NGOs can be particularly vulnerable to attack in retaliation for the actions of UN forces and must therefore be kept informed of developing military situations and offered protection or evacuation if necessary. In return such bodies can be a source of valuable local intelligence.[7]

Guidelines and SOP must be kept updated, used in training and made widely available to peace operations personnel well in advance. The UN already has a collection of these but many are at least five years old and fail to encompass the developments that have occurred since then, most notably the increasing expectations that peacekeepers will afford protection to civilians under threat.[8]

---

[6] Friedrich Ebert Stiftung (Germany), Life and Peace Institute (Sweden), Norwegian Institute of International Affairs (NUPI) and United Nations Department of Peace-keeping Operations, Lessons Learned Unit, 'Comprehensive report on lessons-learned from United Nations Operation in Somalia April 1992–March 1995', Swedish Government, Stockholm, Dec. 1995, p. 7.

[7] For further analysis of civil–military relations see Findlay, T. C., 'UNAMIR and the Rwandan humanitarian catastrophe: marginalization in the midst of mayhem', ed. N. Azimi, *Humanitarian Action and Peacekeeping Operations: Debriefing and Lessons* (Kluwer Law: The Hague, 1997).

[8] United Nations, Department of Peace-keeping Operations, Military Division, Training and Evaluation Service, 'Peacekeeping publications 2001', New York, 2001 (on CD-ROM). It contains sections on peacekeeping training, military observers, medical support, civilian police and logistics. The peacekeeping training section includes the following documents: 'UN peacekeeping training assistance teams: advisor's guidebook'; the UN *Peacekeeping Training Manual*, 2nd edn [1997], incorporating the 1991 Training Guidelines for National or Regional Training Operations; a 'UN peacekeeping handbook for junior ranks'; 'Disarmament, demobilization and reintegration of ex-combatants in a peacekeeping environment'; the 1995 *General Guidelines for Peace-keeping Operations*; a 'Code of conduct'; 'We are peacekeepers'; a

As Brahimi noted, many new and updated versions of peacekeeping guidelines and handbooks 'now sit half finished in a dozen offices all around DPKO, because their authors are busy meeting other needs'.[9]

Proper planning also needs to be done for particular tasks in peace operations, especially those that run the risk of the use of force. They include: the enforced or protected delivery of humanitarian assistance; the protection of civilians at risk; and the disarmament, cantonment and demobilization of armed forces. In the case of humanitarian assistance, the experiences of Somalia and Bosnia should be drawn on to produce SOP and model strategies for different circumstances. In the case of civilian protection, strategies for establishing, maintaining and defending safe areas, safe havens and enclaves should be developed and the advantages and disadvantages of each elucidated for future reference.

For disarmament, cantonment and demobilization, model schemata should be developed for each type of undertaking, including the role of force in implementing and protecting them, drawing on the UN's rich and varied experience. The DPKO announced in December 2001 its intention to include 'comprehensive disarmament, demobilization and reintegration programmes' in the planning for future peace operations, as appropriate.[10] Such plans should take as a given that successful disarmament does not require the removal of every single weapon (there are permanently millions of firearms in private hands in many countries, including the USA), but rather that sufficient disarmament must be achieved and sustained in order for confidence to be built and a peace process facilitated, unburdened by the threat of the use of force by armed factions. This has been the practice followed in Bosnia, Kosovo and Macedonia.

## More capable and rapidly deployable UN forces

Implementation of the Brahimi Report's recommendations and Kofi Annan's follow-on proposals for meeting its 30- and 90-day deployment goals would vastly improve the quality, availability and deployability of contingents for UN peace operations. The most important reforms in this regard include: improvements to UNSAS, including the addition of brigade-size forces; an essential equipment stockpile at the UN Logistics Base; rapid dispatch of field assessment teams to the mission area, implementing the Canadian vanguard concept for the rapid deployment of mission headquarters;[11] standby arrangements for civilian and civilian police deployments; and greater selectivity in the choice of contingents for UN missions, plus training and equipment improvements.

'Hostage incident card'; 'Provisional guidelines for public information components in UN peacekeeping and other field missions'; the 'UN military symbols handbook'; and 'Security awareness: an aide-mémoire'.

[9] Report of the Panel on United Nations Peace Operations (note 5), para. 192.

[10] United Nations, Implementation of the recommendations of the Special Committee on Peacekeeping Operations and the Panel on United Nations Peace Operations: report of the Secretary-General, UN document A/56/732, 21 Dec. 2001, p. 14.

[11] Government of Canada, *Towards a Rapid Reaction Capability for the United Nations* (Government of Canada: Ottawa, Sep. 1995).

Ultimately, it is to be hoped that improvements in the management and operation of UN missions will increase the confidence of all member states, including the most militarily capable, that they can entrust their forces to the UN and that they will be properly commanded and protected. This should increase the willingness of member states to contribute forces to more difficult missions. However, much more will be required before the UN is able to deploy rapidly.

There have been various proposals over the years for the UN to have, on call, its own standing rapid reaction capability. Currently, the political, organizational and financial obstacles to such a development remain insuperable. Exhaustive studies have been done of both the idea of the UN having its own force and the alternative of making available such a capability to the UN on call.[12] Perhaps the most important step in this direction would be for the states which contribute to the Stand-by High-Readiness Brigade (SHIRBRIG) to permit it to be available for inclusion in peace enforcement missions.[13] Norway has supported the idea, but has noted that the decision would have to be taken by the brigade's members on a case-by-case basis with due account being taken of the proposed mandates and ROE, as well as the overall political and military situation.[14] Alternatively, SHIRBRIG could be used as an in-theatre or offshore rapid reaction force to act as a deterrent and in case quick reinforcement is needed, like UNPROFOR's RRF and the marine forces stationed off Somalia and East Timor by the USA. This may become possible if the brigade achieves success in the less challenging missions in which it is currently being tested.

One difficulty with SHIRBRIG is the opposition of the non-aligned countries to its extended use. Speaking on behalf of the non-aligned, Jordan bluntly, if absurdly, told the Special Committee on Peacekeeping Operations in February 2002 that: 'The Movement continued to harbour serious reservations over the multinational initiative because, by referring to a "brigade", the authors of the scheme appropriated for themselves the authority of the Secretary-General to decide the composition of part of or—depending on its size—the entire United Nations peacekeeping force'.[15]

---

[12] Studies include: Dennehy, E. J. (Capt.) *et al.*, 'A Blue Helmet combat force', Policy Analysis Paper no. 93-01, National Security Program, Harvard University, 1993; Conetta, C. and Knight, C., *Vital Force: A Proposal for the Overhaul of the UN Peace Operations System and for the Creation of a UN Legion*, Project on Defense Alternatives Research Monograph no. 4 (Commonwealth Institute: Cambridge, Mass., Sep. 1995); Cox, D. and Legault, A. (eds), Lester B. Pearson Canadian International Peacekeeping Training Centre, *UN Rapid Reaction Capabilities: Requirements and Prospects* (Canadian Peacekeeping Press: Clementsport, 1995); Kaysen, C. and Rathjens, G. W., 'Send in the troops: a UN foreign legion', *Washington Quarterly*, vol. 20, no. 1 (1996); US Congressional Research Service (CRS), '*A UN Rapid Reaction Force? Considerations for US Policymakers*, CRS Report for Congress (Library of Congress, Congressional Research Service: Washington, DC, 29 June 1995); and Haynes, L. and Stanley, T. W., 'To create a United Nations fire brigade', *Comparative Strategy*, vol. 14, no. 1 (Jan./Mar. 1995).

[13] SHIRBRIG, set up to provide the United Nations with a high-readiness peacekeeping force, was declared available to the UN in Jan. 2000. The participating countries at the time of writing are Argentina, Austria, Canada, Denmark, Italy, the Netherlands, Norway, Poland, Romania and Sweden.

[14] United Nations, 'Under-Secretary-General for Peace-keeping Operations tells Special Committee operations must deploy credibly, rapidly to succeed', Press release GA/PK/174, 11 Feb. 2002, p. 8.

[15] 'Under-Secretary-General for Peace-keeping Operations tells Special Committee operations must deploy credibly, rapidly to succeed' (note 14), p. 5.

However SHIRBRIG develops, the UN, when deploying a mission to a dangerous environment, should investigate the possibility of asking a group of states or single state to provide an offshore rapid reaction force to reinforce a UN mission in difficulty or to assist in evacuation, as the UK was willing to do in Sierra Leone. Such an arrangement has the advantage of not overburdening the mission in theatre while at the same time providing deterrence to belligerents and reassurance to troop contributors. At the very least the UN should hone its rather rudimentary existing plans for evacuation and withdrawal and establish contingency plans prior to each mission's deployment.

The practice of deploying a multinational 'coalition of the willing' force when the UN itself is unable to raise a force quickly enough to deal with an emergency—to be succeeded by a UN follow-on force when ready—has evolved more as a pragmatic response to particular cases than as a considered strategy. It is clearly preferable to doing nothing and in most cases has worked well. The Security Council and UN member states could, however, be more creative and less rigid in imagining how UN peace operations might better take advantage of such 'willing' partners. Instead of 'subcontracting out' an entire mission and having it only loosely tethered to UN oversight (to date this has mostly been simply by means of a requirement to report periodically), the Security Council could request a lead nation to provide the force commander, key command personnel and a sizeable troop contribution to create a nucleus of coherence and military capability, but subject all elements to the usual UN command and control structure. 'Coalitions of the willing' would then be left to cases where the Security Council could not agree to deploy a UN mission, or when the potential lead nation was not prepared to accept UN command and control, rather than because the mission was deemed to be beyond UN capabilities.

Given that such mechanisms are likely to be needed for some time to come, it would be useful for the UN to better identify the requirements for smooth transitions from coalition to UN operations: as previous chapters have shown, this is when such undertakings are likely to fall apart under challenge from local 'spoilers'. Transitional planning modules would be a worthwhile innovation.

The special requirements of humanitarian emergencies, where armed conflict might threaten the delivery of urgently needed aid, also need to be considered. Tom Weiss argues that, because political and military enforcement are inconsistent with fundamental humanitarian principles, UN agencies are compromised by association with Chapter VII peace enforcement operations.[16] He proposes a Humanitarian Protection Force (HUMPROFOR), to be established by the Security Council in much the same way as the UN Special Commission on Iraq (UNSCOM), comprising experts and resources siphoned off from existing UN humanitarian agencies, plus troops seconded from national forces experienced in humanitarian operations. In cases where consent was not obtainable or

---

[16] Weiss, T., 'Overcoming the Somalia syndrome: Operation Rekindle Hope?', *Global Governance*, vol. 1, no. 3 (May/Aug. 1995), p. 175.

was shaky, the military forces could, for instance, 'carve out defensible areas within which they could take command without constant friction from combatants and local factions'. The models are Operation Provide Comfort in northern Iraq and Opération Turquoise in Rwanda rather than UNITAF, UNOSOM or UNPROFOR.

## Civilian police

The more rapid deployment of more capable UN CivPols, either to monitor the activities of local police or to assume police functions in cases where the local police have dissolved or are incapable of operating effectively, could help avoid the use of force in UN peace operations by tackling law-and-order problems at an appropriate level. Saul Mendlovitz and John Fousek propose a global constabulary 10 000–15 000 strong comprising volunteers directly recruited and paid for by the UN.[17] It would be the police arm of the International Criminal Court and be mandated to act in a preventive role. If prevention failed it would be authorized to use force to protect threatened groups and apprehend war criminals. The virtue of such a constabulary would be that it was truly international and readily deployable. Its most controversial aspect would be that authority to deploy it would be vested in the Secretary-General. Moreover, if it landed in difficulties it would have to be rescued by a military operation.

Current efforts to improve the management of CivPol deployments (including the separation of the Civilian Police Division from the Military Division in the DPKO in 2001, in part to avoid CivPol operations being swamped by military considerations), should continue. Continuing efforts to improve 'quality control' processes for selecting CivPols and enhanced training are also necessary.[18]

## Command and control

The importance of tight command and control increases exponentially whenever the use of force is envisaged, threatens or eventuates. Two major problems must be avoided. First, allied military forces should not operate outside the UN command structure. If a separate national force is present in the same theatre of operations it must either be brought quickly under UN command or withdraw. Second, forces within the command structure must obey UN command, or they should also withdraw. The authority of the SRSG, acting on the orders of the UN Secretary-General, must be paramount.

Again, many of the Brahimi and follow-up recommendations, if implemented, would strengthen command and control by producing better-selected,

---

[17] Mendlovitz, S. and Fousek, J., 'A UN constabulary to enforce the law on genocide and crimes against humanity', ed. N. Riemer, *Protection Against Genocide: Mission Impossible?* (Praeger: Westport, Ct., 1999), cited in Wheeler, N. J., 'Review article: humanitarian intervention after Kosovo: emergent norm, moral duty or the coming anarchy?', *International Affairs*, vol. 77, no. 1 (Jan. 2001), pp. 124–25.

[18] The DPKO has recently announced the preparation of a model CivPol headquarters, the first time this has ever happened, to enhance rapid deployment of CivPols. Implementation of the recommendations (note 10), p. 7.

-briefed and -prepared SRSGs and force commanders. The UK's proposal for a UN Staff College to prepare senior officers for leadership roles in UN operations would be an excellent innovation in this respect.

Efforts to involve troop-contributing countries more in discussions on mandates, concepts of operation, ROE and any changes after deployment would help to avoid the problem of national contingents second-guessing instructions from UN forces by seeking high-level authorization from their national capitals. An institutional innovation at the UN which could help further alleviate, if not end, the problem would be the establishment for each mission of an equivalent of Hammarskjöld's Congo Advisory Committee, comprising representatives of troop-contributing countries and senior UN Secretariat officials involved in planning and managing the mission. Presumably, as the staff of the DPKO grows, it will become increasingly feasible to service such committees. John Ruggie also proposes that senior officers of the larger troop-contributing countries be made part of the field headquarters staff of a mission, performing liaison and advisory functions outside the operational chain of command.[19]

Clearly, though, the UN needs to avoid micromanagement of its missions by troop contributors, lest its operations become even more unwieldy. During the troop-contributor consultations for the Sierra Leone deployment, it was agreed that, while these consultations were 'indispensable', they should not lead to 'delays in the execution of tasks or prevent the Mission from retaining the necessary operational flexibility'.[20]

At the strategic level, one issue of command and control that was not considered by Brahimi or any of the subsequent reports is the role of the Secretary-General as the supreme commander of UN forces. There have been suggestions, notably by Giandomenico Pico,[21] that the Secretary-General should be relieved of this role lest his command of peace enforcement or more robust missions compromise his impartiality and ability to mediate international disputes. However, the four secretaries-general who have had the closest involvement in commanding UN operations that involved peace enforcement—Hammarskjöld, U Thant, Boutros-Ghali and Annan—seem not to have been so encumbered. Indeed, it could be argued that giving the UN a more powerful military deployment capability might give the Secretary-General more negotiating power. He would have more options available than simply good offices, monitoring and peacekeeping. In any event negotiating theory does not require that effective negotiators are unalloyedly neutral: the pro-Israel bias of the US has never stopped it being an effective negotiator in the Middle East. Finally, it is hard to see who else in the UN system could be entrusted with being UN supreme force commander. The Security Council presidency rotates every month, while the Military Staff Committee remains a dead letter.

[19] Ruggie, J. G., 'The UN and the collective use of force: whither or whether?', ed. M. Pugh, *The UN, Peace and Force* (Frank Cass: London, 1997), p. 16.
[20] United Nations, Sixth report of the Secretary-General on the United Nations Mission in Sierra Leone, UN document S/2000/832, 24 Aug. 2000, p. 7.
[21] Pico, G., 'The UN and the use of force', *Foreign Affairs*, vol. 73, no. 5 (Sep./Oct. 1994), p. 15.

On balance, it is probably better to leave the current structure for strategic command and control of UN forces as it is. A better-informed Security Council and the provision of more substantial and long-range military advice than the current military adviser and various DPKO offices can provide can be expected to help improve the UN command and control structure overall.

## Intelligence

One of the great gaps in the UN's peace operations capability is the acquisition, analysis and effective use of timely intelligence information. Proper intelligence information is essential for the effective and judicious use of force, as the Rwanda case indicated, and vital if ill-judged plans to use force are to be avoided, as the attempted seizure of Aideed demonstrated. Again, the importance of intelligence information rises exponentially once the use of force is contemplated or occurs.

Concerned about the hypersensitivity of some if its members to the issue, the UN has traditionally shied away from openly acknowledging the utility of gathering and using intelligence information. In practice, however, from the very beginning, UN operations have, out of military necessity, unofficially gathered and used such information, albeit at a relatively basic level. UN missions have also cooperated with certain participating countries in obtaining higher-level intelligence information when deemed necessary.

There have been several attempts to establish at UN Headquarters a capacity for intelligence-gathering and analysis, but all have met with opposition from key developing countries. Perhaps experience with the modest EISAS that will now be established as a result of the Brahimi Report will convince the sceptics that such activity does not pose a threat to either their sovereignty or the UN's independence. In any event, the same communications revolution that is making it increasingly difficult for states to keep information from crossing borders will also make it increasingly easy for the UN to obtain access to information previously undreamed of. This will come not from a dedicated intelligence unit in the Secretariat, but from the Internet and via rapid communications with UN global offices, missions and networks. Member states could assist by sharing information derived from what is known in the arms control community as national technical means, most spectacularly satellite photographs (which the USA, for instance, provided to UNSCOM with respect to Iraq, and to the International Atomic Energy Agency (IAEA) with respect to North Korea).

## Rules of engagement

While UN operations have always used rules of engagement to regulate the use of force by their troops, they have not always been called ROE and knowledge of them was largely confined to the military. Since the end of the cold war, largely as a result of US and British participation in Somalia and Bosnia, respectively, ROE have become the subject of intense interest and scrutiny by the media, policy makers, legislators and the general public. The issuing of unclassified ROE on cards carried by UN peacekeepers has increased interest further. Proper preparation of, training in and use of ROE has accordingly become much more important, for these reasons alone, but there are additional reasons why they are critical to the proper functioning of modern UN peace operations.

First, perhaps more than any other UN document—whether Security Council resolution, reports of the Secretary-General, press release or information kit released in the field—the ROE will reveal, both to the UN soldier and to the parties in conflict, the true nature of the UN operation. Second, since the UN relies on voluntary contributions of forces, it needs, perhaps even more than governments, to delineate precisely the circumstances and manner in which contingents under its command might be expected to use force. Third, in a peace operation there will normally be no large-scale military campaign, and the tactical level—which is where ROE are utilized—is the cutting edge of the use of force. The injudicious use of force at this level by a single individual or a small group of UN troops could jeopardize an entire mission, especially if the press is present and news of an incident is transmitted around the world before the UN has begun to receive its own reports. Enormous responsibility is thus placed on the local area commander and individual troops, who are often quite junior. ROE are a vital tool for helping them to act appropriately.

Fourth, peace operations are characterized by restraint in the use of force; ROE for peace operations are therefore arguably even more important than they are in war. According to Lorenz: 'Instant response, junior leader execution, political volatility and local customs add dimensions to ROE not normally encountered in wartime'.[22] Finally, the importance of proper, agreed ROE is magnified in any multinational operation by the national, ethnic and cultural diversity of the military personnel involved. ROE should be an important tool for helping to forge 'unity of effort' in multilateral peace operations, if not 'unity of command'.

## Difficulties with rules of engagement in UN missions

There have been three main problems with ROE in UN peace operations. The first is the way in which they are drafted; the second is their content; and the third is the way they have been implemented.

Even if a mission is conceived correctly, ROE may not be adequately drafted to reflect this understanding. They have often simply been lifted or adapted from Nordic or other national models which were themselves poorly drafted or inappropriate, without consideration for the UN's own precedents established by much trial and error from UNEF I onwards. Usually no effort has been made to consult troop-contributing countries about the content of ROE, either before or after their contingents are deployed, to take into account any particular

[22] Lorenz, F. M. (Col), 'Forging rules of engagement: lessons learned from Operation United Shield', *Military Review*, Nov./Dec. 1995, p. 25.

requirements they might have. Until recently there was no centralized repository of previous ROE, no comprehensive, systematic attempt to draw lessons from their application in different circumstances and no attempt to establish model ROE. These efforts still have not borne fruit. As has been shown, UN ROE have often been sloppily drafted, expressed in poor English (the working language of most UN peace operations) and difficult to comprehend.

UN ROE have usually encapsulated well the use of force in self-defence norm as narrowly defined. They have been less successful in dealing with 'defence of the mission' and other uses of force that might be necessary. They have rarely, for instance, contained guidance on what exactly defence of the mission entails or how to ensure the protection of non-UN personnel and local populations at risk. While an admirable emphasis has been placed on the avoidance of escalation, there has been little recognition that the credibility and therefore safety of an entire mission can be damaged if an over-cautious attitude is taken towards the use of force when it is warranted.[23] Issues such as crowd control have often not been dealt with adequately, reflecting outdated concepts and methods. Increasing Americanization of UN ROE has led to new concepts like 'deadly force', 'perceived threat' and 'proportional response' being introduced without adequate explanations being provided to troops unused to them.

In the field there has often been surprisingly little effort to ensure that the UN's use-of-force rules were widely disseminated and actually superseded national ones, or at least complemented them. Sometimes, as in Somalia, the differences between national ROE were only discovered by serendipity rather than systematically. Even where the force commander tried to achieve harmonization, as in Cambodia and Sierra Leone, he encountered resistance and sometimes insubordination. Joint training in the use of UN ROE has been almost non-existent, and where it has occurred has been localized and unsystematic. The great exception was UNMIH in Haiti, where training was successfully provided and paid dividends in avoiding the use of force.

There may be legal, political, national or cultural reasons for the reluctance of states to follow UN ROE.

Each nation has a different ROE philosophy and interprets the relevant terms, such as 'hostile act', 'hostile intent', in a different way. For some nations ROE are integral to crisis management, the objective being to avoid taking any action that might escalate the situation, and the firing of a weapon, even in self-defence, is very much an action of last resort. For others, conflict is a less complex affair and the threshold for aggressive reaction is much lower . . . This is not a question of being 'trigger happy', or excessively nervous in the face of danger, but is rather the result of training in a different military culture—for example, one that does not expect military men to react in too sophisticated a way when lives are at risk, or where the sole doctrine is winning at any cost.[24]

---

[23] Palin, R. H., International Institute for Strategic Studies (IISS), *Multinational Military Forces: Problems and Prospects. The Problems Facing Multinational Forces and Operations, and Prospects for the Future*, Adelphi Paper no. 294 (Oxford University Press: London, 1995), p. 34.

[24] Palin (note 23), p. 34.

Some militaries, like those of Australia and the USA, regard ROE as orders and soldiers who disobey them are liable to court martial. Others, such as those of Canada and New Zealand, regard them simply as 'guidelines'.[25] Some states have legal difficulties deriving from their domestic law. For instance, the use of force by Canadian troops beyond defending themselves and their colleagues— for instance, to defend property, civilians or 'the mission'—could violate Canadian domestic law and subject them to prosecution. The British Army does not normally allow the use of warning shots before force is used on the grounds that this weakens the deterrent effect of the threat of force and in some situations may endanger the lives of the soldiers involved. Some military forces, such as those of Malaysia, do not use ROE at all.

The difficulties that disparate national policies on the use of force can create in the field are legion. Local factions will soon become aware which UN contingents are reluctant to use force and will attempt to play one off against the other, instinctively testing the limits of the ROE and trying to exploit weakness and inconsistencies.[26] When force commanders, local area commanders or entire units or battalions are replaced during the course of long-term missions, local factions may test the resolve of the newcomers in adhering to their ROE by manufacturing an incident.

Those contingents using more robust ROE than others may endanger the lives of other peacekeepers through crossfire, by aggravating particular incidents or by giving the impression that the operation has moved into a higher gear than intended.[27] On the other hand, contingents following more conservative ROE, by not reacting robustly and consistently when it is justifiable, degrade the credibility of the UN force, thereby compounding its inability to carry out its mission.

### Considerations in devising UN rules of engagement

UN ROE need to be drafted in consultation with all troop-contributing countries and take into account the special needs of peace operations in balancing restrictiveness with permissiveness and conciseness with comprehensiveness. The following elements should be considered in devising UN ROE.[28]

---

[25] Personal communications with Lt-Col Mike Kelly, Legal Advisor, Australian Defence Forces, Canberra, May 1995, and officials of the New Zealand Ministry of External Relations and Trade, Wellington, May 1995. This did not stop the force commander in Bosnia telling the Canadian troops to treat UN ROE as orders (Erwin A. Schmidl, Institute for Military Studies, Vienna, at the Conference on the Use of Force in Peace Operations, Lester B. Pearson Canadian International Peacekeeping Training Centre, Nova Scotia, 16 May 1996).

[26] Lorenz (note 22), p. 24.

[27] In Somalia, when it was discovered that Italian troops operating alongside US Marines were trained to use warning shots, the US Command decided to adapt to the Italian procedure rather than risk Italian warning shots being mistaken for hostile action against US forces. Lorenz (note 22), p. 22. A further complication arose in Haiti, where UN CivPols were armed for the first time in a UN mission. Since they could not be issued with military-style ROE, they were given 'guidelines' instead. Schmidl (note 25).

[28] The following is based in part on a very useful analysis found in Bowens, G. (Capt.), *Legal Guide to Peace Operations* (US Peacekeeping Institute, US Army War College: Carlisle, Pa., 1998).

1. *The UN's political, military and legal purposes.* UN ROE should reflect these faithfully. In the political realm they need to ensure that UN objectives are reflected in the action of commanders in the field. Of special importance for the UN is that its ROE take account of the influence of international public opinion and how the use of force might affect and, in turn, be affected by, the local and international media.

The military purpose of ROE for UN peace operations should be to establish a ceiling on the use of force and ensure that UN actions do not trigger undesired escalation. ROE should be neither too restrictive nor too permissive. For both peacekeeping and peace enforcement operations they should always authorize the use of force in self-defence and to protect non-military UN personnel and civilians at risk. They should also include guidance concerning mutual support by the components of the UN force, such as civilian police or rapid reaction forces.

In legal terms, UN ROE should signify the restraints placed on a force commander's action by international law, to which the UN, above all, must scrupulously adhere. ROE should not be used to convey strategy or doctrine, restate the laws of war or prescribe tactics.[29]

2. *Proportionality and restraint.* Compared with war-fighting, which places a premium on aggressiveness once the enemy has been identified, peace operations should be characterized by restraint in the use of force. For peace enforcement purposes ROE will be more robust, to permit the use of force for wider purposes, but should nonetheless be carefully calibrated to the political and military circumstances. Even the authorization to respond to hostile *intent*, which is prohibited in peacekeeping but likely to be permitted in peace enforcement, should be more constrained than it would be in wartime.[30]

3. *Clarity.* Clarity is necessary not only for the troops that will be using force but for all the local parties involved in the conflict, as well as the local population. The media, which often focus on ROE and can easily misunderstand them, also need to be clear about their meaning. ROE in peace operations should therefore be clearly drafted and unclassified.

4. *Simplicity versus detail.* For similar reasons, simplicity is a virtue. Above all ROE must be readily understandable, easy to memorize and instantly applicable. Allard recommends that ROE be written 'not only with the "KISS" principle (Keep it Simple, Stupid) in mind but also with an appreciation for how they might be applied in tense situations by warfighters rather than lawyers'.[31] Force commanders often have an inclination to control individual conduct by creating detailed ROE—the 'legislative' approach—in an attempt to eliminate

---

[29] Bowens (note 28), pp. 189–90.
[30] Hardesty, J. M. (Col) and Ellis, J. D., 'Training for peace operations: the US Army adapts to the post-cold war world', *Peaceworks* (United States Institute of Peace (USIP), Washington, DC), no. 12 (Feb. 1997), p. 11.
[31] Allard, K., 'Co-operation, command and control: lessons learned or lessons identified?', Lecture to the Swedish War College, reproduced in Ahlquist, L. (ed.), *Co-operation, Command and Control in UN Peace Support Operations: A Pilot Study from the Swedish War College* (Försvarshögskolan, Operativa Institutionen [Swedish National Defence College, Department of Operations]: Stockholm, 1996), p. 38.

doubt as to individual and unit behaviour,[32] for example, placing the phrase 'clearly demonstrated' before 'hostile intent'. The Somalia lessons-learned report favoured ROE 'sufficiently detailed to eliminate doubt as to individual and unit behaviour'.[33] However, detailed, complex and legalistic ROE are useless in military operations in which quick decisions must be made in stressful circumstances. There is thus a continuing tension between the need for simplicity and brevity, on the one hand (especially given the limited size that an ROE card can be), and the need for sufficient detail to provide for all major contingencies, on the other.

5. *Flexibility.* Local commanders must have the flexibility to restrict ROE if necessary. However, frequent changes should be avoided. Allard notes that the old military maxim, 'Order—Counter-order—Disorder', applies to ROE as well.[34] Especially in peace enforcement missions, the ROE must be continually monitored for their appropriateness and relevance, but constant readjustment should be avoided.

## Training in the use of rules of engagement

In an ideal peace operations world all states contributing troops to each mission should commit themselves to common objectives in using force and be involved in drafting common ROE. Even the best ROE will, however, still leave room for ambiguity and will not cover every imaginable situation—which is where training becomes essential. An enduring lesson of UN peace operations is that the ROE should be issued before an operation commences and training must begin as soon as possible in advance to ensure that soldiers truly understand the application of the ROE and do not just memorize them.[35] One serious challenge is ensuring that soldiers do not confuse ROE with other guidelines and understand that ROE take precedence over all other rules governing the use of force.[36] Lieutenant-Colonel William Martinez, who served with the US 10th Mountain Division in Somalia, says: 'Creating different scenarios or situations to help soldiers practice the ROE will help them clarify in their minds the situation in which they can or cannot fire. The time to learn this is before coming under fire or getting into a situation that could cost a life'.[37]

As a direct result of the Brahimi recommendations, the UN has moved recently to meet the need for 'in-mission' training, including in ROE. Its Standard Operating Procedures for Mission Training Cells (MTCs), which have already been established for UNTAET, UNMEE, MONUC and UNAMSIL,

[32] 'Comprehensive report on lessons-learned from United Nations Operation in Somalia' (note 6), p. 15.
[33] 'Comprehensive report on lessons-learned from United Nations Operation in Somalia' (note 6), p. 15.
[34] Allard (note 31), p. 38.
[35] Dworken, J. T., 'Rules of engagement: lessons from Restore Hope', *Military Review*, vol. 74, no. 5 (Sep. 1994), p. 33; and Schroeder, D. (Lt-Gen.), 'Lessons of Rwanda', *Armed Forces Journal*, Dec. 1994, pp. 31–33.
[36] Dworken (note 35), p. 33.
[37] Martinez, W. (Lt-Col), 'Peace operations', *Infantry*, May/June 1994, pp. 39–40.

call for monthly training in ROE and in the use of force by all peace operations in the field.[38]

*Determining mission-specific rules of engagement*

Even when UN models are agreed there are likely to be continuing tussles between the UN Secretariat and some troop contributors over the ROE for any specific mission. The current plan is that, as soon as a mandate for a new or altered mission is mooted, ROE will be drafted by the Office of Planning and Support and submitted to the force commander or commander-designate for approval. The regular meetings that have been instituted between representatives of troop-contributing countries and senior officers of the DPKO are likely to be used to discuss ROE and other use-of-force issues. Differences between the national ROE of participating contingents will be taken into account and an attempt made to adopt a unified set of ROE across the theatre of operations. The Under Secretary-General for Peacekeeping Operations will be given the final right of approval (it is unlikely that the Secretary-General would be involved in the process, unless the ROE are extraordinarily controversial). In the theatre of operations, it will remain up to the force commander whether or not ROE cards are used. He can choose his own method of dissemination.

The danger is that troop contributors will attempt to veto ROE that they perceive to be too robust or unsatisfactory in other ways, thereby holding up the deployment or operation of a mission. To avoid this the Secretary-General has consistently reiterated his view that it remains the UN Secretariat's prerogative ultimately to determine ROE.

The major difficulty that the UN currently confronts in drafting ROE is that there is no consensus among its member states on doctrine, from which the crafting of ROE should automatically flow. Until this missing element is provided, the drafting of UN ROE will be problematic, especially in the case of more robust or complex operations.

## III. Peace enforcement and the UN

Volumes have been written and academic and military reputations staked since the end of the cold war on the question of how to characterize the new type of peace operation known throughout this volume as peace enforcement. This would have remained a mere academic exercise were it not for the fact that, as an increasingly plausible tool of international statecraft, peace enforcement has to be carefully distinguished from other types of endeavour, including peace-keeping and enforcement. States, non-state actors and the UN itself must know what peace enforcement means, particularly with regard to the use of force, if they are to host, participate in, organize or otherwise support such operations.

---

[38] See the DPKO Internet site at URL <http://www.un.org/Depts/dpko/training/MTC>.

## What is peace enforcement?

There seems to be a convergence of view that peace enforcement is an identifiable category of peace operations which is both conceptually and doctrinally conceivable and which can also work in practice. Numerous academic studies, although they may use different terms to describe it, have collectively conceptualized the basic characteristics of what here has been called peace enforcement.[39]

Western militaries, while also using divergent terms, have moved towards a shared conceptualization of peace enforcement. The conservative military reaction to the idea of peace enforcement—that it was synonymous with 'warfighting'—has been discredited. The change in military attitudes may have been due partly to a realization that if the military were not prepared to undertake peace enforcement they would deprive themselves of both political support and resources at a time when the end of the cold war was threatening military budgets. Western militaries also seemed to find comfort in the realization that they have always been asked to undertake missions with political objectives and that there are always significant restraints on the uses to which military force could be put.

Since the end of the cold war the major Western militaries have adopted some form of peace enforcement doctrine.[40] According to Lieutenant-Colonel Philip Wilkinson, an international consensus has developed along the lines of British doctrine.[41] Peter Viggo Jakobsen attributes greater influence to the French *'restauration de la paix'* doctrine.[42] Whatever the case, the development of peace enforcement doctrine occurred initially in and between the major new peace operations players, France, the UK and the USA, and has gradually spread to all of NATO[43] and Western partners like Australia. Even the Nordic countries have been won over, partly because of their experience in Bosnia.[44] Western peace enforcement doctrine has been on display in several missions, including INTERFET, Opération Turquoise, IFOR, the Stabilization Force (SFOR) in Bosnia and the Kosovo Force (KFOR).

[39] See in particular the works, listed in the bibliography in this volume, of Jarat Chopra, Don Daniel, Brad Hayes, John Mackinlay, John Ruggie, Tom Weiss and Philip Wilkinson.

[40] For examples, see appendix 1 in this volume.

[41] Wilkinson, P. R. (Lt-Col), 'The development of the United Kingdom's doctrine on peace-support operations', International Security Information Service (ISIS) Briefing Paper no. 68, London, May 1998, p. 8; and Thornton, R., 'The role of peace support operations doctrine in the British Army', *International Peacekeeping*, vol. 7, no. 2 (summer 2000), p. 57.

[42] Jakobsen, P. V., 'The emerging consensus on grey area peace operations doctrine: will it last and enhance operational effectiveness?', *International Peacekeeping*, vol. 7, no. 3 (autumn 2000), pp. 36–56. On *'restauration de la paix'* see appendix 1, section III, in this volume.

[43] NATO, Bi-MNC [i.e., issued by the 2 major NATO commands] Directive for NATO doctrine for peace support operations, Brussels, Final draft, 27 July 1998. According to Wilkinson, however, NATO still does not have an agreed peace operations doctrine after 6 years of trying. Wilkinson, P. (Lt-Col), Presentation at a Joint Foreign and Commonwealth Office–United Nations Association Seminar on Steps towards Implementation of Conflict Prevention and the Brahimi Report, Lancaster House, London, 28 Mar. 2001.

[44] Swedish Armed Forces, 'Joint military doctrine: peace support operations', Stockholm, Oct. 1997.

The generally shared concept of peace enforcement appears to be that it aims to ensure the implementation of a peace agreement or arrangement (such as a ceasefire), including compliance by all parties with their undertakings, through the judicious application of incentives and disincentives, among them the robust use of force. Any use of force will be closely calibrated with political action, hopefully at the highest level, that of the UN Security Council. While peace enforcement may sound like a military strategy, in essence it must be political, with the military playing a supporting role involving deterrence and compellence as necessary.

A peace enforcement operation may take place in the context of a comprehensive political strategy which may include all or most of the following elements: a ceasefire; the withdrawal and/cantonment of forces; the demobilization, disarmament and reintegration of soldiers into civil society; the establishment or re-establishment of democratic governance; the repatriation and resettlement of refugees and internally displaced persons; humanitarian assistance; the inculcation and protection of human rights; action on landmines; the re-establishment of a judicial system and a civilian police force; encouragement of the growth of civil society; and quick-impact development projects in conjunction with longer-term economic reconstruction and development.

Unlike in peacekeeping, the threat of force and the use of force beyond self-defence are key instruments in the 'tool box' of a peace enforcement operation—although the more impressive the capabilities for using force appear to be to the former belligerents, the less likely they are to be employed. The requirement for the use of force is likely to be high at the beginning of an operation but taper off as the peace settlement takes hold. As in peacekeeping, the degree of consent to or acquiescence in the deployment and operation of a peace enforcement mission that is obtainable from the local parties will be a key consideration.

Unlike peacekeeping operations, peace enforcement operations will by definition be deployed in situations where consent may be extremely tenuous or where only acquiescence can be mustered. In contrast to a pure enforcement operation, a peace enforcement operation would not be expected to fight its way into a theatre of operation (although it might have to fight its way out if consent disappeared completely). A peace enforcement mission would only deploy where a peace agreement or other arrangement, such as permission to protect the distribution of humanitarian assistance—however shaky—had been agreed. Its aim would not be to impose its own will on the country or parties concerned by defeating them in battle, but rather to bolster the chances that an agreement reached by mistrustful parties will succeed. Unlike in peacekeeping operations, where such support is passive and reactive, peace enforcement operations will take a more proactive stance and will not make 'best-case' assumptions about the final outcome of a peace process.

A peace enforcement operation, like a peacekeeping one, should seek from the outset to be impartial in its treatment of the local parties. It should not knowingly take sides, but rather act as an independent, impartial arbiter. Unlike a peacekeeping operation, however, it will have at its disposal the use of military force as the ultimate sanction in case it needs to coerce one side or the other to behave. This tool of 'coercive inducement', as Don Daniel, Brad Hayes and Chantal de Jonge Oudraat call it,[45] should be used after all other reasonable methods, such as negotiation and positive inducements, have been tried, although not necessarily (as in peacekeeping) as a last resort. When it is used it may be robust but must always be judicious, an inducement rather than a punishment, leave the way open for the belligerent party involved to concede without too much loss of face, and be undertaken in full awareness of the consequences of escalation and of the long-term need for reconciliation. It also needs to be used with an awareness of UN and other civilian activities going on in the rest of the mission area, the need to take great pains to avoid civilian casualties or 'collateral damage' to property, and the need for scrupulous compliance with international law.

The main military role of a peace enforcement force will be not in actually using force but in rapidly projecting a military presence into the theatre of operations as soon as possible to: (*a*) signal international resolve; (*b*) reassure parties which are nervous about surrendering their military assets as part of the peace process (thereby leaving them vulnerable and uncertain, and more likely to hedge their bets by only partially fulfilling their obligations)—a reassurance that traditional peacekeepers could not give; and (*c*) provide protection for the other elements of the international operation, especially the civilian components and the civilian police if they are unarmed. The rapid and confident insertion of a Security Council-mandated international force into the field immediately after a peace agreement is signed is now seen as a significant factor in sustaining the momentum of peace and creating a spiral of confidence in compliance that will produce a successful long-term outcome. The tardy, disorganized and tentative deployment of a patched-together UN peacekeeping operation into delicate post-conflict environments is now seen as almost an invitation to the parties to hedge their bets and for 'spoilers' to chance their luck.

Once a peace operation is successfully deployed, the scenarios in which it might be necessary for it to use significant force, apart from in self-defence, are relatively easily identified. They include: (*a*) persistent and/or large-scale viola-tion of a ceasefire line or demilitarized zone; (*b*) a refusal to cooperate in can-tonment, demobilization and/or disarmament; (*c*) an attempt to disrupt an elec-toral process by military or other violent means; (*d*) attempts at genocide and/or the commission of gross violations of human rights; and (*e*) threats to the delivery of humanitarian assistance. It is also clear that, as in peacekeeping operations, a number of these scenarios would involve or be accompanied by attacks on UN forces or their installations. UN forces could thus use force in self-defence or in defence of their mission at whatever level of 'robustness' was required (without peacekeepers' normal fear of overstepping their mandate into

---

[45] Daniel, D. C. F. and Hayes, B. D. (eds) with Chantal de Jonge Oudraat, *Coercive Inducement and the Containment of International Crises* (United States Institute of Peace Press: Washington, DC, 1999).

peace enforcement). Hence in some cases peace enforcement, from a military perspective, may be little different from 'robust' use of force in self-defence.

A peace enforcement mission should be prepared for the likelihood that if punitive military action is taken against one party then that party will accuse the international force of being biased against it and intent on crushing it. Not only will the operation need diplomatic and political skills and high-level political backing from the Security Council to overcome such accusations and bring the recalcitrant party back into the peace process, but significant military strength will also be required to give the impression that resistance is futile. The force will thus need to be designed for something between the best-case and the worst-case scenarios. In current military parlance it will be required to maintain 'escalation dominance', while at the same time employing the types of conflict de-escalation technique for which doctrine now exists and which have been perfected by a number of militaries.[46] If the recalcitrant party is not coerced and resorts to sustained retaliation or even guerrilla or terrorist operations against the peace operation, various options will have to be considered. These may range from bolstering the military capability of the force, to changing the nature of the operation to pure enforcement (which would involve taking sides in the conflict), to withdrawal. These are the same dilemmas that face peacekeeping operations or indeed any military undertaking. The deployment of accompanying rapid reaction or off-shore back-up forces is an increasingly common approach to the need for reinforcements in emergencies.

As with more substantial peacekeeping operations, a peace enforcement operation should not be a purely military affair. To have the greatest chance of success it should comprise the necessary civilian, civilian police, humanitarian and peace-building components. It should operate in close coordination with the non-governmental sector, both international and local, and with civil society generally. It should aim for 'unity of effort' in these relationships. In sum, it should be geared towards a political rather than military end-state.

### Peace enforcement in practice

The above is the theory of peace enforcement. In practice, as the case studies reveal, it is a surprisingly elusive phenomenon. As yet there seems to have been no case of a pure peace enforcement mission in the way it has been conceptualized in theory. The UN missions that have been widely considered to have engaged in peace enforcement (or accused of doing so)—ONUC, UNOSOM II and UNPROFOR—were never mandated to do so comprehensively; they did so only spasmodically and unsystematically; and they lacked the necessary doctrine, concepts of operation and, indeed, comprehensive peace enforcement strategy (including a peace agreement) that the theory would expect. It is not for nothing that such missions became known in the early days of the post-cold war

---

[46] See, e.g., Last, D., *Theory, Doctrine and Practice of Conflict De-Escalation in Peacekeeping Operations* (Canadian Peacekeeping Press: Clementsport, 1997).

debate as 'grey area' operations. While they all hold lessons for peace enforcement in the future, none of them represents a model to be emulated.

ONUC acted mostly in peacekeeping mode, as if it had the consent of all the parties, carrying out most of its tasks using force only in self-defence. Only in the case of military action against the mercenaries and against the Katangan Government could it be said to have engaged in peace enforcement. However, the fact that the UN ultimately used force to bring about the downfall of the Katangan regime suggests Chapter VII enforcement, rather than peace enforcement, and illustrates the fine line between the two. ONUC should, to that extent, be viewed as a mixture of peacekeeping, peace enforcement and enforcement.

Although UNOSOM II Force Commander Çevik Bir says that he saw his operation as Chapter VII peace enforcement,[47] the Somalia commission of inquiry notes that Chapter VII was invoked only to obviate the need for Somalia to give consent to the presence of a UN force and to authorize the use of force, if necessary, to keep aid delivery channels open and disarm the militia.[48] Force was not authorized for imposing peace on Somalia in the sense of coercing the parties to reach a peace settlement or foisting nation-building on it. It might be argued that, once the Security Council expanded UNOSOM II's mandate in order to permit it to deal forcefully with Aideed, it automatically became a peace enforcement operation; but those who see impartiality as a key characteristic of peace enforcement see UNOSOM II more properly as enforcement. William Durch's description of it as a 'quasi-enforcement' operation seems apt.[49] The mission in reality combined elements of peacekeeping, peace enforcement and enforcement, as well as, in its civilian and humanitarian functions, peacemaking and peace-building.

UNPROFOR was similarly a mixed operation, and perhaps the furthest of the three from being pure peace enforcement. Although commonly described as a peacekeeping operation, it lacked key essentials of such missions—the consent of the parties, freedom of movement and a peace agreement, or at least a ceasefire to establish the context of its work. Its peacekeeping-like activities, such as the protection of humanitarian assistance and monitoring of weapon exclusion zones, were all done without the benefit of general consent. To that extent the Security Council was imposing UNPROFOR on the parties. Although it eventually acquired a Chapter VII mandate, this was only ever explicitly designed to bolster its own self-defence (although, as in the ONUC case, it was expected that there would be side-benefits, in this case protection of the safe areas). Even NATO was only mandated to help UNPROFOR protect

[47] Briefing by Lt-Gen. Bir at UN Headquarters, 25 Jan. 1994.

[48] United Nations, Report of the Commission of Inquiry established pursuant to Security Council Resolution 885 (1993) to investigate armed attacks on UNOSOM II personnel which led to casualties among them, 24 Feb. 1994, appended to United Nations, Note by the Secretary-General, UN document S/1994/653, 1 June 1994, paras 195–211.

[49] Durch, W. J., 'Introduction to anarchy: humanitarian intervention and "state building" in Somalia', ed. W. J. Durch, UN Peacekeeping, American Policy, and the Uncivil Wars of the 1990s (St Martin's Press: New York, 1996), p. 350.

itself, not to enforce the sanctity of the enclaves. Only at the very end of the mission, when NATO, the RRF and other elements of UNPROFOR used force to drive the Serbs to the negotiating table, can UNPROFOR be said to have become a peace enforcement operation. However, this last-gasp gamble can hardly be portrayed as a model for future peace enforcement operations.

*Non-UN missions*

Ironically, Chapter VII mandates covering all the activities of a peace operation have been reserved for non-UN (but Security Council-authorized) multinational coalitions. Several of these are widely believed to have demonstrated—albeit not flawlessly—the feasibility of at least some peace enforcement concepts in the field. These include the multinational coalition operation in Northern Iraq after the Gulf War,[50] UNITAF, IFOR and the follow-on SFOR in Bosnia,[51] the MNF in Haiti, Opération Turquoise in Rwanda, the NATO-led KFOR[52] and INTERFET in East Timor.[53]

UNITAF was widely seen at the time an instance of successful peace enforcement. However, there are several reasons why, especially with the benefit of hindsight, this is not convincing. First, its Chapter VII powers only related to the creation of a secure environment for the delivery of humanitarian aid. Second, the USA, ever wary of 'mission creep', deliberately chose to interpret this mandate narrowly, excluding comprehensive and systematic disarmament from its concept of creating a secure environment. Third, even in the execution of its narrowed mandate, UNITAF adopted a defensive posture, was obsessed with force protection, and chose not to use force when its concept of operation and relatively robust ROE would have permitted it to do so. This was principally to avoid being drawn into armed clashes with the Somali factions and thereby avoid US casualties. Had it been engaged in true peace enforcement, UNITAF would have used 'its overwhelming advantages in military

---

[50] Tom Weiss describes it as follows: 'Superior military force was sub-contracted to the allied coalition that secured direct access to civilians', with the mission thereafter turned over to civilian humanitarian organizations (and UN guards), and NATO firepower in reserve in Turkey. Weiss (note 16), p. 173.

[51] SFOR was fielded by NATO but accompanied by UN CivPols and other UN and Organization for Security and Co-operation in Europe (OSCE) civilian components.

[52] UN Security Council Resolution 1244 of 10 June 1999 did not expressly authorize the use of force and did not say that member states could take 'all necessary measures' to carry out its mandate. Instead it authorized member states and relevant international organizations to establish the international security presence in Kosovo 'with all necessary means to fulfill its responsibilities under the resolution'. This was seen by the West as wide enough to cover enforcement action, but by China and Russia as not an authorization to use force. Coray, C., *International Law and the Use of Force* (Oxford University Press: Oxford, 2000), p. 190. KFOR is accompanied by the non-military UN Mission in Kosovo (UNMIK) and OSCE civilian components.

[53] Not included in this list are the Inter-African Mission to Monitor the Implementation of the Bangui Agreements (MISAB) in the Central African Republic and the Italian-led Multinational Protection Force (MPF), both established in 1997, since they were only authorized under Chapter VII to use force in self-defence, to ensure the security and freedom of movement of their own personnel. Findlay, T., 'Armed conflict prevention, management and resolution', *SIPRI Yearbook 1998: Armaments, Disarmament and International Security* (Oxford University Press: Oxford, 1998), p. 53. The replacement force for MISAB, the UN Mission in the Central African Republic (MINURCA), established in 1998, had a similar limitation on its authorization to use force.

force, command and control, logistics, and communications to support a political agenda'.[54] Walter Clarke argues that UNITAF had no idea what it hoped Somalia would look like at the end of its intervention, making the collapse of subsequent UN political and military efforts 'probably inevitable'—again, hardly a model to be emulated.[55]

IFOR, SFOR and KFOR are generally regarded as successful examples of peace enforcement, but these missions were only possible because of a preceding NATO bombing campaign which would be more properly defined as pure enforcement. This meant that the parties were already cowed into compliance before these missions were deployed. The missions were thus able to operate much more like peacekeeping than peace enforcement operations. Indeed, IFOR and SFOR have both been accused of ignoring certain aspects of their peace enforcement role—the detention of suspected war criminals—on the grounds that it was too dangerous and not a role the military were trained for.

The mission that probably comes closest to the theory of peace enforcement is INTERFET, except that as an entirely military operation it lacked the civilian components that are seen as essential to managing and resolving intra-state conflict. These came later with UNTAET, which, even though it did not need to use its enforcement powers, can be regarded as a successful case of peace enforcement—although, again, it had the benefit of INTERFET's good work in securing and pacifying the territory before it arrived.

## Could the UN successfully do peace enforcement?

With each new failure of a peace operation there are assertions that the UN should confine itself to traditional peacekeeping and leave more dangerous missions to others. There are two variations on this theme. One holds that the UN is inherently incapable of peace enforcement and that no amount of organizational reform can give it the required capacity. For Michael Mandelbaum: 'The UN can no more conduct military operations on a large-scale on its own than a trade association of hospitals can conduct heart surgery'.[56] The second variation is that the UN is not currently capable of conducting such operations but might, in time, be able to do so, providing its capabilities are dramatically improved. Robert Oakley concludes of the Somalia episode that it 'cast too great a shadow' over the whole concept of Chapter VII enforcement and 'it would be wrong to conclude that such efforts cannot succeed under other circumstances, or if managed more carefully'.[57] The two camps tend to agree that the preferred option, at least for the foreseeable future, is the contracting out of peace enforcement to 'coalitions of the willing' on an ad hoc basis.

---

[54] Clarke, W., 'Failed visions and uncertain mandates in Somalia', eds W. Clarke and J. Herbst, *Learning from Somalia: The Lessons of Armed Humanitarian Intervention* (Lynne Rienner: Boulder, Colo., 1996), p. 11.

[55] Clarke and Herbst (note 54), p. 4.

[56] Mandelbaum, M., 'The reluctance to intervene', *Foreign Policy*, no. 95 (summer 1994), p. 11.

[57] Hirsch, J. L. and Oakley, R. B., *Somalia and Operation Restore Hope: Reflections on Peacemaking and Peacekeeping* (United States Institute of Peace Press: Washington, DC, 1995), p. 162.

Unfortunately, the debate about whether the UN is capable of peace enforcement or not is still bedevilled by a lack of clarity about what peace enforcement is and disagreement about whether the obstacles to UN involvement in peace enforcement are inherent or remediable given time, commitment and resources. Indeed, the reflections of many observers on this issue are almost tautologous: UN peace enforcement operations could succeed if they were provided with all the elements for success.

The most plausible arguments for the 'inherent incapacity' thesis centre on: (a) the collective character of UN decision making and its alleged consequent inability to command and control a peace enforcement operation; (b) the fact that member states will be unwilling to accept the risks and sacrifices involved in peace enforcement for an 'internationalist' rather than a national cause; and (c) the fact that the UN lacks the 'sovereign legitimacy and authority' which would allow it to build the institutions, structures and procedures necessary for conducting peace enforcement.[58]

However, most of the arguments about the inherent incapacity of the UN to conduct peace enforcement operations also appear to hold true for 'coalitions of the willing' or even military operations conducted by a single state. Contrary to the arguments of John Hillen,[59] it is only the UN, as the supreme organization of international society, that can confer legitimacy and authority on peace enforcement operations. One of the reasons why Russian troops were invited to join KFOR was to help give legitimacy to a 'coalition of the willing' operation that followed a NATO bombing campaign which had not been authorized by the UN and which many observers and states, notably China, argued was illegal under international law. And even though Opération Turquoise and Operation Alba[60] were lent legitimacy by means of Security Council endorsement, this was insufficient to convince many observers that French and Italian national interests, respectively, were not paramount in these operations.

As General Douglas MacArthur's insubordination during the Korean War, which led to his sacking, illustrates, command and control are not foolproof even in coalition operations commanded by one state. The command and control failures in UNOSOM II were as much a product of supposedly more robust national arrangements, in this case those of the USA, as those of the 'inherently' more fallible UN.

Certainly, it is easier for a nation state to mobilize national support for a military operation where national honour and liberty are at stake, and which may call for sacrifices of 'blood and treasure', but even this degree of commitment is not unknown to UN peace operations, as the determination of India and Pakistan to keep their troops in Somalia after the 1994 debacle indicated. The number of casualties in UN peacekeeping operations (more than 1600 by the

[58] Hillen, J., *Blue Helmets: The Strategy of UN Military Operations*, 2nd edn (Brassey's: Washington, DC, 2000), pp. 237, 243.
[59] Hillen (note 58).
[60] See chapter 8, note 101, in this volume.

end of 2000[61]) suggests that states are actually willing to make contributions to dangerous multilateral causes if they perceive the cause to be just and legitimate. Finally, history suggests that the management of communal conflict is inherently difficult, whether it is attempted by states, empires, or regional or global organizations. 'The UN should not be judged too harshly merely for running into difficulties similar to those encountered by other bodies.'[62]

In a sense the debate about whether the UN is capable of and should be allowed to conduct peace enforcement operations is academic. In practical terms the UN is likely to be asked to carry out peace enforcement, whether it is called that or 'robust' or 'complex' peacekeeping', or is afforded no moniker at all. Typically, the Security Council will act pragmatically in seeking solutions to the breakdown or imminent breakdown of peace agreements or to bolster the implementation of shaky ones from the outset. Moreover, Secretary-General Kofi Annan has made increasingly clear that the events in Kigali and Srebrenica mean that the UN can no longer ignore the moral imperatives of humanitarian and human rights situations, especially when there is already an armed UN presence on the scene. The inevitable conclusion is that UN peace forces must, in these circumstances, become involved in this type of peace enforcement, whether they are explicitly mandated to or not.

The argument that the UN should subcontract peace enforcement operations to coalitions of the willing rather than do them itself may also prove to be misleading. The only reason why INTERFET became a multinational force rather than a UN one was that Indonesia opposed a UN operation and rapid deployment seemed to be beyond the UN's capabilities at that stage. If the UN can successfully tackle its rapid deployment challenges, the only remaining barrier will be political will—and in some instances solving the capability problem may solve the political one.

It is not clear why a force along the lines of INTERFET could not be deployed directly under UN command, yet maintain essentially the same characteristics as that operation. Had INTERFET been designated 'UNFET', General Peter Cosgrove would have taken his orders direct from the Security Council, via the Secretary-General, rather than from the Australian Prime Minister. Cosgrove was presumably in any case acutely conscious that he had to act within both the letter and the spirit of the UN's 'mandate' to the multinational force and with the confidence and cooperation of the highly diverse, UN-like multinational force assembled. In many respects INTERFET had the appearance of a UN mission but without the UN. It would have been improved by the addition of UN civilian components. Just two countries, Australia and New Zealand, supplied an unusually high proportion of the troops, headquarters staff and communications personnel compared to a normal UN mission; but UN

---

[61] United Nations, Department of Public Information, 'United Nations peacekeeping from 1991 to 2000: statistical data and charts', UN document DPI/2175, New York, Dec. 2000.

[62] Roberts, A., 'Communal conflict as a challenge to international organization: the case of the former Yugoslavia', eds O. A. Otunnu and M. W. Doyle, *Peacemaking and Peacekeeping for the New Century* (Rowman & Littlefield: Lanham, Md., 1998), p. 50.

missions themselves have been dominated in the past by a small number of large contingents. This includes UNPROFOR, dominated by the NATO states, UNOSOM II, dominated by the South Asian states after the Western countries departed, and most recently UNAMSIL. The model being proposed here is also not too different from those of UNMIH and UNTAES, where US force commanders were able to bring highly capable US command and control and military capabilities to form the core of a UN mission. In some respects these missions looked like multinational operations with a UN cover. Further experimentation with such models may make the argument over the UN's capacity for peace enforcement essentially redundant.

## IV. Towards a UN peace operations doctrine?

The great lacuna in all efforts to improve UN peace operations is doctrine. Despite the current Secretary-General's pleas for an expansive reconsideration of the UN's conduct of peace operations, the support of all member states for strengthening UN capabilities in at least some respects and the existence of virtual doctrinal consensus among Western states, there seems little immediate prospect that the political will exists for a radical new approach to the use of force in UN peace operations and its encapsulation in doctrine. Whenever doctrinal development is mooted, as shown by the reaction to Annan's virtual throwaway line in his report on implementing Brahimi's recommendations,[63] the reaction of some member states can be swift and discouraging.

The difficulties are further illustrated by the reaction to Annan's initiative for tackling the misuse of force by individual UN soldiers and units. On 10 August 1999 he issued an executive order, to coincide with the 50th anniversary of the 1949 Geneva conventions, establishing a code of conduct for peacekeepers with regard to international humanitarian law which obliges them to abide by it in the same way that national armed forces must.[64] The Special Committee on Peacekeeping Operations chided him over the lack of prior consultation with member states over the initiative, questioned the legal status of the document and requested immediate discussions with him.[65]

States opposed to the development of a UN peace operations doctrine believe that it will inevitably imitate Western doctrine, meaning peace enforcement that might be practised against them, or at the very least might set precedents that could affect their cherished independence, sovereignty and territorial integrity. The reports of the Special Committee on Peacekeeping Operations, adopted by consensus, try to ward off doctrinal development by repeating the mantra of traditional peacekeeping. Despite the evolution of peace operations in the past

[63] See chapter 9, section V, in this volume.
[64] United Nations, *Secretary-General's Bulletin*, ST/SGB/1000/13; and 'US to train Africans for Sierra Leone duty', *International Herald Tribune*, 10 Aug. 2000, p. 2.
[65] United Nations, Comprehensive review of the whole question of peacekeeping operations in all their aspects, Report of the Special Committee on Peacekeeping Operations, UN document A/54/839, 20 Mar. 2000, para. 82.

decade and the disasters that have befallen so many missions, not to mention the expansion of the self-defence norm in 1973 to include the use of force to defend the mission, the committee's March 2001 report obliviously noted that 'respect for the basic peacekeeping principles, such as the consent of the parties, impartiality and the non-use of force, except in self-defence' is essential to the success of peacekeeping.[66] Nothing more was said on conceptual or doctrinal issues: it was as if the Srebrenica report had never been written.

One way in which UN peace operations are acquiring de facto doctrine is through the insinuation of Western doctrine into the practice of UN missions in the field. Increasing numbers of non-Western UN troop contributors are adopting Western doctrine as a result both of cooperation with Western countries in UN and non-UN operations and of increased training of developing country peacekeepers by France, the UK and the USA.[67] The military personnel of developing countries tend to be more amenable to adopting the latest doctrinal innovation than their national representatives at the UN, who have other political and ideological agendas.

Some new elements of doctrine can be found in recent Security Council resolutions, most notably those establishing the missions in Sierra Leone and the DRC, and in the most recent concepts of operation for different missions devised for the Security Council's consideration by the Secretariat. Clues might also be expected to be found in the guidelines and SOP for peace operations and the training materials for peacekeepers which the UN Secretariat has been trying to update. However, incorporating them has proved difficult, not only because of staff shortages but because certain developing countries regard the drafting of concepts of operation, guidelines and ROE as an attempt by the Secretariat to introduce doctrine by the back door. Clearly the Secretariat cannot and should not be expected to produce a consensus, through its own efforts, on a UN peace operations doctrine, either through the back door or more openly. It is essential that the UN membership, with leadership from the Security Council, reaches a political consensus on an explicit doctrine, or at least the essential elements of one, from which the work of the Secretariat could flow.

## What would a UN peace operations doctrine look like?

The truth is that a UN peace operations doctrine would, as the critics fear, inevitably draw on Western models, particularly those of France, the UK and the USA, since they are the most advanced, coherent and comprehensive. A UN doctrine would not, however, be identical to Western doctrine, since it would need to reflect the UN's collective character and responsibilities, particularly with regard to the Charter, and take account of the sensitivities of all members.

[66] Comprehensive review of the whole question of peacekeeping operations (note 65), p. 7.

[67] For details see Dwan, R., 'Armed conflict prevention, management and resolution', *SIPRI Yearbook 2000: Armaments, Disarmament and International Security* (Oxford University Press: Oxford, 2000), p. 95. France, the UK and the USA are especially active in training other nations' peacekeepers in South Asia (Bangladesh and Nepal) and Africa (e.g., in the member states of the Southern African Development Community (SADC) and ECOWAS).

*Consonance with the UN Charter*

A UN doctrine would naturally have to be cast in terms of the 'ideology' of the UN Charter. It would have to stress the priorities of that document—conflict prevention and the peaceful settlement of disputes—as well as the ultimate sanction of 'collective measures'. A UN doctrine would need to pay particular attention to the conflict resolution sequence laid down in chapters VI and VII, reiterating that negotiation, mediation and non-military measures such as economic sanctions should be considered before resorting to the deployment of a peace enforcement operation and the use of force. At the same time, a peace enforcement doctrine should not be totally hamstrung by the former tendency of the Security Council to take at face value the declared peaceable intentions of every party and the ability of recalcitrant parties to make a semblance of negotiating in good faith in order to avoid more drastic measures being taken against them.

*Sovereignty versus the right of intervention*

The doctrine would naturally have to pay obeisance to the principle of respect for the sovereignty and territorial integrity of member states, while upholding the right of the Security Council to take binding decisions to deal with threats to the peace, in addition to the 'emerging right of humanitarian intervention'.

Just how such competing principles might be accommodated in a UN peace operations doctrine has been indicated by the report of the International Commission on Intervention and State Sovereignty. It argued that sovereignty implied a primary responsibility on the part of a state to protect its people. Where a population is suffering serious harm as a result of internal war, insurgency, repression or state failure and the state in question is unable or unwilling to halt or avert it, the principle of non-intervention yields, the commission argued, to the 'international responsibility to protect'.[68] Military intervention for human protection purposes, it cautioned, is an exceptional and extraordinary measure warranted only by the occurrence or imminence of 'serious and irreparable harm' to human beings such as large-scale loss of life or ethnic cleansing. Echoing the traditional 'just war' criterion, the commission asserted that such intervention must have the right intention, be a last resort, use proportional

---

[68] International Commission on Intervention and State Sovereignty, *The Responsibility to Protect* (International Development Research Centre: Ottawa, 2001). Its setting up was announced in the UN General Assembly in Sep. 2000 by Canadian Foreign Minister Lloyd Axworthy, in response to Kofi Annan's speech to the General Assembly in Sep. 1999 in which he called on states to confront such difficult dilemmas. It was chaired by former Australian Foreign Minister Gareth Evans and former SRSG for Somalia Mohamed Sahnoun, and its report was submitted to the 2001 UN General Assembly.

Other recent reports include studies commissioned by Denmark, the Netherlands and Sweden, all of which have retained the terminology of 'humanitarian intervention' and argued for a distinction between 'legal' and 'legitimate' interventions. Danish Institute of International Affairs (DUPI), *Humanitarian Intervention: Legal and Political Aspects* (DUPI: Copenhagen, 1999); Netherlands Advisory Council on International Affairs and Advisory Committee on Issues of Public International Law, 'Humanitarian intervention', Advisory Report no. 13, as requested by the government of the Netherlands, AIIV/CAVV, The Hague, Apr. 2000; and Independent Commission on Kosovo, *Kosovo Report: Conflict—International Response—Lessons Learned* (Oxford University Press: Oxford, 2000).

means and have reasonable prospects. The Security Council was identified as the proper authority for authorizing such interventions. The permanent members of the Security Council were exhorted to waive their veto power when their vital state interests are not involved. Alternative means would be a 'Uniting for Peace' authorization by the General Assembly or action by regional or sub-regional bodies under Chapter VIII of the UN Charter.

The commission further identified the need for: (*a*) clear objectives, clear and unambiguous mandates at all times, and resources to match; (*b*) a common military approach among involved partners, unity of command, and clear and unequivocal communications and chain of command; (*c*) acceptance of limitations, incrementalism and gradualism in the application of force, the objective being the protection of a population, not the defeat of a state; (*d*) rules of engagement which fit the operational concept, are precise, reflect the principle of proportionality and adhere to international humanitarian law; (*e*) acceptance that force protection cannot become the principal objective; and (*f*) maximum possible coordination with humanitarian organizations.[69]

While the commission's work is a further useful boost to the move to increase international acceptance of and UN preparedness for humanitarian intervention that may involve the use of force, it will take more than a single report, however well argued, to convince the non-aligned sceptics that less honourable motives do not lie behind (mostly Western) calls for such intervention in specific cases.

### Adjusting the norms of traditional peacekeeping

A UN doctrine would need to carefully delineate the nature of the various types of UN operations—traditional peacekeeping, wider peacekeeping (including humanitarian intervention), and peace enforcement or complex peacekeeping. The terms used would have to be acceptable to the whole UN membership, but the precise terms adopted would not matter so long as a common understanding of their meaning could be established.

The doctrine would necessarily have to confront the norms (some would say shibboleths) of traditional peacekeeping—consent, impartiality and the use of force only in self-defence. The Brahimi Report has already done so, but this now needs to be agreed and encapsulated in doctrine. Clearly, the attempt to obtain the maximum degree of consent will remain important in deploying all types of UN peace operations. However, a UN peace enforcement doctrine will need to concede that consent is not always possible to obtain or maintain in full and that a peace enforcement operation might have to be mounted with little consent or in the face of considerable opposition.

On impartiality, a UN doctrine would emphasize that all UN missions must fulfil their mandates impartially while at the same time upholding the principles of the UN Charter and international law (although this will at times inevitably

---

[69] *The Responsibility to Protect* (note 68), synopsis, pp. xii–xiii.

involve difficult trade-offs between competing principles), but that if parties repeatedly violate agreements they should be subject to forceful measures.

*Principles for the use of force*

On the use-of-force question itself, a UN peace operations doctrine might restrict peacekeeping operations to the use of force in self-defence, while allowing peace enforcement operations to use force in defence of their mission. Since all UN peace operations already have the right to defend their mission (albeit a right simply adopted by fiat of the Secretary-General rather than by the UN membership), and it can be interpreted as encompassing every use of force that a peace enforcement mission might need, this could be a relatively non-controversial way of codifying UN doctrine for missions beyond peacekeeping. The problem, as discussed above, is that 'defence of the mission' is so open-ended and has the potential to lead to uncontrolled escalation. If the concept of defence of the mission continues to be used, it needs to be clearly defined and delineated both in general and for particular missions. The right of freedom of movement and what that entails in terms of the use of force also need to be carefully defined and integrated into doctrine.

UN doctrine must also explicitly encompass the principle that UN troops have a 'duty of care' in protecting other UN and international personnel and civilians at risk and may use force in doing so. This should, however, apply to both peacekeeping and peace enforcement operations; in practical terms an extended definition of right to use force in self-defence could be used to achieve this.

Other important doctrinal issues that the UN must confront relate to the question of 'minimum force', proportionality, pre-emption and the use, when appropriate, of 'overwhelming force' as envisaged in US doctrine.[70] Traditionally the UN has stressed the use of force only as a last resort after all peaceful efforts have failed. This may not be appropriate in some circumstances during a peace enforcement operation. Exhausting peaceful means may simply give respite to those intent on derailing a peace process or, worse, committing atrocities such as genocide. (Accurate assessments of the true intentions of local belligerents will depend on better intelligence and better mission leadership.)

While force is unlikely ever to be an entirely first resort, the UN will have to be more ready to concede, when this point in a crisis has been reached, that further negotiations are not only pointless but dangerous and counterproductive in achieving UN goals. Similarly there will be times when, in order to ensure self-defence or defence of the mission, a pre-emptive offensive military operation in self-defence will be needed. Finally, the UN will probably need to confront the fact that sometimes only a crushing military engagement will end a party's recalcitrance or force it to stop preventing the UN from carrying out its mandate. It may be preferable to launch a robust pre-emptive attack at an early

---

[70] See, e.g., Crawford, T., 'Why minimum force won't work: doctrine and deterrence in Bosnia and beyond', *Global Governance*, vol. 4, no. 2 (Apr./June 1998).

stage rather than watch the credibility of the mission being whittled away by unchallenged pinprick provocations from a determined 'spoiler'.

In all circumstances UN peace operations doctrine needs to emphasize the need for proportionality, and strict adherence to the international laws of war and international humanitarian law.

*Integration into a political strategy*

Perhaps most important of all, a UN peace operations doctrine will have to recognize that the use of force is only likely to be effective if integrated into a political strategy with a clear goal in mind. Even in what may be perceived as strictly humanitarian operations there are always political considerations and consequences that doctrine cannot ignore. The military will perforce have to work closely with those conducting peace negotiations, those managing humanitarian, peace-building or other 'nation-building' activities, and the local population in whose interests the military intervention has presumably been launched.

The UN as a whole has become increasingly cognizant of the need to take a holistic, longer-term attitude towards the attempt to bring peace and security to troubled lands. The comprehensive strategies and plans that it now routinely devises for peace operations, involving civilian police, humanitarian assistance, human rights, economic reconstruction, public information and other components, alongside the military, indicate that lessons have been learned and consciousness raised, even if practice still falls short. Handled properly, the potential to use force can be considered only one small, albeit critical, tool of military strategy for peace operations, and only a minute element of a comprehensive effort to have peace and prosperity prevail. Doctrine must take these necessities and complexities fully into account.

# V. Conclusions

The UN is currently undergoing a fundamental debate about the future of its peace operations, including the use-of-force issue. With its traditional interventionist tool, peacekeeping, now widely deemed inappropriate for the more complex challenges facing it, and the failings of Somalia, Rwanda, Bosnia and Sierra Leone now publicly exposed, the UN is no longer able to carry on as before. Under Annan the debate has become more hard-headed and probing and has drawn on more professional advice than ever before. The language used is increasingly that which national defence ministries would use in assessing the capabilities of their armed forces. The consideration of planning and management issues is increasingly that of management consultants.

Such developments indicate a move away from the amateurism and diplomatic wishful thinking that has so long characterized UN operations. Both the Secretary-General and senior UN officials have been brutally critical of the failings of past missions and honest in putting the dilemmas of such operations before member states, in particular with regard to the use of force. The dilemmas about when and how to intervene for humanitarian purposes and the moral imperatives of UN troops faced with gross violations of human rights have been openly aired for the first time. The conclusion of many is that the UN must de facto become better prepared for peace enforcement operations even if the political will and the conceptual and doctrinal underpinnings appear at present to be missing.

Many of the initiatives mooted by the Brahimi Report, Kofi Annan, various lessons-learned exercises, independent commissions and individual member states for improving the planning and management of UN peace operations generally would indubitably improve their capability to use force if and when required. While implementing all their recommendations will not necessarily produce a UN that is able to conduct substantial peace enforcement operations along the lines outlined in this work, at the very least it will produce a UN that is better able to deploy complex peace operations that can act robustly in self-defence and hence are more credible in attempting to carry out their mission. Paradoxically, if the UN were to develop a vastly improved capability to conduct standard peacekeeping operations, this would go a long way towards providing it with the ability to conduct peace enforcement.

Yet a number of constraints exist which may prevent the UN from making significant advances in its ability to project and use force in peace enforcement mode. Apart from organizational and managerial inadequacies which have yet to be addressed, the most notable obstacle is the reluctance of many developing states and China to permit the UN to acquire appropriate doctrine and planning capabilities matching those of a nation state, lest this facilitates UN intervention in their own affairs or at least sets bad precedents. The underlying fear of the slippery slope towards supranational authority is not confined to these states, moreover; it informs an influential sector of US opinion, including key legislators. One means of reassuring these critics would be for UN doctrine to make absolutely clear that UN forces will continue to be mandated and controlled by the Security Council, and at the same time to begin genuine, long-overdue reform of the Council itself to make it more representative, inclusive and transparent in its operations.

The other significant constraint facing the United Nations in improving its peace operations performance is the unwillingness of its member states, especially the permanent members of the Security Council and the larger Western states, to provide militarily capable forces, finance and other support for individual UN operations. This reluctance usually increases with the probability that force might have to be used. These political constraints on UN peace operations, usually encapsulated by the unenlightening expression 'lack of political will', must be tackled. The task will be made easier if the UN can show itself to be capable of better managing and safeguarding the human and material assets that states put at its disposal. It will be made easier still if it can be demonstrated that enhancing the UN's capability to use force means that UN soldiers are less, rather than more, likely to actually have to use it.

# Appendix 1. National peace operations doctrines

While debate raged in academic and political circles about the United Nations' role in peace enforcement, the national militaries of key participants, with typical military purposefulness and intensity, began to re-examine their own doctrine on the use of force in such operations. The new doctrines took several years to evolve. The UK and the USA began first, in 1992, and made the greatest progress, the first versions of their doctrines appearing in 1994. However, these doctrines were not universally accepted among their own military establishments and they continued to evolve. Australia, Canada, France and Russia also developed new doctrines. The Nordic countries were 'somewhat absent' in the early years of doctrinal experimentation, staying loyal longer than most to the traditional peacekeeping norms, but they too eventually adopted new peace operations doctrines.[1] The elaboration of common doctrine, especially for NATO, was more problematic and has still not been entirely resolved.

This appendix examines the national peace operations doctrines of the USA, the UK, France, Australia, Canada and Russia.

## I. The USA

The development of US military doctrine for peace operations took place against the background of heated political debate about the use of US military power generally.[2] The prevailing Weinberger–Powell doctrine,[3] derived from the lessons of Viet Nam[4] and US 'peacekeeping' in Beirut in 1982–84, had been reinforced by its apparent success in Grenada, Panama and, most impressively, the 1991 Persian Gulf War. In its most exaggerated form, the doctrine has been characterized as follows: 'There should be no use of force . . . unless success is all but guaranteed. Force should be used decisively and its application should preferably be short. As soon as the aims are achieved, American forces should be quickly extracted, less the military fall into a quagmire. Above all, the image of the armed forces is to be protected'.[5]

While General Powell's views are easy to parody and exaggerate, in fact they evolved considerably as the new realities of the post-cold war era dawned on him and

---

[1] Eide, E. B. and Solli, P.-E., *From Blue to Green: The Transition from UNPROFOR to IFOR in Bosnia and Herzegovina*, NUPI Working Paper no. 539 (Norwegian Institute of International Affairs (NUPI): Oslo, Dec. 1995), p. 11, fn. 8.

[2] For the USA, 'doctrine' is the 'capstone' strategic policy from which organization, equipment, training, exercises and rules of engagement are derived. Sewall, J. O. B. (Maj.-Gen.), 'Peacekeeping implications for the US military: supporting the United Nations', ed. D. J. Quinn, *Peace Support Operations and the US Military* (National Defense University Press: Washington, DC, 1994), p. 39.

[3] Named after Casper Weinberger, Secretary of Defense in the administration of President George Bush, and Gen. Colin Powell, Chairman of the Joint Chiefs of Staff during the administration of President George Bush and currently US Secretary of State.

[4] According to Charles Stevenson, the doctrine comprised 'essentially rules for avoiding another Vietnam'. Stevenson, C. A., 'The evolving Clinton doctrine on the use of force', *Armed Forces and Society*, vol. 22, no. 4 (summer 1996), p. 515.

[5] Gordon, M. and Trainor, B., 'Beltway warrior', *New York Times Magazine*, 27 Aug. 1995, p. 40.

others. Just before his retirement as Chairman of the Joint Chiefs of Staff in 1993 he published the fullest elaboration of his views in an official Doctrine for Joint Operations.[6] Notably, he distinguished between war, defined as 'large-scale, sustained combat operations', and 'military operations other than war involving the use or threat of force'. In war the goal was 'to fight and win', whereas in the latter type of operation the goal might only be to 'support national objectives, deter war, and return to a state of peace'. These distinctions sound uncannily like those widely touted by analysts later as the distinctions between war-fighting and peace enforcement. As Charles Stevenson notes: 'In other words, the military may have to settle for something short of victory, and there are likely to be political restraints on weaponry, tactics, and the level of violence. Decisive military action may not even be appropriate if such action could undermine long-term strategic objectives'.[7]

The Powell document also foresaw a need to distinguish between negotiated and imposed settlements—the peacekeeping–peace enforcement divide. It called for 'properly conceived conflict termination criteria and awareness of whether the political objective is an imposed settlement, requiring the domination or overthrow of the opponent, or a negotiated settlement, when both sides necessarily make concessions'.

Powell appears to have absorbed the criticisms of the chairman of the House Armed Services Committee, Les Aspin, later Secretary of Defense in the administration of President Bill Clinton, who compared existing US military doctrine advocating simply the use of overwhelming force to a 'bumper sticker' slogan deriving from the 'all or nothing school'. Aspin deemed this particularly inappropriate to the complex, largely intra-state conflicts that were becoming a feature of the post-cold war environment. He argued that force, including the coercive threat of force, could be used for limited objectives such as preserving peace. The USA could now do this better than ever because of the demise of the Soviet Union, which had freed up US options, and the US military technological revolution which permitted more precise application of military force.[8]

The US military seemed to sense the new situation even before their political masters did. Michael MacKinnon argues that from as early as 1992 senior civilian and military officials at the Department of Defense—despite the vicissitudes of Somalia—pursued 'relatively speaking' a pro-peace operations policy.[9] For the US military, as opposed to successive administrations, debate focused more on how to categorize peace operations in order to determine how to handle them than on whether they should be done or not. Debate on categorization revolved 'primarily around the use of force (combat power), as well as the concomitant issue of the consent of the parties involved in the conflict'.[10]

## Amendment of 'capstone' doctrine FM 100-5

In 1993 the need for new US peace operations doctrine was handled by amending the US Army's 'capstone' military doctrine, FM 100-5, which had been devised primarily

[6] US Joint Chiefs of Staff, *Doctrine for Joint Operations*, Joint Pub 3-0 (Joint Chiefs of Staff: Washington, DC, 1993), pp. 1-3, 1-4.

[7] Stevenson (note 4), p. 517.

[8] Quoted in Hoffman, F. G., *Decisive Force: The New American Way of War* (Praeger: Westport, Ct. and London, 1996), pp. 101–102.

[9] MacKinnon, M. G., *The Evolution of US Peacekeeping Policy under Clinton* (Frank Cass: London, 2000), p. 48.

[10] Quinn, D. J., 'Peace support operations: definitions and implications', ed. Quinn (note 2), p. 20.

for conventional conflict with the former Warsaw Pact in Central Europe.[11] The new version included a separate chapter which established operational principles for 16 separate mission categories of what it called operations other than war (OOTW). This term, which superseded the previous term, 'low-intensity conflicts', became US nomenclature for missions that included not only peace operations but also 'strikes', air raids, shows of force, counter-terrorism, counter-insurgency, peacekeeping, peace enforcement, non-combatant evacuation operations, anti-drug smuggling efforts, and search and rescue.

However, there was criticism of this early approach. According to Michael Hardesty and Jason Ellis, FM 100-5 was the basis for all supporting doctrinal manuals, their tactics and training strategies.[12] Critics claim that FM 100-5 attempted to force OOTW into the 'ill-fitting Clausewitzian war model' and in particular into the prevailing US war-fighting doctrine known as the AirLand Battle.[13] According to Antonia Chayes and George Raach, 'OOTW' was 'not a useful category for analysis' since missions assigned to OOTW were 'ghettoized' and 'somewhat indistinct', leading military planners to regard such operations as diversions.[14]

## Peace operations doctrine, FM 100-23

In December 1994, largely in response to the realization that peace operations were not going to be mere diversions but were to be a major new task for the US military, the US Army published its Field Manual FM 100-23, devoted entirely to peace operations.[15] Developed by the army's Training and Doctrine Command (TRADOC), the document brought peace operations into the military mainstream. It summarized many of the lessons of recent operations, such as Operation Provide Comfort in Iraq and Operation Restore Hope in Somalia, and depicted the 'strategic context, organizational principles and operational imperatives unique to peace operations'.[16] It defined peace operations as encompassing three types of activity—support to diplomacy, peacekeeping and peace enforcement (see table A1). Although it did not include humanitarian assistance in its definition of peace operations, it noted that such programmes would probably be conducted simultaneously in almost every peace operation.

'Support to diplomacy' was taken as including peacemaking, peace-building and preventive diplomacy. The latter could involve preventive deployments, such as UNPREDEP in the Former Yugoslav Republic of Macedonia, other shows of force or 'higher levels of readiness'. Peacekeeping (PK) was defined as military or paramilitary operations undertaken with the consent of the major belligerent parties, designed to monitor and facilitate implementation of an existing truce agreement and support

[11] US Department of the Army, *Field Manual: Operations*, FM 100-5 (Department of the Army: Washington, DC, June 1993). Previously there had been some peacekeeping 'doctrine' implicit in a 1989 document: US Army–Air Force Center for Low-Intensity Conflict, 'Peacekeeping tactics, techniques, and procedures', Langley Air Force Base, Va., 1989.

[12] Hardesty, J. M. (Col) and Ellis, J. D., 'Training for peace operations: the US Army adapts to the post-cold war world', *Peaceworks* (United States Institute of Peace (USIP), Washington, DC), no. 12 (Feb. 1997), p. 4.

[13] Hunt, J. B. (Lt-Col), 'OOTW: a concept in flux', *Military Review*, Sep./Oct. 1996, p. 6.

[14] Chayes, A. H. and Raach, G. T., 'Beyond fighting and winning', eds A. H. Chayes and G. T. Raach, *Peace Operations: Developing an American Strategy* (National Defense University Press: Washington, DC, 1995), pp. 9–10.

[15] US Department of the Army, *Peace Operations*, FM 100-23 (Department of the Army: Washington, DC, Dec. 1994).

[16] Hardesty and Ellis (note 12), p. 4.

**Table A1.** Operational variables in US Army Field Manual FM 100-23

| Variables | Support to diplomacy | Peacekeeping | Peace enforcement |
|---|---|---|---|
| Consent | High | High | Low |
| Force | Low | Low (self-defense/ defense of mandate from interference | Sufficient to compel/ coerce |
| Impartiality | High | High | Low |

*Source:* US Department of the Army, *Peace Operations*, FM 100-23 (Department of the Army: Washington, DC, Dec. 1994), p. 13.

diplomatic efforts to reach a long-term political settlement, including 'observation and monitoring of truces and cease-fires and supervisions of truces'.[17]

Peace enforcement (PE) was defined as the 'application of military force or the threat of its use, normally pursuant to international authorization, to compel compliance with generally accepted resolutions or sanctions'. Its purpose was 'to maintain or restore peace' and, like peacekeeping, 'support diplomatic efforts to reach a long-term political settlement'.[18] As the newest and most troubling type of peace operation, peace enforcement received a great deal of attention in FM 100-23. While it was noted that actions with respect to acts of aggression as defined in Chapter VII of the UN Charter were also sometimes called peace enforcement, from a doctrinal point of view these were 'clearly wars' and should not be confused with the type of peace enforcement considered to be a subset of peace operations.[19] PE, the document noted, may include combat action, the transition to which requires the 'successful application of warfighting skills'.[20] Five 'tenets' of US Army operations, which had already been formulated in FM 100-5, were said to be fundamental to the success of PE operations—versatility, initiative, agility, depth and synchronization.[21] The doctrine also noted, contrary to the assumptions of a number of military leaders, that both combat and non-combat actions might take place simultaneously in the same theatre of operations. The following elements were said to apply to all PE operations:

*Phases.* PE operations are normally conducted in several phases. The first may involve the insertion of rapidly deployable combat forces in order to establish a significant and visible military presence. Subsequent phases will involve the transition from a military presence to support for the development of competent civil authority.

*Forces.* Infantry units, supported by engineer, military police and aviation assets, are most often employed in this role. They are normally reinforced by civil affairs (CA) and psychological operations (PSYOP) assets.

*Missions.* The missions assigned to PE forces include the restoration and maintenance of law and order and stability, protection of humanitarian assistance, guarantee and denial of

---

[17] *Peace Operations*, FM 100-23 (note 15), p. 4.
[18] *Peace Operations*, FM 100-23 (note 15), p. 6.
[19] *Peace Operations*, FM 100-23 (note 15), p. 2.
[20] *Peace Operations*, FM 100-23 (note 15), p. 6.
[21] *Peace Operations*, FM 100-23 (note 15), pp. 18–19.

movement, enforcement of sanctions, establishment and supervision of protected zones, forcible separation of belligerent parties, and other operations as determined by the authorizing body.[22]

The document rehearsed in detail what it saw as the differences between peace-keeping and peace enforcement. It denied that the two were part of a continuum which would allow a 'unit' to move freely from one to the other: 'a broad demarcation separates these operations'.[23] The two types of operation would take place under 'vastly different circumstances', involving the critical variables of consent, force and impartiality. A force tailored for peacekeeping may lack sufficient combat power for peace enforcement, and any change required a review of the 'mission, enemy, troops, terrain and time available (METT-T) and force tailoring'. On the other hand, the doctrine posited that a force tailored for PE could accomplish peacekeeping missions provided the belligerent parties accepted its presence (which is exactly what IFOR would do in Bosnia). Generally, the document said, a contingent that has been conducting operations under a PE mandate should not be used in a PK role in that same mission area 'because the impartiality and consent divides have been crossed during the enforcement operation'.

The variables of consent, force and impartiality were seen as the critical determinant of the nature of the peace operation and 'force-tailoring mix'. It was recognized that they are not constant and may individually or collectively shift during the course of an operation. Success in peace operations, it said, often hinges on the ability to exercise 'situational dominance' with respect to the variables. Reflecting the Somalia experience, commanders were enjoined to 'avoid inadvertently slipping from one type of peace operation to another'.[24]

### Level of consent

FM 100-23 noted that in PK the belligerent parties consent to the presence and operations of the peacekeeping forces, while in PE consent is not absolute and force may be used to compel or coerce. In peacekeeping, loss of consent could lead, the document warned, to an uncontrolled escalation of violence which could profoundly change the nature of the operation. The 'crossing of the *consent divide* from PK to PE' was a 'policy level decision'.[25] Commanders should, the document enjoined, 'avoid hasty or ill-conceived actions that unintentionally cause a degradation of the level and extent of consent'.

### Level of force

While traditional peacekeeping was held to be 'generally nonviolent', PE 'may include violent combat actions'.[26] Of the three variables—consent, force and impartiality—the level of force was said to be usually the only one over which a commander could exert dominant influence. However, the manual warned, in terms reminiscent of Nordic peacekeeping doctrine, that:

[22] *Peace Operations*, FM 100-23 (note 15), p. 7.
[23] *Peace Operations*, FM 100-23 (note 15), p. 12.
[24] *Peace Operations*, FM 100-23 (note 15), pp. 12–13.
[25] *Peace Operations*, FM 100-23 (note 15), p. 13. Emphasis in original.
[26] *Peace Operations*, FM 100-23 (note 15), p. 13.

The proper use of force is critical in a peace operation. The use of force to attain a short-term tactical success could lead to a long-term strategic failure. The use of force may affect other aspects of the operation. The use of force may attract a response in kind, heighten tension, polarize public opinion against the operation and participants, foreclose negotiating opportunities, prejudice the perceived impartiality of the peace operation force, and escalate the overall level of violence . . . In PK, commanders should regard the use of force as a last resort.[27]

## Degree of impartiality

While peacekeeping was seen as requiring an impartial, even-handed approach, so was PE. An 'even-handed and humanitarian' approach to all sides of the conflict could improve the prospects for lasting peace and security, 'even when combat operations are underway'. As in the case of consent, 'compromised impartiality' was seen as liable to trigger an uncontrollable escalation from peacekeeping to PE by 'crossing the consent divide'. In circumstances where the required degree of impartiality was unclear, the commander was enjoined to 'press the authorizing body for clarity since misunderstanding can be disastrous'. While PK and PE were at different poles of consent and impartiality, commanders should, regardless of the type of operation, always strive to increase levels of consent and impartiality and reduce levels of force.[28]

## Principles

FM 100-23 noted that, because many of the tasks of peace operations, especially in PE, required the 'focused and sustained application of force', the following principles for the conduct of war, all of which were contained in FM 100-5, should also guide planning for peace operations: (a) clarity of objective; (b) unity of effort; (c) security; (d) restraint; (e) perseverance; and (f) legitimacy.[29]

The first principle declared: 'Direct every military operation toward a clearly defined, decisive, and attainable objective'. The *objective* was said to comprise the mandate and terms of reference and the 'end state'. In regard to the mandate the following were to be of concern to commanders: the ROE; force protection; geographical limitations; limitations on the duration of the operation; relationships with belligerent parties; relationships with others, such as NGOs or voluntary organizations; and financing and personnel. On the end-state question, since peace operations are intended to 'create or support conditions conducive to a negotiated conflict resolution, they always complement diplomatic, economic, informational, or humanitarian efforts'. A peace operation should 'not be viewed as an end in itself, but as part of a larger process that must take place concurrently'. The aim should be *unity of effort*, derived from the 'unity of command' principle of war.[30]

The principle of *security* was to 'never permit hostile factions to acquire an unexpected advantage' and would involve 'force protection as a dynamic of combat power against virtually any person, element, or hostile group', including terrorists, any group opposed to the operation, criminals and even looters. As in UN peacekeeping 'doctrine', the inherent right of self-defence, 'from unit to individual level', was said to apply in all peace operations at all times. Sensibly, security was perceived as requiring

[27] *Peace Operations*, FM 100-23 (note 15), pp. 33–34.
[28] *Peace Operations*, FM 100-23 (note 15), pp. 13, 14.
[29] *Peace Operations*, FM 100-23 (note 15), p. 15.
[30] *Peace Operations*, FM 100-23 (note 15), pp. 15–16.

more than physical protection measures, and was held to be 'significantly enhanced by perceived legitimacy and impartiality, the mutual respect built between the force and the other parties involved and the force's credibility in the international arena'. In addition, effective public affairs, PsyOps and civil affairs programmes would enhance security. In PE, security involved further measures, notably demonstrations of military capability and preparedness, sustainment training and the 'overt presence of uncommitted mobile combat power available as a reserve'—a mobile ready-reaction force, presumably of the type that had been available in Somalia.[31]

One of the critical principles with regard to the use of force in peace operations was *restraint*.[32] Unlike the case of PK, in PE operations force might be used to coerce, but FM 100-23 cautioned that this might have far-reaching international political consequences. It could attract a response in kind, escalate tension and violence in the local area, and embroil troops in a 'harmful, long-term conflict contrary to their aims'. Hence force should only be used when other means of persuasion, including mediation and negotiation, were exhausted. Other alternatives were: deterrence; control measures such as pre-planned or improvised roadblocks, cordons and checkpoints; warnings; and demonstrations or shows of force. As a rule, to limit escalation, 'conciliatory, deterrent, controlling, and warning actions should be carried out on the spot and at the lowest possible level'.

'The use of force is the primary characteristic that determines the nature of the operation, and authority for its use should be clear and unambiguous in the mandate.' In all cases force should be 'prudently applied proportional to the threat': 'Every soldier must be aware that the goal is to produce conditions that are conducive to peace and not to the destruction of an enemy. The enemy is the conflict, although at times such operations assume the character of more traditional combat operations'. The principle of restraint would ideally permeate considerations concerning ROE and the choice of weapons and equipment, but this 'does not preclude the application of sufficient or overwhelming force when required to establish situational dominance, to display US resolve and commitment, to protect US or indigenous lives and property, or to accomplish other critical objectives'.[33]

As to the principle of *perseverance*, it was to 'prepare for the measured, sustained application of military capability in support of strategic aims'. However, in (sensibly) noting that most peace operations require long-term commitments, FM 100-23 ran directly contrary to US strategic culture, which is predisposed towards the 'quick fix'.[34] The document tried to square this circle by declaring that perseverance should not give the impression of permanency.

Finally, the principle of *legitimacy* was said to 'sustain the willing acceptance by the people of the right of the government to govern or a group or agency to make and carry out decisions'.[35] This would only be possible if operations were 'conducted with scrupulous regard for international norms on the use of military force and regard for humanitarian principles'. Again obviously drawing on the lessons of Somalia, commanders were advised to use 'extreme caution in dealing with individuals and organizations that will avoid inadvertently legitimizing them'.

[31] *Peace Operations*, FM 100-23 (note 15), p. 17.
[32] *Peace Operations*, FM 100-23 (note 15), p. 17.
[33] *Peace Operations*, FM 100-23 (note 15), p. 17.
[34] *Peace Operations*, FM 100-23 (note 15), p. 18.
[35] *Peace Operations*, FM 100-23 (note 15), p. 18.

*Rules of engagement*

FM 100-23 set great store by ROE, noting that in peace operations 'well-crafted ROE can make the difference between success and failure'.[36] While ROE, it said, must reflect the law of armed conflict and 'operational considerations', in peace operations they are principally concerned with restraints on the use of force. FM 100-23 offered the following advice in devising ROE:

ROE are developed by military commanders and must consider the direction and strategy of political leaders. This process must balance mission accomplishment with political considerations while ensuring protection of the force. In all cases, restraint remains a principle of peace operations and should guide ROE development, particularly in light of collateral damage, post-conflict objectives, desired end states, and the legitimacy of the operation and authorities involved.[37]

FM 100-23 noted that ROE seldom anticipate every situation. Commanders and leaders at all levels must understand the intent of the ROE and act accordingly. The commander responsible for ROE formulation should consider including an 'intent portion' that describes the desired end-state of the operation as well as conflict-termination considerations. This seems a rather more expansive notion of what ROE are than is normal. 'Fire support' ROE were judged to be as important as individual weapons ROE. ROE, it was suggested, should be issued in unclassified form to all personnel, who should adhere to them at all times, 'notwithstanding noncompliance by opposing forces'. On the problem of multinational interpretation of ROE, FM 100-23 noted only that: 'ROE in multinational operations can create unique challenges. Commanders must be aware that there will most likely be national interpretations of ROE. Close coordination of ROE with multinational partners may preclude problems'.

ROE, it noted, should change with the changing circumstances of the mission and establish guidance for such situations as the search and seizure of inhabitants; the authority of local security patrols; the prevention of black market operations; the surrender of hostile personnel; and the protection of contractor personnel and equipment in support of US operations.

US doctrine as expounded in FM 100-23 is an impressive work that shows the influence of traditional peacekeeping concepts, as adumbrated in Nordic doctrine. It was also influenced by the UK's wider peacekeeping doctrine, which emphasized the sharp divide between peacekeeping and peace enforcement, compared to the original US view of a continuum.[38] Apart from occasional references to the need for 'overwhelming force', it is surprisingly divorced from the prevailing US doctrine for conventional military operations.

Several documents subsequently elaborated on FM 100-23.[39] In addition, the US Army developed training programmes to prepare its forces for peace operations, while

---

[36] *Peace Operations*, FM 100-23 (note 15), p. 35. It defined ROE as 'directives that delineate the circumstances and limitations under which US forces initiate and/or continue engagement with belligerent forces'.

[37] *Peace Operations*, FM 100-23 (note 15), p. 35.

[38] 'UK, US agree on keeping the peace', *The Independent*, 29 Mar. 1995, p. 14.

[39] US Joint Chiefs of Staff, 'Joint military doctrine for operations other than war', Washington, DC, 16 June 1995; US Joint Chiefs of Staff, 'National military strategy of the United States of America: a strategy of flexible and selective engagement', Washington, DC, Feb. 1995; and US Joint Forces Command, Joint Warfighting Center, *Joint Task Force Commander's Handbook for Peace Operations* (Joint Warfighting Center: Ft Monroe, Va., 28 Feb. 1995).

its branch service schools in infantry, aviation and other areas prepared their own specific peace operations doctrines.[40] In 1993 the US Army Peacekeeping Institute was established as part of the Center for Strategic Leadership at Carlisle Barracks, Pennsylvania. Its mission was to study the strategic and operational implications of peace operations, develop concepts and doctrine for the senior military leadership, and refine inter-agency coordination through studies, conferences, exercises and war games. At the same time the army founded a Center for Lessons Learned at Fort Leavenworth, Kansas.[41] It was to make a continuing contribution to US peace operations doctrine.

## II. The UK

Historically averse to committing doctrine to paper, the UK first produced a peacekeeping field manual in 1988, just before the cold war ended, entitled *Peacekeeping Operations*. It was largely a codification of traditional UN peacekeeping thinking.[42] The attempt at establishing a broader peace operations doctrine began with the publication of *Wider Peacekeeping* in 1994.[43] As well as tapping into the long British experience of colonial and decolonization conflicts and the 'troubles' in Northern Ireland, the document drew heavily on more contemporary British experience in Cambodia and Bosnia, and observation of the US experience in Somalia. It identified three forms of 'UN-sponsored' peace operation—peacekeeping, wider peacekeeping and peace enforcement—but focused on the second and clearly advocated avoiding the third. It defined the three categories as follows:

a. Peacekeeping. Operations carried out with the consent of the belligerent parties in support of efforts to achieve or maintain peace in order to promote security and sustain life in areas of potential or actual conflict.
b. Wider Peacekeeping. The wider aspects of peacekeeping operations carried out with the general consent of the belligerent parties but in an environment that may be highly volatile.
c. Peace Enforcement. Operations carried out to restore peace between belligerent parties who do not all consent to intervention and who may be engaged in combat activities.[44]

Wider peacekeeping was thus seen as an element of peacekeeping, whereas peace enforcement was seen as a distinct and separate activity. The entire conceptualization of *Wider Peacekeeping* was based on the notion that consent was the key differential: 'What divides peacekeeping from peace enforcement . . . is not the level of violence, but the level of consent' (see figure A.1). This was argued in spite of the fact that the manual itself declared that in wider peacekeeping consent would be 'anything but absolute' and that the situation could be 'highly volatile', which could only mean that

---

[40] For details see Hardesty and Ellis (note 12), pp. 17–22.
[41] It has produced such documents as US Army, Center for Lessons Learned, 'US Army operations in support of UNOSOM II', Ft Leavenworth, Kans., 1994.
[42] British Army, *Army Field Manual, Vol. 5. Part 1: Peacekeeping Operations* (AFM/PKO) (Ministry of Defence: London, 1988).
[43] British Army, *Army Field Manual, Vol. 5. Operations Other than War, Part 2: Wider Peacekeeping*, D/HQDT/18/34/30 (Her Majesty's Stationery Office: London, 1994), p. 4. It was largely drafted by Lt-Col Charles Dobbie of the Army Staff College at Camberley. The drafts of the manual were cleared successively at 1-, 2- and 3-star levels and by the Joint Warfare Committee and the Army Board. Mallinson, A. (Lt-Col), 'Wider peacekeeping: an option of difficulties', *British Army Review*, no. 112 (Apr. 1996), p. 6.
[44] *Wider Peacekeeping* (note 43), pp. 2-4–2-5.

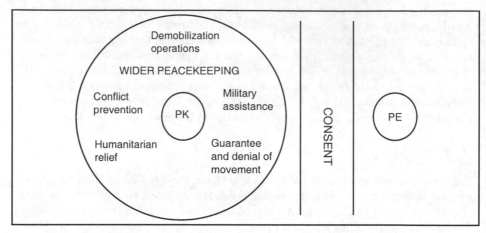

**Figure A1.** The British Army's conceptual model of peace support operations

*Notes*: PK = peacekeeping. PE = peace enforcement.

*Source*: British Army, *Army Field Manual, Vol. 5. Operations Other than War, Part 2: Wider Peacekeeping*, D/HQDT/18/34/30 (Her Majesty's Stationery Office: London, 1994), p. 2-11.

consent was unstable. Thus, 'depending on the volatility of the general environment, [consent] is unlikely ever to be more than partial and could amount to nothing more than tolerance of presence'.[45]

It was difficult to see where the dividing line between wider peacekeeping and peace enforcement really lay. To solve this problem a distinction was drawn between the tactical and operational levels: consent at the tactical level was said to be subject to frequent change and its boundary mobile and poorly defined, while at the operational level it would devolve largely from formal agreements and would be relatively clearcut and easier to discern.

Another critical element of wider peacekeeping was said to be impartiality, deriving from, and in turn sustaining, consent.[46] As Paul Mansell puts it, the British Army placed consent, 'interpreted doctrinally at the tactical level as impartiality', at the 'fulcrum' of peacekeeping and peace enforcement.[47] The doctrine used the analogy of the rugby referee to suggest that peacekeepers' legitimacy and third-party status are guaranteed by the rules and the acceptance of these by the 'players'. Since the referee, like a peacekeeping force, is outnumbered, it is only legitimacy, based on impartiality, that enables punishment to be inflicted for infractions of the rules.

On the use of force, the document made the unremarkable observation that the 'unrestricted use of force in a Wider Peacekeeping operation is likely to cross the consent divide faster than anything else'.[48] However, the need to preserve overall consent did not foreclose the use of force. On the contrary: 'If a strong consensual framework reduces the status of armed opposition to that of maverick banditry, then demonstrably reasonable and proportionate force may be employed against it without

---

[45] *Wider Peacekeeping* (note 43), pp. 2-5, 2-6.
[46] *Wider Peacekeeping* (note 43), p. 2-8.
[47] Mansell, P., *The Ambivalence of the US to United Nations Peacekeeping Operations*, London Defence Studies no. 24 (Centre for Defence Studies, King's College, London: London, Nov. 1994), p. 28.
[48] *Wider Peacekeeping* (note 43), p. 2-9.

fear of fracturing the consent divide'.[49] However, the document warned against cross-ing the consent divide inadvertently, from peacekeeping to peace enforcement: 'If perceived to be taking sides or using force in a way that alienates support, the peace-keeping force loses its credibility as a trustworthy third party, thereby prejudicing its legitimacy and security'. In an expression that was to become the new doctrine's leitmotif (and its bane), the use of excessive force could prove to be a Rubicon from which there was no way back. Withdrawal of the mission would be the only option.

This was not to suggest, the manual argued, that 'a UN force could not or should not undertake peace enforcement operations from the outset if that is demanded by analysis of the mission and conditions on the ground', nor that a 'deployed wider peacekeeping contingent would necessarily be unable to transit to such operations'. The great danger was seen as inadvertent transition.[50]

The UK doctrine did not develop in isolation, but was discussed with 'other major UN players', in the process, according to Colonel Alan Mallinson, revealing a 'formid-able international consensus'.[51] The document itself claims that its terminology was 'similar in substance to US definitions, and compatible with those of most nations'.[52] The British ideas were apparently well received at UN Headquarters and among tra-ditional UN troop contributors, such as the Nordic countries, which interpreted the manual as a validation of their old peacekeeping principles.[53]

In particular the British attempted to coordinate their doctrinal development with that of the USA. In 1993–94, during the crucial stages of drafting the British and US doc-trines, the staff on both sides were reportedly 'at pains to ensure a similarity of approach'.[54] Thus the US and British manuals have an affinity in key areas, including their treatment of the principles and the types of military task to be expected. However, there are key differences. Strangely, given that the USA had experienced Somalia while the UK did not, the problem of 'drift' or 'mission creep' is given much more emphasis in British doctrine than in the US. As Antonia and Abram Chayes argue:

The British argue for a bright-line distinction between peacekeeping and peace enforcement based on the presence or absence of consent while the United States has seemed to envision a more graduated transition from one to the other. UK doctrine contemplates a range of limited coercive actions in support of the force mission . . . , but only if the impartiality of the force and the underlying consensual character of the mission is not impaired. It posits an explicit political (not merely legal) decision to move to peace enforcement, including a decision to provide the necessary forces to impose a solution.[55]

The USA, according to Mansell, put the divide between peacekeeping and peace enforcement where the UK puts the divide between traditional peacekeeping and wider peacekeeping (called peace enforcement in the USA).[56] 'Put crudely', write John

[49] *Wider Peacekeeping* (note 43), p. 2-9.

[50] *Wider Peacekeeping* (note 43), p. 2-13.

[51] Mallinson (note 43), p. 6.

[52] *Wider Peacekeeping* (note 43), p. 2-5.

[53] Jakobsen, P. V., 'The emerging consensus on grey area peace operations doctrine: will it last and enhance operational effectiveness?', *International Peacekeeping*, vol. 7, no. 3 (autumn 2000), p. 38.

[54] Mackinlay, J. and Kent, R., 'Complex emergencies doctrine: the British are still the best', *RUSI Journal*, vol. 142, no. 2 (Apr. 1997), p. 42.

[55] Chayes, A. H. and Chayes, A., 'Alternatives to escalation', in Aspen Institute, *The United States and the Use of Force in the Post-Cold War Era*, Report by the Aspen Strategy Group (Aspen Institute: Queenstown, Md., 1995), p. 215.

[56] Mansell (note 47), p. 29.

Mackinlay and Randolph C. Kent, the difference between the British and US institutional approaches to peace operations was 'the difference between the Weinberger doctrine and the residual influence of fifty years of post-colonial "Keeping the Peace" experiences'.[57] Mallinson, who was responsible for subsequent further development of British doctrine, seemed to nail the differences down better when he pointed out that *Wider Peacekeeping* was a tactical manual which envisaged the loss of consent only at the tactical level, whereas US doctrine focused on the operations level and did foresee, through the use of massive firepower, a crossing of the 'Mogadishu Line' and the loss of consent at the operational level.[58]

Critics of the British doctrine argued that it was 'explicitly status quo and for that reason, since it appears to some to be progressive, it fully deserves the distinction of being recognised as unhelpful and implausible'.[59] Rod Thornton claimed that many army and ex-army officers criticized the doctrine because it seemed to be political in intent, aimed at excusing the military for its inaction, rather than being a guide to action itself.[60] It seemed, he said, to be directed at those in the military, academia, the press and the general public, not to mention the USA, who were pressing the UK to use more force in Bosnia. Thornton notes that *Wider Peacekeeping* self-confessedly contained 'nothing new': 'It had about it the quality of prescription—and particularly prescription for Bosnia—that seemed to detail to all those who advocated the use of force a wealth of qualifying factors that illuminated the pitfalls and dangers of how wider peacekeeping could easily become wider conflict'.[61]

Mackinlay, a persistent critic of the new doctrine, declared that: 'Although "Wider Peacekeeping" and FM 100-23 were developed in response to the problems of intra state conflict, in effect they both turned out to be "stretched versions" of existing peacekeeping doctrine and provided little new insight on how to cope with inter communal violence. Both documents failed to define complex emergencies as a significant issue'.[62] In the new circumstances, Mackinlay and Kent argue, consent had to be purposely forged: 'Factions only consented to the activities of an intervening force when put under pressure and under these circumstances they even accepted when force was used against them. It was therefore a matter of the "consensus" needed to put them under pressure rather than "consent"'.[63] This would involve not just the militaries but also multi-component international operations and the coordinated participation of all the local actors as well as different elements of the international community. While the British and US doctrines recognized some of these special requirements and complexities, they lacked, according to Mackinlay and Kent, a 'concept or an overwhelming logic that could pull the disparate elements of the response together into the same approach'.[64]

---

[57] Mackinlay and Kent (note 54), p. 43.

[58] Mallinson (note 43), p. 7, fn. 4.

[59] Connaughton, R., 'Wider peacekeeping: how wide of the mark?', *British Army Review*, no. 111 (Dec. 1995), p. 55.

[60] Thornton, R., 'The role of peace support operations doctrine in the British Army', *International Peacekeeping*, vol. 7, no. 2 (summer 2000), p. 42.

[61] Thornton (note 60), p. 50.

[62] Mackinlay, J., 'International responses to complex emergencies: why a new approach is needed', *International Peacekeeping News*, vol. 2, no. 5 (Nov./Dec. 1996), p. 36.

[63] Mackinlay and Kent (note 54), p. 41.

[64] Mackinlay and Kent (note 54), p. 42.

In 1998 a new British doctrinal document, *Peace Support Operations* in the Army Field Manual series, was released.[65] The aim was admittedly to 'subsume' the former wider peacekeeping concept into a comprehensive peace support operations doctrine which also included traditional peacekeeping and peace enforcement.[66] It was said to be the product of a thorough analysis of British experience in Bosnia, both in UNPROFOR and subsequently in IFOR and SFOR. It was also undoubtedly a response to criticism of the previous doctrine.

Mackinlay and Kent argue that the new doctrine rectified many of the shortcomings of *Wider Peacekeeping*.[67] It did this in part by acknowledging the relevance of the British Army's long-standing expertise in civil–military operations. Gone is the absolute view of consent. While crossing the 'Rubicon of consent' is still considered dangerous for a lightly armed peacekeeping force, for a combat-capable operation no such Rubicon is considered to exist, even though the level of consent that exists at any particular time is still an important consideration to be taken into account.[68] Peace enforcement operations are expected to cross backwards and forwards across the Rubicon (as IFOR and SFOR have done, and as UNAMSIL did, with British urging and support), while aiming to lower their operational profile towards peacekeeping as soon as possible. Lieutenant-Colonel Philip Wilkinson, the principal author of the doctrine, argues that, since predictions of the level of consent in intra-state conflicts might be 'so problematic as to be worthless', the judicious course of action is to deploy forces at levels sufficient to achieve the mission irrespective of any opposition.[69] Thus there is a need to be prepared for peace enforcement at the outset of missions where consent is questionable. There is also a need, British doctrine holds, for close involvement of humanitarian and other civilian elements to produce a coordinated strategy for gaining and maintaining consent.

With regard to the key peacekeeping principle of impartiality, the new British doctrine holds that peace enforcement operations should aim to be impartial in terms of international law and the mandate, but that inevitably the use of force against one party will be seen by that party as breaching impartiality. This may not matter as much as in peacekeeping, since a peace enforcement operation should have the military capability to impose its will on the recalcitrant party.[70] This is comparable, it notes, to the assumption that the impartiality of a legal system is not compromised because it only punishes the guilty.

As for the use of force, the new British doctrine posits that, while the use of force by a peacekeeping operation will be limited to self-defence, a peace enforcement operation may require the application of the complete range of combat techniques. However, it would be unusual, it asserts, for force to be initiated without first attempting other methods of deterrence and compulsion. When resorted to, force should still be applied prudently and all measures taken to avoid civilian casualties and minimize collateral damage. Nevertheless, 'overwhelming force' may be necessary. Whatever the circumstances, the use of force should, the doctrine opines, be 'seen as a tool to set the con-

[65] British Ministry of Defence, *Peace Support Operations*, Joint Warfare Publication 3-05, document JWP 3-05/PSO (Ministry of Defence: London, 1998).

[66] British Army, 'Peace support operations', Draft Army Field Manual, 1997, p. 1-2 (unpublished).

[67] Mackinlay and Kent (note 54), p. 39.

[68] Wilkinson, P. (Lt-Col), 'The development of the United Kingdom's doctrine on peace-support operations', International Security Information Service (ISIS) Briefing Paper no. 68, London, May 1998, p. 6.

[69] Wilkinson (note 68), p. 5.

[70] *Peace Support Operations* (note 65), p. 4-5.

ditions for the development of peace in the long term, rather than the means of defeating a designated enemy'.[71]

The new doctrine has also not been without its critics. Mackinlay and Kent argue that, while it was to be welcomed, what was also required was a joint army–air force–navy doctrine for peace operations, as well as a joint 'doctrine' for the political, military and civil elements of such operations.[72]

Paradoxically, despite all the heated transatlantic debate about doctrine, neither the British nor the US Army follows a slavish approach to manuals: both rely on recent experience as well. Their respective doctrines provide a 'conceptual framework within which to act rather than a precise agenda for action'.[73] Worryingly for the proper conduct of peace operations, Mackinlay and Kent claim that at the field level 'each army will revert to an individual approach that is not significantly influenced by manuals'.[74]

## III. France

French doctrine divides peace operations into three types—peacekeeping, 'peace restoration' and peace enforcement. It is unusual to the extent that the second type, *restauration de la paix*, is defined as being conducted in an 'ongoing conflict'—presumably one in which there is no peace agreement to enforce.[75] The country concerned will be 'in the throes of a civil war, where serious violations of human rights are being committed and where force may need to be used to establish peace, using a mixture of persuasion and coercion, but not against a defined aggressor'.[76] Don Daniel and Brad Hayes note that the French military General Staff identify peace restoration as an operation under a Chapter VII mandate but with no aggressor identified.[77] For France, peacekeeping is the traditional 'Chapter VI-and-a-half' type of operation, whereas peace enforcement is 'conducted against an aggressor', presumably in a scenario similar to that of the Gulf War.

French doctrine has been portrayed as deriving from France's experiences in both Somalia and Rwanda. Belbutowski claims that their experience in Somalia proved to them 'the need for units capable of carrying out violent action in high intensity engagements with composure, comportment, and the fire mastery necessary to bring about a cessation of hostilities'.[78] What the French military regarded as their supremely successful operation in Rwanda in 1994, Opération Turquoise, inspired them, Mats

[71] *Peace Support Operations* (note 65), pp. 3-9, 4-3.

[72] Mackinlay and Kent (note 54), p. 43.

[73] Mackinlay and Kent (note 54), pp. 42–43.

[74] Mackinlay and Kent (note 54), pp. 42–43.

[75] Stern, B., 'Introduction', ed. B. Stern, *United Nations Peace-keeping Operations: A Guide to French Policies* (United Nations University: Tokyo, 1998), p. 5. See also Raimond, J.-B., 'La politique d'intervention dans les conflits: éléments de doctrine pour la France' [Policy on intervention in conflicts: elements of doctrine for France], Rapport d'information no. 1950, Commission des affaires étrangères, Assemblée Nationale, Paris, 23 Feb. 1995.

[76] Stern (note 75).

[77] Daniel, D. C. F. and Hayes, B. C., 'Securing observance of UN mandates through the employment of military force', ed. M. Pugh, *The UN, Peace and Force* (Frank Cass: London, 1997), pp. 109–110.

[78] Belbutowski, P. M., 'Contemporary French peacekeeping', ed. F. L. Mokhtari, *Peacemaking, Peacekeeping and Coalition Warfare: The Future Role of the United Nations* (National Defense University Press: Washington, DC, 1994), p. 90.

Berdal says, to formalize their 'peace restoration' doctrine.[79] Gérard Prunier argues that Opération Turquoise, in spite of all its ambiguities, was 'a perfect example of French thinking on the matter of armed humanitarian interventions for the future'.[80] Berdal is critical, arguing that, unlike British and US doctrine, French doctrine is 'anything but impartial' and 'a very poor model indeed'.[81]

France, both doctrinally and in practice, in comparison to the USA and especially the UK, seems entirely at home with using force in UN peace operations to enforce the mandate and if necessary abandoning impartiality in the process. Brigitte Stern claims that the most original feature of the French peace operations doctrine is that: 'Unlike the Anglo-Saxon countries, France considers that *there may be a continuum between "Chapter VI and a half" peacekeeping operations and Chapter VII enforcement actions'*—that is, a non-coercive peacekeeping operation may at any time become an operation using force.[82] The influential strategic analyst François Heisbourg has noted that, as a Frenchman, 'I have few inhibitions about scaling up the nature of UN operations. That one should move away from the traditional forms of peacekeeping . . . does not in the slightest disturb me in the philosophical sense, although [this entails] political difficulties'.[83] He is under no illusion that peace enforcement can be done without taking sides:

Seizing an airport in the midst of genocide in Rwanda would have resembled the Foreign Legion's operations in Kolwezi in 1979 rather than a UN peacekeeping operation. Nor could one say that seizing the airport, creating safe areas, would have been 'impartial'. It would have been an extremely partial operation. That does not mean that I would be uncomfortable with it. I would have been delighted if this had happened. But I do not think that it is possible, if one extends the UN's role to those types of tasks, to maintain impartiality.[84]

Espen Eide and Per-Erik Solli claim that France was responsible for developing the concept of 'active partiality' for peace restoration operations for which there was little or no consent.[85] This involves being impartial in applying the rules equally to all parties, but being willing to use force to punish those who transgress the rules, regardless of whether this results in accusations of partiality (which it invariably does).

France has also actively sought to shape UN peace operations to give expression to certain humanitarian norms which it identifies as important.[86] The French approach has combined the pursuit of negotiated settlements at the diplomatic level with the protection of civilian populations, by non-consensual military means if necessary, from aggression by local warring factions. Thus France has been a particularly strong advocate of 'safe areas' within which civilians could be shielded and humanitarian aid distributed, 'humanitarian corridors' through which these areas could be supplied, and

---

[79] Berdal, M., 'Lessons not learned: the use of force in "peace operations" in the 1990s', *International Peacekeeping*, Special issue on Managing Armed Conflicts in the 21st Century, vol. 7, no. 4 (winter 2000), pp. 56, 68–70.

[80] Prunier, G., 'The experience of the European armies in Operation Restore Hope', eds W. Clarke and J. Herbst, *Learning from Somalia: The Lessons of Armed Humanitarian Intervention* (Lynne Rienner: Boulder, Colo., 1996), p. 145

[81] Berdal (note 79), p. 70.

[82] Stern (note 75), pp. 4–5. Emphasis in the original.

[83] Heisbourg, F., 'Response to the case for a rapid response', eds O. A. Otunnu and M. W. Doyle, *Peacemaking and Peacekeeping for the New Century* (Rowman & Littlefield: Lanham, Md., 1998), p. 195.

[84] Heisbourg (note 83), p. 196.

[85] Eide and Solli (note 1), p. 11, fn. 8.

[86] Ruggie, J. G., 'The UN and the collective use of force: whither or whether?', ed. Pugh (note 77), p. 8.

armed protection of humanitarian convoys engaged in 'innocent passage' through the corridors. These ideas were, notably, advocated for Bosnia and Rwanda.

## IV. Australia

The Australian armed forces initially resisted the elaboration of a peace operations doctrine on the grounds that troops that were conventionally trained, armed and led should be capable of mounting any type of operation.[87] They would simply 'ratchet down' their war-fighting capabilities to conduct less threatening missions. There was also a fear that, if 'trained down' to do peacekeeping, they would be unable to handle their primary mission—the mounting of conventional military operations in the defence of Australia and its interests. Eventually, it was realized that doctrine was required for two reasons: to avoid terminological confusion within the Australian forces and between them and other contingents participating in peace operations; and because of the need to cooperate with a wide variety of other players in peace operations, including UN civilian components, UN humanitarian agencies, UN civilian police and NGOs.

Australian peace operations doctrine was created by the Australian Defence Force Peacekeeping Centre at Williamtown, New South Wales, beginning with a draft paper, ADF Pamphlet no. 1, in 1994. By 1996 the draft doctrine had grown from 3 pages to 40 and was still being refined.[88] It covered the full range of peacekeeping and peace enforcement operations, identifying nine separate categories of peace support operation, although recognizing that the distinction between them may sometimes be blurred.[89] The nine categories are 'notionally placed' on a continuum ranging from observer missions to 'the conventional military operations which are implied in peace enforcement'. Across the categories three levels of 'activity' are defined, which equate with traditional peacekeeping, expanded peacekeeping and peace enforcement. Australian Foreign Minister Gareth Evans was one of the first government ministers anywhere to enunciate clearly the distinction between these three activities and to promote them in a coherent way. This undoubtedly helped frame Australian military thinking.[90]

Current Australian peace operations doctrine still uses the concept of a continuum, but now includes only two categories for which a military response is relevant—peacekeeping and peace enforcement. Peacekeeping is defined as 'a non-coercive instrument of diplomacy, where a legitimate, international civil and/or military coalition is employed with the consent of the belligerent parties, in an impartial manner, to implement conflict prevention and/or resolution arrangements'. Peace enforcement, on the other hand, is 'the coercive use of civil and military sanctions and collective security actions, by legitimate, international intervention forces, to assist diplomatic efforts to prevent armed conflict from starting, escalating or spreading or to restore peace between belligerents, who may not consent to that intervention'. Peace enforcement

---

[87] Miles, A. (Director of the Australian Defence Force Peacekeeping Centre), personal communication with the author, Sydney, 30 Apr. 1996.

[88] Miles (note 87).

[89] Waddell, J. G. (Maj.), 'Legal aspects of UN peacekeeping', ed. H. Smith, *The Force of Law: International Law and the Land Commander* (Australian Defence Studies Centre: Canberra, 1994), p. 48.

[90] Evans, G., *Cooperating for Peace: The Global Agenda for the 1990s and Beyond* (Allen & Unwin: Sydney, 1993).

operations, according to Australian doctrine, differ from war: 'In war, the ultimate military aim is to defeat a designated enemy force. In peace enforcement operations, the military aim will normally be to coerce the belligerent(s) or potential belligerent(s) into avoiding or ceasing armed conflict and participating in peaceful settlement of disputes'.[91]

Like British doctrine, Australian doctrine sees the key difference between peace-keeping and peace enforcement as being the level of consent of the parties to the conflict. However, it is cognizant of the subtleties: 'Th[e] distinction can often be complicated by a force gaining consent at the political, strategic and operational levels but, for various reasons, losing it at the local tactical level'.

On the question of self-defence, Australian doctrine appears to be flexible and pragmatic:

Even in peacekeeping operations the force will retain the right of self-defence. This notion can be robustly applied. In some situations, formal guidelines to Force Commanders have defined self-defence as including defence of the mandate itself. A key consideration in the use of force, however, will be the capability of the peace operations force when compared to the task and the capabilities of the belligerents or potential belligerents. A force deployed, structured, trained and equipped to undertake peace enforcement would normally be able to operate in a peacekeeping posture. The reverse is not true.

Australian doctrine has been refined in the course of a number of UN missions—in Cambodia, Somalia and East Timor—and in regional peace operations in Bougainville, Papua New Guinea, and in the Solomon Islands. The Australian forces won widespread praise for their performances in Somalia and East Timor in combining military capabilities with 'hearts and minds' techniques—a legacy, no doubt, of Australia's involvement in counter-insurgency campaigns in Malaya and Viet Nam in the 1950s and 1960s.

## V. Canada

It is surprising that Canada, despite its almost unsurpassed record of participation in peacekeeping since its invention, and indeed the Canadian claim that Lester Pearson invented it, has contributed so little to doctrinal development, particularly with regard to the use of force.[92] Until the mid-1990s Canadian peacekeeping doctrine was almost non-existent, relatively ad hoc and 'reactively adapted to the wide variety of peace-keeping situations'.[93] This doctrinal gap has since been partially addressed by the Canadian Armed Forces as well as through the establishment in 1994 of the Lester B. Pearson International Peacekeeping Training Centre in Nova Scotia. Although the centre tended to concentrate on training rather than pursuing doctrinal innovation, it has stimulated useful discussion of the use of force issue through workshops and

[91] See the Internet site of the Australian Defence Force Peacekeeping Centre, URL <http://www.adfwc.org.au/peacekeeping>.

[92] For background see Jockel, J. T., *Canada and International Peacekeeping*, Significant Issues Series, (Center for Strategic and International Studies (CSIS), Washington, DC, and Canadian Institute of Strategic Studies, Toronto), vol. 16, no. 3 (1994).

[93] Maloney, S. M., 'Insights into Canadian peacekeeping doctrine', *Military Review*, Mar./Apr. 1996, p. 12. See also Jockel (note 92).

conferences and published several studies, including David Last's impressive work on conflict de-escalation.[94]

In 1995 Canada produced a comprehensive doctrinal manual.[95] Like the USA it adopted 'operations other than war' as the doctrinal framework, but its nomenclature differed significantly from other manuals.

Canada used 'peacekeeping operations' as a generic term for four types of operations—peace enforcement (defined as being of the Korean War type), peacekeeping forces, observer missions and humanitarian assistance.[96] Canadian doctrine provided for the 'appropriate use of force in cases of self-defence'.[97] It also established that the use of force, when justified and commensurate with the provocation, contributes to a force's credibility and may act as a deterrent against further provocations.[98] Maloney claims that 'informal' Canadian doctrine put even more emphasis on 'credibility'. This led to Canada rejecting UN force planning parameters for Bosnia and deploying more heavily-armed battalions than the DPKO considered necessary and appropriate.[99] Canada in retrospect feels vindicated, pointing out that its contingent was often accorded respect by the local factions in a way that other UN peacekeepers were not.

Success in OOTW, Canadian doctrine holds, will be determined more by political factors than by military considerations or actions, and will be measured by the degree to which military actions contribute to the achievement of the strategic 'end-state'. The desired military end-state will rarely be a true military victory but rather the achievement of the conditions necessary for the fulfilment of political, diplomatic or social/ humanitarian actions.[100] Unlike war-fighting, the ultimate end-state will be 'normally achieved through negotiation'.[101] As in the case of other national doctrines, Canadian doctrine is said to be 'authoritative but not directive' and commanders on the spot are reportedly given 'great latitude'.[102]

Much of Canadian theorizing seems to have been derived from its troops' experiences in Croatia and Bosnia. Incidents in January 1993 involving the 3rd Battalion, Princess Patricia's Canadian Light Infantry, which had to deal forcibly with Croatian incursions along the Belgrade–Zagreb highway, are portrayed by the Canadians as an example of 'offensive action' in peace operations.[103] The confrontation with Croatian forces in the Medak pocket in September 1993, when Canadian and French peacekeepers used force to interpose themselves between Croat and Serb forces, also appears to have had a significant effect on Canadian thinking.[104]

---

[94] Morrison, A. *et al.*, *Peacekeeping with Muscle: The Use of Force in International Conflict Resolution* (Canadian Peacekeeping Press: Clementsport, 1997); and Last, D. M., *Theory, Doctrine and Practice of Conflict De-escalation in Peacekeeping Operations* (Canadian Peacekeeping Press: Clementsport, 1997).

[95] Canadian Armed Forces, *Operations Land and Tactical Air Vol. 3: Peacekeeping Operations*, Manual B-GL-301-003/FP-001 (Canadian Armed Forces: Ottawa, 1995).

[96] Maloney (note 93), pp. 16–17.

[97] Bergstrand, B. M. (Maj.), 'Operations other than war: the Canadian perspective', eds A. Woodcock and D. David, *Analytic Approaches to the Study of Future Conflict* (Canadian Peacekeeping Press: Clementsport, 1996), p. 106.

[98] Bergstrand (note 97), p. 106.

[99] Maloney (note 93), pp. 20–21.

[100] Bergstrand (note 97), p. 106.

[101] Bergstrand (note 97), p. 112.

[102] Maloney (note 93), p. 15.

[103] Bergstrand (note 97), p. 109.

[104] Last (note 94), pp. 105–107.

The Canadian experience in Somalia was salutary to a nation that had rightly prided itself on making an invaluable contribution to peacekeeping since its inception. The brutal murder of a young Somali who had trespassed on a Canadian compound and the mistreatment of other Somalis by Canadian troops led to the disbanding of the unit responsible and a long-drawn-out controversy in Canadian public life.[105] The conclusion reached was that recruitment, training and leadership were at fault rather than Canada's peacekeeping doctrine.

## VI. Russia

Russian peace operations doctrine emerged from an experience completely different from those of the Western states.[106] It has been coloured not just by Russian participation in UN peacekeeping operations (which has increased significantly since the Soviet Union collapsed) but more profoundly by Russian attempts to prevent or end armed conflicts in the former Soviet states. Russian troops have been deployed for the latter purposes in Abkhazia, Nagorno-Karabakh, South Ossetia, Tajikistan and Trans-Dniester. Although some of these missions were supposed to be collective undertakings by the Commonwealth of Independent States (CIS), while others were meant to be collaborative efforts with the government or parties in conflict, in reality Russia dominated them. Russia launched them without a peacekeeping doctrine, with little prior experience to draw on, and initially 'without a proper mandate, with partiality, and a high level of force'.[107] According to Lieutenant-General Anatoliy Shapovalov, an adviser on peacekeeping to the Russian Defence Minister, Russian peacekeeping forces were 'tasked to pursue, apprehend and destroy by fire groups or individuals who are not following the rules in a given situation'.[108] Shapovalov was also reported to have told an international seminar in Moscow in mid-1995 that: 'All of this definitional debate about peacekeeping, peacemaking, peace enforcement, peace building is irrelevant. These operations are limited war and should be treated as such'.[109]

Nonetheless, in 1992 and 1996 the CIS adopted a series of documents on conflict resolution and peacekeeping, drafted by Russia, which suggested a peacekeeping doctrine close to the UN model.[110] Force was only to be used in self-defence (although that was not defined) and intervention was to be impartial. The involvement of peacekeepers in combat operations was forbidden. The documents also reserved to the CIS, rather than the UN Security Council, the right to decide on measures (including military force) to guarantee peace and stability in the CIS area. Only in the case of

---

[105] See chapter 6, section I and fn90, in this volume.

[106] For useful analyses see Raevsky, A. and Vorob'ev, I. N., *Russian Approaches to Peacekeeping Operations*, Research paper no. 28 (UN Institute for Disarmament Research: Geneva, 1994); Allison, R., *Peacekeeping in the Soviet Successor States*, Chaillot Papers no. 18 (Western European Union, Institute for Security Studies: Paris, 1994); and Trenin, D., 'Russia', ed. T. Findlay, *Challenges for the New Peacekeepers*, SIPRI Research Report no. 12 (Oxford University Press: Oxford, 1996).

[107] Jonson, L., 'In search of a doctrine: Russian interventionism in conflicts in its "near abroad"', *Low Intensity Conflict and Law Enforcement*, vol. 5, no. 3 (winter 1996), p. 440.

[108] Quoted in Davis, M. T., 'Russian "peacekeeping operations"', NATO CDN (93) 577, 20 Sep. 1993, p. 8 (unpublished), cited in Tanner, F., 'Weapons control in semi-permissive environments: a case for compellence', ed. Pugh (note 77), p. 135.

[109] Quoted in Allison, R., 'The military background and context to Russian peacekeeping', eds L. Jonson and C. Archer, *Peacekeeping and the Role of Russia in Eurasia* (Westview Press: Boulder, Colo., 1996), p. 45.

[110] See Jonson (note 107) for details of the various documents.

'peace enforcement' (which apparently meant a Gulf War-type action) would the authority of the Security Council be necessary.

In practice, Russian troops have had little difficulty adapting to UN norms when involved in UN peacekeeping operations, for instance, in Bosnia, presumably because they are under the command of UN force commanders who brief them and monitor their behaviour accordingly. According to a comprehensive study for the Canadian Department of National Defence, 'experience, training and international oversight (however limited) have contributed to a gradual convergence of Russian practice and traditional peacekeeping norms in most of the UN *and* regional missions undertaken by Moscow'.[111] The study concludes that, contrary to the assumptions of international commentators, Russia does not appear to have used 'a great deal of force' in its operations in Abkhazia, South Ossetia or Trans-Dniester. Russian troops have also responded well to joint peace operations training with US forces and others under NATO's Partnership for Peace (PFP) programme, learning in particular to negotiate before shooting.[112]

The CIS mission in Tajikistan remains the greatest departure from international norms, mainly because Russian troops are deployed in the country both as CIS peacekeepers and as partial supporters of the government. The presence since 1994 of a small UN Mission of Observers in Tajikistan (UNMOT) to monitor the CIS force has reportedly restrained Russian behaviour somewhat.

The unique situation of Russia and the gradual evolution of its peacekeeping role and policy have meant that Russian doctrine, unlike the doctrines of Western states, has had little influence, if any, on the UN debate. On the contrary, Russian doctrine and to a lesser extent practice appear to have been influenced by the UN debate and by Western models.

---

[111] Kellett, N. A., 'Russian peacekeeping part IV: Russian goals and methods in the context of international peacekeeping practice', Research note 98/04, Directorate of Strategic Analysis Policy Group, Department of National Defence, Ottawa, Canada, Mar. 1998, p. 121. Emphasis added. In the same series see also 'Russian peacekeeping part I: the Soviet background', Research note 94/17, Oct. 1994; 'Russian peacekeeping part II: the strategic context', Research note 96/08, Dec. 1996; and 'Russian peacekeeping part III: peacekeeping operations since 1991 (revised version)', Research note 98/03, Mar. 1996.

[112] Kellett (note 111), pp. 63, 96–97.

# Appendix 2. Rules of engagement

## 1. Selected ONUC operations directives

**Operations Directive no. 2**
**ONUC policy relating to questions of arrests**

*17 August 1960*

1. The function of the UN Force is to assist in maintaining law and order. In the exercise of this function, the United Nations is not contesting the right of the Government of the Congo to take police or judiciary measures which it considers necessary for the security of the State. In particular, the United Nations Force is not challenging the principle of the right for the Government to proceed to personal arrest.

2. Wherever there may appear, however, to be wrongful, excessive or arbitrary exercise of police authority in any locality, or a special reason for the UN to step into the situation—in particular in relation to its own operations—the UN Command in the locality should employ its good offices toward the end of ensuring just treatment for all. This should be done tactfully and should be approached on the basis of ethics rather than any legal right on our part.

When and where actual disorder occurs or threatens to occur through acts of arbitrary arrest, the UN Force is entitled to intervene directly, by means of establishing a presence at the particular locality, acting as a buffer between disputing parties, seeking to persuade the authorities concerned to place the person or persons arrested under UN safekeeping, trying to disperse unruly crowds, and any other peaceful actions that the Command may find appropriate.

3. Members of the Staff of ONUC, that is of the UN and the Specialized Agencies, and the officers and men of the UN Force in the Congo, have an international status entitling them to special consideration. They can be identified by the UN identity cards which they carry (blue for the military and pink for the civilian). Unless such a person is clearly guilty of some serious breach of the law, every peaceful effort must be exerted to prevent the arrest or to effect his release, on the grounds both of immunity for international officials and non-interference in the work of ONUC.

Iyassu Mengasha, Brigadier General
Chief of Staff, ONUC

**Operations Directive no. 3**
**ONUC policy with regard to inter-tribal conflict**

*17 August 1960. Confidential*

The following are instructions to be followed by all commanding officers with regard to intervention of the UN Force in inter-tribal conflict situations.

1. Inter-tribal conflict is an internal matter with heavy political connotations. But it also often becomes a source of grave public disorder, which ONUC cannot ignore.

2. Responsible officials in the Government of the Republic of the Congo, including the Prime Minister, the President of the Senate, the Minister of the Interior, the Commander of the ANC [Armée Nationale Congolaise] and various other officials, have recently expressed their desire that the UN Force in the Congo should concern itself with the control of inter-tribal conflict, which is particularly troublesome at present in the provinces of Kasai and Equateur.

3. Elements of the UN Force, when confronted with inter-tribal conflict, should pursue the following course

(*a*) Every effort should be made to induce local authorities, political, police and military, to take all possible measures to control the conflict, to the full extent of their authority and resources.

(*b*) If elements of the Armée Nationale are in the area and are sufficiently organized, officered and disciplined to be reasonably effective, they should be induced to intervene to the extent of their capability.

(*c*) UN good offices should be employed with tribal leaders and local authorities toward establishing at least an understanding precluding further resort to violence.

(*d*) The UN Force, at the discretion of the local commander when he considers such action to be called for, and in the light of the manpower available to him, may intervene more directly through the undertaking of patrols, guards and other preventive or protective actions. In this regard, it must be kept in mind that arms are to be fired *only* in self-defence, when all other measures have failed.

Iyassu Mengasha, Brigadier General
Chief of Staff, ONUC

## Operations Directive no. 6
## Security and the maintenance of law and order

*28 October 1960. Confidential*

### Applicability

1. This Directive replaces all previous instructions to commanding officers regarding their responsibilities in ensuring security and the maintenance of law and order in the areas under their command and is in amplification of the various directives on the subject so far issued.

### General

2. The UN Force in the Congo serves as a temporary security force at the request of the Government of the Republic of the Congo. It acts under the mandate of the resolutions of the Security Council of 14 and 22 July and 9 August, and resolution 1474 of the Fourth Emergency Special Session of the General Assembly. Its purpose is to assist the Government in the restoration and maintenance of law and order and particularly to take all possible measures for the protection of life throughout the territory of the Republic of the Congo, with the ultimate purpose of safeguarding international peace and security.

3. The UN Force in the Congo is a peace force. It carries arms in order to lend weight to its authority and as a deterrent, but these arms may be used only in self-defence, as explained in the Directive. The UN force is in no sense an occupying force. It seeks only to help achieve security in which government and administration can function effectively. Thus, its main purpose is to assist the government in creating conditions of peace in which Congolese people may themselves be able to develop

their political freedom and economic prosperity. The UN force therefore must respect the sovereignty, independence and national integrity of the Republic of the Congo.

### Responsibilities of the Congolese authorities

4. The UN Force shall not repeat not be a party to or in any way intervene in or influence the outcome of any internal conflict, constitutional or otherwise. This, of course, does not repeat not preclude the UN from humanitarian measures to prevent bloodshed, such as serving as a buffer in inter-tribal conflict, lending its good offices to local disputants, and arranging cease fires. Where more than one authority claims to exercise the powers of government, at whatever level, the UN can take no position as to which authority should be recognized. The UN Force, in pursuance of its efforts to maintain law and order, may take necessary contacts for this purpose with those officials on the spot who may be exercising authority, without, however, thereby implying any attitude or position with regard to the legal status of such officials.

5. The responsibility for the maintenance of law and order is primarily that of the Congolese authorities. The aim of the UN Force is to assist these authorities in the carrying out of their responsibilities. Therefore, in the event of a disturbance, actual or potential, UN commanders wherever possible, will in the instance rely on the appropriate competent Congolese authorities, administrative, policy or military, to take the necessary lawful measures, or if necessary, try to induce them to do so, and may give them assistance towards that end.

6. Should the Congolese authorities be unable to deal with the situation adequately, or when it is apparent that they intend to apply or when they do apply harsh and repressive measures not sanctioned by law and in violation of humanitarian principles, then and only then will the UN Force take further appropriate steps to fulfil its responsibilities in the protection of life, law and order.

7. As a peace force the UN Force may not take the initiative in the use of armed force. It is however, entitled to use force in self-defence, but only as a last resort after other means viz., negotiation or persuasion, have failed. In the following types of cases UN troops are entitled to respond with force to an armed attack upon them:

(*a*) attempts by force to compel them to withdraw from a position which they occupy under orders from their commanders, or to infiltrate and envelop such positions as are deemed necessary by their commanders for them to hold, thus jeopardising their safety;

(*b*) attempts by force to disarm them;

(*c*) attempts by force to prevent them from carrying out their responsibilities, as ordered by their commanders;

(*d*) violation by force of United Nations' premises and attempts at arrest or abduction of UN personnel, civil or military.

The minimum force necessary will be used in all such cases in order to prevent as far as possible the loss of human life or serious injury to person[s].

8. In the event of firing being resorted to for purposes of selfdefence, the following principles shall apply:

(*a*) the object throughout is to deter and not to cause loss of life;

(*b*) it follows that firing should be low and not aimed at vital parts;

(*c*) in the case of mob attack, the leaders should be picked out for deterrent action;

(*d*) firing must at all times be controlled and not indiscriminate;

(*e*) the officer in charge will keep a record of the number of rounds fired;

(*f*) firing into the air should be avoided as it may be provocative without strengthening respect for the force.

### Protection against marauders or armed bands

9.

(*a*) Whenever a threat of attack develops towards a particular area either by marauders or armed bands, UN commanders will endeavour to pacify the area through the Congolese authorities as described in para. 5 above, or failing that, where possible, by direct approach to the attackers. Mobile patrols should . . . immediately be organized to manifest the presence of UN in the threatened or disturbed area, in whatever strength is available. Loudspeaker vans and other appropriate means may be used to calm and restrain public excitement.

(*b*) If all attempts at peaceful settlement fail, UN commanders may recommend to the Supreme Commander that such threatened areas be declared as under UN protection by means of the deployment of UN troops. In the event of their receiving specific instructions to that effect, the UN commanders will announce that the entry into such area of marauders or armed bands, as the case may be, will be opposed by force, if necessary in the interests of law and order.

(*c*) If, notwithstanding these warnings, attempts are made to attack, envelop or infiltrate the UN positions thus jeopardising the safety of UN troops, they will defend themselves and their positions by resisting and driving off the attackers with such minimum use of force including firing, as may be necessary.

10. It follows from para. 9 that if UN units arrive at the scene of an actual conflict between marauders and civilians or between opposing armed bands, they will, in the interests of law and order, immediately call on the participants to break off the conflict. If the participants fail to comply, UN commanders will immediately take appropriate steps to separate the combatants and to prevent further lawlessness, bloodshed, pillaging or looting. If the UN troops are then attacked, they may use such degree of force as may be necessary for the exercise of their right of self-defence, including firing.

11. Persons observed to be engaged in looting, but not fighting, on the scene of such conflicts will be called upon by UN troops to desist and surrender. If they desist from looting and flee, firing should not be resorted to in order to apprehend them. On the other hand, if they refuse to desist from looting, force may be employed to stop them, and, if they attack, the principle of self-defence applies and resort may be had to the minimum firing necessary.

### Disruption of agencies of public order

12. The obligation of the UN Force to assist in the maintenance of law and order is in no way diminished where it happens that elements of Congolese forces may themselves be engaged in general lawlessness. Where soldiers, gendarmerie or police have broken away from their command and are no longer under the control of the authorities, or where they engage in the unlawful killing of unarmed civilians or the pillaging and burning of towns and villages or in any flagrant violation of elementary human rights, they constitute a danger to public order and society and an immediate report on the situation should be sent to the Supreme Commander. If such units appear to be operating under any form of leadership, UN commanders will use their good offices to stop all such activities, by direct consultation with

that leadership or by reference to the nearest authorities of the civil government, the ANC [Armée Nationale Congolaise] or the gendarmerie. If these endeavours fail, every effort should be made to disarm or neutralise the lawless elements and to confine them to barracks. Any further action should be taken only on receipt of specific instructions from the Supreme Commander.

## UN property and existing installations

13. UN troops are responsible for the protection of UN property. In addition, essential public utilities such as electricity works, waterworks etc., should be given such protection as may be necessary when they are threatened by public disorder, and where any damage or destruction to them would cause hindrance to the UN operation or acute hardship to the civilian population.

14.

(a) Protection of UN or other essential installations may be provided by means of mobile patrols or static guards, as appropriate.

(b) Physical force may be used, if necessary, to protect such installations.

(c) Such force may extend to the minimum degree of firing necessary, as a last resort.

## Conclusions

15. In carrying their responsibilities for assisting in the maintenance of law and order in the Congo, the UN troops are expected to act with tact and moderation at all times. The very presence of armed and disciplined troops, skilfully deployed, can act as a powerful deterrent to the forces of disorder and violence. When force has to be used it should be kept to the minimum required for the attainment of the objective. It is expected that the action of the UN troops will always be inspired by the aims and purposes of the United Nations in Congo.

(Carl Carlson Van Horn) Gen.
Sup Comdr.

## Amendment no. 1

Page 1, para 1, line 1
*Delete* word 'replaces' and substitute 'is in amplification of'. *Insert* after the word 'instructions' as follows 'so far issued'. In *lines 3, 4 and 5 delete* 'and is in amplification . . . so far issued'.

Lt Col S. N. Mitra, Chief Operations Officer
No. 1001/11/OPS

## Operations Directive no. 8
## Outgoing code cable
## OPS 277

*Untitled, [February 1961]*

Para 1. Within the framework of Operational Directive no. 6, all units will continue to try to prevent armed conflict by every means at their disposal other than the use of armed force. If these efforts fail and actual conflict occurs between any two armed factions of the Congolese, UN troops will not participate and will withdraw from the area of fighting.

Para 2. Where feasible, every protection will be afforded to unarmed groups who may be subjected by any armed party to acts of violence likely to lead to loss of life. In such cases, UN troops will interpose themselves, using armed force if necessary, to prevent such loss of life.

Para 3. Refugees, irrespective of nationality, will be afforded the maximum protection by UN troops. If necessary, armed force will be resorted to in affording this protection.

Para 4. Political leaders seeking UN protection will be afforded that protection.

Para 5. Every possible step will be taken to ensure the personal safety of any person or persons held as hostages.

Para 6. In the event of an attempt being made by any outside force (including the use of paratroops) to intervene in the Congo, such attempt will be immediately countered by UN troops, resorting to armed force if necessary. This action will be taken even if it is claimed by the aggressors that their intervention is for the purpose of evacuating their own or other nationals.

Para 7. Operational Directive no 6 remains fully valid, insofar as it is not inconsistent with the present instructions.

. . . .

## Operations Directive no. 9
## Use of force in self defence

*4 March 1961. Confidential*

(This directive is in amplification of the general principles given at paragraphs 7 and 8 of Operation Directive no. 6)

1. The instances of UN military personnel giving up their arms to the Congolese Army are on the increase. Such incidents are most undesirable and have a detrimental effect on

the morale of the troops. I direct that commanders at all levels take immediate steps to stop any recurrence of such incidents.

2. Military personnel are authorized to open fire in self defence. The use of force to prevent being disarmed falls under self defence as directed in para 7(b) of Operation directive No 6. Special measures as outlined in succeeding paragraphs will be taken by all units/sub units of ONUC.

. . .

5. It should be noted that use of force is authorised whenever there is any danger to UN personnel or property. Although discretion is essential in the use of force, whenever the circumstances justify it, commanders at all levels must use their initiative and take bold action.

Lieut General Commander UN Force in the CONGO (S MAC EOIN)
No. 1001/11 (OPS)

**Operational Directive no. 10**
**Action of the United Nations Force in the Congo to prevent armed clashes**

*30 March 1961. Confidential*

1. In compliance with the Security Council resolution of 20/21 February 1961, United Nations troops must prevent armed clashes between different sections of the Congolese. Intervention by United Nations troops can arise under the following circumstances:

(*a*) When the situation indicates the possibility of a civil war developing.

(*b*) In the event of the actual outbreak of an armed clash.

(*c*) When an armed clash has taken place and the hostilities threaten to envelop ONUC forces.

**2. When the situation indicates the possibility of a civil war developing**

The United Nations command should immediately determine the nature and activation of any fresh movements of Congolese troops or armed bands. The first aim of the command should be to satisfy itself whether or not a civil war situation exists and then, if it does, to seek to eliminate it by negotiations. The United Nations commander should avoid making any move with his troops which might jeopardize his attempt to negotiate or might exacerbate the situation; but if there is a likelihood that

during negotiations one or both of the parties should place themselves in an advantageous position vis-à-vis their opponents or make a move which might later prevent United Nations troops from taking effective action, the United Nations commander on the spot should interpose his troops without delay.

**3. In the event of the actual outbreak of an armed clash**

In the event of the actual outbreak of an armed clash despite the steps stated in paragraph 2 above, efforts for a cease-fire should continue. Meanwhile, any United Nations troops interposed or deployed in any other way to prevent a clash may defend themselves from any attack on their position in accordance with existing directives on self-defence. The right of self-defence thus applies to action in support of the measures already taken for the prevention of a clash. If, however, United Nations troops have not been able successfully to interpose themselves, they should at the earliest opportunity attempt either to interpose themselves between the parties or otherwise deploy themselves to stop or limit the clash; in so doing, they continue to have the right to defend themselves by force, if necessary, subject to the reservations in paragraph 4 below.

**4. When an armed clash has taken place and the hostilities threaten to envelop UN forces**

The United Nations commander should attempt to retain his position without getting involved in the fire-fight and maintain contact with both parties so as to be able to negotiate a cease-fire at the first possible opportunity. However if there is a clear risk of United Nations troops becoming a party to the armed clash, or if the United Nations commander considers that the safety of his men will be unduly jeopardized, United Nations troops may be withdrawn. In no case should United Nations troops join with one section against another.

Lieut. General Commander UN Force in the Congo (S. Mac Eoin)
No. 1001/11 (OPS)

*Source:* UN Archives DAG13/1.6.5.0.0, Ops Directives Aug. 1960–Jan. 1964, Box 3.

## 2. Use-of-force instructions for UNEF II

*HQ UNEF, Cairo, undated*

### Aim

1. To specify the circumstances under which force may be used by UNEF troops.

### Definitions

2. FORCE—the general term describing the use of physical means to impose the will of UNEF.

Examples—obstacle, use of bayonet, opening fire.

For the purposes of this instruction FORCE will be divided into two parts:

(*a*) UNARMED FORCE

(*b*) ARMED FORCE

The use of military weapons.

### Principles

3. (*a*) One of the main principles on which UNEF operations are based is that incidents must be prevented and, if necessary, stopped by negotiations and persuasion rather than by the use of force. It therefore follows that force will only be used when all peaceful means of persuasion have failed.

(*b*) The use of force is authorised ONLY in self-defense and as a last resort in the carrying out of the task given to UNEF troops. Only the minimum force to achieve the mission is to be used in order to prevent, as far as possible, the loss of human life or serious injury to persons.

(*c*) The only circumstances in which fire may be opened are:

(i) Self-defence, including defence against attempts by force to disarm UNEF personnel, but only as a last resort.

(ii) In the defense of UNEF posts, premises and vehicles under armed attack.

(iii) In support of other troops of UNEF under armed attack.

### 4. Circumstances in which force may be used

(*a*) By careful planning and foresight commanders at all levels should seek to foresee dangerous situations well in advance and should ask to obtain detailed direction which would include clearance to use force should it be necessary.

(*b*) The decision as to when force may be used rests with the commander on the spot whose main concern will be to distinguish between an incident which merits the use of armed force as opposed to the use of unarmed force.

(*c*) In circumstances where time does not permit reference to higher authority the commander on the spot will use that amount of force which he considers to be required.

(*d*) It is not possible to define all circumstances in which force may be used. However, for the guidance of commanders, the following are given as examples of situations in which troops may be authorized to use force:

(i) When they are compelled to act in self-defence.

(ii) When the safety of the Force or members of it are in jeopardy.

(iii) When attempts by force are made to compel them to withdraw from a position which they occupy under orders from their commanders, or to infiltrate and envelop such positions as are deemed necessary by their commanders for them to hold, thus jeopardizing their safety.

(iv) When attempts by force are made to disarm them.

(v) When attempts by force are made to prevent them from carrying out their responsibilities as ordered by their commanders.

(vi) When violation by force is made of UN premises.

(vii) When attempts are made to arrest or abduct UN Personnel, civil or military.

(viii) When specific arrangements accepted by both communities have been, or in the opinion of the commander on the spot, are about to be violated.

### 5. Degree of force to be used

(*a*) The principle of minimum force will always be applied. All appropriate means of warning will be used whenever possible before fire is opened.

(*b*) Should it become necessary to open fire, two warning shots should be fired before resorting to aimed fire. While aimed fire will be for effect, it should be directed low, at the legs of the attackers, whenever possible.

(*c*) Automatic fire is NOT to be used except in extreme emergency.

(*d*) In all cases fire will continue only as long as is necessary to achieve its immediate aim.

### 6. Protection against individual or armed attack

(*a*) Whenever a threat of attack develops towards a particular area, commanders will endeavour to pacify the area with the co-operation of the local authorities. Mobile patrols should immediately be organized to manifest the presence of UNEF in the threatened or disturbed areas in whatever strength is available.

(*b*) If all attempts at peaceful settlement fail, unit commanders may recommend to their senior commander that such threatened areas be declared under UNEF protection by means of the deployment of UNEF troops.

(*c*) If, despite these warnings, attempts are made to attack, envelop or infiltrate UNEF positions, thus jeopardizing the safety of troops in the area, they will defend themselves and their positions by resisting and driving off the attacks with minimum force, including the use of fire if necessary.

(*d*) The procedure in defending a locality will approximate the following:

(i) A tape or strand of barbed wire will be laid across the various [axes] of approach.

(ii) Signs will be used to announce to all approaching the tape or barbed wire that if they cross over it they will be shot.

(iii) Should an individual or a group of individuals approach the barrier they will be warned to stop. If they try to advance beyond the tape or strand of barbed wire, fire will be opened and aimed shots will be directed low and towards the apparent ring-leaders.

(*e*) If soldiers of either party are passing a UNEF position without danger to the lives of the occupants, UN will NOT use force to STOP such passing, but will remain in their posts until the situation is resolved by negotiations.

### 7. Principles of self-defence

(*a*) In the event of fire being used for purposes of self-defence, the following principles will be observed:

(i) The aim is to deter and NOT to cause loss of life.

(ii) It follows that aimed fire will be low. This does NOT mean that the point of aim will be the ground in front of the attacker. Firing low means aiming at the legs of the attacker.

(iii) Firing must at all times be controlled and not indiscriminate.

(iv) If a soldier opens fire, he will continue to act independently only until an officer or NCO [non-commissioned officer] arrives on the scene. He will then only act under the orders of the officer or NCO.

(v) The commander on the spot will keep a record of the number of rounds fired.

### 8. Action after firing

(*a*) Any wounded will be given medical aid.

(*b*) An endeavour will be made to collect and count empty cartridge cases after each incident.

(*c*) A report will be made out and despatched to HQ UNEF on forms as attached.

### 9. Orders

(*a*) Unit Commanders will prepare orders for their respective units on the use of firearms, these orders are to be based on the principles set out in this directive.

(*b*) Unit Commanders will ensure that all ranks under their command are fully aware of the principles governing the use of force by UNEF personnel.

_____

*Source:* UN Archives DAG13/0.3.14.1.0.0.0 #8 [undated] (UN restricted).

---

## 3. Rules of engagement for UNPROFOR

**Force Commander's Policy Directive 13, Rules of engagement, Part I: Ground forces**

*Issued 24 March 1992, revised 19 July 1993*

### General

1. The conduct of military operations is controlled by the provisions of international and national law. Within this legal framework, the

United Nations (UN) establishes the parameters within which the UN Forces can operate. Rules of Engagement (ROE) are the means by which the UN can provide direction and guidance to commanders at all levels governing the use of force. They are approved by the UN and may only be changed with their authority.

2. The UN has stated, in the Report of the Secretary-General pursuant to Security Council Resolution 721 (1991) dated 11 December 1991, Annex III, para 4: 'Those personnel who were armed would have standing instructions to use force to the minimum extent necessary and normally only in self-defence'. The UNPROFOR is equipped with weapons for defensive purpose only. The use of weapons is authorized normally only in self-defence. Retaliation is forbidden. Self-defence includes resistance to attempts by forceful means to prevent the Force from discharging its duties under the mandate for the UNPROFOR. In applying these rules the principle of minimum force is to be strictly adhered to. The definitions provided at Annex A should be understood and used.

3. The ROE stated in this document apply to all nations contributing to the UNPROFOR. The ROE are written in form of prohibitions or permissions, Annexes B and C refer. Issued as prohibitions, they are orders not to take specific actions. Issues as permissions, they will be guidance to commanders that certain specific actions may be taken if they are judged necessary to achieving the aim of the mission.

4. Changes to these rules will be issued to suit each operational situation as it occurs or to implement changes in the political policy. The classification of these rules is UN RESTRICTED.

**Authority**

5. UNPROFOR personnel may use their weapons:

(*a*) to defend themselves, other UN personnel, or persons and areas under their protection against direct attack, acting always under the order of the senior officer/soldier at the scene;

(*b*) to resist attempts by forceful means to prevent the Force from discharging its duties; or,

(*c*) to resist deliberate military or paramilitary incursions into the United Nations Protected Areas (UNPAs) or Safe Areas.

**Rules of Engagement**

**6. Rule No. 01: Authority to carry arms**

Option A: No authority

Option B: Authority granted to carry weapons.

**7. Rule No. 02: Status of weapons**

Option A: Weapons will be carried with loaded magazines.

Option B: Weapons will be carried charged and made safe.

**8. Rule No. 03: Response to hostile intent (without use of fire)**

Option A: Observe and report, withdraw in order to preserve own Force.

Option B: Observe and report, stay in place. Make contact and establish liaison with opposing Force(s) and/or local authorities concerned.

Option C: Observe and report, stay in place. Warn aggressor of intent to use force and demonstrate resolve by appropriate means without opening fire (i.e.: cock weapons, deploy troops, etc.).

**9. Rule No. 04: Response to hostile act (with use of fire)**

Option A: take immediate protection measures, observe and report. Warn the aggressor of intent to use force and demonstrate resolve by appropriate means. Warning shots are authorized (See paragraph 15 and Annex A). Report action taken. If the hostile act does not cease and life is threatened, Option B can be ordered by the troop commander.

Option B: On order, Open Fire (See paragraph 16 and Annex A). Report action taken.

Note: In both Option A and Option B the following manoeuvres are authorized (Depending on the situation, orders and reports given by the troop commander):

(1) Withdraw in order to preserve own Force,

(2) Stay in place and defend, or

(3) Move through to escape and preserve own force.

## 10. Rule No. 05: Response to hostile act (self-defence)

Anytime, in self-defence situations, take immediate protection measures and/or return fire without challenging (See paragraphs 16, 17 and Annex A). Report action taken.

## 11. Rule No. 06: Disarmament of paramilitary, civilian and soldiers

Option A: No authorization granted.

Option B: Authorization is granted if failure to do so prevents the UNPROFOR from carrying out its task. In doing so use minimum necessary and proportional force up to and including use of fire, if hostile intent so warrants, or a hostile act is committed. Hand over to appropriate authorities at the earliest opportunity.

## 12. Rule No. 07: Control of weapon systems

Option A: Manning, in preparation, movement and firing of weapons in the presence of the forces in conflict is prohibited.

Option B: Designated activity (See Note) in the presence of the forces in conflict is prohibited.

Note: Designated activities in this rule will be signalled from the following list, using the numbered prefix:

(1) Overt manning of weapons.
(2) Movement of weapons.
(3) Firing of weapons.
(4) Others (to be specified).

13. In the normal, daily situation the following ROE status applies:

Rule No. 01, OPTION B
Rule No. 02, OPTION A
Rule No. 03, OPTION B
Rule No. 04, OPTION A
Rule No. 05, PERMANENT
Rule No. 06, OPTION A
Rule No. 07, OPTION A

14. Changes in normal status of ROE as described in para 13 for the Force as a whole will be ordered by the Force Commander. Sector Commanders are authorized to change ROE within their sectors and to delegate the authority to battalion commanders if time does not permit sector Commanders' authorization.

## Challenging procedures

15. The following challenging procedure is to be followed in all cases except as outlined in para 17 unless the requirement to fire immediately in self-defence dictates otherwise:

(a) Warn the aggressor to stop.

(b) Repeat the warnings as many times as possible to ensure that the aggressor has understood the situation.

(c) Charge weapons if not already authorized.

(d) Fire warning shots in the air.

(e) If the warnings are ignored, on order open fire.

(See Annex A).

## Principles of opening fire

16. When it becomes necessary to open fire (Rules 04 and 05), the following principles apply:

(a) Action which may reasonably be expected to cause collateral damage is prohibited.

(b) Fire is to be used only until the aggressor has stopped firing.

(c) Retaliation is forbidden.

(d) Minimum force is to be used at all times.

## Opening fire without challenging

17. The only circumstances in which it is permissible to open fire without challenging in Self-Defence. When an attack by an aggressor comes so unexpectedly that even a moment's delay could:

(a) lead to death or serious injury to the UN personnel;

(b) lead to death or serious injury to persons whom it is the UNPROFOR duty to protect; or,

(c) the property which UNPROFOR has been ordered to guard with firearms is actually under attack.

## Cordon and search operations

18. Cordon and Search Operations are a military responsibility but, in general, the military will establish the Cordon, and the police will conduct the Search. Searches of buildings are not to be conducted at random. They will only be carried out in response to specific evidence that indicates the probable violation of the Vance Plan or the UN Security

Council Resolution. The military have overall responsibility for initiating, and for the command and control of all Cordon and Search Operations. Searches should be carried out by local police. In the event they refuse to cooperate, UNCIVPOL will carry out the Search with a security element (the minimum necessary) from the military inside the building. Cordon and Search Operations will be conducted using the principles outlined at Annex D.

Jean Cot, General, Force Commander

## Annex A: Definitions

*Self Defence*: Action to protect oneself or one's unit, when faced with an instant and overwhelming need, leaving no choice of means and no time for deliberation.

*Hostile Intent*: Hostile intent is an action(s) which appears to be preparatory to an aggressive action against personnel or equipment of Peacekeeping Forces and/or personnel or property placed under their responsibility.

*Hostile Act*: A hostile act is any aggressive action against personnel or equipment of Peacekeeping Forces and/or personnel or property placed under their responsibility. When deciding on appropriate reaction by Peacekeeping Forces, it has to be kept in mind that the use of armed force is only permitted in the presence of an attack or imminent attack.

*Minimum Force*: The minimum authorized degree of force which is necessary, reasonable and lawful in the circumstances.

*Collateral Damage*: Damage to persons or property adjacent to, but not part of an authorized target.

*Positive Identification*: Assured identification by a specific means can be achieved by any of the following methods: visual, electronic support measures, track behavior, flight correlation, thermal imaging, passive acoustic analysis, or IFF [identification, friend or foe] procedures.

*Armed Force*: The use of firearms including warning shots.

*Unarmed Force*: The use of physical force short of firearms, such as stones, batons, shields, CS-gas (when not delivered by firearms). This directive will not discuss further unarmed force.

*Warning Shots*: A warning shot is used in the challenging procedure (See paragraph 15). It is limited to single shots in the air (and not aimed shots above the target).

*Open Fire* (See paragraph 16): Open Fire initially with single armed shots until the protection task is complete. The use of automatic fire is a last resort.

## Annex B: Rules of engagement guidelines

For issue to all personnel authorized to carry arms and ammunition in UNPROFOR

### General rules

1. You have the right to use force in self-defence.
2. In all situations you are to use minimum force necessary. FIRE ARMS MUST ONLY BE USED AS A LAST RESORT.

### Challenging

3. A challenge must be given before opening fire unless:

(*a*) to do so would increase the risk of death or grave injury to you or any other person;

(*b*) you or others in the immediate vicinity are under armed attack.

4. You are to challenge in English by shouting: 'UN! STOP OR I FIRE!' or in Serbo-Croat by shouting: 'UJEDINJENE NACIJE! STAN ILI PUCAM!' (uyedinyene natsiye! stan ili putsam).

### Opening fire

5. You may only open fire against a person if he/she is committing or about to commit an act LIKELY TO ENDANGER LIFE, AND THERE IS NO OTHER WAY TO STOP THE HOSTILE ACT. Dependent always on the circumstances, the following are some examples of such acts:

(*a*) Firing or being about to fire a weapon.

(*b*) Planting, detonating or throwing an explosive device (including a petrol bomb).

(*c*) Deliberately driving a vehicle at a person, where there is no other way of stopping him/her.

6. You may open fire against a person even though the conditions of paragraph 5 are not met if:

(*a*) He/she attempts to take possession of property or installations you are guarding, or to damage or destroy it; and,

(*b*) THERE IS NO OTHER WAY OF PREVENTING THIS.

7. If you have to open fire you should:

(*a*) fire only aimed shots; and

(*b*) fire no more rounds than necessary; and,

(*c*) take all reasonable precautions not to injure anyone other than your target.

**Annex C: Instructions to military personnel**

To:

From: (Note 1)

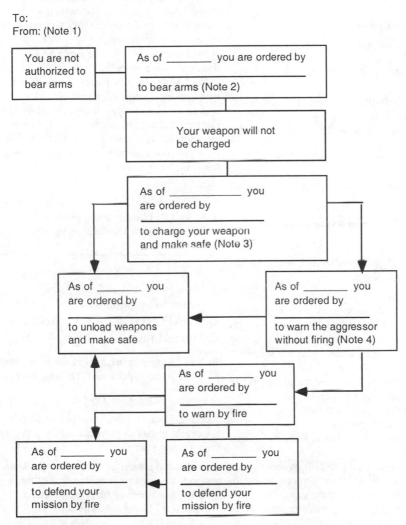

Notes:

1. Normally issued by a Company to a Platoon Commander or detached Section or patrol.
2. Authorization may refer to radio call-sign or other appointments title.
3. Bayonets may be fixed or unfixed at any stage in escalation or de-escalation.
4. See Challenging Procedures.

**Challenging and opening fire procedures**

1. Warn the aggressor to STOP.
2. REPEAT the warnings; ensure UNDER-STANDING.
3. CHARGE or COCK the weapons.
4. Fire WARNING SHOT.
5. If warning shots are ignored, ON ORDER, FIRE SINGLE AIMED ROUNDS until task is accomplished. Automatic fire is a last resort.

**Search procedures**

1. Searchers are not to humiliate nor to embarrass.
2. The object of the search must be clearly stated in orders.
3. Females will be searched by scanners or other females if available.
4. Searchers must be neither overly friendly nor overbearing.
5. A searcher will always be 'covered' by a comrade(s).
6. Searches will be reported promptly and fully.

**Annex D: Cordon and search operations**

**Principles**

1. Principles of cordon and search operations are as follows:

(a) A Cordon and Search must be justified by a clear violation of the Vance Plan or the UN Security Council Resolution. Justification must not be sought through illegal procedures which violate the human rights of citizens in the UNPAs or Safe Areas;

(b) Cordons will only be conducted if the situation warrants isolation of that area. This should be the exception. In most cases, only a search should be required;

(c) Military will not conduct searches inside buildings;

(d) Searches should be done by local police but, in the event they do not respond, UNCIVPOL will conduct the search;

(e) The military will provide the appropriate security force to support . . . UNCIVPOL searches. The requirement for a preliminary search for mines/booby traps etc., is the responsibility of the OC [Officer in Charge] in consultation with UNCIVPOL/local police.

(Engineers may be used in the recce [reconnaissance] party if judged appropriate);

(f) The military officer commanding the operation should accompany the search team;

(g) The search should be conducted in such a manner so as to cause the minimum disruption to the occupants. Damage to property is to be kept to the absolute minimum. Any property damages are to be recorded immediately and signed by the OC of the operation. A copy is to be given to the occupant and the original is to be processed for reimbursement as soon as possible; and,

(h) Every effort will be made to explain, through interpreters, the reason(s) for the search. Those involved, especially inside private houses, must be cognizant of the fact that it is private property. Although security is a priority, it is not an excuse for belligerence or the adoption of a confrontational attitude. All involved should display a highly professional, fair firm, but friendly attitude.

---

*Source*: Berkowitz, B. D., 'Rules of engagement for UN peacekeeping forces in Bosnia', *Orbis*, vol. 38, no. 3 (fall 1994), pp. 637–46.

# 4. Rules of engagement for UNITAF: ROE card for Operation Restore Hope

**Rules of Engagement, Joint Task Force for Somalia Relief Operations, Ground Forces**

*Reproduced December 1994*

Nothing in these rules of engagement limits your right to take appropriate action to defend yourself and your unit.

1. You have the right to use force to defend yourself against attacks or threats of attack.
2. Hostile fire may be returned effectively and promptly to stop a hostile act.
3. When US forces are attacked by *unarmed* hostile elements, mobs, and/or rioters, US forces should used the minimum force necessary under the circumstances and proportional to the threat.

4. You may not seize the property of others to accomplish your mission.

5. Detention of civilians is authorized for security reasons or in self-defense.

Remember

– The United States is not at war.
– Treat all persons with dignity and respect.
– Use minimum force to carry out the mission.
– Always be prepared to act in self-defense.

_____

*Source:* 'Rules of engagement for Operation Restore Hope: sample rules of engagement', in *Peace Operations*, FM 100-23 (Department of the Army: Washington, DC, Dec. 1994) appendix D, p. 95.

_____

# 5. Rules of engagement for UNOSOM II

*May 1993*

**1. UNOSOM personnel may use deadly force:**

(*a*) To defend themselves, other UN lives, or persons and areas under their protection against hostile acts or hostile intent.

(*b*) To resist attempts by forceful means to prevent the Force from discharging its duties.

**2. Challenging**

(*a*) Whenever practicable, a challenge should be given before using deadly force.

(*b*) Challenging is done by:

(i) Shouting in English: 'UN, STOP OR I FIRE' or

(ii) Shouting in Somali 'UN, KA HANAGA JOOGO AMA WAA GUBAN'

(iii) Firing warning shots in the air.

**3. Principles for use of force**

When it becomes necessary to use force, the following principles may apply:

(*a*) Action may be reasonably be expected to cause excessive collateral damage is prohibited.

(*b*) Reprisals [are] forbidden.

(*c*) Minimum force is to be used at all times.

**4. Specific rules**

(*a*) UNOSOM Forces may use deadly force in response to a hostile act or when there is clear evidence of hostile intent.

(*b*) Crew-served weapons are considered a threat to UNOSOM Forces and the relief effort whether or not the crew demonstrates hostile intent. Commanders are authorized to use all necessary force to confiscate and demilitarize crew-served weapons in their area of operations.

(*c*) Within those areas under the control of UNOSOM Forces armed individuals may be considered a threat to UNOSOM and the relief effort whether or not the individual demonstrates hostile intent. Commanders are authorized to use all necessary force to disarm and demilitarize groups or individuals in those areas under the control of UNOSOM. Absent a hostile or criminal act, individuals and associated vehicles will be released after any weapons are removed/demilitarized.

(*d*) If UNOSOM Forces are attacked or threatened by unarmed hostile elements, mobs and/or rioters, UNOSOM Forces are authorized to employ reasonable force to repel the attacks or threats. UNOSOM Forces may also employ the following procedures: verbal warnings to demonstrators, shows of force including use of riot control formations, and warning shots.

(*e*) UNATTENDED MEANS OF FORCE. Unattended means of force, including bobby [*sic*] traps, mines, and trip guns, are not authorized.

(*f*) DETENTION OF PERSONNEL. Personnel who interfere with the accomplishment of the mission or who otherwise use or threaten deadly force against UNOSOM, UN or relief material, distribution sites, or convoys may be detained. Persons who commit criminal acts in areas under the control of UN Forces may likewise be detained. Detained persons will be evacuated to a designated location for turn/over [*sic*] to military police.

**5. Definitions**

The following definitions are used:

(*a*) SELF DEFENCE

Action to protect oneself or one's unit against a hostile act or hostile intent.

(*b*) HOSTILE ACT

The use of force against UNOSOM personnel or mission-essential property, or against personnel in an area under UNOSOM responsibility.

(*c*) HOSTILE INTENT

The threat of imminent use of force against UNOSOM Forces or other persons in those areas under the control of UNOSOM.

(*d*) MINIMUM FORCE

The minimum authorized degree of force which is necessary, reasonable and lawful in the circumstances.

6. Only the Force Commander, UNOSOM, may approve changes to these ROE.

---

*Source:* 'UNOSOM II (1993) rules of engagement (ROE)', Mogadishu (NT3224), 021200C May 1993, appendix 6, annex C to UNOSOM II OPLAN 1, pp. C-61–C-63.

# Appendix 3. The UN master list of numbered rules of engagement

## UN master list of numbered rules of engagement

*Provisional, May 2002*

1. The following ROE, when authorised, permit United Nations armed military personnel to use force in the circumstances specified below. However, the principle of minimum necessary force is to be observed at all times.

2. The United Nations Master List contains five sets of rules: Use of Force (Rule 1), Use of Weapon Systems (Rule 2), Authority to carry Weapons (Rule 3), Authority to Detain, Search and Disarm (Rule 4) and Reaction to Civil Action/Unrest (Rule 5). The list provides various options from which a selection will be made under each of the five rules, to suit a specific UNPKO (see example contained in Annex A of Attachment 2).

### Rule 1. Use of force

#### Rule No. 1.1

Use of force, up to, and including deadly force, to defend oneself and other UN personnel against a hostile act or a hostile intent is authorised.

#### Rule No. 1.2[1]

Use of force, up to, and including deadly force, to defend other international personnel against a hostile act or a hostile intent is authorised.

#### Rule No. 1.3

Use of force, up to, and including deadly force, to resist attempts to abduct or detain oneself and other UN personnel is authorised.

#### Rule No. 1.4[2]

Use of force, up to, and including deadly force, to resist attempts to abduct or detain other international personnel is authorised.

#### Rule No. 1.5

Use of force, up to, and including deadly force, to protect United Nations' installations, areas or goods, designated by the Head of the Mission in consultation with the Force Commander, against a hostile act is authorised.

#### Rule No. 1.6[3]

Use of force, up to and including deadly force, to protect key installations, areas or goods designated by the Head of the Mission in consultation with the Force Commander, against a hostile act is authorised.

**OR:**

#### Rule No. 1.7

Use of force, excluding deadly force, to protect key installations, areas or goods, designated by the Head of the Mission in consultation with the Force Commander, against a hostile act is authorised.

#### Rule No. 1.8

Use of force, up to, and including deadly force, to defend any civilian person who is in need of protection against a hostile act or hostile intent, when competent local authorities are not in a position to render immediate assistance, is authorised. When and where possible, permission to use force should be sought from the immediate superior commander.

---

[1] This Rule can only be included in addition to Rule 1.1 if consistent with the mandate of the UNPKO.

[2] This Rule can only be included in addition to Rule 1.3 if consistent with the mandate of the UNPKO.

[3] This Rule can only be included in addition to Rule 1.5 if consistent with the mandate of the UNPKO.

## Rule No. 1.9

Use of force, excluding deadly force, to pre-vent the escape of any detained person, pending hand-over to appropriate civilian authorities, is authorised.

## Rule No. 1.10

Use of force, up to, and including deadly force, against any person and/or group that limits or intends to limit freedom of movement is authorised. When and where possible, per-mission to use force should be sought from the immediate superior commander.

## Rule 2. Use of weapon systems

### Rule No. 2.1

Use of explosives in order to destroy weapons/ammunition, mines and unexploded ordnance, in the course of the disarmament exercise, is authorised.

### Rule No. 2.2

Indiscriminate pointing of weapons in the direction of any person is prohibited.

### Rule No. 2.3

Firing of all weapons other than for organised training and as authorised in these ROE, is prohibited.

### Rule No. 2.4

Firing of warning shots is authorised.

### Rule No. 2.5

Use of riot control equipment is authorised.

### Rule No. 2.6

Use of lasers for survey, range-finding and targeting is authorised.

## Rule 3. Authority to carry weapons

### Rule No. 3.1

Carriage of weapons is not authorised.

### Rule No. 3.2

Carriage of unloaded personal weapons, whilst on duty, is authorised.

### Rule No. 3.3

Carriage of unloaded personal weapons, both on duty and as designated by the Force Com-mander, is authorised.

## Rule No. 3.4

Carriage of loaded personal weapons is auth-orised.

## Rule No. 3.5

Hand-held support weapons, such as machine guns, light mortars and hand-held anti-tank weapons, may be carried in UN vehicles, but must be obscured from the public's view.

## Rule No. 3.6

Overt carriage by individuals of hand-held support weapons, such as machine guns, light mortars and hand-held anti-tank weapons, is authorised.

## Rule 4. Authority to detain, search and disarm

### Rule No. 4.1

Detention of individuals or groups who com-mit a hostile act or demonstrate a hostile intent against oneself, one's unit or United Nations personnel is authorised.

### Rule No. 4.2[4]

Detention of individuals or groups who com-mit a hostile act or demonstrate a hostile intent against other international personnel is authorised.

### Rule No. 4.3[5]

Detention of individuals or groups who com-mit a hostile act or demonstrate hostile intent against installations and areas or goods desig-nated by the Head of the Mission in con-sultation with the Force Commander, is auth-orised.

### Rule No. 4.4

Searching, including of detained person(s), for weapons, ammunition and explosives is authorised.

### Rule No. 4.5

Disarming individuals, when so directed by the Force Commander, is authorised.

---

[4] This Rule can only be included in addition to Rule 4.3 if consistent with the mandate of the UNPKO.
[5] Idem.

### Rule 5. Reaction to civil action/unrest

**Rule No. 5.1**

Action to counter civil unrest is not authorised.

**Rule No. 5.2**

When competent local authorities are not in a position to render immediate assistance, detention of any person who creates or threatens to create civil unrest with likely serious consequences for life and property is authorised.

_____

*Source*: United Nations, Guidelines for the development of ROE for UNPKO, UN document MD/FGS/0220.0001, May 2002, Attachment 1.

# Appendix 4. The Charter of the United Nations

## The Charter of the United Nations

*Signed at San Francisco, California, 26 June 1945*

*Excerpts*

### 1. Chapter VI
### Pacific settlement of disputes

#### Article 33

The parties to any dispute, the continuance of which is likely to endanger the maintenance of international peace and security, shall, first of all, seek a solution by negotiation, enquiry, mediation, conciliation, arbitration, judicial settlement, resort to regional agencies or arrangements, or other peaceful means of their own choice.

2. The Security Council shall, when it deems necessary, call upon the parties to settle their dispute by such means.

#### Article 34

The Security Council may investigate any dispute, or any situation which might lead to international friction or give rise to a dispute, in order to determine whether the continuance of the dispute or situation is likely to endanger the maintenance of international peace and security.

#### Article 35

1. Any Member of the United Nations may bring any dispute, or any situation of the nature referred to in Article 34, to the attention of the Security Council or of the General Assembly.

2. A state which is not a Member of the United Nations may bring to the attention of the Security Council or of the General Assembly any dispute to which it is a party if it accepts in advance, for the purposes of the dispute, the obligations of pacific settlement provided in the present Charter.

3. The proceedings of the General Assembly in respect of matters brought to its attention under this Article will be subject to the provisions of Articles 11 and 12.

#### Article 36

1. The Security Council may, at any stage of a dispute of the nature referred to in Article 33 or of a situation of like nature, recommend appropriate procedures or methods of adjustment.

2. The Security Council should take into consideration any procedures for the settlement of the dispute which have already been adopted by the parties.

3. In making recommendations under this Article the Security Council should also take into consideration that legal disputes should as a general rule be referred by the parties to the International Court of Justice in accordance with the provisions of the Statute of the Court.

#### Article 37

1. Should the parties to a dispute of the nature referred to in Article 33 fail to settle it by the means indicated in that Article, they shall refer it to the Security Council.

2. If the Security Council deems that the continuance of the dispute is in fact likely to endanger the maintenance of international peace and security, it shall decide whether to take action under Article 36 or to recommend such terms of settlement as it may consider appropriate.

#### Article 38

Without prejudice to the provisions of Articles 33 to 37, the Security Council may, if all the parties to any dispute so request, make recommendations to the parties with a view to a pacific settlement of the dispute.

## 2. Chapter VII
### Action with respect to threats to the peace, breaches of the peace, and acts of aggression

### Article 39

The Security Council shall determine the existence of any threat to the peace, breach of the peace, or act of aggression and shall make recommendations, or decide what measures shall be taken in accordance with Articles 41 and 42, to maintain or restore international peace and security.

### Article 40

In order to prevent an aggravation of the situation, the Security Council may, before making the recommendations or deciding upon the measures provided for in Article 39, call upon the parties concerned to comply with such provisional measures as it deems necessary or desirable. Such provisional measures shall be without prejudice to the rights, claims, or position of the parties concerned. The Security Council shall duly take account of failure to comply with such provisional measures.

### Article 41

The Security Council may decide what measures not involving the use of armed force are to be employed to give effect to its decisions, and it may call upon the Members of the United Nations to apply such measures. These may include complete or partial interruption of economic relations and of rail, sea, air, postal, telegraphic, radio, and other means of communication, and the severance of diplomatic relations.

### Article 42

Should the Security Council consider that measures provided for in Article 41 would be inadequate or have proved to be inadequate, it may take such action by air, sea, or land forces as may be necessary to maintain or restore international peace and security. Such action may include demonstrations, blockade, and other operations by air, sea, or land forces of Members of the United Nations.

### Article 43

1. All Members of the United Nations, in order to contribute to the maintenance of international peace and security, undertake to make available to the Security Council, on its call and in accordance with a special agreement or agreements, armed forces, assistance, and facilities, including rights of passage, necessary for the purpose of maintaining international peace and security.

2. Such agreement or agreements shall govern the numbers and types of forces, their degree of readiness and general location, and the nature of the facilities and assistance to be provided.

3. The agreement or agreements shall be negotiated as soon as possible on the initiative of the Security Council. They shall be concluded between the Security Council and Members or between the Security Council and groups of Members and shall be subject to ratification by the signatory states in accordance with their respective constitutional processes.

### Article 44

When the Security Council has decided to use force it shall, before calling upon a Member not represented on it to provide armed forces in fulfilment of the obligations assumed under Article 43, invite that Member, if the Member so desires, to participate in the decisions of the Security Council concerning the employment of contingents of that Member's armed forces.

### Article 45

In order to enable the United Nations to take urgent military measures, Members shall hold immediately available national air-force contingents for combined international enforcement action. The strength and degree of readiness of these contingents and plans for their combined action shall be determined within the limits laid down in the special agreement or agreements referred to in Article 43, by the Security Council with the assistance of the Military Staff Committee.

## Article 46

Plans for the application of armed force shall be made by the Security Council with the assistance of the Military Staff Committee.

## Article 47

1. There shall be established a Military Staff Committee to advise and assist the Security Council on all questions relating to the Security Council's military requirements for the maintenance of international peace and security, the employment and command of forces placed at its disposal, the regulation of armaments, and possible disarmament.

2. The Military Staff Committee shall consist of the Chiefs of Staff of the permanent members of the Security Council or their representatives. Any Member of the United Nations not permanently represented on the Committee shall be invited by the Committee to be associated with it when the efficient discharge of the Committee's responsibilities requires the participation of that Member in its work.

3. The Military Staff Committee shall be responsible under the Security Council for the strategic direction of any armed forces placed at the disposal of the Security Council. Questions relating to the command of such forces shall be worked out subsequently.

4. The Military Staff Committee, with the authorization of the Security Council and after consultation with appropriate regional agencies, may establish regional sub-committees.

## Article 48

1. The action required to carry out the decisions of the Security Council for the maintenance of international peace and security shall be taken by all the Members of the United Nations or by some of them, as the Security Council may determine.

2. Such decisions shall be carried out by the Members of the United Nations directly and through their action in the appropriate international agencies of which they are members.

## Article 49

The Members of the United Nations shall join in affording mutual assistance in carrying out the measures decided upon by the Security Council.

## Article 50

If preventive or enforcement measures against any state are taken by the Security Council, any other state, whether a Member of the United Nations or not, which finds itself confronted with special economic problems arising from the carrying out of those measures shall have the right to consult the Security Council with regard to a solution of those problems.

## Article 51

Nothing in the present Charter shall impair the inherent right of individual or collective self-defence if an armed attack occurs against a Member of the United Nations, until the Security Council has taken measures necessary to maintain international peace and security. Measures taken by Members in the exercise of this right of self-defence shall be immediately reported to the Security Council and shall not in any way affect the authority and responsibility of the Security Council under the present Charter to take at any time such action as it deems necessary in order to maintain or restore international peace and security.

———

*Source:* URL <http://www.un.org/aboutun/ charter>.

# Bibliography

## I. UN publications and documents

### Publications

United Nations, *The 50th Anniversary Report of the Secretary-General on the Work of the Organization* (UN Department of Public Information: New York, 1996)
—, *An Agenda for Peace: Preventive Diplomacy, Peacemaking and Peace-keeping. Report of the Secretary-General Pursuant to the Statement Adopted by the Summit Meeting of the Security Council on 31 January 1992* (UN Department of Public Information: New York, 1992)
—, *The Blue Helmets: A Review of United Nations Peace-keeping*, 2nd edn (UN Department of Public Information: New York, 1990)
—, *The Blue Helmets: A Review of United Nations Peace-keeping*, 3rd edn (UN Department of Public Information: New York, 1996)
—, *The United Nations and the Congo: Some Salient Facts* (United Nations: New York, 1963)
—, *The United Nations and Rwanda 1993–1996* (UN Department of Public Information: New York, 1996)
—, *The United Nations and the Situation in the Former Yugoslavia*, Reference paper, Department of Public Information, DPI/1312/Rev. 2, 15 Mar 1994 (reprint)
—, *The United Nations and the Situation in the Former Yugoslavia*, Reference paper, Department of Public Information, DPI/1312/Rev. 3, Add. 1, 23 Jan. 1995
—, *The United Nations and the Situation in the Former Yugoslavia*, Reference paper, Department of Public Information, DPI/1312/Rev. 4, July 1995
—, *The United Nations and Somalia 1992–1996* (UN Department of Public Information: New York, 1996)
— *United Nations Peace-keeping* (UN Department of Public Information: New York, Sep. 1996)
—, *Yearbook of the United Nations 1992* (United Nations: New York, 1993)
—, *Yearbook of the United Nations: Special Edition, UN Fiftieth Anniversary 1945–1995* (United Nations: The Hague, 1995)
—, Department of Peace-keeping Operations, *General Guidelines for Peace-keeping Operations*, UN document 95-38147 (United Nations: New York, Oct. 1995)
—, —, *A Peace-keeping Training Manual*, 2nd edn (United Nations: New York, [1997])
—, —, Lessons Learned Unit, *Multidisciplinary Peacekeeping: Lessons from Recent Experience* (United Nations: New York, Dec. 1996)
—, Office of Legal Affairs, Codification Division, *Handbook on the Peaceful Settlement of Disputes Between States* (United Nations: New York, 1992)
United Nations Institute for Disarmament Research (UNIDIR), *Managing Arms in Peace Processes: Croatia and Bosnia-Herzegovina* (UNIDIR: Geneva, 1996)
—, *Managing Arms in Peace Processes: Somalia* (UNIDIR: Geneva, 1995)

## Documents

*1956*

Report of the Secretary-General on basic points for the presence and functioning in Egypt of the United Nations Emergency Force, UN document A/3302, 6 Nov. 1956

Aide-memoire on the basis for the presence and functioning of UNEF in Egypt, UN document A/3375, 20 Nov. 1956

Verbatim record, Meeting of the Advisory Committee for UNEF, UN Secretariat, New York, 18 Dec. 1956

*1957*

Report of the Secretary-General in pursuance of General Assembly Resolution 1123 (XI), UN document A/3512, 24 Jan. 1957

Incoming code cable no. UNEF 294, from Burns, Ballah to SecGen, 1 Feb. 1957, 1655 EST, UN Archives DAG1/2.2.5.5.0, #2

Letter dated 8 February 1957 from the Secretary-General to the minister for foreign affairs of Egypt and Letter dated 8 February 1957 from the minister for foreign affairs of Egypt to the Secretary-General, UN document A/3526, 8 Feb. 1957

Report of the Secretary-General in pursuance of General Assembly resolutions 1124 (XI) and 1125 (XI), UN document A/3527, 11 Feb. 1957

Incoming code cable no. UNEF 554, from Bunche, Gaza to Secretary-General, 11 Mar. 1957, 1133 EST, UN Archives DAG1/2.2.5.5.0, #2

Verbatim records, Meeting of the Advisory Committee for UNEF, UN Secretariat, New York, 15 Mar. 1957, 16 Mar. 1957

Incoming code cable no. UNEF 609, to Secretary-General from Burns, Gaza, 16 Mar. 1957, 1300 EST, UN Archives DAG1/2.2.5.5.0, #2

Outgoing code cable no. 503, from SecGen to Bunche, Burns, Gaza, 16 Mar. 1957, UN Archives DAG1/2.2.5.5.0, #2

Incoming code cable [unnumbered], from Reddy, Cairo to Cordier, 16 Mar. 1957, 1446 EST, UN Archives DAG1/2.2.5.5.0, #2

Verbatim record, Meeting of the Advisory Committee for UNEF, UN Secretariat, New York, 18 Mar. 1957

Incoming code cable no. UNEFCA 153, from Bunche, Cairo to Cordier, 26 Mar. 1957, 2310 (25th)-1129 (26th) EST, UN Archives DAG1/2.2.5.5.0, #2

Letter from Commander UNEF to Secretary-General, 27 Mar. 1957, UN Archives DAG1/2.2.5.5.2, #13

Memorandum concerning the functions, rights and responsibilities of the UNEF following the withdrawal of Israeli forces behind the armistice demarcation line, 27 Mar. 1957, UN Archives DAG1/2.2.5.5.2, #13

Verbatim record, Meeting of the Advisory Committee for UNEF, UN Secretariat, New York, 28 Mar. 1957

Danor Battalion, Beit Hanun, 'In self defence', Memorandum no. 1199 to Commander, HQ, UNEF, Gaza, 25 May 1957, UN Archives DAG1/2.2.5.5.1, #19

Commander UNEF, Gaza, 'Right of UNEF troops to fire in self-defence', Memorandum to Lt Col J. Berg, Commander DANOR Battalion, 11 June 1957, UN Archives DAG1/2.2.5.5.1, #19

Report of the Secretary-General, UN document A/3694 and Add. 1, 9 Oct. 1957

*1958*

UNEF Headquarters, Gaza, 'Use of force by UNEF personnel', HQ UNEF,1911/12-4 (OPS), 6 Feb. 1958, UN Archives DAG13/3.11.1.1, #4

Letter from Under-Secretary-General Ralph Bunche to Lt General E. L. M. Burns, UNEF Commander, 28 Feb. 1958, UN Archives DAG1/2.2.5.5.1, #19

Summary study of the experience derived from the establishment and operation of the force, report of the Secretary-General, UN document A/3943, 9 Oct. 1958

*1960*

Security Council, *Official Records* (SCOR), 15th year, 873rd meeting, 13–14 July

First report of the Secretary-General on the implementation of Security Council Resolution S/4387 of 14 July 1960, UN document S/4389, 18 July 1960 (SCOR, Supplement for July–Sep. 1960, pp. 16–24)

Security Council, Verbatim records (provisional), 884th meeting, UN document S/PV.884, 8 Aug. 1960

UN document S/4426, 9 Aug. 1960

Telegram dated 10 August 1960 from the Secretary-General to the president of the provincial government of Katanga, UN document S/4417/Add. 4, 10 Aug. 1960 (SCOR, 15th year, Supplement for July, Aug. and Sep. 1960, p. 45)

Report by Major-General H. T. Alexander, UN document S/4445, 19 Aug. 1960, annex II (SCOR, Supplement for July, Aug. and Sep. 1960, pp. 101–102)

Observations by the Special Representative of the Secretary-General in the Congo on the report by Major-General Alexander (S/4445, Annex II), UN document S/4451, 21 Aug. 1960 (SCOR, Supplement for July, Aug. and Sep. 1960, pp. 113, 114)

Security Council, Verbatim records (provisional), 896th meeting, UN document S/PV.896, 9–10 Sep. 1960

First progress report to the Secretary-General from his Special Representative in the Congo, Mr Rajeshwar Dayal, UN document S/4531, 21 Sep. 1960

Second progress report to the Secretary-General from his Special Pepresentative in the Congo, Mr Rajeshwar Dayal, UN document S/4557, 2 Nov. 1960 (SCOR, Supplement for Oct., Nov. and Dec. 1960, pp. 22–23)

Situation in the Republic of the Congo, report to the Secretary-General from his Acting Special Representative in the Republic of the Congo, General Rikhye, 22 Nov. 1960, UN Archives DAG13/1.6.5.0.0, #4

Verbatim record, United Nations Advisory Committee on the Congo, meeting no. 15, 24 Nov. 1960

*1961*

Security Council, *Official Records (SCOR)*, 935th meeting, 15 Feb. 1961

Progress report of the Secretary-General, UN document A/4837, 30 Aug. 1961

Message from HQ Katanga Command Elisabethville to ONUC Leopoldville, 13 Sep. 1961, UN Archives DAG13/1.6.5.7.1.0, #4

Flash message from HQ Katanga Command to HQ Sector A, 14 Sep. 1961, UN Archives DAG13/1.6.5.7.1.0, #4

Report of the officer-in-charge of the United Nations Operation in the Congo, UN document S/4940, 14 Sep. 1961 (SCOR, Supplement for July, Aug. and Sep. 1961, p. 103) and Addenda 1–11, 14 Sep.–24 Oct. 1961

Interoffice memorandum from Oscar Schachter, Director, General Legal Division to Dr Ralph Bunche, Under-Secretary-General, 14 Nov. 1961, UN Archives, Box 2, file 8

Security Council, Verbatim records (provisional), 982nd meeting, UN document S/PV.982, 24 Nov. 1961

Code cable L-179, 30 Nov. 1961 from Acting Secretary-General to Linnér and MacFarquhar, Leopoldville, UN Archives DAG1/2.2.1, #10

Telex Conversation Leopoldville–New York, 5 Dec. 1961, UN Archives DAG1/2.2.1, #34

[ONUC], Chief of Military Operations, Elisabethville, Summary of major events, 6–7 Dec. 1961, UN Archives DAG13/1.6.5.2.0

Secret code message from the force commander to ONUC in Elisabethville, 5 Dec. 1961, UN Archives DAG13/1.6.5.2.0, #41

*1962*

Progress report of the Secretary-General, UN document A/5172, 22 Aug. 1962

*1963*

Report by the Secretary-General on the implementation of the Security Council resolutions of 14 July 1960, 21 Feb. and 24 Nov. 1961, UN document S/5240, 4 Feb. 1963 (SCOR, Supplement for Jan., Feb. and Mar. 1963, p. 95)

Progress report of the Secretary-General, UN document A/5494, 12 Sep. 1963

*1964*

Interoffice memorandum, Standard Operating Procedures from Dr Ralph J. Bunche, Under-Secretary [General] for Special Political Affairs to Major-General J. T. U. Aguiyi-Ironsi, Force Commander, ONUC and Major-General C. F. Paiva Chaves, Force Commander, UNEF, 16 Jan. 1964, UN Archives DAG13/3.11.0.0, #9

Note by Secretary-General concerning certain aspects of the function and operation of the United Nations Peacekeeping Force in Cyprus, UN document S/5653, 11 Apr. 1964

Report by the Secretary-General on the United Nations Operation in Cyprus, UN document S/5950, 10 Sep. 1964

Progress report of the Secretary-General, UN document A/5736, 29 Sep. 1964

*1967*

United Nations Emergency Force: special report of the Secretary-General, UN document A/6669, 18 May 1967

Report of the Secretary-General, UN document S/7896, 19 May 1967

United Nations Emergency Force: special report of the Secretary-General, addendum, UN document A/6669/Add. 2, 19 June 1967

United Nations Emergency Force: special report of the Secretary-General, addendum, UN document A/6669, Add. 3, 26 June 1967

Final report by Secretary-General U Thant on UNEF, UN document A/6672, 12 July 1967

*1973*

Report of the Secretary-General on the implementation of Security Council Resolution 340 (1973), UN document S/11052/Rev. 1, 27 Oct. 1973

*1978*

Report of the Secretary-General on the implementation of Security Council Resolution 425 (1978), UN document S/12611, 19 Mar. 1978
Progress report of the Secretary-General on the United Nations Interim Force in Lebanon, UN document S/12620/Add. 5, 13 June 1978

*1979*

Letter dated 7 May 1979 from the Permanent Representative of Lebanon to the United Nations addressed to the President of the Security Council, UN document S/13301, 7 May 1979

*1980*

Security Council, Verbatim records (provisional), 2218th meeting, UN document S/PV.2218, 18 Apr. 1980
Report of the Secretary-General on the United Nations Interim Force in Lebanon, for the period from 11 December 1979 to 12 June 1980, UN document S/13994, 12 June 1980
Security Council, Verbatim records (provisional), 2232nd meeting, UN document S/PV.2232, 17 June 1980

*1985*

Report of the Secretary-General, UN document S/17093, 11 Apr. 1985

*1986*

Report of the Secretary-General, UN document S/18348, 18 Sep. 1986

*1992*

Report of the Secretary-General on the situation in Somalia, UN document S/23829, 21 Apr. 1992
Report of the Secretary-General pursuant to Security Council Resolution 749 (1992), UN document S/23836, 24 Apr. 1992
Further report of the Secretary-General pursuant to Security Council Resolution 749 (1992), UN document S/23900, 12 May 1992
Statement by the President of the Security Council, 17 July 1992
Report of the Secretary-General on the situation in Somalia, UN document S/24343, 22 July 1992
Letter dated 8 September 1992 from the President of the Security Council to the Secretary-General, UN document S/24532, 8 Sep. 1992
Report of the Secretary-General, UN document S/24540, 10 Sep. 1992
Second progress report of the Secretary-General on the United Nations Transitional Authority in Cambodia, UN document S/24578, 21 Sep. 1992

Note by the President of the Security Council, UN document S/24872, 30 Nov. 1992
Letter dated 8 December 1992 from the Secretary-General to President Bush of the
    United States, reproduced in *The United Nations and Somalia 1992–1996* (UN
    Department of Public Information, New York, 1996)
Report of the Secretary-General submitted in pursuance of paragraphs 18 and 19 of
    Security Council Resolution 794 (1992), UN document S/24992, 19 Dec. 1992
Note by the President of the Security Council, UN document S/25036, 30 Dec. 1992

*1993*

UNTAC Electoral Component, Phnom Penh, *Free Choice: Electoral Component
    Newsletter*, no. 11 (15 Jan. 1993)
Progress report of the Secretary-General on the situation in Somalia, including annexes
    containing the texts of the agreements reached by the Somali factions in Addis
    Ababa from 4 to 15 January 1993, UN document S/25168, 26 Jan. 1993, Annex III,
    . Agreement on implementing the cease-fire and on modalities of disarmament
    (supplement to the General Agreement signed in Addis Ababa on 8 January 1993)
Note by the President of the Security Council, UN document S/25184, 29 Jan. 1993
Notes by the President of the Security Council, UN document S/25344, 26 Feb. 1993
Further report of the Secretary-General submitted in pursuance of paragraphs 18 and
    19 of Resolution 794 (1992), UN document S/25354, 3 Mar. 1993, and addenda
    S/25354/Add. 1, 11 Mar. 1993, and S/25354/Add. 2, 22 Mar. 1993
Note by the President of the Security Council, UN document S/25493, 31 Mar. 1993
Note by the President of the Security Council, UN document S/25696, 30 Apr. 1993
Fourth progress report of the Secretary-General on the UN Transitional Authority in
    Cambodia, UN document S/25719, 3 May 1993
Comprehensive review of the whole question of peace-keeping operations in all their
    aspects, UN document A/48/173, 25 May 1993
Note by the President of the Security Council, UN document S/25859, 28 May 1993
'Statement by the President of the Security Council endorsing the actions of
    UNOSOM II', UN Press release SC/5647-SOM/24, 14 June 1993
Report of the Secretary-General pursuant to Security Council Resolution 836 (1993),
    UN document S/25939, 14 June 1993
Report on the situation of human rights in Rwanda submitted by Mr R. Degni-Ségui,
    Special Rapporteur of the Commission on Human Rights, 25 May 1993, UN
    document E/CN.4/1994/7/Add. 1, 11 Aug. 1993
Further report of the Secretary-General submitted in pursuance of paragraph 18 of
    Resolution 814 (1993), UN document S/26317, 17 Aug. 1993
Report on the work of the organization from the 47th to the 48th session of the General
    Assembly, New York, Sep. 1993
Further report of the Secretary-General submitted in pursuance of paragraph 19 of
    Resolution 814 (1993) and paragraph 5 of Resolution 865 (1993) on the situation in
    Somalia, UN document S/26738, 12 Nov. 1993

*1994*

'UNOSOM II: Review of the model for Chapter VII interventions', Briefing by
    Lt Gen. Bir to troop-contributing nations, United Nations, 25 Jan. 1994

Improving the capacity of the United Nations for peace-keeping: report of the Secretary-General, UN document A/48/403, S/26450, 14 Mar. 1994

Report of the Secretary-General pursuant to Resolution 871 (1993), UN document S/1994/300, 16 Mar. 1994

Report of the Secretary-General pursuant to Resolution 844 (1993), UN document S/1994/555, 9 May 1994

Report of the commission of inquiry established pursuant to Security Council Resolution 885 (1993) to investigate armed attacks on UNOSOM II personnel which led to casualties among them, New York, 24 Feb. 1994, appended to UN, Note by the Secretary-General, UN document S/1994/653, 1 June 1994

Report of the Secretary-General pursuant to Resolution 908 (1994), UN document S/1994/1067, 17 Sep. 1994

Press release DH/1716, Geneva, 25 Aug. 1994

Report of the Secretary-General on the work of the organization, UN document A/49/1, 2 Sep. 1994

Report of the Security Council mission to Somalia (26–27 October 1994), UN document S/1994/1245, 3 Nov. 1994

Report of the Secretary-General pursuant to Security Council Resolution 959, UN document S/1994/1389, 1 Dec. 1994


*1995*

Supplement to *An Agenda for Peace*: position paper of the Secretary-General on the occasion of the 50th anniversary of the United Nations, UN document A/50/60, S/19951, 3 Jan. 1995

UN Mission in Haiti, 'United Nations Forces in Haiti Force Training Program', Port-au-Prince, 3 Mar. 1995

Report of the Secretary-General, UN document S/1995/444, 30 May 1995

Report of the Seminar on Lessons Learned from the United Nations Operation in Somalia at the Strategic and Operational Levels, 19–20 June 1995, New York

Letter dated 95/07/26 from the Secretary-General addressed to the President of the Security Council, UN document S/1995/623, 27 July 1995

Statement by the Secretary-General, UN document SG/SM/5712, 29 Aug. 1995

Press Conference, UN Secretary-General Boutros Boutros-Ghali, UN headquarters, UN document SG/SM/95/331, 18 Dec. 1995

Comprehensive report on lessons learned from United Nations Operation in Somalia April 1992–March 1995, Dec. 1995 (unnumbered)


*1996*

Report of the Working Group on a Multinational United Nations Stand-by Forces High Readiness Brigade, Annex to letter dated 29 February 1996 from the Permanent Representative of Denmark to the United Nations addressed to the Secretary-General, UN document A/51/75, 5 Mar. 1996

Annex to Letter dated 7 May 1996 from the Secretary-General addressed to the President of the Security Council, UN document S/1996/337, 7 May 1996

Letter of intent concerning cooperation on the Multinational United Nations Stand-by Forces High Readiness Brigade, Denmark, 15 Dec. 1996

Department of Peace-keeping Operations, Lessons Learned Unit, Comprehensive report on lessons learned from United Nations Assistance Mission for Rwanda (UNAMIR), October 1993–April 1996, New York, Dec. 1996

*1999*

Report of the Security Council mission to Jakarta and Dili, 8–12 September 1999, UN document S/1999/976, 14 Sep. 1999

'Secretary-general presents his annual report to General Assembly', Press release SG/SM/7136 and GA/95920, 20 Sep. 1999

General Assembly Official Records, 54th session: 4th Plenary Meeting, Monday, 20 September 1999, UN document A/54/PV.4, 20 Sep. 1999

Report of the Secretary-General on the situation in East Timor, UN document S/1999/1024, 4 Oct. 1999

Report of the Secretary-General pursuant to General Assembly Resolution 53/35: the fall of Srebrenica, UN document A/54/549, 15 Nov. 1999

Report of the Independent Inquiry into the Actions of the United Nations during the 1994 Genocide in Rwanda, UN document S/1999/1257, 15 Dec. 1999

Letter dated 23 December 1999 from the Secretary-General addressed to the President of the Security Council, UN document S/1999/1285, 28 Dec. 1999

*2000*

Second report of the Secretary-General pursuant to Security Council Resolution 1270 (1999) on the United Nations Mission in Sierra Leone, UN document S/2000/13, 11 Jan. 2000

Report of the Secretary-General on the United Nations Transitional Administration in East Timor, UN document S/2000/53, 26 Jan. 2000

Comprehensive review of the whole question of peacekeeping operations in all their aspects: report of the Special Committee on Peacekeeping Operations, UN document A/54/839, 20 Mar. 2000

'We the peoples: the role of the United Nations in the twenty-first century', Report of the Secretary-General, UN document A/54/2000, 27 Mar. 2000

Fourth report of the Secretary-General pursuant to Security Council Resolution 1270 (1999) on the United Nations Mission in Sierra Leone, UN document S/2000/455, 19 May 2000

Office of the Spokesman for the Secretary-General, Daily Press Briefing, New York, 5 June 2000

Report of the Secretary-General on the United Nations Transitional Administration in East Timor, UN document S/2000/738, 26 July 2000

Fifth report of the Secretary-General on the United Nations Mission in Sierra Leone, UN document S/2000/455, 31 July 2000

Statement by the President of the Security Council, UN document S/PRST/2000/26, 3 Aug. 2000

'We the peoples: Millennium Forum declaration and agenda for action. Strengthening the United Nations for the 21st century', in UN document A/54/959, 8 Aug. 2000

Report of the Panel on United Nations Peace Operations, UN document A/55/305, S/2000/809, 21 Aug. 2000 (the Brahimi Report)

Identical letters dated 21 August 2000 from the Secretary-General to the President of the General Assembly and the President of the Security Council, UN document A/55/305, S/2000/809, 21 Aug. 2000

Sixth report of the Secretary-General on the United Nations Mission in Sierra Leone, UN document S/2000/832, 24 Aug. 2000

'Security Council holds open meeting on latest developments in East Timor', Press release SC/6915, 29 Aug. 2000

Report of the Secretary-General on the work of the organization, UN document A/55/1, 30 Aug. 2000

United Nations Millennium Declaration, resolution adopted by the General Assembly, UN document A/Res/55/2, 18 Sep. 2000

Report of the Secretary-General on Ethiopia and Eritrea, UN document S/2000/879, 18 Sep. 2000

Report of the Secretary-General on the situation in East Timor, UN document S/1999/1024, 4 Oct. 1999

Report of the Security Council mission to Sierra Leone, UN document S/2000/992, 16 Oct. 2000

Report of the Secretary-General on the implementation of the report of the Panel on United Nations Peace Operations, UN document A/55/502, 20 Oct. 2000

Seventh report of the Secretary-General on the United Nations Mission in Sierra Leone, UN document S/2000/1055, 31 Oct. 2000

'Security Council discusses exit strategies for peacekeeping operations', Press release SC/6951, 15 Nov. 2000

Department of Public Information, United Nations peacekeeping from 1991 to 2000: statistical data and charts, document DPI/2175, New York, Dec. 2000

Comprehensive review of the whole question of peacekeeping operations in all their aspects, report of the Special Committee on Peacekeeping Operations, UN document A/C.4/55/6, 4 Dec. 2000

'Special Committee on Peacekeeping adopts report on Brahimi recommendations', Press release GA/PK/169, 4 Dec. 2000

'Fifth Committee approves draft texts on scale of assessments, peacekeeping finance, Brahimi Report implementation', Press release GA/AB/3425, 23 Dec. 2000

*2001*

Ninth report of the Secretary-General on the situation in Sierra Leone, UN document S/2001/228, 14 Mar. 2001

Implementation of the recommendations of the Special Committee on Peacekeeping Operations and the Panel on United Nations Peace Operations, report of the Secretary-General, UN document A/55/977, 1 June 2001, Annex D

Tenth report of the Secretary-General on the situation in Sierra Leone, UN document S/2001/627, 25 June 2001

Implementation of the recommendations of the Special Committee on Peacekeeping Operations and the Panel on United Nations Peace Operations: report of the Secretary-General, UN document A/56/732, 21 Dec. 2001

*2002*

Note by President of the Security Council, UN document S/2002/56, 14 Jan. 2002

'Under-Secretary-General for Peace-keeping Operations tells Special Committee operations must deploy credibly, rapidly to succeed', Press release GA/PK/174, 11 Feb. 2002

Statement of Mr Jean-Marie Guéhenno, Under Secretary-General for Peace-keeping Operations, to the Special Committee on Peacekeeping Operations, in 'Special Committee on Peacekeeping Operations ends two-day debate on need for rapid deployment of peace operations', Press release, GA/PK/175, 12 Feb. 2002

## General Assembly resolutions

General Assembly Resolution 998 (ES-1), 4 Nov. 1956
General Assembly Resolution 1000 (ES-1), 5 Nov. 1956
General Assembly Resolution 47/120A, 18 Dec. 1992
General Assembly Resolution 47/120 B, 8 Oct. 1993

## Security Council resolutions

Resolution adopted by the Security Council at its 873rd meeting on 14 July 1960 [Resolution 143], UN document S/4387, 14 July 1960 (SCOR, Supplement for July–Sep. 1960, p. 16)
Resolution adopted by the Security Council at its 879th meeting on 22 July 1960 [Resolution 145], UN document S/4405, 22 July 1960
Security Council Resolution 146, 9 Aug. 1960
Resolution adopted by the Security Council at its 942nd meeting on 20–21 February 1961 [Resolution 161], UN document S/4741, 21 Feb. 1961
Resolution adopted by the Security Council at its 982nd meeting on 24 Nov. 1961 [Resolution 169], UN document S/5002, 24 Nov. 1961
Security Council Resolution 186, 4 Mar. 1964
Security Council Resolution 355, 1 Aug. 1974
Security Council Resolution 425, 19 Mar. 1978
Security Council Resolution 426, 19 Mar. 1978
Security Council Resolution 467, 24 Apr. 1980
Security Council Resolution 501, 25 Feb. 1982
ecurity Council Resolution 743, 21 Feb. 1992
Security Council Resolution 745, 28 Feb. 1992
Security Council Resolution 751, 24 Apr. 1992
Security Council Resolution 752, 15 May 1992
Security Council Resolution 758, 5 June 1992
Security Council Resolution 762, 30 June 1992
Security Council Resolution 767, 27 July 1992
Security Council Resolution 769, 7 Aug. 1992
Security Council Resolution 770, 13 Aug. 1992
Security Council Resolution 775, 28 Aug. 1992
Security Council Resolution 776, 14 Sep. 1992
Security Council Resolution 779, 6 Oct. 1992
Security Council Resolution 781, 9 Oct. 1992
Security Council Resolution 794, 19 Dec. 1992
Security Council Resolution 795, 11 Dec. 1992

Security Council Resolution 814, 26 Mar. 1993
Security Council Resolution 816, 31 March 1993
Security Council Resolution 819, 16 Apr. 1993
Security Council Resolution 824, 6 May 1993
Security Council Resolution 836, 4 June 1993
Security Council Resolution 837, 6 June 1993
Security Council Resolution 844, 18 June 1993
Security Council Resolution 846, 22 June 1993
Security Council Resolution 865, 22 Sep. 1993
Security Council Resolution 871, 4 Oct. 1993
Security Council Resolution 872, 5 Oct. 1993
Security Council Resolution 885, 16 Nov. 1993
Security Council Resolution 897, 4 Feb. 1994
Security Council Resolution 908, 31 Mar. 1994
Security Council Resolution 912, 21 Apr. 1994
Security Council Resolution 918, 17 May 1994
Security Council Resolution 929, 22 June 1994
Security Council Resolution 940, 31 July 1994
Security Council Resolution 954, 4 Nov. 1994
Security Council Resolution 958, 19 Nov. 1994
Security Council Resolution 975, 30 Jan. 1995
Security Council Resolution 981, 31 Mar. 1995
Security Council Resolution 982, 31 Mar. 1995
Security Council Resolution 983, 31 Mar. 1995
Security Council Resolution 998, 16 June 1995
Security Council Resolution 1004, 12 July 1995
Security Council Resolution 1031, 15 Dec. 1995
Security Council Resolution 1037, 15 Jan. 1996
Security Council Resolution 1246, 11 June 1999
Security Council Resolution 1264, 15 Sep. 1999
Security Council Resolution 1265, 17 Sep. 1999
Security Council Resolution 1270, 22 Oct. 1999
Security Council Resolution 1272, 25 Oct. 1999
Security Council Resolution 1289, 7 Feb. 2000
Security Council Resolution 1291, 24 Feb. 2000
Security Council Resolution 1299, 19 May 2000
Security Council Resolution 1318, 7 Sep. 2000
Security Council Resolution 1327, 13 Nov. 2000
Security Council Resolution 1343, 7 Mar. 2001
Security Council Resolution 1346, 30 Mar. 2001

## Operations documents

UNEF Headquarters, Operations Instruction no. 10 [untitled], HQ UNEF 1-0 (OPS),
   El Ballah, 2 Mar. 1957, UN Archives DAG13/3.11.1.1, #4
UNEF Headquarters, Gaza, Operations Instruction no. 36 [untitled], no. 65/5-3 (OPS)
   12 Jan. 1960, UN Archives DAG13/3.11.0.0, #9

ONUC, Operations Directive no. 1 [untitled and undated], UN Archives DAG13/1.6.5.0.0, Ops directives Aug. 1960–Jan. 1964, Box 3

ONUC, Directive on the protection of internal security, 2 Aug. 1960, UN Archives DAG13/1.6.5.0.0, Ops directives Aug. 1960–Jan. 1964, Box 3

ONUC, Operations Directive no. 3, 'ONUC policy with regard to inter-tribal conflict', 17 Aug. 1960, UN Archives DAG13/1.6.5.0.0, Ops directives Aug. 1960–Jan. 1964

ONUC, Operations Directive no. 6, 'Security and the maintenance of law and order', 28 Oct. 1960, UN Archives DAG13/1.6.5.0.0, Ops directives Aug. 1960–Jan. 1964, Box 3

ONUC, Operations Directive no. 7, 'Security measures at airports', document no. 1001/11/OPS, 5 Nov. 1960, UN Archives DAG13/1.6.5.0.0, Ops directives Aug. 1960–Jan. 1964, Box 3

ONUC, Operations Directive no. 8 [untitled, Feb. 1961], UN Archives DAG13/1.6.5.0.0, Ops directives Aug. 1960–Jan. 1964, Box 3

ONUC, Operational [sic] Directive no. 10, 'Action of the United Nations Force in the Congo to prevent armed clashes', 30 Mar. 1961, UN Archives DAG13/1.6.5.0.0, Ops directives Aug. 1960–Jan. 1964, Box 3

UNEF Headquarters, Gaza, 'Instructions for the guidance of troops for protective duty tasks', ref. 2131/7(OPS), 1 Sep. 1962

ONUC, Undated instruction to UN forces in Katanga Area, no. 3330/Katanga/ops, UN Archives DAG13/1.6.5.2.0, #41

ONUC Headquarters, Leopoldville, Fighter Operations Order no. 16, 27 Dec. 1962, AHQ/6600/1/F-OPS, UN Archives DAG13/1.6.5.0.0., #9

[ONUC], HQ Indian Independent Brigade Group, Operation Instruction no. 3, 'Op Grand Slam', document no. 1013/4/G S (0), 31 Dec. 1962, UN Archives DAG13/1.6.5.7.1.0, #9

UNEF Headquarters, Operations Section, 'Standing orders' (revised up to April 1966), UN Archives DAG13/3.11.0.0, #9

## II. National government documents

### Australia

Australian Defence Force, Amber Card, called OFOF [Orders for Opening Fire] Low Level Ops in Australia, Unopposed Deployment Overseas, Jan. 1991, 7690-66 136 3620

'Report by Australia to the Comprehensive Seminar on Lessons-Learned from United Nations Operation in Somalia (UNOSOM)', Plainsboro, N.J., 13–15 Sep. 1995

Evans, Gareth (Australian Minister for Foreign Affairs), 'The United Nations: Cooperating for Peace', address to the UN General Assembly, 27 Sep. 1993

### Canada

Government of Canada, *Towards a Rapid Reaction Capability for the United Nations* (Government of Canada: Ottawa, Sep. 1995)

Canadian Armed Forces, *Operations Land and Tactical Air Vol. 3: Peacekeeping Operations*, Manual B-GL-301-003/FP-001 (Canadian Armed Forces: Ottawa, 1995)

## Netherlands

Netherlands Ministry of Defence, 'Debriefing report on Srebrenica to the Speaker of the Lower House of the States-General', The Hague, 30 Oct. 1995

## UK

British Army, *Army Field Manual, Vol. 5. Operations Other than War, Part 2: Wider Peacekeeping*, D/HQDT/18/34/30 (Her Majesty's Stationery Office: London, 1994)
—, *Army Field Manual, Vol. 5, Part 1, Peacekeeping Operations* (AFM/PKO) (Ministry of Defence: London, 1988)
—, 'Peace support operations', Draft Army Field Manual, 1997 (unpublished)
*Government Reply to the Fourth Report from the Defence Committee, Session 1992–93*, HC 988 (Her Majesty's Stationery Office: London, 3 Nov. 1993)
House of Commons, Foreign Affairs Committee, *The Expanding Role of the United Nations and its Implications for United Kingdom Policy, Third Report, Vol. I*, HC 1992/93 235-1 (Her Majesty's Stationery Office: London, 23 June 1993)
Ministry of Defence, *Land Operations, Vol. 3: Counter-Revolutionary Operations* (Ministry of Defence: London, 1977)
—, *Peace Support Operations*, Joint Warfare Publication 3-05, document JWP 3-05/PSO (Ministry of Defence: London, 1998)
—, *Strategic Defence Review* (Ministry of Defence: London, July 1998)

## USA

Army, 'Operation Uphold Democracy: initial impressions', D-20 to D+40, Center for Army Lessons Learned, Fort Leavenworth, Kans., Dec. 1994
— Center for Lessons Learned, 'US Army operations in support of UNOSOM II', Ft Leavenworth, Kansas, 1994
Army–Air Force Center for Low-Intensity Conflict, 'Peacekeeping tactics, techniques, and procedures', Langley Air Force Base, Va., 1989
Aspin, Les, 'Remarks prepared for delivery by Secretary of Defense Les Aspin at the Center for Strategic and International Studies, Washington, DC, August 27, 1993', News release, Office of the Assistant Secretary of Defense, Washington, DC, 27 Aug. 1993
Albright, Madeleine K. (US Permanent Representative to the United Nations), 'Building a consensus on international peace-keeping', Statement before the Senate Foreign Relations Committee, Washington, DC, 20 Oct. 1993, *US Department of State Dispatch*, vol. 4, no. 46 (15 Nov. 1993)
Clinton, W. J. (Pres.), 'Confronting the challenges of a broader world', Address to the UN General Assembly by President Bill Clinton, 27 Sep. 1993, *US Department of State Dispatch*, vol. 4, no. 39 (27 Sep. 1993)
—, 'A national security strategy of engagement and enlargement', White House: Washington, DC, Feb. 1995
Congressional Research Service (CRS), *A UN Rapid Reaction Force? Considerations for US Policymakers*, CRS Report for Congress (Library of Congress, Congressional Research Service: Washington, DC, 29 June 1995)
Department of State, *The Clinton Administration's Policy on Reforming Multilateral Peace Operations*, Department of State Publication 10161 (Department of State,

Bureau of International Organization Affairs: Washington, DC, May 1994) (Presidential Decision Directive 25)

Department of the Army, Army, *Field Manual: Operations*, FM 100-5 (Department of the Army, Washington, DC, June 1993)

—, *Peace Operations*, FM 100-23 (Department of the Army: Washington, DC, Dec. 1994)

—, 'Rules of engagement for Operation Restore Hope: sample rules of engagement' in *Peace Operations*, FM 100-23 (Department of the Army: Washington, DC, Dec. 1994), appendix D

General Accounting Office (GAO), 'United Nations: reform initiatives have strengthened operations, but overall objectives have not yet been achieved', report to congressional requesters, GAO/NSIAD-00-150, Washington, DC, 10 May 2000

Joint Chiefs of Staff, *Doctrine for Joint Operations*, Joint Pub 3-0 (Joint Chiefs of Staff: Washington, DC, 1993)

—, 'Joint military doctrine for operations other than war', Washington, DC, 16 June 1995

—, 'National military strategy of the United States of America: a strategy of flexible and selective engagement', Washington, DC, Feb. 1995

—, Standing Rules of Engagement for US Forces, Chairman of the Joint Chiefs of Staff Instruction 3121.01 of 1, Enclosure A, Unclassified, Office of the Joint Chiefs of Staff, Washington, DC, 1 Oct. 1994

Joint Forces Command, Joint Warfighting Center, *Joint Task Force Commander's Handbook for Peace Operations* (Joint Warfighting Center: Ft Monroe, Va., 28 Feb. 1995)

Office of Technology Assessment, 'Improving the prospects for future international peace operations: workshop proceedings', document OTA-BP-ISS-67, Washington, DC, Sep. 1995

Senate, Committee on Armed Services, 'Review of the circumstances surrounding the Ranger raid on October 3–4, 1993 in Mogadishu, Somalia', Memorandum for Senator Thurmond and Senator Nunn from Senator Warner and Senator Levin, Washington, DC, 29 Sep. 1995

## III. Other

*NATO Doctrine for Peace Support Operations*, Change 1, Draft, SHAPE, 28 Feb. 1994

Memorandum of Understanding (MOU) between CINCSOUTH and FC UNPF pursuant to the North Atlantic Council (NAC) decisions of 25 July 1995 and 1 August 1995 and the direction of the UN Secretary-General, Camp Pleso, Croatia, 19 Aug. 1995

## IV. Books and reports

Abi-Saab, G., *The United Nations Operation in the Congo 1960–1964* (Oxford University Press: Oxford, 1978)

Ahlquist, L. (ed.), *Co-operation, Command and Control in UN Peace Support Operations: A Case Study on Haiti from the National Defence College* (Försvarshögskolan, Operativa Institutionen [Swedish National Defence College, Department of Operations]: Stockholm, 1998

—, *Co-operation, Command and Control in UN Peace Support Operations: A Pilot Study from the Swedish War College* (Försvarshögskolan, Operativa Institutionen [Swedish National Defence College, Department of Operations]: Stockholm, 1996)

Alexandrov, S. A., *Self-Defense Against the Use of Force in International Law* (Kluwer Law International: The Hague, 1996)

Allard, K., *Somalia Operations: Lessons Learned* (National Defense University, Institute for National Strategic Studies: Washington, DC, 1995)

Allison, R., *Peacekeeping in the Soviet Successor States*, Chaillot Papers no. 18 (Western European Union, Institute for Security Studies: Paris, 1994)

Arend, A. C. and Beck, R. J., *International Law and the Use of Force* (Routledge: London and New York, 1993)

Aspen Institute, *The United States and the Use of Force in the Post-Cold War Era*, Report by the Aspen Strategy Group (Aspen Institute: Queenstown, Md., 1995)

Azimi, N. (ed.), *Humanitarian Action and Peacekeeping Operations: Debriefing and Lessons* (Kluwer Law: The Hague, 1997)

Biermann, W. and Vadset, M., *Peacekeeping Principles in a Civil War-Like Conflict*, Working Paper no. 563 (Norwegian Institute of International Affairs (NUPI): Oslo, Nov. 1996)

Bingham, J., *U Thant: The Search for Peace* (Alfred A. Knopf: New York, 1967)

Bodansky, Y., *Bin Laden: The Man Who Declared War on America* (Random House: New York, 1999)

Boulden, J., *The United Nations and Mandate Enforcement: Congo, Somalia, and Bosnia*, Martello Papers no. 20 (Centre for International Relations, Queen's University: Kingston, Ont., 1999)

—, *Prometheus Unborn: The History of the Military Staff Committee*, Aurora Papers no. 19 (Canadian Centre for Global Security: Ottawa, 1993)

Boutros-Ghali, B., *Unvanquished: A US–UN Saga* (I. B. Tauris: New York, 1999)

Bowens, G. (Capt.), *Legal Guide to Peace Operations* (US Peacekeeping Institute, US Army War College: Carlisle, Pa., 1998)

Boyd, A., *United Nations: Piety, Myth, and Truth* (Penguin: Harmondsworth, 1964)

Burns, A. L. and Heathcote, N., *Peacekeeping by UN Forces: From Suez to the Congo*, Princeton Studies in World Politics no. 4 (Praeger for the Center for International Studies, Princeton: New York, 1963)

Burns, E. L. M. (Lt-Gen.), *Between Arab and Israeli* (George G. Harrap: London, 1962)

Caplan, R. D., *Post-Mortem on UNPROFOR*, London Defence Studies no. 33 (Brassey's for the Centre for Defence Studies, King's College, London: London, Feb. 1996)

Chayes, A. C. and Chayes, A. H., *The New Sovereignty: Compliance with International Regulatory Agreements* (Harvard University Press: Cambridge, Mass., 1995)

Chayes, A. H. and Raach, G. T. (eds), *Peace Operations: Developing an American Strategy* (National Defense University Press: Washington, DC, 1995)

Chopra, J., Eknes, Å. and Nordbø, T., *Fighting for Hope in Somalia*, Peacekeeping and Multinational Operations no. 6 (Norwegian Institute of International Affairs (NUPI): Oslo, 1995)

Cilliers, J. and Mills, G. (eds), *Peacekeeping in Africa*, vol. 2 (Institute for Defence Policy and South African Institute of International Affairs: Braamfontein, 1995)

Clarke, W. and Herbst, J. (eds), *Learning from Somalia: The Lessons of Armed Humanitarian Intervention* (Lynne Rienner: Boulder, Colo., 1996)

Clements, K. and Ward, R. (eds), *Building International Community: Cooperating for Peace Case Studies* (Allen & Unwin: St Leonard's, 1994)

Cohen, B. and Stamkoski, G. (eds), *With No Peace to Keep: United Nations Peace-keeping and the War in the Former Yugoslavia* (Grainpress Ltd: London, 1995)

Conetta, C. and Knight, C., *Vital Force: A Proposal for the Overhaul of the UN Peace Operations System and for the Creation of a UN Legion*, Project on Defense Alternatives Research Monograph no. 4 (Commonwealth Institute: Cambridge, Mass., Sep. 1995)

Coray, C., *International Law and the Use of Force* (Oxford University Press: Oxford, 2000)

Cox, D., *Exploring* An Agenda for Peace: *Issues Arising from the Report of the Secretary-General*, Aurora Papers no. 20 (Canadian Centre for Global Security: Ottawa, 1993)

— and Legault, A. (eds), Lester B. Pearson Canadian International Peacekeeping Training Centre, *UN Rapid Reaction Capabilities: Requirements and Prospects* (Canadian Peacekeeping Press: Clementsport, 1995)

Crocker, C., Hampson, F. O. and Aall, P. (eds), *Managing Global Chaos: Sources of and Responses to International Conflict* (United States Institute of Peace Press: Washington, DC, 1996)

Damrosch, L. F. and Scheffer, D. J. (eds), *Law and Force in the New International Order* (Westview Press: Boulder, Colo., 1991)

Daniel, D. C. F. and Hayes, B. C. (eds), *Beyond Traditional Peacekeeping* (Macmillan: London, 1995)

— with de Jonge Oudraat, C., *Coercive Inducement and the Containment of International Crises* (United States Institute of Peace Press: Washington, DC, 1999)

Danish Institute of International Affairs (DUPI), *Humanitarian Intervention: Legal and Political Aspects* (DUPI: Copenhagen, 1999)

Dayal, R., *Mission for Hammarskjöld: The Congo Crisis* (Oxford University Press: London, 1976)

Dixon, A. M. and Wigge, M. A., *Military Support to Complex Humanitarian Emergencies: From Practice to Policy. 1995 Annual Conference Proceedings* (Center for Naval Analyses: Alexandria, Va., 1995)

Durch, W. J. (ed.), *The Evolution of UN Peaceekping: Case Studies and Comparative Analysis* (St Martin's Press for the Henry L. Stimson Center: Washington, DC, 1993)

— (ed.), *UN Peacekeeping, American Policy, and the Uncivil Wars of the 1990s* (St Martin's Press: New York, 1996)

Eide, E. B. and Solli, P.-E., *From Blue to Green: The Transition from UNPROFOR to IFOR in Bosnia and Herzegovina*, Working Paper no. 539 (Norwegian Institute of International Affairs (NUPI): Oslo, Dec. 1995)

Ericson, L. (ed.), *Solidarity and Defence: Sweden's Armed Forces in International Peace-keeping Operations During the 19th and 20th Centuries* (Swedish Military History Commission: Stockholm, 1995)

Erskine, E. A. (Lt-Gen.), *Mission with UNIFIL: An African Soldier's Reflections* (St Martin's Press: New York, 1989)

Evans, G., *Co-operating for Peace: The Global Agenda for the 1990s and Beyond* (Allen & Unwin: Sydney, 1994)

Fetherston, A. B., *Toward a Theory of United Nations Peacekeeping*, Peace Research Report no. 31 (Department of Peace Studies, University of Bradford: Bradford, Feb. 1993)

Findlay, T. C., *The Blue Helmets' First War? Use of Force by the UN in the Congo 1960–64* (Canadian Peacekeeping Press: Clementsport, 1999)

—, *Cambodia: The Legacy and Lessons of UNTAC*, SIPRI Research Report no. 9 (Oxford University Press: Oxford, 1995)

—, *Challenges for the New Peacekeepers*, SIPRI Research Report no. 12 (Oxford University Press: Oxford, 1996)

Fondation pour les Études de Défense, *Operations des Nations Unies: Leçons de Terrain* [United Nations operations: lessons on the ground] (Fondation pour les Études de Défense: Paris, 1995)

George, A. L., *Forceful Persuasion: Coercive Diplomacy as an Alternative to War* (United States Institute of Peace Press: Washington, DC, 1991)

Goldmann, K., *Peacekeeping and Self-Defence*, Monograph no. 7 (International Information Center on Peace-Keeping Operations: Paris, Mar. 1968)

Gordon, K., *The United Nations in the Congo: A Quest for Peace* (Carnegie Endowment for International Peace: Washington, DC, 1962)

Goulding, M., *Peacemonger* (John Murray: London, 2002)

Haass, R. N., *Intervention: The Use of American Military Force in the Post-Cold War World* (Carnegie Endowment for International Peace: Washington, DC, 1994)

Hampson, F. O., *Why Peace Settlements Fail* (United States Institute of Peace (USIP): Washington, DC, 1996)

Harbottle, M., *The Blue Berets* (Stackpole Books: Harrisburg, Pa., 1972)

Hayes, M. D. and Wheatley, G. F. (eds), *Peace Operations: Haiti—A Case Study* (National Defense University, Institute for National Strategic Studies: Washington, DC, Feb. 1996)

Heiberg, M., *Peacekeeping in Southern Lebanon*, NUPI Paper no. 453 (Norwegian Institute of International Affairs (NUPI): Oslo, Nov. 1991)

Henry L. Stimson Center, *Handbook on United Nations Peace Operations*, Handbook no. 3 (Henry L. Stimson Press: Washington, DC, Apr. 1995)

Higgins, R., *United Nations Peacekeeping 1946–1967: Documents and Commentary. Vol. 1: The Middle East* (Oxford University Press: Oxford, 1969)

Hillen, J., *Blue Helmets: The Strategy of UN Military Operations*, 2nd edn (Brassey's: Washington, DC, 2000)

Hirsch, J. L. and Oakley, R. B., *Somalia and Operation Restore Hope: Reflections on Peacemaking and Peacekeeping* (United States Institute of Peace Press: Washington, DC, 1995)

Hoffman, F. G., *Decisive Force: The New American Way of War* (Praeger: Westport, Ct. and London, 1996)

Holbrooke, R., *To End A War* (Random House: New York, 1998)

Honig, J. W. and Both, N., *Srebrenica: Record of a War Crime* (Penguin: London, 1996)

von Horn, C. (Maj.-Gen.), *Soldiering for Peace* (Cassell: London, 1966)

Hoskyns, C., *The Congo Since Independence* (Oxford University Press: London, 1965)

Hymoff, E., *Stig von Bayer* (James A. Heineman: New York, 1965)

Independent Commission on Kosovo, *Kosovo Report: Conflict—International Response—Lessons Learned* (Oxford University Press: Oxford, 2000)

Institute for National Strategic Studies (INSS), *Strategic Assessment 1996: Instruments of US Power* (INSS/National Defense University Press: Washington, DC, 1996)

International Commission on the Balkans, *Unfinished Peace* (Brookings Institution Press for the Aspen Institute, Berlin, and the Carnegie Endowment for International Peace: Washington, DC, 1996)

International Commission on Intervention and State Sovereignty, *The Responsibility to Protect* (International Development Research Centre: Ottawa, 2001)

International Peace Academy, *Peacekeeper's Handbook* (Pergamon Press: New York, 1984)

James, A., *Britain and the Congo Crisis, 1960–63* (St Martin's Press: London, 1996)

—, *The Politics of Peace-keeping* (Chatto & Windus for the Institute for Strategic Studies: London, 1960)

Janovitz, M., *The Professional Soldier* (Free Press: Glencoe, Ill, 1960)

Joint Nordic Committee for Military UN Matters (NORDSAMFN), *Nordic UN Tactical Manual* (Gummerus Kirjapaino Oy: Jyväskylä, 1992), vols 1 and 2

Kanza, T., *Conflict in the Congo* (Penguin: Harmondsworth, 1972)

Kyle, K., *The UN in the Congo*, Occasional Paper no. 2, Initiative on Conflict Resolution and Ethnicity (INCORE) (University of Ulster and United Nations University: Coleraine, 1995)

Last, D., *Theory, Doctrine and Practice of Conflict De-Escalation in Peacekeeping Operations* (Canadian Peacekeeping Press: Clementsport, 1997)

Lefever, E. W., *Crisis in the Congo: A United Nations Force in Action* (Brookings Institution: Washington, DC, 1965)

— and Joshua, W., *United Nations Peacekeeping in the Congo, 1960–1964: An Analysis of Political, Executive and Military Control, Vols 1–4* (Brookings Institution for the US Arms Control and Disarmament Agency (ACDA): Washington, DC, 30 June 1966)

Leurdijk, D. A., *The United Nations and NATO in Former Yugoslavia, 1991–1996: Limits to Diplomacy and Force* (Netherlands Atlantic Commission: The Hague, 1996)

—, *The United Nations and NATO in Former Yugoslavia: Partners in International Cooperation* (Netherlands Atlantic Commission and Netherlands Institute of International Relations 'Clingendael': The Hague, 1994)

Lewis, W. H. (ed.), *Military Implications of United Nations Peacekeeping Operations* (National Defense University, Institute for National Strategic Studies: Washington, DC, June 1993)

— (ed.), *Peacekeeping: The Way Ahead? Report of a Special Conference* (National Defense University, Institute for National Strategic Studies: Washington, DC, 1993)

Linnér, S., *Min Odyssé* [My Odyssey] (P. A. Norstedt & Söner: Stockholm, 1982)

Liu, F. T., *United Nations Peacekeeping and the Non-Use of Force*, Occasional Paper, International Peace Academy (Lynne Rienner: Boulder, Colo., 1992)

Lyons, T. and Samatur, A. I., *Somalia: State Collapse, Multilateral Intervention, and Strategies for Political Reconstruction*, Brookings Occasional Papers (Brookings Institution: Washington, DC, 1995)

McCoubrey, H. and White, N. D., *The Blue Helmets: Legal Regulation of United Nations Military Operations* (Dartmouth: Aldershot, 1996)

MacKenzie, L. (Maj.-Gen.), *Peacekeeper: The Road to Sarajevo* (HarperCollins: London, 1994)

Mackinlay, J., *The Peacekeepers: Peacekeeping Operations at the Arab–Israeli Interface* (Unwin Hyman: London, 1989)

— (ed.), *A Guide to Peace Support Operations* (Thomas J. Watson Institute for International Studies, Brown University: Providence, R.I., 1996)

MacKinnon, M. G., *The Evolution of US Peacekeeping Policy under Clinton* (Frank Cass: London, 2000)

McLean, D., *Peace Operations and Common Sense: Replacing Rhetoric with Realism*, Peaceworks Paper no. 9 (United States Institute of Peace (USIP): Washington, DC, 1996)

Makinda, S., *Seeking Peace from Chaos: Humanitarian Intervention in Somalia*, Occasional Paper (International Peace Academy: New York, 1993)

Malan, M., *Surveying the Middle Ground: Conceptual Issues and Peace-keeping in Southern Africa*, IDP Papers no. 2 (Institute for Defence Policy: Johannesburg, Mar. 1996)

Mansell, P., *The Ambivalence of the US to United Nations Peacekeeping Operations*, London Defence Studies no. 24 (Centre for Defence Studies, King's College, London: London, Nov. 1994)

Martelli, G., *Experiment in World Government: An Account of the United Nations Operation in the Congo 1960–1964* (Johnson Publications: London, 1966)

Martinkus, J., *A Dirty Little War: An Eyewitness Account of East Timor's Descent into Hell, 1997–2000* (Random House Australia: Sydney, 2001)

Melvern, L., *The Ultimate Crime: Who Betrayed the UN and Why* (Allison & Busby: London, 1995)

Minear, L. and Guillot, P., *Soldiers to the Rescue: Humanitarian Lessons from Rwanda* (Organisation for Economic Co-operation and Development (OECD) Development Centre: Paris, 1996)

Mokhtari, F. L. (ed.), *Peacemaking, Peacekeeping and Coalition Warfare: The Future Role of the United Nations* (National Defense University: Washington, DC, 1994)

Morrison, A. (ed.), *The New Peacekeeping Partnership* (Canadian Peacekeeping Press: Clementsport, 1994)

—, Fraser, D. A. and Kiras, J. D. (eds), *Peacekeeping with Muscle: The Use of Force in International Conflict Resolution* (Canadian Peacekeeping Press: Clementsport, 1997)

Moskos, C. C., Jr, *Peace Soldiers: The Sociology of a United Nations Military Force* (University of Chicago Press: Chicago, Ill. and London, 1976)

Munro, J. A. and Inglis, A. I. (eds), *Mike: The Memoirs of the Right Honourable Lester B. Pearson. Vol. 2, 1948–1957* (University of Toronto Press: Toronto, 1973)

Nassif, R., *U Thant in New York 1961–1971: A Portrait of the Third UN Secretary-General* (Hurst: London, 1988)

O'Brien, C. C., *Murderous Angels: A Political Tragedy and Comedy in Black and White* (Hutchinson: London, 1969)

— *To Katanga and Back: A UN Case History* (Hutchinson: London, 1962)

Ocaya-Lakidi, D., *UN and the US Military in Regional Organizations in Africa and the Middle East* (Institute for National Strategic Studies, National Defense University Press: Washington, DC, 1994)

Otunnu, O. A. and Doyle, M. W. (eds), *Peacemaking and Peacekeeping for the New Century* (Rowman & Littlefield: Lanham, Md., 1998)

Overseas Development Council, *Conflict Resolution, Humanitarian Assistance and Development in Somalia: Lessons Learned*, Conference Report, Washington, DC, 1994

Palin, R. H., International Institute for Strategic Studies (IISS), *Multinational Military Forces: Problems and Prospects. The Problems Facing Multinational Forces and Operations, and Prospects for the Future*, Adelphi Paper no. 294 (Oxford University Press: London, 1995)

*Peacemaking and Peacekeeping for the Next Century*, Report of the 25th Vienna Seminar, International Peace Academy, New York, 1995

Pearson, L. B., *Memoirs* (Gollancz: London, 1973–75), 3 vols

Prunier, G., *The Rwanda Crisis: History of a Genocide 1959–1994* (Hurst: London, 1995)

Pugh, M. (ed.), *The UN, Peace and Force* (Frank Cass: London, 1997)

Quinn, D. J. (ed.), *Peace Support Operations and the US Military* (National Defense University Press: Washington, DC, 1994)

Raevsky, A. and Vorob'ev, I. N., *Russian Approaches to Peacekeeping Operations*, UNIDIR Research Paper no. 28 (UN Institute for Disarmament Research: Geneva, 1994)

Raimond, J.-B., *La Politique d'Intervention dans les Conflits: Éléments de Doctrine pour la France* [The politics of intervention in conflicts: elements of a doctrine for France], Rapport d'information no. 1950 (Commission des affaires étrangères, Assemblée Nationale: Paris, 23 Feb. 1995)

Ratner, S., *The New UN Peacekeeping* (Macmillan: London, 1995)

Rikhye, I. J., *Military Advisor to the Secretary General: UN Peacekeeping and the Congo Crisis* (St Martin's Press: New York, 1993)

—, *The Theory and Practice of Peacekeeping* (St Martin's Press for the International Peace Academy: New York, 1984)

Rohde, D., *A Safe Area* (Simon & Schuster/Pocket Books: London, 1997)

Rønnfeldt, C. F. and Solli, P.-E. (eds), *Use of Air Power in Peace Operations*, Peacekeeping and Multinational Operations no. 7 (Norwegian Institute of International Affairs (NUPI): Oslo, 1997)

Rose, M. (Lt-Gen.), *Fighting for Peace: Bosnia 1994* (Harvill Press: London, 1998)

de Rossanet, B., *Peacemaking and Peacekeeping in Yugoslavia* (Kluwer Law International: The Hague, 1996)

Sahnoun, M., *Somalia: The Missed Opportunities* (United States Institute of Peace (USIP): Washington, DC, 1994)

Schmidl, E. A. (ed.), *Peace Operations: Between War and Peace* (Frank Cass: London, 2000)

Schultz, G. P., *Turmoil and Triumph* (Macmillan: New York, 1993)

Seyersted, F., *United Nations Forces in the Law of Peace and War* (Sijthoff: Leyden, 1966)

Shevchenko, A., *Breaking with Moscow* (Alfred A. Knopf: New York, 1985)

Simmonds, R., *Legal Problems Arising from the United Nations Military Operations in the Congo* (Nijhoff: The Hague, 1968)

Skogmo, B., *UNIFIL: International Peacekeeping in Lebanon 1978–1988* (Lynne Rienner: Boulder, Colo. and London, 1989)

Sköld, N., *Med FN i Kongo: Sveriges medverkan i den fredsbevarande operationen 1960–1964* [With the UN in the Congo: Sweden's participation in the peacekeeping operation 1960–64] (Probus: Stockholm, 1994)

Smith, H. (ed.), *The Force of Law: International Law and the Land Commander* (Australian Defence Studies Centre: Canberra, 1994)

— (ed.), *International Peacekeeping: Building on the Cambodian Experience* (Australian Defence Studies Centre: Canberra, 1994)

Solli, P.-E., *UN and NATO Air Power in the Former Yugoslavia*, NUPI Report no. 209 (Norwegian Institute of International Affairs (NUPI): Oslo, Oct. 1996)

Stern, B. (ed.), *United Nations Peace-keeping Operations: A Guide to French Policies* (United Nations University: Tokyo, 1998)

Stewart, B. (Lt-Col), *Broken Lives: A Personal Vew of the Bosnian Conflict* (HarperCollins: London, 1993)

Stjernfelt, B., *The Sinai Peace Front: UN Peacekeeping Operations in the Middle East, 1973–1980* (Hurst: London, 1992)

Sutterlin, J., *Military Force in the Service of Peace*, Aurora Papers no. 18 (Canadian Centre for Global Security: Ottawa, 1993)

Thakur, R. and Thayer, C. A. (eds), *A Crisis of Expectations: UN Peacekeeping in the 1990s* (Westview Press: Boulder, Colo., 1995)

Tharoor, S., *Peace-keeping: Principles, Problems, Prospects*, Research Report 9-93 (Strategic Research Department, Center for Naval Warfare Studies, US Naval War College: Newport, R.I., Dec. 1993)

Trilateral Commission, *Keeping the Peace in the Post-Cold War Era: Strengthening Multilateral Peacekeeping* (Trilateral Commission: New York, Mar. 1993)

U Thant, *View from the UN* (David & Charles: London, 1978)

United Nations Association of the United States of America, *The Preparedness Gap: Making Peace Operations Work in the 21st Century* (United Nations Association of the United States of America: New York, 2001)

United States Institute of Peace (USIP), *Restoring Hope: The Real Lessons of Somalia for the Future of Intervention*, Special Report (USIP: Washington, DC, 1994)

—, *Peacekeeping in Africa*, Special Report (USIP: Washington, DC, Feb. 2001)

Urquhart, B., *A Life in Peace and War* (Weidenfeld & Nicolson: London, 1987)

—, *Hammarskjold* (Alfred A. Knopf: New York, 1972)

—, *Ralph Bunche: An American Life* (W. W. Norton: New York, 1993)

Waern, Jonas, *Katanga: Svensk FN-trupp i Kongo 1961–62* [Katanga: Swedish troops in the Congo 1961–62] (Atlantis: Stockholm, 1980)

Weiland, H. and Braham, M., *The Namibian Peace Process: Implications and Lessons for the Future. Report of the Freiburg Symposium, 1–4 July 1992* (Arnold Bergstraesser Institut for Socio-Cultural Research and International Peace Academy: Freiburg and New York, 1994)

Weinberger, C., *Fighting for Peace* (Warner Books: New York, 1990)

White, N. D., *The United Nations and the Maintenance of International Peace and Security* (Manchester University Press: New York, 1990)

Woodcock, A. and David, D. (eds), *Analytic Approaches to the Study of Conflict* (Canadian Peacekeeping Press: Clementsport, 1996)

Woodward, S. L., *Balkan Tragedy: Chaos and Dissolution after the Cold War* (Brookings Institution: Washington, DC, 1995)

Wurmser, D. and Dyke, N. B., *The Professionalization of Peacekeeping: a Study Group Report* (United States Institute of Peace (USIP): Washington, DC, Aug. 1993)

Zurick, T., *Army Dictionary and Desk Reference* (Stackpole Books: Harrisburg, Pa., 1992)

# V. Articles and papers

Abizaid, J. P. (Lt-Col), 'Lessons for peacekeepers', *Military Review*, Mar. 1993

Adams, G., Oxfam, 'Rwanda: an agenda for international action', Oxford, 1994

— and Human Rights Watch/Africa, 'Genocide in Rwanda April–May 1994', London, May 1994

Adams, M. P., 'Peace enforcement versus American strategic culture', *Strategic Review*, vol. 23, no. 1 (winter 1995)

Adibe, C., 'Part I: Case Study' in United Nations Institute for Disarmament Research (UNIDIR), *Managing Arms in Peace Processes: Somalia* (UNIDIR: Geneva, 1995)

Akashi, Y., 'The challenges faced by UNTAC', *Japan Review of International Affairs*, summer 1993

—, 'The challenges of peacekeeping in Cambodia: lessons to be learned', Paper presented to the School of International and Public Affairs, Columbia University, New York, Nov. 1993

Allard, K., 'Co-operation, command and control: lessons learned or lessons identified?', Lecture to the Swedish National Defence College, reproduced in Ahlquist, L. (ed.), *Co-operation, Command and Control in UN Peace Support Operations: A Pilot Study from the Swedish War College* (Försvarshögskolan, Operativa Institutionen [Swedish National Defence College, Department of Operations]: Stockholm, 1996)

Allen, W. W. A. (Col), Johnson, A. D. (Col) and Nelson, J. T. (Col), 'Peacekeeping and peace enforcement operations', *Military Review*, vol. 73, no. 10 (Oct. 1993)

Anderson, G., 'UNOSOM II: not failure, not success', eds D. C. F. Daniel and B. C. Hayes, *Beyond Traditional Peacekeeping* (Macmillan: London, 1995)

Annan, K. A., 'UN peacekeeping operations and cooperation with NATO', *NATO Review*, vol. 41, no. 5 (Oct. 1993)

—, 'Challenges of the new peacekeeping', eds O. A. Otunnu and M. W. Doyle, *Peacemaking and Peacekeeping for the New Century* (Rowman & Littlefield: Lanham, Md., 1998)

Art, R. J., 'American foreign policy and the fungibility of force', *Security Studies*, vol. 5, no. 4 (summer 1996)

Avant, D. D., 'Are the reluctant warriors out of control? Why the US military is averse to responding to post-cold war low-level threats', *Security Studies*, vol. 6, no. 2 (winter 1996/97)

Barnett, M., 'The new United Nations politics of peace: from juridical sovereignty to empirical soveriegnty', *Global Governance*, vol. 1, no. 1 (winter 1995)

Belbutowski, P. M., 'Contemporary French peacekeeping', ed. F. L. Mokhtari, *Peacemaking, Peacekeeping and Coalition Warfare: The Future Role of the United Nations* (National Defense University Press: Washington, DC, 1994)

Berdal, M., 'Fateful encounter: the United States and UN peacekeeping', *Survival*, vol. 36, no. 1 (spring 1994)

—, 'Lessons not learned: the use of force in "peace operations" in the 1990s', *International Peacekeeping,* Special issue on Managing Armed Conflicts in the 21st Century, vol. 7, no. 4 (winter 2000)

—, 'United Nations peacekeeping in the former Yugoslavia', eds D. C. F. Daniel and B. C. Hayes, *Beyond Traditional Peacekeeping* (Macmillan: London, 1995)

—, *Whither UN Peace-keeping?*, Adelphi Paper no. 281 (Brassey's for the International Institute for Strategic Studies (IISS): London, 1993)

Bergstrand, B. M. (Maj.), 'Operations other than war: the Canadian perspective', eds A. Woodcock and D. David, *Analytic Approaches to the Study of Future Conflict* (Canadian Peacekeeping Press: Clementsport, 1996)

Berkowitz, B. D., 'Rules of engagement for UN peacekeeping forces in Bosnia', *Orbis,* vol. 38, no. 3 (fall 1994)

Betts, R. K., 'The delusion of impartial intervention', *Foreign Affairs,* vol. 73, no. 6 (1994)

—, 'The delusion of impartial intervention', eds C. Crocker, F. O. Hampson and P. Aall, *Managing Global Chaos: Sources of and Responses to International Conflict* (United States Institute of Peace Press: Washington, DC, 1996)

Bolton, J. R., 'Wrong turn in Somalia', *Foreign Affairs,* vol. 73, no. 1 (Jan./Feb. 1994)

Bostock, I., 'By the book: East Timor: an operational evaluation', *Jane's Defence Weekly,* 3 May 2000

Boutros-Ghali, B., 'Empowering the UN', *Foreign Affairs,* vol. 71 (winter 1992/1993)

Brown, S. D., 'Psyop in Operation Uphold Democracy', *Military Review,* Sep./Oct. 1996

Bryant, L. and Loza, T., 'Expectations and realities', eds B. Cohen and G. Stamkoski, *With No Peace to Keep: United Nations Peacekeeping and the War in the Former Yugoslavia* (Grainpress, Ltd: London, 1995)

Bryden, M., 'Somalia: the wages of failure', *Current History,* vol. 94, no. 591 (Apr. 1995)

Burns, E. L. M., 'Observations of General E. L. M. Burns, First Commander of UNEF and presently advisor to the Canadian Government on disarmament', *International Journal* (Canadian Institute of International Affairs, Ottawa), vol. 23, no. 1 (winter 1967/68), reprinted in Mezerik, A. G. (ed.), *The United Nations Emergency Force (UNEF): 1956—Creation, Evolution, End of Mission—1967,* International Review Service, vol. 13, no. 97 (1969)

—, 'Pearson and the Gaza Strip, 1957', ed. M. G. Fry, *Freedom and Change: Essays in Honour of Lester B. Pearson* (McLelland & Steward: Toronto, 1975)

Caplan, R. D., 'The former Yugoslavia', eds J. Tessitore and S. Woolfson, *A Global Agenda: Issues Before the 49th General Assembly,* 1993/94 edn (University Press of America: New York, Sep. 1994)

Carnegie Commission on Preventing Deadly Conflict, 'Preventing deadly conflict: executive summary of the final report', New York, Dec. 1997

Cervenak, C. M., 'Lessons of the past: experiences in peace operations', eds A. H. Chayes and G. T. Raach, *Peace Operations: Developing an American Strategy* (National Defense University Press: Washington, DC, 1995)

Chayes, A. H. and Chayes, A., 'Alternatives to escalation' in Aspen Institute, *The United States and the Use of Force in the Post-Cold War Era: A Report by the Aspen Strategy Group* (Aspen Institute: Queenstown, Md., 1995)

Chayes, A. H. and Raach, G. T., 'Beyond fighting and winning', eds A. H. Chayes and G. T. Raach, *Peace Operations: Developing an American Strategy* (National Defense University Press: Washington, DC, 1995)

Chilton, P., 'French policy on peacekeeping', *Brassey's Defence Yearbook 1995* (Brassey's for the Centre for Defence Studies, King's College, London: London, 1995)

Chopra, J., 'Back to the drawing board', *Bulletin of the Atomic Scientists*, Mar./Apr. 1995

—, 'The UN's kingdom of East Timor', *Survival*, vol. 42, no. 3 (autumn 2000)

Cilliers, J., 'Peace support operations', eds J. Cilliers and G. Mills, *Peacekeeping in Africa*, vol. 2 (Institute for Defence Policy and South African Institute of International Affairs: Braamfontein, 1995)

Clapham, C., 'Problems of peace enforcement: some lessons from operations in Africa', eds J. Cilliers and G. Mills, *Peacekeeping in Africa*, vol. 2 (Institute for Defence Policy and South African Institute of International Affairs: Braamfontein, 1995)

Clarke, W., 'Failed visions and uncertain mandates in Somalia', eds W. Clarke and J. Herbst, *Learning from Somalia: The Lessons of Armed Humanitarian Intervention* (Lynne Rienner: Boulder, Colo., 1996)

— and Herbst, J., 'Somalia and the future of humanitarian intervention', eds W. Clarke and J. Herbst, *Learning from Somalia: The Lessons of Armed Humanitarian Intervention* (Lynne Rienner: Boulder, Colo., 1996)

Claude, I. L., Jr, 'The new international security order: changing concepts', *Naval War College Review*, vol. 47, no. 1 (winter 1994)

Cohen, M., 'The United Nations Emergency Force: a preliminary view', *International Journal*, no. 12 (spring 1957)

Collins, J. M., 'Military options in Bosnia', *US Naval Institute Proceedings*, vol. 121, no. 8 (Aug. 1995)

Connaughton, R., 'Wider peacekeeping: how wide of the mark?', *British Army Review*, no. 111 (Dec. 1995)

Cordy-Simpson, R. A. (Maj.-Gen.), 'Keynote address', ed. A. Morrison, *The New Peacekeeping Partnership* (Canadian Peacekeeping Press: Clementsport, 1994)

—, Speech by Maj.-Gen. R. A. Cordy-Simpson, Chief of Staff, HQ, British Army on the Rhine, former Chief of Staff, United Nations, Bosnia (date and place unknown)

Cox, D. (ed.), 'The use of force by the Security Council for enforcement and deterrent purposes: a conference report', Canadian Centre for Arms Control and Disarmament, Ottawa, 1991

Crawford, T. W., 'Why minimum force won't work: doctrine and deterrence in Bosnia and beyond', *Global Governance*, vol. 4, no. 2 (Apr./June 1998)

'Crisis in Sierra Leone: the failure of UN peacekeeping', *Strategic Comment* (International Institute for Strategic Studies (IISS), London), vol. 6, no. 9 (Nov. 2000)

Crocker, C. A., 'The lessons of Somalia: not everything went wrong', *Foreign Affairs,* vol. 74, no. 3 (May/June 1995)

Daalder, I. H., 'Knowing when to say no: the development of US peacekeeping policy in the 1990s', unpublished research paper, Jan. 1995

Dalsjö, R., 'Sweden and Balkan Blue Helmet operations', ed. L. Ericson, *Solidarity and Defence: Sweden's Armed Forces in International Peace-keeping Operations*

*During the 19th and 20th Centuries* (Swedish Military History Commission: Stockholm, 1995)

Daniel, D. C. F., 'Issues and considerations in UN gray area and enforcement operations', Occasional Paper, Centre for Naval War Studies, Strategic Research Department Research Memorandum 4-94, US Naval War College, Newport, R.I., 1994

—, 'The United States', ed. T. Findlay, *Challenges for the New Peacekeepers*, SIPRI Research Report no. 12 (Oxford University Press: Oxford, 1996)

—, 'US perspectives on peacekeeping: putting PDD25 in context', Occasional paper, Center for Naval Warfare Studies, Strategic Research Department Memorandum 3-94, US Naval War College, Newport, R.I., 1994

—, 'Wandering out of the void? Conceptualizing practicable peace enforcement', eds A. Morrison, D. A. Fraser and J. D. Kiras, *Peacekeeping with Muscle: The Use of Force in International Conflict Resolution* (Canadian Peacekeeping Press: Clementsport, 1997)

— and Hayes, B. C., 'Securing observance of UN mandates through the employment of military force', ed. M. Pugh, *The UN, Peace and Force* (Frank Cass: London, 1997)

Dennehy, E. J. (Capt.) *et al.*, 'A Blue Helmet combat force', Policy Analysis Paper no. 93-01, National Security Program, Harvard University, 1993

Dobbie, C., 'A concept for post-cold war peacekeeping', *Survival*, vol. 36, no. 3 (autumn 1994)

Donald, D., 'The right man gets it wrong', *Time*, 19 Nov. 1998

Dorn, A. W. and Bell, D. J. H., 'Intelligence and peacekeeping: the UN Operation in the Congo, 1960–64', *International Peacekeeping*, vol. 2, no. 1 (spring 1995)

Doyle, M. W., 'Discovering the limits and potential of peacekeeping', eds O. A. Otunnu and M. W. Doyle, *Peacemaking and Peacekeeping for the New Century* (Rowman & Littlefield: Lanham, Md., 1998)

—, 'UNTAC: sources of success and failure', ed. H. Smith, *International Peacekeeping: Building on the Cambodian Experience* (Australian Defence Studies Centre: Canberra, 1994)

Draper, G. I. A. D., 'The legal limitations upon the employment of weapons by the United Nations in the Congo', *International and Comparative Law Quarterly*, vol. 12 (1963)

Duncan, A. D. (Col), 'Operating in Bosnia', *IBRU Boundary and Security Bulletin* (International Boundaries Research Unit, University of Durham), vol. 2, no. 3 (Oct. 1994)

Durch, W. J., 'Introduction to anarchy: humanitarian intervention and "state building" in Somalia', ed. W. J. Durch, *UN Peacekeeping, American Policy, and the Uncivil Wars of the 1990s* (St Martin's Press: New York, 1996)

— and Schear, J. A., 'Faultlines: UN operations in the former Yugoslavia', ed. W. J. Durch, *UN Peacekeeping, American Policy, and the Uncivil Wars of the 1990s* (St Martin's Press: New York, 1996)

— and Vaccaro, J. M., 'The environment and tasks of peace operations', ed. W. J. Durch, *UN Peacekeeping, American Policy, and the Uncivil Wars of the 1990s* (St Martin's Press: New York, 1996)

Dwan, R., 'Armed conflict prevention, management and resolution', *SIPRI Yearbook 2000: Armaments, Disarmament and International Security* (Oxford University Press: Oxford, 2000)

—, 'Armed conflict prevention, management and resolution', *SIPRI Yearbook 2001: Armaments, Disarmament and International Security* (Oxford University Press: Oxford, 2001)

Dworken, J. T., 'Rules of engagement: lessons from Restore Hope', *Military Review*, vol. 74, no. 5 (Sep. 1994)

Eikenberry, K. W., 'Take no casualties', *Parameters*, vol. 26, no. 2 (summer 1996)

Eliasson, J., 'Humanitarian action and peacekeeping', eds O. A. Otunnu and M. W. Doyle, *Peacemaking and Peacekeeping for the New Century* (Rowman & Littlefield: Lanham, Md., 1998)

Evans, G. and Sahnoun, M., 'Intervention and state sovereignty: breaking new ground', *Global Governance*, vol. 7, no. 2 (Apr.–June 2001)

Eyal, J., 'Sierra Leone: saving Africa from another disaster?', *RUSI Newsbrief*, vol. 20, no. 40 (June 2000)

Fafo Institute for Applied Social Science, Programme for Co-operation and Conflict Resolution, Peace Implementation Network, 'Command from the saddle: managing United Nations peace-building missions. Recommendations. Report of the Forum on the Special Representative of the Secretary-General: shaping the UN's role in peace implementation', Fafo Report no. 266, Oslo, 1999

Farer, T., 'United States military participation in UN operations in Somalia: roots of conflict with General Mohamed Farah Aideed and a basis for accommodation and renewed progress', testimony for submission to the Committee on Armed Services, US House of Representatives, US Congress, 14 Oct. 1993

Farris, K., 'UN peacekeeping in Cambodia: on balance, a success', *Parameters*, vol. 24, no. 1 (1994)

Feil, S. R., 'Preventing genocide: how the early use of force might have succeeded in Rwanda', A report to the Carnegie Commission on Preventing Deadly Conflict, Carnegie Corporation of New York, New York, Apr. 1998, URL <http://www.ccpdc.org/pubs/rwanda/rwanda.htm>

Fergusson, J. and Levesque, B., 'The best laid plans: Canada's proposal for a United Nations rapid reaction capability', *International Journal*, vol. 52, no. 1 (winter 1996/97)

Findlay, T. C., 'Armed conflict prevention, management and resolution', *SIPRI Yearbook 1995: Armaments, Disarmament and International Security* (Oxford University Press: Oxford, 1995)

—, 'Armed conflict prevention, management and resolution', *SIPRI Yearbook 1996 Armaments, Disarmament and International Security* (Oxford University Press: Oxford, 1996)

—, 'Armed conflict prevention, management and resolution', *SIPRI Yearbook 1997: Armaments, Disarmament and International Security* (Oxford University Press: Oxford, 1997)

—, 'Armed conflict prevention, management and resolution', *SIPRI Yearbook 1998: Armaments, Disarmament and International Security* (Oxford University Press: Oxford, 1998)

—, 'Multilateral conflict prevention, management and resolution', *SIPRI Yearbook 1994* (Oxford University Press: Oxford, 1994)

—, 'UNAMIR and the Rwandan humanitarian catastrophe: marginalization in the midst of mayhem', ed. N. Azimi, *Humanitarian Action and Peacekeeping Operations: Debriefing and Lessons* (Kluwer Law: The Hague, 1997)

—, 'The use of force in self-defence: theory and practice', eds A. Morrison, D. A. Fraser and J. D. Kiras, *Peacekeeping with Muscle: The Use of Force in International Conflict Resolution* (Canadian Peacekeeping Press: Clementsport, 1997)

Fortna, V. P., 'United Nations Transition Assistance Group', ed. W. J. Durch, *The Evolution of UN Peacekeping: Case Studies and Comparative Analysis* (St Martin's Press for the Henry L. Stimson Center: Washington, DC, 1993)

Foster, L. M., 'Clear mandate: reforming US and UN peace operations', *Harvard International Review*, vol. 18, no. 3 (summer 1996)

Franck, T. M. and Carey, J., 'Working paper: the role of the United Nations in the Congo. A retrospective perspective', ed. L. M. Tondel, Jr, *The Legal Aspects of the United Nations Action in the Congo*, Background Papers and Proceedings of the Second Hammarskjöld Forum (Oceana Publications for the Association of the Bar of the City of New York: New York, 1963)

Friedrich Ebert Stiftung (Germany), Life and Peace Institute (Sweden), Norwegian Institute of International Affairs (NUPI) and United Nations, Department of Peace-keeping Operations, Lessons Learned Unit, 'Comprehensive report on lessons-learned from United Nations Operation in Somalia April 1992–March 1995', Swedish Government, Stockholm, Dec. 1995

Gaudreau, R. (Maj.-Gen.) and Liu, F. T., 'Peacekeeping in internal conflicts: the dilemmas of the use of force', IPA Seminar Report, International Peace Academy Seminar on Peacemaking and Peacekeeping, New York, 3–8 Sep. 1996

George, A. L., 'The role of force in diplomacy: a continuing dilemma for US foreign policy', eds C. Crocker, F. O. Hampson and P. Aall, *Managing Global Chaos: Sources of and Responses to International Conflict* (United States Institute of Peace Press: Washington, DC, 1996)

Ghali, M., 'United Nations Emergency Force I: 1956–1967', ed. W. J. Durch, *The Evolution of UN Peacekeeping: Case Studies and Comparative Analysis* (St Martin's Press for the Henry L. Stimson Center: Washington, DC, 1993)

Gill, B. and Reilly, J., 'Sovereignty, intervention and peacekeeping: the view from Beijing', *Survival*, vol. 42, no. 3 (autumn 2000)

Goulding, M., 'The evolution of United Nations peacekeeping', *International Affairs*, vol. 69, no. 3 (1993)

—, 'The use of force by the United Nations', *International Peacekeeping*, vol. 3, no. 1 (spring 1996)

Greco, E., 'New trends in peace-keeping: the experience of Operation Alba', *Security Dialogue*, vol. 29, no. 2 (June 1998)

Greenberg, K. E., 'The essential art of empathy', *Soldiers for Peace*, Supplement to *Military History Quarterly*, vol. 5, no. 1 (autumn 1992)

Guillot, P., 'France, peacekeeping and humanitarian intervention', *International Peacekeeping*, vol. 1, no. 1 (spring 1994)

Haass, R. N., 'Military force: a user's guide', *Foreign Policy*, no. 96 (fall 1994)

—, 'Military intervention: a taxonomy of challenges and responses', *The United States and the Use of Force in the Post-Cold War Era*, a report by the Aspen Strategy Group, Aspen Institute, Queenstown, Md., 1995

—, 'Using force: lessons and choices for US foreign policy', eds C. Crocker, F. O. Hampson and P. Aall, *Managing Global Chaos: Sources of and Responses to International Conflict* (United States Institute of Peace Press: Washington, DC, 1996)

Hardesty, J. M. (Col) and Ellis, J. D., 'Training for peace operations: the US Army adapts to the post-cold war world', *Peaceworks* (United States Institute of Peace (USIP), Washington, DC), no. 12 (Feb. 1997)

Harrell, M. C. and Howe, R., 'Military issues in multinational operations', eds D. C. F. Daniel and B. C. Hayes, *Beyond Traditional Peacekeeping* (Macmillan: London, 1995)

Haynes, L. and Stanley, T. W., 'To create a United Nations fire brigade', *Comparative Strategy*, vol. 14, no. 1 (Jan./Mar. 1995)

Hedl, D. and Magas, B., 'The unfulfilled mandate', eds B. Cohen and G. Stamkoski, *With No Peace to Keep: United Nations Peacekeeping and the War in the Former Yugoslavia* (Grainpress Ltd: London, 1995)

Heisbourg, F., 'Reponse to the case for a rapid response', eds O. A. Otunnu and M. W. Doyle, *Peacemaking and Peacekeeping for the New Century* (Rowman & Littlefield: Lanham, Md., 1998)

Henn, F., 'Eyewitness: the Nicosia Airport incident of 1974: a peacekeeping gamble', *International Peacekeeping*, vol. 1, no. 1 (spring 1994)

Higgins, R., 'The new United Nations and the former Yugoslavia', *International Affairs*, vol. 69, no. 3 (1993)

Hill, R., 'Preventive diplomacy, peace-making and peace-keeping', *SIPRI Yearbook 1993: World Armaments and Disarmament* (Oxford University Press: Oxford, 1993)

Hoar, J. P., 'Humanitarian assistance operations challenges: the CENTCOM perspective on Somalia', *Joint Forces Quarterly*, vol. 1, no. 2 (Nov. 1993)

Holmes, J., 'The United Nations in the Congo', *International Journal*, vol. 16 (1960/61)

Howe, J., 'Relations between the United States and United Nations in dealing with Somalia', eds W. Clarke and J. Herbst, *Learning from Somalia: The Lessons of Armed Humanitarian Intervention* (Lynne Rienner: Boulder, Colo., 1996)

—, 'The United States and United Nations in Somalia: the limits of involvement', *Washington Quarterly*, vol. 18, no. 3 (summer 1995)

Human Rights Watch/Africa, 'Genocide in Rwanda April–May 1994', London, May 1994

Hunt, J. B. (Lt-Col), 'OOTW: a concept in flux', *Military Review*, Sep./Oct. 1996

International Court of Justice, 'Certain expenses of the United Nations (article 17, para. 1), Advisory Opinion of 20 July 1962', *Reports of Judgements, Advisory Opinions and Orders* (International Court of Justice: The Hague, 1962)

International Crisis Group (ICG), 'Sierra Leone: time for a new military and political strategy', ICG Africa Report no. 28, ICG, Freetown, London and Brussels, 11 Apr. 2001

'Interview: Major-General Peter Cosgrove, Commander International Force East Timor', *Jane's Defence Weekly*, 23 Feb. 2000

Ito, T., 'UN authorized use of force: recent changes in UN practice', IFS Info 5/1995, Institutt for Forsvarsstudier [Institute of Defence Studies], Oslo, 1995

Jakobsen, P. V., 'The emerging consensus on grey area peace operations doctrine: will it last and enhance operational effectiveness?', *International Peacekeeping*, vol. 7, no. 3 (autumn 2000)

—, 'Overload, not marginalization, threatens UN peacekeeping', *Security Dialogue*, vol. 31, no. 2 (June 2000)

James, A., 'The Congo controversies', *International Peacekeeping*, vol. 1, no. 1 (spring 1994)

—, 'Internal peacekeeping: a dead end for the UN?', *Security Dialogue*, vol. 24, no. 4 (1993)

—, 'The international politics of peacekeeping', ed. A. Morrison, *The New Peacekeeping Partnership* (Canadian Peacekeeping Press: Clementsport, 1994)

—, 'Is there a second generation of peacekeeping?', *International Peacekeeping*, vol. 1, no. 4 (Sep./Nov. 1994)

—, 'Peacekeeping in the post-cold war era', *International Journal*, vol. 30, no. 2 (spring 1995)

—, 'A review of UN peacekeeping', *Internationale Spectator*, vol. 18, no. 11 (Nov. 1993)

Jan, A., 'Peacebuilding in Somalia', IPA Policy Briefing Series, International Peace Academy, New York, July 1996

Jockel, J. T., 'Canada and international peacekeeping', Significant Issues Series (Center for Strategic and International Studies (CSIS), Washington, DC and Canadian Institute of Strategic Studies, Toronto), vol. 16, no. 3 (1994)

Joint Evaluation of Emergency Assistance to Rwanda, 'The international response to conflict and genocide: lessons from the Rwanda experience', Studies 1–4 and Synthesis Report, Copenhagen, 1996, URL <http://www.reliefweb.int/library/nordic>

Kaldor, M., 'Towards a strategy of peace enforcement', *War Report*, Dec. 1994/Jan. 1995

Karhilo, J., 'Case study on peacekeeping: Rwanda', *SIPRI Yearbook 1995: Armaments, Disarmament and International Security* (Oxford University Press: Oxford, 1995), appendix 2C

—, 'Conflict prevention, management and resolution', *SIPRI Yearbook 1999: Armaments, Disarmament and International Security* (Oxford University Press: Oxford, 1999)

Kaysen, C. and Rathjens, G. W., 'Send in the troops: a UN foreign legion', *Washington Quarterly*, vol. 20, no. 1 (1996)

Kellett, N. A., 'Russian peacekeeping part IV: Russian goals and methods in the context of international peacekeepng practice', Research note no. 98/04, Department of National Defence, Ottawa, Mar. 1998

Kennedy, K. M., 'The relationship between the military and humanitarian organizations in Operation Restore Hope', *International Peacekeeping*, vol. 3, no. 1 (spring 1996)

Kinloch, S. P., 'Utopian or pragmatic? A UN permanent military volunteer force', ed. M. Pugh, *The UN, Peace and Force* (Frank Cass: London, 1997)

Klep, C. and Winslow, D., 'Learning lessons the hard way: Somalia and Srebrenica compared', ed. E. A. Schmidl, *Peace Operations: Between War and Peace* (Frank Cass: London, 2000)

Knudsen, T. B., 'Humanitarian intervention revisited: post-cold war responses to classical problems', ed. M. Pugh, *The UN, Peace and Force* (Frank Cass: London, 1997)

Kühne, W., 'Fragmenting states and the need for enlarged peacekeeping', Stiftung Wissenschaft und Politik, Berlin, Oct. 1994

Lalande, S., 'Somalia: major issues for future UN peacekeeping', ed. D. Warner, *New Dimensions of Peacekeeping* (Dordrecht Nijhoff: The Hague, 1995)

Leurdijk, D. A., 'The rapid reaction force', *International Peacekeeping*, Oct./Nov. 1995

Lewis, I. and Mayall, J., 'Somalia', ed. J. Mayall, *The New Interventionism 1991–1994*, London School of Economics Monograph series (Cambridge University Press: Cambridge, 1996)

Lewis, P., 'A short history of United Nations peacekeeping', *Soldiers for Peace*, Supplement to *Military History Quarterly*, vol. 5, no. 1 (autumn 1992)

Liu, F. T., 'The use of force in UN peacekeeping operations: a historical perspective', Paper prepared for the Tokyo Symposium on New Dimensions of United Nations Peacekeeping, Tokyo, 19–20 Jan. 1995

Longworth, R. C., 'Phantom forces, diminished dreams', *Bulletin of the Atomic Scientists*, Mar./Apr. 1995

Lorenz, F. M. (Col), 'Forging rules of engagement: lessons learned from Operation United Shield', *Military Review*, Nov./Dec. 1995

—, 'Law and anarchy in Somalia', *Parameters: US Army War College Quarterly*, vol. 23, no. 4 (winter 1993/94)

—, 'Rules of engagement in Somalia: were they effective?', *Naval Law Review*, May 1995

McCormick, S. H., 'The lessons of intervention in Africa', *Current History*, vol. 94, no. 591 (Apr. 1995)

MacInnis, J. A. (Maj.-Gen.), 'Lessons from UNPROFOR: peacekeeping from a force commander's perspective', ed. A. Morrison, *The New Peacekeeping Partnership* (Canadian Peacekeeping Press: Clementsport, 1994)

—, 'Peacekeeping and postmodern conflict: a soldier's view', *Mediterranean Quarterly*, vol. 6, no. 2 (spring 1995)

Mackinlay, J., 'Defining a role beyond peacekeeping', ed. W. H. Lewis, *Military Implications of United Nations Peacekeeping Operations*, McNair Paper no. 17 (National Defense University Press: Washington, DC, June 1993)

—, 'Improving multifunctional forces', *Survival*, vol. 36, no. 3 (Aug. 1994)

—, 'International reponses to complex emergencies: why a new approach is needed', *International Peacekeeping News*, vol. 2, no. 5 (Nov./Dec. 1996)

—, 'Mission failure', *World Today*, vol. 56, no. 11 (Nov. 2000)

—, 'Problems for US forces in operations beyond peacekeeping', ed. W. H. Lewis, *Peacekeeping: The Way Ahead* (National Defense University Press: Washington, DC, 1993)

—, 'Successful intervention', *International Spectator*, Nov. 1993

— and Chopra, J., 'A draft concept of second generation multinational operations 1993', Thomas J. Watson Jr Institute for International Studies, Brown University, Providence, R.I., 1993

— and Chopra, J., 'Second generation multilateral operations', *Washington Quarterly*, summer 1992

— and Kent, R., 'Complex emergencies doctrine: the British are still the best', *RUSI Journal*, vol. 142, no. 2 (Apr. 1997)

Madden, J., 'Namibia: a lesson for success', eds K. Clements and R. Ward, *Building International Community: Cooperating for Peace. Case Studies* (Allen & Unwin in association with the Australian National University Peace Research Centre: St Leonard's and Canberra, 1994)

Maley, M., 'The UN and East Timor', *Pacific Review*, vol. 12, no. 1 (Feb. 2000)

Mallinson, A. (Col), 'Wider peacekeeping: an option of difficulties', *British Army Review*, no. 112 (Apr. 1996)

Malone, D. and Wermester, K., 'Boom and bust? The changing nature of UN peacekeeping', *International Peacekeeping*, Special issue on Managing Armed Conflicts in the 21st Century, vol. 7, no. 4 (winter 2000)

Maloney, S. M., 'Insights into Canadian peacekeeping doctrine', *Military Review*, Mar./Apr. 1996

Mandelbaum, M., 'The reluctance to intervene', *Foreign Policy*, vol. 95, no. 11 (summer 1994)

Martin, L., 'Peacekeeping as a growth industry', *The National Interest*, summer 1993

Martinez, W. (Lt-Col), 'Peace operations', *Infantry*, May/June 1994

Mearsheimer, J. J., 'The false promise of international institutions', *International Security*, vol. 19, no. 3 (winter 1994/95)

Mehic, D., '"We are dying of your protection"', *Bulletin of the Atomic Scientists*, Mar./Apr. 1995

Meister, S., 'Crisis in Katanga', *Soldiers for Peace*, Supplement to *Military History Quarterly*, vol. 5, no. 1 (autumn 1992)

Mellor, W. J. A. (Col), 'Somalia: a catalyst for change in the command and control of UN operations', ed. H. Smith, *International Peacekeeping: Building on the Cambodian Experience* (Australian Defence Studies Centre: Canberra, 1994)

Melvern, L., 'The Security Council: behind the scenes', *International Affairs*, vol. 77, no. 1 (Jan. 2001)

Mendlovitz, S. and Fousek, J., 'A UN constabulary to enforce the law on genocide and crimes against humanity', ed. N. Riemer, *Protection Against Genocide: Mission Impossible?* (Praeger: Westport, Ct., 1999), cited in Wheeler, N. J., 'Review article: humanitarian intervention after Kosovo: emergent norm, moral duty or the coming anarchy?', *International Affairs*, vol. 77, no. 1 (Jan. 2001)

Mezerik, A. G. (ed.), *The United Nations Emergency Force (UNEF): 1956–Creation, Evolution, End of Mission–1967*, International Review Service, vol. 13, no. 97 (1969)

Miller, E. M., 'Legal aspects of the United Nations action in the Congo', *American Journal of International Law*, vol. 55, no. 1 (Jan. 1961)

Minear, L. *et al.*, 'Caught in a vice', eds B. Cohen and G. Stamkoski, *With No Peace to Keep: United Nations Peacekeeping and the War in the Former Yugoslavia* (Grainpress Ltd: London, 1995)

Morillon, P. (Lt-Gen.), 'UN operations in Bosnia: lessons and realities', *RUSI Journal*, Dec. 1993

Morrow, L., 'An interview: the man in the middle', *Soldiers for Peace*, Supplement to *Military History Quarterly*, vol. 5, no. 1 (autumn 1992)

Mortimer, E., 'Under what circumstances should the UN intervene?', eds O. A. Otunnu and M. W. Doyle, *Peacemaking and Peacekeeping for the New Century* (Rowman & Littlefield: Lanham, Md., 1998)

Muldoon, J. P., 'What happened to humanitarian intervention?', *Bulletin of the Atomic Scientists*, Mar./Apr. 1995

Netherlands Advisory Council on International Affairs and Advisory Committee on Issues of Public International Law, 'Humanitarian intervention', Advisory Report no. 13, as requested by the government of the Netherlands, AIIV/CAVV, The Hague, Apr. 2000

Oakley, R. and Bentley, D., 'Peace operations: a comparison of Somalia and Haiti', *Strategic Forum* (National Defense University, Institute for National Strategic Studies, Washington, DC), no. 30 (May 1995)

Oakley, R. and Dziedzic, M., 'Sustaining success in Haiti', *Strategic Forum* (National Defense University, Institute for National Strategic Studies, Washington, DC), no. 77 (June 1996)

Ocaya-Lakidi, D., 'Regional conflicts, regional coalitions and security co-operation in Africa and the Middle East: the roles of the UN and the US military', Paper presented at 1993 Topical Symposium on Military Coalitions and the United Nations: implications for the US Military, National Defense College, Washington, DC, 2–3 Nov. 1995

Ogata, S., 'Humanitarian responses to international emergencies', eds O. A. Otunnu and M. W. Doyle, *Peacemaking and Peacekeeping for the New Century* (Rowman & Littlefield: Lanham, Md., 1998)

Ord, R. L. (Lt-Gen.), 'Rules of engagement: a template for interoperability', ed. H. Smith, *The Force of Law: International Law and the Land Commander* (Australian Defence Studies Centre: Canberra, 1994)

Organization of African Unity, 'Executive summary, Report of the International Panel of Eminent Personalities to Investigate the 1994 Genocide in Rwanda and the Surrounding Events', Addis Ababa, 11 July 2000

Otunnu, O. A., 'The peace-and-security agenda of the United Nations: some critical issues for the next century', IPA Seminar Report, International Peace Academy Seminar on Peacemaking and Peacekeeping, New York, 3–8 Sep. 1996

—, 'The peace-and-security agenda of the United Nations: from a crossroads into the new century', eds O. A. Otunnu and M. W. Doyle, *Peacemaking and Peacekeeping for the New Century* (Rowman & Littlefield: Lanham, Md., 1998)

Paschall, R., 'UN peacekeeping tactics', *Soldiers for Peace*, Supplement to *Military History Quarterly*, vol. 5, no. 1 (autumn 1992)

Patman, R. G., 'The UN Operation in Somalia', eds R. Thakur and C. A. Thayer, *A Crisis of Expectations: UN Peacekeeping in the 1990s* (Westview Press: Boulder, Colo., 1995)

Pearson, L. P. (Rt Hon.), 'Keeping the Peace', Lecture in the Dag Hammarskjöld Memorial Series, Carlton University, 7 May 1964, in *Survival*, vol. 6, no. 5 (July/Aug. 1964)

Pellnäs, B., 'Peacekeeping: Jonas Waern and the first battle experience', ed. Svenska Institutet [Swedish Institute], *Sweden and the UN* (Swedish Institute: Stockholm, 1996)

Pico, G., 'The UN and the use of force', *Foreign Affairs*, vol. 73, no. 5 (Sep./Oct. 1994)

Prager, K., 'The limits of peacekeeping', *Time*, 23 Oct. 1995

Prunier, G., 'The experience of the European armies in Operation Restore Hope', eds W. Clarke and J. Herbst, *Learning from Somalia: The Lessons of Armed Humanitarian Intervention* (Lynne Rienner: Boulder, Colo., 1996)

Prutsalis, M., 'Too little, too late', eds M. Cohen and G. Stamkoski, *With No Peace to Keep: United Nations Peacekeeping and the War in the Former Yugoslavia* (Grainpress Ltd: London, 1995)

Quinn, D. J., 'Peace support operations: definitions and implications' ed. D. J. Quinn, *Peace Support Operations and the US Military* (National Defense University Press: Washington, DC, 1994)

'Report by Australia to the Comprehensive Seminar on Lessons-Learned from United Nations Operation in Somalia (UNOSOM)', Plainsboro, N.J., 13–15 Sep. 1995

Righter, R., 'A marriage made in hell', eds B. Cohen and G. Stamkoski, *With No Peace to Keep: United Nations Peacekeeping and the War in the Former Yugoslavia* (Grainpress Ltd: London, 1995)

Rikhye, I. J. (Maj.-Gen.), 'Lessons of experience', *Soldiers for Peace*, Supplement to *Military History Quarterly*, vol. 5, no. 1 (autumn 1992)

Ripley, T., 'Bosnia mission forces UN to grow with the times', *International Defence Review*, no. 5 (1994)

Roberts, A., 'Communal conflict as a challenge to international organization: the case of the former Yugoslavia', eds O. A. Otunnu and M. W. Doyle, *Peacemaking and Peacekeeping for the New Century* (Rowman & Littlefield: Lanham, Md., 1998)

—, 'The crisis in UN peacekeeping', *Survival*, vol. 36, no. 3 (autumn 1994)

—, 'The crisis in UN peacekeeping', eds C. Crocker, F. O. Hampson and P. Aall, P., *Managing Global Chaos: Sources of and Responses to International Conflict* (United States Institute of Peace Press: Washington, DC, 1996)

Roos, J. G., 'The perils of peacekeeping', *Armed Forces Journal International*, Dec. 1993

Rosenau, J. N., 'Governance in the 21st century', *Global Governance*, vol. 1, no. 1 (winter 1995)

Rosenau, P. W., 'Peace operations, emergency law enforcement, and constabulary forces', eds A. H. Chayes and G. T. Raach, *Peace Operations: Developing an American Strategy* (National Defense University Press: Washington, DC, 1995)

Rotberg, R., 'The lessons of Somalia for the future of US foreign policy', eds W. Clarke and J. Herbst, J., *Learning from Somalia: The Lessons of Armed Humanitarian Intervention* (Lynne Rienner: Boulder, Colo., 1996)

Ruggie, J. G., 'Peacekeeping and US interests', *Washington Quarterly*, vol. 17, no. 4 (1993)

—, 'The UN and the collective use of force: whither or whether?', ed. M. Pugh, *The UN, Peace and Force* (Frank Cass: London, 1997)

—, 'Wandering in the void: charting the UN's new strategic role', *Foreign Affairs*, Nov./Dec. 1993

Sanderson, J. M. (Lt-Gen.), 'Australia, the United Nations and the emerging world order', the 28th Alfred Deakin Lecture, Melbourne, 5 Sep. 1994

—, 'Preparations for, deployment and conduct of peacekeeping operations: a Cambodia snapshot', Paper presented at the conference on UN Peacekeeping at the Crossroads, Canberra, 21–24 May 1993

—, Presentation to the Australian Peacekeeping Training Centre, Williamtown Air Base, New South Wales, Australia, 8 May 1996

—, 'A review of recent peacekeeping operations', Paper presented to the Pacific Armies Management Seminar (PAMS) 18th Conference, Dacca, Jan. 1994

Schachter, O., 'Dag Hammarskjold and the relation of law to politics', *American Journal of International Law*, vol. 56, no. 1 (1962)

—, 'Authorized uses of force by the UN and regional organizations', eds L. F. Damrosch and D. J. Scheffer, *Law and Force in the New International Order* (Westview Press: Boulder, Colo., 1991)

Schear, J. A., 'The case of Cambodia', eds D. C. F. Daniel and B. C. Hayes, *Beyond Traditional Peacekeeping* (Macmillan: London, 1995)

Scheffer, D. J., 'Commentary on collective security', eds L. F. Damrosch and D. J. Scheffer, D.J., *Law and Force in the New International Order* (Boulder, Colo.: Westview Press, 1991)

Schneider, S. J., 'Congo force and standing UN force: legal experience with ONUC', *Indian Journal of International Law*, vol. 4, no. 2 (Apr. 1964)

Schroeder, D. (Lt-Gen.), 'Lessons of Rwanda', *Armed Forces Journal International*, Dec. 1994

Segal, G. and Berdal, M., 'The Cambodian dilemma', *Jane's Intelligence Review*, vol. 5, no. 3 (Mar. 1993)

Semb, A. J., 'The new practice of UN-authorized interventions: a slippery slope of forcible intervention?', *Journal of Peace Research*, vol. 37, no. 4 (July 2000)

Sewall, J. O. B. (Maj.-Gen.), 'Peacekeeping implications for the US military: supporting the United Nations', ed. D. J. Quinn, *Peace Support Operations and the US Military* (National Defense University Press: Washington, DC, 1994)

Sewall, Sarah, 'Peace enforcement and the United Nations', ed. D. J. Quinn, *Peace Support Operations and the US Military* (National Defense University Press: Washington, DC, 1994)

Sköld, N., 'The Congo 1960–1964', ed. L. Ericson, *Solidarity and Defence* (AB C. O. Ekblad for the Swedish Military History Commission: Stockholm, 1995)

Smith, D., 'Are there any options left?', *War Report*, Dec. 1994/Jan. 1995

Smouts, M.-C., 'The political aspects of peace-keeping operations', ed. B. Stern, *United Nations Peace-keeping Operations: A Guide to French Policies* (United Nations University: Tokyo, 1998)

Sokolsky, J. J., 'Great ideals and uneasy compromises: the United States approach to peacekeeping', *International Journal*, vol. 50, no. 2 (spring 1995)

Solli, P.-E., 'In Bosnia, deterrence failed and coercion worked', eds C. F. Rønnfeldt and P.-E. Solli, *Use of Air Power in Peace Operations*, Peacekeeping and Multinational Operations no. 7 (Norwegian Institute of International Affairs (NUPI): Oslo, 1997)

Stedman, S. J., 'Spoiler problems in peace processes', *International Security*, vol. 22, no. 2 (fall 1997)

—, 'UN intervention in civil wars: imperatives of choice and strategy', eds D. C. F. Daniel and B. C. Hayes, *Beyond Traditional Peacekeeping* (Macmillan: London, 1995)

Stevenson, C. A., 'The evolving Clinton doctrine on the use of force', *Armed Forces and Society*, vol. 22, no. 4 (summer 1996)

Suhrke, A., 'Facing genocide: the record of the Belgian battalion in Rwanda', *Security Dialogue*, vol. 29, no. 1 (1998)

Sweetman, A. D. (Group Capt.), 'Close air support over Bosnia-Hercegovina', *RUSI Journal*, Aug. 1994

Tanner, F., 'Weapons control in semi-permissive environments: a case for compellence', ed. M. Pugh, *The UN, Peace and Force* (Frank Cass: London, 1997)

Thakur, R., 'From peacekeeping to peace enforcement: the UN Operation in Somalia', *Journal of Modern African Studies*, vol. 32, no. 3 (1994)

Tharoor, S., 'The future of peacekeeping', *Brown Journal of World Affairs*, vol. 3, no. 1 (winter/spring 1996)

—, 'Should UN peacekeeping go "back to basics"?', *Survival*, vol. 37, no. 4 (winter 1995/96)

—, 'United Nations peacekeeping in Europe', *Survival*, vol. 37, no. 2 (summer 1995)

Thornton, R., 'The role of peace support operations doctrine in the British Army', *International Peacekeeping*, vol. 7, no. 2 (summer 2000)

Torstensson, J., 'Pioneers in Bosnia', *Försvarets Forum* [Defence forum], special ed. 1996

Turbiville, G. H., Jr, 'Operations other than war: organized crime dimension', *Military Review*, Jan. 1994

'A UN volunteer military force: four views', *New York Review of Books*, 24 June 1993

'A UN volunteer force: the prospects', *New York Review of Books*, 15 July 1993

Urquhart, B., 'For a UN volunteer military force', *New York Review of Books*, 10 June 1993

—, 'Prospects for a rapid response capability', eds O. A. Otunnu and M. W. Doyle, *Peacemaking and Peacekeeping for the New Century* (Rowman & Littlefield: Lanham, Md., 1998)

Waddell, J. G. (Maj.), 'Legal aspects of UN peacekeeping', ed. H. Smith, *The Force of Law. International Law and the Land Commander* (Australian Defence Studies Centre: Canberra, 1994)

Warbrick, C., 'Current developments: public international law', *International and Comparative Law Quarterly*, vol. 43 (Oct. 1994)

Warner, N., 'Cambodia: lessons of UNTAC for future peacekeeping operations', Paper presented to the conference on UN Peacekeeping at the Crossroads, Canberra, 21–24 Mar. 1993

Warrington, R. D., 'The helmets may be blue, but the blood's still red: the dilemma of US participation in UN peace operations', *Comparative Strategy*, vol. 14 (1995)

Weiss, T. G., 'Intervention: whither the United Nations?', *Washington Quarterly*, vol. 17, no. 1 (winter 1994)

—, 'Overcoming the Somalia syndrome: Operation Rekindle Hope?', *Global Governance*, vol. 1, no. 2 (May/Aug. 1995)

Whitman, J. and Bartholomew, I., 'UN peace support operations: political–military considerations', eds D. C. F. Daniel and B. C. Hayes, *Beyond Traditional Peacekeeping* (Macmillan: London, 1995)

Wilkinson, P. R. (Lt-Col), 'Developing doctrine for peace-support operations', eds A. Woodcock and D. David, *Analytic Approaches to the Study of Conflict* (Canadian Peacekeeping Press: Clementsport, 1996)

—, 'The development of the United Kingdom's doctrine on peace-support operations', International Security Information Service (ISIS) Briefing Paper no. 68, London, May 1998

—, 'Peace support under fire: lessons from Sierra Leone', International Security Information Service (ISIS) Briefing Paper on Humanitarian Intervention no. 2, London, June 2000

Williams, P. and Scharf, M., 'The letter of the law', eds B. Cohen and G. Stamkoski, *With No Peace to Keep: United Nations Peacekeeping and the War in the Former Yugoslavia* (Grainpress, Ltd: London, 1995)

Windsor, L., 'Rwanda 1994: historian rebuts *Saturday Night* view', *Vanguard*, vol. 2, no. 6 (1996)

Woodhouse, T. and Ramsbotham, O., 'Terra incognita: here be dragons. Peacekeeping and conflict resolution in contemporary conflict: some relationships considered', Initiative on Conflict Resolution and Ethnicity (INCORE), Londonderry, 1996

Zinni, A. (Lt-Gen), 'It's not nice and neat', *Proceedings, US Naval Institute*, vol. 121, no. 8 (Aug. 1995)

Zucconi, M., 'The former Yugoslavia: lessons of war and diplomacy', *SIPRI Yearbook 1995: Armaments, Disarmament and International Security* (Oxford University Press: Oxford, 1995)

# VI. Interviews, discussions and personal communications

Lieutenant-General John Sanderson, Australian Defence Force, in Stockholm, 26 Sep. 1994

Don Daniel and Brad Hayes, US Naval War College, in Stockholm, 21 Oct. 1994

Superintendant Bill Kirk, Australian Federal Police, Canberra, in Kuala Lumpur, 12 Dec. 1995

Abdul Razak Abdulla Baginda, Executive Director, Malaysia Strategic Research Centre, in Kuala Lumpur, 13 Dec. 1995

Brigadier-General Soon Lian Cheng, Royal Malaysian Air Force; Major-General Datuk Jelani HJ Asmawi, Malaysian Ministry of Defence; Mak Joon Num, Director of Research, Malaysian Institute of Maritime Affairs; Colonel Mohamed Yunus Long, Head of Strategic Studies and International Relations, Malaysian Armed Forces Defence College (MPATI); Colonel Hadi Abdul Razak, Malaysian Ministry of Defence; and Mohamed Jawhar Hassan, Deputy Director-General, Institute for Strategic and International Studies (ISIS) Malaysia, in Kuala Lumpur, 14 Dec. 1995

David Stuart and Ruth Pearce, Australian Department of Foreign Affairs and Trade, in Canberra, 15 Dec. 1994

Lieutenant-Colonel Rick Dobie, Officer in Charge, Australian Defence Force Recruiting Unit, Sydney; Lieutenant-Colonel Tony Miles, Director, Australian Defence Force Peacekeeping Centre; and Squadron Leader Michael V. O'Brien, Staff Officer, Australian Defence Force Peacekeeping Centre, in Sydney, 18 Dec. 1995

Colonel Jonas Waern, Chief, Sector B, ONUC Katanga Command, in Stockholm, 24 Nov. 1995

David McBrien, UN Political and Commonwealth Section; Matthew Neuhaus, Director, International Organisations Branch; and Luke Williams, UN Political and Commonwealth Section, Australian Department of Foreign Affairs and Trade, in Canberra, 21 Dec. 1995

Lieutenant-Colonel Damien Healy, United Nations and Peacekeeping Policy, Australian Department of Defence, in Canberra, 21 Dec. 1995

Major Mike Kelly, Australian Department of Defence, in Canberra, 21 Dec. 1995

John McKinnon, Director, External Assessments Bureau, New Zealand Department of the Prime Minister and Cabinet; Peter J. Noble, Deputy Director, Strategic Developments, Directorate of Stategic Policy, New Zealand Defence Force; Andrew

Renton-Green, Manager, Policy Coordination, New Zealand Ministry of Defence; and Roundtable with officials of the New Zealand Ministry of External Relations and Trade, in Wellington, 16 Jan. 1996

Lieutenant-Colonel David Phillips, Australian High Commission, in Nadi, Fiji, 18 Jan. 1996

Brigadier-General J. K. Konrote; Lieutenant-Colonel Filipo Tarakinikini; Lieutenant-Colonel Peni Jikoiono, Lieutenant-Colonel Meli Bainimarama; Lieutenant-Colonel Isaac Mattiakabara; Captain Tui Gucake; and Captain Fred Naceba, Headquarters, Royal Fiji Military Force, in Nabua, Fiji, 18 Jan. 1996

Japanese peacekeeping experts at the SIPRI/Research Institute for Peace and Security (RIPS) workshop, Tokyo, 25–26 Jan. 1996: Major Shinichi Tsurada, Japan Self-Defence Force (JSDF); Shigeki Sumi, Director, International Peace Cooperation Division, Foreign Policy Bureau, Japanese Ministry of Foreign Affairs; and Dr Yoshio Katayama, Senior Researcher, National Institute for Defence Studies, Tokyo

Lieutenant-General Sir Michael Rose, British Army, at the Australian Peacekeeping Centre, Williamtown, New South Wales, 8 May 1996

Lieutenant-General Indar Jit Rikhye, former Military Adviser to the UN Secretary-General, at the Lester B. Pearson Canadian International Peacekeeping Training Centre, Nova Scotia, 15 May 1996

Colonel P. Leentjes, Chief Training Unit, UN Department of Peace-keeping Operations (DPKO), New York, at the Lester B. Pearson Canadian International Peacekeeping Training Centre, Nova Scotia, 15 May 1996

Lieutenant-Colonel Mike Bailey, US Army, Office of Peacekeeping and Humanitarian Operations, US State Department, Washington, DC, 18 June 1996

Lieutenant-Colonel G. Chesley Harris, Office of the Deputy Assistant Secretary of Defense for Peacekeeping and Peace Enforcement, in Washington, DC, 18 June 1996

Matthew Vaccaro, Allan Langland and Aphar Sidhu, Political/Military Bureau, US State Department, in Washington, DC, 18 June 1996

Lieutenant-Colonel Phil Wilkinson, Directorate General of Development and Doctrine, British Army, in Stockholm, 21 Aug. 1996

Leonard T. Kapunga, Chief, Lessons-Learned Mechanism, UN Department of Peace-keeping Operations (DPKO), at SIPRI, Stockholm, 31 Jan. 1997

Jarat Chopra and Tom Weiss, Thomas J. Watson Jr Institute for International Studies, Brown University, Providence, RI, 20 June 1997

Brendan Corcoran, UN Institute for Training and Research (UNITAR), New York, 17 Apr. 1998

Lieutenant-Colonel Mark Lavender and Roger Little, Mission Planning Service, UN DPKO, New York, 28 May 1998

Andrew Grrene, Deputy Head, Policy Unit, UN DPKO, in New York, June 1998

Susan Woodward, Visiting Fellow, King's College, London, 28 Nov. 2000

Salman Ahmed, UN DPKO, in New York, 5 Feb. 2001

Runo Bergstrom, Coordination Office, Lessons-Learned Unit, Department of Peace-Keeping Operations, UN DPKO, in New York, 5 Feb. 2001

Andrew Mack, Advisor to UN Secretary-General Kofi Annan, New York, 5 Feb. 2001

## VII. Conferences

Joint FCO–UNA Seminar: Steps towards Implementation of Conflict Prevention and
the Brahimi Report, Lancaster House, London, 28 Mar. 2001
Conference on the Use of Force in Peace Operations, Lester B. Pearson Canadian
International Peacekeeping Training Centre, Nova Scotia, Canada, 16 May 1996
Workshop on Implementation of the Dayton–Paris Peace Agreement and Options for
Follow-on Forces to IFOR, organized by the Centre for Defence Studies, King's
College, London, the Swedish Defence Research Organization and the Swedish
Ministry of Foreign Affairs, Stockholm, 28–29 Oct. 1996

## VIII. News sources

The following newspapers and journals have been consulted.

Africa Watch
The Age (Melbourne)
Armed Forces Journal International
Atlantic News
The Australian
Bangkok Post
British Army Review
Bulletin of the Atomic Scientists
Canberra Times
Comparative Strategy
Contemporary History
Defense and Foreign Policy
European Wall Street Journal
Financial Times
Foreign Affairs
Försvarets forum
Global Governance
The Guardian
Guardian Weekly
Harvard International Review
IBRU Boundary and Security Bulletin
   (International Boundaries Research
   Unit, University of Durham)
The Independent
International Affairs
International and Comparative Law
   Quarterly
International Herald Tribune
International Journal
International Peacekeeping
International Security
Jane's Defence Weekly

Jane's Intelligence Review
Joint Forces Quarterly
Journal of Peace Research
Los Angeles Times
Maclean's (Toronto)
Military Review
Moscow News
National Interest
Naval War College Review
New York Review of Books
The New York Times
Nouvelles Atlantiques
Orbis
Parameters: US Army War College
   Quarterly
Peacekeeping News
Phnom Penh Post
La Répubblica
RUSI Journal
Security Dialogue
Security Studies
Sydney Morning Herald
Sunday Times (London)
Survival
Time
Times of India
The Times
War Report
Washington Quarterly
Weekend Australian
UN and Conflict Monitor
UN Chronicle

# Index